*Assessment Centres and
Global Talent Management*

To my parents who are sadly no longer with us, my wife Gill and my children Lucy, Jonathan and Caroline who have all given me much pride and joy and a rewarding sense of purpose.

Nigel Povah

To my grandchildren, never-ending sources of joy and stimulation: Caley, Haydn, Jerett, Tyler, Jacob, Cheyenne, Jillian, Payson, Bowen and Jace.

George C. Thornton III

Assessment Centres and Global Talent Management

Edited by

NIGEL POVAH and
GEORGE C. THORNTON III

GOWER

Published by
Gower Publishing Limited
Wey Court East
Union Road
Farnham
Surrey
GU9 7PT
England

Gower Publishing Company
Suite 420
101 Cherry Street
Burlington
VT 05401-4405
USA

www.gowerpublishing.com

Nigel Povah and George C. Thornton III have asserted their moral right under the Copyright, Designs and Patents Act, 1988, to be identified as the editors of this work.

British Library Cataloguing in Publication Data
Assessment centres and global talent management.
    1. Assessment centers (Personnel management procedure) 2. Assessment centers (Personnel management procedure) – Cross-cultural studies. 3. Assessment centers (Personnel management procedure) – Evaluation.
    I. Povah, Nigel. II. Thornton, George C., 1940–
    658.3'125–dc22

Library of Congress Cataloging-in-Publication Data
Assessment centres and global talent management / [edited by] Nigel Povah and George Thornton.
    p. cm.
    Includes bibliographical references and index.
    ISBN 978-1-4094-0386-9 (hbk. : alk. paper) – ISBN 978-1-4094-0387-6 (ebook)
  1. Assessment centers (Personnel management procedure) 2. Personnel management – Cross-cultural studies. I. Povah, Nigel. II. Thornton, George C., 1940–

    HF5549.5.A78A79 2011
    658.3–dc23
                                2011022431

ISBN 9781409403869 (hbk)
ISBN 9781409403876 (ebk)

Printed and bound in Great Britain by the
MPG Books Group, UK

Contents

List of Figures

List of Tables

About the Editors

Nigel Povah, MSc, CPsychol, AFBPsS

Nigel Povah is a Chartered Occupational Psychologist and an Associate Fellow of the British Psychological Society. He is also a Founder Member of the Association of Business Psychologists. He has a degree in Psychology from the University of Leeds and a Masters in Occupational Psychology from Birkbeck College, University of London.

He is the CEO and founder in 1988 of Assessment and Development Consultants Ltd (A&DC®), which is one of the UK's leading firms of Occupational Psychologists. A&DC® have established themselves as one of the best-known names in the Assessment Centre field, in which Nigel is widely regarded as one of the UK's leading experts. He has over 30 years experience in this field, having designed and run hundreds of Assessment or Development Centres ranging in duration and format.

Nigel has authored or co-authored a number of books and articles on assessment centres, including some of the earliest articles on the concept of Development Centres in 1985. His previous books include *Assessment & Development Centres*, (with Iain Ballantyne, 1st edition in 1995 and 2nd edition in 2004) and *Succeeding at Assessment Centres for Dummies* (with his daughter Lucy Povah in 2009).

He has presented various papers at numerous conferences and events at different locations around the world. He was also a member of the committee responsible for the British Psychological Society's Best Practice Guidelines on the *Design, Implementation and Evaluation of Assessment and Development Centres*, which was published in November 2003.

As a Chartered Occupational Psychologist, Nigel has broad experience in conducting psychometric assessments, designing competency frameworks, designing and delivering training in competency-based interviewing, assessor skills, performance-appraisal techniques and many other behaviourally based topics. However, his greatest passion continues to be in the richly complex world of assessment centres.

Prior to founding A&DC® Nigel had brief spells in recruitment and training and before embarking on his career as an Occupational Psychologist he spent five years as a professional chess player. During this time he played for England, wrote four books on chess and coached a number of England's top players. He holds the title of International Master for over-the-board play and is a Grandmaster at Correspondence Chess and at his peak he was ranked 11th in the World.

As the CEO of A&DC, Nigel is no longer able to spend much time as an active practitioner, having to focus instead on writing, advising and coaching some of his colleagues in the areas of his expertise and managing the business. Nor does he find much time to pursue his interest in chess, although he still tries to remain an active competitor for his local club, whenever the opportunity arises. Nigel can be contacted by email at nigel.povah@adc.uk.com

George C. Thornton III, Ph.D.

Dr. Thornton is Professor Emeritus of Psychology, Colorado State University, Fort Collins, Colorado, USA. Dr. Thornton earned his Ph.D. from Purdue University in 1966. He is a Diplomate in Industrial/Organizational Psychology awarded by the American Board of Industrial/Organizational Psychology, and a Fellow of the Society of Industrial and Organizational Psychology.

Dr. Thornton specializes in assessment centers (ACs) and implications of employment discrimination law for personnel psychology. He has developed and validated ACs for numerous jobs in corporations and government agencies. He has advanced theory, research, and practice on using simulations to assess, diagnose, and develop performance competencies.

Dr. Thornton has been an active participant in the International Congress on Assessment Center Methods for the past 35 years. He has presented keynote addresses, reported research findings, served on the program and planning committee, and chaired the Congress. He has been instrumental in writing the *Guidelines and Ethical Considerations for Assessment Center Operations*, now in its fifth edition. He chaired the international task force which wrote the third edition. On two occasions, he worked with colleagues in Indonesia who wrote a set of guidelines on assessment centers for that country.

At Colorado State University, Dr. Thornton has taught courses and advised doctoral students studying the assessment center method. His students have completed seminal research on assessment centers for selection, promotion, diagnosis, and development. Many of his graduates have gone on to prominent positions in academia, HR management, contract research institutes, and consulting firms where they have advanced the research on and practice of the assessment center method.

Dr. Thornton is the author of numerous publications on ACs. His 1982 book (with William Byham), *Assessment Centers and Managerial Performance*, has been labelled the 'bible' on assessment centers. His recent books include *Assessment Centers in Human Resource Management* (2006 with Deborah Rupp) and *Developing Organizational Simulations: A Guide for Practitioners and Students* (2004 with Rose Mueller-Hanson).

Dr. Thornton has made presentations on the AC method to professional audiences throughout the United States, and in Germany, Switzerland, England, Belgium, Israel, South Africa, Indonesia, Korea, Singapore, Brazil, Costa Rica, Dubai, Russia, and China. He has provided advice to and served on advisory committees for student research on the assessment center method in Germany, Holland, India, Belgium, Israel, and South Africa.

Even in his 'retired' status, Dr. Thornton reports to work almost every day. But this does not interfere with his regular sports activities including winter skiing and year-round participation in endurance sports, namely triathlons and swimming.

He can be contacted at George.Thornton@colostate.edu

Notes on Contributors

Mohd Hanafiah Ahmad, MA, is a Lecturer of Management at Universiti Malaysia Pahang, Malaysia and is also completing his PhD at Massey University, New Zealand. His research focuses on how national cultural values are reflected in the design and implementation of assessment centers in Malaysia. He can be contacted by email at hanafiah@ump.edu.my

Sean P. Baldwin, MS, is a doctoral candidate at the University of Georgia studying industrial and organizational psychology and his principal research interest is measuring leadership in the workplace. He has authored and co-authored manuscripts addressing the validity and psychometric quality of AC ratings and performance ratings in general. Sean has experience creating measures of leadership, providing developmental feedback to practicing managers, and administering and interpreting employee engagement surveys. Sean can be contacted by email at seanpbaldwin@gmail.com

Eva Bergvall obtained a degree in Psychology from the University of Lund, before becoming a Research Assistant in the Department for Educational Psychology, followed by working in a number of local schools and social institutions. In 1992 she moved to Gothenburg where she managed a group of 30 psychologists, before taking charge of Administration for Human Resources for a local municipality within the City. In 2002 she was given the task of running an Assessment and Development Center service for Gothenburg and 12 smaller cities. The Assessment Center has evoked a lot of interest and many articles have been published in a number of Swedish Magazines. Eva has delivered a number of presentations at the Swedish 'Testdagarna', the International Congress on Assessment Center Methods, and the Assessment Centre Study Group in Stellenbosch, South Africa. Since 2009 Eva's work has focused on the recruitment and development of top level executives in Gothenburg. Eva can be reached by email at eva.bergvall@stadshuset.goteborg.se

Sandra Betti graduated from the *Pontificia Universidade Católica* of *São Paulo* (PUC-SP) as a psychologist. She has a master's degree in Social Psychology from the same university, a specialization in Human Resource Development from Harvard University and another specialization in HR Strategy from the University of Michigan Business School. As a specialist in Management Development, Coaching, Mentoring, Team Building, Assessment Centers and Talent Identification she has extensive HR experience and has filled executive positions in large companies. She is also a professor in the post-graduate and MBA programs at *Fundação Dom Cabral* and UNICENP (a division of *Grupo Positivo*). Actively engaged in pro-bono activities, she is a mentor at the FGV-SP Junior Enterprise, *Fundação Estudar*, *Fundação Brava*, *Brasil Junior* (Brazilian Association of Junior Enterprises), and is a volunteer at *Empreender Endeavor Brasil*. She is also a certified

xvi   Assessment Centres and Global Talent Management

international Master Coach through the New York Behavioral Coaching Institute. Email: Sandrabetti@mbaempresarial.com.br

Raimund Birri, PhD, in Neuropsychology from the University of Zürich, Switzerland. He trained software developers and specialists for human-computer interfaces and their evaluation in usability-labs. He became a Research Fellow in HUSAT (Human Sciences and Advanced Technology) at Loughborough University of Technology, England. He has broad experience as a manager of software development units in Credit Suisse, progressing to the Head of a team of AC specialists in Credit Suisse, before becoming the Global Head of Human Capital Evaluation and Management, responsible for performance management, engagement surveys, talent management, ACs, 360°, and so on. Dr Birri has made several contributions to International Conferences on Assessment Centers and Human Capital Management. Since retiring in 2008, he enjoys travelling, sports, and reading and writing. Contact information: Dr. Raimund Birri, Schiffbaustr. 12, 8005 Zürich, Switzerland. Tel: +41 79 2161679 Email: raimund.birri@gmx.ch

Seán Boyle, MSc, CPsychol, AFBPsS, MCIPD, is an independent business psychologist and a former partner in one of the UK's most admired psychology consulting firms. He has advised and supported many blue-chip organizations on varied aspects of talent management, concentrating on the identification, development and coaching of senior management potential. Designing and implementing assessment and development centres, and conducting individual assessments for senior management positions are regular aspects of his work. Earlier in his career, having trained in occupational psychology he held research posts at Queen's University Belfast and Birkbeck College (University of London). Seán was an internal specialist in assessment, development and change management for a number of public and private sector organizations in Britain and Ireland. Seán can be contacted by email at psychology@sboyle.eu

Anne Buckett, MCom, is a qualified Industrial Psychologist in South Africa with extensive experience in assessment and development in industry. She is presently the Managing Consultant of Precision HR with specialist expertise in the areas of HR competency-based assessment and development. She has worked at and with several large international consulting firms acquiring consolidated experience in a wide range of HR interventions. In addition, she is trained on a variety of tools, techniques and methodologies across a large number of well-established test publishers. Her experience covers both private and public sector organizations. Anne has served as a member of the executive committee of People Assessment in Industry (PAI) in 2006–2007. She was Regional Chairperson for the Society of Industrial and Organisational Psychology of South Africa (SIOPSA) Pretoria Branch (2007–2009) and the Chairperson of the Assessment Centre Study Group of South Africa (ACSG) from 2008–2009. She can be reached by email at anne@precisionhr.co.za

Olexander (Sasha) Chernyshenko is currently an associate professor at Nanyang Technological University School of Business. His research focuses on applications of psychometric methods in the areas of personality and job attitudes, and he teaches graduate level courses including advanced industrial organizational psychology, research methods, human resource management, performance management, and organizational development. He can be reached by email at Chernyshenko@ntu.edu.sg

Tony Cockerill is currently a visiting research fellow at Goldsmiths, University of London. He was formerly at London Business School and he co-founded the business that is now Kenexa Leadership Solutions. He has expertise in the application of innovative approaches to assessment of leadership capability, strategic talent management, and organizational design. He can be contacted by email at Tony.Cockerill@HighPerform.co

Chris Dewberry, PhD, was educated at Plymouth Polytechnic where he graduated with a BA in Psychology and he then went on to University College London, where he gained a PhD in Psychology. Chris has lectured at several institutions including University of London Goldsmiths and Roehampton University and he has worked in the Department of Organizational Psychology at Birkbeck College, University of London, for over 20 years, where he teaches research methods and personnel selection and assessment, to students studying Occupational Psychology and Organizational Behaviour. Chris's research interests are principally in the areas of assessment and self-regulation. He is particularly interested in the psychological processes which affect the evaluation of human performance and in individual differences in self-regulatory styles and ability. Chris can be contacted by email at c.dewberry@bbk.ac.uk

Fritz Dragow is currently a professor of Psychology and of Labor and Employment Relations at the University of Illinois at Urbana-Champaign. His research focuses on psychological measurement. He has conducted research designed to identify individuals mis-measured by tests. He has used multimedia computer technology to assess social and interpersonal skills not easily measured by paper-and-pencil tests, and explored psychometric models for non-cognitive assessment. He can be reached by email at fdrasgow@illinois.edu

Madeleine Dunford, BA, MSc, is the Managing Director of Career Connections, an assessment consultancy in Kenya, which she founded in 1997. She has extensive experience in the areas of psychometric testing and assessment centres. For the past 6 years Career Connections has been instrumental in the introduction of Assessment and Development Centres into East Africa. Career Connections is primarily focused in providing these services for the regional head quarters of global multinationals, and large local companies, including fast moving consumer good manufacturers, banking and telecommunication organizations. Madeleine received a BA (Hons) from the University of York, UK, and an MSc from Edinburgh University, UK. She is an accredited executive coach. Madeleine can be contacted at Career Connections Ltd, P.O. Box 25118, 00603, Nairobi, Kenya, or by email at madeleine@careerconnections.co.ke

Clive Fletcher, BA, PhD, CPsychol, FBPsS, FRSM, is Professor Emeritus in Psychology at Goldsmiths College, University of London, an Honorary Professor at Warwick Business School and Managing Director of Personnel Assessment Ltd. Clive is a Fellow of both the British Psychological Society and the Royal Society of Medicine. He has been involved in research in the fields of performance appraisal and leadership assessment and development for more than 30 years, and has authored over 200 publications and conference papers in this area. He is a consultant to a wide range of organizations on psychological assessment of candidates for top management positions. His knowledge and experience in the assessment field is recognised internationally; he has held visiting professorial posts in other European countries and serves on the Advisory Boards of a number of UK and overseas companies working in the assessment field. He can be contacted at c.fletcher@personnel-assessment.com

Shaul Fox, PhD, is a Professor of Industrial-Organizational Psychology in the Department of Psychology at Bar-Ilan University in Ramat-Gan, Israel, where he also completed his doctorate. His research interests span a broad spectrum, including personnel selection, cognitive biases in decision-making, organizational changes, and performance appraisal. He has published a large number of articles in both Israeli and international scientific journals, such as *Journal of Applied Psychology, Personnel Psychology, International Journal of Selection and Assessment, Journal of Occupational and Organizational Psychology, and Journal of Business and Psychology.* He is also the author of a book (in Hebrew) on Resistance to Organizational Changes and has published numerous technical reports. He has extensive experience in the field of organizational consultation, OD projects, and in developing, implementing, administering, and researching assessment centres at several leading organizations in Israel. Shaul can be contacted by email at Shaul.Fox@biu.ac.il

Gary Grace, MSc, is a consultant for PeopleCentric Associates and specializes in the field of applied psychology and psychometric testing. He has an active role in the psychological society in New Zealand, acting as the professional development coordinator and I-O editor of the psychological society biannual magazine. Gary has a keen interest in the use of task-based assessment centres in New Zealand organizations and is considering undertaking a PhD in this area. He can be contacted by email at gary@peoplecentric.co.nz

Nigel Guenole is currently the Kenexa High Performance Institute's research director for the United Kingdom. He is also a lecturer in work psychology and programme director for the MSc Occupational Psychology at Goldsmiths College, University of London. His work focuses on applications of modern psychometric approaches like structural equation modeling to the study of personality and work attitudes. Nigel can be reached by email at n.guenole@gold.ac.uk.

Soly Haboucha, MA, from City University of New York, USA, is an Industrial-Organizational Psychologist with 30 years of research and practical experience in the fields of personnel selection, test development, performance appraisal and organizational consulting. Among the pioneers of managerial ACs in Israel, he has been instrumental in introducing ACs in several Israeli organizations and maintains a hands-on approach in everyday practice. His professional experience spans a broad spectrum of organizations, including the military, government and public institutions, as well as business firms. From 1988 to 1996 he served as head of the Israeli Air Force Personnel Selection Branch, before joining Top-C, a leading provider of personnel testing and organizational consulting services, as chief psychologist. His international projects include the development and application of selection systems in two African countries. He has published numerous technical reports. Soly can be reached by email at sires@smile.net.il

Shinichi Hirose is a Research Associate at the Graduate School of Business Administration, Keio University in Yokohama, Japan. His business experience includes management consulting at McKinsey Tokyo, Osaka, and Seoul Offices, and the role of

Director of Human Resources at Electronic Data Systems (EDS, currently a division of Hewlett-Packard), among others. In recent years he served as an assessor in the assessment center programs for Japanese branches of global corporations. He received a Master of Management from J.L. Kellogg Graduate School of Management at Northwestern University and BA in Letters from the University of Tokyo. Shinichi can be contacted by email at hirose@kk.iij4u.or.jp

Brian J. Hoffman, PhD, is Assistant Professor on the Industrial and Organizational Psychology Program at the University of Georgia. He earned his doctorate from the University of Tennessee. His primary research interest is leadership assessment, with an emphasis on understanding the quality of information received from assessment centers and multisource performance ratings. Brian's research has been published in *Personnel Psychology*, *Journal of Applied Psychology*, and *Academy of Management Journal,* and he was the recipient of the 2011 Douglas Bray/Ann Howard award. He has served on the program committee of the International Congress on the Assessment Center Method and has co-edited a book on ACs, 'The Psychology of Assessment Centers.' Over the past ten years, Brian has served as an AC designer, administrator, and assessor / role player for a variety of large and small companies. He can be reached by email at hoffmanb@uga.edu

Duncan Jackson, PhD, works as an Assistant Professor at the University of Seoul, South Korea. He has experience researching and developing assessment centers in New Zealand and in Korea and has published in some of the leading journals in Industrial-Organizational Psychology, including the *International Journal of Selection and Assessment* and *Human Performance*. His experience in the assessment center domain spans a range of industries in both the public and private sectors. This includes applications at executive, managerial, and entry levels. He has worked with assessment centers for employee selection and development purposes in retail, service, military, government, and agricultural industries. Duncan's expertise ranges from the design of assessment center exercises to scoring approaches and psychometric analyses. Duncan can be contacted by email at duncanjackson@gmail.com

Myungjoon (Marco) Kim, PhD, MBA, is a very experienced senior consultant in personnel development and organizational behavior and is expert in the use of psychometric instruments and the assessment center method. He has strong facilitation skills in management development programs, particularly using the Strong Interest Inventory and MBTI® applications, and other aptitude tests and selection and development tools within Korea. He has delivered assessment and development centers within both the public and private sectors for government and global companies. Dr. Kim is Managing Director of the ASSESTA Corp. in Seoul (www.assesta.com). He has an MBA from Yonsei University and a PhD in Human Resource Management from Kwangwoon University. He recently spent three years as a visiting scholar at the University of Illinois at Urbana-Champaign, conducting research on developmental assessment centers. He is a well known researcher and writes frequently for academic journals. He can be reached by email at marcok@unitel.co.kr.

Dr. Diana E. Krause is a tenured Professor of Human Resource Management and Organizational Behavior at the Alpen-Adria University Klagenfurt (Austria) (www.uni-klu. ac.at/opm/inhalt/1.htm or http://kinderbali.ki.funpic.de/). She is the head of the team on Personnel, Organization, and Management Development. She had several professorships at University Paderborn (Germany), University of Medical Informatics and Technology (Austria), University Speyer (Germany), Humboldt University Berlin (Germany), and University of Western Ontario (Canada). Dr. Krause intensified her research on Assessment Center Programs during her Visiting fellowship at Colorado State University (USA) in 2004 and 2005 where she worked closely together with Professor George C. Thornton III. In 2005, she finished her Habilitation (*Venia legendi* for Psychology) at Ludwig-Maximillians University Munich. In 2003, she received her Ph.D. in Economics and Management at Technical University Berlin. She can be contacted by email at DianaEva.Krause@uni-klu.ac.at

Dr. Kai-Guang (Carl) Liang is the managing director of C&D Management Consulting. He received an M.S. in Managerial Psychology (1986) from Zhejiang University, an M.A. from the Central Michigan University (1994) and a Ph.D. from the Old Dominion University in Industrial-Organizational Psychology (1999). Previously Dr. Liang worked at PDI Shanghai Office, AT&T's Sourcing & Selection Group in New Jersey, and Renmin University of China in Beijing. He and his colleagues had set up one of the earliest assessment centers in 1990 and conducted a pioneering validation research on assessment centers in China. Dr. Liang works with multinational and local companies as well as government agencies in China in the areas of competency modeling, leadership assessment and development, and organizational development. He is an active contributor at the Society for Industrial and Organizational Psychology and the International Congress of Assessment Center Methods. He can be reached by email at carl.liang@cndgroup.com

Filip Lievens received his PhD from Ghent University, Belgium and is currently Professor at the Department of Personnel Management and Work and Organizational Psychology at the same university. He is the author of over 100 articles in the areas of organizational attractiveness, high-stakes testing, and selection including assessment centers, situational judgment tests, and web-based assessment. He has also delivered over 200 presentations, workshops and invited keynote presentations across all continents (Europe, USA, Asia, Africa, and Australia). Filip serves as an editorial board member of both the *Journal of Applied Psychology* and *Personnel Psychology* and was a past book review editor of the *International Journal of Selection and Assessment*. Dr. Lievens has also received several awards, such as being the first European winner of the Distinguished Early Career Award of the Society for Industrial and Organizational Psychology (2006) and the first industrial and organizational psychologist to be laureate of the Royal Flemish Academy of Sciences and Arts (2008). He can be contacted by email at Filip.Lievens@UGent.be or by telephone on +32-9-2646453.

Ying Liu, PhD, is assistant professor in the School of Public Administration at Renmin University of China. She received her M.S. and PhD. in Industrial/Organizational Psychology from Old Dominion University. Her research interests include team performance and team leadership, leadership development as well as cross-cultural management. Her research has appeared in the *Journal of Cross-cultural Management*, *International Journal of Intercultural*

Relations, and *International Journal of Psychology*. She is a member of the Society of Industrial and Organizational Psychology and the Academy of Management. Dr. Liu can be reached by email at lylw.liu@gmail.com or liuying@mparuc.edu.cn.

Natalie Livings, MSc, CPsychol, AFBPsS, MCIPD, is a Consultant for YSC Ltd, a global business psychology consultancy. She is a chartered occupational psychologist, a member of the Chartered Institute of Personnel and Development and an associate fellow of the British Psychological Society. After graduating with an MSc in Occupational Psychology, Natalie started her career working for Marks & Spencer. She then moved to QinetiQ where she spent a number of years undertaking research for the military and government. Natalie then joined A&DC Ltd, a Surrey-based consultancy. There she designed and delivered a variety of assessment and development centre solutions to UK-based and international organizations. At YSC she is involved in the assessment and development of senior leaders, high-potential identification, executive coaching and assessment and development centre design and delivery. A qualified coach and counsellor, Natalie's passion is helping individuals to understand and achieve their potential. Natalie can be reached at natalie.livings@ysc.com

Zia Manji, BCom, is a Director of Career Connections, an assessment consultancy which he joined in 2002, after nearly seven years in general management in a large food manufacturing company. He has extensive experience in executive recruitment and was involved in the introduction of Assessment and Development Centres, including marketing and assessor training. For the last 9 years he has specialized in working with companies to design and conduct assessment centres, selection programmes, 360-degree feedback programmes, and executive coaching. He received his BCom from the University of Edinburgh, and is an accredited executive coach and facilitator for the Academy of Executive Coaching. Zia can be contacted at Career Connections Ltd, P.O. Box 25118, 00603, Nairobi, Kenya. Email: zia@careerconnections.co.ke

Deon Meiring, PhD, is an Associate Professor at the University of Pretoria, Department of Human Resource Management. He completed his PhD at the Tilburg University, Netherlands under Prof Fons van de Vijver in 2007 one of the leading Cross-Cultural Psychologists. Deon's field of specialisation is in advanced assessment practice and he has extensive experience in assessment and development centre design, situational judgment testing and personality test construction. He was the chairperson of the Assessment Centre Study Group (ACSG) in 2007–2008 and in 2010 he received an honorary membership from the ACSG for his work in assessment centres in South Africa (www.acsg.co.za). His research can be viewed at www.meiringd.co.za.

Andreas Melcher, Diplom, in Psychology from the University of Kiel, Germany. He then joined SHL Deutschland GmbH, where he gained broad experience in the development and validation of psychometric products, implementation of personnel selection solutions and management assessments. He then moved to Credit Suisse where he became an AC specialist, before heading up a team of Human Capital specialists, responsible for varying topic areas such as the bank-wide Talent Development Process, Performance Management, 360° feedback, competency modelling. He was promoted to Head of Assessments and Human Capital Metrics at Credit Suisse with responsibility for the global assessment practice and overarching topics related to the human capital management framework and metrics. He has made several contributions to International Conferences on Human Capital Management with a key focus on measurement approaches and quantifying the impact of human capital practices on the bottom-line. Contact information: Andreas Melcher, Credit Suisse AG, HLLC, 8070 Zürich, +41 44 332 1093, andreas.melcher@credit-suisse.com

Will Mitchell, BSc, MSc, CPsychol, heads up the consultancy practice of over 20 psychologists at A&DC Ltd. He has over 15 years of experience in consulting and is a Chartered Occupational Psychologist and Assessor on the Board of the BPS Occupational Psychology Division. He has specific expertise in the development of talent management strategy based on the use of assessment and development centres and building the business case based on ROI evidence. He has written widely on talent development, positive psychology, work-life balance, 360° feedback and learning agility in specialist journals and media such as the Sunday Times. He regularly speaks at HR practitioner conferences and has designed and delivered a number of programmes for both public sector and private sector clients. He coaches senior executives in how to deal with change and transition, utilising the principles of positive psychology to aid personal development. Will has held previous consulting roles with Mercer and International Survey Research as well as with the Outward Bound Trust. He can be contacted by email at will.mitchell@adc.uk.com

Satiko Monobe graduated from the *Pontifícia Universidade Católica* of *São Paulo* (PUC-SP) as a psychologist and has a masters degree in Social Psychology from the same university. She holds the Certificate of Advanced Studies in Cross-Cultural Communication by the Thunderbird School of Global Management. Her extensive professional HR experience was obtained in management positions in large companies. Her specialties are Executive Recruitment, Coaching, and Assessment Centers. She coordinates projects to identify new talents, and selects MBA candidates for company sponsorship. Actively engaged in pro-bono activities, she is a mentor at the *Fundação Estudar*, *Fundação Brava* and FGV-SP Junior Enterprise. Email: satikomonobe@mbaempresarial.com.br

Ee-Ling Ng, MA, is a Senior Consultant with the Centre for Leadership Development at the Civil Service College in Singapore. She graduated with honours from the University of Nottingham, UK, and obtained her MA (Psychometrics) degree from the University of British Columbia, Canada. She started her career in the Singapore Civil Service with a focus on providing selection and assessment solutions for various public sector organisations. Specifically, her work revolved around conducting assessments for early identification of talent, and the design and implementation of assessment programmes for senior personnel. In recent years, her interest in developing people and nurturing talent has resulted in a career shift towards providing consultancy in leadership development. Currently, she provides assistance to public sector clients in defining, designing and implementing appropriate leadership development strategies. She also facilitates leadership development programmes, and provides leadership feedback and coaching. She can be contacted by email at ng_ee_ling@cscollege.gov.sg

Glenn J. Nosworthy, PhD, is an Independent Consultant and Adjunct Associate Professor at the National University of Singapore Business School. He obtained his

PhD in 1993 in Basic and Applied Psychology at Queen's University, Canada. For 9 years he worked as an occupational psychologist in the Canadian Public Service and the Royal Canadian Mounted Police specialising in assessment largely for recruitment and promotion purposes (for example, participating in the design of cognitive ability tests, structured interviews, situational judgment tests, assessment centres, and so on). He moved to Singapore in 1999 and took up a faculty position at the National University of Singapore Business School where he became Head of the Department of Management and Organisation. He subsequently joined SHL, an international consultancy, as VP Assessment for the Asia Pacific region. For the past 6 years, he has been an independent consultant offering assessment services to various public and private sector organizations in Singapore. Glenn can be reached by email at glennj@starhub.net.sg

Vina G. Pendit, Bachelor Degree (S1) in Psychology, University of Indonesia. She is a Director and co-founder of PT Daya Dimensi Indonesia, a human resources company which supports the preparation of human capital via selection and assessment, learning and development, and human resources strategic consulting. Clients include multi-national organizations, state-owned and government institutions, and private organizations in various industrial sectors. Ms. Pendit has a keen interest in the development and implementation of assessment centers for various levels of staff, and she coordinated the national committee which wrote Indonesia's 'Ethical Guidelines for Assessment Center Implementation.' She has presented many workshops and seminars on the assessment center method, including presentations to the International Congress on Assessment Center Methods. She established and is now Vice Chair of PASSTI (Perkumpulan Assessment Center Indonesia), a non-profit organization that promotes the integrity of the assessment center method through communication sessions to different communities and practitioners. Contact information: vina.pendit@dayadimensi.co.id

R.K. Premarajan, PhD, currently works as Professor in the Organizational Behavior and Human Resources areas at XLRI Jamshedpur, India. He is also a member of the Governing Board of XLRI. He completed his Masters in Psychology at the University of Calicut, and his PhD in Organizational Behavior at the Indian Institute of Technology, Bombay. He teaches, researches and consults in the areas of Competency Based HRM, Organizational Career Development, and Measuring HR. At XLRI he held the Chair position of L&T Scholar of HR during 2002–2005. Prior to joining XLRI he held positions with the Corporate HRD department of Larsen & Toubro Limited (L&T) in Bombay, as well as Executive Assistant to Chairman, National Dairy Development Board (NDDB) India. Contact information: XLRI, Jamshedpur, CH Area (E) P.O. Box No 222, Jamshedpur 831 001 India. Tel: +91-657-3983149. Email: prem@xlri.ac.in

Sophie Pritchard, MSc, MSc, CPsychol, is currently Head of Talent for a global financial services organization. Previously, Sophie worked as a Senior Consultant at A&DC. She has extensive experience designing and using simulation exercises in Assessment and Development Centres, working with clients across a range of industry sectors. Sophie holds a Bachelor's degree in Psychology from the University of Sheffield and Masters degrees in Occupational and Forensic Psychology from the University of Surrey and University of Kent. Sophie can be contacted by email at either Sophie.Pritchard@barclays.com or Pritchard_Sophie@hotmail.com

David C. Purdy, CMC, is President of Psychological Consultants, Inc. (www.pciassessments.com), having joined the firm in 1977. He has extensive experience in leadership assessment and is responsible for the development and conduct of assessment center programs for major US organizations as well as international companies. For the past 20 years, he has specialized in working with companies in the pharmaceutical, biotech, and medical device industry, designing and conducting assessment center programs for aspiring sales managers as well as current managers and executives. He is a Certified Management Consultant. Mr. Purdy received his BA from the College of William and Mary and his MA from the University of Richmond. Contact information: Psychological Consultants, Inc., 6724 Patterson Avenue, Richmond, VA 23226, USA. Tel: +1-804-288-4125. Email: david.purdy@pciassessments.com

Philippa Riley, MSc, CPsychol, is currently working as a Senior Consultant in the Product Development team at A&DC, having previously worked as a Consultant for QinetiQ Ltd. Philippa holds a Bachelor's degree in Psychology and Sociology from the University of Durham, and a Masters degree in Occupational Psychology from the University of Sheffield. Philippa has extensive experience as an exercise designer, assessor and centre manager and is responsible for managing A&DC's assessment and development centre exercise range, AC-EXS™, the world's largest range of ready-to-use assessment and development centre exercises. Philippa can be contacted by email at philippa.riley@adc.uk.com

Deborah E. Rupp, PhD, from Colorado State University, is the William C. Byham Chair in Industrial/Organizational Psychology in the Department of Psychological Sciences at Purdue University. She was formerly Associate Professor of Labor/Employment Relations, Psychology, and Law at the University of Illinois at Urbana-Champaign (www.psychology.illinois.edu/people/derupp). Her assessment-related research focuses on validation, developmental assessment centers, and the use of technology to enhance assessment and development. She co-authored the latest edition (2006) of *Assessment Centers in Human Resource Management* with George Thornton and was the first recipient of the Douglas Bray/Ann Howard Award for research on leadership assessment and development. She also conducts research on organizational justice, corporate social responsibility, and emotions at work, and has published over 60 scholarly papers. She is currently Editor of the *Journal of Management,* and recently co-chaired the International Congress on Assessment Center Methods, where she co-led the taskforce that prepared/published a revision to the *Guidelines and Ethical Considerations for Assessment Center Operations*. Her assessment center research was also cited in proceedings surrounding US Supreme Court case *Ricci* v. *DeStefano et al.* She can be reached at ruppd@purdue.edu

Eveline Schollaert is a PhD student at Ghent University, Belgium. She is an academic assistant in Human Resources Management at the Department of Personnel Management and Work and Organizational Psychology. Her main area of interest involves psychometric characteristics of assessment centres. She is currently exploring this issue in the context of her dissertation about validity and reliability of assessment centres. She is also interested in the development and use of situational judgment tests and she has contributed to research focusing on their psychometric characteristics, which enabled her to write a practical handbook about this topic with Professor Filip Lievens. Besides her interests in assessment centres and situational judgment tests, she also focuses on other selections tools (such as personality questionnaires, emotional intelligence tests) and other research areas (such as recruitment, response rates, and performance feedback) which have resulted in a number of related presentations and publications. Eveline can be contacted by email at Eveline.Schollaert@UGent.be or by telephone on +32-9-2646459.

Rosalind H. Searle, PhD, MBA, Dip Opsy, CPsychol, AFBPsS, is currently Senior Lecturer in Organizational Psychology at the Open University, UK, and Hon Sen Visiting Fellow, Centre for Performance at Work, City University, UK. She specialises in and has written a number of journal articles, books, chapters and reports on recruitment and selection, trust and HRM, political trust, and the evaluation of performance and training initiatives. Her most recent book is a co-edited collection looking at Trust and HRM. She is co-convenor of the EGOS Standing Working Group on Organizational Trust, Co-chair of the British Academy of Management's Organisational Psychology Group, Chair of the British Psychological Society, Division of Occupational Psychology's International Strategy Group. She also sits on the editorial board of the *Journal of Trust Research* and advises a number of organizations about their Recruitment and Selection processes, as well as their change programmes. She can be contacted by Email: r.searle@open.ac.uk; Tel: +44 7776 303 580; Skype: rossearle

Svetlana Simonenko, PhD, is the Business Development Director and co-founder of DeTech, a consultancy specialising in the assessment and development field. The company was established in 2004 and now operates in Russia and the Commonwealth of Independent States (CIS). She has over 15 years experience in human resources consulting. During the last 10 years she mainly focuses on assessment methods of personnel. Her primary areas of interest are the adoption of British personnel assessment methods within Russia, Ukraine, Belorussia and Kazakhstan; research on leadership effectiveness in different social and economic environments; and developing new assessment tools such as personality questionnaires and ability tests. Svetlana is one of the authors of the Russian generic competency model '20 Dimensions' and 'Palette of Competencies'. She is a recognized authority in competency modelling, assessment and development centres, psychometric testing and leadership development in Russia, Ukraine and Kazakhstan. Svetlana can be contacted by email at simonenko@detech-group.com

Stephen Stark is currently an associate professor of Psychology at the University of South Florida. His research focuses on the development and application of item response theory methods to practical problems in organizations with an emphasis on non-cognitive assessment, computerized adaptive testing, and the detection of differential item functioning. He can be reached by email at sestark@usf.edu

Jan H. van der Westhuizen is the MD of Experiential Technologies Pty Ltd, (www.experttech.com) a global Assessment and Learning Solutions Company. He completed his post graduate degree at the University of South Africa (UNISA). Jan's field of specialisation is in Organizational Development with emphasis on the use of computer based simulation technology in assessment and development centres. Jan has membership from the Assessment Centre Study Group (ACSG); he is Chartered Human Resources Practitioner with the South African Board for Personnel Practice (SABPP) and a Fellow member of the *Australian Institute for Management* (AIM). In 2009 he won the

APPETD award for Innovation in recognition of his work in the use of technology in assessment centres. Jan delivered papers at the annual ACSG conferences in South Africa and the International Congress on Assessment Center Methods in Singapore 2010, where his paper was on *The use of CBST in ADC: a Global Perspective.* Jan can be contacted by email at jan@experttech.com or by telephone on +32-27-83- 468-6750.

Charles Woodruffe PhD, CPsychol, AFBPsS, FCIPD, is Managing Director of Human Assets Limited, a London-based firm of business psychologists. Charles and his colleagues specialise in creating and implementing strategies to ensure that clients have the leadership pipeline they need to fulfil their business strategies. Charles has published widely, based on his 30 years experience working on development and assessment centres, competencies and talent management. He has worked with a range of private and public sector clients including Shell, Exxon-Mobil, HSBC, Ernst and Young, the Security Service and the Cabinet Office. Charles emphasizes taking a tailored approach to clients' needs and he has built a reputation for ensuring the diversity credentials of his solutions. Charles can be contacted by email at charles.woodruffe@humanassets.co.uk

Jeeyun Yoon, MS, is a Graduate Student at the Georgia Institute of Technology. Her PhD research focuses on cross-cultural issues related to attributions in Leadership Studies. Jeeyun has experience working in Assessment Centers in South Korea with the Assesta organization. Jeeyun can be reached by email at jyoon@gatech.edu

Reviews of Assessment Centres and Global Talent Management

Destined to be a classic for both practitioners and researchers that will take the assessment center method to new levels of efficiency and accuracy. Really new insights and research that answer questions about assessment center design, validity, arithmetic data integration, and new techniques and simulations based on research from 18 countries. Easy to read and to focus in on specific areas of interest.
    William C. Byham, Ph.D.Chairman & CEO, Development Dimensions International, Inc.

Since the innovative work by Doug Bray and his colleagues at AT&T in the early 1960's, Assessment Centers have been a valuable tool for talent management. In today's hyper-competitive, global world, Assessment Centers have not only stood the test of time, but become an invaluable talent management tool. Povah and Thornton offer the definitive work on modern Assessment Centers.

This comprehensive anthology integrates and extends theory, research, and practice; it shows how Assessment Centers may be used to build corporate strategies of globalization, innovation, and customer service; and it clearly demonstrates the global reach of Assessment Centers. They have purposefully collected insights from 48 thought leaders in 18 countries, and each of the 32 chapters stands alone, but they have gone further to discern and deliver observations across these chapters. This work will become an instant foundation review of the modern Assessment Center.
    Dave Ulrich Professor, Ross School of Business, University of Michigan,
    Partner, the RBL Group (www.rbl.net)

This is an important book which combines theoretical models of best practice in Assessment and Development Centre design with practical guidance on implementation. The Authors have produced chapters that are accessible to interested stakeholders who are not necessarily Assessment Centre practitioners, yet they are sufficiently detailed and referenced such that those requiring more detail can easily delve deeper.

The book asks some critical questions, challenging accepted wisdom regarding the implementation of Assessment Centres, considering such issues as the relative merits of consensus meetings compared to more pragmatically straightforward arithmetic scoring and off-the shelf versus bespoke exercise simulations. Issues rarely considered in the design of Assessment Centres are also considered, such as the potential effect on self-awareness and motivation of candidates; the authors arguing that as Psychologists and practitioners greater emphasis should be given to individual candidates' welfare than may have been demonstrated in the past.

An important theme throughout the central chapters of the book is the need to implement Assessment and Development Centres within the context of the organisations they are designed to help. In addition to implementing empirically valid Assessment and Development Centres, as practitioners the requirement to carefully align the organisation's aims at strategic, operational and individual levels is emphasised. To this end, practical help is provided which will be invaluable to both practitioners and those commissioning Assessment and Development Centres alike.

Professor Peter Saville, BA, MPhil, PhD, FBPsS, C.Psychol, CSci, FRSA,
International Chairman and CEO, Saville Consulting Group Limited

Preface

The assessment centre method has been around for over 50 years, and even longer if you consider its clear ancestors operating under different names and guises. Hundreds of articles, chapters, books, and technical reports have been written – many of which we have contributed to or authored. Why then is there a need for another book? Well, several reasons. The method continues to evolve; much is happening around the world that has not been documented; old devotees are seeking to understand new developments and learn about new applications; new initiates in developing countries are coming to the field. Assessment centres are thriving in both traditional sites and new locations.

The goal of this book is to take a different perspective on the many applications of this versatile human resource management intervention. The unique contribution of this book is its focus on three themes that cut across much of the older and newer work on ACs: the roles of ACs in the broader talent management efforts of organizations; the cross-cultural issues arising as ACs are installed in organizations in emerging economies; and the continued interface of theory, research, and practice of the AC method. We asked contributors to focus on these themes.

The assessment centre method has been a major part of our professional lives for many years. For Nigel, the method has been a core part of his consulting, writing, supervising and coaching colleagues for around 30 years. For George, the method has been a focus of his university career including teaching, advising, researching, writing, and consulting for over 40 years. He continues to be active in the field even in his ostensible state of 'retirement' from many university duties.

We wish to express deep appreciation to the 48 authors from 18 countries who have provided special contributions to understanding the valuable and unique implementation of the assessment centre method. We solicited these contributors because we were familiar with some of their work through our prior association with them, their writings, and/or their eminence in the field. We thank them for their patience with us as we explained our objectives for the book and steered them into writing about the themes of the book. We gave more direction, prodding, and cajoling than is typical of editors of contributed chapters to ensure the authors addressed the themes of the book. We also provided hefty amounts of input on grammar, punctuation, word choice, style, and format to ensure the writing was accessible to diverse readers around the world. We thank the authors for their patience for this somewhat unusual form of 'editing' as we went through more revisions than is typical with chapters for a professional book.

We thank our wives for their forbearance in the 2 years this project consumed. At certain pressure points in the process, we did little else outside normal business activities.

We also thank our editor, Jonathan Norman, at Gower Publishing for showing confidence to undertake this monumental project. He has been instrumental in shaping our seminal ideas, advising on critical points, and showing flexibility as the project evolved.

We would also like to thank some of the team at A&DC for their administrative support with some of the formatting requirements and the re-formatting of some of the figures. Nigel would also like to thank a number of his colleagues for taking on certain activities whilst he was 'away from the office' and for their tolerance and patience when he was less accessible than usual. Particular thanks on these matters go to Jenny Goad, Andy Gorton, Shane McGarrigle, Lucy Povah, Chris Rawlinson, Kate Sobczak, Nigel Thomas, Isobel Venner and David Williams.

At Colorado State University, we thank Kyle Sandell for his insightful and conscientious help in preparing the author and subject indexes. As an informed reader, he was able to contribute to the logic and usefulness of the subject headings and organization.

Nigel Povah
Guildford, Surrey, UK

George Thornton
Fort Collins, Colorado, USA

AC Best Practice

Three Themes that Explain Our Passion for Assessment Centres as Tools for Talent Management

NIGEL POVAH AND GEORGE C. THORNTON III

The purpose of this chapter is to introduce the reader to a unique book aimed at those with a keen interest in assessment centres (ACs). It is unique for a number of distinct reasons.

Firstly, unlike most books on ACs which aim to cover every conceivable aspect of AC design and practice in equal measure, we have chosen to focus on three major themes which are becoming increasingly important in how ACs are deployed in the modern world, namely corporate strategy and talent management, cross-cultural implications of international human resources (HR) practices, and the interplay of science and practice. In this respect we have assumed that the reader already has a good grasp of the basic principles of AC practice and is interested in some of the critical factors that impact on how ACs are implemented within a global organizational context. Readers who are less familiar with the basics of theory, research, and practice related to the AC method may wish to refer to books by Ballantyne and Povah (2004), Thornton and Rupp (2006) and Schlebusch and Roodt (2008).

Secondly, it moves beyond the traditional treatment of published material on ACs, which is either the production of highly technical material for the academic researcher or a sterile, highly practical 'how to' guide for the practitioner. This book aims to plug a gap in the literature by creating a unique blend between these two different approaches. This is exemplified in the theme of the book showing the reciprocal interplay between scientific research and practical implementation. Another source that explores theory, research, and practice in alternative approaches of the AC method is Jackson, Lance, and Hoffman (in press).

Thirdly, and perhaps most important of all, this book is able to boast a significant number of the world's leading authorities on ACs amongst its contributors, either in their capacity as highly-regarded academics and/or highly experienced practitioners. In addition to this extensive level of knowledge and experience (collectively around 1,000 years) they bring a truly global appreciation of AC practice, as our 48 contributors come from 18 different countries spanning all continents.

Finally, we selected contributors on the basis of their reputations and expertise or experience with regard to a number of key AC-related issues. These included things such as:

- different approaches to centre design and implementation;
- exercise simulation design;
- diversity challenges;
- candidate motivation;
- the use of ACs to support different Talent Management strategies;
- establishing AC practice in different countries with varying levels of maturity in the world of assessment.

However, all of our contributors had one thing in common: their undeniable passion and enthusiasm for their work in the AC field, which we hope will be passed on to you!

The Three Themes and Why We Chose Them

We have chosen to focus on three major themes for this book and we now explain what they are and our rationale for choosing them.

THE INTERPLAY OF SCIENCE AND PRACTICE

This theme tackles the productive interplay of science and practice and how it helps to create top quality assessment centres and it is therefore featured throughout the whole book. Authors were asked to describe their own research and its implications or how they have used the research of others to design and implement specific assessment and development centres. In addition, researchers and practitioners alike propose research that is needed to provide guidance for new applications of the assessment centre method, especially how assessment and development centres contribute to corporate strategy and talent management. This theme perpetuates the long history of basic and applied research into the assessment centre method. Specific questions that contributors were asked to address included:

- What theories of psychology, management, leadership, organizational development, learning, and so forth, guided your development and implementation of the AC?
- What prior research studies or theories gave you guidance in designing the essential features of the AC?
  - Dimensions;
  - exercises;
  - observation and evaluation procedures;
  - method of integrating the observations;
  - feedback to assessees;
  - integration of the behavioural observations with other assessment information.

- What challenges did you face that have not been addressed in prior research? What future research would you like to see conducted to provide guidance for issues you faced?

The theme also exemplifies a more recent and broader emphasis on evidence-based management (Pfeffer and Sutton 2006). Practitioners will see how science informs good practice; scholars will find the chapters a rich source of ideas for conducting research into emerging issues in the field.

CORPORATE STRATEGY AND TALENT MANAGEMENT

This theme describes the use of assessment and development centres which are linked to corporate strategy and in particular talent management. These corporate strategies will often relate to issues or topics such as:

- globalization;
- innovation (products and markets);
- increased competition (for market share, the 'war for talent' and so forth);
- identifying leaders who are visionary, inspirational and/or entrepreneurial;
- customer service (greater focus on service or knowledge-based economies) and so forth.

The book focuses on how these strategies influence the design of the assessment centre in terms of the competencies, exercises and nature of the event, so that they can deliver what is required. Some of the questions that the contributors were asked to address included:

- What was the impetus for your development of the AC?
- What organizational problems were you trying to address?
- What opportunities were you trying to capitalize on?
- What business challenge(s) was the AC designed to meet?
- What top level executives or boards were involved in deciding to use the AC and shape its direction and scope?
- How did you get their support for this admittedly complex and costly human resource practice?
- What other HR practices was your AC linked with?
- How does your AC impact other HR interventions?
- What follow-up HR activities were needed for your AC to be successful?

Typical applications involve the use of assessment and development centres to screen external applicants, promote internal managers, diagnose developmental needs, or develop behavioural skills, often with the intention of changing organizational culture and values. It becomes clear as we read these accounts, that no matter what the ostensible reason for the AC, the intervention often results in a broader 'OD' (organization development) process. Practical examples/case studies are sprinkled throughout the book.

CROSS-CULTURAL IMPLICATIONS OF INTERNATIONAL AC PRACTICE

The third theme explores cross-cultural implications for the design of assessment centres and development centres. We are fortunate to have an impressive cross-section of international contributors from around the world who have described the special issues faced when designing an assessment or development centre in non-traditional cultures, moving an AC from one country to another, or assessing persons from different countries in the same assessment programme. Some of these issues relate to questions such as:

- How did the specific characteristics of the culture/country influence the ways you designed and implemented the essential features of the AC in relation to the:
  - dimensions;
  - exercises;
  - observation and evaluation procedures;
  - method of integrating the observations;
  - feedback to assessees;
  - integration of the behavioural observations with other assessment information.
- If your AC was carried out in two different cultural settings, how did you deal with any cross cultural considerations? In particular:
  - Did you produce materials (such as exercises) in different languages and how did you ensure linguistic and conceptual equivalence?
  - What training did you provide assessors to make reliable and valid observations and evaluations when faced with cultural differences?
- What special challenges did you face in your cultural setting to demonstrate the effectiveness of this AC in different countries?

A Brief Word About Language and Nomenclature

With an international set of contributors we needed to make some arbitrary decisions about the language and terminology that would be adopted. In order to cater to a global readership we decided that each chapter would be written in either UK or US English, depending on the author's preference, so you will find both centre and center and other words with different UK and US spellings used throughout the book.

Also the assessment centre (center) and its various derivatives are often referred to in a variety of different ways, so we have adopted a set of standard abbreviations throughout the book to refer to the different types of programmes, generally with their different primary purposes (see Table 1.1). However, we hasten to point out that the actual purpose does not always match the ostensible purpose.

Table 1.1   Overview of the different types of Assessment Centres

Type of Assessment Centre	Abbreviation	Typical purpose
Assessment Centre (er)	AC	Selection or promotion
Development Centre (er)	DC	Development; either during or after the centre
Developmental Assessment Center (re)	DAC	Development; either during or after the centre
Assessment Development Centre (er)	ADC	Unspecified so needs to be defined in each case

Otherwise we have left the contributor to explain their own choice of terminology as appropriate.

Structural Outline

The book is divided into three parts, with each part principally focusing on one of the three themes described above. Each part contains 10 or more chapters covering a wide range of issues relating to that particular theme. However, it should be noted that the content of many of the chapters naturally relates to more than one of the themes.

We would also like to point out that this is not the type of book that you need to read from cover to cover. You should feel free to dip in and out of the different chapters, depending on your interest. Each chapter can be read independently of the others, although we have asked our contributors to highlight relevant links with other chapters.

We briefly describe each part below and highlight some of the issues covered within each chapter.

PART I: AC BEST PRACTICE

This part addresses specific technical matters and best practice principles, as well as highlighting some of the most interesting recent research, such as the debate around the relative merits of a dimensions-based approach versus a task-based approach. Although the interplay between science and practice is a recurring theme throughout the book, it is clearly most evident in Part I.

Chapter 2 by an international team of Guenole, Chernyshenko, Stark, Cockerill, and Drasgow provides evidence that ratings in an AC demonstrate construct validity to measure intended dimensions. The authors describe a large international assessment programme which provided extensive assessor training and certified assessor competence to assess distinct competencies. Using unique analytic procedures, the results reveal that dimension ratings show considerable evidence of convergent and discriminant validity of post-exercise dimension ratings. The reasons why these results differ from the results of previous studies finding a lack of this form of construct validity are described in the chapter.

In Chapter 3, Jackson, Ahmad, Grace, and Yoon describe task-based assessment centres (TBACs), which adopt a different approach to research and practice of the AC method by focusing on task lists and roles within exercises, rather than dimensions across exercises. Although TBACs are designed in much the same way as traditional dimension-based assessment centres (DBACs), the authors argue that performance on the tasks is as important (if not more so) than performance on the dimensions. The authors' claims are supported by a case study describing a TBAC employed within a New Zealand-based organization and some further examples of similar practices employed in South Korea.

In Chapter 4, Lievens and Schollaert show how the concepts of Trait Activation Theory (TAT) can guide the development of assessment simulations and the actions of role players to ensure that participants display behaviours relevant to specified assessment dimensions. The theory of TAT explains that behaviours relevant to traits (that is, dimensions in the case of ACs) will be displayed if the situation (that is, exercises in the case of ACs) provides cues to elicit such behaviour. Situations can be made relatively 'strong' or 'weak' and thus provide different insights into individual differences in performance on dimensions. Practical examples are given, along with results of research studies showing the effects of different AC designs.

In Chapter 5, Prichard and Riley discuss the pros and cons of using off-the-shelf versus customized exercise simulations and highlight a range of factors that should be considered when deciding between the two options. Central to the decision is the concept of fidelity and the legitimacy of this approach is discussed and brought into question. In short they question the usual stance that customized exercise simulations are always best and reveal that the decision isn't quite as straightforward as had previously been thought. Thirteen questions provide the framework for considering when these two options are appropriate.

Chapter 6 by Meiring and van der Westhuizen provides insight into the long history of the applications of the AC method in South Africa and the recent challenges of human resource management in a diverse population. They show how computer-based technology can be used as a part of an AC programme to identify and develop individuals for a newly created role of service advisor in a financial institution. The chapter gives details on the process of working with IT colleagues to develop methods of presenting exercise materials, recording responses, scoring performance, integrating objective and behavioural judgements, and preparing reports. Other chapters that provide information on the history and culture of South Africa and how ACs have been implemented there include Chapters 13 by Buckett and 23 by Krause.

Chapter 7 by Dewberry discusses the relative merits of consensus meetings as opposed to pure arithmetic scoring, as a means of determining participant performance in an AC. It raises some interesting issues around the informal, latent processes that can occur within a consensus meeting which can have unforeseen impacts on the outcome, despite the use of a formal methodology within the meeting. It goes on to suggest ways of mitigating these effects and debates the relative merits of the two different approaches.

In Chapter 8, Fletcher covers the impact that an AC or DC can have on a candidate's motivation, well-being and self-awareness. It examines how attending an AC or DC can impact the candidate's emotional state (for example anxiety) during the event and how it can affect his/her performance. It also reviews the longer term effects on candidates of having been through an AC and how this can impact their psychological well-being, motivation and self perceptions.

Chapter 9 by Woodruffe raises the question as to whether ACs do enough to ensure they are sufficiently diversity-friendly. It looks at how ACs compare with other assessment methods in terms of addressing typical diversity concerns and reviews how certain aspects of diversity are unique to ACs, such as the diversity awareness of assessors, given the critical nature of their role in determining final AC outcomes. This is one particular topic where the often stated need for more focused research is strongly justified.

Hoffman and Baldwin, in Chapter 10, provide an integration of research and practice on assessment centres and multi-source performance rating (MSPR) systems. Similarities and differences in the two interventions are described. The strengths in the approaches and research findings of both ACs and MSPRs are highlighted. Lessons from MSPRs that can improve AC methodology are noted.

Chapter 11 by Thornton traces the 50-year history of reciprocal influences of theory, research, and practice of ACs and DCs. It shows how practice has been influenced by laboratory and field research in measurement, social cognition, judgement, and learning in four time-periods. In return, researchers have been stimulated by practices in job analysis, exercise development, ratings, and feedback, and issues of fairness and efficiency in ACs operations. Questions about the construct validity of AC ratings have stimulated an exchange of research studies and practice innovations in an attempt to improve the accuracy of diagnosis of performance on distinct dimensions of performance. A call for research on current challenges is intended to perpetuate this healthy interface of evidence-based human resource management.

PART II: CORPORATE STRATEGY AND TALENT MANAGEMENT

This part focuses on how ACs and DCs are used to further Corporate Strategy and to foster Talent Management in modern organizations. This part is sub-divided into two sections. One set of chapters describes the more traditional applications of ACs for selection and promotion. Here administrative consistency in implementation is essential and predictive accuracy is paramount. The second section includes chapters about DCs used for diagnosis, developmental planning, and development per se. In these instances differential diagnosis is essential and learning/training principles are paramount.

Many chapters deal with issues relevant to both selection/promotion and development. The placement in one or the other section may not represent the full contribution of the chapter. The reader will quickly realize that chapters in the first section often deal with issues related to development, and chapters in the second section often deal with issues of selection and promotion.

Chapter 12 by Birri and Melcher shows how the AC method has played a major role in the broader human capital management in Credit Suisse for over 30 years. ACs have been used in a variety of ways for individual contributor and managerial levels. While these ACs have involved different participants, assessors, assessment methods, feedback processes, and so forth, the common theme is that they all contribute unique information to talent management. For example, the dimensions dovetail with competencies tied to corporate strategy; middle managers who themselves have been assessed serve as assessors in subsequent years; new metrics are used to determine the contribution of ACs to human capital management. These and other discussions provide lessons on how to sustain ACs in organizations over time.

Chapter 13 by Buckett describes a very large-scale AC in South Africa designed to provide a skills audit of candidates seeking positions in a large government organization. The chapter shows how the designers incorporated a number of AC design features intended to improve the accuracy of assessments in the context of a nationwide programme carried out under strict time constraints and in a potentially volatile climate. The programme succeeded in providing useful, and bias-free, assessment for hundreds of candidates. Other chapters that provide information on the history and culture of South Africa and how ACs have been implemented there, include Chapters 6 by Meiring and van der Westhuizen and 23 by Krause.

Chapter 14, by an international team of Rupp and Searle, describes the application of the AC method to a special occupation, namely the placement of medical doctors to hospitals for medical specialty training across multiple settings in the UK. Challenges included the coordination of multiple stakeholders, the administration of mass repeated assessments in a tight timeframe, and the high stakes implications for both doctors and hospitals. The authors discuss how the programme can contribute to assessing relevant non-medical dimensions, provide standardized information for different host settings, and meet the demands of numerous stakeholders.

In Chapter 15 Premarajan describes an innovative programme capitalizing on the strengths of the AC method to assess candidates for certification as human resource (HR) managers in India. This national-level programme uses a combination of knowledge tests and behavioural exercises to test the competencies required by HR managers. The author discusses the need for talent in India's growing economy and the resultant need for skilled HR professionals to assess, select, and develop such talent. The HR assessment programme, designed by a national committee, included an HR competency model, the design of tests and behavioural assessment tools, assessor training, and the design of a deployment strategy.

Chapter 16 by Bergvall describes how ACs were introduced into Swedish Local Government within the city of Gothenburg to select future leaders. The process of convincing the City's Executive Board and designing the AC commenced in 2000 and a series of centres have been run at various levels during the last decade, with some 2,000 people attending the centres. This chapter provides a classic public sector case study (see Chapters 25 by Kim, 26 by Nosworthy and Ng and 28 by Liang and Liu for others) describing the complete process of designing an AC from scratch and implementing it over many years, culminating with a validation exercise to illustrate its worth.

In Chapter 17 Livings and Mitchell describe how a global manufacturing organization used an AC to develop a talent management solution aimed at stimulating cultural change in order to implement an innovation strategy over the next 15 years. A further challenge was the need to cater to different types of talents, Leaders, Innovators and Specialists, within the same AC, where they had to demonstrate their ability to perform within a rapidly changing environment. This had a major impact on the competencies being assessed, which included Learning Agility, and the types of simulation exercises required to measure them.

In Chapter 18, Betti and Monobe provide four case studies showing how a system of assessment and development, based on principles of the AC method, make contributions to a complex system of the corporations' strategic and operational decisions about promotion, career management, and employee development. Initiated in Brazil and then extended to other countries, these case studies show the cross-national relevance of many of the traditional practices of the AC method. Lessons learned include how to influence corporate decisions about the use of ACs, how to integrate ACs into a complex talent management system, and what alterations, if any, need to be made to implement ACs in a new culture.

Chapter 19 by Purdy describes the evolution of a series of AC initiatives within a large pharmaceutical sales organization over a period of 15 years aimed at accomplishing various talent management objectives in a commercial environment (see Chapters 12 by Birri and Melcher and 16 by Bergvall for some similar challenges). These include identifying and developing emerging leaders, determining their training needs, and planning for leadership succession. To date some 1,200 participants have attended the ACs or DCs with many progressing to director and senior executive positions, making this a truly effective, long-term programme.

Boyle in Chapter 20 reviews the influencing process used to gain acceptance of assessment and development centres (ADCs) as effective components of a talent management strategy within different organizations. This interesting challenge is investigated by the unusual approach of interviewing a panel of 10 highly experienced ADC practitioners, some of whom were in-house experts, with others being external consultants. The research examines three particular issues: ensuring alignment with the organization's strategic direction; getting buy-in from stakeholders and achieving organizational fit and maintaining support. The views expressed by the different panel members provide a valuable insight to some of the subtleties that need to be considered when trying to advocate an ADC programme. This chapter has widespread relevance to the successful implementation of any AC programme and thus it relates to many of the other chapters in this book, with particular links to Parts II and III and Boyle makes specific reference to Chapters 8 by Fletcher, 12 by Birri and Melcher and 21 by Thornton and Birri.

In Chapter 21, Thornton and Birri summarize their collective experiences over 50 years of seeing ACs come and go in organizations. They address the factors that lead to failure and success and provide suggestions for sustaining ACs over time. Ten factors leading to failure can be summarized as failures to comply with the state-of-the-art technical aspects of AC design and implementation. Making these mistakes often leads to the early demise of an AC, but do not necessarily lead to a long life. Other factors lead to sustainability over the long haul. These factors have to do with the conduct and context of the broader talent management programmes in each organization.

PART III: INTERNATIONAL ISSUES AND IMPLICATIONS

This part includes chapters emphasizing international implications. Authors describe the special issues encountered in designing and implementing assessment and development centres in multicultural settings. Whereas centres have operated for decades in North America, Western Europe, Israel, and South Africa, in recent years they have sprung up in developing countries. They have also been used more frequently when assessees come from more than one country.

Chapter 22 by Povah provides a summary of one of the most extensive global surveys into AC practices that has ever been conducted, with 443 respondents from a total of 43 countries spanning 5 continents. With ACs being conducted in every corner of the globe, it is more important than ever to maintain consistency by advocating the best practice standards that have made the AC the successful tool that it is. There is no doubt that cultural differences have influenced the design of some of these ACs in different parts of the World and this chapter examines some of those different features and approaches.

Chapter 23 by Krause is another survey of AC practices, in this case a comparison of operations in South Africa, Western Europe, and North America. The findings help us understand how ACs are being adapted in various countries in response to cultural differences and local concerns. ACs are not new to South Africa; in fact, they were first set up around 40 years ago. Their usage has expanded to the extent that a conference on ACs has been held annually since 1981. This survey documents the objectives, job analysis techniques, job requirements and dimensions, exercises and simulations, data integration processes, and feedback methods in the comparison region. Other chapters that provide information on the history and culture of South Africa and how ACs have been implemented there include Chapters 6 by Meiring and van der Westhuizen and 13 by Buckett.

In Chapter 24 Pendit shows how ACs have played a role in introducing transparency into HR processes in Indonesia as a part of general reform of government and business practices in the late 1990s and the 2000s. Amidst political and economic turmoil, organizations started to use the AC method to make selection and promotion decisions more open and merit-based. The author describes the special cultural characteristics that have required modification of some AC practices, for example, due to a lack of experience of reading complex written material, participants may need more time and pictorial displays to aid their understanding in the more analytical exercises.

Kim, in Chapter 25, provides the first comprehensive summary of AC practices in South Korea's government agencies. He describes the geographical, historical, political, and cultural context that shaped traditional personnel practices. He then shows how ACs have played an integral role in making selection, promotion, and developmental decisions more valid and fair. The implementation of ACs in South Korea hasn't been without its challenges and the author describes how these were tackled in two federal ministries and the city of Seoul.

In Chapter 26 Nosworthy and Ng describe ACs in four departments of the Singapore public service. ACs have been used in the Ministry of Education for appointment to school principalships, and in the Ministry of Foreign Affairs for graduate recruitment and more recently for selection. ACs have also been used to select young high-potential scholars to receive scholarships to attend the best universities around the world and to design developmental activities for high-potential officers for future leadership positions. Challenges to implementing ACs in Singapore are described, including lack of familiarity with the method, diversity in languages, and leakage of content in the AC process. Lessons learned from these and other experiences reinforce the need to build support for the programme and actions to sustain the method over time while making adaptations to meet changing conditions in the government.

In Chapter 27 Manji and Dunford provide insight into how ACs were first used in East Africa (principally Kenya and Uganda) and some of the challenges that this posed in trying to introduce the methodology to a developing HR community. These challenges included being aware of the key cultural differences that determine acceptable norms of behaviour, such as the attitude towards timekeeping and how this manifests itself in the performance of both assessors and participants. It highlights a number of interesting observations made by local HR professionals within organizations using ACs and how these have influenced their design and implementation.

Liang and Liu, in Chapter 28, provide one of the first insights into AC practices in China. For centuries, candidates for the civil service have been assessed for selection and promotion, and as early as World War II, ACs were used to select and train intelligence agents. But it was not until the 1980s that ACs were reintroduced for assessment in government organizations. Subsequently ACs spread to other types of organizations. The authors describe the differences in AC applications in the public sector, state-owned companies, multinational companies, and private Chinese companies.

In Chapter 29, Simonenko reveals some of the issues faced in trying to establish ACs in the former USSR, with a particular focus on Russia. ACs are relatively new to Russia, having only been in use for the last 20 years, so a challenge faced by the local AC experts, is how to get the wider HR and business community to accept the importance of adopting best practice. Thus the challenges are similar to those being faced in East Africa (see Chapter 27 by Manji and Dunford), Indonesia (see Chapter 24 by Pendit), or China (see Chapter 28 by Liang and Liu) and this is another example of the classic situation where 'a little knowledge is a dangerous thing'. The chapter explains the nature of some of these challenges and how they are tackled.

In Chapter 30, Hirose provides one of the first published summaries of AC practices in the private and public sectors in Japan in the past 40 years. Unique practices which suit Japanese national and corporate culture are described. For example, at the junior management level, group exercises are common, and group feedback is given. Both assessors and participants give feedback in group settings after the exercises. Assessors also watch the process of peer feedback in these group settings, because this is relevant to expectations of teamwork in organizational settings in Japan.

Chapter 31 by Fox and Haboucha describes AC practices in Israel, a country which has a long history of psychological assessment, including the AC, primarily for personnel selection. They provide an in-depth analysis of several professional challenges when ACs are trimmed down and yield poor results. They compare and contrast AC practices in Israel, Europe, and the United States. They challenge the commonly accepted requirement of strict standardization by pointing out that rigid structuring of assessment activities may sacrifice the insight assessors may get from more individualized assessment. The question is whether strict standardization limits validity. More important for these authors, is the amount of stage time for candidates and observation time for assessors when relevant behaviours can be assessed.

Finally, in Chapter 32 we provide an overview of all of the preceding chapters by summarizing some of the lessons learned from the contributions of our array of international authors. In the spirit of continuous improvement, we explore several critical questions raised about AC applications. That scrutiny leads naturally to suggestions for new research studies. We close by posing and providing a preliminary answer to the question: 'To what extent is the AC field evidence-based?' (Briner and Rousseau 2011). We conclude that considerable evidence has been accumulated over 50 or more years that the assessment centre method is a valuable intervention to select, promote, and develop human resource talent in diverse organizations in diverse countries.

Summary

Few, if any of the chapters deal with all three major themes, but a number make diverse contributions to understanding how assessment and development centres contribute to talent management in the global business world through the interface of science and practice. Thus, the reader will want to be alert to multiple contributions of chapters in various parts of the book. Certainly many chapters in Part III: 'International Issues and Implications', discuss how their applications have been guided by and are in need of good theory and research; and they discuss how applications contribute to talent management. Likewise, some of the more research oriented chapters in Part I: 'AC Best Practice', have direct application to improvement for selection/promotion and development. Finally, chapters in Part II: 'Corporate Strategy and Talent Management' often describe research findings and cross-cultural issues and how these impact the execution of various Talent Management initiatives and influence wider HR practices, in pursuit of an organization's Corporate Strategy.

Our hope is that the diverse contributions of the authors will stimulate interest amongst those who are just starting to learn about the AC method, provide new ideas for practice and research amongst current users and reinforce the passion for ACs amongst established adherents.

References

Ballantyne, I. and Povah, N. 2004. *Assessment and Development Centres* (2nd Edition). Aldershot: Gower.

Briner, R.B. and Rousseau, D.M. 2011. Evidence-based I-O psychology: Not there yet. *Industrial and Organizational Psychology: Perspectives on Science and Practice*, 4, 3–22.

Jackson, D.J.R., Lance, C.E. and Hoffman, B.J. (eds). In Press. *The Psychology of Assessment Centers*. New York, NY: Routledge.

Pfeffer, J. and Sutton, R.I. 2006. *Hard Facts, Dangerous Half-Truths and Total Nonsense: Profiting from Evidence-Based Management*. Boston: Harvard Business School Press.

Schlebusch, S. and Roodt, G. (eds). 2008. *Assessment Centres*. Randburg: Knowres.

Thornton, G.C. III, and Rupp, D.R. 2006. *Assessment Centers in Human Resource Management: Strategies for Prediction, Diagnosis, and Development*. Mahwah, NJ: Lawrence Erlbaum.

2

We're Doing Better than You Might Think: A Large-Scale Demonstration of Assessment Centre Convergent and Discriminant Validity

NIGEL GUENOLE, OLEXANDER CHERNYSHENKO,
STEPHEN STARK, TONY COCKERILL AND FRITZ DRASGOW

An assessment centre (AC) is a standardized evaluation of behaviour based on inputs from multiple assessment methods (International Taskforce 2009). In a typical AC, trained assessors rate candidates' performance on a predetermined set of behavioural dimensions across several exercises. Ratings for the same dimensions in different exercises, known as post exercise dimension ratings (PEDRs), are then combined into a set of dimension scores, as well as into a single performance score, known as the overall assessment rating (OAR). Because ACs are believed to measure managerial-level skills and abilities, and are known to predict future job performance, their use for personnel selection and executive development is widespread in applied settings (Thornton and Gibbons 2009). Despite their popularity, an increasing number of academic researchers in recent years have raised concerns over findings that ACs do not seem to measure what they purport to measure.

Studies of PEDRs reveal that ratings of the same dimension taken in different exercises are only weakly related and *should not* be aggregated into a specific dimension score. On the other hand, some studies found that ratings of different behaviours within the same exercise are almost always strongly related and *should* be aggregated into a specific exercise score. This conclusion has been substantiated by examining correlations between ratings organized into a multi-trait multi-method (MTMM) matrix (Campbell and Fiske 1959) and, more formally, by fitting a hierarchical confirmatory factor analytic (CFA) model where each rating is specified as a function of latent factors representing dimensions, exercises, and measurement error (Eid, Lischetzke and Nussbeck 2006, Marsh and Bailey 1991, Widaman 1985).[1]

Several meta-analytic reviews that summarize the problems with dimension ratings have been published in well-respected applied psychology journals (Bowler and Woehr 2006, Lance, Lambert, Gewin, Lievens and Conway 2004, Lievens and Conway 2001, Woehr and Arthur 2003). Perhaps the best illustration of the importance of this issue is a recent special section of the journal *Industrial and Organizational Psychology* on assessment centres. In the featured article, Lance (2008) argued that the weak evidence for dimensions to date is an accurate reflection of candidate behaviour, which is specific to each exercise rather than consistent across situations, as it was originally believed to be. He concluded that, based on the existing evidence, the current practice of giving dimension ratings within exercises should be abandoned in favour of scoring the performance of candidates on the exercises themselves. Curiously, in a series of critical commentaries that followed the article, authors pointed out that such a move would be impractical, or that AC ratings should not be analyzed with MTMM methods, but there was little conviction that assessment centres could ever be designed in a way that would yield data supporting scores for dimensions (Connelly, Ones, Ramesh and Goff 2008, Howard 2008, Rupp, Thornton and Gibbons 2008). Other authors too have previously advocated scoring exercises rather than dimensions (for example, Jackson, Barney, Stillman and Kirkley 2007).

In this chapter, we adopt a more direct stance in defending the use of dimensions in ACs as measures of important skills and abilities. We will point out that (a) most meta-analyses have relied extensively on studies conducted prior to 1998, (b) many of the earlier studies did not use currently recommended AC design features or inadequately implemented design features, (c) more recent data tend to show stronger evidence for dimensions, and (d) methodological improvements in applications of CFA would likely lead to stronger evidence of dimensions. We then introduce a large new data set involving a well-designed developmental AC that measures leadership behaviours and show that dimension factors are stronger than exercise factors, and the dimensions can be further strengthened by examining the results of the CFA MTMM analyses and by eliminating a handful of poorly performing PEDRs.

The Impact of Strong Design Features on PEDRs

The source of much of the momentum behind the move by Lance (2008) to reinterpret the historical pattern of AC results is a series of meta-analytic reviews that summarized the convergent and divergent validity from AC PEDRs over the last 30 years (Bowler and Woehr 2006, Lance, Lambert, Gewin, Lievens and Conway 2004, Lievens and Conway 2001, Woehr and Arthur 2003). From these meta-analyses, it is very clear that PEDRs are mutually determined by the individual and the exercise, it is only the relative contribution of each that is at issue. On the basis of these studies it appears that, at best, PEDRs are equally determined by both the individual and the exercise within which PEDRs are collected. These meta-analyses seem comprehensive by almost any standard,

---

1   Our discussion of assessment centre research is restricted to MTMM analyses of assessment centre PEDRs. However, MTMM analyses of assessment centre data can be also be made without ever making PEDRs if OARs are used as the basis of analyses. In this case, the 'exercise' is the assessment centre itself in relation to other selection methods, such as interviews or other psychological tests.

in relation to the breadth of studies synthesized, the timeframe over which the data were collected, and size of the samples included. This has suggested to many, including Lance (2008) and the authors of commentaries on his paper, that attempts to use design features have been largely unsuccessful at improving AC convergent and discriminant validity. However, we believe there is a compelling alternative view of the picture presented by these meta-analyses.

A time when we expect that Industrial and Organizational (IO) psychologists in industry became widely aware of the steps that could be taken to improve AC convergent and divergent validity, is when Lievens (1998) published his qualitative review of the literature on design features. Since this time, numerous developments have occurred in AC practice that point to the conclusion that older AC data sets might not be representative of ACs as they are run today. First of all, in part due to the work of Lievens (1998), there are now numerous refinements and improvements in the way that assessment centres are implemented (Howard 2008). For example, we better understand the most effective way to train assessors. We know that frame-of-reference training outperforms data-driven assessor training methods (Lievens 2001). We know that use of a behavioural observation checklist facilitates assessor accuracy, and that other things being equal, fewer dimensions seem easier to rate accurately than more, and so on (Lievens 1998, Woehr and Arthur 2003). There has also been an increase in the use of ACs for purely developmental purposes, in which a focus on the individual dimension score is more important than an overall score (Rupp et al. 2006). Both of these points suggest an increase in the quality of dimension measurement over recent years.

But each of the recent meta-analyses in the dimensions versus exercises debate that have swayed the opinion of so many IO psychologists did not analyze data representative of these new forms of AC. To illustrate, we examined the mean publication year of the studies in each of the four meta-analyses. This showed that the publication year of the majority of studies included in each meta-analysis is well before when Lievens (1998) published his qualitative review. In the Lievens and Conway (2001) study, the mean publication year was 1994, and 80 per cent of studies pre-1998. In the Woehr and Arthur (2003) meta-analysis, the mean publication year was 1990, and 93 per cent of studies came from before 1998. In the Lance et al. (2004) meta-analysis, the mean publication year was 1995, and 73 per cent of studies were from before 1998; and in the Bowler and Woehr (2006) study, the mean publication year was 1996, and 64 per cent of studies were from before 1998. The latter study, with the smallest proportion of studies from before 1998, showed the strongest evidence of dimensions. Further, there was substantial overlap across all of these meta-analyses with regard to the studies analyzed, and the total sample size across all meta-analyses was approximately 7,000. With these points in mind, from our perspective, several very important unanswered questions remain. Namely, would a more thorough examination of design features in a modern AC setting yield stronger evidence of dimensions than exercise effects? And can the application of rigorous methodology to analysis of data collected in such a setting help to refine the effectiveness of our measurement of dimensions? We turn to these issues now.

Design Features That Promote Convergent and Divergent Validity

The design features that have been shown to have some impact on the convergent and divergent validity of assessment centres are by now well known. These features include using job related dimensions, using well trained assessors, using carefully chosen dimension exercise combinations, providing assessors with observational aids, rotating assessors, keeping a low assessor to participant ratio, and applying a within-exercise rating approach (Lievens 1998, Woehr and Arthur 2003). But just like a closer look at the recent meta-analyses revealed a slightly different interpretation of cumulative AC findings, so too does a closer look at psychologists' typical implementation of design improvements. We will focus here on assessor training methods, which we believe show the greatest promise for improving convergent and divergent AC validity. To illustrate why typical assessor training approaches are not satisfactory, it is worth describing in detail the most advanced assessor training methods we identified in the literature, and outlining ways that this training could be adapted or improved. Such an assessor training method will then be coupled with other design features thought to lead to dimension measurement and implemented in our large scale AC study in the next section of our paper.

THE IMPORTANCE OF ADVANCED ASSESSOR TRAINING METHODS

Lievens (2001) conducted an experimental comparison of the effectiveness of schema-driven (that is, frame of reference) and behaviour-oriented (that is, data driven, or bottom up) assessor training approaches. We do not expect training of the standard applied in Lieven's paper is common in applied settings. The behaviour-oriented training workshop emphasized the importance of separating behavioural observation, behavioural classification, and evaluation of behaviour. The schema-driven training emphasized to participants that rater accuracy could be improved by knowing what ineffective, average, and effective behaviour looked like for each dimension, and that this mental framework should be used to scan and rate the stream of behaviours of AC candidates. Training for both conditions lasted 6 hours. This training duration is twice as long as the 3 hours for the frame of reference delivered by Noonan and Sulsky (2001), four times longer than the 90 minutes required for the frame-of-reference training in studies described by Schleicher, Day, Mayes and Riggio (2002) and Schleicher and Day (1998). However, we expect that such brief exposure to the principles of assessor training is unlikely to sufficiently ingrain the rigour required of assessors for effective candidate assessment.

Moreover, examining Lievens' (2001) training process in relation to the principles of modern instructional design systems (for example, Goldstein and Ford 2002) indicates several other areas that might be improved. For instance, the assessors do not appear to have received exercise-specific frame-of-reference training. In other words, they were not trained to rate behaviour in every exercise that would eventually be used in the ACs separately. While this lack of correspondence between the training conditions and ultimate assessment conditions is probably common in practice, rater training would ideally include instruction on assessing all forms of the AC exercise taxonomy described by Thornton (1992), that is, in-baskets, role plays, group exercises, presentations, and strategy exercises. This is an important point, because the form that an expression of a dimension takes in an in-basket could be very different from, for example, a role play exercise. In the schema-driven training, assessors only practiced rating the dimensions at three levels rather than the five levels that they were asked to use. This lowered the fidelity of the training by reducing the correspondence between the training and performance conditions. It would be better to train assessors to rate all levels of performance.

The training in the studies described probably reflects the reality of AC practice in relation to another area of instructional design, namely training evaluation. Although the goals of many of these studies actually *required* that everyone who completed training go on to act as assessors, this should not necessarily occur. Trainees may or may not acquire the knowledge, skills and ability to accurately assess behaviour. Therefore, there needs to be an evaluation of the competence of trainee assessors, and those who fail to meet requisite standards for accurate assessment should be required to retake training, or disqualified from assessing candidates. Otherwise, the quality of ratings is compromised. However, we have found that in applied settings, it is more common than not to simply assume that anyone who has completed assessor training is sufficiently competent to serve as an assessor. The training we describe in our AC study below will address these typical shortcomings by being longer in duration, specific to each AC exercise, combining dimension and frame-of reference training across two stages, and including an examination after each stage with a pre-specified pass mark.

Approaches to Analysis in Assessment Centre Research

Since Campbell and Fiske's (1959) landmark paper, one of the principal ways AC data sets are analyzed has been to visually examine the correlation matrix that results from correlating each PEDR column in the data set with every other PEDR column in the data set. Under this approach of inspecting the PEDR correlation matrix, convergent and discriminant validity exists for the data matrix of the AC if, *on average*, the correlations between the same dimensions measured in different exercises are greater than the correlations between different dimensions measured in the same exercise. But, authors have criticized this method for its subjectivity. Instead, today it is recommended that MTMM data matrices are analyzed with confirmatory factor analysis (CFA). Under CFA representations of AC data, the variances and co-variances of PEDRs are described as a function of underlying latent variables representing the hypothesized behavioural dimensions, the exercises within which the dimensions were measured, and error terms representing systematic and random measurement error. This corrects for unreliability of the PEDRs, allows broader links to other variables external to the assessment centre, and importantly, permits formal statistical evaluations of model fit (or in other words, an assessment of how well the observed relationships among the ratings agree with the hypothesized relations among the variables). A number of models have been proposed that describe hypothesized relationships of PEDRs, some of which propose correlated or uncorrelated dimensions and/or correlated or uncorrelated exercises. Typically, the best fitting from a series of models is selected. The models vary according to whether the dependencies amongst PEDRs made within the same exercises are accounted for using residual correlations or 'exercise factors'. Today the latter approach is considered more methodologically appropriate (Conway, Lievens, Scullen, and Lance 2004). And within this approach, a series of models is estimated that vary in the number of dimensions, the number of exercises, and whether or not the dimensions and exercises are correlated amongst themselves. Note, however, that the dimension factors and exercise factors are usually assumed to be mutually uncorrelated. Convergent validity for dimensions exists if the average dimension loading is greater than the average exercise loading, and divergent validity exists if the correlations amongst dimensions are low (Marsh and Bailey 1991, Widaman 1985). While the CFA method and its application to MTMM data has been labelled inappropriate and a cause of the assessment centre paradox (Lance 2008), in this paper we show strong evidence of dimension measurement using precisely this approach.

A Large-Scale Examination of Design Features on Convergent and Divergent Validity

We have presented the case that existing and oft-quoted meta-analyses do not accurately portray the effect of sound design features in improving dimension measurement. The data these meta-analyses synthesize are too old and AC structures have changed radically since these data sets were collected. We have further argued that typical assessor training is not sufficiently well implemented to permit assessors to provide accurate PEDRs. Our final proposition is that a large new data set that incorporates other design features, PEDRs made by better trained assessors, and is analyzed using appropriate MTMM CFA approaches can improve dimension measurement. To demonstrate the effect of these steps, we now present results from analyses of developmental ACs run for Fortune 500 firms in a leadership development context. The developmental ACs on which these data are based relate to the High Performance Behaviour (HPB) leadership competency model (Cockerill 1989). The HPB model contains 12 dimensions of leadership behaviour, and was developed based on a qualitative review of the academic literature on effective leadership behaviour. This review included seminal research including the Ohio State studies (Stogdill 1950), the Michigan studies (Likert 1961), and studies carried out at Harvard (Bales 1950). We provide a brief definition of each HPB competency in Table 2.1.

Table 2.1   Brief descriptions of high-performance behaviour

Dimension		Description
Information search	IS	Gathering a rich variety of information from many different sources about events
Concept formation	CF	Linking information to form new ideas that explain the underlying causes of events
Conceptual flexibility	CX	Seeing issues from many different perspectives to compare options prior to taking action
Empathy	EM	Encouraging others to express openly their real thoughts and feelings
Teamwork	TW	Creating effective teams within the unit and across related departments or functions
Developing people	DP	Providing staff with the resources, coaching, feedback, and training to develop their capability
Influence	IN	Using persuasive arguments and the goals and interests of others to build support for ideas

Building confidence	BC	Making your stance on issues clear
Presentation	PR	Making clear and concise presentations and establishing effective communication processes
Proactivity	PO	Designing implementation plans and outlining actions and responsibilities
Continuous improvement	CI	Setting goals and targets, and monitoring progress, in order to improve performance
Customer focus	CU	Setting targets focused on adding value for the customer

Design Features to Improve the Measurement of Dimensions

We based our developmental AC design on the principle that the more design features we implemented that were thought to improve dimension measurement, the better the quality of measurement was likely to be. We expect that this is consistent with the suggestions of Arthur, Woehr and Maldegen (2000), that while these design aspects have been shown to independently increase the construct validity of assessment centres, their combined use is likely to lead to the greatest evidence of construct validity in assessment centres. One common recommendation we did not follow was to reveal the dimensions to participants, as we felt that revealing the dimensions to them would be contrary to the notion of leadership. Leadership refers to a process of social influence (Chemers 2000) and revealing the dimensions to be assessed would create a situation in which the participants *are* socially influenced. Those design steps we did follow are described now.

JOB-RELATED DIMENSIONS

The HPB dimensions in the current study were defined in job related language and grounded in job analysis, as recommended by Lievens (1998). While there is actually a good case for using fewer dimensions than 12 in AC design to minimize cognitive demands on assessors, it was more important to examine evidence for the 12 competency structure because this was the structure all of our assessors were trained to observe. If convergent and discriminant validity is demonstrated with a relatively large number of dimensions, it is even more likely that such evidence will be found with fewer dimensions.

APPROPRIATELY SELECTED EXERCISE-DIMENSION COMBINATIONS

The exercise to dimension mapping, presented in Table 2.2, was based on discussions with subject matter experts (SMEs) and subsequent consensus among three further subject matter experts of the likelihood that different exercises would elicit the different behaviours. For example, it was unanimously agreed difficult by the judges for empathy to be displayed in the in-basket exercise. Hence, the in-basket was not used to assess Empathy.

AN OBSERVATIONAL AID

The assessors were all provided with a table of dimension descriptions and indicators corresponding to five levels that ranged from highly ineffective to highly effective.

Similar dimensions were grouped together. This corresponds directly to the schema learned during frame-of-reference training.

LOW PARTICIPANT-TO-ASSESSOR RATIO WITH ASSESSOR ROTATION

The assessor-participant ratio was always one assessor to two participants. Each AC included 6 participants. Assessors each observed two participants per exercise, and rotated to another pairing of candidates in a subsequent exercise. Because there were three assessors, six participants, and six exercises, each participant was rated by each assessor twice.

ASSESSOR TRAINING

The assessor training used in the current study was a combination of performance dimension training (for example, Woehr and Huffcutt 1994) and frame-of-reference training (for example, Lievens 2001, Woehr and Huffcutt 1994) delivered in two stages, spread over 4–6 weeks and 2–6 months, respectively. At the end of stage one, a 30-minute examination was held where trainees were required to accurately classify a minimum of 40 out of 50 statements into the dimension that subject matter expert consensus indicated they belonged. Importantly, performance dimension training was dispersed over a considerably longer period than even the schema driven training outlined by Lievens (2001), it required substantial self-study, and was subsequently tested to see whether minimum proficiency levels had been met. During the frame of reference training in stage two, the performance dimensions learned in stage one were elaborated to include levels of performance within each dimension. Importantly, assessors practiced rating behaviour in each of the exercises that were ultimately used in our assessment centres, that is, role plays, in-baskets, presentations, and group exercises. This occurred across five two-hour face-to-face sessions over the course of training. Prospective assessors were also required to achieve 80 per cent correct in an exam where they classified 60 short descriptions and 20 long descriptions of behaviour from past assessment centres into dimensions and levels that SMEs have agreed they belong. As part of the exam, the trainee assessors were required to successfully role play the interview with the examiner acting as an interviewee, and score the in-basket to 80 per cent accuracy against SME defined standards.

Method

PARTICIPANTS

Participants in the development centres were 1,205 executives from a wide variety of white-collar occupations in banking, pharmaceuticals, manufacturing and transport industries. The sample was two-thirds male; age and ethnicity were not recorded. Participants were of varying levels of managerial experience, though all were responsible for the performance of other staff, or thought to be capable of moving into such roles. Scores were used solely for personal development planning and not for personnel-related decisions.

EXERCISES

The simulations used in the current research all related to situations relevant to the running of an arm of an international business. The simulations are all derived from the exercise typology proposed by Thornton (1992). In the in-basket simulation, participants responded in paper and pencil format to 12 internal pieces of correspondence representative of the work that arrives in a typical manager's inbox. In the role play, participants took part in a one-to-one interview to elicit information from a laconic employee portrayed by an assessor. The first cooperative group exercise involved working to agree on a global brand strategy to present to the board for a new product. The second cooperative group exercise required the participants to develop a business strategy to address sales problems for presentation to the board. In the competitive group exercise, participants represented different geographical regions of a business and promoted an idea that they had been given beforehand which conflicted with ideas of other participants. In the presentation exercise, participants were given 30 minutes preparation time before talking for between 5 and 10 minutes on a business simulation topic. The dimensions assessed in each exercise are presented in Table 2.2.

Table 2.2   Dimensions assessed in each exercise

Dimension	In-basket	Interview	Group 1	Group 2	Group 3	Presentation
IS	✓	✓	✓			
CF	✓	✓	✓	✓	✓	
CX	✓	✓	✓	✓	✓	
EM			✓	✓	✓	
TW			✓	✓	✓	
DP	✓	✓	✓	✓		
IN			✓	✓	✓	✓
BC	✓	✓	✓	✓	✓	✓
PR		✓	✓	✓	✓	✓
PO	✓	✓	✓	✓	✓	
CI	✓	✓	✓	✓	✓	
CU	✓	✓	✓	✓	✓	

IS = Information Search; CF = Concept Formation; CX = Conceptual Flexibility; EM = Empathy; TW = Teamwork; DP = Developing People; IN = Influence; BC = Building Confidence; PR = Presentation; PO = Proactivity; CI = Continuous Improvement; Cu = Customer Focus.

ASSESSORS

Assessors in the current study were drawn from an international pool of HPB accredited consultants on an as needed basis from around the world. All potential consultants were thoroughly screened to ensure they had a suitable background, often, but not always including a psychology degree. Assessors were subsequently trained in the HPB framework. Assessors were not permitted to serve as assessors until they had met the accreditation requirements described above, including passing the accreditation exam.

ANALYSIS

Because each candidate was assessed by a single assessor in each exercise, we fitted a series of CFA models that are appropriate when each candidate is assessed by a single rater in any given exercise (Eid et al. 2006). We used the MPlus computer programme (Muthén and Muthén, 2006). We report multiple indices in addition to the model x^2, because the sensitivity of x^2 to sample size can lead to rejection of theoretically appropriate models (see, for example, Bentler and Bonnet 1980). Additional indices included the root mean square error of approximation (RMSEA; Steiger 1990); Bentler's (1990) Comparative Fit Index (CFI); and the Tucker and Lewis (1973) Index (TLI). The RMSEA is a measure of badness of fit per degree of freedom, and conventionally values less than .05 are considered indicative of good fit (Browne and Cudeck 1993). The CFI and TLI are incremental fit indices which range between 0 and 1. Values over .9 are considered acceptable fit, while values over .95 indicate excellent fit (Hu and Bentler 1999).

Following selection of the best model, we examined the variance in PEDRs that could be explained by dimension and exercise factors, respectively, by inspecting the mean standardized loading for dimensions and comparing it to the mean standardized loading for exercises. In the current context, standardized loadings can be thought of as indications of how well ratings made within exercises assess their intended competencies. As noted by Lievens and Conway (2001), standardized parameter estimates of loadings are particularly useful for this purpose, as they represent proportions of true variance explained in PEDRs by dimensions and exercises. In addition, we amended our initial model to remove poorly performing PEDRs. This process is similar to removing poor items in test development. The result provides a final measurement model for further validation, and yields a better estimate of the ratio of dimension to exercise variance.

Results

The best fitting model among all of the models Eid et al. (2006) suggested are appropriate for situations where a single observation is taken on the participant in each exercise was the correlated dimensions correlated exercises (CDCE) model. This model showed excellent fit by conventional standards (see, for example, Hu and Bentler 1999), with x^2 = 1541.67, df = 1191, CFI = .94, TLI = .93, and RMSEA = .02. Fit for other models estimated is available from the authors. Under MTMM CFA analyses, strong dimension factor loadings are an indicator of convergent validity, and low inter-dimension correlations are an indicator of discriminant validity (Eid, Lischetzke and Nussbeck 2006, Marsh and Bailey 1991, Widaman 1985). Table 2.3 shows factor loadings for dimensions and exercises in the original model. Results from computing the mean of the factor loadings for dimensions and exercises in Table 2.3 showed that the mean loading for dimensions was .43, while the mean factor loading for exercises was .32. This result is distinguished from past work in the AC area because there is more variance in PEDRs explained by dimensions than by exercises. The only published study previously to demonstrate this effect previously was by Arthur, Woehr and Maldegen (2000). However, that study was based on a small sample and its results have not been replicated in any study since of which we are aware.

It is also important to look at the average loadings within dimensions to examine the quality of measurement by dimension, rather than the quality of measurement of all dimensions overall. The final row of Table 2.3 contains the average loading for each dimension and the average loading for each exercise. This row of Table 2.3 shows that every PEDR made in the presentation exercise yields a loading on its target factor that is below the mean loading for its target dimension. The mean loading for Influence is .41, while the PEDR loading for Influence from the presentation exercise is just .25. The mean loading for Building Confidence is .37, while the loading for the Building Confidence PEDR from the presentation exercise is just .32. Finally, the mean loading for the Presentation behaviour is .47, and the loading of the Presentation PEDR taken from the Presentation exercise is only .31. Removal of the entire presentation exercise, therefore, could improve the precision of measurement for each of the dimensions that is currently measured by the presentation exercise, while concurrently shortening the time required of candidates in the actual AC. We decided to remove the entire presentation exercise from this model, and to consider removal of the PEDR of the Presentation dimension from future assessment centres.

Importantly, we recommend that analysts do not include fewer than three ratings from different exercises per competency in the model, and ideally, include four ratings per competency. This is because three ratings are needed to estimate a model for any given competency, but four are required to estimate the appropriateness of the model (see, for example, Bollen 1989). It can be seen from Table 2.3 that each of the dimensions that a Presentation PEDR contributes to is already well defined by at least three, and usually four other PEDRs from other exercises. For example, the Information Search competency is measured in three exercises, namely, the in-basket, the interview, and the second group exercise. This can be seen from the first three rows of Table 2.3 under the Information Search competency column that read IS-IB, IS-I, and IS-G2.

We re-estimated the best fitting model (that is, the CDCE model) from our previous series of analyses without the PEDRs taken in the Presentation exercise. Note that while the fit of the original and modified CFA models cannot technically be compared due to omission of variables in the second model, the fit of our new model was also excellent, with x^2 = 1338.82, df = 1044, CFI = .95, TLI = .94 and RMSEA = .02. The impact of these changes on dimension measurement is illustrated in Table 2.4, in the form of substantial increases in the size of the average loading for all dimensions that had a PEDR removed, with little change in the average loading for exercise factors. In particular, the average dimension loading for Influence increased from .41 to .46, the average loading for Building Confidence improved from .37 to .39, and the average dimension loading for Presentation improved from .47 to .55. Importantly, this targeted improvement of dimensions occurred while simultaneously reducing the length of the AC process.

Table 2.3   Factor loadings for dimensions and exercises in the original model

	Dimensions parameter loadings												Exercise parameter loadings					
	IS	CF	CX	EM	TW	DP	IN	BC	PR	PO	CI	CU	IB	I	G1	G2	G3	PR
IS-IB	.35												.39					
IS-I	.30													.16				
IS-G2	.33															.29		
CF-IB		.37											.33					
CF-I		.46												.31				
CF-G1		.52													.06			
CF-G2		.41														.34		
CF-G3		.32															.33	
CX-IB			.19										.29					
CX-I			.31											.21				
CX-G1			.44												.35			
CX-G2			.48													.29		
CX-G3			.42														.30	
EM-G1				.56										.27				
EM-G2				.57											.10			
EM-G3				.46												.29		
TW-G1					.62									.28				
TW-G2					.59											.21		
TW-G3					.39												.34	
DP-IB						.32							.22					
DP-I						.43								.32				
DP-G1						.55									.23			
DP-G2						.22										.38		
IN-G1							.53								.24			
IN-G2							.52									.25		
IN-G3							.32										.41	
IN-PR							**.25**											**.48**
BC-IB								.31					.29					
BC-I								.35						.44				
BC-G1								.49							.21			
BC-G2								.42								.35		
BC-G3								.36									.46	
BC-PR								**.32**										**.58**
PR-I									.45					.45				
PR-G1									.54						.22			
PR-G2									.61							.14		
PR-G3									.46								.59	
PR-PR									**.31**									**.63**
PO-IB										.17			.48					
PO-I										.45				.43				
PO-G1										.56					.23			
PO-G2										.41						.29		
PO-G3										.38							.39	
CI-IB											.16		.34					
CI-I											.38			.39				
CI-G1											.53				.03			
CI-G2											.49					.23		

	Dimensions parameter loadings												Exercise parameter loadings					
	IS	CF	CX	EM	TW	DP	IN	BC	PR	PO	CI	CU	IB	I	G1	G2	G3	PR
CI-G3											.41						.31	
CU-IB												.32	.53					
CU-I												.51		.35				
CU-G1												.77			.19			
CU-G2												.28				.38		
CU-G3												.36					.33	
Mean	.32	.42	.37	.53	.53	.38	.41	.37	.17	.39	.39	.45	.36	.34	.21	.27	.37	.56

IS = Information Search; CF = Concept Formation; CX = Conceptual Flexibility; EM = Empathy; TW = Teamwork; DP = Developing People; IN = Influence; BC = Building Confidence; PR = Presentation; PO = Proactivity; CI = Continuous Improvement; CuF = Customer Focus. IB = In-basket; I = Interview; G1 = First Group Exercise; G2 = Second Group Exercise; G3 = Third Group Exercise; PR = Presentation.

Table 2.4   Factor loadings for dimensions and exercises in the revised model

	Dimensions parameter loadings												Exercise parameter loadings					
	IS	CF	CX	EM	TW	DP	IN	BC	PR	PO	CI	CU	IB	I	G1	G2	G3	PR
IS-IB	.348												.39					
IS-I	.30													.17				
IS-G2	.34															.29		
CF-IB		.36											.33					
CF-I		.46												.31				
CF-G1		.52													.06			
CF-G2		.42														.33		
CF-G3		.33															.33	
CX-IB			.19										.29					
CX-I			.31											.21				
CX-G1			.43												.35			
CX-G2			.48													.27		
CX-G3			.42														.30	
EM-G1				.55									.		28			
EM-G2				.58												.09		
EM-G3				.45													.30	
TW-G1					.60										.30			
TW-G2					.60											.20		
TW-G3					.39												.32	
DP-IB						.31							.22					
DP-I						.44								.31				
DP-G1						.54									.23			
DP-G2						.23										.40		
IN-G1							.51								.25			
IN-G2							.56									.26		
IN-G3							.30										.40	
IN-PR							R											R
BC-IB								.30					.29					
BC-I								.35						.44				
BC-G1								.50							.21			
BC-G2								.43								.36		
BC-G3								.35									.47	

Table 2.4   Factor loadings for dimensions and exercises in the revised model *concluded*

	Dimensions parameter loadings												Exercise parameter loadings					
	IS	CF	CX	EM	TW	DP	IN	BC	PR	PO	CI	CU	IB	I	G1	G2	G3	PR
BC-PR								R										R
PR-I									.50					.51				
PR-G1									.56						.24			
PR-G2									.66							.14		
PR-G3									.48								.65	
PR-PR									R									R
PO-IB										.16			.49					
PO-I										.44				.43				
PO-G1										.56					.22			
PO-G2										.41						.28		
PO-G3										.38							.39	
CI-IB											.16		.34					
CI-I											.39			.39				
CI-G1											.53				.04			
CI-G2											.49					.23		
CI-G3											.41						.32	
CU-IB												.32	.54					
CU-I												.52		.33				
CU-G1												.76			.18			
CU-G2												.28				.38		
CU-G3												.35					.35	
Mean	.32	.42	.37	.52	.53	.38	.46	.38	.55	.39	.39	.44	.36	.34	.21	.27	.38	R

IS = Information Search; CF = Concept Formation; CX = Conceptual Flexibility; EM = Empathy; TW = Teamwork; DP = Developing People; IN = Influence; BC = Building Confidence; PR = Presentation; PO = Proactivity; CI = Continuous Improvement; CuF = Customer Focus. IB = In-basket; I = Interview; G1 = First Group Exercise; G2 = Second Group Exercise; G3 = Third Group Exercise; PR = Presentation.

We stress here that these model modifications are post hoc, and because they are empirically driven, such decisions need to be balanced with construct coverage issues and they require cross-validation. But we also wish to emphasize that such an interactive development process, which sits at the heart of traditional scale development (Clark and Watson 1995), can substantially improve the quality of dimension measurement in ACs. Nevertheless, typical scale development approaches such as this are rarely discussed or applied in the AC literature.

Conclusion

To us, the dimension versus exercise debate that has recently received considerable attention in the I/O community is reminiscent of tensions about the relative influence of the person and the situation in personality assessment literature (See Mischel 1973). Social psychologists have also shown on numerous occasions that situations do matter (for example, Milgram 1963). If the situations are structured and strong, as they are in the AC design, we should actually expect fairly strong exercise factors. Yet, as argued here and elsewhere (Lievens 1998; Woehr and Arthur 2003), by carefully training assessors, using fewer dimensions, providing behavioural observation checklists, and so on, it is possible to observe cross-situational consistency in a person's behaviour, which justifies the use of dimension scores without recourse to arguments based on the impracticality of not using dimensions. We showed this by presenting data from a large new sample of developmental AC candidates, because recent meta-analyses analyzed data sets that are too old and are not representative of ACs as they can be run today, following state-of-the-art prescriptions of design improvement.

While this study was correlational, precluding causal interpretations in relation to the current findings, certain prominent features of the design seem likely explanations. First, our data set was collected since the millennium and was collected using modern AC design features. The data summarized by past meta-analyses often do not. Second, the training that we described was more comprehensive than training usually implemented, covering all exercises that are used in an actual assessment centre. In addition to including both performance dimension and frame-of-reference training, the duration of the training was considerably longer than typical AC training, and length of training has been shown to be a moderator of rater effectiveness (Woehr and Arthur 2003). The assessors were also required to pass an assessor exam before being permitted to participate in live development centres, and a minimum standard of proficiency is required before assessors are considered accredited. While some might think that the assessor training we presented is impractical, we have found that a model where a network of highly trained and accredited assessors is used around the world, as and when required, is a model that suits both the lifestyles of independent IO psychologists, and the needs of an international consulting business.

Another important reason why the current study shows greater levels of convergent and discriminant validity among PEDRs is possibly because frame-of-reference training was used here, but was not used in a large proportion of previous studies. A meta-analysis by Woehr and Huffcutt (1994) indicated that while frame of reference training is the single most effective assessor training method, it is used in AC research only half as much as the most frequently described assessor training method namely, rater bias training. Given that this meta-analysis was conducted at around the time of the average publication year of most of the studies included in recent meta-analyses on the dimension versus exercise debate (as described in the introduction), it would appear much of the data on which earlier construct validity conclusions regarding AC validity were based on data generated using assessors with less than optimal training.

This chapter has also shown how an iterative psychometric development process, similar to that used in traditional scale development, can be adapted to improve the measurement precision of ACs. By carefully selecting the PEDRs that are made within each exercise, both in the design of the AC and on the basis of empirical considerations, measurement of dimensions can be improved considerably. This was demonstrated by looking at the average factor loadings for dimensions, identifying poorly performing PEDRs and removing them from the model. While these steps are routine in traditional scale development (Clark and Watson 1995), their use in AC design is not so prominent. However, by adopting these practices, we have shown that measurement of dimensions can be improved markedly. Finally, it is important to note that despite the stronger evidence of dimension measurement than exercise measurement, exercise effects were still present and need to be modelled by exercise factors for adequate model fit. This chapter has simply demonstrated how the variation due to dimensions might be increased. In our view, embracing the coexistence of dimension and exercise factors, and studying the determinants of both, will provide the richest and most accurate understanding of the determinants of candidate performance in ACs.

References

Arthur, W., Jr., Woehr, D.J., and Maldegen, R. 2000. Convergent and discriminant validity of assessment center dimensions: A conceptual and empirical reexamination of the assessment center constructrelated validity paradox. *Journal of Management*, 26, 813–835.

Bales, R.F. 1950. A set of categories for the analysis of small group interaction, *American Sociological Review*, 15, 257–263.

Bentler, P.M. 1990. Comparative fit indexes in structural models. *Psychological Bulletin*, 107, 238–246.

Bentler, P.M. and Bonnet, D.C. 1980. Significance tests and goodness of fit in the analysis of covariance structures. *Psychological Bulletin*, 88, 588–606.

Bollen, K.A. 1989. *Structural Equations with Latent Variables*. Wiley Series in Probability and Mathematical Statistics. New York: Wiley.

Bowler, M.C. and Woehr, D.J. 2006. A meta-analytic evaluation of the impact of dimension and exercise factors on assessment center ratings. *Journal of Applied Psychology*, 91, 1114–1124.

Browne, M.W. and Cudeck, R. 1993. Alternative ways of assessing model fit, in *Testing Structural Equation Models*, edited by K.A. Bollen and J.S. Long. Beverly Hills, CA: Sage, 136–162.

Campbell, D.T. and Fiske, D.W. 1959. Convergent and discriminant validation by the multitrait-multimethod matrix. *Psychological Bulletin*. 56, 81–105.

Clark, L.A., and Watson, D.W. 1995. Constructing validity: Basic issues in objective scale development. *Psychological Assessment*, 7, 309–319.

Chemers, M. 2000. Leadership research and theory: A functional integration. *Organizational Behavior and Human Decision Processes*, 13, 46–78.

Cockerill 1989. Managerial competence as a determinant of organizational performance. Unpublished doctoral dissertation. London Business School, London.

Connelly, B.S., Ones, D.S., Ramesh, A. and Goff, M. 2008. A pragmatic view of assessment center exercises and dimensions. *Industrial and Organizational Psychology: Perspectives on Science and Practice*, 1, 87–100.

Conway, J.M., Lievens, F., Scullen, S., and Lance, C. 2004. Bias in the correlated uniqueness model for MTMM data. *Structural Equation Modeling*, 11, 535–559.

Eid, M., Lischetzke, T. and Nussbeck, F.W. 2006. Structural equation models for multitrait-multimethod data. In *Handbook of Multimethod Measurement in Psychology*, edited by M. Eid and E. Diener. Washington, DC: American Psychological Association, 283–299.

Goldstein, I., and Ford, K. 2002. *Training in Organizations*. Belmont, CA: Wadsworth.

Howard, A. 2008. Making assessment centers work the way they are supposed to. *Industrial and Organizational Psychology: Perspectives on Science and Practice*, 1, 98–104.

Hu, L.T., and Bentler, P.M. 1999. Cutoff criteria for fit indexes in covariance structure analysis. *Structural Equation Modeling*, 6, 1–55.

International Task Force on Assessment Center Guidelines 2009. Guidelines and ethical considerations for assessment center operations. *International Journal of Selection and Assessment*, 17, 24 –253.

Jackson, D.J.R., Barney, A., Stillman, J. and Kirkley, W. 2007. When traits are behaviors: The relationship between behavioral responses and trait-based overall assessment center ratings. *Human Performance*, 20, 415–432.

Lance, C.E. 2008. Why assessment centers (ACs) don't work the way they're supposed to. *Industrial and Organizational Psychology: Perspectives on Science and Practice*, 1, 87–100.

Lance, C.E., Lambert, T.A., Gewin, A.G., Lievens, F. and Conway, J.M. 2004. Revised estimates of dimension and exercise variance components in assessment center post-exercise dimension ratings. *Journal of Applied Psychology*, 09, 377–385.

Lievens, F. 1998. Factors which improve the construct validity of assessment centers: A review. *International Journal of Selection and Assessment*, 3, 141–152.

Lievens, F. 2001. Assessor training strategies and their effects on accuracy, interrater reliability, and discriminant validity. *Journal of Applied Psychology*, 86, 255–264.

Lievens, F., and Conway, J.M. 2001. Dimensions and exercise variance in assessment center scores: A large-scale evaluation of multitrait-multimethod studies. *Journal of Applied Psychology*, 86, 1202–1222.

Likert, R. 1961. *New Patterns of Management*, New York, NY: McGraw-Hill.

Marsh, H.W., and Bailey, M. 1991. Confirmatory factor analysis of multitrait-multimethod data: A comparison of the behavior of alternative models. *Applied Psychological Measurement*, 15, 47–70.

Milgram. S. 1963. Behavioural Study of Obedience. *Journal of Abnormal and Social Psychology*, 67, 371–78.

Mischel, W. 1973. Toward a cognitive social learning theory of personality. *Psychological Review*, 80, 252–283.

Muthén, L. and Muthén, B. 2006. *Mplus User's Guide*. 4th Edition. Los Angeles, CA: Muthén and Muthén.

Noonan, L.E., Sulsky, L.M. 2001. Impact of frame of reference and behavioural observation training on alternate training effectiveness criteria in a Canadian military sample. *Human Performance*, 14, 3–26.

Rupp, D.E., Gibbons, A.M., Baldwin, A.M., Snyder, L.A., Spain, S.M., Woo, S.E., Brummel, B.J., Sims, C., and Kim, M.J. 2006. An initial validation of developmental assessment centers as accurate assessments and effective training interventions. *The Psychologist-Manager Journal*, 9, 171–200.

Rupp, D., Thornton, G.C., and Gibbons, A.M. 2008. The construct validity of the assessment center method and usefulness of dimensions as focal constructs. *Industrial and Organizational Psychology: An exchange of Perspectives on Science and Practice*, 1, 87–100.

Schleicher, D.J., Day, D.V. 1998. A cognitive evaluation of frame of reference rater training. Content and process issues. *Organizational Behavior and Human Decision Processes*, 73, 76–101.

Schleicher, D.J., Day, D.V., Mayes, B.T., and Riggio, R.E. 2002. A new frame-of-reference training: Enhancing the construct validity of assessment centers. *Journal of Applied Psychology*, 4, 735–746.

Steiger, J.H. 1990. Structural model evaluation and modification, *Multivariate Behavioral Research*, 25, 214–12.

Stogdill, R.M. 1950. Leadership, membership, and organization. *Psychological Bulletin*, 47, 1–14.

Thornton, G.C. III. 1992. *Assessment Centers and Human Resource Management*. Reading, MA: Addison Wesley.

Thornton, G.C. III, and Gibbons, A.M. 2009. Validity of assessment centers for personnel selection. *Human Resource Management Review*, 19, 169–187.

Tucker, L.R, and Lewis, C. 1973. The reliability coefficient for maximum likelihood factor analysis. *Psychometrika*, 38, 1–10.

Widaman, K.F. 1985. Hierarchically nested covariance structure models for multitrait-multimethod data. *Applied Psychological Measurement*, 9, 1–26.

Woehr, D.J. and Arthur, W., Jr. 2003. The construct-related validity of assessment center ratings: A review and meta-analysis of the role of methodological factors. *Journal of Management*, 29, 231–258.

Woehr, D.J., and Huffcutt, A.I. 1994. Rater training for performance appraisal: A quantitative review. *Journal of Occupational and Organizational Psychology*, 67, 189–205.

3 An Alternative Take on AC Research and Practice: Task-Based Assessment Centers[1]

DUNCAN JACKSON, MOHD HANAFIAH AHMAD,
GARY GRACE AND JEEYUN YOON

Assessment centers (ACs) are often designed to provide information about individuals with respect to scores on dimensions. Howard (1997) defines dimensions as collections of traits, learned skills, readily demonstrable behaviors, basic abilities, attitudes, motives, knowledge, and other characteristics. While this definition includes a plethora of variables, our contention is that most of them are united by an allusion to characteristics of an underlying nature. Importantly, some authors, such as Howard (2008), have suggested that dimensions were never intended as trait measures. Despite this, in practice, we argue that dimensions (aka competencies) are often treated, at least at the conclusion of an AC, as though they are constructs that can be meaningfully aggregated across exercises. In this respect, common dimensions such as oral communication, written communication, influencing others, and stress tolerance (from Arthur, Woehr and Maldegen 2000: 821) are routinely summarized across multiple AC exercises. In this sense, dimensions take on a primary role in ACs whereas exercises often take on the role of a method used to arrive at dimension scores (Arthur and Villado 2008).

But what if exercises play a much more important role than merely acting as methods for arriving at dimension scores? This is a question posed by proponents of Task-Based ACs (TBACs). TBACs represent an alternative perspective on ACs and are defined as an approach to the assessment of performance based on multiple job-related simulations or work roles. More traditional dimension-based ACs (DBACs) are very similar to TBACs in many ways. Table 3.1 shows that DBACs and TBACs are equivalent on several design features. However, a major distinction between the approaches is that, in TBACs, behavior is primarily assessed within simulation exercises rather than on dimensions assessed across exercises.

---

1   The authors would like to thank SangHee Kim, SunKyung Lee and Brian Hoffman for their assistance in developing this chapter.

Table 3.1   Similarities and differences between two assessment center approaches

Design feature		Assessment center type	
		Dimension-based	Task-based
1.	Job analysis/ competency modeling	Analysis of tasks, job requirements, and attributes	Emphasis on tasks and job roles and requirements, however attributes can provide supplementary information
2.	Focus of observation	Behavioral responses	Behavioral responses
3.	Variables to be assessed	Dimensions across exercises	Task lists/roles within exercises
4.	Exercises	Simulations with varying degrees of fidelity, depending on job requirements	Simulations with varying degrees of fidelity, depending on job requirements
5.	Potential assessors	Managers, HR Specialists, psychologists	Managers, HR Specialists, psychologists
6.	Assessor training	Frame of reference (FOR) with an emphasis on rating dimensions	Frame of reference (FOR) with an emphasis on rating tasks or roles
7.	Rating forms	Can potentially include task lists but always include dimensions	Include task lists and exercises are treated as measures of work roles
8.	Feedback	Based on performance on dimensions with examples of behavior in exercises	Based on work role performance within exercises
9.	Integration discussion	Emphasizes dimensions across exercises	Emphasizes performance within exercises
10.	Specific scoring	Summarizes dimension scores	Summarizes exercise/role scores
11.	Overall scoring	Based on dimensions	Based on exercise/role scores

In this chapter, TBACs are introduced with respect to their background, theoretical underpinnings, comparisons with traditional dimension-based assessment centers (DBACs), and guidelines for development. Reference is made to a real world TBAC case study in New Zealand and, additionally, we explore an application of TBAC features in South Korea.

Where Do Task-Based Assessment Centers Come From?

TBACs arise out of criticisms of dimensions. Surprisingly, such criticisms are almost as old as the AC technique itself. In discussing military precursors to modern ACs, Vernon and Parry (1949) state that the aim of AC-akin techniques was to get away from atomistic, trait-based descriptions of human behavior. Yet, even in the 1930s, it was likely that users of such techniques "continued to treat them as tests of leadership, cooperativeness, and the like" (Vernon and Parry 1949: 65).

In the organizational realm, Gorham (1978) suggested that dimensions were best considered merely as labels for sets of behavioral descriptors. However, such labels, according to Gorham, often gained a status elevated above any behavioral information gathered during an AC and ended up forming the basis for many employment decisions. Later, Sackett and Dreher (1982) and Turnage and Muchinsky (1982), among others, found empirical evidence against the measurement of AC dimensions as stable constructs and showed evidence that different dimensions correlated strongly within exercises. They also found that correlations among measures of the same dimensions across exercises were relatively weak. Taken together, this phenomenon is commonly referred to as *the exercise effect* and has been repeated ad nauseum ever since (Lance 2008a, 2008b).

The exercise effect is often regarded as a criticism of dimension-based measurement. From a different perspective, however, it provides empirical evidence in favor of the TBAC approach. From a TBAC perspective, the exercise effect suggests that AC scores should be aggregated within exercises as opposed to indicating measurement problems. A key component of the TBAC framework is a focus on behavior that is tied to particular exercises. Strong within-exercise correlations provide support for this idea.

With regard to formalizing TBAC concepts, Goodge (1988) published a pioneering AC article endorsing the use of checklists indicating whether participants either performed or did not perform a given task in a particular exercise. Several other key suggestions were proposed, including the endorsement of job-relevant exercises akin to work samples. In keeping with empirical findings surrounding relatively strong within-exercise correlations, Goodge also suggested that candidate performance commonly varies by exercise and that assessment procedures should reflect this. Moreover, in line with more recent research, Goodge suggested that rating overall task performance is valuable and, in addition, that integration discussions can, in some cases, be replaced by using arithmetically aggregated scores such as averages.

Subsequent to Goodge, little or nothing was written on TBACs until an article almost a decade later by Lowry (1997), who produced a set of developmental guidelines. Lowry's article reinforced many of the ideas mentioned by Goodge and was even more profound in terms of its task focus. Expanding upon Goodge, Lowry emphasized the use of task-analysis to help ensure the job-relevance of exercises and suggested formally scoring TBACs on the basis of exercise-specific task lists, with the added enhancement of rating the quality of performance on each task via a scaled response.

Theory and Research Related to Task-Based Assessment Centers

Available empirical research on TBACs is currently limited to around six journal articles (Jackson, Atkins, Fletcher, and Stillman 2005; Jackson, Barney, Stillman, and Kirkley 2007; Jackson, Stillman, and Atkins 2005; Jackson, Stillman, Burke, and Englert 2007; Jackson, Stillman, and Englert 2010; Russell and Domm 1995) and a small collection of conference publications (see Lance, in press). Preliminary research has focused on two major theoretical threads for TBACs, namely *systems theory* and *behavioral consistency* (Jackson 2007, in press; Jackson, Stillman et al. 2010). Rather than focusing solely on subcomponents of human behavior, systems theory acknowledges that a multitude of variables interact in concert to produce behavioral output (Kast and Rosenzweig 1972).

In this respect, Jackson et al. (2010) suggest that participant factors such as traits, AC design factors such as the amount of job analysis, rater factors such as levels of bias, and organizational factors such as culture, all interact during an AC to produce a manifest exercise-specific work role performance (discussed later) as well as a general performance (GP). GP represents the occurrence where, for example, a participant tends to perform well across a range of exercises. While, in TBAC mode, GP is based on exercise performance, it has traditionally been assumed that overall assessment ratings (OARs) are based on performance on dimensions. Some evidence exists, however, to suggest that GP based on exercises and the traditional OAR based on discussions about dimensions are very strongly correlated (Jackson, Barney et al. 2007). Participants, design, raters, and organizational factors all serve as inputs into a system. These input factors interact and, in turn, influence the production of output behavior.

While systems theory may help to explain some of the inner workings of TBACs and ACs generally, behavioral consistency is regarded as a useful way of explaining why TBAC scores might be related to such outcomes as job performance (Jackson 2007, in press). The principle underlying behavioral consistency simply states that behavior in a particular situation will be consistent with behavior in similar situations (Wernimont and Campbell 1968). In fact, this idea is congruent with systems theory, in that the behavioral output from a job-relevant set of TBAC simulation exercises should be consistent with behavioral output on the job. Thus, the relationship is theorized to be between two systems; the AC system and the job performance system, both of which should bear similar features.

Only one known study has specifically investigated the criterion-related validity of TBACs. Jackson (2007) found a task-based overall exercise rating (OER) correlated $r = .42$ (uncorrected for range restriction and attenuation) with supervisory ratings of job performance for a managerial position taken a year later. This represents a promising start, however, further studies are needed on the criterion-related validity of TBACs. Other related research suggests that developmental feedback based on tasks is at least as effective as dimension-based feedback (Thornton et al. 1995). Additionally, Kluger and Denisi (1996) suggest that specific behavioral feedback is more adaptive than feedback which focuses attention on personal characteristics. Task-based feedback highlights the influence of the situation on behavior. Moreover, Lance (in press) reports evidence of meaningful nomological network relationships with TBAC-based scores and other measures, as well as reliability estimates in the region of the .80s to .90s.

Given the research findings, when is it more appropriate to apply a DBAC or a TBAC for the purposes of selection or development? The answer to this question, as yet, remains uncertain because of the modest TBAC research database that has, as yet, accumulated. The information so far obtained suggests that TBACs are at least as useful as DBACs for a range of purposes. This probably isn't surprising, given how many similarities there are between the two approaches (see Table 3.1).

How are Task-Based Assessment Centers Developed?

In this section, we cover general principles on how to develop TBACs. In some cases, this can be achieved by altering an existing bespoke or off-the-shelf DBAC. In other situations, it may be necessary to develop a TBAC from scratch. Whatever the approach, the architect will be aided by an understanding of the fundamental elements of a TBAC: namely, the job-analysis strategy underlying the process; exercise design principles, scoring; and rater training strategies, each of which are described below.

EXERCISES ASSESS WORK ROLES

Probably the most obvious practical difference between DBACs and TBACs relates to an absence of individual cross-exercise dimensions in the latter. Rather than assessing on the basis of such dimensions, TBACs are scored on the basis of task lists that are specific to each exercise (Lowry 1997). Thus, in a TBAC, each exercise is treated as though it is a substantive measure, in and of itself. Here, exercises are measures of work-related roles, akin to the classic work on managerial roles by Mintzberg (1973). In this respect, a presentation exercise could be thought of as an assessment of the *liaison* role, where a manager is required to maintain a rapport with the audience. Likewise, a fact-finding exercise involving an employee dispute could be thought of as an assessment of the *disturbance handler* role, where a manager takes corrective action to resolve a crisis.

To assess contextualized work roles in a TBAC, each exercise carries an associated task-list associated, such that the number of task lists equals the number of exercises included in the entire AC. A simplified example of one such exercise is shown in Tables 3.2 and 3.3. Note, however, that TBACs are *always* defined by the presence of multiple exercises and a comprehensive example would show multiple exercises and their associated task-lists. A single exercise does not allow for the assessment of GP, which TBAC research, so far, suggests is an important element of the process (Jackson, Stillman et al. 2010, Lance et al. 2007). Also, a single exercise does not constitute an AC, but is better defined as an individual performance test (see Gatewood, Feild, and Barrick 2008).

In Table 3.2, instructions are given for an example exercise, which involves a group discussion and individual presentation based on three videos showing an employee engaging in potentially maladaptive behavior. This exercise is relevant to Mintzberg's (1973) *disturbance handler* role. As the example implies, the exercises used in TBACs are often similar to those used in traditional DBACs. An obvious practical difference, however, occurs with respect to the manner in which the exercises are scored at the end of the process. Here, each candidate receives item-level scores, for which the associated task list can be used as a development aid. Candidates also receive aggregate scores on each exercise and a GP score, which is formed by an aggregate of performance on all exercises.

Table 3.2   Example of an instruction guide

Managing challenging employees exercise
Instructions: This exercise is intended for managerial level participants. In the exercise, the participant is exposed to a series of three videos that have been taken from security cameras within the organization. The first video shows an example of the employee apparently taking company property without permission. The second video shows what could be an example of the employee participating in the sexual harassment of another employee. The third video shows an example of the employee ostensibly engaging in a violent episode whilst at work. Formal complaints have been laid against the employee, with relation to the second and third videos. The participant needs to discuss the videos with other group members for 10 minutes. In turn, each group member needs to prepare a 10-minute presentation on how they think the current situation should be managed with respect to the video evidence that has been collected. As the assessor for this exercise, your job is to rate the performance of the participant in terms of their capacity to offer suggestions about how to best manage the employee under scrutiny. Rate the quality of these suggestions using the rating scale that follows. Note that standards for performance have been previously established through training. 1.   Certainly below standard 2.   Somewhat below standard 3.   Unsure, probably below standard 4.   Unsure, probably above standard 5.   Somewhat above standard 6.   Certainly above standard

Table 3.3 shows an example of a rating form for a TBAC exercise. This includes a list of tasks that a participant needs to complete in order to be successful on the exercise. Note that the tasks are specified with a level of generality so as to allow for multiple manifestations of appropriate behavior. For example, there could be a number of different ways in which a participant could respond to other group members in an affable manner. Although oriented towards an assessment of observable responses, this process is, however, not completely free of inference. As with any judgmental behavioral measure, raters in TBACs must still make a judgment about the quality of a response. However, an advantage here is that there is no requirement to make judgments beyond these observable behaviors (for example, into high-level dimensions).

The quality of performance on each task is rated in terms of the extent to which it meets a standard, in this case on a scale ranging from 1 to 6 (see Table 3.2). Schemata around standards for performance are established during assessor training. Note, also, the presence of an overall task score at the end of the task list in Table 3.3, which can be derived simply by averaging all individual task scores, creating a weighted average, or, if necessary, by discussion (Jackson, Stillman et al. 2005; Lowry 1997). Overall within-exercise task scores can then be similarly aggregated across exercises to produce an OER. Thus, each individual task score represents performance specific to each exercise (work role), while the OER represents GP (Jackson 2007; Jackson, Stillman et al. 2010; Lance et al. 2007).

Table 3.3   Example of a task-checklist

Managing challenging employees exercise		
	Task item	**Task score**
1.	Gives priority to seeking appropriate legal advice with a view to protecting the rights of the organization and the employee.	
2.	Suggests actions that would not be regarded as threatening to the employee or that would not exacerbate the situation (for example, speaking harshly to the employee).	
3.	Makes suggestions that are conducive to maintaining the confidentiality of all parties involved.	
4.	Makes suggestions around compiling as much evidence as possible whilst maintaining confidentiality.	
5.	Given that some of the evidence may involve criminal activity, makes suggestions around involving the police (as opposed to taking the law into their own hands).	
6.	Suggests that actions should have been taken to ensure the health, safety, and well-being of any potential victims involved in these events.	
7.	Makes suggestions around involving senior members of staff and ensuring that executives are aware of the situation and how it is being managed.	
8.	Makes suggestions around how to manage the company reputation and how to mitigate any potential damage in that regard.	
9.	Responds to other group members in an affable manner (for example, using positive body language, smiling, welcoming others).	
10.	Encourages other group members where appropriate (for example, asks questions of others, attempts to elicit responses from less forthcoming members of the group).	
11.	Speaks clearly and uses language that is appropriate for the audience.	
12.	Presents items of interest in a manner that is logical and easy to understand.	
Overall task score		

JOB ANALYSIS FOR TASK-BASED ASSESSMENT CENTERS

The aim, for a TBAC, is to derive a set of behavioral measures that are as job-relevant as possible. The degree of job relevance is crucial because, as stated above, the hypothesis is that any relationship between task scores and job performance is due to consistency between behavior in a job simulation and the actual job. Following this logic, greater content similarities between simulations and actual jobs create better conditions for prediction. Job analysis is, therefore, important to this approach, and, given that the aim in a TBAC is to assess task performance related to work roles, task analysis has been argued as presenting an effective basis. The task analysis methods used in TBACs do not differ from those observed in other areas in psychology and detailed guidance in this regard is available through a range of sources (see Lowry 1997; Pearlman and Sanchez 2010; Williams and Crafts 1997). In developing TBACs, however, it would often be impractical to create exercises for every work situation that could be identified through a task analysis. Rather, the suggestion is to simulate only the most challenging situations that a worker may face. The assumption here is that if the participant is able to succeed on a small set of the most challenging work situations then, logically, they should also be able to succeed on the range of less challenging situations that might be encountered on the job.

A concern for practitioners could stem from how TBAC information can be integrated into a competency framework for an organization. A solution to this arises from the idea that, in TBACs, each exercise is considered to be a measure of a work role or multiple work roles. Frameworks are available to help guide decisions about the selection of appropriate roles and include the classic management role framework from Mintzberg (1973), which covers three major roles (*informational, decision-making,* and *interpersonal roles*) along with seven more specific roles (*monitor, disseminator, spokesperson, disturbance handler, entrepreneur, negotiator, resource allocator, figurehead, leader,* and *liaison roles*). Russell and Domm (1995) also provide a role framework covering eight roles (*judgment, organization and planning, forcefulness, initiative, energy, decisiveness, behavioral flexibility, impact, leadership, oral communication,* and *social sensitivity*). Based on its content, a given exercise could be regarded as a measure of one or even multiple roles. The role titles provide a language that is congruent with that often expressed in competency models and provides an impetus for integration between TBACs and competencies. For example, the competency *decision-making* (defined as "uses good judgment in resolving problems," Tett et al. 2000: 218) is conceptually similar to the role *judgment* (defined as the "degree to which decisions of high quality are made as required on the job," Russell and Domm 1995: 30).

EXERCISE DESIGN FOR TASK-BASED ASSESSMENT CENTERS

Exercises for use in TBACs can vary with respect to their level of fidelity. In line with Lowry's (1997) suggestions, a desirable outcome is to include exercises that are samples of an actual job. However, TBACs in the research literature have successfully involved lower-fidelity situational exercises (for example, Jackson, Stillman et al. 2005, Jackson, Stillman et al. 2010), and, as such, they can be used for a range of blue- and white-collar positions. In fact, the exercises used in traditional ACs are often the same as those used in TBACs, except that TBACs place more emphasis on the importance of these exercises and their job relevance.

Thornton and Mueller-Hanson's (2004) guidelines on simulation development are pertinent to TBACs. Adapting from these guidelines, development should cover:

- the purpose of the assessment and the resources that are available;
- the use of the task analysis information to assist in determining the types of situations that are job-relevant;
- establishing the level of difficulty for the TBAC and the extent to which it assumes prior knowledge of the job;
- consultation with subject matter experts about what form the exercises should take and how many should be used;
- preparing materials such as instruction sheets and rating forms;
- piloting exercises and revising their content;
- conducting a psychometric evaluation on obtained ratings.

The number of exercises selected, as a rough guide, should be three or more, in order to reasonably assess GP. Examples of instructions and scoring sheets are shown in Tables 3.2 and 3.3. Of reassurance is that within-exercise scoring approaches are deemed acceptable under current international guidelines on AC development (International Task Force on Assessment Center Guidelines 2009). As such, TBACs represent bone fide ACs. A number of different AC exercise types can be used for a TBAC, but the overall goal should be for the exercises to be as job-relevant as possible. Examples of such exercises include group discussions, oral presentations, problem-solving exercises, group discussions, role plays, in-basket exercises, and business games (see Thornton and Mueller-Hanson 2004). In some circumstances, work samples may also be appropriate, depending on work characteristics and job level.

TRAINING FOR TASK-BASED ASSESSMENT CENTERS

It has long been suggested that it is potentially easier to train raters on TBAC task lists than on dimensions (Goodge 1988, Jackson, Stillman et al. 2005, Lowry 1997). This idea is predicated on the notion that TBACs do not require raters to make inferences about dimensions on the basis of behavioral output. Rather, raters make a quality judgment of the behavior itself without drawing further inferences. In keeping with this focus, rater training in TBACs focuses, primarily, on task checklists (see Tables 3.2 and 3.3 for an example).

A typical training procedure for a TBAC might cover (a) familiarizing assessors and role players with exercise content, assessment materials, and rating scales, (b) allowing time for role players (if used) to rehearse their parts, (c) familiarization with common rater errors, and (d) standard-setting training involving practice assessments. Standard-setting training involves developing shared schemata for raters vis-à-vis standards for performance. The goal is to have all assessors sharing similar standards when they see participants performing in the AC. Similar to DBACs, frame of reference (FOR) training principles are often recommended for use in TBACs for standard-setting purposes (Jackson, Atkins et al. 2005, Jackson, Barney et al. 2007, Jackson, Stillman et al. 2005).

From Dimensions to Tasks: A Case Study of a New Zealand Organization

TBAC scoring approaches, like those described above, have been used in several organizations in New Zealand (Jackson, Ahmad, and Grace 2010, Jackson, Atkins et al. 2005, Jackson, Stillman et al. 2010). A nationwide retail organization based in New Zealand made the recent step of converting their existing DBAC scoring approach into that of a TBAC. The organization under scrutiny is one of the largest of its kind in New Zealand and employs around 8,500 individuals in 86 outlets. Their AC was used for the selection of high-potential candidates into management programs and had been in existence for around 10 years in the traditional DBAC mode where dimension scores were aggregated across exercises. A year after the organization switched to a TBAC scoring approach, we conducted structured interviews with three members of the executive team to gauge their reactions to the change. There is currently an absence of research in terms of practitioner perceptions of TBACs (Lance, in press) and the present, qualitative case study provides preliminary, albeit anecdotal, insights in this regard. Key themes and direct quotes are summarized below from these interviews.

In the original DBAC, six to eight dimensions were assessed in five exercises over a 2-day period. The assessor group was mainly composed of managerial staff. DBAC training lasted one day and covered observation skills as well as practice and familiarization with exercises and dimensions. In training for TBAC mode, more emphasis was given to behavioral observation skills and each exercise was considered to be a measure of a managerial role. Executives commented that time spent on integration discussions during ACs had reduced from a day in DBAC mode to around just 2 hours in TBAC mode. Between six and eight task list items were used per exercise in TBAC mode and the exercises constituted a mix of off-the-shelf and bespoke approaches. The latter were developed to reflect "real work experience." In terms of changes vis-à-vis feedback, two executive managers commented that the feedback system had not really changed and that, previously, candidates had been provided with feedback that focused on exercise performance. This is concordant with Howard's (2008) comments that dimensions are not treated like traits in practice.

The executive panel was asked how the DBAC and TBAC modes differed from a practical perspective. On the integration discussion at the end of the AC, they stated that this was the "area that has changed the most." The session had become much shorter and performance was summarized by exercises rather than by dimensions. They stated that the integration was easier and more enjoyable. The new focus was also oriented toward "performance overall rather than a focus on smaller aspects of their performance." This observation is in keeping with research on the importance of GP in TBACs and, perhaps, the idea that managers are sensitive to such information (see Jackson, Stillman et al. 2010, Stillman and Jackson 2005).

With regard to resistance to change, the executives tended to state that this was minimal and, after trying TBAC scoring, they were open to the new approach. In terms of impact on participants and assessors, the general reflection was that the biggest affect had been on the assessors. The process was considered to be more user-friendly and less time-consuming. Feedback was considered to be more easily deliverable. A manager also commented that TBACs were "much easier for our non-expert observers (for example, line managers) to understand and participate in." This comment corresponds to similar suggestions in the literature (Jackson, Stillman et al. 2005).

To summarize, in this qualitative case study of a New Zealand-based organization, switching from a DBAC to a TBAC mode resulted in few or no changes to the way in which feedback was delivered. Feedback had traditionally been communicated on the basis of within-exercise performance. The major difference noted by the executive managers surrounded the integration discussions at the end of the process. Such discussions were found to be less complex and of a shorter duration in TBAC mode. Little or no resistance to change was experienced when changing to the TBAC mode and, in fact, was generally accepted by assessors and participants in the focal organization. Although information on disadvantages was requested in this study, no such information was provided. Larger studies are required to ascertain, in greater detail and from a broader perspective, the advantages and, particularly, the disadvantages when moving from a DBAC to a TBAC approach.

Within-Exercise Assessment Center Scoring in Korea

Another country that has implemented aspects of the TBAC scoring approach is South Korea (Heo and Shin 2010). According to Lim (2004), Korean organizations often apply ACs for selection purposes where a large number of applicants are involved. In this regard, Heo and Shin (2010) state that a number of practitioners in South Korea score different dimensions within exercises to save time and cost. Heo and Shin also reported evidence, in a Korean context, for the reliability of a within-exercise scoring approach in ACs.

Further issues about content were raised in another study of a South Korean AC that was used to select government directors in Seoul (Lee 2007). In this AC, five different types of exercise (in-basket, group discussion, analysis and presentation, and a role play with an additional interview) were developed to assess four dimensions (*change management, problem analysis, persuasiveness,* and *communication skills*). Exercises were designed following international guidelines (International Task Force on Assessment Center Guidelines, 2009), but the definitions and details of the dimensions differed slightly from those that are typically used. For example, the AC guidelines for the Civil Service Commission in Korea define dimensions as behaviors that are performance-related, job-specific, anchored to situations, and observable. Moreover, they state that assessors should provide feedback on specific behavioral responses from participants. In a similar vein, although developmental ACs have rarely been used in South Korea, there is evidence to suggest that assessors in such procedures tend to give exercise-specific feedback even when they are trained to give dimension-based feedback (Kim 2010).

The above findings suggest that there are content issues and design details that are unique to Korean ACs, many of which focus on the specificity of behavior in particular contexts. However, none of these studies explain why these differences exist and how to improve ACs in South Korea. There are several possible explanations for these differences, including cross-cultural issues and cost-saving efforts driven by large-scale assessment programs.

As in other East Asian countries, people in Korea tend to show high collectivism, power distance, and a culture driven by context (Hofstede 1980). In this regard, Yoon (2009) compared two different cultural groups, North American and South Korean people, on their concepts of leadership characteristics. She found that Korean respondents had difficulty in constructing a list of leader attributes or verbalizing their thoughts or concepts in this respect when compared to American respondents. Korean respondents reported that this was because a focus on leader attributes underemphasizes the role of contextual factors. Thus, the within-exercise emphasis described in Heo and Shin's work on ACs appears to fit well with Korean cultural norms that accentuate contextual influences.

Conclusion

TBACs represent an approach to ACs that treats each exercise as a substantive measure of a work role (or roles), such as the managerial roles described by Mintzberg (1973). TBACs are also characterized by the fact that they do not involve scoring dimensions across exercises and, rather, they use task lists that are specific to each exercise. The output from a TBAC includes exercise-specific scores representing performance on work roles and GP, the latter of which offers suggestions on performance tendencies on a range of work roles. Behavioral consistency provides a basis for the criterion-related validity of TBACs, whereby performance on a job-relevant simulation is intended to predict behavior in similar situations. As exercises are regarded as measures of work roles in TBACs, when choosing roles for assessment, the AC architect needs to be cognizant of which roles are likely to be important to an organization in the future. Thus a strategic approach to job analysis and role selection is necessary. In an anecdotal case study presented in this chapter, a New Zealand-based organization found the TBAC approach to be less time consuming and less complex than a traditional DBAC approach. In South Korea, where aspects of TBAC scoring are also used, TBACs appear to be well suited to cultures that emphasize context. To echo Lance's (2008a, 2008b) calls, while initial studies have shown some promising results, further studies of TBACs are warranted from a broad range of perspectives.

References

Arthur, W. Jr. and Villado, A.J. 2008. The importance of distinguishing between constructs and methods when comparing predictors in personnel selection research and practice. *Journal of Applied Psychology*, 93, 435–442.

Arthur, W. Jr., Woehr, D.J. and Maldegen, R. 2000. Convergent and discriminant validity of assessment center dimensions: A conceptual and empirical reexamination of the assessment center construct-related validity paradox. *Journal of Management*, 26, 813–835.

Gatewood, R.D., Feild, H.S. and Barrick, M.R. 2008. *Human Resource Selection*. 6th Edition. Mason, OH: Thomson South-Western.

Goodge, P. 1988. Task-based assessment. *Journal of European Industrial Training*, 12, 22–27.

Gorham, W.A. 1978. Federal executive agency guidelines and their impact on the assessment center method. *Journal of Assessment Center Technology*, 1, 2–8.

Heo, C.G. and Shin, K.H. 2010. *Reliability and validity of nested-designed assessment center*. Paper to the Korean Society for Industrial Organizational Psychology, Daejon, Korea, June.

Hofstede, G. 1980. *Culture's Consequences: International Differences in Work-Related Values*. Beverly Hills, CA: Sage.

Howard, A. 1997. A reassessment of assessment centers, challenges for the twenty-first century. *Journal of Social Behavior and Personality*, 12, 13–52.

Howard, A. 2008. Making assessment centers work the way they are supposed to. *Industrial and Organizational Psychology: Perspectives on Science and Practice*, 1, 98–104.

International Task Force on Assessment Center Guidelines. 2009. Guidelines and ethical considerations for assessment center operations. *International Journal of Selection and Assessment*, 17, 243–253.

Jackson, D.J.R. 2007. *Task-specific assessment centers: Evidence of predictive validity and fairness*. Paper to the Society for Industrial and Organizational Psychology, New York, NY, April.

Jackson, D.J.R. (in press). Theoretical perspectives on task-based assessment centers. In *The Psychology of Assessment Centers*, edited by D.J.R. Jackson, C.E. Lance and B.J. Hoffman. New York: Routledge.

Jackson, D.J.R., Ahmad, M.H. and Grace, G.M. 2010. *Are Task-Based Assessments Best Represented by Absolute Situational-Specificity?* Paper to the Society for Industrial Organizational Psychology, Atlanta, Georgia.

Jackson, D.J.R., Atkins, S.G., Fletcher, R.B. and Stillman, J.A. 2005. Frame of reference training for assessment centers: Effects on interrater reliability when rating behaviors and ability traits. *Public Personnel Management*, 34, 17–30.

Jackson, D.J.R., Barney, A.R., Stillman, J.A. and Kirkley, W. 2007. When traits are behaviors: The relationship between behavioral responses and trait-based overall assessment center ratings. *Human Performance*, 20, 415–432.

Jackson, D.J.R., Stillman, J.A. and Atkins, S.G. 2005. Rating tasks versus dimensions in assessment centers: A psychometric comparison. *Human Performance*, 18, 213–241.

Jackson, D.J.R., Stillman, J.A., Burke, S. and Englert, P. 2007. Self versus assessor ratings and their classification in assessment centers: Profiling the self-rater. *New Zealand Journal of Psychology*, 36, 93–99.

Jackson, D.J.R., Stillman, J.A. and Englert, P. 2010. Task-based assessment centers: Empirical support for a systems model. *International Journal of Selection and Assessment*, 18, 141–154.

Kast, F. and Rosenzweig, J.E. 1972. General systems theory: Applications for organization and management. *Academy of Management Journal*, 15, 447–465.

Kim, M. 2010. *The present and future of development centers – Central officials training institute case.* Paper to the Korean Society for Industrial Organizational Psychology, Daejon, Korea, June.

Kluger, A.N. and DeNisi, A. 1996. The effects of feedback interventions on performance: A historical review, a meta-analysis, and preliminary feedback theory. *Psychological Bulletin*, 119, 254–284.

Lance, C.E. 2008a. Why assessment centers do not work the way they are supposed to. *Industrial and Organizational Psychology: Perspectives on Science and Practice*, 1, 84–97.

Lance, C.E. 2008b. Where have we been, how did we get there, and where shall we go? *Industrial and Organizational Psychology: Perspectives on Science and Practice*, 1, 140–146.

Lance, C.E. (in press). Research into task-based assessment centers. In *The Psychology of Assessment Centers*, edited by D.J.R. Jackson, C.E. Lance and B.J. Hoffman. New York: Routledge.

Lance, C.E., Foster, M.R., Nemeth, Y.M., Gentry, W.A. and Drollinger, S. 2007. Extending the nomological network of assessment center construct validity: Prediction of cross-situationally consistent and specific aspects of assessment center performance. *Human Performance*, 20, 345–362.

Lee, S. 2007. *Research on assessment centers on department settings*. Seoul: Korean Civil Service Commission.

Lim, D.Y. 2004. *Developing and demonstrating assessment centers programs*. Paper to the Korean Society for Industrial Organizational Psychology, Seoul, November.

Lowry, P.E. 1997. The assessment center process: New directions. *Journal of Social Behavior and Personality*, 12, 53–62.

Mintzberg, H. 1973. *The Nature of Managerial Work*. New York: Harper & Row.

Pearlman, K. and Sanchez, J.I. 2010. Work analysis. In *Handbook of Employee Selection*, edited by J.L. Farr and N.T. Tippins. New York: Routledge, 73–98.

Russell, C.J. and Domm, D.R. 1995. Two field tests of an explanation of assessment centre validity. *Journal of Occupational and Organizational Psychology*, 68, 25–47.

Sackett, P.R. and Dreher, G.F. 1982. Constructs and assessment center dimensions: Some troubling empirical findings. *Journal of Applied Psychology*, 67, 401–410.

Stillman, J.A. and Jackson, D.J.R. 2005. A detection theory approach to the evaluation of assessors in assessment centres. *Journal of Occupational and Organizational Psychology*, 78, 581–594.

Tett, R.P., Guterman, H.A., Bleier, A. and Murphy, P.J. 2000. Development and content validation of a "hyperdimensional" taxonomy of managerial competence. *Human Performance*, 13, 205–251.

Thornton, G.C., III., Kaman, V., Layer, S. and Larsh, S. 1995. *Effectiveness of two forms of assessment center feedback: Attribute feedback and task feedback*. Paper to the 23rd International Congress: the Assessment Center Method, Kansas City, KS.

Thornton, G.C., III. and Mueller-Hanson, R.A. 2004. *Developing Organizational Simulations: A Guide for Practitioners and Students*. Mahwah, NJ: Routledge.

Turnage, J.J. and Muchinsky, P.M. 1982. Trans-situational variability in human performance with assessment centers. *Organizational Behavior and Human Performance*, 30, 174–200.

Vernon, P.E. and Parry, J.B. 1949. *Personnel Selection in the British Forces*. London: University of London Press.

Wernimont, P.F. and Campbell, J.P. 1968. Signs, samples, and criteria. *Journal of Applied Psychology*, 52, 372–376.

Williams, K.M. and Crafts, J.L. 1997. Inductive job analysis: The job/task inventory method. In *Applied Measurement Methods in Industrial Psychology*, edited by D.L. Whetzel and G.R. Wheaton. Palo Alto, CA: Davies-Black Publishing, 51–88.

Yoon, J. 2009. Leadership perception in South Korea and the United States. Unpublished manuscript. Georgia Institute of Technology. Atlanta, GA.

4 *Adjusting Exercise Design in Assessment Centers: Theory, Practice, and Research*

FILIP LIEVENS AND EVELINE SCHOLLAERT

Upon looking at this title, an obvious question is whether assessment center (AC) exercises need to be designed differently from what was done in the past. AC exercises have been around since World War I and their longevity attests to their success. So why propose some changes to this monument in personnel selection and development?

Let us first acknowledge that we concur that ACs are in still in good shape. However, every good brand needs some adjustments (which is a more appropriate term than "changes" in this context) once in a while, based on new theoretical insights and empirical research. Therefore we build our novel exercise design approach on recent insights in person-situation interactionism to make a good tool even better.

The structure of this chapter is as follows: we start with delineating the reasons behind our revised exercise design approach in ACs. Next we explain the theory behind the revised exercise design approach. In a third section, we report on our program of research related to this new approach. The fourth part discusses some other possible applications in the AC domain that are congruent with this revised exercise design approach.

Why Adjust AC Exercise Design?

Generally, ACs show a record of success: first, meta-analytic research confirmed that AC ratings were predictive of a variety of criterion measures. The meta-analysis of AC criterion-related validity studies at the dimension level (Arthur et al. 2003) contained 258 validity coefficients from 34 studies. In each study, the criterion was job-related (for example, job performance ratings, promotion, and salary). On the basis of a set of 6 dimensions Arthur et al. found a range of estimated true criterion-related validities from .25 to .39, indicating the predictive power of ACs. Second, applicants react positively to ACs. The meta-analysis of Hausknecht, Day and Thomas (2004) showed that behavior sample-based selection procedures were perceived more favorably than, for instance, cognitive ability tests and personality inventories. In particular applicants view ACs as more face valid than most other selection procedures. Third, a recent meta-analysis demonstrated that different assessors tend to agree when they are asked to evaluate candidates (Connelly and Ones 2008). Fourth, the majority of AC studies on adverse impact attest to the widely held view that ACs are reasonably unbiased regarding race and gender. According to the meta-analysis of Dean, Roth and Bobko (2008), positive results were reported, in particular for females and Hispanics. For Blacks, however, their results suggested that ACs may be associated with more adverse impact than was previously thought in the literature, but still have less adverse impact than the typical cognitive ability test.

Besides these benefits leading to the popularity of ACs, one of the main advantages of ACs is that assessors have the opportunity to observe actual behavior in a simulated work setting. This key focus on behavior in ACs is also well reflected in the most recent *Guidelines and Ethical Considerations of Assessment Center Operations*, in which the observation of overt behavioral responses is described as a necessary and fundamental component of ACs (International Task Force on Assessment Center Guidelines 2009). The *Guidelines* further state that AC designers should attempt to design exercises that evoke a large number of job-related behaviors because this should give assessors enough opportunities to observe job-related behavior. Generating more job-related behaviors in an exercise is quintessential for developmental ACs, because these behaviors serve as a basis for providing participants with detailed developmental feedback about their strengths and weaknesses. The more behavioral examples one can assemble, the more convincing the feedback will likely be. In addition, regardless of how that behavior is then captured and evaluated by assessors (for example, in exercise/task-based models, dimension-based models), eliciting and observing behavior is key to effective assessment and development centers.

Although the AC *Guidelines* and the literature emphasize the importance of exercises providing sufficient opportunities for observing job-related behavior, various authors have emphasized that AC exercises score not that well in terms of observability of behavior:

- First, Bycio, Alvares, and Hahn (1987: 472) noted that "assessors within an exercise are sometimes, if not usually, forced to base *all* of their judgments on *four* or *five* behaviors."
- Next, Brannick, Michaels, and Baker (1989) mentioned that assessors often need to rely on *one* particular behavioral reaction ("red hot" item) to score candidates on *several* dimensions.
- Third, Reilly, Henry and Smither (1990) pointed out that assessors sometimes have too few observations on which to base their ratings for some dimensions, when not enough behaviors are evoked.
- Furthermore, Kudisch, Ladd and Dobbins (1997) suggested that consistency of AC ratings across exercises may be enhanced when dimensions are easier to observe. For example, the dimension Communication (which is overt in most exercises) produced more convergent validity, as opposed to Problem Analysis (which is less observable in most exercises).
- Although the meta-analysis of Connelly and Ones (2008) revealed good inter-rater reliability coefficients for AC ratings, reliability was lowest for so-called within-exercise dimension ratings (ratings made on one dimension within a specific exercise). The main argument is that such ratings are often based on rather limited behavioral evidence.

In sum, it seems that it is not always guaranteed that AC exercises enable assessors to collect enough behavioral observations per dimension (see Brannick 2008, Howard 2008, Lievens 2008, Lievens, Tett and Schleicher 2009). An explanation can be found in the traditional AC paradigm which focuses on the exercise as a whole. In this holistic approach, the exercise as a whole is seen as a vehicle for evoking behavior (Howard 2008, Lievens et al. 2009, McFarland et al. 2005). However, as noted above, research has shown that this holistic exercise approach might occasionally be problematic in that an insufficient number of behaviors are elicited. That is the reason why we argue for a more molecular approach by planting situational stimuli within exercises to enhance the observability of dimensions across a variety of dimensions in ACs. Upfront we acknowledge that practitioners might already have intuitively attempted to elicit dimension relevant behavior by building context, content, personnel, problems into exercises or by instructing role players to use prompts in response to paths chosen by participants. However, our point is that theory and research has not shown systematically how the behavioral elicitation process works and has not provided empirical evidence of its effectiveness

Theoretical Background

It is generally acknowledged that behavior of candidates in ACs is determined neither solely by dispositional factors (stable personal characteristics of candidates) nor solely by situational factors (AC exercises) but by the interaction of the person and the situation. Therefore, it is relevant to conceptualize the occurrence of candidate behavior in ACs in terms of a recent interactionist theory such as trait activation theory (Lievens et al. 2009; Tett and Burnett 2003). Trait activation theory focuses on the person-situation interaction to explain behavior based on responses to trait-relevant cues found in situations (Tett and Guterman 2000). These observable responses serve as the basis for behavioral ratings in a variety of assessments such as ACs (Tett and Burnett 2003).

According to trait activation theory, two factors are important to understand in which situations a trait is likely to manifest itself in behavior. First, trait activation theory emphasizes the importance of *situation trait relevance*. A situation is considered relevant to a trait if it provides cues for the expression of trait relevant behavior (Tett and Guterman 2000). Thus, situation trait relevance is a qualitative feature of situations that is essentially trait specific; it is informative with regard to which cues are present to elicit behavior for a given latent trait. Relatedly, trait activation theory states that situations should provide ample opportunities for behavior to be expressed. This idea builds on the well-known principle of aggregation (Epstein 1979) in social psychology, which states that the sum of a set of measurements is more stable than any single measurement from the set. For example, when someone is having an accident and is confronted with an angry driver, this situation provides cues for traits such as Emotional Stability. Conversely, this situation is less relevant to evoke traits such as Imagination (Openness).

Situation strength is the second relevant factor from the trait activation perspective. Situation strength is more of a continuum that refers to how much clarity there is with regard to how the situation is perceived. Strong situations involve unambiguous behavioral demands and are therefore likely to negate almost all individual differences in behavior without regard to any specific trait. Conversely, weak situations are characterized by more ambiguous expectations, enabling much more variability in behavioral responses to be observed (Meyer, Dalal and Hermida 2010). For instance, at the end of a busy day a shop assistant may be confronted with a messy shop full of odds and ends left by the customers. When the supervisor instructs the shop assistant to clean the mess in the shop, it will be much more difficult to observe individual differences related to the trait order, whereas the opposite might be true in the absence of such clear-cut supervisory instructions (without instructions some shop assistants will immediately start to clean the shop, others will not notice the mess).

Thus, trait activation theory has key implications for AC exercises (see Lievens et al. 2009). That is, the application of trait activation theory involves recognition of the importance of building multiple stimuli into the AC exercises. Accordingly, exercises can be explicitly designed to increase their situation trait relevance. In this respect, Brannick (2008: 132) cogently argued to "deliberately introduce multiple dimension-relevant items or problems within the exercise and to score such items." Apart from increasing the situation trait relevance of AC exercises, trait activation theory also suggests taking situation strength into account when planting stimuli in AC exercises. That is, behavior elicitation should avoid presenting the candidate with a too strong situation (in terms of behavioral demands). For example, role players might create a relatively weak situation by showing for a moment a sad facial expression (prompt to evoke Interpersonal Sensitivity). Some candidates will ask what is bothering the role player, whereas other candidates will ignore the expression or even will not notice the expression, leading to variability in candidate reactions. On the other hand, to evoke Interpersonal Sensitivity the role player might also start to sob. Almost every candidate will notice this and will react on it. This is probably too strong of a situation so that variability in candidate reactions will be masked.

Examples of Situational Stimuli

In the previous section, we outlined some general principles for eliciting candidate behavior in ACs. In this section, we provide five different examples of how to put this general logic into practice.

The first approach entails adapting the content of the exercise. Let us take an oral presentation with challenging questions as an example. Examples of stimuli to elicit behavior relevant to a dimension such as Resistance to Stress (a facet of the broader trait of Emotional Stability) might be the inclusion of a stringent time limit, sudden obstacles, or information overload. In a more systematic way, AC designers might ensure that several content cues are embedded at the task, social, and organizational levels within a given exercise (if job-related, of course).

A second way to elicit job-related behavior is through exercise instructions. In ACs, exercise instructions provide information and set expectations for candidates about what behavior to show or not to show. For example, exercise instructions might be vague (for example, "solve the problem") or more concrete (for example, "motivate the problem subordinate"). Similarly, exercise instructions might be unidimensional (for example, reach consensus) or multidimensional (for example, reach consensus and make the company more profitable). To date, we know little about how such exercise instruction variations might affect the behavior demonstrated, in terms of either direct effects or in interactions with underlying personality traits.

Thirdly, when interpersonal exercises are used, role-player cues are an additional means of eliciting job-related behavior. In current AC practice, role players are typically given a specific list of things to do and to avoid. Role players are also trained to perform realistically and consistently across candidates. Although these best practices have proven their usefulness over the years, a key function of trained role players consists of evoking behavior from candidates (Thornton and Mueller-Hanson 2004). Trait activation theory can help identify which specific behaviors might be evoked by specific role-player stimuli (prompts). Prompts are defined as predetermined statements that a role player consistently mentions in an AC across candidates to elicit behaviors related to specific job-related dimensions. For example, to arouse behavior related to Interpersonal Sensitivity, the role player might state that he feels bad about a candidate's decision. Similarly, role players might trigger behavior related to Planning and Organizing (deeper trait of Conscientiousness) by asking how the candidate will implement his or her solution.

It is important that these role-player cues should *subtly* elicit assessee behavior because the situations might otherwise become too strong. Indeed, role-player prompts might vary from being very explicit (strong) to being very implicit (weak) in eliciting the dimensions targeted. We illustrate this notion of situation strength in role-player prompts again with the dimension of Interpersonal Sensitivity. That is, role players might react to a decision made by the candidate by showing momentarily a distressed expression on their face (weak situation) or might start to sob (extremely strong situation).

Fourthly, one might consider including a large number of shorter exercises (exercise "vignettes") in the AC. For example, Brannick (2008) recommends using five 6-minute role plays instead of a single 30-minute role play (for example, with a problem subordinate) so that one obtains samples of performance on a large number of independent tasks that are each exclusively designed to elicit behavior related to a specific trait (see also Motowidlo, Hooper and Jackson 2006, for the use of 1- or 2- minute role plays). As another example, one could aim to measure communication by including "speed" role plays with a boss, peers, colleagues, customers, and subordinates.

Finally, stimuli could also be presented via videotape, PC, or even virtual reality. In the videotape approach, resembling earlier social intelligence measures (Stricker and Rock 1990), candidates are shown short scenes and asked to react to what they saw. Recent applications even enable creation of avatar-based simulation exercises wherein participants take on a virtual identity and are confronted with standardized stimuli in a virtual workplace (Rupp, Gibbons and Snyder 2008).

Overview of Empirical Research

Let us start by acknowledging that some earlier studies have already scrutinized the effects of specific characteristics of AC exercises (Highhouse and Harris 1993, Schneider and Schmitt 1992). For instance, Schneider and Schmitt (1992) experimentally manipulated the effects of exercise content (competitive vs. cooperative demands) and exercise form (for example, role play vs. group discussion) on candidate ratings. The form of the exercise emerged as the most important exercise factor in leading candidates to perform differently across exercises.

So, the focus of this limited number of prior studies on AC exercise characteristics has typically been the *exercise as a whole*. Specific situational stimuli *within exercises* were not investigated. To fill this gap in empirical research and to put our aforementioned theory to the test we set up a research program. So far, the following questions have been addressed:

1. Is it possible to build situational stimuli in AC exercises?
2. What are the effects of building situational stimuli in AC exercises on observability?
3. What are the effects of building situational stimuli in AC exercises on inter-rater reliability?
4. What are the effects of building situational stimuli in AC exercises on construct-related validity?
5. What are the effects of building situational stimuli in AC exercises on applicant reactions?

The remainder of this section provides an overview of the available empirical research evidence. Note that most of the studies are still ongoing and that only preliminary research evidence is presented.

IS IT POSSIBLE TO BUILD SITUATIONAL STIMULI IN AC EXERCISES?

Some situational stimuli (for example, exercise instructions, video-based stimuli or stimuli in virtual reality) can be used and implemented independently of the candidate. In that case, it is relatively straightforward that the answer to this question is "Yes." However, other situational stimuli (role-player prompts) are given in a constantly changing situation. In that case, the answer to this question might be more complex. Prompts create a situational stimulus for evoking job-relevant behavior. Role players are taught to use multiple standardized prompts for each dimension in a consistent fashion across candidates. These prompts provide a framework for responding as every conversation is different. By using prompts a situational stimulus for evoking job-relevant behavior is created. In role-player training, role players are then taught to use multiple standardized prompts per dimension in a consistent fashion across candidates. These prompts are framed in a script as every conversation is different. On the one hand role players need to follow this script as strictly as possible, thereby being expected to use enough prompts per dimension. Yet, on the other hand they also need to play their role in a credible way. Each candidate reacts differently so that the role player often has to pursue several dissimilar strategies to maintain the script. These opposing demands might put some pressure on role players. Consequently, the question is whether role players are actually able to use prompts in a standardized way despite those opposing demands.

Schollaert and Lievens (in press) sought to examine this. Their focal question was whether role players were able to use prompts. A sample of role players was randomly assigned to one of the following two conditions: role-player training without prompts and role-player training with prompts. Generally, the results indicated that attending training with prompts substantially increased the number of prompts used by role players during the assessment exercises. Effect sizes were large. In the role-play exercise, the average proportion of prompts increased fivefold. In the presentation exercise, the proportion of prompts quadrupled. Thus, these results support the view that role players might serve as a practical means of structuring AC exercises to consistently evoke job-relevant behavior. Despite this positive evidence, using prompts is not straightforward as results also showed that after attending role-player training with prompts, half of the interactions still failed to show any prompts.

WHAT ARE THE EFFECTS OF BUILDING SITUATIONAL STIMULI INTO AC EXERCISES ON OBSERVABILITY?

As noted above, the AC *Guidelines* have underscored the importance of the observability of behavior. Hence, an important argument for using situational stimuli is based on the key assumption that they should increase the number of observations per dimension noted down by assessors.

Schollaert and Lievens (2009) tested this assumption of the increased situational relevance of AC exercises by contrasting two vehicles for increasing behavior observability, namely instructions to role players prior to a role play and role-player prompts during the role play. No main effect was found for exercise instructions. Apparently, providing specific exercise instructions did not influence the number of good observations. However, results showed a clear effect for prompt-training, with the use of role-player prompts leading to greater observability of dimension-relevant behavior. Thus, the inclusion of situational stimuli and especially the use of prompts might serve as a practical vehicle to avoid that assessors need to rely on too few behavioral reactions to score candidates (Brannick et al. 1989).

WHAT ARE THE EFFECTS OF BUILDING SITUATIONAL STIMULI IN AC EXERCISES ON INTER-RATER RELIABILITY?

If situational stimuli are built into AC exercises, one might expect that this has beneficial effects on inter-rater reliability for several reasons. First, evoking more candidate behavior should increase the standardization of those exercises. Second, the opportunity to observe and take notes on dimension-related behavior should also increase the reliability of the ratings made in light of the aforementioned principle of aggregation (Epstein 1979). Just as the reliability and content representation of a test increases with the addition of items from the same domain, assessing a given dimension in an AC exercise might improve with the addition of dimension-specific cues. Third, the use of standardized situational cues in ACs can be compared to the use of standardized questions among interviewers. Research in the interview domain has shown that the inter-rater reliability of structured interviews is higher than that of unstructured interviews (Conway, Jako and Goodman 1995). Thus the use of standardized dimension-related stimuli across candidates might increase the standardization, the structure, and the consistency of AC ratings.

In our research, we found empirical support for these hypotheses only when assessors were also familiar with the situational stimuli built into the AC exercises. For example, Lievens, Keen, and Schollaert (2010) compared three conditions. In the low behavior elicitation condition, no formal attempts were implemented to evoke dimension-related behavior. In the medium behavior elicitation condition, role players were trained to use specific prompts for evoking candidate behavior. The high behavior elicitation condition was similarly designed as the medium behavior elicitation condition, with the addition that assessors were also familiarized with the prompts for eliciting behavior. In that condition, assessors knew which prompts were related to which dimensions. Inter-rater reliability was highest in the third condition, where role players used prompts for evoking behavior and where assessors were also familiar with the prompts used by role players.

Taken together, these results make sense as they indicate that it is not enough that exercises generate more behavior. In addition, it seems important that assessors receive information about the cues that elicit behavior in order to consistently observe, classify, and rate that behavior.

WHAT ARE THE EFFECTS OF BUILDING SITUATIONAL STIMULI IN AC EXERCISES ON CONSTRUCT-RELATED VALIDITY?

When situational stimuli are used to elicit a higher number of behaviors in AC exercises, it can be expected that dimensions are also better measured in AC exercises. Thus, one might anticipate beneficial effects on the construct-related validity of AC exercises. Given the higher number of behaviors available per dimension, assessors should be less prone to using a couple of behavioral items per dimension to rate these dimensions. In other words, their ratings should be less susceptible to halo. The convergence of their ratings across exercises might also increase due to the higher observability of the dimensions. This might be an important advantage of the use of situational stimuli as the construct-related validity of AC ratings has traditionally been identified as one of the weaker points of AC technology, especially when within-exercise dimension ratings are used (Bowler and Woehr 2006; Lance 2008; Lievens and Conway 2001).

In recent years, some studies have put these expectations to the test. Schollaert and Lievens (in press) found that Problem-solving and Interpersonal Sensitivity dimensions were better measured in AC exercises when role players used prompts for evoking these dimensions. This was evidenced by higher correlations between Problem-solving and Interpersonal Sensitivity ratings and Cognitive Ability and Agreeableness, respectively. Lievens et al. (2010) focused on behavior elicitation via role-player prompts in a sample of actual candidates for a managerial job. As noted above, they distinguished between three levels of behavior elicitation (high, medium and low). Results showed that construct-related validity (convergent and discriminant correlations) was highest in the high behavior elicitation condition. That is, significantly more evidence for convergent and discriminant validity was established when role players used prompts for eliciting behavior and when assessors were familiar with these prompts.

Two other studies experimented with the use of video-based vignettes for eliciting dimension-related behavior. In Lievens (2009), candidates for police-officer jobs watched video-based scenes. Each of these scenes triggered a specific dimension. At the end of each scene, the character in the video spoke directly into the camera. Candidates were next required to answer the character directly, with their verbal and non-verbal reply being captured by a webcam. These reactions were then coded by trained assessors. One set of analyses examined the consistency of assessors' dimensional ratings across scenes (convergent validity). That is, did scenes that triggered a similar dimension provide a consistent measurement of that specific dimension? In line with expectations, the consistency in assessor ratings was acceptable (only a more ambiguous dimension such as Integrity scored a bit lower), confirming that the use of multiple videotaped scenes for measuring one dimension might serve as a good vehicle for obtaining a more consistent measurement of the targeted dimension. Brink et al. (2008) also showed candidates short video scenes and asked them to react to what they saw. They focused on the discriminant validity of assessor ratings and found that assessors were able to make good differentiations among the various dimensions.

WHAT ARE THE EFFECTS OF BUILDING SITUATIONAL STIMULI IN AC EXERCISES ON APPLICANT REACTIONS?

Traditionally, AC exercises are held in high regard by participants. However, the use of situational stimuli might also have an impact on how participants perceive AC exercises. On the one hand, the use of situational stimuli might lead to more favorable applicant perceptions because candidates might appreciate that prompts aim to elicit job-related behavior. That is, the use of stimuli that evoke relevant behavior might be perceived as increasing the overlap with behavior on the job. As candidates prefer job-related selection procedures (Hausknecht et al. 2004) the inclusion of situational stimuli might lead to higher perceptions of job-relatedness.

On the other hand, the use of situational stimuli might also have some negative effects on applicant perceptions. Possibly it reduces the realism and interpersonal warmth of AC exercises because it might detract from the natural flow of the exercise. In fact, prior research in the interview domain has shown that the use of structure in interviews led to less favorable candidate perceptions as compared to unstructured interviews (Conway and Peneno 1999).

So far, only one study has examined the impact of the use of situational stimuli (in this case role-player prompts) on applicant perceptions. Schollaert and Lievens (in press) examined the effects of situational stimuli in the form of role-player prompts on perceptions of job-relatedness, two-way communication, and interpersonal treatment. They hypothesized that the use of prompts led to higher perceptions of job-relatedness and to decreases in the perceptions of two-way communication and interpersonal treatment. Half of the candidates were confronted with role players not using prompts and half of the candidates were confronted with role players using prompts. For interpersonal treatment and job-relatedness, no significant effects were found. This could be due to a ceiling effect as previous research showed that candidates already react highly favorable to AC exercises. For two-way communication, a significant effect was reported. Contrary to expectations, candidates had the perception of having more opportunities to give their opinion in the condition with prompts. Candidates might have considered prompts as providing them with more opportunity to converse with the role player. In any case, these results suggest that the use of prompts does not have a negative influence on candidate reactions. However, a caveat is warranted as this study was not conducted in a real selection setting and the sample consisted of final year university students without AC experience. So, future research with experienced applicants is needed. In addition, the effects of the use of situational cues on participants' acceptance of AC feedback should be scrutinized.

SUMMARY AND FUTURE RESEARCH

So far, researchers have experimented with three types of situational stimuli: exercise instructions, role-player prompts, and videotaped stimuli. Generally, this overview of the growing empirical evidence shows that it is possible to build situational stimuli into AC exercises. Incorporating multiple situational stimuli is also found to generate the anticipated effects in terms of increasing the number of behaviors to be observed. That is, assessors noted down more behaviors on their observation forms in the case where situational stimuli were built into the exercises. However, situational stimuli do not guarantee that assessors are taking them into account in their ratings. Only if assessors are familiarized with the situational cues do they have effects on inter-rater reliability, convergent validity, and discriminant validity. Finally, applicants do not seem to notice any negative effects of the use of situational cues in AC exercises.

Future research should extend these results. A key issue consists of investigating whether the use of situational cues also increases the criterion-related validity of the AC exercise; the rationale being that as more dimension-relevant behavior will be elicited, the use of situational stimuli might increase the overlap with the criterion.

Another issue is whether the provision of cues changes the dimension that is actually being measured. That is, does it change from a measure of maximum performance to typical performance, or vice versa? The provision of cues in AC exercises may make the situation stronger, and suggest to participants what they should do, rather than allow them to choose what to do. Interestingly, the effects might differ depending on the type of dimensions (personality-like dimensions versus ability-like dimensions). For example, consider a role play where the candidate is a manager and the role player is a supervisor having a problem with an employee. With no cues, the candidate may or may not engage in coaching behaviors; with cues from the role player (for example, "Well, what can you do to help me with my problem?"), the candidate may start giving suggestions. The exercise then provides behavior relevant to coaching (maximum performance or "can do"), but at the cost of denying the candidate the opportunity of proactively displaying any inclination to provide coaching to the subordinate (typical performance or "will do"). So, giving cues might change the dimensions being measured from a measure of tendency to coach to a measure of ability to coach (see also McDaniel, Hartman, Whetzel and Grubb, 2007).

The same sort of analysis should be applied to dimensions like problem-solving. With minimal cues, the candidate may do very little systematic problem analysis and decision analysis. But the role player might give a series of cues in follow-up questions after the presentation: "What led you to say you would do … ?" "What other solutions did you consider … ?" The situation then may become stronger, and the candidate would give answers that he did not really consider in his initial preparation. Thus, one could evaluate their ability at problem-solving because more of those behaviors would be displayed. In summary, to measure "personality-like" traits, providing cues might make the situation stronger and reduce individual differences in the behavior one wants to observe. To measure "cognitive ability-like" traits, providing cues may ensure that relevant behaviors are displayed, and thus enhance measurement accuracy. In future studies, we plan to test these ideas.

Other Implications

So far, we have focused on the use of situational cues in AC exercises. However, the inclusion of situational cues not only has implications for AC exercises, but also for at least the following three other components of AC technology, namely the design of behavioral checklists, assessor training, and alternate AC exercises.

BEHAVIORAL CHECKLISTS

As noted above, initial research with the inclusion of predetermined situational cues in AC exercises suggests that it is important that assessors are familiar with the cues used. To accomplish this, a practical approach might consist of including the situational cues that were designed to elicit candidate behavior (for example, the role-player statements) in the behavioral checklists provided to the assessors. In an even more structured format, these cues could be presented in their anticipated chronological order, with the candidate behaviors to be observed arranged around them. Accordingly, assessors are reminded and prompted by the situational cues when attending to candidate behavior. It might help them to "see the forest for the trees" in the complex stimuli triggered by AC exercises. Brannick (2008) refers to this approach as aligning the stimulus content of the exercises with the scoring rubric (as is sometimes done in in-baskets, wherein they are provided behaviorally anchored rating scales which show, for each in-basket item, the types of responses that would be considered high/medium/low performance).

ASSESSOR TRAINING

A related implication consists of familiarizing assessors with the situational cues in assessor training. In current assessor training practice, the focus is placed on imposing a consistent frame-of-reference on assessors (Lievens 2001). In such training programs, the dimensions and the accompanying behaviors logically play a crucial role. However, it is equally important that assessors know when specific behavior is potentially being activated by various situational stimuli. We are not aware of studies that have examined such a comprehensive assessor training approach. Apart from teaching assessors the cues in a lecture, other options are possible. For example, when the same individuals serve as assessors and role players in the AC, they also learn to use the cues. This might be especially helpful in cross cultural settings where candidates and assessors come from different backgrounds.

ALTERNATE AC EXERCISES

One potential benefit of incorporating situational cues in AC exercises is that the AC exercise is no longer a "black box"; that is, the development and inclusion of situational cues within an AC exercise breaks it down into different parts and components. Thus, the identification of situational cues might guide the determination of the deeper structural aspects (the so-called radicals, to use a term from item generation theory; Irvine, Dann and Anderson 1990; Lievens and Sackett 2007) of an AC exercise, in terms of providing a template of what aspects of the exercise map onto which dimensions, and should be kept constant across exercises.

Such a more molecular approach to AC exercise design might make it easier to develop alternate forms of AC exercises (Brummel, Rupp and Spain 2009). For example, one might develop several role-player cues to evoke behavior related to the dimension of Interpersonal Sensitivity in a series of role plays. Superficial differences among the cues would be incidental to their deeper similarities (as radicals) in targeting the same dimension. The same might be done for other dimensions. Thus, more generally, to construct alternate forms of AC exercises, we suggest changing the surface features of an AC exercise, while keeping the deep structure of the exercise intact.

Epilogue

In this paper, we proposed to build multiple situational stimuli in AC exercises. We also reported on various studies that have implemented this approach. We want to emphasize that we do not suggest that current best practices of exercise development (and AC design in general) should be abandoned. Rather, we argue that our approach should also play a more prominent role in such development, with the goal of making a good tool even better. Whereas current practices typically simulate key task, social, and organizational demands of the job, we see untapped potential in planting multiple stimuli within exercises as a systematic and structured means of increasing the frequency and variability of job-related behavior in AC exercises.

References

Arthur, W. Jr., Day, E.A., McNelly, T.L. and Edens, P.S. 2003. A meta-analysis of the criterion-related validity of assessment center dimensions. *Personnel Psychology*, 56, 125–154.

Bowler, M.C. and Woehr, D.J. 2006. A meta-analytic evaluation of the impact of dimension and exercise factors on assessment center ratings. *Journal of Applied Psychology*, 91, 1114–1124.

Brannick, M.T. 2008. Back to basics of test construction and scoring. *Industrial and Organizational Psychology*, 1, 131–133.

Brannick, M.T., Michaels, C.E. and Baker, D.P. 1989. Construct validity of in-basket scores. *Journal of Applied Psychology*, 74, 957–963.

Brink, K.E., Lance, C.E., Bellenger, B.L., Morrison, M.A., Scharlau, E.A. and Crenshaw, J.L. 2008, April. Discriminant validity of a "next generation" assessment center. In: B.J. Hoffman (Chair), *Reexamining assessment centers: Alternate approaches*. Symposium conducted at the Annual Conference of the Society for Industrial and Organizational Psychology, San Francisco, CA.

Brummel, B.J., Rupp, D.E. and Spain, S.M. 2009. Constructing parallel simulation exercises for assessment centers and other forms of behavioral assessment. *Personnel Psychology*, 62, 137–170.

Bycio, P., Alvares, K.M. and Hahn, J. 1987. Situational specificity in assessment center ratings: A confirmatory factor analysis. *Journal of Applied Psychology*, 72, 463–474.

Connelly, B.S. and Ones, D.S. 2008. *Interrater unreliability in assessment center ratings: A meta-analysis.* Paper presented at the Annual Conference of the Society for Industrial and Organizational Psychology, April, San Francisco, CA.

Conway, J.M., Jako, R.A. and Goodman, D.F. 1995. A meta-analysis of interrater and internal consistency reliability of selection interviews. *Journal of Applied Psychology*, 80, 565–579.

Conway, J.M. and Peneno, G.M. 1999. Comparing structured interview question types: Construct validity and applicant reactions. *Journal of Business and Psychology*, 13, 485–506.

Dean, M.A., Roth, P.L. and Bobko, P. 2008. Ethnic and gender subgroup differences in assessment center ratings: a meta-analysis. *Journal of Applied Psychology*, 93, 685–691.

Epstein, S. 1979. The stability of behavior: I. On predicting most of the people much of the time. *Journal of Personality and Social Psychology*, 37, 1097–1126.

Hauskneckt, J.P., Day, D.V. and Thomas, S.C. 2004. Applicant reactions to selection procedures: An updated model and meta-analysis. *Personnel Psychology,* 57, 639–683.

Highhouse, S. and Harris, M.M. 1993. The measurement of assessment center situations: Bem's template matching technique for examining exercise similarity. *Journal of Applied Social Psychology,* 23, 140–155.

Howard, A. 2008. Making assessment centers work the way they are supposed to. *Industrial and Organizational Psychology,* 1, 98–104.

International Taskforce on Assessment Centers Guidelines. 2009. Guidelines and ethical considerations for assessment center operations. *International Journal of Selection and Assessment,* 17, 243–253.

Irvine, S.H., Dann, P.L. and Anderson, J.D. 1990. Towards a theory of algorithm-determined cognitive test construction. *British Journal of Psychology,* 81, 173–195.

Kudisch, J.D., Ladd, R.T. and Dobbins, G.H. 1997. New evidence on the construct validity of diagnostic assessment centers: The findings may not be so troubling after all. *Journal of Social Behavior and Personality,* 12, 129–144.

Lance, C.E. 2008. Why assessment centers do not work the way they are supposed to. *Industrial and Organizational Psychology,* 1, 84–97.

Lievens, F. 2009, February. Effects of response fidelity on test performance and validity. Paper presented at the 23rd Meeting of the Personnel and Human Resources Research Group, College Station, TX.

Lievens, F. 2008. What does exercise-based assessment really mean? *Industrial and Organizational Psychology: Perspectives on Science and Practice,* 1, 117–120.

Lievens, F. 2001. Assessor training strategies and their effects on accuracy, inter-rater reliability, and discriminant validity. *Journal of Applied Psychology,* 86, 255–264.

Lievens, F. and Conway, J.M. 2001. Dimension and exercise variance in assessment center scores: A large-scale evaluation of multitrait-multimethod studies. *Journal of Applied Psychology,* 86, 1202–1222.

Lievens, F., Keen, G. and Schollaert, E. 2010, April. *A novel look at behavior elicitation in assessment center exercises.* Poster session presented at the 25th Annual Conference of the Society for Industrial and Organizational Psychology, Atlanta, United States.

Lievens, F. and Sackett, P.R. 2007. Situational judgment tests in high stakes settings: Issues and strategies with generating alternate forms. *Journal of Applied Psychology,* 92, 1043–1055.

Lievens, F., Tett, R.P. and Schleicher, D.J. 2009. Assessment centers at the crossroads: Toward a reconceptualization of assessment center exercises. In *Research in Personnel and Human Resources Management,* edited by J.J. Martocchio and H. Liao. Bingley: JAI Press, 99–152.

McDaniel, M.A., Hartman, N.S., Whetzel, D.L. and Grubb, W.L. 2007. Situational judgment tests, response instructions, and validity: A meta-analysis. *Personnel Psychology,* 60, 63–91.

McFarland, L.A., Yun, G.J., Harold, C.M., Viera, L. and Moore, L.G. 2005. An examination of impression management use and effectiveness across assessment center exercises: The role of competency demands. *Personnel Psychology,* 58, 949–980.

Meyer R.D., Dalal, R.S. and Hermida, R. 2010. A review and synthesis of situational strength in the organizational sciences. *Journal of Management,* 36, 121–140.

Motowidlo, S.J., Hooper, A.C. and Jackson, H.L. 2006. Implicit policies about relations between personality traits and behavioral effectiveness in situational judgment items. *Journal of Applied Psychology,* 91, 749–761.

Reilly, R.R., Henry, S. and Smither, J.W. 1990. An examination of the effects of using behavior checklists on the construct validity of assessment center dimensions. *Personnel Psychology*, 43, 71–84.

Rupp, D.E., Gibbons, A.M. and Snyder, L.A. 2008. Transforming our models of learning and development: Web-based instruction as enabler of third-generation instruction. *Industrial and Organizational Psychology: Perspectives on Science and Practice*, 1, 454–467.

Schneider, J.R. and Schmitt, N. 1992. An exercise design approach to understanding assessment-center dimension and exercise constructs. *Journal of Applied Psychology*, 77, 32–41.

Schollaert, E. and Lievens, F. in press. The use of role-player prompts in assessment center exercises. *International Journal of Selection and Assessment*.

Schollaert, E. and Lievens, F. 2009, October. *Using trait activation theory to increase the amount of candidate behaviors elicited in assessment center exercises?* Paper session presented at the 4th Dutch-Flemish Research Meeting on Personnel Recruitment and Selection, Amsterdam, The Netherlands.

Stricker, L.J. and Rock, D.A. 1990. Interpersonal competence, social intelligence, and general ability. *Personality and Individual Differences*, 11, 833–839.

Tett, R.P. and Burnett, D.D. 2003. A personality trait-based interactionist model of job performance. *Journal of Applied Psychology*, 88, 500–517.

Tett, R.P. and Guterman, H.A. 2000. Situation trait relevance, trait expression, and cross-situational consistency: Testing a principle of trait activation. *Journal of Research in Personality*, 34, 397–423.

Thornton, G.C. III and Mueller-Hanson, R.A. 2004. *Developing Organizational Simulations: A Guide for Practitioners and Students*. Mahwah, NJ: Lawrence Erlbaum Associates, Inc.

5 *Fit For Purpose? Considerations when using 'Off-the-shelf' versus 'Customized' Simulation Exercises*

SOPHIE PRITCHARD AND PHILIPPA RILEY

Introduction

The purpose of this chapter is to identify and discuss the criteria practitioners should consider when determining whether to use 'off-the-shelf' versus 'customized' simulation exercises. While a great deal has been written about simulation exercises in general, there has been little discussion in the literature about the merits of each approach and specifically when one approach may be preferable over another. In this chapter, off-the-shelf and customized exercises are defined. A broad range of factors that impact the choice of approach are discussed in relation to the concept of 'fit for purpose.' This discussion is intended to help guide practitioners in the decision-making process. Additionally, a framework is provided for determining if an exercise, either off-the-shelf or customized, is valid for use for a particular purpose.

Defining Simulation Exercises

Behavioural simulation exercises are 'designed to elicit behaviours related to dimensions of performance on the job requiring the participants to respond behaviourally to situational stimuli' (International Task Force on Assessment Centre Guidelines 2009: 246). Common types of simulation exercises include in-basket exercises, analysis exercises, role plays, presentations and group exercises. Simulation exercises differ in the extent to which they replicate the job role being assessed (referred to as fidelity). Fidelity in this context means 'the similarity of the assessment situation to the job situation' (Thornton and Mueller-Hanson 2004: 6). High fidelity simulations are those which are very similar to the requirements of the job role and which measure specific observable skills and behaviours required for the role in question. The highest level of fidelity is found in work samples, which typically take the form of a subset of tasks that are performed on the job (for example, a typing test or proof reading exercise for a secretarial position). 'Low fidelity' simulations include assessment methods which require individuals to choose from predetermined alternative responses or which ask them to indicate their behavioural intentions. These do not strictly qualify as behavioural simulations, as instead of displaying behaviour, the candidate is required to recognize what behaviour would be appropriate in a predetermined situation.

Behavioural simulation exercises are available off-the-shelf or customized. Off-the-shelf exercises are typically purchased from an exercise publisher and are not designed to be specific to one organization; however, customized exercises are designed specifically for a given purpose and context. These different alternatives are described in detail below and the remainder of this chapter discusses the degree to which the two options are suited to different contexts.

OFF-THE-SHELF EXERCISES

A number of assessment services providers offer off-the-shelf Assessment and Development Centre exercises. These exercises have typically been developed by, and are therefore owned by, the provider. The diversity of exercises offered is dependent upon the individual provider's range, but most include a variety of exercise types set in different working contexts (such as working alone, one-to-one, or in groups), operating at different levels (such as administrative through to senior executive) and within different industry sectors (such as the not-for-profit, public or private sectors, with further sub-divisions within those sectors). Additionally exercises may also focus on particular issues, such as data storage/handling, diversity or outsourcing. A recent study indicated that, in the UK, 17 per cent of those running Assessment Centres were using off-the-shelf materials (Rankin 2007), compared to 22 per cent in the US (Eurich, Krause, Cigularov and Thornton 2009).

Whilst off-the-shelf exercises are purchased in a pre-existing format, some providers build flexibility into this format to allow for variations in purchasers' requirements in terms of timings, competencies and technology. For example, a user may be able to select a subset of the list of potential competencies that could be assessed by an exercise. They may also be able to choose to include or omit certain exercise components, for example an optional presentation at the end of a written analysis exercise. Additionally, purchasers may opt to ask candidates to complete presentations or reports on computer or conduct a role play remotely, for example via the telephone. In order to purchase off-the-shelf exercises, many providers will require users to meet minimum qualification criteria, which aim to ensure they are competent in the use of these exercises. These criteria may take the form of an assessment of knowledge or skills, or in some cases a requirement to undertake formal training.

CUSTOMIZED EXERCISES

A customized exercise is one that has been designed for a specific purpose within a particular organization. Typically the design of customized exercises is driven by focused research which informs the type of exercise, the industry setting and the issues under consideration. Customized exercises may be designed to assess one specific job role (such as a contact centre representative within a specified organization) or a category of job roles (for example first line managers). Whether developed externally or by an 'in house' team, customized exercises are typically owned by the commissioning organization. The associated benefits of this ownership are discussed later in this chapter.

TAILORED EXERCISES

While off-the-shelf and customized exercises have been presented as a dichotomy, 'tailored exercises' represent a third option which sits between the two. A tailored exercise is an off-the-shelf exercise that has been adapted. There is a huge variety of tailoring options available. Some of the most common types of tailoring are outlined here.

At the most basic level, the surface details of the exercise can be amended. In this instance, the fundamental structure of the exercise would remain the same; however, superficial details such as names, currencies and specific terminology could be changed. Making this type of amendment is generally relatively simple and will help to ensure that the exercise content is more closely aligned to the specific need. These changes are usually inexpensive and may enhance the perceived relevance of the exercise.

Exercises can also be tailored at a more in-depth level where changes are made to the actual structure and fundamental basis of the exercise. This type of tailoring might include changing the competencies being assessed, amending timings or changing the setting by altering the industry sector, role or task responsibilities. Undertaking any of these changes is likely to entail significant alterations to the content of the candidate (and possibly role player) instructions, as well as the assessor marking guide. For example, in the case of changing the competencies to be assessed, updates would need to be made to the behavioural indicators, competency titles and definitions included in the assessor marking guide. It might also be necessary to amend the candidate or role-player information, to build in the measurement of an additional competency, if this competency is not readily measurable within the existing exercise structure.

As illustrated, there is a large array of tailoring options available which can help to make a standard off-the-shelf exercise more closely aligned to a particular requirement. Whereas a highly tailored exercise may closely resemble a customized exercise, an exercise with only superficial changes may be very similar to the off-the-shelf version. Because of the breadth of possibilities for tailored exercises, the discussion in this chapter focuses primarily on off-the-shelf and customized options.

Having defined off-the-shelf, customized and tailored exercises, the remainder of this chapter details the key criteria that exercise users should consider when deciding which approach is most appropriate for a given situation. Within this chapter, reference is made to the use of simulation exercises within Assessment Centres (ACs). The same arguments, however, apply when using simulation exercises during Development Centres (DCs), unless specifically stated otherwise.

Objectives for Exercise Selection/Design

Before detailing the criteria influencing the selection of off-the-shelf versus customized exercises, it is helpful to consider the main objectives that a practitioner should have in mind when identifying or developing a suitable exercise. Whilst other factors may influence the extent to which a particular approach is favoured, the selection of an off-the-shelf approach should not be seen as an opportunity to cut corners. The key objectives to be met are outlined in Table 5.1 below, along with details of how they should be accounted for in exercise design or selection.

Table 5.1   Objectives for exercise selection/design

Objective	Customized exercise development	Selection of off-the-shelf exercise
1. Ensure task relevance	Design the exercise around the output of the task analysis	Evaluate the comparability of the tasks to available off-the-shelf exercises
2. Ensure relevant competencies/ dimensions are elicited	Base exercise design on competency/dimension analysis	Determine the suitability of the exercise to elicit relevant competencies/dimensions
3. Ensure appropriate level of difficulty	Design in appropriate level of difficulty and trial to confirm	Determine suitability of exercise level and content (trial if necessary)
4. Ensure quality of exercise documentation	Design all documentation and forms to meet Candidates' and Assessors' requirements	Evaluate documentation to determine suitability to Candidates' and Assessors' requirements
5. Ensure content (and face) validity of exercise	Involve subject matter experts in the design process	Involve subject matter experts in the exercise selection process

The Issue of Exercise Fidelity

Much of the debate about the relative merits of off-the-shelf versus customized exercises has concerned the issue of exercise fidelity, and specifically the extent to which high fidelity is desirable and the factors that influence this.

A key assumption underpinning this debate is that off-the-shelf exercises have lower fidelity than customized exercises, and that consequently ACs designed specifically for a given organization (that is, customized) are likely to more accurately reflect the organization's needs and context (Krause and Gebert 2003). The current authors argue that it is not *necessarily* the case that off-the-shelf exercises will have lower fidelity than customized ones as, from larger collections of off-the-shelf exercises it may well be possible to identify an exercise which bears a close resemblance to key elements of the job role that is being assessed (which may be enhanced by tailoring). Furthermore, this depends upon what have been identified as the 'key elements' of a given job role that need to be reflected in a particular exercise. As Thornton and Mueller Hanson (2004) identify, 'fidelity' can refer to a variety of different elements in the context of exercise selection, such as industry setting, the problems at the heart of the simulation, the importance of tasks, the medium for presenting materials and the response mode. Additionally, aspects such as timings, the role the candidate assumes in the exercise, the size and nature of the organizational setting (over and above industry sector) and the national and market context may also be relevant. Whilst it is unlikely that an off-the-shelf exercise is able to exactly match all of these elements in terms of fidelity, for a given context some aspects of fidelity may be more important than others, in which case identifying an appropriate off-the-shelf exercise in relation to these key aspects may well be possible. 'Fidelity' in its broadest sense may also encompass the job relevance of the behaviours or attributes elicited during the exercise, in addition to the context, which is also known as 'behavioural' or 'psychological' fidelity (Thornton and Kedharnath, in press). Commonalities have been identified in the competencies measured in ACs across a wide range of different organizations (Eurich et al. 2009; Arthur et al. 2003; Lievens 1998), and consequently behavioural fidelity may be more easily achieved than fidelity in relation to the specific context of the exercise. In some cases, achieving fidelity on this level may be sufficient. The instances in which competencies may be favoured over tasks and vice versa are discussed later in this chapter.

If we are to accept the premise that taking an off-the-shelf approach will, in general, result in lower levels of fidelity than a customized approach, the second issue is the extent to which high fidelity is always desirable. Critical to this debate is the issue of whether high fidelity always results in higher criterion-related validity. Whilst this assumption is implicit in some discussions (Krause and Gebert 2003; Thornton and Gruys 2003), the current authors have not found any studies that have experimentally manipulated a variety of different dimensions of exercise fidelity across a variety of contexts in relation to criterion-related validity. Neither does there appear to be evidence to indicate at what point there may be diminishing returns on higher levels of fidelity in terms of validity gains. Where research has been conducted in this area, it has typically focused on the design features contributing to construct as opposed to criterion-related validity (Lievens 1998) and has concerned the support, guidance and instruction provided to the Assessor (Woehr and Arthur 2003) rather than the specific instructions provided to the candidate that result in particular behaviours being demonstrated during an exercise. However, more recently, the use of Trait Activation Theory to consider the 'cues' within an exercise that influence a candidate's behaviour, has provided a promising framework by which aspects of fidelity may be viewed and evaluated (Lievens, Tett and Schleicher 2009).

Despite the absence of specific studies examining exercise fidelity, best practice guidance is clear in this area. The most recent International Task Force Assessment Centre Guidelines state that whilst the 'stimuli contained in a simulation [should] parallel or resemble stimuli in the work situation ... the desirable degree of fidelity is a function of the purpose of the Assessment Centre' (2009: 246). The authors also suggest that not only is the desirable degree of fidelity dependent on the purpose of the AC, but also that the aspects of fidelity which impact validity will also vary on this basis.

Considerations When Choosing Off-the-Shelf versus Customized Exercises

The following section details the considerations which influence the extent to which off-the-shelf and customized exercises are appropriate in a given situation. Many of these considerations relate to the criteria that influence whether exercise fidelity is more or less important, although additional considerations, unrelated to exercise fidelity, are also discussed. A table summarizing 13 factors to consider when choosing between off-the-shelf or customized exercises is presented near the end of this chapter.

CONSIDERATION 1 – IS POTENTIAL OR PERFORMANCE BEING ASSESSED?

A key consideration in terms of exercise fidelity is the extent to which the exercise/AC is concerned with assessing potential for future roles versus current levels of job performance. Whilst identifying exercises for the assessment of current levels of job performance may lend itself to job and task specific exercises, it is likely when assessing potential that task requirements are broader due to the unknown nature of future tasks, as well as the need to capture competencies related to a wider variety of different contexts. Consequently when assessing potential for future roles, lower fidelity simulations in terms of the specific tasks within the exercise may be more appropriate, as the competencies being elicited may become more important than the specifics of the task itself (Thornton and Mueller-Hanson 2004; Lievens and Conway 2001). The distinction between performance and potential loosely parallels that between Development and Assessment Centres, specifically when Development Centres are focused on performance gaps in relation to future roles (rather than current ones); hence, on this basis, off-the-shelf exercises may be more appropriate in a development context where competencies are the priority, than in a selection context where the fidelity of the task itself may take precedence.

CONSIDERATION 2 – HOW CRITICAL IS THE ROLE?

The criticality of the job role may influence the decision about whether an off-the-shelf or customized approach is taken, with the premise in this case being that a customized exercise is likely to have higher validity. In such circumstances the decision is less about what is the most valid approach to take in the context, and more about allocating budget and resources on the basis of business impact. Whilst less than optimal relevance and validity may be acceptable for lower level roles with limited bottom line impact (ignoring the obvious issues around litigation), for higher level roles with a high level of impact and hence potential risk, the identification of the most appropriate and focused exercises with the highest level of validity may be required. Additionally, for roles that are safety critical, customized exercises may be more appropriate, regardless of the level of role, because of the significant 'costs' of failure associated with these roles.

CONSIDERATION 3 – WHAT IS THE FORMAT OF THE AC?

The extent to which the timings and structure of the AC correspond to available off-the-shelf exercises will also influence whether relevant off-the-shelf exercises can be identified. The number of candidates that need to be assessed could affect the choice of approach if, for example, an off-the-shelf group exercise requires a minimum of four candidates and only three will be attending a given AC. Similarly, if the AC timetable means that only 45 minutes is available for a specific exercise, and no off-the-shelf exercises of that type are available of less than 60 minutes, this would necessitate either a tailored or customized approach, or potentially restructuring the AC to make it fit with the available off-the-shelf exercises. The decision to use linked exercises may also have an influence. Whilst some providers of off-the-shelf exercises do have suites of interlinked exercises, sometimes called 'day in the life' suites, the potential for all the linked exercises in a suite to be relevant is less likely than for a single exercise. Additionally, while these suites of exercises exist, they are not commonplace and the choice may be limited. Therefore if linking exercises, it may well be necessary to develop a customized set of exercises, or tailor a set of appropriate off-the-shelf exercises. A similar approach would need to be taken if a 'non-standard' exercise type was required, for example an integrated role play and analysis exercise.

CONSIDERATION 4 – ARE APPLICANTS INTERNAL/EXTERNAL OR A MIXTURE OF BOTH?

It is important to consider who will be attending the AC. The main consideration in this respect is whether candidates will be internal or external to the organization. Whilst it might seem desirable to design the exercise suite in the actual organization, having the exercises set in this context could unfairly disadvantage external applicants as they do not have a working knowledge of the organization. Similarly, for internal candidates, it is also important to consider the extent to which the level of knowledge of the organization may impact on performance on the exercises. Even within a group of internal candidates, it is likely that there will be differing levels of knowledge and experience of the organization. If these are not elements that are explicitly being assessed in the process, it is important to factor this into exercise design to avoid unfairly disadvantaging candidates with less experience. Where situations are too similar to the real organizational context, there is a risk that internal assessors may also apply real life rules and standards rather than focusing on the requirements of the assessment. Where such issues are likely, it is common to use off-the-shelf exercises, or to design such exercises in a parallel organization and industry, which faces similar challenges to the actual one. For example it might be appropriate to set exercises in a generic 'professional services' context if designing exercises for a financial services organization. The situations faced by individuals in both contexts would be similar enough to ensure realism and face validity, but different enough to ensure that there was no unfair advantage for specific groups. Either approach will ensure that there is a level playing field for all candidates whether internal or external and regardless of organizational knowledge.

CONSIDERATION 5 – HOW SPECIFIC ARE THE ROLE REQUIREMENTS?

For roles that are more generic and are likely to be similar across a range of organizations (for example, sales and marketing, general management), it is more likely that an off-the-shelf exercise may be identified that assesses relevant competencies and has face validity (Adams 1987). However, for specialist roles (in particular where job knowledge is a key part of the assessment), suitable exercises may simply not exist in an off-the-shelf format, and a customized approach may be necessary. Thornton and Gibbons (2009: 26) extend this point, suggesting that a task-based approach to exercise design, that is where the nature of the exercise tasks takes precedence over the competencies to be measured, may be more appropriate 'when selecting for a specific, well-defined position' and 'when the job consists of a small set of repeated tasks'.

CONSIDERATION 6 – HOW IMPORTANT IS IT TO ASSESS JOB KNOWLEDGE AND CURRENT JOB PERFORMANCE?

As highlighted previously, the highest level of exercise fidelity is where the exercise very closely resembles or replicates a specific job task, as is the case with work samples.

These high fidelity simulations may be appropriate where job knowledge and current job performance are being assessed (Thornton and Rupp 2006; Fowler 1988). In such circumstances, it is unlikely that this information would be elicited in an off-the-shelf exercise, and hence a customized approach may be necessary.

CONSIDERATION 7 – HOW IMPORTANT IS IT THAT THE AC COMMUNICATES BRAND AND ORGANIZATION/ROLE CHARACTERISTICS?

For many organizations, attracting the right people to apply for a given role is a key focus for recruitment activities. Whilst for many organizations attraction concerns an almost exclusive focus on recruitment literature and websites, ACs can also play their part. They can serve as a Realistic Job Preview (Premack and Wanous 1985), which assists the candidate with the self-selection process, both in terms of whether they want to join the organization and whether the role is suitable for them. Where this is important, a customized approach is likely to be more appropriate, where exercises can be designed to communicate key information about the role and organization.

The communication of this information will be more important for some organizations and roles than others. For example, roles where there may be high levels of attrition due to unmet or unrealistic expectations about job requirements, or roles with particularly unique requirements, may lend themselves to exercises which communicate key role characteristics, both positive and negative. Conversely, where suitably qualified candidates are few and far between, it may be critical that the selection process itself serves to further engage future employees and hence maximize the probability that they will accept a job offer if one is made.

For many organizations with particularly strong external brands, or strong and unique cultures or values, AC exercises may provide a means to communicate this information. For example, if an organization promotes its ethical work practices, or operates in a potentially controversial area such as tobacco or alcohol manufacture, or defence, the organization may wish to ensure that the selection process openly presents their stance on these factors, so applicants can carefully evaluate the extent of the fit. As previously stated, if this requirement is important, a customized approach is likely to be necessary to ensure that the exercises are appropriate and communicate these messages.

CONSIDERATION 8 – WHAT IS THE ANTICIPATED VOLUME OF USAGE?

The anticipated volume and frequency of use are likely to be key factors in determining which approach is taken. Gratton (1985) argues that one of the main reasons for the widespread use of generic exercises is the absence of development costs associated with these exercises. For off-the-shelf exercises, the development costs are commonly absorbed by the exercise developer and are then typically sold on a 'per use' basis. Therefore, whilst there are no upfront development costs for the exercise purchaser, there are likely to be ongoing fees per use, the extent of which will be dependent upon the specific exercises purchased and the usage volumes. Conversely, for customized exercises, a fee is typically paid upfront for the cost of developing the exercise(s) with no further ongoing fees for usage. For tailored exercises, the position is less clear and is likely to be dependent upon the ownership of the Intellectual Property and legal copyright of the content. This issue is discussed further in a later section.

The varying levels of investment (upfront versus ongoing) are, as Gratton suggests, usually a strong determinant in the choice of approach. If exercises are to be used for a small one-off assessment or administered to a minimal number of candidates, there may be limited logic in investing time and money in the development of customized exercises. The greater the volume of candidates, the more likely it is that the 'per use' fees will outweigh the costs of developing a customized exercise. Table 5.2 below shows a possible comparison of the equivalent costs associated with use of an off-the-shelf exercise versus a customized exercise.

Table 5.2   A cost comparison of using off-the-shelf versus customized exercises

Approach	Upfront development cost of one exercise	Ongoing costs
Off-the-shelf	No upfront costs	£100 per candidate
Customized	£7,500	Limited or no ongoing costs

In this example it would become more cost effective to opt for the customized approach if volumes of more than 75 candidates were anticipated (£100 × 75 candidates). This is not a particularly high volume and may be common for many organizations. For example those which run large scale recruitment campaigns, such as graduate programmes, or where turnover is high and frequent ongoing recruitment is required, for example in a contact centre environment. It is common for ongoing costs to be overlooked, with the focus tending to be on the upfront development costs. This often leads to the decision to opt for off-the-shelf exercises, which appear on the face of it to be the cheaper option. However, when considered more holistically, a customized solution may actually prove to be more cost effective.

CONSIDERATION 9 – WHAT IS THE ANTICIPATED SHELF LIFE OF THE EXERCISE?

When estimating volumes of usage and the consequent cost effectiveness, another key consideration is the likely *shelf life* of an exercise, that is, the length of time for which an exercise remains fit for use. Shelf life is impacted by a number of factors, notably content relevance, content exposure and leakage.

In considering shelf life, thought should be given to the continued content relevance of exercises. Questions should be asked about whether external or internal organizational changes are imminent and what impact these will have on the organization and role requirements depicted in the exercise.

Content exposure and leakage are the other key concerns when considering shelf life. Content exposure refers to instances where individuals have previously experienced the exercise. Content exposure can occur in a number of ways. For off-the-shelf exercises, the exercise content is available to anyone who purchases the exercise and therefore the same off-the-shelf exercise may be used in a number of different organizations. Additionally, as off-the-shelf materials are publicly available, albeit usually with purchase restrictions, there is a possibility that they could be accessed inappropriately by candidates seeking to gain an unfair advantage. Content exposure may also occur if unsuccessful candidates are able to reapply for a position and repeat the same assessment process. In such circumstances, consideration needs to be given as to how repeat applications should be dealt with. At the very least a 'practice effect' will be present for a candidate completing the exercise for a second time, whereby repeated exposure is linked to enhanced performance (Lievens, Buyse and Sackett 2005). This effect may be particularly strong for exercises with a 'speed' component (such as Analysis Exercises) where prior experience of the content will provide a significant advantage, or in interactive exercises (that is, Role plays / Fact Finds) where the candidate will be aware of and prepared to deal with information that is 'revealed' during the exercise. Research suggests that such performance gains are due to memory of content rather than increases in knowledge or skill (Lievens, Reeve and Heggestad 2007). In some instances, candidates may also have received feedback on their performance on the particular exercise, which could give them a further advantage if undertaking the exercise again. This is likely to be a particular issue when internal candidates are assessed for promotion, and feedback is standard practice, or forms part of the employee's ongoing development plan. For a more detailed discussion of the impact of coaching and practice effects on performance, please see Chapter 14 by Rupp and Searle in this volume.

Leakage refers to the release of information about the exercise into the public domain, usually from candidates who have undertaken the assessment process sharing details with others. Leakage over time is inevitable and may advantage later candidates who obtain prior knowledge about the exercise, which could allow a candidate to prepare possible response strategies in advance. Thornton and Gibbons (2009) call for research to address the effects of different levels of knowledge about exercise content on the performance of AC candidates on different competencies. They hypothesize that performance on administrative competencies such as delegation may be enhanced due to this prior knowledge, but performance on basic aptitude competencies such as decision-making abilities or leadership skill may not increase with prior knowledge.

Considering these issues will help to quantify the likely shelf life of an exercise. Once the likely shelf life has been determined, it is possible to calculate the anticipated volume of use within this timeframe. Using the example referred to previously where the development cost of a customized exercise is £7,500 and the equivalent off-the-shelf exercise is £100 per use, if the shelf life of this exercise was 3 years, around 25 candidates would need to be assessed each year over the 3-year period in order to make the customized approach more cost effective than an off-the-shelf approach. However, it is likely cost will not be the only driver of decision-making in many cases, and hence there may well be occasions where a customized approach is selected even when it is not the most cost effective.

CONSIDERATION 10 – HOW IMPORTANT IS LEGAL OWNERSHIP OF THE EXERCISE MATERIALS TO THE ORGANIZATION?

'Intellectual property rights' (IPR) typically cover copyrights, trademarks, design rights and patents. Whilst there are variations in the detail of copyright law between countries, the Berne Convention and Universal Copyright Convention lay down a common set of rights around intellectual property which has been signed up to by the majority of nation states (UK Copyright Service 2010).

According to these IPR conventions, copyright for 'literary works' such as off-the-shelf exercises will in virtually all cases reside with the supplier, and typically the supplier will grant a non-exclusive license for use of these exercises to the user at the point of purchase. The purchaser may therefore be one amongst a number of users of that exercise, and they will not be able to copy, adapt, publish or sell the content to others. Whilst for many users these constraints may not be a cause for concern, for others they may be an issue, the implications of which have been highlighted previously in relation to content exposure.

Conversely, in the case of customized exercises, copyright may be vested with the commissioning organization or individual, or with a supplier, where applicable. This will clearly be the case if an exercise is written by an internal design team, in which case copyright will typically lie with the employing organization or authors. However, in the case of an external consultancy developing an exercise for a client, the exact arrangements are likely to depend upon the particular terms and conditions of the contract. For most organizations commissioning a customized exercise, ownership of copyright may be a key driver for their decision to opt for the customized route, driven by a requirement for the exclusive and unlimited use of that exercise within their organization. This approach may be necessary for particular types of roles, and may actually be more cost effective for certain volumes, as discussed previously in relation to volume of usage. In relation to tailored exercises, the issue of copyright is likely to be less clear. It will be up to the exercise supplier and client to determine the extent to which copyright is shared. For a more detailed discussion of the issues concerning exercise copyright see Owen (1988). Notably, while purchasers of off-the-shelf exercises are usually subject to some kind of pre-qualification criteria, this is often not the case for tailored or customized exercises. Regardless of the approach taken, organizations should ensure that appropriate training is given to those using the materials.

CONSIDERATION 11 – WHAT RESOURCE EXPERTISE IS AVAILABLE FOR DEVELOPING EXERCISES?

In deciding which approach to take, consideration should be given to the resources available, in particular time and expertise. The development of effective simulation exercises is a carefully crafted skill (Caldwell, Thornton and Gruys 2003). This point is emphasized in the Guidelines and Ethical Considerations for Assessment Centre Operations (International Task Force on Assessment Centre Guidelines 2009), which state that those who are involved in developing exercises must be technically qualified to do so. Despite the importance of this, Ahmed, Payne and Whiddett (1997: 62) note that 'there is surprisingly little guidance for designing exercises in either academic or practitioners literature'. It is suggested that this lack of step by step guidance may be a cause for the general widespread use of off-the-shelf exercises. Being skilled in the design of exercises is therefore a prerequisite to ensuring the design and validation of high quality simulation exercises. Where organizations choose to develop their own exercises, they need to question whether they have the internal expertise to do so. Unfortunately Caldwell, Thornton and Gruys (2003) note that an increasing number of individuals who lack training in methods of validation believe that they can become self educated in the AC process and develop exercises based upon examples of what they have seen in other ACs.

In addition to resource expertise, resource availability should also be considered in determining which approach to take. The development of customized exercises will without doubt incur a more significant time investment than using off-the-shelf simulations, even where external expertise is used to develop customized exercises. Organizations should be clear about the resource commitment involved in designing customized simulation exercises before deciding which approach to take.

CONSIDERATION 12 – WHAT IS THE CLIMATE AROUND LITIGATION?

A key influence in recruitment and selection practice is the requirement to provide an organizational defence against potential claims of unequal treatment of candidates. The approach taken should therefore aim to ensure that all candidates experience 'sameness of treatment.' As highlighted previously, the selection of a high fidelity exercise may not always be preferable if this is likely to result in differential treatment of certain groups, such as internal candidates with prior job knowledge versus external candidates without this knowledge.

As well as fairness itself, perceptions of fairness are important and have also been shown to influence intentions to initiate litigation (Fodchuk and Sidebotham 2005; Goldman 2003). Critical to the perception of fairness is the concept of procedural justice (Gilliland 1993). A number of characteristics of selection process design have been identified as contributing to procedural justice perceptions, with the most notable from the perspective of exercise design being 'job relatedness', that is 'the extent to which an assessment appears to measure content relevant to the job situation or appears to be valid' (Gilliland 1993: 703). Research has indicated that candidates perceive simulation exercises in general to be 'job related' and therefore fair (Smither et al. 1993). This finding can arguably be extended *within* the category of simulation exercises, with exercises that are more job-related, such as customized exercises, being perceived as fairer than off-the-shelf exercises, which may not represent the job to the same extent.

Therefore, in situations where litigation is more likely, taking an approach which increases job relatedness may be preferable in order to increase perceived fairness and consequently acceptance of the process by candidates. In such instances, it may be preferable to use customized exercises to ensure that the specific job context is accurately reflected. However, as a note of caution it should be highlighted that candidate perceptions of fairness do not necessarily equate to actual levels of validity, with evidence indicating that high perceived fairness may on occasion coincide with low levels of validity and vice versa (Fodchuk and Sidebotham 2005).

CONSIDERATION 13 – WHAT ARE THE REQUIREMENTS FOR INCORPORATING TECHNOLOGY?

The extent to which technology is to be deployed in a particular assessment may impact the choice of approach. Technological advances mean that more realistic methods can be used for the presentation of exercises and response formats (Lievens and Thornton 2005), for example electronic inbox simulations, provision of information by video stream and so on. In general, the initial outlay for a customized exercise sitting on a software platform that is proprietary or has been designed for the organization is likely to be higher than a paper-based exercise. The costs associated with this are likely to include both content development and software implementation, rather than content development alone. Hence the decision to utilize technology may for financial reasons necessitate an 'off-the-shelf' approach, or alternatively the need to leverage greater budget to develop a customized solution.

The decision around whether to use technology may also interact with the extent to which ownership of Intellectual Property is a key criterion. In the case of using a pre-existing platform, whilst it may be possible for the exercise user to own the exercise content, it will be unlikely that they are able to purchase the software in its entirety, and hence there will be the need for an ongoing reliance on and commercial arrangement with a supplier, which would not be the case for a paper-based exercise.

Table 5.3 below summarizes the information presented in this chapter in relation to selecting off-the-shelf and customized exercises. As any given requirement is likely to consist of a number of potentially conflicting criteria, with some supporting an off-the-shelf approach and others a customized approach, these criteria should be prioritized when considering which approach to take. As the table provides a simplified summary of the information in this chapter, it should not be used in isolation and the reader is advised to examine the more detailed information provided in the relevant sections.

Table 5.3   Factors to consider when choosing off-the-shelf or customized exercises

Consideration	Off-the-shelf	Customized
1. Is potential or performance being assessed?	Potential	Performance
2. How critical is the role?	Non-critical	Critical
3. What is the format of the AC?	Standard	Non-standard
4. Are applicants internal/external or a mixture of both?	Mixture	Only internal or only external
5. How specific are the role requirements?	Generic	Specific
6. How important is it to assess job knowledge and current job performance?	Unimportant/ irrelevant	Important
7. How important is it that the AC communicates brand, organization and role characteristics?	Unimportant	Important
8. What are the anticipated volumes of usage?	Low	High
9. What is the anticipated shelf life of the exercise?	Short	Long
10. How important is legal ownership of the exercise materials to the organization?	Unimportant	Important
11. What resource expertise is available for developing exercises?	Limited resource	Significant resource
12. What is the climate around litigation?	Non-litigious	Litigious
13. What are the requirements for incorporating technology?	Required or not-required (to be judged on a case by case basis)	Required or not-required (to be judged on a case by case basis)

Summary

This chapter has discussed the considerations that Assessment and Development Centre practitioners should take into account when determining whether to choose off-the-shelf or customized simulation exercises. It highlights the importance of the concept of 'fit for purpose' when deciding which of these options to select, and has taken the position that the decision about whether to adopt off-the-shelf or customized exercises will depend on a variety of factors.

The chapter questions the elements underpinning the view that customized exercises are in virtually every case preferable to off-the-shelf exercises. In doing this the following assumptions are challenged: firstly that lower fidelity is always a consequence of selecting off-the-shelf exercises and secondly that high fidelity is always desirable. It is notable, however, that very little specific research was found to support this discussion, with no research having systematically evaluated whether there really is a difference between off-the-shelf and customized exercises in terms of validity. At a more detailed level, neither is there research to indicate which aspects of fidelity contribute to key outcomes. When deciding which approach to take, it is recommended that practitioners use the framework presented within this chapter to determine, on the basis of the specific circumstances in question, whether an off-the-shelf, customized or tailored approach is preferable.

In conclusion, despite best practice guidance highlighting a preference for the use of customized over off-the-shelf exercises, there is little evidence available to support this position. As a starting point it is recommended that the elements of fidelity that can be achieved in a given exercise are identified so that they can be systematically manipulated. Additionally broad consideration should be given to outcome variables in terms of both validity and applicant reactions.

References

Adams, D. 1987. Assessment centre exercises – bespoke or ready to wear. *Guidance and Assessment Review*, 3, 6–7.

Ahmed, A., Payne, T. and Whiddett, S. 1997. A process for assessment exercise design: A model of best practice. *International Journal of Selection and Assessment*, 5, 62–68.

Arthur, W. Jr., Day, E.A., McNelly, T.L. and Edens, P.S. 2003. A meta-analysis of the criterion-related validity of assessment center competencies. *Personnel Psychology*, 56, 125–154.

Caldwell, C., Thornton, G.C. III and Gruys, M.L. 2003. Ten classic assessment center errors: Challenges to selection validity. *Public Personnel Management*, 32, 73–88.

Eurich, T.L., Krause, D.E., Cigularov, K. and Thornton, G.C. III. 2009. Assessment centers: Current practices in the United States. *Journal of Business Psychology*, 24, 387–407.

Fodchuk, K.M. and Sidebotham, E.J. 2005. Procedural justice in the selection process: A review of research and suggestions for practical applications. *The Psychologist Manager Journal*, 8, 105–120.

Fowler, A. 1998. Role rehearsal. *People Management*, June, 52–55.

Gilliland, S.W. 1993. The perceived fairness of selection systems: An organizational justice perspective. *Academy of Management Review*, 18, 694–734.

Goldman, B.M. 2003. The application of referent cognitions theory to legal-claiming by terminated workers: The role of organizational justice and anger, *Journal of Management*, 29, 705–728.

Gratton, L. 1985. Assessment centers: Theory, research and practice. *Human Resource Management Australia*, 23, 10–14.

International Task Force on Assessment Centre Guidelines. 2009. Guidelines and Ethical Considerations for Assessment Centre Operations. *International Journal of Selection and Assessment*. 17, 243–253.

Krause, D.E. and Gebert, D. 2003. A comparison of assessment center practices in organizations in German-speaking regions and the United States. *International Journal of Selection and Assessment*, 11, 297–312.

Lievens, F. 1998. Factors which improve the construct validity of assessment centers: A review. *International Journal of Selection and Assessment*, 6, 141–152.

Lievens, F., Buyse, T. and Sackett, P. 2005. The operational validity of a video-based situational judgment test for medical college admissions: Illustrating the importance of matching predictor and criterion construct domains. *Journal of Applied Psychology*, 90, 442–452.

Lievens, F. and Conway, J.M. 2001. Competency and exercise variance in assessment center scores: A large-scale evaluation of multitrait-multimethod studies. *Journal of Applied Psychology*, 86, 1202–1222.

Lievens, F., Reeve, C. and Heggestad, E. 2007. An examination of psychometric bias due to retesting on cognitive ability tests in selection settings. *Journal of Applied Psychology*, 92, 1672–1682.

Lievens, F. and Thornton, G.C.III. 2005. Assessment centers: Recent developments in practice and research. In *Handbook of Personnel Selection*, edited by A. Evers, N. Anderson and O. Voskuijl. Malden, MA: Blackwell, 243–264.

Lievens, F., Tett, R.P. and Schleicher, D.J. 2009. Assessment centers at the crossroads: Toward a reconceptualization of assessment center exercises. *Research in Personnel and Human Resources Management*, 28, 99–152.

Owen, L. 1988. Assessment centre exercises: The question of copyright. *Guidance and Assessment Review*, 4, 1–3.

Premack, S.L. and J.P. Wanous. 1985. A meta-analysis of realistic job preview experiments. *Journal of Applied Psychology*, 70, 706–719.

Rankin, N. 2007. Assessment centres: The IRS report, *IRS. Employment Review*, 877 [Online]. Available at: http://www.xperthr.co.uk/article/77770/assessment-centres–the-irs-reports-data-in-full.aspx [accessed: 15 November 2010].

Smither, J.W., Reilly, R.R., Millsap, R.E., Pearlman, K. and Stoffey, R.W. 1993. Applicant reactions to selection procedures. *Personnel Psychology*, 46, 49–76.

Thornton, G.C. III and Rupp, D.E. 2006. *Assessment Centers in Human Resource Management: Strategies for Prediction, Diagnosis and Development*. Mahwah, NJ, Lawrence Erlbaum Associates.

Thornton, G.C. III and Gibbons, A.M. 2009. Validity of assessment centers for personnel selection. *Human Resource Management Review*, 93, 169–187.

Thornton, G.C. III and Gruys, M.L. 2003. Ten classic assessment center errors: Challenges to selection validity. *Public Personnel Management*, 32, 73–88.

Thornton, G.C. III and Kedharnath, U. In press. Work sample tests, in *Handbook of Testing and Assessment in Psychology*, edited by K.F. Geisinger. Washington, D.C.: American Psychological Association.

Thornton, G.C. III and Mueller-Hanson, R. 2004. *Developing organizational simulations: A guide for practitioners and students*. Mahwah, NJ: Lawrence Erlbaum.

United Kingdom Copyright Service. 2010. *Fact Sheet P-08: The Berne Convention*. [Online]. Available at: http://www.copyrightservice.co.uk/copyright/p08_berne_convention [accessed: 9 November 2010].

United Kingdom Copyright Service. 2010. *Fact Sheet P-10: The Universal Copyright Convention.* [Online]. Available at: http://www.copyrightservice.co.uk/copyright/p14_universal_copyright_convention [accessed: 9 November 2010].

Woehr, D.J. and Arthur, W. 2003. The construct-related validity of assessment center ratings: A review and meta-analysis of the role of methodological factors. *Journal of Management,* 29, 231–258.

6 Using Computer-Based Simulation Technology within an ADC: A South African Case Study

DEON MEIRING AND JAN H. VAN DER WESTHUIZEN

The Assessment Centre (AC) technique has been used in South Africa since the 1970s. ACs in South Africa were generally closely aligned to the United States model, with a strong influence from Doug Bray and Bill Byham, who introduced the AC technique when visiting South Africa. In 1974 Byham was instrumental in introducing one of the first ACs to the Old Mutual Group, the largest and most well-established financial services provider in Southern Africa. This trend continued in South Africa and soon other organizations adopted the AC model and techniques in their businesses (Meiring 2008). Since the 1980s, Assessment Centres (ACs) and Development Centres (DCs) have gone from strength to strength with the Assessment Centre Study Group (ACSG) leading the way in South Africa. The ACSG is a special-interest group of practitioners and professionals who have presented annual conferences on ACs and DCs for the past 31 years in Stellenbosch. The Study Group promotes the professional use of AC and DC techniques and facilitates the exchange of experience and skills with regard to AC practice (www.acsg.co.za).

Political Factors Impacting the Development of Assessment Centres in South Africa

Research and development of ACs and DCs in South Africa centred on important and relevant socio-political debates of the time. From the mid 1980s there was a strong focus on ACs to identify black managerial potential (Charoux 1986; 1987; 1990; 1991; 1992; Shaw and Human 1989). With confirmation that the AC is predictive of managerial potential amongst black applicants (Hurst 1992; Charoux and Hurst 1992; Kriek, Hurst and Charoux 1994), researchers started to focus on issues of culture fairness (Kriek and Thornton 1989), the cross-cultural application of AC techniques (Charoux and Hurst 1992; Shaw and Human 1989), the assessment of managerial potential (Shaw and Human 1989; Sakinofsky and Raubenheimer 1982) and the better differentiation of criteria in order to advance affirmative action and economic goals (Kriek, Hurst and Charoux 1994).

ACs and DCs cannot be separated from South African political, economic and social history, and the mainstream research agenda was led by socio-political transformation.

After the abolition of apartheid in 1994, various Acts were introduced to address the development and advancement of the majority black groups in South Africa which had lagged behind due to the injustice of apartheid. The Labour Relations Act No. 66 (Republic of South Africa 1995), the Employment Equity Act No. 55 (Republic of South Africa 1998) and the Promotion of Equality and Prevention of Unfair Discrimination Act No. 4 (Republic of South Africa 2000) are all directed at increasing workplace democracy and equality. Under the apartheid regime, black people were to a large extent excluded from the economically active population, from ownership of productive assets and from the possession of advanced skills. To a large extent, the Employment Equity Act No. 55 (Republic of South Africa 1998) in general, and the Affirmative Action Subsection in particular (Section 15), have therefore been earmarked to proactively spearhead employment equity in South Africa (Becker 2009). The Skills Development Act No. 97 (Republic of South Africa 1998) also seeks to provide an institutional framework aimed at developing and improving the skills of the South African workforce, which, in turn, made it easier for employers to recruit, select and develop individuals from previously disadvantaged backgrounds (Becker 2009). The Broad-based Black Economic Empowerment Act No.53 (Republic of South Africa 2003) was also promulgated to increase the participation of black ownership in private organizations, subsequently leading to black economic empowerment.

On a macro-level, South African organizations were grappling with the implementation of the above-mentioned legislative frameworks, which at the same time impacted on sustainability, the stability of markets, and the attraction and retention of human capital. Organizations in South Africa are required to manage the implementation of this legislation and at the same time compete internationally while protecting their local markets from international competitors. In the recent World Competitiveness Scoreboard (IDM 2010), South Africa was ranked 44th in terms of competitiveness out of 58 nations around the world, with Singapore and Hong Kong in positions one and two respectively, followed by the United States of America. A critical component of competitiveness is having the appropriate skills across a range of occupations and professions as well as the skill to drive leadership in organizations (Phillips and Thomas 2009). South Africa is experiencing a general crisis, especially pertaining to the retention of its top talent and knowledge workers (Du Preez 2002). The 'brain drain' of these resources had a negative impact on the economic and social growth of the country. South Africa experienced three peak periods of emigration, namely in 1977 after the Soweto riots, in 1986 during the State of Emergency and in 1994 during the election of the ANC government. In the past 20 years since democracy, South Africa has witnessed dramatic increases in emigration to countries such as Australia, New Zealand and the United Kingdom (Statistics South Africa 2005).While retaining talent is a macro-challenge, South African organizations are also faced with micro-challenges of retaining top talent (Phillips and Thomas 2009). South African business leaders have to acquire the skills to effectively manage post-apartheid organizations and business dynamics. Rood (1997) indicates that ethnic and language diversity, affirmative action and the gaps in income levels, education and opportunities influence the complexity of organizational culture in the South African workplace. In managing such diversity, leaders of South African organizations are challenged to create organizational cultures in which the mix of diverse individuals needs to be harnessed in order to gain a competitive advantage locally and internationally. In developing ACs for the multicultural South Africa, the cross-cultural application of ACs is becoming increasingly important. The fourth edition of the Assessment Centre and Development Assessment Centre Guidelines for South Africa elaborates on the cross-cultural application of ACs in South Africa (ACSG, 2007). ACs will be subject to close scrutiny as stronger demands for the cultural appropriateness of assessment measures will be required by the Employment Equity Act, 1998 (Act No.55 of 1998) (Government Gazette, 1998). Refer to Chapters 13 and 23 by Buckett and Krause respectively in this volume for more information on South Africa, its culture and the evolution of ACs.

The case study in this chapter focuses on a financial institution that had to operate in a new, democratic South Africa amid exposure to both the macro- and micro-challenges. We start by providing the background to the case study with an overview of the financial institution and its restructuring initiatives. We describe how this led to the need to create a new service advisor (SA) role to enhance customer-service excellence. We provide an overview of the newly created job profile of the SA along with the integrated competency profile consisting of both behavioural and organizational competencies. We then elaborate on the development of an Assessment Development Centre (ADC) using computer-based simulations (CBSs) and exercises, and we provide insight into the development phases of both the CBSs and the ADC exercises. We then describe the scoring of the CBSs and exercises and provide information on how the results were used to inform talent management processes in the financial institution. Finally, we conclude the chapter by sharing the lessons that were learned.

Financial Institution Case Study

The aim of the present case study was to use computer-based simulation technology (CBST) along with more typical exercises to develop computer-based simulations (CBSs) for an Assessment Development Centre (ADC) for a financial institution in South Africa. The primary purpose of the ADC was to identify individuals who fitted the profile of the newly created role of a service advisor (SA) and to redeploy individuals who did not fit the profile within the financial institution. The secondary purpose of the ADC was to offer individuals a learning and development experience by exposing them to a realistic business environment with business simulations and to assess the behavioural and organizational competencies required for success.

BACKGROUND AND DESCRIPTION

The South African banking sector is well developed and highly modernized. It is indeed one of the largest and most deregulated sectors within the emerging markets. The sector is experiencing significant growth, defying the global economic slowdown. This case study focuses on a financial institution that operates throughout South Africa, with more than 500 branches that underwent a major change strategy of its business operations. Although the financial institution strives to provide superior and excellent customer service, the reality appears to be one in which customers do not always experience this kind of service. The importance of a superior customer experience cannot be overemphasized, as experience has shown that service remains the only differentiator between financial institutions and their competitors. In 2004, the financial institution embarked on a huge restructuring drive of its business operations, striving to build enduring and rewarding relationships with all its customers, providing them not only with a wide range of cutting-edge banking products, but also superior customer service. Traditionally, organizational performance and efficiency measurements have been focused on cost containment in the banking industry. Today, however, performance-measurement systems of world-class organizations are tailored to drive customer and service business excellence. Business-excellence models are based on the premise that customer satisfaction, people (employee) satisfaction, and impact on society are all achieved through leadership driving the policy and strategy, people management, resources and processes, leading ultimately to excellence in business results (Williams 2008). The financial institution embarked on the implementation of the South African Excellence Model using a slightly modified version of the Kaplan–Norton Balanced Scorecard approach (Kaplan and Norton 2001) in their restructuring drive. The South African Excellence Model provides a snapshot of the financial institution's strengths and areas for improvement and 'scores' the organization in relation to other financial institutions. The Balanced Scorecard aligns the organization's strengths and areas for improvement with the key objectives of the organization to ensure that its strategic outcomes are achieved. According to Botha (2008), the South African Excellence Model brings to the organization improvements to its strategic direction and processes, its relationships with its customers and employees, and ultimately its bottom line and ability to compete.

The '60 in 90 Project' was launched in 2004 as part of the financial institution's change strategy with the focus on revamping 60 bank branches in 90 days throughout South Africa to improve the financial institution's competitive edge in order to ensure that it not only kept up with its competitors, but also exceeded its customers' expectations. The revamping was furthermore part and parcel of ensuring that the financial institution continuously created and improved enduring and rewarding relationships with its customers by listening to and addressing their needs. In order to live up to the brand promise, the financial institution offered a more comprehensive banking experience to its customers through the revamping of its branches.

THE SERVICE ADVISOR'S ROLE

In order to achieve the above-mentioned goals, the institution started off by identifying key roles for change. The first were those of the area managers, branch managers and administration managers, whereof all changed to the role of customer care consultant (CCC). Achieving the goals of excellent customer service means retaining and developing high-quality employees who will deliver great service. Today's challenging financial industry system calls for carefully constructed methods of selecting, preparing and developing staff to deliver exceptional customer service (Blaney, Hobson, Meade and Scodro 1993). To execute the financial institution strategy, the institution had to focus on critical key roles to execute its change strategy.

The CCC position was identified as one of the key strategic roles to be changed and reintegrated, as the role had been in existence since 2001. The role was seen as that of a floorwalker (meeter and greeter). The CCC position was initially a senior position in the branch, but over time the position had been filled by junior and inexperienced staff, which diminished the role. Branch management changed the role and job description to suit the needs of the branch. A need was identified to reposition the role of CCC in branches to manage the customer experience more effectively, especially in the welcoming zone (banking hall) of the bank.

The repositioning of this key role was in line with the financial institution's customer and service business-excellence strategy. The repositioning included a name change, from CCC to Service Advisor (SA). A new role description was formulated and focused on the SA managing the experience of customers in the welcoming zone and ensuring prompt and superior service to customers by correctly determining their needs and facilitating the resolution thereof. This function was a key contributor to building enduring and rewarding relationships with customers.

The position of SA was created at all the financial institution's branches. Some branches could have more than one such position, depending on the size and complexity of the branch as well as the volume of customers visiting the branch.

THE COMPETENCY PROFILE OF THE SERVICE ADVISOR

Based on the redefinition of the role from CCC to that of SA, a first-phase competency-design strategy was used to develop a set of behaviour-based competencies for the role. In a second phase, a more elaborate, blended competency modelling design was adopted, focusing on both behavioural and organizational competencies. This mixed-model design was followed because the project team and custodians of the financial institution felt that the purpose of the assessment was not only to identify people to fit the job, but also to indicate where people could possibly be placed elsewhere in the financial institution. Other considerations focused on training, development, performance contracting and the future direction in which the role would grow. A final consideration entailed the design of both CBS ADC exercises to be futuristic in terms of the business-excellence model. This entailed ensuring that the CBS ADC exercises were developed taking into account variables such as the environment, the organization and human resources, and linking them to reach the most appropriate action, given certain contingencies. It meant making the most of people, finances and technologies in order to achieve the objectives.

The project team created the ideal profile for the SA role and mapped existing competencies against the newly developed skills as well as the new role criteria and outcomes of the job. Role clarity was an important factor and entailed the alignment of roles within the business with leaders who functioned at the right level with the right competence. Tables 6.1 and 6.2 represent the new blended-competency model for the SA role consisting of both behavioural and organizational competencies.

Table 6.1   Behavioural competencies for the service advisor role

Behavioural competencies	
Performance-motivation	**1. Innovation:** willingness and ingenuity to generate original ideas and to initiate matters without being urged; being resourceful, original and creative. **2. Energy:** persevering with a task despite opposition or obstacles; time and energy spent in an attempt to accomplish tasks successfully.
Decision-making	**3. Analytical thinking:** grasping a problem by delving to the root causes thereof; considering all relevant information collected, and analysing it in detail. **4. Decision-making and business acumen:** carefully contemplating the consequences of various alternatives (positive as well as negative) before a decision is made; handling other partners in business dealings tactfully. **5. Flexibility:** displaying a readiness to listen and contemplate new ideas, policies, work methods or circumstances; being prepared to consider the credibility of others' opinions and if necessary, adjusting own standpoint accordingly and adapting to unforeseen or changed circumstances.
Leadership	**6. Utilizing teamwork:** effectively handling, utilizing and developing team members by leading them to goal attainment. **7. Task structuring:** structuring tasks effectively to attain goals. **8. Impact and conflict resolution:** making decisions adequately and decisively without unnecessary hesitation; willingness to accept responsibility for the consequences and risks involved in the decisions, and dealing with conflict. **9. Sensitivity:** being sensitive to and having a genuine concern for the needs and feelings of others, and looking out for the community and one's environment.
Communication	**10. Interpersonal influence:** putting forward logical and convincing arguments spontaneously in order to achieve a purpose. **11. Persuasive presentation:** communicating effectively with others, whether it is in a group situation, a one-on-one situation, or in the form of a formal presentation.
Administrative	**12. Planning and organizing:** setting objectives for the short and long term, determining priorities, linking variables, developing and evaluating alternatives and choosing the best course of action in order to achieve the set objectives.

Table 6.2   Organizational competencies for the service advisor role

Organizational competencies	
Financial perspective	**1. Branch resource management:** managing resources to improve the branch's performance, which includes capacity management, merchandising and the physical environment. **2. Business acumen:** understanding the local business environment.
Internal processes	**3. Operational efficiency and risk:** understanding the Operating Model and maintaining organizational policies and procedures in the branch. **4. Analytical thinking:** Applying analytical thinking to solve problems and make decisions with regard to the welcoming-zone environment.
People perspective	**5. Coaching:** providing coaching support to an identified mentee(s) in the branch **6. Identify development capability:** having the ability to identify positive and negative behaviour. **7. Communication:** facilitating the flow of communication in the branch; communicating effectively. **8. Self-development:** accepting accountability for own development **9. Decision-making:** identifying customer needs and conflict situations in the welcoming zone; ensuring that material is available.
Customer perspective	**10. Branch opportunities and service planning:** ensuring the implementation of a service-improvement plan to meet branch targets and demonstrating an understanding of customer measurements. **11. Management of customer-service experience:** facilitating performance motivations and service innovations in the branch as well as service excellence; managing the Visitor's Comments Book; handling service recovery. **12. Understanding customer profile in local market:** identifying and using opportunities to increase market share in the local business environment; applying results from market analyses to identify potential market segments.

Computer-Based Simulation Technology (CBST)

Between 1998 and 2004, the competitive landscape of financial industries in South Africa exploded with new advances in information technology (IT) being incorporated into financial institutions' business models. This change in the business environment, the sophistication of a new-generation employee corps, and customer service and competitiveness in the market, brought early exploration of CBST and ADCs to the fore (Van der Westhuizen 2009).

Business simulation is a dynamic, competitive and exciting computer-based tool that replicates the entire interaction occurring between the role it simulates and other roles within the organization, in this case the financial institution. The end result is a true reflection of what people are doing in the workplace and the experiences they might encounter. It depicts the business issues, the technical job-related skills issues as well as the people issues. The powerful learning experienced by using business simulation, exposes candidates to a realistic business environment and enables them to recognize the trade-offs surrounding major strategic business decisions at both strategic and tactical levels.

Transformation from ADC exercises to integrated business-process business simulations calls for more than mere assessment of the traditional behavioural competencies. CBST integrates organizational processes and business issues on a simulation platform where candidates are given the opportunity to demonstrate both behavioural and organizational competencies needed for success. Owing to the change strategy followed by the financial institution in revamping its branches, new functions and structures and a futuristic approach to simulation exercises were called for by the financial institution. CBST was used as the platform from which the CBS ADC exercises for the role of SA in the financial institution were developed.

Although a description of the technical aspects of working with the IT team to design and implement the CBST provides a valuable contribution, an overview of the overall ADC process provides a framework for understanding the technical issues within the context of the ADC. The development of the CBST was initiated by refocusing the project team's attention to the definition of an ADC, namely evaluation of behaviour, based on multiple inputs, together with specially developed simulation exercises and techniques whereby judgements about the candidate's behaviour are made and then reported and discussed by numerous trained observers. Observers then reach consensus on the behaviour of the candidate.

Therefore, in order to adhere to good standard practice regarding the ADC process, our ADC had to follow suit. Exercises used mostly in the traditional ADC are: the Case Study and/or Analysis Problem; the In-Basket; the Interactive Group Exercise; and One-on-One Interview with some type of Presentation.

Thus far the understanding was that the In-Basket exercise was the most common ADC exercise that lent itself to CBST, while the Analysis Problem and interactive exercises would not. The challenge for the Project Team was incorporating all these exercises into the ADC process and capitalizing on the input and output of some or all of these exercises. Therefore the welcoming address of the ADC not only explained the objective of the CBST ADC but also provided an overview of which exercises to expect. The Case Study or Analysis Problem at the same time laid the foundation for the background of the new role. The key analysis, proposals and other deliverables requested during the Case Study exercises were also used during the 'To Do' In-Basket item and provided immediate self-discovery and feedback to participants. That also applied to the Group Discussion and One-on-One Interview which provided input into the In-Basket through their outcome. For example, during the Group Discussion participants would discuss the service standards and service inputs and use this as input for In-Basket items, explaining how they would most beneficially utilize the outcome of the meeting.

Development of Computerized Business Simulations (CBSs)

The success of CBS lies in the development methodology and the project management of this intervention with the client. The development of the CBS followed the four-phase design approach depicted in Figure 6.1.

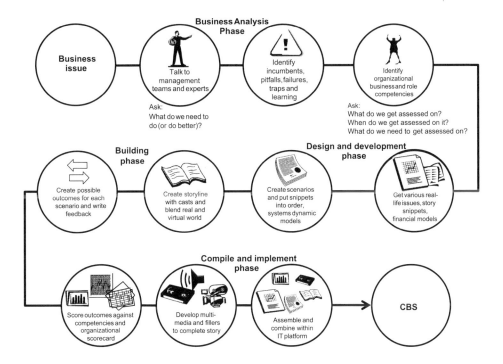

Figure 6.1   The four-phase design approach of the CBS

BUSINESS ANALYSIS PHASE

The Business Analysis Phase is the most important phase in the development of CBSs and entails meeting and consulting with the client's project team. The team consisted of consultants and the internal project team members of the financial institution, namely representation from learning and development, recruitment and organizational development, talent management, branch managers, risk management, business strategy and IT. The development of project goals with specific project deliverables and timelines is essential in this phase. Detailed tasks and activities were assigned to members of the project team, amongst others arranging venues, scheduling meetings and liaising with stakeholders. The project team gathered information on the role of the SA in the organization, its environment, and dilemmas the incumbent would face. It also included spending actual time with the incumbents to discuss key organizational issues and challenges of the role. Extensive meetings on processes of the role were held with the aim of identifying procedures, structures, challenges, pitfalls, duplication and the uniqueness of the role. The project team spent approximately three weeks and held two project meetings to obtain a clear picture of the role of an SA. Once the role description was compiled, the project team categorized job-relevant samples of challenges, pitfalls and critical incidents as played out in real time in the workplace.

The next steps in the Business Analysis Phase were to identify learning and training needs in the new SA role. New aspects of technical processes, desired behaviour, business culture and typical learning interventions were explored and brainstormed. The aim of the learning interventions was to enhance the benefit of the simulation experience and to align these interventions with existing training efforts in the organization. The last important step in this phase was to identify what the project team wanted to assess. As the competencies of the current CCC role were no longer sufficient, a new competency profile was developed for the SA role, as discussed earlier.

The project team also had to identify how the assessment would be rolled out on the financial institution's local area network (Intranet) as well as the technological challenges it would face. Finally, how and where the actual CBST ADC should be administered, namely on a stand-alone platform or on the local area network, also had to be envisaged.

DESIGN AND DEVELOPMENT PHASE

This phase focused on the project goal, with the project team creating real-life workplace scenarios. It started with a basic storyline, using the assessment criteria and competency framework and conforming to learning-development and experiential outcomes. Figure 6.2 depicts the delivery process on the day of assessment.

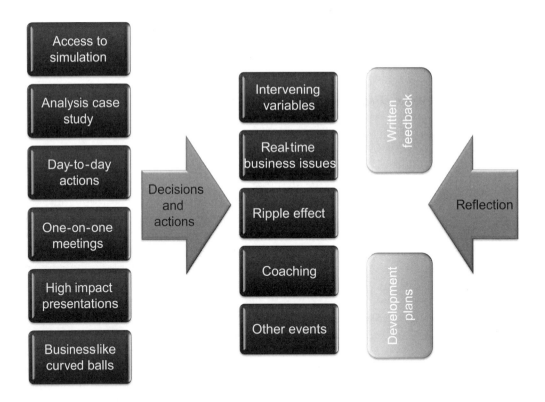

Figure 6.2   Delivery process of a CBS in an AC

- **Welcoming address:** The candidates were provided with a set of instructions on how to 'play' through the simulation and manage their way around, how to obtain help and how to ask frequent questions.

- **Introduction:** The candidates were introduced by the branch manager in the simulation to the new role, new colleagues and people they would interact with most frequently within the simulation. The simulation consisted of various rounds and is the central element of the other exercises in the assessment, integrating all the other exercises. Various scenarios were depicted during each round, requiring the SA to make judgements of the processes and situations within a specific scenario.
- **Simulation round 1:** This round dealt with a typical day in the new role as an SA in a virtual branch simply called the 'Good 2 Great' branch. The candidates had to deal with five scenarios with multiple-choice questions. The candidates could elaborate on each answer in an open text box on the simulation. Each question had a time limit of 4 minutes. This formed part of the computerized In-Basket that simulates all the day-to-day administrative and managing tasks of an SA. As with any typical branch, this branch also faces complex business problems, which the candidate must help solve. As the computerized In-Basket forms an integral part of the financial institution, the candidate must make interactive, strategic decisions by means of a dynamic-systems model, and then apply these disciplines in practice. Immediate feedback is received in the form of automated feedback reports and graphs, which reinforce the specified experiential objectives.
  - **Exercise 1:** The candidates received an email from the branch manager requesting them to submit a service-improvement plan as an input to the branch's business plan. The candidates could choose to either type or handwrite their service-improvement plan. This exercise served as the analysis problem – a typical case study in which the candidate is provided with a considerable amount of information concerning service in a branch. Background to the branch was provided through the financial institution's Intranet as well as hard copies, with the request that the service problem areas in the branch be analysed and formal recommendations made in order to improve the overall service levels and effectiveness. The candidates had to analyse the current situation of the branch in terms of its service plan, customer profiles in its micro market, service efficiency and Visitors' Comments Book, taking into account the problem situations they might encounter. The candidates had to submit a formal written report on their service-improvement plan within one hour, clearly identifying all service problems within the branch, stating the long- and short-term actions they would take, and assigning responsibilities to specific persons.
- **Simulation round 2:** This round entailed scenarios in the welcoming zone in which the candidates had to interact with virtual customers and colleagues. Each scenario called for a decision to be made by choosing the most appropriate option, almost like the case with a situational judgement test, and each decision in turn led to a new scenario. The scenarios followed a logical decision tree. In some cases candidates avoided making decisions. However, owing to the logical sequence in the decision tree, they eventually had to make decisions. One such aspect was the option of meeting with the branch manager on personal-performance contracting and performance discussions. Should the candidate indefinitely postpone this meeting, a phone call would be received from the branch manager saying that they needed to meet to discuss the said issues. This simulation round had 10 scenarios each with its own logical sequence, questions and answers. What differentiated this from the situational judgement test was that it provided an open-ended free-text option for

own behaviour on each scenario that called for a decision. The benefit of this 'free-text for own behaviour' option is that if someone could indeed identify the most appropriate option, they still had to demonstrate the accompanying behaviour and/or elaborate on their option. With that approach, the project team felt that simply identifying the most appropriate answer was not such valuable behavioural evidence as elaborating on that same answer.

  - **Exercise 2:** Toward the end of simulation round 2, the candidates received a phone call from the branch manager inviting 10 candidates to conduct a team meeting during which they would discuss the service standards and service inputs for the welcoming zone. Agreement had to be reached while representing their branch as team leaders of the service-improvement team. In the course of the discussion, behaviours are observed and each candidate had to attempt to convince the other candidates that his/her ideas were the best and at the same time reach consensus on the best ideas for service improvement.

- **Simulation round 3:** This round started with a scenario whereby the SA was requested to give feedback on the outcome of the team meeting. The feedback had to be sent to his/her virtual branch manager in the simulation via email. The branch manager used some of the discussion points in follow-up scenarios. More welcoming-zone scenarios were introduced in which the SA had to interact with virtual clients and colleagues. As the simulated branch became busier, the SA role also became more hectic, and scenarios had to be handled more effectively and within a shorter space of time, that is, 3 minutes per question. There were 20 scenarios with questions and answers. These scenarios, just like the others during the previous simulation rounds, were all depicted as various situations in which the candidates needed to make judgements on the processes of the job and not on the stand-alone situations *per se*.

  - **Exercise 3:** This exercise forms an important part of the SA's managerial repertoire. The art of conducting a one-on-one interview plays a crucial role in solving conflict with customers. In this scenario, the candidates had to meet one on one with an irritated customer, try to solve the conflict and enhance the customer-service experience. The one-on-one meeting was followed by a general feedback and coaching session during which the candidates received feedback on their performance from an administrator.

- **Simulation round 4:** In this round, the candidates were required to give feedback to the virtual branch manager via email on the outcome of the one-on-one interview and the feedback session. A further 20 welcoming-zone scenarios were introduced with different customers and colleagues, building up towards a formal presentation by the candidates to the branch management team on service improvement and the management of the welcoming zone. The candidates had to present an 8-minute motivational talk, for which they had 30 minutes to prepare, on their recommendations for the branch and their suggested initiatives for the service plan. They were required to use a PowerPoint slideshow or any other visual aids.

  - **Exercise 4:** In this exercise, the candidates had to prepare a formal presentation to the branch management team on how they could improve service. A number of assessees were grouped together and the presentation was done in real life. This was not a computerized exercise.

- **Simulation round 5:** In this round, a feedback email was sent from the branch management team to all the candidates on their presentations done in Exercise 4.

Thereafter 10 more scenarios were presented, bringing the simulation experience to a logical closure. The simulation concluded by the virtual branch manager congratulating the candidates on their effort and indicating that they would shortly receive feedback on their inputs.

The computerized scoring assessment and the assessment are covered over 2 days, with various behavioural exercises and multiple simulation scenarios allowing ample time to assess behaviour as well as the number of scenarios that simulated the process of the SA role.

TECHNICAL SOFTWARE DEVELOPMENT PHASE

The technical software development phase involved the consultant team updating the storyline on their simulation platform. Capturing the competencies, linking the scenarios with each other and further developing the storyline were some of the main activities performed in this phase. Multimedia was used to depict various scenarios and video shoots were arranged. Videos included a message from the bank's CEO as well as the project sponsor.

This phase entailed developing hard copies of the assessment and experiential material, including a simulation-background guide, technical-requirement documentation, terms and acronym guides, easy reference guides and instructions for the various assessment exercises. Once all the information (data) and content had been captured onto the simulation software platform, it was exported and the simulation then ran on a stand-alone platform and/or a closed local area network.

IMPLEMENTATION PHASE

To ensure that the implementation ran smoothly, a pilot run was conducted with six people in the SA role and with consultants acting as the primary observers and administrators of the process. Pre-pilot training and orientation took place, and since the observers and administrators formed part of the project team, only minor issues needed to be addressed. During this phase, individual coaching and development took place, for those members of the financial institution's personnel who were going to take over the administration of the CBS. A final feedback report also had to be incorporated into the learning and development platform of the organization, in order to facilitate the targeted development needs of each individual, as well as feedback on the final assessment of each candidate in the new SA role.

Scoring of the Computer-Based Simulation

The scoring of possible options for the computer-based simulation was initially very similar to that of a situational judgement test, and it was done as part of the development phase of the CBS. That entailed the identification of various possible answers to a particular scenario which on the day of the ADC, the SA needed to identify which of the options they regarded as the most appropriate. One factor that differentiated that from the situational judgement test, however, was the fact that the SA could also, apart from choosing the most appropriate answer, indicate by means of own behaviour what he/she would do in a similar situation.

Scoring of the online answers against the SA-blended competencies and the criteria the organization desired, was a major task in the project, as 64 scenarios had to be assessed. Each scenario had at least four options to choose from and needed to be scored against both the behavioural and organizational competencies. Deciding which competencies should be assessed in a particular scenario and which actions were called for was a challenging assignment. There were no correct or incorrect answers, only most appropriate or least appropriate options. The project team took the following steps to develop a scoring key:

Step 1: Select the most appropriate option.
Step 2: Identify the primary as well as the secondary competencies evidenced by a response to the scenario.
Step 3: Score the responses to the scenarios. The primary competencies were scored firstly, using a 10-point scale, where the most appropriate answer was scored a +5 and the least appropriate answer a -5. Secondary competencies were also scored and ranged from +3 to -3. Table 6.3 indicates the scoring criteria for the CBS ADC.
Step 4: Aligning the scores with AC practice while still allowing each SA to answer a particular scenario in his/her own words. By answering what he/she would do, contributed to the behavioural information from the various behavioural exercises.

Table 6.3   Scoring criteria for the CBS ADC

If an answer is the most appropriate	Competencies are scored highest (+4, +5)
If an answer is in the middle appropriate	Competencies are scored towards the middle (+2, +3 or -2, -3)
If an answer is less appropriate	Competencies are scored towards the middle (+1 or -1)
If an answer is the least appropriate	Competencies are scored lowest (-4, -5)

The next step in the scoring was to evaluate the four options of behaviour against the norm of effective management practices and against the norm of an effective SA. The candidate's overall performance during the exercises was rated against the selections he/she made, as well as the answers given per scenario. The following five-point rating scale describes this assessment:

1. **Development:** Some elements of behaviour appropriate to the required standard are present, but there is insufficient quality of strength. Skills are promising, but require further development. Behaviour tends to react to situations/events as they occur. Coaching is needed to bring behaviour up to the required level. On track, but not yet there. Medium-term development is needed.

2. **Development with potential:** Elements of behaviour meeting the required standard are present, but insufficient quality of strength. Nevertheless, good potential is displayed.
3. **Merely requires rounding off:** Behaviour frequently exceeds the required standard, and seldom fails to meet it. Skills are well developed, although showing some opportunity for improvement through additional practice and/or increased insight. The approach is generally proactive. Behaviour is consistent as a rule, but some errors occur. Short-term development, or rounding off, is needed.
4. **Adequate:** Behaviour is adequate in relation to the norm of an effective SA. Skills are highly developed and polished, showing only little, if any, opportunity for improvement. The approach is constantly proactive: thinking ahead, anticipating matters and taking action to anticipate or influence events. Very few, if any errors are made.
   4C. Adequate: Behaviour is adequate in relation to the norm of an effective SA – but the candidate could benefit from coaching and counselling to fully comply with the norm.
5. **More than adequate:** Behaviour is outstanding, consistently exceeding the required standard. Skills are highly developed and polished, showing only little, if any, opportunity for improvement. The approach is constantly proactive: thinking ahead, anticipating matters and taking action to anticipate or influence events. Very few, if any, errors are made.

Training of Assessors and Administrators

Before any form of assessment could take place, personnel in the financial institution had to be trained in the CBS ADC. A key challenge was to select personnel of the financial institution to become either assessors or administrators. Two groups were trained over a period of five days by the consultants, with one group trained to act as assessors and the other group as administrators, who would manage the process. The training included both groups completing the CBS ADC themselves over a period of two days. The next three days were dedicated to the orientation to the CBS ADC, introduction to and discussion of exercises, scenarios within the simulation and the competency framework. Assessors were also trained in the rating scales, rating of behaviour, classifying competencies, giving feedback, reflecting on outcomes of behaviour, integrating results and report writing. Table 6.4 shows a portion of the scoring key with some of the competencies and associated behavioural indicators of an SA and illustrates how the five-point rating scale is used for assessment.

Table 6.4   Scoring key extract illustrating use of the five-point rating scale

Performance-motivation competence					
Innovation (problem analysis, service-improvement plan, written report)	1	2	3	4	5
Nature and extent of proposals: Reactive (Rating: 1) Reactive/Proactive (Rating: 2–3) Proactive (Rating: 4–5)					
Rating for innovation (problem analysis, service-improvement plan)					
Innovation (group discussion)	1	2	3	4	5
Original ideas					
Provides stimulus					
Points out advantages					
Links with others' arguments (value adding)					
Meets innovation					
Rating for innovation (group discussion)					
Final rating for innovation					
Energy (group discussion)	1	2	3	4	5
Frequency of participation					
Quality of inputs					
Perseveres with standpoints/arguments					
Final rating for energy					
Decision-making competence					
Analytical thinking (problem analysis, service-improvement plan, written report)	1	2	3	4	5
Gathering of information Rough work, calculations, graphs and tables, identifies main problem areas and sub-areas					
Integration of information Problem-solving techniques, updates processes, conclusions, in-depth analysis					
Rating for analytical thinking (problem analysis, service-improvement plan)					
Analytical thinking (group discussion)	1	2	3	4	5
Gathering of information Preparation and rough work prior to meeting, calculations, in-depth questions, analysis of background information					
Integration of information Employs problem-solving techniques, proposes a norm(s)/criteria, combinations/couplings Points out advantages, in-depth questions					
Rating for analytical thinking (group discussion)					
Final rating for analytical thinking					

The CBS ADC was now ready to be rolled out to the 60 branches of the financial institution across the 9 provinces in South Africa. Each assessment took place over 2 days, and 403 candidates were assessed in 4 months. After the assessment, data on selection of options and behaviour displayed had to be integrated. To this end, the technical members of the project team built an extractor module to the CBS programme to extract all options per competencies from the simulation database and put them into an open-source database, whereby the assessors and administrators could integrate their scores on the competencies during the exercises. Once this was completed, the extractor module of the simulation extracted all these behavioural and organizational role competencies and input of the assessors and administrators to generate an automated feedback report for the SA from the simulations.

The integration of behavioural scores was undertaken through consensus and discussion during an assessment-integration session. Recommendations had to be made regarding individuals who fit the profile of an SA and individuals who had to be redeployed within the financial institution.

Using the CBS ADC Results for Talent Management

The CBS ADC adopts a holistic approach to the management of talent by employing a series of interlinked strategies. The first strategy dealt with the candidate being exposed to the simulation itself, as this experience was a major stepping stone in self-discovery of one's own talent as well as comparing people across the organization by the same method and on the basis of the same standard. After each simulation round, the candidate received individual feedback on his/her performance, as indicated by the decisions made during the round. The feedback could be used in the following simulation round. Thus the CBS ADC was a learning experience in which the candidate was confronted with the real business issues of his/her role. The candidate's strengths and areas for development in terms of the role of an SA were also identified. The CBS ADC changed the candidates' perspective of the role and led to self-development and alignment of individual and organizational goals.

A comprehensive, consolidated feedback report was generated for each candidate from the extractor module and focused on the behavioural and organizational competencies' results. The feedback report was used as a discussion document during the individual feedback sessions, highlighting only a few specific development actions as part of the individual's development plan. This feedback and subsequent development discussions took place with each candidate's manager within one or two weeks of the actual CBS ADC experience. Refer to Figure 6.2.

Apart from receiving feedback on the competencies, feedback was also given on the overall job fit, in terms of the new SA role. The following rating scale was used as an indication of job fit:

5: Fit with high potential	The candidate's performance exceeded the required standard of the competencies assessed for the role. Appointment is highly recommended.
4: Fit	The candidate's performance met the required standard of the competencies assessed for the role. Appointment is recommended.
3: Moderate match	The candidate's performance moderately matched the required standard of the competencies assessed for the role. Appointment can be made with reservations, and immediate coaching and development may be required. Alternative matches to other lower-complexity roles can be investigated, where applicable.
2: Weak match	The candidate's performance has a weak match to the required standard of the competencies assessed for the role. No appointment is recommended to the role in question. Alternative matches to other roles may be investigated.
1: No fit	The candidate's performance did not match the required standard of the competencies assessed for the role. Appointment is not recommended.

Management also received feedback by means of a performance matrix with a discussion on each individual's performance as well as the outcomes on the overall job fit. Each SA's direct manager was also involved. The final data were sent to a central database at the Talent Office of the financial institution head office to compile statistics on roles, regions and branches.

Conclusions and Lessons Learned

ACs have a rich history of development and implementation in organizations in South Africa. These developments are strongly imbedded in the political, economic and social history of the country. In a new, democratic South Africa, organizations are exposed to macro- and micro-challenges in a multicultural and ethnic workplace. This case study focused on a financial institution that had to adapt to the macro- and micro-environment to remain competitive. CBST was used to develop a CBS for an ADC to achieve this aim.

Both behavioural and organizational competencies of the SA role were assessed by means of CBS and ADC exercises. Individuals who fit the profile were placed into the role of SA and others who did not fit the profile were redeployed in the financial institution. The business simulations exposed individuals to a realistic business environment and enabled them to recognize the trade-offs surrounding major strategic business decisions at both strategic and tactical levels and created a powerful learning experience.

As the organizational environment is rapidly moving away from paper-based correspondence towards voice mail, email messages and new business technologies, so too will ADCs and ACs have to shift from bundles of paper defining each exercise to web-based applications that simulate a day in the life of a modern manager or employee. This case study is a good example where change in the business environment, the sophistication of a new-generation employee corps and customer service and competitiveness in the market brought early exploration of CBS and ADCs to the fore. Important lessons learned from adopting an integrated approach call for the AC practitioner to take risks and explore the unknown, to understand how a particular role and organization coexist and how he/she can effectively assess the interaction. A new set of skills are required from the AC practitioner in terms of using information technology in the domain of workplace assessment.

References

Assessment Center Study Group Guidelines. (2007). The fourth edition of the Assessment Centre and Development Assessment Centre Guidelines for South Africa. Retrieved 13 March 2011: wwww.acsg.co.za.

Becker, J.R. 2009. *Influence of Values on the Attitude towards Cultural Diversity.* Unpublished Master's thesis, Stellenbosch University, Stellenbosch.

Blaney, D.R., Hobson, C.J., Meade, M.E. and Scodro, J. 1993. The assessment center: Evaluating managerial potential. *Nursing Management*, 24, 54–59.

Botha, A.P. 2008. *Knowledge: Living and Working With It.* Cape Town: Juta.

Charoux, J.A.E. 1986. *The Integration of Black Managers into South African Organisations.* Cape Town: Juta.

Charoux, J.A.E. 1987. Assessment Centres and Equal Employment Opportunity in South Africa. Unpublished manuscript.

Charoux, J.A.E. 1990. Assessment Centres: A route to black advancement. *Human Resource Management*, 6, 30–32.

Charoux, J.A.E. 1991. Assessment Centres: A partial but objective look. *Human Resource Management*, 7, 28–29.

Charoux, J.A.E. 1992. Identifying black leadership potential. *Human Resources Management*, 8, 20–22.

Charoux, J.A.E. and Hurst, D. 1992. Future potential. *People Dynamics*, 10, 35–36.

Du Preez, J. 2002. The depletion of the human resource pool in South Africa. *Acta Commercii*, 2, 80–84.

Government Gazette, Republic of South Africa, vol. 400, No. 19370. Cape Town, 19 October 1998.

Hurst, D. 1992. Assessment Centres: Identifying Black Leadership Potential. Unpublished Master's thesis, Rand Afrikaans University. Johannesburg.

IDM. 2010. *World Competitiveness Yearbook Results* [Online, May 2010]. Available at: http://www.imd.ch/research/publications/wcy/World-Competitiveness-Yearbook-Results/ [accessed: 10 August 2010].

Kaplan, R.S. and Norton, D.P. 1993. Putting the Balanced Scorecard to work, *Harvard Business Review*, Sept–Oct, 2–16.

Kriek, H.J., Hurst D.N. and Charoux, J.A.E. 1994. The assessment centre: Testing the fairness hypothesis. *Journal of Industrial Psychology*, 20, 21–25.

Kriek, H.J. and Thornton, G.C. 1989. Culture fairness of the assessment centre. *IPM Journal*, 7, 27–29.

Meiring, D. 2008. Assessment centres in South Africa. In *Assessment Centres: Unlocking Potential for Growth*, edited by S. Schlebusch and G. Roodt. Johannesburg: Knowres Publishing, 21–31.

Phillips, B.K. and Thomas, A. 2009. Macro and micro challenges for talent retention in South Africa. *SA Journal of Human Resource Management*, 7, 1–10.

Republic of South Africa. 1995. Labour Relations Act No. 66. *Government Gazette*, 400(1877), Cape Town, 13 December.

Republic of South Africa. 1998. Employment Equity Act No. 55. *Government Gazette*, 400(19370), Cape Town, 19 October.

Republic of South Africa. 1998. Skills Development Act No. 97. *Government Gazette*, 401(19420), Cape Town, 17 January.

Republic of South Africa. 2000. Promotion of Equality and Prevention of Unfair Discrimination Act No. 4. *Government Gazette*, 416(20876), Cape Town, 9 February.

Republic of South Africa. 2003. Broad-based Black Economic Empowerment Act No. 53. *Government Gazette*, 4063(25899), Cape Town, 7 January.

Rood, A. 1997. In search of a South African corporate culture. *Management Today*, 13, 14–16.

Sakinofsky, I.G. and Raubenheimer, I.W. 1982. The validity of the assessment centre method as a predictor of managerial potential. *Perspectives in Industrial Psychology*, 8, 23–41.

Shaw, D. and Human, L. 1989. Assessment of managerial potential among black employees in selected South African companies: Methods, perceived problems and concerns. *South African Journal of Labour Relations*, 13, 4–19.

Statistics South Africa. 2005. *Documented Migration*. Report No. 03–51–03 [Online]. Available at: http://www.statssa.gov.za/publications/statsdownload.asp?PPN=Report-03–51–03andSCH=3352 [accessed: 10 August 2010].

Van der Westhuizen, J.H. 2009. Simulation Technology as Part of the Assessment Center: A South African Review. Paper to the 29th Annual Assessment Centre Study Group Conference: Stellenbosch, 18–20 March.

Williams, J.C. 2008. South African Business Excellence Models: A. Retrospective View of the *South African Excellence Model* [Online: University of Stellenbosch SUNScholar]. Available at: http://scholar.sun.ac.za/handle/10019.1/783 [accessed: 5 August 2010].

CHAPTER 7

Integrating Candidate Data: Consensus or Arithmetic?

CHRIS DEWBERRY

In assessment centres information is produced about the performance of each candidate on several competency dimensions across a number of different exercises. A selection decision is made after this information has been pulled together and integrated in some way. There are essentially two ways in which this can be achieved. The first is to discuss each candidate's performance in a consensus meeting. The second is to use some form of arithmetic to combine a candidate's performance data. This can yield a grade or score for each dimension, for each exercise, or an overall score. These two techniques, the consensus meeting and arithmetic, are not mutually exclusive. For example, each candidate's grade on each exercise and dimension might first be discussed (and possibly revised) by assessors, and then these grades might be converted to scores and added together. However, in this chapter I will distinguish between two forms of data integration: an *arithmetic only* approach in which no discussion of candidates takes place, and a *consensus meeting* approach in which candidate data are integrated in part, or in full, though discussion in a consensus meeting.

What is a consensus meeting, a meeting which is often referred to as 'the assessor discussion' or more colloquially as 'the wash-up'? The format of these meetings varies across organizations, but usually assessors meet after the candidate to be discussed has completed all of his or her exercises. In this chaired session, all the scores given to the candidate are presented, possibly on a board or screen, and often in a matrix with exercises in rows and dimensions/competencies in columns, or vice versa. Assessors may be required to explain and justify the reasons for the grades they have given the candidate on each dimension for the exercise they have been involved with. The assessors may then attempt to reconcile apparent inconsistencies in the ratings awarded to a candidate on a given dimension through discussion. At the end of this meeting an overall assessment rating (OAR) is often produced either through mutual verbal agreement between the assessors or by some combination of verbal and arithmetical methods such as adding together revised candidate scores (Krause and Thornton 2009).

By contrast, the arithmetic approach to data integration is relatively quick, inexpensive, and demands little in the way of human resources. If necessary the grades awarded to a candidate are converted into a numerical format and then a spreadsheet or some other form of software can be used to simply add together, or average, the scores awarded to a candidate across exercises or dimensions. This provides an overall score per exercise, per dimension, or overall. Alternatively, some more sophisticated technique might be used to establish the arithmetic process of data integration. One technique would be to derive specific weights for each dimension by regressing the job performance of previous candidates on their competency scores. Whatever the specific form of arithmetical technique used, whether or not a candidate is selected depends on whether their score(s) reaches some pre-assigned threshold(s).

Of the two ways of integrating candidate data and making selection decisions, consensus meetings are by far the most widely used, with surveys suggesting that they are operated in approximately 90 per cent of ACs run in Europe and the United States (Boyle, Fullerton and Wood 1995, Krause and Gebert 2003, Krause and Thornton 2009, Spychalski, Quiñones, Gaugler and Pohley 1997. See also Povah, Chapter 22 this volume). Since running these consensus meetings requires considerable organizational resources (Gilbert 1981), certainly far more than arithmetic data integration, it is necessary to justify their use. What is the evidence that they contribute significantly to the criterion-related validity of assessments? That is, to what extent, if at all, do assessment centres that use consensus meetings predict the future job performance of candidates better than assessment centres in which candidate data is integrated with an arithmetical (otherwise known as mechanical or actuarial) technique? Surprisingly, relatively little research has been specifically designed to address this issue, and most that has is at least 20 years old. Nevertheless the results of this research are helpful. In a study of military recruitment, Borman et al. (1982) compared the effectiveness of (a) consensus ratings and (b) unweighted composites of all relevant assessment exercises in predicting three indices of training performance. For all three criteria measures the consensus ratings were less effective than the averaged ratings in predicting training performance. However, this study was based on a small sample (n=50), and an examination of the 95 per cent confidence intervals for the validity coefficients indicates overlap between the overall assessment ratings and averaged ratings in all three cases. Therefore the study does not provide compelling evidence for the superiority of either overall assessment ratings or averaged ratings in predicting training performance. Another study of the relative effectiveness of the mechanical and consensus methods of predicting training performance of military personnel with assessment centres was carried out by Tziner and Dolan (1982). They found the validity coefficients for (a) averaged dimension ratings, and (b) consensus meeting overall ratings, to be .36 and .38 respectively. The sample size was 193 in this research, and the 95 per cent confidence intervals for these correlations have a large measure of overlap. Hence once again there is no persuasive evidence that either the mechanical or the consensus meeting method for combining information and predicting candidate success are more effective.

A third study of the consensus versus mechanical prediction of training performance was undertaken by Feltham (1988). Feltham focused on an assessment centre used to choose police constables for an accelerated promotion scheme. There were five outcome measures here: overall training performance, a composite of supervisor performance ratings on 17 dimensions, supervisor's rating of potential in the police force, a rating of overall job performance, and rank in the police force attained by candidates at follow-up. The sample size used here (n = 126–156) was larger than in the Borman et al. study. For all five criteria measures the mechanically derived index of performance was more predictive than the overall assessment ratings made in consensus meetings, though once again an examination of the 95 per cent confidence intervals for the consensus and mechanically derived validity coefficients shows overlap in all five cases. As in the Borman et al. and the Tziner and Dolan studies there is therefore no clear evidence for the superiority of either the mechanical or the consensus meeting method in predicting candidate performance.

In the three studies considered above, the effectiveness of the mechanical and consensus meeting approaches were compared using (a) the overall ratings of candidates derived from consensus meetings and (b) the average of the ratings they achieved across assessment centre dimensions or exercises. However, the index of performance derived from the mechanical approach can potentially be improved. Rather than simply averaging ratings across dimensions (or exercises), multiple regression can be used to find the best weighted average of these ratings. In principle such weighted averages can provide better predictions of the future performance of job candidates than unweighted ones because they place more emphasis on dimensions (or exercises) which are relatively good at predicting candidate performance and less emphasis on those which are less good at doing so. The potential of multiple regression in assessment centre data integration was investigated by Wollowick and McNamara (1969). They examined an assessment centre designed for lower and middle management positions. The validity coefficient of the overall consensus rating in predicting the extent to which the managerial responsibility of the candidates had increased 3 years after the assessment centre was .37. By using stepwise multiple regression based on 14 test scores, 6 exercise ratings and 12 characteristic ratings, the authors were able to increase this validity coefficient very considerably to .62. However, given the large ratio of predictors (32) to candidates (n = 94) in this study it is likely that this high validity coefficient capitalizes heavily on sampling error and it should therefore be treated with considerable caution.

Mitchel (1975) further investigated the effectiveness of multiple regression as a means to effectively predict candidate performance in an assessment centre involving 254 managers. The criterion measure was the managers' growth in salary over 1, 3 and 5 years after the centre. Mitchel found the mean validity of the consensus ratings to be .22. In contrast, the average validity of the predictors derived from multiple regression, at .42, was considerably greater. However, when these regression equations were cross-validated on other samples their mean validity fell to .28. Based on a sample size of 254, the 95 per cent confidence intervals for validities of .22 (consensus meeting overall ratings) and .28 (mean cross-validated values derived from multiple regression) overlap. Consequently it is again necessary to conclude that there is no compelling evidence from this study of a difference in the predictiveness of consensus and mechanically derived indices of candidate ability.

None of the five studies discussed above, all of which compare the relative predictiveness of mechanically derived candidate ratings with those derived from consensus meetings, clearly demonstrates the superiority of one of these methods of data integration over the other. However, a more recent meta-analytic study (Dilchert and Ones 2009) based on a sample of nearly 5,000 managers is more revealing. Rather than using a single study to investigate this issue, Dilchert and Ones compared the results of meta-analyses in which the predictive validity of overall assessment ratings had been examined, with the results of meta-analyses in which the predictiveness of arithmetically combined scores had been examined. Specifically, they compared the validity of (a) overall assessment centre ratings, (b) summed assessment centre dimension scores, and (c) optimally weighted and then summed assessment centre dimension scores, in predicting job performance. The operational validity of these three scoring methods was .36 for overall assessment ratings, .44 for unweighted summed ratings, and .45 for optimally weighted summed dimension scores. This indicates that using simple arithmetic to sum scores across dimensions, rather than overall candidate ratings derived partly or wholly from consensus discussions, increases the variation in job performance explained by the assessment centre by about 50 per cent. As Dilchert and Ones put it: 'both unit and optimally weighted, mechanically combined AC dimension composites yield validity estimates well above overall AC ratings, which are often obtained, at least in part, using subjective information combination on the part of assessors' (p. 261). Furthermore, whilst the unweighted, and optimally weighted, assessment scores resulted in a modest but useful amount of incremental validity over personality and cognitive ability test results in predicting job performance ($r = .09$ and $.12$ respectively), overall assessment ratings showed no such incremental validity at all ($r = .00$). Put simply, if the purpose of an assessment centre is simply to select job candidates, Dilchert and Ones' meta-analysis suggests that summing the scores obtained by candidates on each dimension measured in an assessment centre provides a more accurate indication of their future job performance than deriving an overall assessment score through discussion in a consensus meeting.

Considering the very substantial resources required to operate consensus meetings this issue clearly deserves further research. Such research needs to not only focus on the relative predictiveness of different methods of data integration, but also on the processes operating in consensus meetings which serve to enhance, or reduce, the effectiveness of such discussions in deriving an overall assessment rating for each candidate. The purpose of this chapter is to draw together several strands of theoretical and empirical material in order to provide some guidance as to the processes that may be taking place in consensus meetings which have a bearing on their effectiveness. Because there is little empirical research on consensus meetings (Lievens and Klimoski 2001), and what is available is patchy in focus, lacking in an underlying theoretical framework, and generally over 25 years old, these answers will necessarily be tentative. However, there is sufficient theory and research to identify several processes likely to impact on the effectiveness of consensus meetings.

In examining this issue it would appear that there are two sorts of processes occurring simultaneously in consensus meetings: overt and explicit processes, and latent and informal ones.

Explicit versus Latent Processes in Consensus Meetings

At present there are no published or generally agreed procedures for running consensus meetings (Lowry 1997). As a result the formal and explicit processes used in these meetings are probably quite varied. However, we might expect the training generally provided to those attending ACs (Spychalski et al. 1997) to include some explicit guidance on how to behave in consensus meetings, probably stressing the importance of rational processes, such as requiring assessors to provide evidence for their ratings and using information from various sources to test competing hypotheses about candidates. It is these formal and explicit processes which provide the rationale for consensus meetings. If assessors are required to give evidence supporting their candidate assessments, if inconsistencies in the ratings given to candidates by different assessors on the same dimension are discussed and resolved openly and logically, and if an overall picture of the candidate's likely competencies are built up through informed and reasoned discussion, this would appear to increase the likelihood that the best candidates are selected. However, research carried out by social and organizational psychologists, suggests that alongside such laudable attempts to provide a rational and consensual basis for candidate selection, run a variety of dysfunctional hidden processes. These include majority influence, the differential weighting of exercises, the introduction of inappropriate information and criteria, and the differential impact of assessors. Each of these is discussed below and then a qualitative study is described in which evidence for the operation of a number of these processes was examined.

MAJORITY INFLUENCE

There is considerable evidence in the social psychological literature that people in groups often conform to the views of the majority. There are two reasons for this. The first is a need to feel accepted by the group, or fear of rejection by it (Deutsch and Gerrard 1955; Wood, Lundgren, Ouellette, Busceme and Blackstone 1994). This process is known as normative influence. The second process occurs when the judgements of individuals in groups are based not only on information obtained directly through their own experience, but also indirectly through the opinions of other group members (Bishop and Myers 1974; Kaplan and Miller 1987; O'Reilly and Caldwell 1979; Turner, Wetherell and Hogg 1989). This is known as informational influence. Herriot (2003) suggests that both of these social conformity processes are likely to take place in consensus meetings. In this context, the consequence of both normative and informational influence would be to lead assessors who grade a given candidate lower (or higher) than most others, to alter their grade to conform to the majority view. Assuming that their initial grade was actually a fair reflection of the candidate's performance in the exercise they observed, the consequence of majority influence here would be to throw away useful and predictive information about the candidate's potential. The cumulative effect of discarding valuable data about candidates would be a reduction in the predictive validity of the assessment centre.

THE DIFFERENTIAL AND INAPPROPRIATE WEIGHTING OF EXERCISES

When an arithmetic process is used to integrate data about candidates the various exercises will probably be weighted equally or will have weightings based on empirical evidence, such as the use of multiple regression in predicting job performance. However, when assessors discuss the performance of a candidate in a consensus meeting it is possible for other factors to influence the weight given to exercises in arriving at an overall judgement about whether a candidate should be selected. For example, Goldstein, Yusko, Braverman, Smith and Chung (1988) found that the predictive validity of an assessment centre group discussion exercise was .17 (95 per cent CI = .11 to .26) whereas the equivalent figure for a cognitive ability test was .29 (95 per cent CI = .22 to 36). This suggests that the cognitive ability test was at least as useful (and probably more useful) than the group discussion exercise in predicting job performance. However, in a consensus meeting the group discussion exercise might be given more weight than the results of the cognitive ability test because assessors have directly observed the candidates and are overconfident about their ability to generalize from small samples of behaviour (Klayman, Soll, Gonzalez-Vallejo and Barlas 1999; Moore and Healy 2008; Tversky and Kahneman 1971), or because their observation of candidates is recent and salient. If, when deriving an overall assessment centre rating, assessors place an inappropriately high weight on some exercises or psychometric test results and an inappropriately low weight on other exercises or test results the predictive validity of the assessment centre will almost certainly be undermined.

THE INTRODUCTION OF INAPPROPRIATE INFORMATION AND CRITERIA

When assessment ratings are simply summed, the overall score obtained by a candidate is influenced only by the ratings that he or she is given by assessors in exercises. However, in consensus discussions the opportunity exists for other information or criteria to enter the evaluation process. For example, Herriot (2003) argues that where organizational identity is salient, assessors may be more likely to select candidates who fit the organizational prototype of the ideal employee. That is, instead of basing judgements strictly on the dimensions specified in the design of the AC, assessors may also refer (explicitly or covertly) to the criterion of whether they think the candidate would 'fit in' with the team or organization they would work in if selected. If perceived fit is included in the overall evaluation of a candidate in this way, the validity of the AC may be undermined. Arthur et al.'s (2006) meta-analysis of the relation between perceived organizational fit on the one hand, and job performance and turnover on the other, found that the lower 95 per cent credibility values for both job performance and turnover included zero. Therefore the hypotheses that there is no relationship at all between perceived organizational fit and job performance, and organizational fit and turnover, cannot be rejected. If perceived fit is used openly or covertly as part of the process of evaluating candidates in consensus meetings, and, as the study by Arthur and his colleagues suggests, fit is not associated with job performance or turnover, the predictive power of ACs is likely to be diminished.Perceived fit may sometimes act as a latent criterion in assessing candidates in ACs. In addition to this, inappropriate candidate information may be communicated and acted upon in consensus meetings. For example, in justifying the marks or grades awarded to a candidate, an assessor may reveal information about the organization in which he or she has worked, the specific roles that he or she has played (including non-work roles), and experiences that he or she has had, and this information may set up assumptions and prejudices in the minds of other assessors.

THE DIFFERENTIAL INFLUENCE OF ASSESSORS

Sackett and Wilson (1982) studied consensus meetings in a single organization, and found that when disagreement amongst raters required a consensus discussion, assessors sometimes varied in the degree of influence that they exerted. The existence of differentials in the influence of assessors is also supported by a laboratory simulation study of consensus meetings, carried out by Klimoski et al. (1980), in which they found that chairpersons exerted a relatively large influence on ratings, and by the results of a field experiment by Lowry (1992) which indicated that when there are differences in assessor seniority, and it is possible for assessors both to announce their scores publicly and to present arguments against the scores of other assessors, seniors can have a disproportionate impact on the overall ratings given to candidates. Where there are differences in the experience, age, and/or status of people in the consensus meeting, we might expect these to intensify conformity effects, as assessors with greater power are likely to influence the ratings of others (French and Raven 1959; Raven 1965; 1993). As well as possibly having the perceived or actual power to punish juniors who disagree with them (for example via the organizational appraisal or promotion process) juniors may view their seniors' greater experience of personnel assessment as meaning that their judgements should carry more weight than their own. Thus more junior staff may defer to senior ones.

If, as a result of power and status differentials, relatively junior assessors defer to more senior ones in consensus meetings, and particularly if they readily adjust their grades to conform to those of their senior colleagues, then this is yet another way in which valuable candidate data can be lost.

THE COMMUNICATION OF OVERALL IMPRESSIONS OF CANDIDATES

A study by Russell (1985) indicated that when observing candidates in exercises, assessors' initial ratings were dominated by a single general factor, and that this was usually based either on a candidate's perceived interpersonal skills, or on their perceived problem-solving skills. Similarly, and as mentioned earlier, Lance et al. (2000) found evidence that assessors begin by forming a general impression of a candidate, and that this overall impression then drives their ratings of that candidate on specific, formally defined, dimensions. If assessors form impressions of candidates not only on the basis of their evaluations on specific competency dimensions but also as general impressions, such general impressions are liable to be used when the candidates are discussed. For example, an assessor might describe a candidate as 'very good'. The communication of these global impressions to other assessors may result in a shift away from an exclusive focus on the performance of candidates on specific competencies, potentially undermining a core component of assessment centre architecture – the idea that candidates are evaluated strictly against a clearly defined set of competencies.

Qualitative Research on Latent Processes in Consensus Meetings

The implication of the theory and research discussed above is that the formal and explicit procedure which assessors have been trained to employ in consensus meetings is shadowed by a set of informal processes, such as assessors actively seeking to persuade others whether or not a candidate should be appointed, and sometimes using their position power to do so. These informal processes will differ in the extent to which they are, on the one hand, explicit and obvious to all present and on the other, covert and hidden. One reason why little research has been carried out to date on latent processes in consensus meetings is probably that common survey methods, such as those previously used to examine AC processes and procedures (Boyle et al. 1995; Krause and Gebert 2003; Krause and Thornton 2009; Spychalski et al. 1997. See also Chapter 22 by Povah and Chapter 23 by Krause), require respondents to answer questions about processes that can be easily observed. Such methods are not appropriate for the study of latent processes in consensus meetings, because assessors cannot be expected to respond reliably to questions about, for example, the frequency of power and influence processes, when these processes are, by their nature, subtle and hidden rather than explicit and easily observed. This section presents some qualitative data which demonstrates the operation of such hidden processes in a modern and well-run AC, utilizing well-trained assessors. In particular it shows how the informal use of language and latent social processes associated with the use of such language, can influence the outcome of consensus meeting discussions.

In order to examine the nature of latent processes in consensus meetings, the author carried out non-participative observation in a multinational financial organization. Auditory recordings were made in two of these meetings and these recordings were later transcribed. The transcripts were reviewed using template analysis (King 2004), which involves the production of a set of codes (collectively referred to as a template), with each code representing a different theme identified in textual data. Usually at least some of the codes are specified a priori, and then these may be revised and others added, in the process of analysis. Generally the codes are organized hierarchically, with some more inclusive than others. In the analysis carried out here, the central aim was to identify text revealing the active and explicit use of general impressions of candidates, persuasion, and position power, rather than to develop a complex hierarchical representation of the types of persuasion, general impressions and power used. For this reason a simple and flat set of codes representing these three categories was utilized. A *general impression code* was used if the assessor described a candidate globally as good or bad rather than describing and evaluating him or her in relation to specific competencies. A *persuasion code* was used if an assessor used language which was specifically and solely designed to influence the facilitator or other assessors about whether or not a candidate should be selected, rather than to feed back information about the performance or characteristics of that candidate. A *power code* was used for text in which the interchange between a more senior and more junior assessor in a consensus meeting about a particular candidate indicated that the power differential between these assessors significantly influenced the evaluation of that candidate.

The transcripts were examined in order to see whether clear and unambiguous examples of language consistent with these three processes could be found. Clear exemplars of all three were found and in addition, the use of language relevant to a fourth social influence process was also identified and a new *use of social groups code* was added for this. This fourth process is concerned with assessors describing candidates as being members of social groups, such as Indian, or working class. The communication of such social groups between assessors is important because it provides the raw material for candidate stereotyping.

The consensus meetings in this study took place in an assessment centre designed to select graduates. The organization had approximately 12,000 applicants each year for about 400 graduate posts. The selection process began with an application form completed either on paper or on the Internet. When evaluating the application those involved in this initial stage of selection focused primarily on each applicant's academic record at school and university. About 3,000 applicants were then invited to the second stage of the selection process in which they attended a first interview with a relatively junior member of the organization and completed a cognitive ability test.

Approximately one third of these applicants were then asked to attend an AC in which they were evaluated against eight competency dimensions. The exercises used to evaluate the applicants were a case study (for which they were given 90 minutes), a leaderless group discussion (40 minutes) and a second interview (approximately 60 minutes). The second interview was always carried out with a senior member of the organization, who would lead the team in which successful candidates would work. The assessors for the other two exercises were comparatively junior members of the organization. All assessors had a minimum of 2 days training. Assessors who evaluated the candidate gave a rating of 1 (poor), 2 (marginal), 3 (good), or 4 (strong) against each of the dimensions considered relevant to the exercise they observed or conducted.

At a subsequent consensus meeting, facilitated either by a senior member of the human resources department or by a member of the graduate recruitment team, each candidate was discussed in turn. Assessors announced the marks they had given to the candidate for each dimension and these were written up by the facilitator on a board which was visible to all. Immediately after announcing their marks, assessors were required to present evidence for each one. During this process assessors had access to the candidate's performance at the second stage of the selection process: their scores on the cognitive ability test (verbal, numerical, and spatial ability) and the scores they had obtained in the first (pre-AC) interview.

GENERAL IMPRESSIONS OF THE CANDIDATE AND THE COMMUNICATION OF SOCIAL CATEGORIES

The following extract is from a second interviewer announcing the marks given to a particular candidate and providing supporting evidence for them. The country of origin of the candidate has been altered here to protect the anonymity of both the assessor and the candidate, and some sections of text have been replaced by ellipses.

Extract 1

I thought she was excellent … one of the best candidates I've interviewed in a long time … She is Vietnamese, she came to the UK when she was 15 or 16, and she has the most fluent English of any Vietnamese person I have ever interviewed. Her English is just impeccable, couldn't fault it. She's at Oxford, She is, ah, tremendously driven she is … with the Oxford boat, women's boat team … I mean I thought she was great … she is also a musician and has started a string quartet … She, she, very hard working, very driven, spoke a lot about her sort of study, study style, which passed, I think it was very driven, very balanced as well because she fits in lots of extra curricular activities as well, as well as studying … so, I thought she was great.

In the above extract the interviewer begins by expressing a general impression of the candidate 'I thought she was excellent' and then repeats this general impression twice again, once in the middle of the feedback, and again at the end. Clearly there is evidence here that the assessor is following aspects of the formal consensus meeting procedure, in that an evaluation against the required dimensions is provided (for example the two references to being 'driven' are relevant to the competency of personal drive), and a justification for that evaluation is presented also. However, in the process of providing this justification, the assessor also engages in behaviour that is consistent with the operation of social influence processes. Not only is the assessor's general impression of the candidate communicated to co-assessors, but information which might lead to the use of stereotypes of the candidate (for example that she is from south-east Asia and a musician) is also communicated. Furthermore, the assessor's overall enthusiasm about the candidate, 'one of the best candidates I've interviewed in a long time', can also be construed as actively persuading other assessors that this candidate should be selected rather than merely expressing information about her performance against the dimensions in a detached and objective manner. However, even clearer examples of the operation of active persuasion are provided in the following extracts.

EVIDENCE OF THE USE OF ACTIVE PERSUASION

In the following extract, the second interviewer and the leaderless group discussion assessor have given their feedback on a candidate, but the case study assessor is unavailable. For this reason, the meeting facilitator rightly seeks to move on to a discussion of the next candidate, with the intention of obtaining the case study assessor's feedback later on.

Extract 2

> Facilitator: *OK, we'll come back to that one.*
> Second interviewer: *Definitely an offer, definitely an offer.*
> Facilitator: *OK we've got to come back to that one.*
> Second interviewer: *Well based on what I saw …*
> Facilitator: *OK.*
> Second interviewer: *… I think we'd be very silly not to make her an offer.*
> Facilitator: *Well, we will wait to see what the case study says, but based on what you two have said it looks like it will be an offer, yeah.*

This is a clear example of active persuasion by an assessor.

EVIDENCE OF THE EFFECT OF POWER

The observation of consensus meetings suggested that the use of assessor power and influence often took the form of differences in how much was said about a candidate and the force and confidence with which it was expressed. The force and confidence of a contribution is partly manifested in the exact intonation of what is said and in the non-verbal behaviour of the speaker and it is not possible to convey this fully in written extracts. However, it is possible to give an example of differences in the nature (and volume) of words used by relatively senior and junior assessors, and the effect this appears to have on the junior assessor's judgement. In the following extract, the leaderless group discussion (LGD) assessor begins by giving a score of 2 (marginal) for communication skills to a candidate and this is followed by the (more senior) second interviewer who has given the candidate a good score of 4 (strong) on this dimension. A discussion then ensues. Note that the name of the town the candidate comes from and the names of the competency dimensions have been changed to protect the anonymity of the candidate and the organization respectively.

Extract 3

> LGD assessor: *Applied intelligence 3, team orientation 3, familiarity with business 4 … 3 to 4, and communication skills 2.*
> Facilitator: *All right, okay, take me through the interview first.*
> Second interviewer: *Again someone who is very comfortable in driving to get good results. She is someone who I think is trying to help herself pay through getting through university, so she*

does a part time job most evenings, goes to university gets some good results, and on top of that also does some voluntary work on the weekends so someone in terms of trying to get good results and commitment, I see no problem there, in there, at all. In terms of adaptability – it was alright – she, she described herself, her biggest issue if you like in terms of change was when she went to university she is someone who grew up in Hertford, has never left Hertford, was very sort of quiet and reserved at school, and, for her the big change was she went to university in a sense it was exposed if you like, and she realized that she needed to do something about that, so the first thing she did was she went and got herself elected to the first year rep for economics which is a pretty bold step actually because for exactly that reason she needed to, to like to come out of herself which err, certainly in the interview she obviously had, its interesting the comment you made in terms of communication skills in terms of whether she was really outward.

LGD assessor: *Hmm.*

Second interviewer: *'Cause certainly in interview she was, but that was one-on-one.*

LGD assessor: *Yeah.*

Second interviewer: *So, so it would be useful to get some communication skills in the group feedback.*

LGD assessor: *Yeah.*

Second interviewer: *Because that might demonstrate that actually she is comfortable one-on-one but was less comfortable when she was in a group environment*

LGD assessor: *Well I did have, I had 3s scrubbed out and put 2.*

Facilitator: *Communication is this?*

LGD assessor: *Yeah, I thought, I mean she did, really, withdraw from the meeting, um, it was quite a large period where she didn't actually say anything at all, certainly towards the end of the last um … And yeah it was a quiet group, anyway there wasn't any sort of some spark, there was no catalyst there to maybe get people discussing things properly, um, I mean what she said she said it clearly confidently, and so I think I maybe have been a bit harsh on her, um …*

Facilitator (to interviewer): *Would you be happy to go down to a 3?*

Second interviewer: *On communication skills? Not in terms of what I was seeing and the examples we had. One-on-one she was very confident, very comfortable, and the example she gave of where she had had to use her communication skills was, you know, as a representative of the first year economics class she had to attend board meetings of the faculty, and present, and she was quite comfortable doing that and that was why she put herself in that situation. So, I mean if that she giving that as a example so …*

LGD assessor: *I'll happy, I'll happily change mine to a 3 or more.*

Here the second interviewer utters approximately four times as many words as the younger and more junior LGD assessor. Furthermore, the senior assessor's speech is clear and confident whereas that of the LGD assessor appears unsure of his evaluation ('Well I did have, I had 3s scrubbed out and put 2'). In his penultimate contribution, the LGD assessor does appear to rally, and provides a sound justification for his low mark, but after the interviewer's subsequent firm pronouncement that he is unwilling to change his evaluation of the candidate, the LGD assessor capitulates, saying that he is willing to change his mark of 2 (marginal) to 3 (good), or 4 (strong).

Summary and Conclusions

Most of the literature on ACs focuses on an assessment of their criterion-related validity (Arthur, Day, McNelly and Edens 2003; Byham 1970; Cohen, Moses and Byham 1977; Howard 1974; Meriac, Hoffman, Woehr and Fleisher 2008; Muchinsky 1986; Thornton and Byham 1982), and their construct validity. For the most thorough and recent discussion of the issues related to construct validity, the reader is referred to the March 2008 issue of *Industrial and Organizational Psychology: Perspectives on Science and Practice* in which Lance and 19 commentators conduct a lively debate. In focusing on these issues researchers often examine associations between candidates' scores on the different dimensions and exercises within ACs, and their scores on various measures of job performance (Chan 1996; Lievens 2001; Rolland 1999). The auditory recordings of a consensus meeting presented here show how, in addition to formal and explicit processes in which assessors have been trained to engage, including evidence-based ratings of candidates against carefully-defined and performance-relevant dimensions, several informal/latent processes can also have an influential impact on the decision-making process operating in consensus meetings. First, assessors may not merely bring to a consensus meeting a set of scores, and evidence for those scores, but also an overall impression of the quality of the candidate (Lance et al. 2000; Russell 1985). Second, at least some assessors are not merely acting as 'information processing machines', or scientists, carefully testing hypotheses by examining evidence from several sources and arriving at a detached and balanced overall view of the suitability of candidates. Whilst they may try to be objective and detached (or at least present themselves as such), assessors can also use the consensus meeting in general and the opportunity they are given to provide evidence for their scores in particular, to actively persuade others about the strengths (or weaknesses) of the candidates they have assessed. Furthermore, in the process of trying to persuade other assessors, they may present information about the candidate which is not directly relevant to the dimensions being examined. Such extraneous information brings an attendant risk of unwarranted inferences, stereotyping and bias, which is liable to reinforce the tendency of assessors to adjust their ratings of candidates on the pre-specified dimensions to fit their overall impressions, rather than to strictly adhere to evaluations based on observed behaviours. The formal and informal processes operating in consensus meetings may often be closely interlinked. For example the assessor in Extract 1, consistent with the formal and proper consensus meeting procedure, provides a rationale and justification for the positive ratings she has given to the candidate. In doing so she draws attention to several things that the candidate has achieved, particularly given her Vietnamese background, giving as examples her 'impeccable' English, her position in the Oxford University rowing team and her role as a musician in a string quartet. In doing so the assessor may be interpreted as providing sound evidence that the candidate is strong on relevant competency dimensions. However, in furnishing this evidence the assessor is simultaneously positioning the candidate as a member of several social groups (that is a female, Vietnamese, an Oxford University student, a trained musician, and a member of a rowing team), transmitting this information to all others present at the consensus meeting and in doing so potentially triggering the operation of one or more stereotypes which may affect the evaluations that other assessors give to the candidate. In this way the operation of a formal consensus meeting process, where the purpose is typically to justify the ratings given to a candidate and to resolve through rational discussion any striking differences in the ratings given to a candidate by different raters, may unwittingly and simultaneously lead to the operation of an informal and latent process in which assessors are influenced by stereotypes. Whilst this study was not designed to detect whether such stereotypes were formed by assessors, or whether they affected candidate ratings, it nevertheless demonstrates how a formal process operating within a consensus meeting can potentially promote, and provide the raw material for, informal processes with the potential to affect selection decisions made about candidates. The study described above is of small scale. The language recorded in the assessment centre may be atypical, and the processes discussed above may be rare. However, it should be noted that the small amount of previous work on these latent/informal processes in the AC context also detected such phenomena (Klimoski et al. 1980; Lowry 1992;, Russell 1985; Sackett and Wilson 1982) and such findings are consistent with the effects of well-established social psychological phenomena such as informational influence, normative influence and the influence of power (Bishop and Myers 1974; Deutsch and Gerrard 1955; French and Raven 1959; Kaplan and Miller 1987; O'Reilly and Caldwell 1979; Raven 1965; 1993; Turner et al. 1989; Wood et al. 1994).

The preceding sections describe some of the dysfunctions that can occur in group decision-making, and which may take place in the consensus discussions typically run in assessment centres. Equally, and in contrast to these dysfunctional processes, it is possible that consensus discussions can provide benefits and gains over mechanical data integration by offering a set of checks and balances that capitalize on the 'group gains' (Steiner 1972) and 'assembly bonuses' (Nisbett and Ross 1980), and result in a pattern of 'truth supported wins' (McGraw and Kravitz 1982). Reviews of this literature can be found in Thornton (1992) and Thornton and Rupp (2006). Consensus meetings may therefore influence the outcomes of assessment centres positively as well as negatively. Overall, there is a strong case for more research on the nature and frequency of both formal and informal practices and processes in consensus meetings and the influence which such practices may have on the criterion-related validity of ACs.

What are the practical implications of the issues discussed in this chapter? It is possible that consensus meetings are currently undermined by a variety of processes, including those discussed in this chapter and that by reducing or eliminating such processes the predictive validity of assessment centres integrating data partly or wholly through discussion might be substantially improved. This raises an important question – what steps might be taken to maximize the effectiveness and fairness of consensus meetings? As a first step the following set of guidelines, designed to reduce dysfunctional processes in consensus meetings, are worthy of consideration:

- All assessors in a consensus meeting should be of similar and ideally of equal, seniority in the organization.
- At least two assessors should observe each exercise.
- Consensus meeting facilitators should be at least as senior in the organization as the most senior assessor.
- Consensus meeting facilitators should be trained to detect and stop any observed attempts by assessors to actively persuade one another, or the meeting as a whole, about the level of performance of candidates, the rating they should be given, or whether or not they should be selected. Consensus meeting facilitators should try to ensure that the amount of time assessors speak is reasonably similar to each other.

- Consensus meeting facilitators should prevent assessors revealing information about candidates, or presenting them in ways, which might activate stereotypes or prejudice about those candidates in other assessors.
- Consensus meeting facilitators should ensure that all assessors focus exclusively on their observations of the candidate and/or their interpretation of the candidate's performance in relation to the formal set of dimensions used in the centre.
- Consensus meeting facilitators should try to ensure that assessors are not overconfident in the way that they generalize from the small samples of behaviour typically observed in the artificial and simulated assessment centre exercises to the candidate's likely behaviour at work.
- Consensus meeting facilitators should ensure that assessors are aware that candidates may perform well on some exercises and poorly on others and that discrepancies between ratings given to a particular candidate by different assessors, observing different exercises, but rating the same dimensions, may simply reflect differing performance levels by the candidate, rather than rater error.
- Unless there are clear grounds to do otherwise, consensus meeting facilitators should ensure that all exercises and dimensions are given equal weighting when a candidate is discussed.

The adoption of these recommendations should help to restrict the impact of dysfunctional processes on consensus meeting outcomes, and ensure that the meetings are evidence-based, rational, and objective. However, for a variety of reasons it may not be possible for many organizations to fully implement and enforce these recommendations and even if they did so, the effectiveness of the recommendations is currently unknown. In these circumstances a more radical response would be to recommend that consensus meetings should no longer be used. As we have seen, consensus meetings are not essential: information about candidates can be combined in a variety of arithmetical ways, from simply summing the scores obtained by a candidate and examining whether it meets some pre-assigned threshold, to the use of sophisticated weighted-averaging systems developed by regressing measures of job performance on the results of AC exercises. Given the current lack of evidence that consensus meetings contribute to the criterion-related validity of ACs as much as, or more than, arithmetic-based procedures (Borman 1982; Feltham 1988; Mitchel 1975; Dilchert and Ones 2009; Tziner and Dolan 1982; Wollowick and McNamara 1969), the considerable resources and time devoted to them, and the practical difficulties of operating consensus meetings which are not subject to the potentially dysfunctional effects of the latent processes discussed in this chapter, the case for abandoning consensus meetings altogether and replacing them with arithmetical methods of data integration is certainly worthy of consideration. Perhaps the principal argument for the retention of consensus meetings is that they are helpful in producing relevant and helpful feedback to candidates on their assessment centre performance. Such feedback may be particularly critical in a development centre setting. This raises another important question. To what extent is candidate feedback based on consensus meeting discussions more helpful and productive than feedback based simply on the ratings that a candidate has been given on each dimension? There doesn't appear to be any research on this important issue, and without it an answer to this question is currently unavailable.

In conclusion, the process of integrating the information collected on candidates in assessment centres, and the process of making a final judgment about whether or not a candidate should be selected based on this integrated data, has a critical bearing on the effectiveness of the centres. Based on the best evidence currently available (Dilchert and Ones 2009), the simple, cheap, and expeditious use of arithmetic to combine information about candidate performance on various competency dimensions is more effective in predicting the future performance of candidates than the more complex, expensive, and time-consuming use of consensus meetings. Whether certain types of consensus meeting can outperform arithmetic in the integration of candidate data is currently unknown and certainly worthy of future research. Such research should not discount the potentially powerful effects of subtle and hidden social processes in consensus meetings, running alongside the explicit procedures and processes in which assessors have been trained.

References

Arthur, W., Bell, S.T., Villado, A.J. and Doverspike, D. 2006. The use of person-organization fit in employment decision-making: An assessment of its criterion-related validity. *Journal of Applied Psychology*, 91, 786–801.

Arthur, W., Day, E.A., McNelly, T.L. and Edens, P.S. 2003. A meta-analysis of the criterion-related validity of assessment center dimensions. *Personnel Psychology*, 56, 125–154.

Bishop, G.D. and Myers, D.G. 1974. Informational influence in group discussion. *Organizational Behavior and Human Performance*, 12, 92–104.

Borman, W.C. 1982. Validity of behavioral-assessment for predicting military recruiter performance. *Journal of Applied Psychology*, 67, 3–9.

Boyle, S., Fullerton, J. and Wood, R. 1995. Do assessment/development centers use optimum evaluation procedures? A survey of practice in UK organizations. *International Journal of Selection and Assessment*, 3, 132–140.

Byham, W.C. 1970. Assessment center for spotting future managers. *Harvard Business Review*, 48, 150–160.

Chan, D. 1996. Criterion and construct validation of an assessment centre. *Journal of Occupational and Organizational Psychology*, 69, 167–181.

Cohen, B.M., Moses, J.L. and Byham, W.C. 1977. *The Validity of Assessment Centers: A Literature Review*. Pittsburgh, PA: Development Dimensions Press.

Dilchert, S. and Ones, D.S. 2009. Assessment center dimensions: Individual difference correlates and meta-analytic incremental validity. *International Journal of Selection and Assessment*, 17, 254–270.

Deutsch, M. and Gerrard, H.B. 1955. A study of normative and informational social influence upon individual judgement. *Journal of Abnormal and Social Psychology*, 5, 629–636.

Feltham, R. 1988. Assessment centre decision-making – judgemental vs mechanical. *Journal of Occupational Psychology*, 61, 237–241.

French, J.R.J. and Raven, B.H. 1959. The bases of social power, in *Studies in Social Psychology*, edited by D. Cartwright. Ann Arbour, MI: Institute for Social Research, 150–167.

Gilbert, P.J. 1981. An investigation of clinical and mechanical combination of assessment center data. *Journal of Assessment Center Technology*, 4, 1–10.

Goldstein, H.W., Yusko, K.P., Braverman, E.P., Smith, D.B. and Chung, B. 1998. The role of cognitive ability in the subgroup differences and incremental validity of assessment center exercises. *Personnel Psychology*, 51, 357–374.

Herriot, P. 2003. Assessment by groups: Can value be added? *European Journal of Work and Organizational Psychology*, 12, 131–145.

Howard, A. 1974. An assessment of assessment centers. *Academy of Management Journal*, 17, 115–134.

Kaplan, M.F. and Miller, C.E. 1987. Group decision-making and normative versus informational influence – effects of type of issue and assigned decision rule. *Journal of Personality and Social Psychology*, 53, 306–313.

King, N. 2004. Using templates in thematic analysis of text. In *Essential Guide to Qualitative Methods in Organizational Research*, edited by G. Symon and C. Cassell. London: Sage, 11–22.

Klayman, J., Soll, J.B., Gonzalez-Vallejo, C. and Barlas, S. 1999. Overconfidence: It depends on how, what, and whom you ask. *Organizational Behavior and Human Decision Processes*, 79, 216–247.

Klimoski, R.J., Friedman, B. and Weldon, E. 1980. Leader influence in the assessment of performance. *Personnel Psychology*, 33, 389–401.

Krause, D.E. and Gebert, D. 2003. A comparison of assessment center practices in organizations in German-speaking regions and the United States. *International Journal of Selection and Assessment*, 11, 297–312.

Krause, D.E. and Thornton, G.C. III. 2009. A cross-cultural look at assessment center practices: Survey results from Western Europe and North America. *Applied Psychology-An International Review-Psychologie Appliquee-Revue Internationale*, 58, 557–585.

Lance, C.E., Newbolt, W.H., Gatewood, R.D., Foster, M.R., French, N.R. and Smith, D.E. 2000. Assessment center exercise factors represent cross-situational specificity, not method bias. *Human Performance*, 13, 323–353.

Lievens, F. 2001. Assessors and use of assessment centre dimensions: A fresh look at a troubling issue. *Journal of Organizational Behavior*, 22, 203–221.

Lievens, F. and Klimoski, R.J. 2001. Understanding the assessment centre process: Where are we now? *International Review of Industrial and Organizational Psychology* (vol. 16), edited by C.L. Cooper and I.T. Robertson. New York: Wiley, 245–286.

Lowry, P.E. 1992. The assessment center: Effects of varying procedures. *Public Personnel Management*, 21, 171–183.

Lowry, P.E. 1997. The assessment center process: New directions. *Journal of Social Behavior and Personality*, 12, 53–62.

McGraw, J.E. and Kravitz, D.A. 1982. Group research, *Annual Review of Psychology*, 33, 195–230.

Meriac, J.P., Hoffman, B.J., Woehr, D.J. and Fleisher, M.S. 2008. Further evidence for the validity of assessment center dimensions: A meta-analysis of the incremental criterion-related validity of dimension ratings. *Journal of Applied Psychology*, 93, 1042–1052.

Mitchel, J.O. 1975. Assessment-center validity – A longitudinal study. *Journal of Applied Psychology*, 60, 573–579.

Moore, D.A. and Healy, P.J. 2008. The trouble with overconfidence. *Psychological Review*, 115, 502–517.

Muchinsky, P.M. 1986. Personnel selection methods. In *International Review of Industrial and Organizational Psychology* edited by C.L. Cooper and I.T. Robertson. New York: Wiley, 37–70.

Nisbett, R.E. and Ross, L. 1980. *Human Influence Strategies and Shortcomings of Social Judgment?* Englewood Cliffs, NJ: Prentice-Hall.

O'Reilly, C.A. and Caldwell, D.F. 1979. Informational influence as a determinant of perceived task characteristics and job-satisfaction. *Journal of Applied Psychology*, 642, 157–165.

Raven, B.H. 1965. Social influence and power. In *Current Studies in Social Psychology* edited by I.D. Steiner and M. Fishbein. New York: Holt, Rinehart and Winston, 371–381.

Raven, B.H. 1993. The bases of social power: Origins and recent developments. *Journal of Social Issues*, 49, 227–252.

Rolland, J.P. 1999. Construct validity of in-basket dimensions. *European Review of Applied Psychology-Revue Européenne De Psychologie Appliquée*, 49, 251–259.

Roth, P.L., Bobko, P. and McFarland, L.A. 2005. A meta-analysis of work sample test validity: Updating and integrating some classic literature. *Personnel Psychology*, 58, 1009–1037.

Russell, C.J. 1985. Individual decision-processes in an assessment center. *Journal of Applied Psychology*, 70, 737–746.

Sackett, P.R. and Dreher, G.F. 1982. Constructs and assessment-center dimensions – some troubling empirical-findings. *Journal of Applied Psychology*, 67, 401–410.

Sackett, P.R. and Wilson, M.A. 1982. Factors affecting the consensus judgment process in managerial assessment-centers. *Journal of Applied Psychology*, 67, 10–17.

Schmidt, F.L. and Hunter, J. 2004. General mental ability in the world of work: Occupational attainment and job performance. *Journal of Personality and Social Psychology*, 86, 162–173.

Spychalski, A.C., Quiñones, M.A., Gaugler, B.B. and Pohley, K. 1997. A survey of assessment center practices in organizations in the United States. *Personnel Psychology*, 50, 71–90.

Steiner, I. 1972. *Group Process and Productivity*. New York: Academic Press.

Thornton, G.C. III. and Byham, W.C. 1982. *Assessment Centers and Managerial Performance*. New York: Academic Press.

Thornton, G.C. III 1992. *Assessment Centers in Human Resource Management*. Reading, MA: Addison-Wesley.

Thornton, G.C. III and Rupp, D.E. Rupp 2006. *Assessment Centers in Human Resource Management: Strategies for Prediction, Diagnosis, and Development*. Mahwah, New Jersey: Lawrence Erlbaum.

Turner, J.C., Wetherell, M.S. and Hogg, M.A. 1989. Referent informational influence and group polarization. *British Journal of Social Psychology*, 28, 135–147.

Tversky, A. and Kahneman, D. 1971. Belief in the law of small numbers. *Psychological Bulletin*, 76, 105–110.

Tziner, A. and Dolan, S. 1982. Validity of an assessment-center for identifying future female officers in the military. *Journal of Applied Psychology*, 67, 728–736.

Wollowick, H. and McNamara, W.J. 1969. Relationship of the components of an assessment center to management success. *Journal of Applied Psychology*, 53, 348–352.

Wood, W., Lundgren, S., Ouellette, J.A., Busceme, S. and Blackstone, T. 1994. Minority influence: A meta-analytic review of social influence processes. *Psychological Bulletin*, 115, 323–345.

8 The Impact of ACs and DCs on Candidates

CLIVE FLETCHER

Both ethical practice and utility demand that ACs and DCs be run in such a manner as to make attending them a positive experience for candidates. Clearly, organizations would not want their assessment processes to be damaging to candidates in any way. Moreover, it is important that the assessment methods are applied so as to facilitate candidates to give a realistic representation of their performance and potential. In the case of DCs, and ACs run to assess potential in existing employees, a further objective is that candidates should get the maximum benefit and learning potential from their participation. However, in comparison with the substantial AC literature overall, relatively few studies have looked at AC/DCs from the perspective of the candidate, other than to focus on candidate perceptions of fairness, procedural justice and the extent to which ACs are seen as realistic and job relevant by those being assessed. There is, though, a small but growing body of research that has gone beyond this and begun to probe the feelings and reactions that candidates report they have experienced during or after an AC, and the effects on candidates of having been through an AC. The latter can include aspects of their motivation (both personal and towards the organization), self-esteem and other self-perceptions.

There is good reason to look carefully at the impact of ACs in this way. It has been pointed out (Fletcher 1986) that assessment centres are likely to be particularly potent in their effects on candidates precisely because they typically have high face validity and are promoted as being fair, give insights into candidates, are less subject to trainability effects, and so on (Lievens 2002). The sophistication of ACs, the comprehensive range of methods they use and their duration make them highly credible to candidates. Consequently it is more difficult for the latter to rationalize away rejection for a job that results from participating in an AC. If you have been deemed not satisfactory for a job or a place on a high potential scheme after such a thorough assessment, there is simply nowhere to hide. In addition, the demanding nature of ACs, with their range of tests, interviews and simulations, may be fairly daunting to some candidates, which may in itself impact on their performance while going through the AC.

This chapter seeks to pull together the evidence we have on the impact of ACs and DCs on candidates, firstly in terms of initial reactions (specifically, various forms of anxiety) while going through the assessment process, and then in relation to any subsequent changes in those candidates. The latter will be broken down into changes in motivation and well-being on the one hand and changes in self-perceptions of competence on the other. The purpose in reviewing this literature, though, is practical: what can we do to ameliorate dysfunctional reactions during assessment and any potential negative post-assessment consequences? The second part of the chapter will address those issues. What will not be included here is the stream of research mentioned above, on the perceived fairness of ACs and other assessment methods; for that the reader is referred to Hausknecht, Day and Thomas (2004).

Candidate Anxiety and Assessment Centres

The fact that some individuals experience test anxiety has long been recognized (Mandler and Sarason 1952). Typically, this causes them to focus on non-task relevant cognitions (for example, how other candidates are performing, or on the consequences of failure) which interfere with effective performance. Whilst most of this literature centres on reactions to exams or psychological tests, the phenomenon it is describing goes wider and can be construed as a more generalized evaluation apprehension (Skinner and Brewer 1999); some people just get nervous when they feel they are being formally evaluated. The social facilitation literature suggests that having teams of assessors and groups of candidates magnifies evaluation apprehension because there are more sources of evaluation (Zajonc 1980). Should this be of concern for ACs? After all, is that not one of the important things that ACs tell us, whether an individual can perform under pressure? Clearly, if one is dealing with a potentially high stress role, such as a police officer in a tactical firearms unit who may be dealing with a life-and-death situation, then this is very relevant. But most occupational roles are not in this territory and if they are, then the assessment process should be tailored to that requirement, as Lievens (2009: 111) suggests 'if organizations want to assess candidates on a dimension such as resistance to stress that is related to the trait of emotional stability, they must use exercises that put people in a situation that might activate behaviour relevant to the trait of interest'. He goes on to suggest using an oral presentation with challenging questions, and setting stringent time limits, sudden obstacles, or information overload in exercises as a way of testing out this level of resilience. The problem is that the kind of anxiety we are focusing on here, namely evaluation anxiety, is rather situation-specific. In other words, a candidate may exhibit these reactions in the formal assessment situation but perform well in all other circumstances. Thus we might be rejecting someone whose performance in the AC is adversely affected but who might potentially be an excellent employee in normal occupational roles.

A significant proportion of candidates do seem to experience negative psychological effects of one form or another in ACs, as has been demonstrated in a number of studies. Probably the highest figure came from a study by Fletcher, Lovatt and Baldry (1997) who found 47 per cent of candidates reported on a post-AC questionnaire, which was used only for research and not passed on to the employing organization, that their performance had been affected by 'stress and tension'. Le Blanc, de Jonge and Schaufeli (2008: 121) observe that in everyday language as well as the scientific literature the term 'stress' is used to refer to the state of tension, to the consequences of this state and to its cause. So we cannot say what proportion of these 47 per cent consistently suffered from evaluation anxiety or any other particular form of anxiety. Some might simply be individuals who had high general anxiety, or who tended to react emotionally under pressure. Some might also fall into the category identified by Dodd (1977), who found that 14 per cent of candidates said external pressures and problems affected their performance. The limitation of these few (mostly early) studies is that they are usually based on simple reaction questionnaire items, asking *after* an AC whether the candidates felt, anxious, stressed and so on, and usually without defining those terms. They did not differentiate whether, or what kind of, anxiety had been experienced, and they did not use validated, standard measures.

One study that asked *before* an AC whether the thought of going through it made the candidate anxious found that more than 43 per cent said they were very anxious or anxious (Fletcher and Kerslake 1993). Anxiety level did not correlate with self-esteem, with the perceived fairness of the AC procedure, or with the amount of preparation done. It did correlate with pre-AC self-assessment on just one of the AC competencies, with more anxious candidates seeing themselves as more innovative. Post-AC was rather different, however, with a much stronger tendency for candidates who had higher anxiety to assess their performance (rated post-AC) more positively but for the assessors to see things very differently, with a negative correlation ($-.32$ $p<.01$) between OAR and anxiety level. This suggests that although anxiety was associated with candidates taking a more optimistic view of their performance over the course of the AC, it may have had a distorting effect on self-assessment accuracy and a negative effect on AC performance. But, again, this study did not probe the nature of the anxiety or use standard measures.

A further study that did seek to differentiate between anxiety sources was reported by Fletcher et al. (1997). They used a test anxiety questionnaire adapted for the AC context and the Spielberger State-Trait Anxiety Inventory (STAI), which candidates completed pre-AC. Test anxiety was associated with poorer performance on a numerical test and a written exercise. State anxiety, which by definition is more short-lived and situation specific, showed a curvilinear relationship with performance such that high or low state anxiety were both related to doing less well in the AC. This is easily understood, since too little arousal in an assessment situation is probably not helpful, any more than too much, as one needs to be a little keyed-up to do one's best! The same reasoning applies to the rather surprising finding that higher trait anxiety was correlated with better AC performance. Closer examination showed that the overall level of Trait anxiety was low, so it seems possible that those who were higher on this dimension were operating at a more optimum level. Overall, there was nothing in this study to indicate high levels of state or trait anxiety prior to the AC, though as indicated in the first reference to this study above, 47 per cent of candidates reported post-AC that they felt they were affected by stress and tension, which rather suggests that if there were no negative psychological reactions beforehand, the AC experience itself generated them. Interestingly, there was some tendency found for the more familiar elements of an AC (principally, the Interview) to elicit less anxiety effects. This fits with other, general findings suggesting that candidates feel more in control when faced with familiar assessment methods (Fletcher 1997a).

Tovey (2004), following on from this work, examined the relationship of test, state and trait anxiety to AC performance in a series of studies carried out across public and private sector organizations. In her first study, the only correlation between any of the anxiety measures and performance were positive ones, as state anxiety measured pre-AC was associated with better scores and ratings on several elements of the AC. In an echo of Fletcher et al. (1997) above, the pre-AC anxiety levels were very low indeed, thus contributing to the conflicting pattern of findings on pre-AC anxiety indications. However, this study again raises the possibility that the higher (but still medium) levels of anxiety were likely to facilitate rather than disrupt performance. In her second and third studies, she used a measure that separated the two main components of test anxiety, emotionality and worry. The former deals with physiological symptoms, for example perceived elevated heart rate, and the latter reflects distracting cognitions such as 'I feel others will be disappointed in me.' Also included was a checklist of positive and negative thoughts, which included items such as 'Think how good I will feel if I do well,' and 'I feel in control of my reactions.' Summarizing a complex set of findings, Tovey found that test anxiety did correlate with AC outcome (higher anxiety, lower OAR), and that the worry element of the measure used was most predictive. Pre-AC positive thoughts were also correlated with the outcome in the form of a better OAR. This relationship between pre-AC positive thoughts and AC success was replicated in a third study.

CONCLUSIONS

Research findings are seldom completely consistent and clear cut, and with ACs this is particularly so, given that ACs featuring in research studies are usually in different organizations, with different content and structure, different duration, different aims, different assessors (whose training will have varied widely) and different candidates. Despite all these variables, a number of conclusions seem justified on the basis of the studies mentioned here:

- In some instances, a significant proportion of candidates retrospectively report experiencing anxiety, or report stress or tension, when going through ACs. In one case, 43 per cent of candidates said before the AC that the thought of going through it made them anxious. In others, it is less clear whether these candidates were reporting feelings generated as a result of the AC experience itself.
- A moderate degree of state or trait anxiety seems to facilitate performance, though very low levels do not.
- Pre-existing high state anxiety can sometimes disrupt performance during an AC and lead to less accurate self-assessment, though its impact appears to be somewhat variable.
- Test anxiety, particularly that element of it that consists of worry, can detract from an individual's performance and lead them to be less successful in terms of final outcome.
- Positive cognitions, such as 'Think how good I will feel if I do well' pre-assessment seem to exert a beneficial effect.

These conclusions suggest we should give serious attention to the role of anxiety and related cognitions in running ACs. In some instances, candidate trait anxiety coming in to an AC may act as an independent, causal variable, whilst state anxiety may be a dependent variable impacted by participation in the AC. The influence of test anxiety should probably be construed as an interaction of an existing tendency with the experience of being assessed.

Quite apart from anything else, the literature shows that assessors do assess personality traits in an AC and use those judgements in making assessment decisions (Lievens, De Fruyt and Van Dam 2001). Thus, an assessor picking up on a candidate's test anxiety may well make a dispositional attribution and see it as an expression of an enduring rather than transient characteristic of the individual, or make an unsound inference that the anxiety is indicative of lower ability. Overall, anxiety in various forms may disrupt candidate performance and detract from our accuracy in assessing an individual's potential in other, more every-day work settings. Later in the chapter, we will examine what steps might be taken to reduce or otherwise take account of anxiety effects.

The Impact of ACs on Candidates' Subsequent Feelings and Self-Perceptions

As was pointed out in the introduction to this chapter, there are many reasons for believing that extended and thorough assessment processes may have more impact on candidates than simpler, shorter and more familiar assessment methods. Numerous writers have discussed this subject, and have given varying names to it. Iles and Robertson (1997) referred to it as 'Impact Validity', though it is difficult to see how it can be construed as a form of validity as such – rather, it is a factor (like quality of assessor training) that may influence validity. Anderson and Goltsi (2006) refer to it more simply as 'Negative Psychological Effects'. Is there any evidence to support these ideas, though? Probably the first two studies that opened up this area were those by Robertson, Iles, Gratton and Sharpley (1991) and Fletcher (1991). The former compared successful and unsuccessful candidates' responses immediately after the AC. They found no differences on psychological health (measured by the GHQ) or self-esteem between the groups. However, the unsuccessful candidates showed lower organizational commitment and increased career withdrawal thoughts post AC; in other words, their motivation in relation to their employing organization and their own careers seemed to have taken a dip.

Fletcher (1991) conducted a longitudinal study with measures being taken before, immediately after and 6 months after the AC. The results showed that going through the AC did have an impact on candidates, but this tended to reduce over time. For unsuccessful candidates, though, there was a long-term drop in self-esteem and in some aspects of achievement motivation. Given that self-esteem is usually found to correlate with job performance and is generally viewed as a key element of psychological well-being, this is a worrying finding. Most selection processes result in a minority of candidates being accepted. However, where that process is being run for internal candidates, for promotion or entry on to a fast track development programme as is often the case for ACs, organizations cannot afford for the majority who were not successful to be 'switched off'.

Anderson and Goltsi (2006) similarly followed a longitudinal design, with the final post-AC measurement point again being 6 months after attendance, yet found no significant differences between pass and fail candidates in terms of their psychological well-being (they used the GHQ as a measure of this construct, though the same questionnaire was used by Robertson et al. as a measure of psychological health) over time. The contrast between these findings and those of Fletcher (1991) may well lie in differences between candidate groups and the purpose of the AC. In the Fletcher study, the AC was being run to identify potential within an existing employee group, and unusually, more candidates passed than failed. In the Anderson and Goltsi research, not only was the AC for graduate level entry, with candidates consequently being younger, but it also had a rather low pass-rate. The interpretation of failure and its implications are thus likely to be very different for the two groups. For young graduates, recognizing it was a highly competitive AC and the chances were stacked against them in the first place, there is always the comfort of knowing there will be other, perhaps less demanding ACs and other opportunities. Anderson and Goltsi (2006: 244) point out that attributional and other biases may have allowed unsuccessful candidates to persuade themselves, for example: 'so many other applicants were also unsuccessful that I knew all along that this was a long-shot'.

In contrast, for existing employees who have been deemed not to have fast-track potential, the future looks less rosy, and whilst they still have a job, they may begin to suffer some deficit in self-esteem and their personal motivation and/or their organizational commitment. The point made at the beginning of this chapter is relevant here – the fact that ACs are seen as being fair and as having strong face validity may make the psychological impact of 'failure' at the AC all the more powerful.

The three studies mentioned above seem to constitute the only substantial investigations in terms of AC effects on self-esteem, motivation and so on. There is, however, a larger group of investigations that have examined the extent to which ACs and DCs influence candidates' assessments of their competence, and it to these we now turn.

THE IMPACT OF ACs AND DCs ON CANDIDATE SELF-PERCEPTION AND SELF-ASSESSMENT

In theory, the experience of going through a well-designed, extended assessment process should offer the opportunity for individuals to benchmark their existing self-assessment against the observations of trained assessors working to an objective set of criteria. The feedback should facilitate a more accurate self-view, both implicitly enabling the individuals to see how they perform against peers being assessed alongside them and explicitly from direct and formal feedback given by assessors in or after the event. This might be indicated by a shift in self-ratings from pre to post-AC/DC towards closer agreement with assessor ratings, and also by an increasing correlation between self-rating and assessor ratings by the end of an AC. Again, the research presents some mixed and far from reassuring findings.

Schmitt, Ford and Stults (1986) found the correlation between candidate and assessor ratings post-AC to be generally low (<.20). Fletcher and Kerslake (1992) collected self-ratings before, immediately after and 6 months after an AC. On the positive side, they found that while candidates self-assessments made pre-AC did not correlate at all with the assessors' ratings awarded in the AC, immediately post-AC self-assessments correlated (averaging .27) on four of the seven assessment dimensions, suggesting a more realistic self-appraisal. The most striking finding here, though, is the difference between successful and unsuccessful candidates. Both show no pre-AC correlations with assessor ratings, but whereas the former show three post-AC correlations (averaging .35) with assessor ratings, the latter show quite large negative correlations with assessor ratings post-AC on two dimensions (Decision-making, –.48, and Assertiveness, –.52) and no correlation at all on the remainder. It seems that many of the unsuccessful candidates had completely misread their performance in the AC. This failure to accurately self-assess and to pick up cues on their performance may well be one of the reasons they did not do well in the AC, as will be seen below.

Randall, Ferguson and Patterson (2000) studied candidates at a graduate assessment centre. They found that there were reliable self-assessment differences between accepted and rejected candidates for all of the AC exercises. Those candidates who were rejected consistently overestimated their own performance, and Randall et al. concluded that the overestimation of scores by unsuccessful candidates was more consistent and pronounced than had been indicated by previous research. This is where there is congruence between the research on ACs and multi-source feedback. One of the consistent observations from the latter is that people have consistent self-rating styles, with some being overraters, some accurate raters, and some underraters; the differentiation is a little more complex than that, but it is not necessary to go into this in more depth here. Equally, what comes through is that self-awareness – usually operationalized by agreement between self-ratings and colleague/peer/boss ratings – is associated with better performance (Fletcher, 1997b). More than this, people who tend to consistently overrate themselves tend to be poor performers (Ostroff, Atwater and Feinberg 2004; Atwater, Ostroff, Waldman, Robie and Johnson 2005; Jackson, Stillman, Burke, and Englert 2007).

The potential effects of this are illustrated in a study by Halman and Fletcher (2000). This was carried out on a DC and as with other studies, pre- and post- self-ratings were collected and compared with assessor ratings. As before, it was found that congruence between self- and assessor ratings increased from pre- to post-DC. The difference here, though, is that using the methodology deployed in multi-source feedback studies, candidates were divided into overraters, accurate raters and underraters. Analysis showed that underraters actually became more accurate (that is, more congruent with the assessors' ratings) in their self-assessments as a result of going through the DC, but overraters did not; indeed, the latter group had a high opinion of their ability (and high self-esteem) before the DC and despite getting feedback during the process, they emerged at the other end with an equally inflated view of their abilities and their self-esteem was unchanged! Similarly, a later study by Woo, Sims, Rupp, and Gibbons (2008) found overraters were less likely to engage with DC feedback. This perhaps gives an insight into why DCs have all too often not seemed to live up to their potential (Jones and Whitmore 1995; Carrick and Williams 1999) for developing those who go through them; because the impact on under and accurate self-raters is masked by the lack of impact on the overraters. For a discussion of other aspects of this, see Woo, Sims, Rupp, and Gibbons (2008).

One passing observation that might be made from this literature in general is that the lack of correlation between candidates' self-assessments pre-event with the ratings they are given during the process is very consistent and somewhat alarming – perhaps showing up the discrepancy between the high quality of assessment offered through ACs with what is provided for employees through performance appraisal and day to day feedback, the latter suffering by comparison! This also highlights one of the difficulties in gaining acceptance of the feedback; namely its discrepancy with the pre-existing self-evaluation. As ever with feedback, the credibility of the source is crucial to acceptance (Anseel and Lievens 2009), and one might hope that the high face validity of ACs should make them a more credible source than performance appraisal judgements, which are notoriously influenced by non-performance factors (Arvey and Murphy 1998; Fletcher 2002).

CONCLUSIONS

There is a limited amount of varying evidence that the experience of going through an AC may have some deleterious consequences for the self-esteem, commitment and motivation of some, but not all, candidates who are unsuccessful. The extent to which this happens may be influenced by the real or perceived selection ratio, by the age group of the candidates – unfortunately there is no evidence as yet as to impact on diversity in other respects, such as gender, ethnicity and so on – and by the purpose of the AC (selection or identifying potential). There is rather more evidence on the impact of attending an AC or DC on participants' self-assessments. A fair amount of it shows some increase in correlation between self-assessments and assessor ratings at the end of the assessment event, which is a very positive outcome. However, this may be markedly less true for unsuccessful candidates. One of the main reasons for this is probably that lack of self-awareness, perhaps reflected in a tendency to overrate oneself, is actually a direct contributor to poor AC performance.

Improving the Effectiveness of ACs by Enhancing Their Value for Candidates

We should have two broad aims in mind in reviewing these findings. One is purely utilitarian: making these assessment processes more effective in their primary purpose. The other is perhaps best thought of as ethical: how can we make attending ACs and DCs a more positive experience for candidates? However, the author would argue that the second contributes to the first, allowing candidates to give of their best in ACs and helping them use the feedback they get from them is ultimately in the organization's interests.

ANXIETY AND RELATED COGNITIONS

In theory, it would be possible to use or adapt one or more of the numerous measures that exist to identify those individuals who habitually suffer evaluation anxiety before they attend. In an ideal world, they could then be offered some pre-AC counselling and support to reduce their apprehension. It is beyond the scope of this chapter to go into detail on methods, but, for example, cognitive-behavioural therapy techniques can be applied very quickly. As well as seeking to assess evaluation anxiety, one might seek to measure the extent to which candidates have more general positive or negative cognitions pre-AC (see Tovey 2004) and take steps to enhance the former and minimize the latter, boosting self-efficacy where necessary. The relevance of sport psychology can hardly be overstated here. It has long been recognized in that field that pre-event cognitions have a crucial impact on success and failure (Williams and Leffingwell 2002).

This, however, raises the issue of fairness. Such a selective coaching strategy might be considered unacceptable to the affected candidates, to other candidates or to the organization. It could also be seen as illegal, in terms of equal opportunities legislation, to give some candidates additional assistance. There is, of course, nothing to stop a candidate seeking assessment coaching on a personal basis, and organizations, individuals, books and websites offering such coaching are in plentiful supply (for example, Povah and Povah 2009). It is interesting to note that Thornton and Gibbon (2009) conclude that virtually no studies have been conducted to evaluate the efficacy of various techniques to train candidates to perform in ACs. The question of whether the organization running the AC can fairly make such help available is probably dependent on the legislation in the country concerned. One might argue, for example, that if evaluation anxiety is not relevant to actual job performance and hence detracts from validity, then failing to take account of it in some manner is itself inequitable, and that not making coaching support available could unfairly disadvantage some individuals and groups. A number of well-established ACs already, via hard copy or online, give a kind of coaching in the form of advice that seeks to familiarize candidates with the process in advance.

If this kind of personal coaching support is not possible because of practical/resource constraints, then at least the assessors can be alerted to individuals who have these problems when they consider them in the wash-up. Indeed, assessors, in their training, can be sensitized to identify anxiety cues given by candidates, and to evaluate both their impact on the performance of the candidates they are observing and the implications for future behaviour in the job (see also the comments made earlier in this respect). It is not possible to be prescriptive about how this information might be used, as so much would depend on the candidate profile, the AC and the role being selected for. But if a candidate is showing signs of anxiety, it may well be possible to question them about their reactions to the AC during the event, their previous experience of assessment situations and how they felt in them and to probe for any discrepancies between how they are responding in the assessment and how they have coped in stressful situations in their jobs or other aspects of life. Some organizations do this routinely in a candidate debriefing interview at the end of the AC which is a practice that should perhaps be adopted more widely.

In some cases, where anxiety and negative cognitions reach a level that cause concern and suggest that chances of success at the AC are remote, as well as the possibility of it being a potentially damaging experience for the individual, it may be better to sift them out of the process. Again, this potentially raises legal issues, and they will vary from country to country. Certainly, a screening stage, using personality questionnaires and cognitive tests to identify candidates who are less likely to succeed and reject them before they reach the assessment centre, is quite common in UK graduate recruitment. Even in the case of ACs for internal candidates being assessed for fast-track potential, there is very often a nomination process that, with varying degrees of explicitness, is based on a preliminary assessment of candidates that eliminates some from further consideration. It could be argued that organizations running demanding and potentially stressful assessment events have a duty of care to candidates: there is, after all, a widespread acceptance that exam failure can lead to para-suicide and suicide (for example, Neyra, Range and Goggin 1990; BBC 2006) and anecdotal evidence suggests that receiving unfavourable assessment in organizations, for example from critical multi-source feedback, can sometimes lead to very adverse psychological consequences. Exposing vulnerable candidates to an assessment process that might do them more harm than good could be costly to both organization and candidate.

More generally, it probably helps if the organization is able to offer more than one chance at attending an AC, albeit after a period for the candidate to work on their development. If candidates know that it is not an 'all or nothing' opportunity and that after a suitable period they may attend the AC again, then this should help to reduce some of the pressure. Of course, many ACs are one-off events and this is simply not possible.

PSYCHOLOGICAL WELL-BEING AND MOTIVATION

Moving on to the impact of ACs on psychological well-being and motivation, the focus is clearly on candidates who have not been successful at the AC. For employees attending an AC to identify potential for fast-tracking, feedback to those who have 'failed' the AC needs careful handling. As it is, feedback is too often delayed until quite some time after the event and after candidates have heard the outcome. Krause and Thornton (2009) report that only a quarter of organizations in North America and only half in Western Europe provide feedback to participants immediately after AC completion. Although feedback is most effective in general when given immediately after behaviour (Thornton and Rupp 2006), it will be especially important for those who have not succeeded to have their feedback discussion as quickly as possible, both to take them over the detail of their performance while it is fresh in their minds and to deal with their understandable issues about where this leaves them in terms of their career. This implies face-to-face feedback; as Krause and Thornton (2009) observe, because AC feedback is generally complex, written feedback alone could lead to frustration, confusion, and lack of understanding.

The organization needs to have a clear plan as to how it is going to maintain the motivation and commitment of those who are not successful. It is too easy for this group to feel they will now be forgotten about, left to stagnate in some way, with the possible result of them thinking in terms of career withdrawal (Roberston et al. 1991). Indeed, arguably, they are the ones who need more development resources devoted to them than the candidates who actually passed the AC! The post-AC process for handling the unsuccessful group needs to be sensitive to any damage to the individual's self-esteem. In that respect, it might be useful to have self-esteem measures taken pre, post and 6 months after the AC to monitor any signs of a decreasing sense of self-worth. Again, it is not sensible to seek to be prescriptive in how unsuccessful candidates are managed, but the most immediate requirement is to have the resource in place to counsel and help them formulate their career strategy – in terms of how they can play to their strengths, look at possible development activities and to think through the options they have in terms of future progression, above all, to make them feel they are still valued and supported.

Where an AC has been used for external recruitment, extensive follow up support is clearly less feasible. But organizations should not shrug off their responsibilities for the well-being of the candidates too readily. If the author may resort to anecdotal evidence for a moment, I once met a very able individual (in terms of IQ scores, degree class and career progression) who on first graduating had attended one of the toughest ACs in the UK, where as many as 10,000 graduates apply and many are sifted out by earlier stages of the assessment process prior to the AC, with perhaps as few as 150 finally being accepted. He progressed all the way through to the AC, but was not offered a job. He carried round a very strong (but actually rather distorted) sense of failure for literally years afterwards, which affected his subsequent career choices. Some brief post-AC counselling would probably have put his 'failure' in a more realistic context and helped him rationalize it. Some telephone and written feedback should routinely be offered, and those giving it should be trained to pick up on indications of any more severe reactions and have a range of support options available, such as being able to refer the candidate to a counselling service if appropriate.

SELF-ASSESSMENT

Finally, we can look at the practical implications of the work examining the impact of AC attendance on self-assessments. Receiving clear and detailed feedback as soon as possible after the assessment event is likely to be important for the candidate to understand and accept that feedback, which is a necessary precursor to them revising their self-assessment and actually doing anything about it. Clearly, as indicated above, this is especially important in the case of unsuccessful candidates.

In the context of DCs, it is often feasible and potentially desirable for feedback to be given during the event as noted by a number of writers (Thornton 1992; Thornton and Rupp 2006) so that candidates can use it actively. Indeed, the extent to which they demonstrate that they *are* able to learn from feedback and apply that learning as they progress through the DC may be an important input to the assessment of them.

The well-established fact that individuals have consistent self-assessment styles and yet differences in self-awareness needs to be recognized and consideration should be given to how this might feature in ACs and particularly DCs. It is likely to be especially useful, pre-event, to identify individuals who habitually overrate themselves. At its simplest, this entails asking all participants to assess themselves on the AC dimensions pre- and post-AC and comparing these with the ratings given them by assessors. However, if multi-source feedback data is available pre-AC this can also be very useful in picking out people who consistently rate themselves higher than their colleagues. Indeed one might suggest that if they do, they should be screened out beforehand anyway, although this is probably unlikely to be possible for legal reasons.

Whichever method is used, it seems likely that candidates whose self-assessments remain unjustifiably positive and whose self-esteem remains very buoyant post-AC, despite poor performance, may need a different approach taken to their feedback. For example, it may be appropriate to take an approach that is rather tougher in tone if they are to really engage with the feedback and learn from it.

Looking at the other side of the coin, individuals who tend to underrate themselves might benefit from feedback counselling that boosts their self-esteem and self-efficacy, because their unrealistically modest self-assessment may be holding them back and also detracting from the organization getting the best from them.

Self-awareness, defined here as congruence between self-assessment and external evaluation, has a demonstrable relationship to performance (Fletcher 1997b, Atwater et al. 2005). ACs offer an opportunity to gather such data, comparing self-assessments with assessor ratings. Making explicit use of this information in the final AC assessment process, as an indication of candidate self-awareness, could make a valuable contribution to the overall assessment of an individual. One caveat worth noting here is that all the studies mentioned in this chapter were done in a western cultural context; it may well be that in other cultural settings, different patterns of response to assessment apply (Bailey and Fletcher 2008).

In summary, then, there are steps that organizations can take before and after an AC to maximize utility and candidate well-being:

- *Setting up the AC:* Assessors can be sensitized to recognize and evaluate candidate anxiety cues in their training.
- *Immediately before the AC*: Measures of anxiety, positive/negative cognitions, self-esteem, can be taken (all of which are very quick to administer) along with candidates' self-assessments on the AC dimensions.
- *Immediately after the AC*: Feedback should be given quickly, and tailored both to the candidate's self-assessment style and to the outcome, and unsuccessful candidates need to be reassured and supported.

- *Longer term post-AC:* Self-esteem and motivation of candidates who were unsuccessful in an AC aimed at identifying potential in existing staff should be monitored and support given where necessary.

In Conclusion

Thornton and Krause (2009) in their international survey of development assessment centres conclude 'there is an insufficient degree of evaluation of participants' reaction' to DACs, and that asking participants about 'consequences for self-concept and motivation' was very rarely done. One can only agree. Indeed, one practitioner (Maldé 2006) asks rather plaintively 'do assessment centres really care about the candidate?' to which his answer is – not enough. The very influential International Task Force's Assessment Centre Guidelines (2009) has relatively little to say on this, confining itself largely to the need for informed consent, the need to give feedback, offering some rationale for a selection decision when asked for and ensuring a degree of confidentiality. Indeed there is no discussion in the Guidelines focused directly on the psychological well-being of the candidates other than a very general statement that there should be mechanisms for follow-up support and monitoring. Nor is there any overt recognition of responsibility for this outside the areas mentioned above, which is surprising, given that so many psychologists are involved in AC applications and all of them presumably have a professional code of ethics to guide them. Much the same is true of the UK Best Practice Guidelines (British Psychological Society 2006). It would be desirable for future editions of both sets of Guidelines to make more specific and formal recommendations on the consideration and evaluation of candidate responses to assessment as a routine element in setting up and running ACs and perhaps most importantly to recommend that there should be a debriefing session with each candidate, carried out by a member of the AC staff at the end of the AC, and for the observations from this to be fed into the assessment wash-up discussion.

There may be barriers in time and resources to implementing some of the suggestions made in this chapter, but there is no reason why AC practitioners should not at least give greater consideration to these issues than has been the case hitherto, especially as tackling some of them may well enhance the effectiveness of ACs in identifying potential. And for researchers in particular, more attention can and should be given to research on the candidate perspective. At present, the bulk of the research effort is directed towards making ACs more effective from a rather utilitarian, organizational/employer viewpoint, an imbalance that psychologists should not feel entirely comfortable with.

References

Anderson, N. and Goltsi, V. 2006. Negative psychological effects of selection methods: Construct formulation and an empirical investigation into an assessment center. *International Journal of Selection and Assessment*, 14, 236–255.

Anseel, F. and Lievens, F. 2009. The mediating role of feedback acceptance in the relationship between feedback and attitudinal and performance outcomes. *International Journal of Selection and Assessment*, 17, 362–376.

Arvey, R.D. and Murphy, K.R. 1998. Performance evaluation in work settings. *Annual Review Psychology*, 49, 141–168.

Atwater, L., Ostroff, C, Waldman, D., Robie, C. and Johnson, K.M. 2005. Self-other agreement: Comparing its relationship with performance in the US and Europe. *International Journal of Selection and Assessment*, 13, 25–40.

Bailey, C. and Fletcher, C. 2008. Performance management and appraisal – an international perspective. In *The Handbook of Research in International Human Resource Management*, edited by M.M. Harris. Organization Management Series, Erlbaum 125–143.

BBC News: Education (Justin Parkinson). 2006. When exam stress becomes too much. 16 August 2006.

British Psychological Society. 2006. Design, implementation and evaluation of assessment and development centres: Best practice guidelines. BPS Psychological Testing Centre, Leicester.

Carrick, P. and Williams, R. 1999. Development centres: A review of assumptions. *Human Resource Management Journal*, 9, 77–92.

Dodd, W.E. 1977. Attitudes to assessment centre programs. In *Applying the Assessment Center Method*, edited by J.L. Moses and W.C. Byham. New York: Pergamon, 161–183.

Fletcher, C. 1986. Should the test score be kept a secret? *Personnel Management*, April, 44–46.

Fletcher, C. 1991. Candidates' reactions to assessment centres and their outcomes: A longitudinal study. *Journal of Occupational Psychology*, 64, 117–127.

Fletcher, C. and Kerslake, C. 1992. The impact of Assessment Centres and their outcomes on participants' self-assessments. *Human Relations*, 45, 73–81.

Fletcher, C. and Kerslake, C. 1993. Candidate anxiety level and assessment centre performance. *Journal of Managerial Psychology*, 8, 19–23.

Fletcher, C. 1997a. The impact of psychometric assessment: Fostering positive candidate attitudes and reactions. *Selection and Development Review*, 13, 8–11.

Fletcher, C. 1997b. Self-awareness – a neglected attribute in selection and assessment. *International Journal of Selection and Assessment*, 5, 183–187.

Fletcher, C., Lovatt, C. and Baldry, C. 1997. A study of State, Trait and Test Anxiety and their relationship to assessment centre performance. *Journal of Social Behaviour & Personality*, 12, 205–214.

Fletcher, C. 2002. Appraisal – an individual psychological analysis. In *The Psychological Management of Individual Performance: A Handbook in the Psychology of Management in Organizations*, edited by S. Sonnentag. Wiley: Chichester, 115–135.

Halman, F. and Fletcher, C. 2000. The impact of development centre participation and the role of individual differences in changing self assessments. *Journal of Occupational and Organizational Psychology*, 73, 423–442.

Hausknecht, J.P., Day, D.V. and Thomas, S.C. 2004. Applicant reactions to selection procedures: An updated model and meta-analysis. *Personnel Psychology*, 57, 639–683.

Iles, P.A. and Robertson, I.T. 1997. The impact of personnel selection procedures on candidates. In *International Handbook of Selection and Assessment*, edited by N. Anderson and P. Herriot. Wiley: Chichester, 543–566.

International Task Force on Assessment Center Guidelines. 2009. Guidelines and ethical considerations for Assessment Center Operations. *International Journal of Selection and Assessment*, 17, 243–253.

Jackson, D.J.R., Stillman, J.A., Burke, S. and Englert, P. 2007. Self versus assessor ratings and their classification in assessment centres: Profiling the self-rater. *New Zealand Journal of Psychology*, 36, 93–99.

Jones, R.G. and Whitmore, M.D. 1995. Evaluating developmental assessment centers as interventions. *Personnel Psychology*, 48, 377–388.

Krause, D.E. and Thornton, G.C. III. 2009. A cross-cultural look at assessment center practices: Survey results from Western Europe and North America. *Applied Psychology: An International Review*, 58, 557–585.

Le Blanc, P., de Jonge, J. and Schaufeli, W. 2008. Job stress and occupational health. In *An introduction to Work and Organizational Psychology: A European Perspective*, edited by N. Chmiel. Blackwell: Oxford, 119–147.

Lievens, F. De Fruyt, F. and Van Dam, K. 2001. Assessors' use of personality traits in descriptions of assessment centre candidates: A five factor model perspective. *Journal of Occupational and Organizational Psychology*, 74, 623–636.

Lievens, F. 2002. An examination of the accuracy of slogans related to assessment centres. *Personnel Review*, 31, 86–102.

Lievens, F. 2009. Assessment Centres: A tale about dimensions, exercises and dancing bears. *European Journal of Work and Organizational Psychology*, 18, 102–121.

Maldé, B. 2006. Do assessment centres really care about the candidate? *British Journal of Guidance & Counselling*, 34, 539–549.

Mandler, G. and Sarason, S.B. 1952. A study of anxiety and learning. *Journal Abnormal and Social Psychology*, 47, 166–173.

Neyra, C.J., Range, L.M. and Goggin, W.C. 1990. Reasons for living following success and failure in suicidal and nonsuicidal college students. *Journal of Applied Social Psychology*, 20, 861–868.

Ostroff, C., Atwater, L.E. and Feinberg, B.J. 2004. Understanding self-other agreement: A look at rater and ratee characteristics, context and outcomes. *Personnel Psychology*, 57, 333–376.

Povah, N. and Povah, L. 2009. *Succeeding at Assessment Centres for Dummies*. London: John Wiley and Son.

Randall, R., Ferguson, E. and Patterson, F. 2000. Self assessment accuracy and assessment centre decisions. *Journal of Occupational and Organizational Psychology*, 73, 443–459.

Robertson, I.T., Iles, P.A., Gratton, L. and Sharpley, D.S. 1991. The impact of personnel selection and assessment methods on candidates. *Human Relations*, 44, 963–982.

Schmitt, N., Ford, L.K. and Stults, D.M. 1986. Changes in self-perceived ability as a function of performance in an assessment centre. *Journal of Occupational Psychology*, 59, 327–335.

Skinner, N. and Brewer, N. 1999. Temporal characteristics of evaluation anxiety. *Journal of Anxiety Disorders*, 13, 293–314.

Thornton, G.C. III 1992. *Assessment Centers in Human Resource Management*. Reading, MA: Addison-Wesley.

Thornton, G.C. III and Rupp, D.R. 2006. *Assessment Centers in Human Resource Management: Strategies for Prediction, Diagnosis, and Development*. Mahway, NJ: Erlbaum.

Thornton, G.C., III and Krause, D.E. 2009. Selection versus development assessment centers: An international survey of design, execution, and evaluation. *The International Journal of Human Resource Management*, 20 478–498.

Thornton, G. C III and Gibbons, A.M. 2009. Validity of assessment centers for personnel selection *Human Resource Management Review*, 19, 169–187.

Tovey, R.C. 2004. *The role of anxiety in assessment centre performance*. Unpublished PhD thesis, University of London.

Williams, J.M. and Leffingwell, T.R. 2002. Cognitive strategies in sport and exercise psychology. In *Exploring Sport and Exercise Psychology*, edited by J.L. Van Raalte and B.W. Brewer. Washington: APA, 75–98.

Woo, S.E., Sims, C.S., Rupp, D.E. and Gibbons, A.M. 2008. Development engagement within and following developmental assessment centers: Considering feedback favourability and self-assessor agreement. *Personnel Psychology*, 61, 727–759.

Zajonc, R.B. 1980. Compresence. In *Psychology of Group Influence*, edited by P.B. Paulus. Hillsdale, NJ: Erlbaum, 35–60.

9 Whiter than White? The Diversity Credentials of Assessment and Development Centres

CHARLES WOODRUFFE

Introduction

The purpose of this chapter is to give assessment centres a stress test with respect to their diversity friendliness. Cognitive tests are well known for their adverse impact with respect to ethnicity. Assessment centres enjoy a far cleaner image. As noted by Dean, Roth and Bobko (2008), they are generally thought of as being even-handed across the conventional axes of diversity, maybe showing a slight favouring towards females. But is this image of fairness solidly based? In this chapter, I want to carry out a qualitative analysis that examines how an assessment centre might not be fair. I then want to see what quantitative evidence there is on whether assessment centres currently have adverse impact or not.

In writing this chapter, my aim is to help those using an assessment centre consider ways in which the centre might be unfair and take the necessary corrective measures. I am not seeking to suggest that there is anything inherently unfair in the assessment centre method. Indeed, I have made assessment and development centres my specialist area of consultancy for the past quarter of a century and very much believe in the basic fairness and validity of the approach and in its superiority over other methods of assessment (Woodruffe, 2007). Based on that experience, I want to consider how an assessment centre might have adverse impact unless great care is taken in its design and implementation.

The importance of these matters hardly needs explaining. Apart from the legal and professional imperative of using methods that are fair, there is the straightforward business case. Diversity is at the heart of talent management. It is a truism that talent management is about securing the services of the best people from the entire – diverse – population. Having less than the best people will render an organization at a disadvantage and this will impact on business performance. If you couple this business imperative that an organization needs to secure the best people – whatever their demographic characteristics – with the ubiquity of assessment centres as the selection method for talent pools, then the crucial requirement that assessment centres are fair is obvious. Quite simply, assessment and development centres sit at the core of many talent management strategies. Assessment centres are widely held to offer the best way of identifying people's strengths and weaknesses for selecting the most suitable people. Likewise development centres borrow assessment centre 'technology' to identify people's strengths and development needs and help them prepare for future roles.

The acid test on whether centres operate without adverse impact would be empirical evidence. However, as we shall see, there is generally a lack of good quantitative studies on the impact of centres. Such studies are bedevilled by difficulties, particularly the low numbers available for many comparisons (ethnicity, disability and so on). How many reports have we read, or indeed written, that describe how the small number of ethnic minority or disabled applicants preclude a statistical comparison of assessment centre scores with the white or non-disabled majority?

This lack of evidence should not be taken as equivalent to an all-clear and the end of the matter. Instead, we should enquire as to whether there are any reasons – obvious or not – to be worried about whether assessment centres are acting in synchronization with organizations' talent agendas. It is with this theoretical, qualitative enquiry that I will start.

A Qualitative Analysis

It would, in fact, be easy to denigrate assessment centres if one chose the many so-called centres that diverge wildly from best practice. The terms assessment and development centre are used by some people to cover a multitude of methods from test batteries masquerading as assessment centres to assessment centres masquerading as development centres. Centres that are well behind best practice have obvious diversity problems. Without itemising every possibility, here are just four of the regular failings.

TEST-BASED CENTRES

Centres that consist mainly of tests inevitably incorporate the widely established adverse impact of ability tests. To quote from one of the main research papers on this subject by Ployhart, Ziegert, and McFarland (2003):

> *Nearly every study of general cognitive ability finds that Whites score higher than Blacks (Sackett, Schmitt, Ellingson, and Kabin, 2001), with the magnitude of such differences ranging from two-thirds to 1 SD unit (for example, Hough, Oswald, and Ployhart, 2001; Jensen, 1998; Roth, Bevier, Bobko, Switzer, and Tyler, 2001). These differences are so large that, with realistic selection ratios, adverse impact against Blacks is nearly guaranteed (Bobko, Roth, and Potosky, 1999; Sackett and Roth, 1996).*

POORLY FOCUSED CENTRES

Then, there are centres that measure ill-researched competencies. Many competency frameworks (that provide the assessment centre dimensions) have not been properly diversity-proofed. Frequently, they are derived by asking a sample of the 'ruling class' in the organization what is required for success. It is an easy target but also fair to observe that generally this means the competencies encapsulate aspects of behaviours that white males regard as important. Little thought appears to be given on whether these qualities are truly necessary for the organization to be successful or whether they might act against some groups in society. For example, in March 2010 Cadbury had the following list of leadership imperatives on its website: Accountable, Aggressive, Adaptable, Forward Thinking, Motivating, Growing People, Collaborative and Living our Values.

Whilst they explain that by aggressive they 'mean the drive and passion to succeed – nothing unfriendly' they leave the feeling that they are likely to appeal more to the caricature alpha white male than the caricature Asian female. If they really mean drive, why not use that word? Of course, this observation can be shrugged off with the claim that being aggressive is what they need to succeed. But is it? There must be many successful businesses populated by leaders for whom the word 'aggressive' would not spring to mind as an obvious descriptor. Perhaps Cadbury could have been one of them, removing any concern about the diversity impact of its stipulations.

INSENSITIVE CENTRES

A third way in which centres can easily drift from best practice is in how welcoming they are to diverse groups. There are obvious points like disabled access but also less obvious ones like the middle class/slightly public school tone of some centres. Ideally, centres should be designed by a diverse group who can spot problems in advance; at the very least, a diverse group should scrutinize and sign off the content and administration of the centre. A further consideration is whether the assessors or observers are a diverse group with whom people from different backgrounds can identify. Likewise it will add to the diversity credibility of an internal centre if it is sponsored by and therefore embraced by a diverse group of leaders in the organization.

CENTRES WITH ILL-TRAINED ASSESSORS

As a final example of how centres can run along diversity-unfriendly lines, there are many centres with poorly trained assessors. As the pressure on managers' time increases, there is an enormous temptation to cut back or even cut out assessor training. Unfortunately, untrained managers are almost bound to fall prey to the pitfalls in interpersonal perception such as stereotypes that are a key part of the training that they have truncated. The untrained observer/assessor will most likely use the many shortcuts that people employ when reaching rapid, if discriminatory, judgements.

Anyone reading this book will be able to add to these examples with other ways that assessment and development centres frequently diverge from best practice. In their divergence, they are almost bound to risk operating in a less than diversity-friendly manner. Yet, the truth is that many organizations host centres that cut corners without the consequences being entirely obvious. For example, the centre still seems to run adequately with ill-briefed assessors or with exercises that bear little relevance to the role (for example, outdoor, bridge-building type exercises for a commercial undertaking) or with over-reliance on psychometric tests.

But what about 'best practice' centres? Could even they have features that might not be fully diversity friendly? I believe that a stern examination might well come out with a worrying affirmative answer. As noted at the outset, the problems are not inherent in the assessment centre approach. They come from the context within which assessment and development centres operate or from seemingly innocuous aspects of the centres themselves.

To start with, it is quite easy for talent strategies that should in theory embody diversity, in practice to fall short of really seeking out and welcoming the best people wherever they might be. Two specific examples are:

- Many graduate recruitment schemes that culminate in a graduate assessment centre start by targeting students at the 'best' universities. In the United Kingdom at least, these universities tend to be the less ethnically diverse. According to the 2008/09 Higher Education Statistics Agency (HESA) Student Returns, the percentage of UK-domiciled students at Russell Group institutions (the top 20 UK Universities) that were reported as being from an ethnic minority was 15.4 per cent and the percentage of UK-domiciled students at non-Russell Group institutions that were reported as being from an ethnic minority was 18.4 per cent. Moreover, the percentage of students known to have a disability at Russell Group institutions was 6.1 per cent and the percentage of students known to have a disability at non-Russell Group institutions was 8.5 per cent. [Please note: in providing these data, HESA requested the statement that they cannot accept responsibility for any inferences or conclusions derived from the data by third parties.]
- Many talent programmes strongly emphasize the level of commitment that they require, a requirement that might be off-putting for people with domestic responsibilities.

The general failure to integrate diversity within talent management is discussed in detail in a Chartered Institute for Personnel and Development (CIPD) (2010) research paper that identifies 10 reasons. These include implicit bias still operating against demographic groups, the economic climate appearing to make diversity too costly and the belief that diversity is only really a concern for large organizations. Probably most of us have heard one objection or another to the arguments for diversity. A selection of these and possible ripostes were quoted by Woodruffe, Lyons and Silver, (2009) and are presented in Table 9.1.

Table 9.1   Why bother? Arguments and counter-arguments for worrying about diversity

Argument	Objection	Comment
You need the best people and therefore must include all talented people	We have plenty of applicants of the right quality without bothering to be inclusive	Might be true for low level jobs. But for top jobs you need the best people, not just 'good enough' people
You need your people to reflect your customer base	Our customers are not that diverse	That's the argument! A more diverse workforce might attract more – and more diverse – customers

If you do not include people, they will not give their best	I won't allow them to be that disengaged	It is a lot less effort to have staff voluntarily engaged to 'go the extra mile' than having to coerce them to perform
All staff want to see corporate social responsibility (CSR) credentials and inclusion is part of that	We are perfectly ethical and principled. If you want more, we will support a local charity.	People are extremely vigilant to hypocrisy and lack of authenticity. If you want to engage people you have to really believe your message.
Exclusion is a social ill	Social ills are not the concern of business	The larger you are in your community the greater the positive impact will be on your business of doing the right thing. Doing nothing undermines any claim to corporate social responsibility

So the assessment or development centre can go wrong from the outset because an inadequate commitment to diversity in the talent strategy has the consequence that the candidate or delegate pool does not reflect diversity. However, the focus of this chapter is, of course, on the more specific issue of whether there is adverse impact attributable to the centre itself. There might well be and problems can arise in relation to a number of key features of the centre, each of which I will look at in turn.

COMPETENCIES AND DIVERSITY

The natural starting point is the competencies against which people are assessed. Obvious pitfalls in poor competency frameworks have already been discussed; but are there inherent problems with all competency frameworks? Woodruffe, Lyons and Silver (2009) believe that competencies are, by their nature, over-prescriptive and therefore act against a diversity of approach. To the extent that different demographic groups adopt different approaches to achieving success in their role (for example, the female versus male approach to establishing good client relations), the competencies used in assessment centres might be loaded against one group or another. Indeed, with the current emphasis on emotional intelligence, perhaps the odds are stacked in favour of females, a notion that correlates with the tendency for females to perform better at centres.

The heart of the problem is that competencies do not simply deal with the performance that is required of people. They prescribe personality differences that are imputed to lead to performance. Competencies are elicited by asking what behaviours a successful person exhibits in comparison to a less successful performer. In deriving a competency matrix, the behaviours are clustered with the aim of producing a model of the person who will be a high performer – essentially, a model of the traits that they will exhibit. As such, they have an inherently restricted rather than diverse bias and, if there are personality differences that run along the demographic axes of diversity, there is an obvious problem.

There is definite evidence of personality differences associated with ethnicity but the stronger differences are between cultures. Personality differences between five US racial groups (Black, White, Hispanic, Asian and American Indian) were investigated in a meta-analysis by Foldes, Duehr and Ones (2008). They showed that differences between White and Black and between White and Asian on the big 5 factors were 'modest' and 'generally quite small' respectively. However, at the facet level for the five factors, some more pronounced differences emerged. For example, White samples scored higher than black samples on 'low anxiety' and higher than Asian samples on 'even tempered'. On the other hand Asians scored higher than Whites on 'self-esteem' and 'low anxiety' as well as the overall trait of agreeableness.

A study by Tett et al. (2009) also refers to the 'diverse array' of demographic factors that may be related to personality scores and some further concrete data come from the Occupational Personality Questionnaire (OPQ) technical manuals (SHL, 2006). Echoing Foldes et al. (2008), the OPQ exhibits few score differences between different ethnic groups that reach statistical significance. However, with the same instrument (the OPQ), greater differences emerged between genders and between cultures. For example, the Chinese came somewhat below the international norm on 'outspoken' and 'vigorous' but somewhat above on 'forward thinking'. The Japanese were below the international norm on 'achieving' but above on 'adaptable'. The Koreans were below on 'conscientious' but above on 'worrying'. Finally, with respect to gender, the OPQ carries gender differences in line with common stereotypes. Females have lower scores than males on 'data rational' and 'tough minded' and higher scores on 'affiliative' and 'caring'.

There is no need to cite every difference. The point that I am making is that there is good reason to believe that people from different demographic groups and particularly different genders and cultures exhibit differences in personality. To the extent that the competencies being used at assessment centres are prescriptive of personality differences – and many, such as Cadbury's aggression are – we can expect the centre (and of course, any other competency based intervention) not to operate even-handedly across the demographic groups. Moreover, to the extent that personality dimensions are indistinguishable from competencies, evidence of demographic differences in the former will also apply to the latter. For example, data on the OPQ from the UK showed 'Asian and Black groups describe themselves as a little more Competitive and Achieving than the White group' (p. 203). This bias in competencies might be tolerable if the competencies are absolutely necessary to performance. However, the link between competencies and performance is often far from direct and obvious.

In contrast to traditional competencies, Woodruffe et al. (2009) advocate an approach that diverges as little as possible from simply focusing upon performing to deliver the organization's strategy, by and large without specifying how this performance is achieved – the male or female way; the Asian or African way; the younger or older way. So the focus is on achieving sales, providing leadership or building relationships and not on how these outputs are achieved. Of course, the organization might put some limit on people's methods – for example, demonstrating integrity might be an output in itself. However, the objective of the approach is to limit as far as possible being prescriptive and restrictive with the obvious limitations to diversity that such restrictions bring about.

The core question is whether it is the end-goal that matters or the routes to the end-goal. The way that many assessment centres operate is to focus on people's ways of achieving the goal, for example, asking open questions and not over-talking, rather than achieving the goal, namely winning the client over. This is because the competencies tend to prescribe an approach, as discussed above. Embracing a diversity of ways to success is, on the face of it, limited by the tolerance of the organization's culture to a diversity of approach. But, if organizations are really to embrace diversity, they have to make their cultures at least go to the limit of what their customers regard as acceptable. As it is, many assessment centres err in the direction of allowing too little rather than too much difference.

The issue of cultural differences in approach becomes of particular importance with assessment centres aimed at a global candidate base who are serving a global customer base. The conundrum such centres have to face is that behaviours that might be appropriate in one culture might be inappropriate in another and vice versa. Such centres should surely recruit a maximum diversity of approaches and the qualities or competencies against which people are assessed need to reflect this. The difficulty, of course, is that the person with acceptable behaviour in one culture might be unacceptable in another. So, the organization needs to select for a meta-competency of cultural sensitivity. However, many organizations solve the problem by taking a less diverse approach and imposing a 'head office' competency set on their global operations. The result might be termed an assessment centre imperialism. The New York, London or Tokyo approach is the global approach for the organization and any commitment to diversity has to fit within these parameters.

Interestingly, the more any society becomes itself multicultural, the more any assessment centre faces the conundrum of the global assessment centre. I would suggest multiculturalism has infused our thinking so that most of us in the United Kingdom, at least, are generally tolerant of a diversity of approaches and styles. Assessment centres should not straight-jacket people to produce the right approach, particularly at a micro-level of detailed behaviours. The first debate for the United Kingdom's 2010 general election featured one questioner from the audience who addressed the Prime Minister and his two contenders with the opening 'Hi, guys'. This sums up the latitude of acceptable behaviour nowadays and illustrates the inappropriateness of imposing one 'right way' on approaching exercises in an assessment centre. Doing so acts against diversity in a needless way.

EXERCISES AND DIVERSITY

So, many organizations will have competencies that restrict diversity but the frameworks can be modified to make them more open. What about the centre itself and in particular its exercises? Best practice centres will have simulation exercises that replicate key elements of the target role. We know that people's behaviour varies across situations and so the centre needs to contain situations that are as similar as possible to the actual situations for which one is trying to make predictions. In itself, this does not seem problematic from a diversity perspective. However, it might become problematic if one or more of the simulations are more familiar situations for one group than another. For example, with a graduate assessment centre, it is quite possible that a group exercise will be more 'home territory' for some demographic groups than others. It is not entirely fanciful to suggest that the public school, Oxbridge track prepares people better for a confident and sophisticated self-presentation in a group than other backgrounds and these differences in backgrounds will correlate with demographic differences. Of course, the confident performance of one group will indicate their readiness for such situations in the role itself. However, the effect will be to restrict diversity and this will act against a talent agenda if people could be quite readily trained to perform the required behaviours.

The issue of familiarity with the simulations and indeed with centres themselves is attested to by the books that are now in demand by those going to centres, for example Povah and Povah (2009). There is every reason to suppose that familiarity will yield a differential advantage to some demographic groups over others and that this will act against diversity. To counter the effect, it is important that as much information as possible about the centre is given to all candidates, perhaps including the possibility of practice sessions. Otherwise, those with more talent but less familiarity in, say, a group discussion might be rejected in favour of people who are familiar with the setting but actually have less to offer the organization in the longer term.

ASSESSORS AND DIVERSITY

Aside from the exercises and competencies, the other obvious way in which assessment centres could have an 'institutional' bias is through the assessors. Best practice centres are well-aware of this flaw. The assessor pool is made up of as diverse a group as possible but, in reality, this is not very diverse at all. Many readers will be familiar with the imploring requests made for senior female leaders, let alone senior ethnic minority leaders to serve as assessors or observers. Yet, with all the best efforts, many assessor panels are simply not that diverse. As such, they serve as poor advertisements to candidates of the possibilities for minority groups to succeed in the organization.

The failure of assessor panels to embody diversity might extend beyond mere window dressing. A group of white male assessors is much less likely to really 'get' diversity than a more diverse group. They might well be perfectly liberal in their attitudes but see harping on about diversity as unnecessary political correctness. Yet as I am hoping to show in this chapter, there are several, relatively subtle ways in which assessment and development centres can operate against the organization's diversity objectives. A more homogeneous group of assessors is perhaps less likely than a more diverse group to endorse the scale of the adaptations necessary to keep the centre on track for diversity. These might be adaptations in the design of the centre as well as its operation, such as making it easy for a Muslim to attend prayers, or taking proper account of a candidate's disability.

THE ASSESSOR CONFERENCE AND DIVERSITY

Having considered various aspects of the context, design and operation of centres, we finally need to consider their end-point. The assessor conference generally operates an 'appoint on merit' principle, offering posts to the candidates who have done best. At first sight this seems unarguable. However, if the odds were somewhat stacked against some groups, those getting the best marks might not, of course, be the best candidates. On the other hand, appointing on any other principle would be contentious and probably illegal. The right time to make any necessary corrections is in the design and operation of the centre rather than appearing to fiddle the marks at the end.

However, an aspect of the assessor conference that definitely does call for attention is the subtle influencing that can very easily take place. Many organizations have a disparity of seniority in the pool of assessors and it can easily be that a powerful senior assessor influences the rest. At a stroke all the efforts to achieve a diverse pool of assessors are nullified by there being one super-assessor who will quite likely be from the dominant group rather than a minority. I certainly have been witness to a centre where the chair of the assessors' group exerted considerable sway over the decisions. This issue should be addressed in assessor training and efforts should be made to ensure the conference is chaired by someone who understands the potential problem (see Dewberry Chapter 7).

Finally, there is the follow through to the centre. The first aspect of this is feedback to the candidates or participants. This affords a minefield for misunderstanding which could attack the centre's credibility, particularly its credibility as being diversity friendly. It is extremely easy for a piece of feedback to appear to show a lack of understanding of the perspective of a candidate that could be seen as insensitive. One way that this could come about is through the issue of the intrusion of cultural preferences into the way that people tackle the exercises. For example, a younger person might be criticized for a less deferential style towards seniors and this might lead to the conclusion that the whole centre is biased against the young.

A quite different aspect of the follow through to the centre is the evaluation of it. The evaluation might act against diversity quite simply by masking any problems that exist. From my experience, I have gained the impression that organizations generally do not want to hear bad news about their centres. It would be politically inconvenient to have any evidence that the centre has not been identifying the best people. As noted earlier, many evaluations simply cannot draw any conclusions about the diversity impact because of the numbers in the minority comparison groups. Often it feels as if this is quite a relief to those carrying out the evaluation. They tend not to dwell for long on indicative but statistically insignificant results.

But it is to such evidence that I will now turn. My conclusion from the qualitative review is that even a best practice centre has various Achilles heels by which it might be less than diversity friendly. My particular concern is with the competencies which might well put an unjustified straight-jacket on the range of acceptable responses. The concerns about diversity can only increase when it comes to 'in practice' centres with their lack of assessor training, off-the-shelf exercises and omitted evaluation. So what is the empirical evidence?

Quantitative Evidence

At the start, it is important to acknowledge that there is a scarcity of data. Perhaps this is unsurprising. What, after all, is the motivation for an employer to make available a study showing that their centre has adverse impact? For the researcher on assessment centres, no news is perhaps bad news. Furthermore, there is the pervasive problem of a lack of reasonable numbers in ethnic minority and disabled people attending centres, although the same is, of course, not the case with respect to gender comparisons.

Notwithstanding these points, studies have begun to appear in the last few years. In particular, Dean, Roth and Bobko (2008) published a meta-analysis of 27 studies (16 published and 11 unpublished) that enabled them to draw some conclusions on ethnic and gender differences in overall assessment centre ratings. In their own words, this was a 'first-of-its-kind quantitative summary' (p. 685). Their basic unit of analysis was the d statistic. This is the magnitude of the difference in the mean scores obtained by the two groups that are being compared divided by the pooled standard deviation. So a d of one denotes that the two means differ by one standard deviation. For the less statistically minded, Cohen (1977) provides the guidance that a d of 0.2 can be considered small;

0.5 is medium; 0.8 and above is large. As a rule of thumb, if the statistic exceeds 0.5, it would appear to me to become a definite cause for concern.

The meta-analysis yielded a d of 0.52 for the Black–White comparison, indicating that the scores of people in the White group were higher than the Black group by half a standard deviation. Restricting the comparison to studies involving external applicants resulted in this statistic increasing to 0.56, whereas for incumbent samples it was 0.32. As Dean et al. note, this level of adverse impact against Blacks would be sufficient for an assessment centre to fail the commonly applied 4/5ths rule when the centre is used with fresh applicants and a 10 per cent selection ratio. The 4/5ths rule requires that the less successful group is nevertheless at least 80 per cent as successful as the more successful group; otherwise the method is seen to create disadvantage.

In comparison to the above ethnic differences, gender differences were more modest. The female–male d of 0.19 represents a slight outperformance by females.

Dean et al. note that their analyses were not able to zoom in on particular exercises or competencies. They deal only with the overall assessment ratings. On the other hand, a paper by Roth, Bobko, McFarland and Buster (2008) looks at Black–White differences broken down by both exercises and competencies for work sample tests. Roth et al. obtained an overall d of 0.36 for incumbents and 0.67 for early stage applicants. The d for the different exercises ranged from 0.54 for in-baskets to 0.22 for oral briefing and 0.16 for role play. The statistics for the early stage applicants, in basket and role play are after the exclusion of one or more studies with particularly large d statistics which could be claimed to distort the results. Technical exercises had a d of 0.76 and for scheduling exercises the statistic was 0.52.

Roth et al. were also able to look at the d for different competencies. They found it to be 0.8 for cognitive ability and job knowledge and 0.70 for written skills. On the other hand, it was 0.21 for oral communication and interpersonal skills and 0.23 for leadership and persuasion.

The meta-analyses that have just been considered are a cause for concern. They suggest that the popular image of assessment centres as diversity-friendly might by more myth than reality. This conclusion is certainly not countered by plenty of other unpublished studies showing that differences between, say Black and White were statistically non-significant or could not be made because of the low number in the minority group.

Conclusions and Recommendations

One consoling thought on the meta-analyses reviewed above is that we do not know the precise quality of the assessment centres and work samples that went into the studies. If these were not aligned with best practice then perhaps the adverse impact is unsurprising. Nonetheless, as the earlier qualitative review has suggested, even an apparently well-designed and operated centre might well have some inbuilt biases. These can be countered and we should remember that some of these biases are not peculiar to assessment and development centres but apply to other methods of assessment.

The particular basic source of bias that I have emphasized is insistence on culture-centric competencies that specify not only what the job-holder should do but also how to do it. The practical way forward is to allow more latitude in the range of acceptable behaviours. In addition, there are possible issues with differential familiarity with exercises, assessors and the assessment conference.

However, can we be sure that the adverse impact seen in the quantitative studies comes from the sources addressed in the qualitative review? There seems to be a clear implication in the article by Roth et al. (2008) that the differences are largely attributable to well-documented disadvantage by people from Black groups in cognitive tasks. This opens up a different area for debate and one that is potentially highly contentious. The specific nature, scale and causes of adverse impact of assessment centres is surely an area crying out for research. Yet, research is limited by the understandable reluctance of organizations to publish or make data available, which would raise any doubts about the even-handedness of their centres. While acknowledging the political pressures, it is nonetheless vital that organizations at least carry out internal, confidential validations of their centres. In my experience, many organizations, both private and public sector, are quite reluctant to hold their centres up to thorough scrutiny or to confront the possibility of adverse impact. They are too ready to seek the 'get out clause' of low numbers and therefore statistical non-significance.

At the same time as urging organizations to validate their centres, the only realistic source of publicly available research on adverse impact will be from university research. It is urgent that we find out the extent and causes of differences in performance by different demographic groups. That seems a suitable point to end a chapter in a book that is bridging the divide between research and practice. Currently, we lack the research that practitioners would dearly love to put into practice.

References

Bobko, P., Roth, P.L., and Potosky, D. 1999. Derivation and implications of a meta-analytic matrix incorporating cognitive ability, alternative predictors, and job performance. *Personnel Psychology*, 52, 561–589.

Cohen, J. 1977. *Statistical Power Analysis for the Behavioural Sciences*. Revised Edition. New York: Academic Press.

Dean, M.A., Roth, P.L. and Bobko, P. 2008. Ethnic and gender subgroup differences in assessment center ratings: A meta-analysis. *Journal of Applied Psychology*, 93, 685–691.

Foldes, H.J., Duehr, E.E. and Ones, D.S. 2008. Group differences in personality: Meta-analyses comparing five US Racial groups. *Personnel Psychology*, 61, 579–616.

HESA 2010. Personal Communication. Data extracted from HESA Student Record 2008/09

Hough, L.M., Oswald, F.L. and Ployhart, R.E. 2001. Determinants, detection, and amelioration of adverse impact in personnel selection procedures: Issues, evidence and lessons learned. *International Journal of Selection and Assessment*, 9, 152–194.

Jensen, A.R. 1998. *The g Factor*. Westport, CT: Praeger.

Povah, N. and Povah, L. 2009. *Succeeding at Assessment Centres for Dummies*. Chichester: John Wiley & Sons.

Ployhart, R.E., Ziegert, J.C. and McFarland, L.A. 2003. Understanding racial differences on cognitive ability tests in selection contexts: An integration of stereotype threat and applicant reactions research. *Human Performance*, 16, 231–259.

Roth, P.L., Bevier, C.A., Bobko, P., Switzer, F.S. III and Tyler, P. 2001. Ethnic group differences in cognitive ability in employment and educational settings. A meta-analysis. *Personnel Psychology*, 54, 297–330.

Roth, P.L., Bobko, P., McFarland, L and Buster, M. 2008. Work sample tests in personnel selection: A meta-analysis of black-white differences in overall and exercise scores. *Personnel Psychology*, 61, 637–662.

Sackett, P.R. and Roth, L. 1996. Multi-stage selection strategies: A monte carlo investigation of effects on performance and minority hiring. *Personnel Psychology*, 49, 549–572.

Sackett, P.R., Schmitt, N., Ellingson, J.E. and Kabin, M.B. 2001. High stakes testing in employment, credentialing and higher education. *American Psychologist*, 56, 302–318.

SHL Group. 2006. *OPQ. Technical Manual*. Thames Ditton: SHL Group.

Tett, R.P., Fitzke, J.R., Wadlington, P.L., Davies, S.A. Anderson, M.G. and Foster, J. 2009. The use of personality test norms in work settings: Effects of sample size and relevance. *Journal of Occupational and Organizational Psychology*, 82, 639–659.

Woodruffe, C. 2007. *Development and Assessment Centres: Identifying and Developing Competence* (4th Edition). London: Human Assets.

Woodruffe, C. Lyons, W. and Silver, J. 2009. *Holding on While Letting Go: A Director's Guide to Contemporary Talent Management*. London: Human Assets.

10 The Assessment of Managers: A Review and Integration of Assessment Center and Multisource Performance Rating Research and Practice

BRIAN J. HOFFMAN AND SEAN P. BALDWIN

The assessment stage is a critical component of any talent management program because it informs numerous HR activities and serves as the first step in the employee development process (Goldstein 1986). Given the prominence of the managerial role in modern organizations and the diversity of skills needed to effectively perform this role, diagnostic tools focusing on managers are a staple of modern organizations. Among these managerial diagnostic tools, few occupy a more prominent role than assessment centers (ACs) and multisource performance ratings (MSPRs), also called 360° feedback (Landy and Conte 2007). In addition to providing a tool to distinguish effective from ineffective managers, ACs and MSPRs overlap in terms of the competencies they assess, and the research methods, research focus, and in many cases, research findings.

Despite the substantial overlap, the literature on these techniques has largely run parallel, with few attempts toward integration. This chapter integrates the literature on ACs and MSPRs in an effort to highlight consistencies and inconsistencies, inform implications for practitioners, and identify avenues for future research. Specific emphasis will be given to areas in which MSPR research and practice can be used to inform AC research and practice and vice versa. Our comparison centers on (a) applications of ACs and MSPRs, (b) measurement focus, (c) components of performance in ACs and MSPRs, and (d) empirical evidence for administrative and developmental applications.

Applications of ACs and MSPRs

We initially planned to present a section comparing applications of ACs and MSPRs; however, we were able to locate only one study that examined common practices associated with MSPRs (London and Smither 1995). We find this lack of benchmarking work interesting in and of itself, particularly when considering that multiple studies over the past 15 years summarize organizational uses of ACs (including two in the present volume). A key lesson MSPR researchers can learn from AC research is the importance of accounting for the popularity, uses, and administration of the assessment tool. Given the wide variability of MSPR practice in terms of scale design and purpose of assessment, gathering such information should be particularly informative.

PARTIES INVOLVED

Both ACs and MSPRs utilize assessors and assessees in evaluative contexts. These roles can be held by a wide variety of individuals and mark a substantive difference between ACs and MSPRs. As described in the AC Guidelines (International Task Force 2009), ACs use trained assessors who usually don't have a prior relationship with the assessees. On the other hand, MSPRs use individuals with whom the manager definitely has a working relationship. MSPR raters are specifically selected because of their organizational level, typically including manager, peer, and subordinate raters. A key difference in ACs and MSPRs is that whereas AC participants can be either incumbents or applicants, MSPRs are generally restricted to incumbent samples, given that the stimulus is behaviors on the job.

THE LOGISTICS OF ASSESSMENT

Below we discuss the basic assessment processes of MSPRs and ACs, such as the use of job analysis, rater training, and technology.

Basic assessment process

ACs and MSPRs both measure behavior using ratings of multiple behavioral dimensions taken in multiple contexts. Given their focus on measuring job relevant behaviors in similar performance domains, the underlying dimensions assessed overlap substantially between ACs and MSPRs. Moreover, ACs and MSPRs both differ from the majority of other measures because they are both behavioral in nature. The process of ACs and MSPRs is distinct from other popular measures (for example, personality and intelligence tests) in that they are behavioral measures, and behaviors are evaluated in multiple measurement contexts (namely exercises in ACs and different sources with MSPRs).

Job analysis

The AC literature emphasizes the importance of job analysis in determining the skills, situations, and demands for a given position (Eurich et al. 2009). In contrast, MSPRs are often not based on a specific job analysis and are more likely to assess general managerial competencies and skills that are pertinent to the entire organization. The relatively infrequent use of job analysis in MSPRs is typified by the widespread use of off-the-shelf

MSPR instruments, such as the Center for Creative Leadership's BENCHMARKS® assessment, which assesses constructs typically found in these more general taxonomies of managerial performance (McCauley and Lombardo 1990).

Rater training

Rater training occupies a central place in the AC method (Lievens 2001; Schleicher, Day, Mayes and Riggio 2002) and focuses on teaching raters about the performance dimensions being rated, common rating errors, behavioral observation and recording techniques, behavioral evaluation, and specific scoring guidelines. In contrast, owing largely to logistic and financial constraints, MSPRs rarely benefit from the implementation of rater training. It would be very difficult and expensive to train multiple raters from multiple organizational levels for each manager. In addition, comprehensive training across organizational levels is cost prohibitive. Moreover, in the context of MSPR, where some raters potentially have limited experience rating others' performance (for example, subordinates), rater training could be particularly beneficial.

Technology

Advances in technology have the potential to greatly increase the efficiency of administering both evaluation systems. For instance, feedback reports are now generated quickly and efficiently using computers for both ACs and MSPRs (Eurich et al. 2009; Summers 2001). In addition, both ACs and MSPRs can be administered via computers. In contrast to ACs where technology has the potential to fundamentally change the nature of the assessment, technology applied to MSPRs primarily increases the efficiency of collecting performance information, leaving the nature of assessment fundamentally unchanged. By presenting AC exercises on computers, the AC experience can be of much higher levels of stimulus and response fidelity, and online applications have the potential to drastically reduce the cost of assessment. However, it is crucial that research keep up with practice by investigating the psychometric implications of these changes.

HOW ARE ACs AND MSPRs USED?

Both ACs and MSPRs have been widely adopted in recent years. Below we discuss reasons for their widespread adoption, including estimates of cost and the typical uses of assessment ratings.

Purpose of the assessment

A key difference in the use of ACs and MSPRs is their application in developmental versus decision-making contexts. Although early ACs were largely used as administrative tools, ACs are now commonly used for multiple purposes, including selection, placement, identification of potential/succession management, and developmental feedback (Thornton and Krause 2009). Alternatively, in the US, 85–93 percent of MSPRs are used exclusively for feedback purposes (Timmreck and Bracken 1997). The primary concern with using MSPRs for administrative purposes (such as selection and promotion) is the potential for rater bias and negative user reactions. Because the raters in MSPRs have a working relationship with the individual being evaluated, there is concern that raters will distort their rating for their own goals (Waldman and Atwater 2001). The relative objectivity associated with ACs in comparison with MSPRs accounts for their more frequent use in administrative contexts as described above, and the ability to implement ACs in both administrative and developmental contexts is a key advantage of the AC method.

Use and cost

The popularity of MSPRs and ACs is on the rise. It has been reported that between 20 (Armour 2003) and 29 percent (Church 2000) of US organizations use MSPRs. Similarly, ACs are used to assess thousands of individuals each year from around the world (Krause and Thornton 2009, Thornton and Krause 2009). In 1992 it was estimated that MSPR systems cost approximately $100–250 per person, (Romano 1994); on the other hand, ACs are one of the most expensive assessment tools on the market, with a per assessee cost estimated at $1,730 per day (Spychalski et al. 1997).

Scores and interpretation

AC and MSPR scores are often converted to a single composite score for decision-making. In developmental settings, AC feedback is usually organized by dimensions and includes specific behavioral examples gleaned from the exercises. The *Guidelines* (International Task Force 2009) state that all ACs must have an integration phase, during which dimension ratings are combined across exercises. This method results in a single performance rating score per dimension, eliminating the potential for making inferences about the rating context (exercise). In contrast, 75 percent of MSPRs separate dimension by source (London and Smither 1995), which focuses ratee attention on differences in evaluations across different sources. Thus, the interpretation of MSPRs emphasizes the context of the ratings, whereas this is often not a formal part of the interpretation of AC performance in ACs used for selection and placement. The lesson for AC practice is that interpretation of the context may enhance benefits for the individual and organization.

Measurement Focus

This section discusses the two key components of ACs and MSPRs: the performance dimensions being measured and the context (exercise and source) in which those dimensions are evaluated. This discussion focuses on the design of ACs and MSPRs; later we discuss the empirical evidence with respect to whether dimensions and context effects are actually present in AC data.

FOCAL CONSTRUCTS

The focal constructs in both ACs and MSPRs are performance dimensions that are thought to be critical to effective job performance. The performance dimensions are largely behaviorally based, skill-type constructs, and there is substantial overlap in the dimensions measured with ACs and MSPRs (Thornton and Byham 1982; Morgeson,

Mumford and Campion 2005). This should not be surprising, given that ACs are designed as content valid simulations of the criterion domain, managerial performance.

Yet, despite this overlap, consensus on the definition of the dimensions of managerial performance has been elusive (Austin and Villanova 1992). For instance, Arthur, Day, McNelly and Edens' (2003) survey of AC dimension labels used in past research revealed 168 different dimension labels assessed across ACs. Similarly, Borman and Brush's (1993) content analysis of the managerial performance literature revealed 178 dimension labels used in past research. Thus, a core similarity between ACs and MSPRs is that the vast number of dimensions has prohibited generalizable research findings and subsequently, actionable implications for practice.

Structure of performance dimensions

Whereas both ACs and MSPRs are characterized by inconsistency in the dimensions measured across administrations and arguably a larger number of dimensions than can be empirically supported, MSPRs have benefited from taxonomic efforts stemming from the broader job performance literature (for example, Borman and Brush 1993). On the other hand, AC research has progressed in a relatively unsystematic manner with little effort to determine the underlying constructs assessed (Arthur and Villado 2008). From this perspective, the lesson is that AC research and practice can benefit from MSPR research that has investigated the structure of managerial performance.

MSPR research and practice has benefited from advances in conceptual models of performance (see Hoffman, Lance, Bynum and Gentry 2010). For instance, the Center for Creative Leadership's popular BENCHMARKS® measure assesses 18 narrow dimensions that were factor analyzed into three broad dimensions factors, including management skills, leadership skills and interpersonal skills. Subsequent feedback is based on the original 18 dimensions, but these dimensions are organized into the three associated broad dimension factors.

In contrast, AC research and practice has been somewhat slower to adopt this approach. Nevertheless, early AC research recognized the importance of devising a general taxonomy. Thornton and Byham (1982) reviewed earlier factor analytic work and pointed to three broad factors that consistently emerge in AC ratings: Administrative skills, Interpersonal skills, and Drive. However, taxonomic work did not seem to gain momentum until Arthur et al. (2003) revisited the use of dimension taxonomies on ACs with their specification of seven broad AC dimensions. Others have followed suit (Bowler and Woehr 2006, Hoffman, Melchers et al. in press; Lievens, Dilchert and Ones 2009). Unfortunately, more often than not, AC research tends to move forward with whatever dimensions were assessed in a given AC, with limited consideration for the adequacy of their measurement or their representation in a broader, more generalizable performance domain (Arthur, Day and Woehr 2008). We suspect that this is due to the belief that reducing the number of dimensions prohibits tailoring the AC to organizational demands. But this need not be the case.

Instead, as is done with MSPRs (for example McCauley and Lombardo 1990) narrow manifest dimensions can still be measured. However, for the purposes of feedback, interpretation, and research, the narrow manifest dimensions should be categorized onto their broader, empirically supported factors. Doing so has many advantages, including: enhanced empirical support for the measurement instrument, facilitating more accurate feedback, increasing the content validity of ACs, and giving AC researchers a common language. Given these advantages, we encourage AC researchers and practitioners to investigate the broad dimension structure of their ACs.

BEHAVIORAL OBSERVATION CONTEXT

The context is defined by the nature of the situation and has implications for the traits activated, the nature of the behaviors displayed, and finally the dimensions evaluated. Whereas other popular measures, such as personality, intelligence, and formal organizational performance evaluations typically use one approach to measurement, both ACs and MSPRs have in common the utilization of multiple approaches to measuring the constructs of interest. In ACs, assessee performance dimensions are observed in multiple moderate-to-high fidelity simulations, such as an in-basket or leaderless group discussion. On the other hand, in MSPRs, performance on the job is evaluated by a manager's co-workers occupying different organizational levels. Thus, the context is defined by the relationship that the ratee has with the evaluator and has implications for the type of performance information observed, attended to, recalled, and valued (Borman 1974; Hoffman et al. 2010).

On the other hand, the context of assessment distinguishes the type of behavioral information obtained in ACs compared to MSPRs. In ACs, present performance is evaluated in the brief, highly controlled context of a simulation exercise; in MSPRs, past performance is evaluated on the job over a relatively long period of time by raters with different relationships with the ratee. Thus, in ACs, the characteristics of the different exercises form the measurement context, and in MSPRs, the context is defined by the rater's relationship with the ratee. This difference in the measurement context plays a central role in the nature of behavioral information obtained. Consistent with Sackett, Zedeck and Fogli (1988), performance in MSPRs is best viewed as a form of typical performance, where performance is measured over a prolonged time period, with both motivation and ability influencing assessee performance. Alternatively, performance measured in ACs is conceptually similar to maximum performance. Specifically, the duration of AC performance is relatively brief, and the performer gives maximum effort. Under these circumstances, individuals are expected to achieve the maximum level of performance possible, given their underlying ability.

Both ACs and MSPRs have been criticized over the lack of convergence of performance dimensions across measurement contexts (for example, the low correlations among the same dimension measured by different sources/exercises). Further complicating matters, arriving at the appropriate analytical model has been a source of confusion and debate in the AC (Lance, Woehr and Meade 2007) and to a lesser extent, the MSPR literature (Lance, Hoffman, Gentry and Baranik 2008). AC research, in particular, has devoted substantial attention to understanding the weaker than expected cross exercise correlations. Indeed, Lievens (2009) referred to this issue as the Achilles heel of ACs.

This interpretation differs sharply from that of context effects associated with MSPRs. Specifically, although weak cross-source correlations have occasionally been interpreted as an indicator of low quality ratings (Viswesvaran, Schmitt and Ones 2005), this common finding is more often interpreted as evidence that different sources capture unique aspects of performance information (Borman 1974; Hoffman and Woehr 2009). Thus, when examining MSPRs, strong context effects are both expected and desired.

There is now a sizeable body of evidence substantiating the conceptual and empirical appropriateness of considering context effects as meaningful variance in ACs. We believe that this is a key lesson that AC research and practice can learn from MSPR research and practice. Specifically, although AC exercises are explicitly designed to reflect unique situations (Howard 2008; Lievens 2009), AC researchers have been resistant to studying exercise effects in ACs (Arthur and Villado 2008; Arthur et al. 2008).

Components of Performance in ACs and MSPRs

Substantial research using a variety of methodological approaches has investigated the internal structure of ACs and MSPRs. Despite the diversity in methods, a common underpinning of much of the AC and MSPR psychometric research is the incorporation of multitrait-multimethod (MTMM) analyses (Campbell and Fiske 1959). In such analyses, construct validity evidence is provided to the degree that the same trait (performance dimension) measured across different methods (exercises and sources) is more strongly correlated than different traits measured using the same method.

The more general MTMM approach has given way to advanced analytical techniques, including confirmatory factor analysis and generalizability theory. These techniques are useful because they allow for a more nuanced and accurate view of the components of ratings (Lance, Dawson, Birkelbach and Hoffman in press). This multifaceted view of AC and MSPR scores allows for a richer understanding of assessee performance than could be gained by focusing on raw MTMM analyses. Below we discuss the empirically supported components common to ACs and MSPRs, including (a) cross-context consistent dimension effects, (b) within-context specific dimension effects, (c) context effects, and (d) general performance. These components are combined into a model of ACs and MSPRs in Figure 10.1.

The column headed manifest ratings depicts the observed ratings coming from a given dimension rated in a given context (for example, dimension 1 rated in an in-basket). The column labeled general context performance proposes that those being rated have an overall level of performance associated with a given context (for example, overall level of effectiveness in a role play). The column labeled context specific dimensions proposes there will be clusters of dimensions within each context: in the in-basket, Communication and Sensitivity will be correlated and form a cluster of interpersonal skills. Column 4 proposes that cross-context consistent dimensions will also characterize AC and MSPR ratings. These reflect consistent performance on a given dimension across all measurement contexts and are conceptually similar to dimension effects found in MTMM analyses.

EVIDENCE FOR DIMENSIONS

As previously mentioned, ACs and MSPRs are designed around core competencies needed for effective job performance. The application of MTMM analyses resulted in the widespread (mis)interpretation of AC dimensions as traits (Howard 2008) that should be consistent across measurement contexts (exercises). Indeed, by relying primarily on MTMM analyses, AC research has implicitly assumed that to be considered dimension variance, the competency must manifest similarly in different measurement contexts

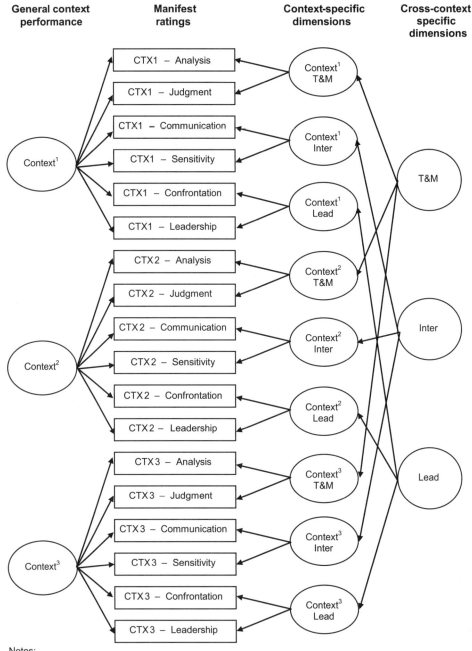

Figure 10.1 Model of the components of performance in ACs and MSPRs

(it must be trait variance in MTMM parlance). We propose that this view of dimensions is unnecessarily narrow. Specifically, although a part of dimensions should be consistent across contexts, an additional aspect of dimensions is expected to be specific to a given context. By pulling back from the interpretation of dimensions as traits, a clear picture of the nature of AC dimensions comes into focus, one that allows for both situationally specific and cross-situationally consistent aspects of dimensions.

Cross-context consistent dimensions

The cross-context consistent aspect of dimensions reflects similar performance on a given dimension across multiple contexts. This component of performance is analogous to the "trait" factors in traditional MTMM-type analyses. Both AC (Lance et al. 2004) and MSPR (Hoffman et al. 2010) research has found that cross-context consistent dimensions explain less than 15 percent of the variance in performance. However, they often explain more variance in ACs than MPSRs (Bowler and Woehr 2009; Hoffman, Melchers et al. in press). It is ironic then that the construct validity of MSPR dimensions has rarely been questioned, while it seems at times that AC research has focused on little else. The finding that context consistent dimensions explain more variance in ACs relative to MSPRs should not be surprising given that AC raters regularly undergo training, whereas it is rare for MSPRs. In addition, being that maximum performance, as measured in ACs, is based on ability rather than motivation, AC performance is presumed to be more consistent across situations.

Context-specific dimensions

We propose that context specific aspects of dimensions also play a role in ACs and MSPRs. These aspects of performance represent distinguishable dimensions of performance that are specific to a given context (for example, leadership in group settings vs. leadership in one-on-one settings). The reader will note that this concept diverges sharply from the way that AC dimensions have been conceptualized by past AC research (Sackett and Dreher 1982; Bowler and Woehr 2006). Ultimately, the use of MTMM analyses has led to the false assumption that dimensions are analogous to trait factors. However, as mentioned above, both ACs and MSPRs are designed to assess somewhat different aspects of a given dimension in different contexts (Howard 2008).

Toward this end, some MSPR research has operationalized performance using within source dimensions, such as peer perceptions of interpersonal skills versus supervisor perceptions of interpersonal skills (Blair, Hoffman and Helland 2008). Of course, this is nothing new to MSPR practice. MSPR feedback recipients are encouraged to attend to cross source discrepancies when interpreting their feedback and devising developmental plans. Implicit in this practice is the importance of examining dimensions in the context of the source providing the rating, rather than interpreting inconsistency across sources as an indicator of poor psychometric quality, as would be implied by a strict reliance on MTMM analyses.

Despite the recognized importance of context effects (Thornton and Byham 1982; Lievens, Chasteen, Day and Christiansen 2006), AC research has rarely attended to the context-specific aspects of dimensions. Instead, AC research has conceptualized dimensions using across-exercise dimension ratings (Arthur et al. 2003) and occasionally, investigated the "trait" variance in MTMM analyses (Hoffman, Melchers et al. in press; Lievens, Dilchert and Ones 2009). As stated previously, we believe that an important lesson that AC research can learn from MSPR research is that the context exerts a substantively meaningful influence on performance.

According to Howard (2008: 99), "If each exercise is equally capable of measuring each dimension, why measure [a given dimension] five different times? Given the costs associated with assessment centers, is this redundancy not an unnecessary waste of resources?" From this perspective, forcing the same dimension to load on a latent factor across exercises ignores the fact that different exercises capture unique aspects of dimensions. For instance, effective "influence" in a cooperative LGD entails persuading other group members to adopt a given proposal, building consensus among other group members, and diffusing disagreements among other group members, whereas effective influence in a role play with a subordinate would include motivating the subordinate to achieve higher levels of performance, offering developmental guidance, or tactfully addressing sensitive topics, such as the subordinate's weaknesses. Although influence is a core component of all of these behaviors, the behavioral manifestation differs because behavior is bounded by the surrounding context, that is, the exercise.

Therefore, a strong correlation among these different aspects of influence should not be expected, it should not have been expected by researchers in MTMM analyses, and never was expected by AC designers. We are aware of only two studies that have investigated the within exercise structure of ACs; both found that performance within a given exercise is characterized by multiple broad performance dimensions (Hoffman and Meade 2007, Rupp, Baldwin and Bashshur 2006). These findings support the relevance of within exercise dimensions to understanding AC performance. Despite preliminary supportive evidence, more work must be done in this area.

MEASUREMENT CONTEXT

Although we have argued that a portion of variance previously attributed to rating context factors actually captures situationally specific dimensional information, to some extent, general context factors also play an important role in understanding assessee performance. In essence, some people just perform better across the board in a given situation; for example, they perform well in group settings or in working with peers, but are ineffective in one-on-one settings or when dealing with their direct reports (Gibbons and Rupp 2009). For this reason, it is probable that an overall context effect will be present in ratings, even after controlling for within-context dimensional performance. In this sense, the context effect is cosmetically similar to a method effect in MTMM analyses, reflecting covariance among all dimensions assessed using a given method. In ACs, this variance is referred to as exercise effects and in MSPRs it is referred to as source effects. Factor analytic work has consistently found that source and exercise effects introduce the largest degree of variance to ACs (Bowler and Woehr 2006; Lance et al. 2004) and MSPRs (Hoffman and Woehr 2009). Although the pervasiveness of context effects was originally viewed as problematic for these tools, there is now evidence that rating context effects do not reflect method bias at all (see Lance et al. 2008); instead, exercise and source effects reflect valid information that is important to understanding performance.

It is clear that both ACs and MSPRs are characterized by pervasive rating context effects and that to some extent, these effects reflect valid, performance relevant variance;

however, the etiology of these effects is unclear. Numerous theoretical propositions have been put forward to account for both exercise and source factors. One explanation for rating context effects associated with both ACs and MSPRs is situational specificity in performance. In ACs, exercise effects have been interpreted as assessees' ability to perform effectively or ineffectively in a given situation (Lance et al. 2008). From this perspective, some individuals are just more effective in certain situations. For instance, more dominant assessees tend to be viewed as more competent and thus, are evaluated more favorably across dimensions in LGDs (Hoffman et al., in press). Similarly, more dominant managers tend to be viewed as more effective by their subordinates, but not their supervisors (Hoffman and Woehr 2009). Thus, preliminary research shows that individual differences partly account for the common findings of overall performance in a given context.

Finally, ACs generally allow a single behavior to inform multiple dimensions in a given exercise. For instance, complimenting a role player on their performance would be indicative of Analysis (because they recognize the strength), Sensitivity (because they complimented the role player), and Confrontation (if they complimented the role player as a way to ease into offering negative feedback). Certainly, this behavior is relevant to all these dimensions, so this would not be a source of bias; instead, if a scoring rubric for a given exercise allows for the same behavior to be a component of multiple dimensions within an exercise, performance in the dimensions should overlap more at the true-score level, resulting in a larger exercise effect. Additional research is needed investigating these and other interpretations of the meaning and theoretical underpinnings of the exercise effect.

General performance

The idea of a *valid* general factor in performance ratings has persisted almost as long as ratings have been used to assess human performance (see Guildford 1954). Intelligent and conscientious ratees are proposed to perform effectively across contexts and aspects of performance (Viswesvaran et al. 2005), resulting in the emergence of a general performance factor. The last decade has seen consistent support for a general performance factor in the MSPR (Hoffman, Lance et al. 2010) and AC literature (Hoffman, Melchers et al. in press, Lance et al. 2000, Lance et al. 2004, Lance et al. 2007). Hoffman, Melchers et al. (in press) estimated that the general performance factor accounted for an average of 14 percent of the variance in AC performance across four independent ACs. In addition, general AC performance was significantly correlated with intelligence, conscientiousness, and extraversion. On the other hand, general performance appears to account for less variance in MSPRs. Hoffman, Lance et al. (2010) used the same analytic model as did Hoffman, Melchers et al. (in press) and estimated that the general performance factor accounted for an average of 4 percent of the variance in MSPRs in two large independent samples. Further research is needed to investigate other ratee antecedents (such as behavioral flexibility, experience, and social awareness) and design characteristics (for example AC exercise similarity) that are related to the general factor.

SUMMARY

The parallels between the components found in ACs and MSPRs are striking. Specifically, both ACs and MSPRs are characterized by large context effects that represent valid variance rather than bias, modest cross-context consistent dimension effects, and modest general performance factors. In addition, the relative importance of these components is consistent across MSPRs and ACs; however, in an absolute sense, cross-context consistent dimensions and general performance appear to be larger in ACs relative to MSPRs. AC researchers are encouraged to apply lessons learned from MSPR research by investigating the role that within context dimensions play in performance. On the other hand, MSPR researchers are encouraged to give stronger consideration to the evidence for context-consistent dimensions in MSPRs.

Empirical Evidence for Selection and Developmental Applications

Given their frequent use in administrative settings, AC research has focused on validity to a greater extent than has MSPR research. On the other hand, given their use in developmental settings, MSPR research has largely focused on developmental applications. Below we review the evidentiary basis underlying developmental and administrative applications of ACs and MSPRs.

VALIDITY OF ACs AND MSPRs

Substantial attention has been paid to the criterion-related validity of ACs, and the results have been almost uniformly positive (Arthur et al. 2003, Gaugler, Rosenthal, Thornton and Bentson 1987, Meriac, Hoffman, Woehr and Fleisher 2008). Gaugler et al.'s meta-analysis estimated that the overall assessment rating has a moderate relationship (rho = .37) with criterion variables. More recently, Arthur et al. (2003) presented a meta-analysis of the relationship between ACs and performance when multiple dimensions were included in regression analyses. Their results indicated even stronger evidence for the validity of ACs, with the group of AC dimensions explaining 20 percent of the variance in criterion variables (note that these results are corrected for criterion unreliability). Meriac et al. (2008) meta-analytically demonstrated that AC dimensions explained incremental variance beyond personality and intelligence. Three studies have taken Arthur et al. and Meriac et al.'s approach of validating specific dimensions a step further and investigated the validity of the components of AC ratings (dimensions and exercises). Connelly, Ones, Ramesh and Goff (2008), Lievens, Dilchert and Ones (2009), and Hoffman, Melchers et al. (in press) each found that exercises and dimensions account for meaningful criterion variance and that dimensions explain variance in outcomes beyond exercises.

On the other hand, far less research has investigated the validity of MSPRs. By validating MSPRs with traditional downward performance ratings, there is an increased potential of finding inflated correlations, because the same raters are completing both the MSPR and the performance criterion. To counteract this problem, Conway, Lombardo and Sanders (2001) presented a meta-analysis of MSPRs and objective performance, which is less likely to be biased by having the same rater(s) complete both measures. Together the three rating sources explained 15 percent of objective performance variance. Thus, when an uncontaminated criterion is used, ACs demonstrated slightly higher validity than MSPRs. In the only study of which we are aware that directly compared the validity of ACs to that of MSPRs in predicting supervisor ratings, Hagan, Konopaske, Bernardin and Tyler (2006) found that ACs explain unique variance in supervisor ratings beyond MSPRs.

Although it is difficult to directly determine which tool is "more" valid based on existing research, past work consistently supports the validity of both MSPRs and ACs. Thus, it appears that both capture important information on constructs relevant to effective management. Moreover, skill-based predictors measured in ACs and MSPRs compare very favorably relative to other predictors (such as paper and pencil measures of personality) of leader effectiveness (Hoffman, Woehr, Maldegen, and Lyons, in press).

DEVELOPMENTAL APPLICATIONS

Rather than predicting effectiveness, the ultimate criterion in developmental settings is performance improvement. Research has begun to flesh out the efficacy of MSPRs and to a much lesser extent ACs for use in managerial development. Smither, London and Reilly (2005) presented a meta-analysis of 24 longitudinal studies that investigated the influence of multisource feedback on performance improvement and found consistently positive, albeit weak effects. On the other hand, very little research has sought to determine whether performance improves following feedback from ACs. In an important exception, Rupp et al. (2006) used multiple criterion variables to evaluate the efficacy of developmental assessment centers (DACs) in two independent samples. Consistent with the MSPR findings, when change in performance was evaluated by others (subordinates), the effects were largely weak and non-significant. The weak effects across MSPRs and ACs should not be surprising. Although accurate feedback is logically a necessary first step in development, solely receiving feedback does not necessarily yield performance improvement. MSPR research has begun to flesh out antecedents, substantive moderators, and explanatory variables of the feedback process. Integrating advances in the MSPR arena with investigations of DACs has the potential to provide a road map for research and give realistic expectations in terms of the magnitude of findings.

MSPR research has investigated a variety of antecedents of performance improvement. Although too numerous to outline here, a few key antecedents are particularly noteworthy. Self-other (SO) agreement is at the heart of the MSPR feedback process. The comparison between self and others' ratings effectively performs a "shock to the system" by alerting participants to discrepancies in their self-view and others' perceptions of their performance. Forcing participants to confront discrepancies in their self-view can be a powerful voice for motivating change. This suggestion is supported by Johnson and Ferstl's (1999) large scale study that showed that individuals who overrated themselves tended to see the most improvement in performance a year after the assessment. To our knowledge, AC research has not investigated SO agreement as an input to developmental activities. Presenting AC participants with SO discrepancies might be a useful approach to ensure that assessees are invested in the feedback derived from ACs.

The primary proximal outcome of feedback is initial reactions to the feedback, such as perceptions of accuracy, perceptions of usefulness, and feedback acceptance (Kirkpatrick 1979). This is because if the feedback recipient does not accept the feedback as accurate, it is highly unlikely that they will put effort into improving the areas identified as weaknesses (Brett and Atwater 2001). Although user reactions to ACs and MSPRs are quite positive, a variety of factors have been shown to influence user reactions to MSPRs. For instance, perceptions of MSPR accuracy, feedback recipient self-efficacy (Bailey and Austin 2006), organizational support for development (Smither et al. 2005), and the availability of an executive coach (Luthans and Peterson 2003) have been shown to increase the potential for feedback acceptance and in some cases, performance improvement. In short, the rich literature on factors influencing the efficacy of MSPRs is ripe to apply to the DAC literature.

A critical question to evaluating the relative efficacy of ACs and MSPRs is the extent to which they engender different levels of feedback acceptance. Although work samples are among the most face valid predictors in selection contexts, it remains to be seen how ACs will fare relative to MSPRs in terms of reactions. Rupp et al. (2006) argued that a key advantage of feedback derived from ACs is increased perceptions of workplace fairness. Clearly, rater bias is less of a concern in ACs relative to MSPRs; however, AC ratings are less externally valid relative to MSPRs. Given these respective strengths and weaknesses, it is not clear at this point which measurement approach will be viewed more positively by feedback recipients.

INTERNATIONAL APPLICATIONS

Although calls to investigate culture's influence on ACs and MSPR systems are not particularly new (Briscoe 1997, Tornow 1993), the literature on international issues associated with ACs is in its infancy. Existing AC research has primarily investigated differences in AC practices across cultures (Krause and Thornton 2009), rather than more substantive questions. On the other hand, while a burgeoning literature base has highlighted important cultural considerations associated with MSPRs, there remains a dearth of knowledge on cultural differences in MSPR practice. The limited knowledge on cultural differences in MSPRs negates a comparison with international applications of ACs, so this section will necessarily focus on substantive issues associated with ACs and MSPRs. Finally, MSPRs and ACs are argued to be useful tools in the selection and development of managers in their role as members of the international community.

Shipper, Hoffman and Rotondo (2007) conducted a longitudinal study of the effectiveness of MSPRs in a multinational sample. They found that when a culture has less stratification between high and low status individuals (low power distance), MSPRs tend to be more effective in improving feedback outcomes. Thus raters from high power distance cultures are sometimes reluctant to openly evaluate their supervisors and peers (Harzing 1997), in which case it is unlikely that MSPRs will be a valid measure of performance and their value will be undermined. We propose that in high power distance cultures, ACs may be particularly valuable for developmental reasons because assessors are independent observers that have no power differential with the assessee. On the other hand, Brutus, Leslie and McDonald-Mann (2001) argued that because of their focus on measuring individual characteristics, MSPRs are unlikely to be effective in collectivist relative to individualistic cultures. Given that ACs also focus on measuring individual characteristics, this criticism of MSPRs would also apply to ACs. Future research investigating user and organizational reactions to ACs in collectivistic cultures is needed.

In addition, there is also evidence stemming from the broader managerial performance literature that the dimensions essential to success differ across cultures. For instance, subordinate ratings of task and interpersonal style leadership have been shown to mean something different to those in collectivistic (Japan and Hong Kong) compared to individualistic (Great Britain and the United States) cultures (Gillespie 2005). According to Javidan and House (2001), in high power distance cultures, communication is expected to be top-down, and input from subordinates is not generally socially acceptable. Aditya and House (2001) invoked cultural differences in implicit leadership theories to explain cultural differences in the appropriateness of various forms of interpersonal facilitation behaviors. Importantly, there is evidence that differences in the conceptualization of leadership impact the bottom line. Newman and Nollen (1996) found that using management practices that are congruent with national culture yielded higher work unit financial performance. In short, evidence for differences in the importance and appropriateness of leadership behaviors across cultures is substantial (for a more in depth review, see Dickson, Hartog and Mitchelson 2003). Collectively, this research can be applied to better understand issues with cross-cultural applications of ACs and MSPRs.

ACs and MSPRs both have the potential to aid organizations in effectively navigating the complexities of operating globally. For instance, given the increased frequency of expatriate assignments, the high cost of expatriate failure, and the importance of adjustment to expatriate success (Thomas and Lazarova 2006), identifying approaches of predicting expatriate success and providing diagnostic feedback on skills needed to effectively negotiate the challenges of expatriate assignments is particularly important. Luthans and Farner (2002) proposed that MSPR systems could be used to culturally train expatriates. In addition, ACs may be particularly well suited to evaluating readiness for expatriate assignment prior to the start of the job. Observing performance with culturally diverse role players in situations that cue the ability to work with those from other cultures might be particularly valuable in the context of ACs. Toward this end, Lievens, Harris, Van Keer and Bisqueret (2003) found that AC performance is an effective predictor of cross-cultural training performance.

SUMMARY

Whereas AC research has heavily emphasized criterion-related validity, far less work has been done to flesh out their value as developmental interventions. On the other hand, a solid literature base has accumulated substantiating the validity and developmental process associated with MSPRs. The accumulated research underscores the criterion-related validity of both ACs and MSPRs and although a direct comparison of their validity can be difficult, initial evidence suggests similar criterion-related validity associated with ACs and MSPRs. In addition, it appears that the components outlined above (context-consistent dimensions, context-specific dimensions, context effects, and general performance) are important to understanding the "active ingredients" of ACs and MSPRs. Another key similarity is that in isolation, neither ACs nor MSPRs yield substantial gains in manager development. We borrow from the MSPR literature in proposing a variety of factors that might help enhance performance improvement associated with ACs.

Summary and Conclusions

MSPRs and ACs have become "the" measures of managerial skills and competencies over the past 30 years. Despite their common goal, the AC and MSPR literature have run parallel, with little attempt at integration. This chapter remedies this issue by highlighting consistencies and inconsistencies between AC research and practice in hopes of finding common ground and more importantly, areas where AC research and practice can learn from MSPR research and practice and vice versa. Key areas of overlap include

(a) the underlying measurement approach which nests skill dimensions within multiple measurement contexts, (b) heavy psychometric focus and the statistical methods used, (c) underlying internal structure of the ratings, (d) relative importance of the various structural components of ratings, (e) controversy over the meaning and magnitude of the measurement context effect, (f) magnitude of their criterion related validity, and g) their small effects on performance improvement when used in isolation.

Perhaps more interestingly, there are a variety of inconsistencies in research and practices associated with the respective measurement tools. First, ACs are more readily applicable to selection settings, despite the somewhat higher validity associated with MSPRs. A related distinction is that MSPRs measure typical performance, whereas ACs are conceptually similar to maximal performance. Second, whereas AC research is characterized by a plethora of systematic reviews of common applications of the AC method, there is a frustrating dearth of research recording common practices associated with MSPRs.

Third, despite the controversy surrounding AC dimensions, it appears that MSPRs are characterized by smaller dimension effects than ACs. Yet, research has rarely seriously questioned the ability of MSPRs to measure cross-context consistent dimensions. One reason for the limited attention to the construct validity of MSPR dimensions is that by nature, MSPRs allow for the presence of context-specific behaviors. On the other hand, AC researchers and practitioners have been slow to acknowledge the importance of measurement-context effects, instead opting to simply combine dimensions across contexts. Integrating the practices and interpretations of measurement context effects stemming from the MSPR literature could curtail the current deadlock associated with the exercises vs. dimensions debate.

Fourth, AC research has lagged behind MSPR research in term of evaluating the usefulness of ACs in developmental contexts. MSPR research has developed a rich literature base highlighting concepts and boundary conditions that present an opportunity to AC researchers. Finally, although neither AC nor MSPR research has devoted considerable resources to understanding cultural issues, the MSPR literature has generated knowledge that is pertinent to cross-cultural applications of ACs. We hope that these insights inspire AC and MSPR researchers and practitioners to look beyond their own boundaries to consider lessons that can be learned from their methodology's contemporary.

References

Aditya, R.N. and House, R.J. 2002. Interpersonal acumen and leadership across cultures: Pointers from the GLOBE study. In *Multiple Intelligences and Leadership*, edited by R.E. Riggio, S.E. Murphy and F.J. Pirozzolo. Mahwah, NJ: Erlbaum, 215–240.

Armour, S. 2003. Job reviews take on added significance in a down economy. *USA Today*, 23 July, 6A–7A.

Arthur, W. Jr., Day, E.A., McNelly, T.L. and Edens, P.S. 2003. A meta-analysis of the criterion-related validity of assessment center dimensions. *Personnel Psychology*, 56, 125–154.

Arthur, W., Jr., Day, E.A. and Woehr, D.J. 2008. Mend it, don't end it: An alternate view of assessment center construct-related validity evidence. *Industrial and Organizational Psychology: Perspectives on Science and Practice*, 1, 105–111.

Arthur, W., Jr. and Villado, A.J. 2008. The importance of distinguishing between constructs and methods when comparing predictors in personnel selection research and practice. *Journal of Applied Psychology*, 93, 435–442.

Austin, J.T. and Villanova, P. 1992. The criterion problem: 1917–1992. *Journal of Applied Psychology*, 77, 836–874.

Bailey, C. and Austin, M. 2006. 360 degree feedback and developmental outcomes: The role of feedback characteristics, self-efficacy and importance of feedback dimensions to focal managers' current role. *International Journal of Selection and Assessment*, 14, 51–66.

Blair, C.A., Hoffman, B.J. and Helland, K.R. 2008. Narcissism in organizations: A multisource appraisal reflects different perspectives. *Human Performance*, 21, 254–276.

Borman, W.C. 1974. The rating of individuals in organizations: An alternative approach. *Organizational Behavior and Human Performance*, 12, 105–124.

Borman, W.C. and Brush, D.H. 1993. More progress toward a taxonomy of managerial performance requirements. *Human Performance*, 6, 1–21.

Bowler, M.C. and Woehr, D.J. 2006. A meta-analytic evaluation of the impact of dimension and exercise factors on assessment center ratings. *Journal of Applied Psychology*, 91, 1114–1124.

Bowler, M.C. and Woehr, D.J. 2009. Assessment center construct-related validity: Stepping beyond the MTMM matrix. *Journal of Vocational Behavior*, 75, 173–182.

Brett, J.F. and Atwater, L.E. 2001. 360° feedback: Accuracy, reactions, and perceptions of usefulness. *Journal of Applied Psychology*, 86, 930–942.

Briscoe, D.R. 1997. Assessment centers: Cross-cultural and cross-national issues. *Journal of Social Behavior & Personality*, 12, 261–270.

Brutus, S., Leslie, J.B. and McDonald-Mann, D. 2001. Cross-cultural issues in multisource feedback. In *The Handbook of Multisource Feedback: The Comprehensive Resource for Designing and Implementing MSF Processes*, edited by D.W. Bracken, C.W. Timmreck and A.H. Church. San Francisco, CA: Jossey-Bass, 433–446.

Campbell, D.T. and Fiske, D.W. 1959. Convergent and discriminant validation by the multitrait-multimethod matrix. *Psychological Bulletin*, 56, 81–105.

Church, A.H. 2000. Do higher performing managers actually receive better ratings? A validation of multirater assessment methodology. *Consulting Psychology Journal: Practice and Research*, 52, 99–116.

Connelly, B.S., Ones, D.S., Ramesh, A. and Goff, M. (2008). A pragmatic view of dimensions and exercises in assessment center ratings. *Industrial and Organizational Psychology Perspectives on Science and Practice*, 1, 127–130.

Conway, J.M., Lombardo, K. and Sanders, K.C. 2001. A meta-analysis of incremental validity and nomological networks for subordinate and peer rating. *Human Performance*, 14, 267–303.

Dickson, M.W., Hartog, D.N. and Mitchelson, J.K. 2003. Research on leadership in a cross-cultural context: Making progress, and raising new questions. *The Leadership Quarterly*, 14, 729–768.

Eurich, T.L., Krause, D.E., Cigularov, K. and Thornton, G.C. III. 2009. Assessment centers: Current practices in the United States. *Journal of Business and Psychology*, 24, 387–407.

Gaugler, B.B., Rosenthal, D.B., Thornton, G.C. and Bentson, C. 1987. Meta-analysis of assessment center validity. *Journal of Applied Psychology*, 72, 493–511.

Gibbons, A.M. and Rupp, D.E. 2009. Dimension consistency as an individual difference: A new (old) perspective on the assessment center construct validity debate. *Journal of Management*, 35, 1154–1180.

Gillespie, T.L. 2005. Internationalizing 360-degree feedback: Are subordinate ratings comparable? *Journal of Business and Psychology*, 19, 361–382.

Goldstein, I.L. 1986. *Training in Organizations: Needs Assessment, Design, and Evaluation*. Monterey, CA: Brooks/Cole.

Guidelines and ethical considerations for assessment center operations. 2009. *International Journal of Selection and Assessment*, 17, 243–253.

Hagan, C.M., Konopaske, R., Bernardin, H.J. and Tyler, C.L. 2006. Predicting assessment center performance with 360-degree, top-down, and customer-based competency assessments. *Human Resource Management*, 45, 357–390.

Harzing, A.-W. 1997. Response rates in international mail surveys: Results of a 22-country study. *International Business Review*, 6, 641.

Hoffman, B., Lance, C.E., Bynum, B. and Gentry, W.A. 2010. Rater source effects are alive and well after all. *Personnel Psychology*, 63, 119–151.

Hoffman, B.J. and Meade, A.W. 2007. *Invariance tests as Assessment Center Construct Validity Evidence*. Symposium presented at the 22nd annual conference of the Society for Industrial and Organizational Psychology, New York, NY.

Hoffman, B.J., Melchers, K., Blair, C.A., Kleinmann, M. and Ladd, R.T. In press. Exercises and dimensions are the currency of Assessment Centers. *Personnel Psychology*.

Hoffman, B.J. and Woehr, D.J. 2009. Disentangling the meaning of multisource performance rating source and dimension factors. *Personnel Psychology*, 62, 735–765.

Hoffman, B.J., Woehr, D.J., Maldegen, R. and Lyons, B. In press. Great man or great myth? A meta-analysis of the relationship between traits and leader effectiveness. *Journal of Occupational and Organizational Psychology*.

Howard, A.N.N. 2008. Making assessment centers work the way they are supposed to. *Industrial & Organizational Psychology*, 1, 98–104.

International Task Force on Assessment Center Guidelines. 2009. Guidelines and ethical considerations for assessment center operations. *International Journal of Selection and Assessment*, 17, 243–254.

Javidan, M. and House, R.J. 2001. Cultural acumen for the global manager: Lessons from Project GLOBE. *Organizational Dynamics*, 29, 289–305.

Johnson, J.W. and Ferstl, K.L. 1999. The effects of interrater and self-other agreement on performance improvement following upward feedback. *Personnel Psychology*, 52, 272–303.

Kirkpatrick, D.L. 1979. Techniques for evaluating training programs. *Training & Development Journal*, 33, 78–92.

Krause, D.E. and Thornton, G.C., III. 2009. A cross-cultural look at assessment center practices: Survey results from Western Europe and North America. *Applied Psychology: An International Review*, 58, 557–585.

Lance, C.L., Dawson, B., Birkelbach, D. and Hoffman, B. In press. A review of the magnitude of common method variance in organizational research. *Organizational Research Methods*.

Lance, C.E., Hoffman, B.J., Gentry, W.A. and Baranik, L.E. 2008. Rater source factors represent important subcomponents of the criterion construct space, not rater bias. *Human Resource Management Review*, 18, 223–232.

Lance, C.E., Lambert, T.A., Gewin, A.G., Lievens, F. and Conway, J.M. 2004. Revised estimates of dimension and exercise variance components in assessment center postexercise dimension ratings. *Journal of Applied Psychology*, 89, 377–385.

Lance, C.E., Woehr, D.J. and Meade, A.W. 2007. Case study: A monte carlo investigation of assessment center construct validity models. *Organizational Research Methods*, 10, 430–448.

Landy, F.J. and Conte, J.M. 2007. *Work in the Twenty-First Century: An Introduction to Industrial and Organizational Psychology* (2nd Edition). Malden: Blackwell Publishing.

Lievens, F. 2001. Assessor training strategies and their effects on accuracy, interrater reliability, and discriminant validity. *Journal of Applied Psychology*, 86, 255–264.

Lievens, F. 2009. Assessment centres: A tale about dimensions, exercises, and dancing bears. *European Journal of Work and Organizational Psychology*, 18, 102–121.

Lievens, F., Chasteen, C.S., Day, E.A. and Christiansen, N.D. 2006. Large-scale investigation of the role of trait activation theory for understanding assessment center convergent and discriminant validity. *Journal of Applied Psychology*, 91, 247–258.

Lievens, F., Dilchert, S. and Ones, D.S. 2009. The importance of exercise and dimension factors in assessment centers: Simultaneous examinations of construct-related and criterion-related validity. *Human Performance*, 22, 375–390.

Lievens, F., Harris, M.M., Van Keer, E. and Bisqueret, C. 2003. Predicting cross-cultural training performance: The validity of personality, cognitive ability, and dimensions measured by an assessment center and a behavior description interview. *Journal of Applied Psychology*, 88, 476–489.

London, M. and Smither, J.W. 1995. Can multi-source feedback change perceptions of goal accomplishment, self-evaluations, and performance-related outcomes? Theory-based applications and directions for research. *Personnel Psychology*, 48, 803–839.

Luthans, F. and Peterson, S.J. 2003. 360 degree feedback with systematic coaching: Empirical analysis suggests a winning combination. *Human Resource Management*, 42, 243–256.

Luthans, K.W. and Farner, S. 2002. Expatriate development: The use of 360-degree feedback. *Journal of Management Development*, 21, 780–793.

McCauley, C.D. and Lombardo, M.M. 1990. BENCHMARKS: An instrument for diagnosing managerial strengths and weaknesses. In *Measures of Leadership*, edited by K.E. Clark and M.B. Clark. West Orange, NJ: Leadership Library of America, 535–545.

Meriac, J.P., Hoffman, B.J., Woehr, D.J. and Fleisher, M.S. 2008. Further evidence for the validity of assessment center dimensions: A meta-analysis of the incremental criterion-related validity of dimension ratings. *Journal of Applied Psychology*, 93, 1042–1052.

Morgeson, F.P., Mumford, T.V. and Campion, M.A. 2005. Coming full circle: Using research and practice to address 27 questions about 360-degree feedback programs. *Consulting Psychology Journal: Practice and Research*, 57, 196–209.

Newman, K.L. and Nollen, S.D. 1996. Culture and congruence: The fit between management practices and national culture. *Journal of International Business Studies*, 27, 753–779.

Romano, C. 1994. Conquering the fear of feedback. *HR Focus*, 71, 9–19.

Rupp, D.E., Baldwin, A. and Bashshur, M. 2006. Using developmental assessment centers to foster workplace fairness. *Psychologist-Manager Journal*, 9, 145–170.

Sackett, P.R. and Dreher, G.F. 1982. Constructs and assessment center dimensions: Some troubling empirical findings. *Journal of Applied Psychology*, 67, 401–410.

Sackett, P.R., Zedeck, S. and Fogli, L. 1988. Relations between measures of typical and maximum job performance. *Journal of Applied Psychology*, 73, 482–486.

Schleicher, D.J., Day, D.V., Mayes, B.T. and Riggio, R.E. 2002. A new frame for frame-of-reference training: Enhancing the construct validity of assessment centers. *Journal of Applied Psychology*, 87, 735–746.

Schmidt, F.L. and Kaplan, L.B. 1971. Composite vs multiple criteria: A review and resolution of the controversy. *Personnel Psychology*, 24, 419–434.

Shipper, F., Hoffman, R.C. and Rotondo, D.M. 2007. Does the 360 feedback process create actionable knowledge equally across cultures? *Academy of Management Learning & Education*, 6, 33–50.

Smither, J.W., London, M. and Reilly, R.R. 2005. Does performance improve following multisource feedback? A theoretical model, meta-analysis, and review of empirical findings. *Personnel Psychology*, 58, 33–66.

Spychalski, A.C., Quiñones, M.A., Gaugler, B.B. and Pohley, K. 1997. A survey of assessment center practices in organizations in the United States. *Personnel Psychology*, 50, 71–90.

Summers, L. 2001. Web technologies for administering multisource feedback programs. In *The Handbook of Multisource Feedback: The Comprehensive Resource for Designing and Implementing MSF Processes*, edited by D.W. Bracken, C.W. Timmreck and A.H. Church. San Francisco, CA: Jossey-Bass, 165–180.

Thomas, D.C. and Lazarova, M.B. 2006. Expatriate adjustment and performance: A critical review. In *Handbook of Research in International Human Resource Management*, edited by G.K. Stahl and I. Björkman. Northampton, MA: Edward Elgar Publishing, 247–264.

Thornton, G.C. and Byham, W.C. 1982. *Assessment Centers and Managerial Performance*. New York, NY: Academic Press.

Thornton, G.C. III and Krause, D.E. 2009. Selection versus development assessment centers: An international survey of design, execution, and evaluation. *The International Journal of Human Resource Management*, 20, 478–498.

Timmreck CW, Bracken DW. 1997. Multisource feedback: A study of its use in decision-making. *Employee Relations*, 24, 21–27.

Tornow, W.W. 1993. Perceptions or reality: Is multi-perspective measurement a means or an end? *Human Resource Management*, 32, 221–229.

Viswesvaran, C., Schmidt, F.L. and Ones, D.S. 2005. Is there a general factor in ratings of job performance? A meta-analytic framework for disentangling substantive and error influences. *Journal of Applied Psychology*, 90, 108–131.

Waldman, D.A. and Atwater, L.E. 2001. Confronting barriers to successful implementation of multisource feedback. In *The Handbook of Multisource Feedback: The Comprehensive Resource for Designing and Implementing MSF Processes*, edited by D.W. Bracken, C.W. Timmreck and A.H. Church. San Francisco, CA: Jossey-Bass, 463–477.

11 Fifty Years On: The Ongoing Reciprocal Impact of Science and Practice on the Assessment Center Method

GEORGE C. THORNTON III

The long history of the assessment center (AC) method is a revealing story of the benefits that derive from a healthy interface of science and practice. What started as a basic research investigation using the AC to study adult development evolved into a range of worldwide talent management applications. Along the way, repeated exchanges took place: practical questions and challenges in the work place led researchers to undertake further research studies, and ideas arising in basic psychological theory and empirical research findings led to revisions and augmentations in practice.

In this chapter, I summarize the 55-year history of reciprocal influences of science and practice on the design and implementation of the AC method. Science contributed to the advancement and sustainability of AC practice with theories and research related to validity, adverse impact, social cognition and judgment, and learning principles. Research was stimulated by issues in the work place and society such as different applications of the method, use of and availability of different types of assessors, equal employment opportunity legislation, pressures to streamline the method, cross-cultural and cross-national applications, the use of information technology, and the desire to assess complex competencies. To this day, the AC method evolves as a function of developments in science and practice.

After a brief description of the basic elements of the AC method and the scientist/practitioner model, I review examples of reciprocity in four, admittedly somewhat arbitrary, time periods. Beginning with the Early Period (1965–1980), I review the seminal American Telephone and Telegraph (AT&T) Management Progress Study and early research and uses of the AC method by I/O psychologists to make promotions in large hierarchical organizations. Organizations investigated whether the method was fair to minorities and women. Next I describe the Middle Period (1980–1990) in which researchers studied many components of the AC method, while practitioners initiated new applications including diagnosis of patterns of developmental needs.

In the Recent Period (1990–2005) we saw applications designed to maximize the actual development of managers in the AC context itself. This necessitated drawing on different theories to guide implementation and different research designs to evaluate impact on diverse outcomes. During this period controversial research into relationships of ratings of dimensions after each exercise led some to question the "construct validity" of the method. Criticisms of that narrow stream of research accompanied by exercise-based AC designs emerged in the Current Period (2005 to present). After years of skepticism, new research affirming that ACs do measure postulated dimensions was conducted. In addition, this period saw ACs going global, and going online in conjunction with advancing technology. These and other developments are being guided by both pressing organizational needs, a war for talent, and new theories and, in turn, they are spurring additional research.

The Assessment Center Method

The basic elements of the AC method need little explanation at this point; they are well documented in extensive sources, including the principal accepted authoritative documents, that is, various versions of sets of guidelines on the AC method. The longest standing such document is the *Guidelines and Ethical Considerations for Assessment Center Operations*, originating in 1975, and now in its fourth edition (Task Force 2009). Similar documents have been produced in individual countries such as Germany (Arbeitskreis Assessment Center e.V. 2004), Indonesia (Ethical Guidelines for Assessment Center Operations in Indonesia 2002), South Africa (Assessment Centre Study Group, 2007), and the United Kingdom (British Psychological Society: Psychological Testing Centre 2003). While the guidelines from these individual countries have some unique features to emphasize special considerations for that culture, the basic elements remain constant:

- Job analysis or competency modeling identifies dimensions or other variables to assess.
- Multiple assessment techniques are used to elicit relevant information.
- The assessment techniques include simulations of job-relevant situations.
- Multiple, trained assessors are used.
- Overt behavior demonstrated by participants is classified into dimensions or other variables.
- Systematic procedures are used to record, classify, report, and sometimes rate behavior.
- Integration of the data across assessors, exercises, and categories is carried out sometime after observation by a systematic process.

Part of the continuing success of the AC method has been its versatility and adaptability. While adhering to the essential elements, AC developers have introduced variations on each. Different dimensions, simulation exercises, types of assessors, methods of recording and sharing observations, and methods of aggregating the data have been used. The variations have been used as a response to different purposes of the AC, the emergence of new psychological theory and research, and organizational, societal, and cultural demands.

Scientist/Practitioner Model

The profession of industrial/organizational psychology prides itself in subscribing to and following the scientist/practitioner model. This model drives many masters' and doctoral graduate-level educational programs. Many I/O psychologists who work in educational, consulting, and organizational settings identify with the model. While not all I/O psychologists carry out research and practice at the same time, many have engaged in each discipline at different times in their career. Furthermore, some have observed that the collective field of I/O psychology contains a healthy balance of individuals doing science and practice (Landy and Conte 2007).

The scientist persona of I/O psychology places a great emphasis on using psychological theories to guide practice, conducting basic and applied research, gathering empirical data to address organizational problems, and evaluating various outcomes of interventions.

There is the general belief in I/O psychology in the reciprocal influences of science and practice: science informs practice, and practice informs science. Interventions in selection, training, performance management, and so forth, are shaped by theories and research in personality, assessment, learning and training, social perception, judgment, and many other sub-areas of psychology. The processes of attracting, selecting, socializing, and managing humans in organizations are studied empirically to determine what works. In like manner, research into these fields is stimulated and made relevant by practitioners engaging in realistic organizational settings as they attempt to better understand actual problems and challenges in organizational life and broader societal settings. Examples of the ways science and practice have influenced each other in ACs in the four periods referred to earlier are presented next.

Early Period: 1965 to 1980

In the early period, two longitudinal validity studies in American Telephone and Telegraph (AT&T) established the value of the AC method through its ability to predict managerial performance. The Management Progress Study tracked men for 20 years from the mid 1950s; the Management Continuity Study tracked women from the mid 1970s (Howard and Bray 1988). Several other longitudinal, true predictive validity studies were carried out in the United States in the early period by large corporations such as SOHIO, IBM, and Sears (Thornton and Byham 1982). These studies gave organizations confidence that AC scores predicted various criteria of managerial effectiveness. The application of the AC method spread, first to various companies in the Bell system, then to other large organizations in the United States and Canada, and ultimately to medium and small companies and public agencies. In this early period the main purpose was identification of potential for advancement and the output of interest was the overall assessment rating (OAR).

During the prosperous economy in this period, organizations had relatively hierarchical organizational structures with several layers of management. Thus there was a need for mechanisms to aid in making promotion decisions. At first the applications assessed non-supervisory personnel (for example, manufacturing employees or sales persons) for promotion into first level supervision. Later, ACs were used to promote staff into middle management and top level executive positions. Many large organizations employed industrial psychologists who conducted research into the psychometric qualities of the

AC method, with primary interest in the correlation of the overall assessment rating (OAR) with various criteria of managerial performance. Early meta-analyses showed the OAR predicted success at about .38.

The civil rights movement in the US led to many questions about whether human resource management techniques provided equal employment opportunities for racial minorities, women, and older workers. Researchers at this time had developed the measurement and statistical methods to investigate various related indicators of fairness, namely adverse impact, differential validity, measurement bias, and prediction bias (Guion 1998, Society for Industrial and Organizational Psychology 2003). These methods were used to investigate the fairness of the AC method. Studies determined that the AC method led to smaller ethnic differences in AC scores in comparison with differences observed on cognitive ability tests. In addition, it was determined no differential validity existed for racial and gender subgroups: the AC method predicted success for Whites and Blacks and for men and women. Much of this early research is described in detail in Thornton and Byham (1982) and summarized and updated in Thornton and Rupp (2006).

Middle Period: 1980 to 1990

During the middle period, a number of changes in organizations and United States society led to changes in the AC method and subsequent research to investigate the effectiveness of these new applications. The structure of organizations became less hierarchical, with fewer layers of middle level managers. Consequently there were fewer opportunities for promotions of managers upward in the organization. There was a need for managers to develop skills in their current, ever-changing positions. Thus, an added emphasis in some ACs was the diagnosis of strengths and weaknesses. ACs were used to lay out plans for development of skills on and off the job. For these different applications, the design and implementation of ACs differed (Thornton 1992).

Research during this period investigated the various components of the AC method. For example, it was established that it was not feasible or even necessary to assess the long lists of 13 to 15 dimensions typically assessed in the early period. Research, guided by principles of social cognition and judgment, established that assessors could not make meaningful distinctions among more than 6 to 8 dimensions (Gaugler and Thornton 1989). The practical payoff of this research was the simplification of the observation and rating processes for assessors.

This period saw considerable research into the methods assessors used to observe, record, rate, and integrate behavior. Behavior checklists, behavioral anchored rating scales, and behavior observation scales were investigated. Spurred by research into the basic processes of human judgment and group decision-making, a healthy debate ensued over whether judgmental or statistical methods should be used to integrate assessment information across exercises, dimensions, and assessors. Mixed findings from studies comparing "clinical/consensual" vs "statistical" integration led to the conclusion that each method offered benefits. When a single, final OAR is paramount for making fine distinctions among candidates for promotion, statistical integration may be preferred; when insights into the idiosyncratic tendencies of individuals who may be part of a process of promotion, placement, and development, a consensus discussion among assessors may be preferred.

Research into group decision-making showed how to maximize group gains and minimize group losses. These studies reinforced the efficacy of the process of the integration discussion in the AC method (Thornton 1992).

Recent Period: 1990 to 2005

In this period, a number of other new applications emerged and additional research studies were undertaken to explore new issues with the AC method. The most severe and complicated questions were asked about the so-called "construct validity problem" with the AC method. Research using the multi-trait multi-method matrix investigated convergent and discriminant correlations among post-exercise dimension ratings (PEDRs) began in the early 1980s (for example, Sackett and Dreher 1982) and continued into this period with studies by Lance and colleagues (see Reference list for citations). Studies found relatively large correlations among dimension ratings within an exercise and relatively small correlations between the ratings of the same dimension in different exercises. In response to these findings, a number of efforts were undertaken to "fix" this supposed problem, including reducing the number of dimensions observed in any one exercise, training assessors to observe behavior more accurately, the use of various observation and rating aids, and the application of frame-of-reference training (a method used to improve performance appraisals). While none of these "design fixes" had appreciable effects on the relationships of PEDRs, the studies and broader debate sharpened our thinking about the judgmental processes inherent in the AC method. In addition, developments in the science of analyzing complex structural equation models (Kaplan 2000; Schumacker and Lomax 2004) enabled researchers to determine the impact of both dimensions and exercises on AC ratings. In the next period, emphasis was placed on the validity of what some believe is the more proper unit of analysis, namely final dimension ratings derived after integration across assessors and exercises.

During this recent period, the AC method was refined to maximize the learning that participants experience. While it had long been recognized that participants often gained personal insights during the assessment activities and subsequent feedback (Ballantyne and Povah 2004), the traditional AC method was based on measurement and assessment principles but not on learning principles. Thus, in this period, developmental assessment centers (DACs), also known as development centers (DCs), were developed using adult and social learning principles (Thornton and Rupp 2006). DACs retain the same basic essential elements of the AC method, but special variations of these elements emerged: assessment mainly of developable dimensions, repeated participation in parallel exercises with immediate feedback and practice, and a program climate emphasizing change rather than solely psychometric precision.

During this period, applications of the AC method spread to more and more countries around the world. To be sure, from their inception, ACs were conducted in Canada, the UK, Israel, Japan, and South Africa. But, global applications expanded markedly during the recent period, with programs appearing in other countries in Europe, South America, and Asia (Lievens and Thornton 2005). This expansion can be explained by the combination of practical matters such as globalization of business, growth of international consulting organizations, and scientific research conducted in diverse countries.

Current Period: 2005 to Present

The investigation of the relationships among post-exercise dimension ratings led to a re-examination of the basic premises of the AC method, alternative methods of studying PEDRs, exercise-based designs of ACs, and studies of the validity of final dimension ratings resulting from integration across ratings by multiple assessors in multiple exercises. These validity studies during the recent and current period have clarified that, when studying the validity of dimension ratings, the correct unit of analysis is the final dimension rating (across exercises and assessors), and not dimension ratings by a single assessor after an individual exercise. The theory of the AC method never intended to make any inference from a PEDR; after all, they are typically a rating by one assessor observing behavior in one exercise. PEDRs are like items on a test; psychometricians would usually not put credence in single item measures.

Studies of across-exercise dimension ratings have generated considerable evidence of their validity, and provide support for the inference that assessment centers measure intended dimensions (Thornton and Rupp, in press). Research shows that these final dimension ratings are related to assessments of the same and similar attributes measured by other methods and to criteria of job performance on the same dimensions, which is evidence of convergent validity. Furthermore, final dimension ratings provide incremental predictive correlation beyond measures of cognitive ability and personality, which is evidence of discriminant validity.

A completely different approach to the design and implementation of ACs has been the proposal for task based or exercise-based ACs. In this method, assessors observe behavior and rate performance on tasks or exercises but not dimensions of performance. Explorations of the theory, research, and practice of both exercise-based and dimension-based ACs are contained in a book edited by Jackson, Lance, and Hoffman (in press).

A new line of research into exercise design based on Trait Activation Theory is leading to practical payoffs (Lievens, Tett, and Schleicher 2009, see also Chapter 4 in this volume by Lievens and Schollaert). Behavior related to different dimensions will be displayed if the situation activates the trait being measured. Thus, dimension-relevant behavior will be displayed, depending on the instructions given, specific material in the exercise, questions asked by the assessors, and behavior of role players in one-on-one situational exercises.

The trend toward analyzing "organizational competency models" has spurred both changes in practice and research in ACs. Organizations have pressed practitioners to incorporate competencies into AC design in place of or in addition to traditional dimensions. The challenge here is to deal with the sometimes lack of clarity in what is meant by a *competency*. Competency lists are often a combination of broad organizational objectives, ill-defined human attributes, and specific technical skills. Some competencies, as stated in some organizational competency models, are not amenable to assessment by most assessment methods, including the AC method. The challenge has been to operationalize complex competencies into human behaviors and attributes that can be observed and assessed with an adequate degree of reliability. Here is where the principles of psychology have contributed to provide the terminology to translate organizational constructs into human behavior and attributes, and the methodologies to create complex organizational simulations. A symposium at the 2009 conference of the Society for Industrial and Organizational Psychology explored these knotty issues (Thornton 2009).

The human capital management (HCM) movement has also presented opportunities and challenges for the AC method, particularly with regard to how they can play an effective part in the talent management lifecycle. HCM strives to integrate many sources of data and actions about human capital into the strategic planning of the organization. The AC method can help translate corporate strategy and organizational competency models into human dimensions, assess potential of key individuals as a supplement to assessments of past performance and experience, train managers to observe and evaluate performance in assessment settings and on the job, and provide methods of gathering and integrating human capital information in systematic ways. In return, involvement of the AC method in HCM processes has provided AC practitioners opportunities to participate in high level strategic planning, to learn about new ways of evaluating the impact of their interventions, and to adapt the AC method in ways that contribute to the organization's strategic objectives.

Advances in information technology have played a prominent role in recent research and practice of ACs. "Dis-assembled" ACs are being run with candidates completing exercises online in disperse locations, specialists scoring in-baskets and video-recorded interview simulations in different locations, and assessors integrating inputs in even different locations. Researchers are investigating the standardization, inter-rater agreement, and validity of the method, as well as participants' reactions, some of which may be positive (for example, they may be more user friendly and hasten feedback) or negative (for example, they may appear "low touch" and dehumanizing).

Advances in technology have helped organizations make assessments more user-friendly and thus attract good people in the war for talent precipitated by a dearth of good people due to declining birth rates and increased global competition for good people. Making the AC method more streamlined and a better depiction of the job opportunity hopefully sells the recruiting process, the job, and the organization to prospective recruits. Research is needed to investigate these alleged advantages.

Summary and Conclusions

The assessment center method has survived and evolved over the past 50 years as a function of numerous mutually beneficial interactions of science and practice. As the method has been used for different purposes over the years, theory and research has contributed to the design and evaluation of the AC method. As the practice of ACs has spread and evolved in response to challenges in organizations and cultures in industrial and governmental organizations around the world, new opportunities for basic and applied research have arisen. To this day, we see instances of both the long-standing and thoroughly validated applications of the method and the yet-to-be- studied innovations in all elements of the method and new applications. All of the historical forms of ACs continue to operate in organizations around the world. For example, traditional paper-and-pencil materials to assess classic management dimensions are being used in police and fire department promotional examinations across the US. All over the world, ACs use the original integration discussion to diagnose strengths and weaknesses, discern development needs, and lay out developmental plans for individuals. Programs to develop managerial skills using AC principles are being set up in government, business, and educational settings. The history of the AC method is the exemplar of the scientist/

practitioner model of the disciplines of industrial psychology and human resource management in the service of talent management.

References

Arbeitskreis Assessment Center e.V. 2004. *German Standards of Assessment Center Procedures.*

Assessment Centre Study Group. 2007. *Guidelines for Assessment and Development Centres in South Africa.*

Ballantyne, I. and Povah, N. 2004. *Assessment and Development Centres* (2nd Edition). Aldershot: Gower.

British Psychological Society: Psychological Testing Centre. 2003. *Design, implementation and evaluation of Assessment and Development Centres. Best Practice Guidelines.* [Online]. Available at: http://www.psychtesting.org.uk/the-ptc/guidelinesandinformation.cfm [accessed: 19 April 2010].

Gaugler, B.B. and Thornton, G.C. III. 1989. Number of assessment center dimensions as a determinant of assessor accuracy. *Journal of Applied Psychology*, 74, 611–618.

Guion, R.M. 1998. *Assessment, Measurement, and Prediction for Personnel Decisions.* Mahwah, NJ: Lawrence Erlbaum.

Howard, A. and Bray, D.W. 1988. *Managerial Lives in Transition: Advancing Age and Changing Times.* New York: Guilford Press.

International Task Force on Assessment Center Guidelines. 2009. Guidelines and ethical considerations for assessment center operations. *International Journal of Selection and Assessment*, 17, 243–254.

Jackson, D.J.R., Lance, C.E. and Hoffman, B.J. In press. *The Psychology of Assessment Centers.*

Kaplan, D. 2000. *Structural Equation Modeling: Foundations and Extensions.* Thousand Oaks, CA: Sage Publications.

Lance, C.E. 2008. Where have we been, how did we get there, and where shall we go? *Industrial and Organizational Psychology: Perspectives on Science and Practice*, 1, 140–146.

Lance, C.E., Foster, M.R., Gentry, W.A. and Thoresen, J.D. 2004. Assessor cognitive processes in an operational assessment center. *Journal of Applied Psychology*, 89, 22–35.

Lance, C.E., Lambert, T.A., Gewin, A.G., Lievens, F. and Conway, J.M. 2004. Revised estimates of dimension and exercise variance components in assessment center post-exercise dimension ratings. *Journal of Applied Psychology*, 89, 377–385.

Lance, C.E., Newbolt, W.H., Gatewood, R.D., Foster, M.R., French, N.R. and Smith, D.E. 2000. Assessment center exercise factors represent cross-situational specificity, not method bias. *Human Performance*, 13, 323–353.

Landy, F.J. and Conti, J.M. 2007. *Work in the Twenty-First Century* (2nd Edition). Malden, MA: Blackwell.

Lievens, F., Tett, R.P. and Schleicher, D.J. 2009. Assessment centers at the crossroads: Toward a reconceptualization of assessment center exercises. In *Research in Personnel and Human Resource Management*, edited by J.J. Martocchio and H. Liao. Bingley: JAI Press, 99–152.

Lievens, F. and Thornton, G.C. III. 2005. Assessment centers: Recent developments in practice and research. In *Handbook of Selection*, edited by A. Evers, O. Voskuijl and N. Anderson. London: Blackwell, 243–264.

Sackett, P.R. and Dreher, G.F. 1982. Constructs and assessment center dimensions: Some troubling empirical findings. *Journal of Applied Psychology*, 67, 401–410.

Schumacker, R.E. and Lomax, R.G. 2004. *A Beginner's Guide to Structural Equation Modeling* (2nd Edition). Mahwah, NJ: Lawrence Erlbaum.

Society for Industrial and Organizational Psychology. 2003. *Principles for the Validation and Use of Personnel Psychology*. Bowling Green, OH: Author.

Thornton, G.C.III. 1992. *Assessment Centers in Human Resource Management*. Reading, MA: Addison-Wesley.

Thornton, G.C. III. 2009. Panelist, *Measuring complex dimensions with executive assessment centers: Challenges and limitations*. Panel Discussion at the 24th Annual Conference of the Society for Industrial and Organizational Psychology, New Orleans, LA. April.

Thornton, G.C. III and Byham, W.C. 1982. *Assessment Centers and Managerial Performance*. New York: Academic Press.

Thornton, G.C. III and Rupp, D.E. In press. Research into dimension-based assessment centers. In *The Psychology of Assessment Centers*, edited by D.J.R. Jackson, C.E. Lance, and B.J. Hoffman.

Corporate Strategy and Talent Management

12 *Building a Talent for Talent*

RAIMUND BIRRI AND ANDREAS MELCHER

This chapter will show how Credit Suisse's deep and long experience with assessment centers (ACs), including 30 years of practice, hundreds of line managers as assessors, and several thousand participations has contributed to building a high quality Human Capital Management (HCM) practice in recent years, and vice versa, how ACs are taking advantage of their integration in a broader suite of instruments and processes of HCM.

ACs are an established and well-accepted instrument for assessing relevant behavioral skills in organizations. Their use is widespread and international.

Human Capital Management, sometimes called Talent Management, is a much newer topic. In many organizations it is not yet much more than a buzzword. Although more and more chief executive officers (CEOs) recognize and stress the importance of human capital for business performance, there is still a long way to go for most organizations in order to understand and professionally manage their human capital (see for example, the annual IBM report on Talent Management by Ringo, DeMarco and Lesser 2008).

In the 1970s some leading edge companies introduced ACs for assuring high level quality of their management. In the 1990s the challenges of the "War for Talent" and the concept of "Human Capital" stimulated a deeper look at how talent and leadership should be addressed with a strategic view. Many companies started to build up or improve their management of human capital. New instruments, processes, and evaluations were targeted at getting the best talent, selecting and developing the right employees for critical positions, and evaluating the existing teams in order to improve their performance.

Today talent or human capital is widely recognized as the main sustainable competitive advantage. However, effectively leveraging human capital to increase business performance creates serious challenges for an organization that are more significant and complex than managing physical and financial assets. Business performance is now so dependent on outstanding Human Capital Management (HCM) that it has become a fundamental element of business management. Business centric HCM shifts the focus from HR ownership to HCM ownership by business users. This shift is difficult to harness. A widespread and established use of ACs with business managers as assessors can substantially ease or even drive this shift and improve the management of human capital.

This case study will provide some insights and hints on how to combine positive AC experiences with evolving talent management processes and how to take full advantage of ACs when introducing or expanding an HCM practice.

To provide the necessary background, we first briefly describe the type of ACs used in Credit Suisse and the history and elements of the HCM in place today. Then we describe the emergence of Human Capital Management in Credit Suisse. We follow that with descriptions of how assessment centers help build talent, and in return, how assessment centers profit from this role.

The History and Types of Assessments in Credit Suisse

Credit Suisse introduced ACs in the late 1970s, after it had gone through a nearly lethal crisis caused mainly by management failures. One lesson learned from this crisis was to improve the selection of middle and top management. HR was asked to come up with valid selection techniques and procedures. The solution was the design of an AC for senior managers, based on a set of newly developed leadership dimensions. Unlike many of its competitors, Credit Suisse has been running ACs uninterruptedly from 1979 until today, even though strategy, leadership style and market conditions have changed several times and substantially in these 30 years. The assessments have always been developed, managed and evaluated by an internal group of assessment specialists, comprising 5 to 10 psychologists each with some leadership experience.

In the 1970s and 1980s the AC team had a rather special status, reporting directly to the head of HR, acting as an audit unit for the management bench. The program of an AC and the dimensions assessed were to a large extent secret. Since 2000, accompanied by the introduction of a formal Talent Development Process (TDP), the AC Team opened up and has become a part of the evaluation services of human capital in the Leadership Institute of the HR-managed Business School of Credit Suisse.

In 2008, this specialist group went through an outsourcing process and is now run by a former head of the internal assessment team. The reason for this outsourcing was a global human resources transformation process to improve efficiency and productivity of the HR function.

THREE TYPES OF ASSESSMENTS

Three different types of assessment programs have been used for different purposes. Each type follows the basic elements of the assessment center method, but is tailor-made for the different applications. Table 12.1 provides an overview of these programs.

Table 12.1 Key features of the assessment programs

	Group assessment (AC-G)	Individual assessment (AC-I)	Assessment for supervisors (AC-G-S/AC-I-S)
Purpose	Assessment of potential to assume a senior role	Same as AC-G – plus: informing hiring decision; focusing development investments	Same as AC-G or AC-I
Target job	Senior role as manager or expert	Senior role as manager or expert	First-level supervisor
Assessees	12 internal candidates	1 (external or internal) candidate	8 internal/1 external candidate
Assessors	6 executive line managers	2 assessment specialists	4 senior managers (AC-I-S)/2 assessment specialists (AC-I-S)
Role of AC-specialists	Facilitator, role player, feedback provider	Assessor, role player, feedback provider	Auditor/assessor
Dimensions/competencies	6 dimensions: interpersonal, conceptual and motivational competencies	Same as AC-G	Same as AC-G
Length	2½ days	1 day	AC-G-S: 2 days / AC-I-S: 1 day
Assessment techniques	Interactive simulations, case studies, in-basket, critical reasoning test	Interactive simulations, case study, in-basket, interview, critical reasoning tests	Interactive simulations, case study, in-basket, interview, critical reasoning tests

Group Assessment (AC-G)

The Group Assessment Center (AC-G) is aimed at internal participants who want to assume a senior role in Credit Suisse. A senior role can be a managerial role where the person leads other managers or an expert role where the person manages a team of specialists or a complex project. The assessment is designed to analyze the potential to be successful in a senior role. An AC-G lasts 2½ days with exercises developed in-house and following an overall business scenario which is not banking specific but near to a banking business. Recently, critical reasoning tests have been added, used for supplementing the measurement of conceptual and analytical skills. One AC-G runs with 12 participants and 6 executive line managers as assessors, monitored by four assessment specialists. Between 60 and 90 executive line managers per year, selected from a pool of around 150 trained assessors, act as assessors for 3 days. Around one quarter of the pool rejuvenates each year. New assessors are selected by senior executive management, based on criteria set by the AC team (upper management tier, good people leadership skills, positive AC result if available).

In an additional day after the candidates have left, the report is written and integrated entirely by the assessors themselves. Strengths and development areas of each candidate are discussed and a final rating for each assessed competency is agreed amongst all assessors. The final assessment report is structured around five competencies: three for interpersonal behavior (Collaboration, Leadership, Diversity and Inclusion), one for conceptual skills (Problem-solving and Implementation) and one for behaviors around drive, learning and managing emotions (Personal Excellence). Each competency is rated on a 4-point rating scale, except for Diversity and Inclusion, where observed behavior is only described with text comments, but not rated. Recently, in alignment with an evolved brand positioning, a sixth competency (Focusing on Clients) has been added to give critical behaviors for successfully managing client relationships explicitly more emphasis. The report now consists of 6 competencies – Focusing on Clients, Delivering Solutions, Pursuing Excellence, Providing Leadership, Fostering Collaboration, and Engaging Differences (which is not rated).

Individual Assessment (AC-I)

An Individual Assessment can serve various purposes. It is used for (a) informing selection decisions when hiring external candidates at a senior level, (b) assessing the potential of internal candidates to assume a senior role, and (c) profiling strengths and development areas of internal candidates who already perform at a senior level in order to support their development and career planning. An AC-I is a one-day assessment with one-on-one exercises and case studies based on a unifying scenario (the same as in the AC-G), critical reasoning tests, and an interview. The report is written by two equally engaged assessors, both chosen from the group of assessment specialists (the ones who also run and monitor AC-Gs). The competencies and the report format are the same as in the AC-G.

AC-G-S and AC-I-S

Before these programs were cancelled, they were assessments in the same style as above but targeted at assessing the potential of employees for a first supervisory role. They lasted only 2 days and the assessors were senior managers. The AC specialist team designed and audited these assessments with the administration and monitoring mainly being done by HR. More than 1,500 candidates went through these assessments in the years 1998 to 2002. After these assessments were cancelled for cost reasons, only some units still use the AC-I-S for recruiting supervisors or team leaders in private banking.

REPORT, FEEDBACK SESSION AND USE OF AC RESULTS

For all assessments in Credit Suisse the reports are sent within a couple of days after the assessment took place to the direct manager (for internal candidates) or to the recruiting manager (for external candidates). A thorough feedback session is offered and highly recommended to each candidate. Around two thirds of the internal candidates take advantage of this feedback. An assessment specialist who had a role in the candidate's assessment explains the report with its ratings, answers questions and assists in interpreting the results in relation to the career development of the candidate. The direct manager of the candidate also takes part in this feedback session, in order to facilitate a "reality check" and to identify and sponsor appropriate development actions.

The use of the assessment reports for internal candidates has slightly changed over time. In the 1980s and 1990s promotion decisions relied exclusively on the AC result. Subsequently the influence of the AC result in the promotion process became less rigorous and was used more as a source for individual development planning. But still, internal longitudinal studies show that practically no executive manager in Credit Suisse had a negative AC result early in his career, despite many major reorganizations sometimes leading to unexpected moves for a number of managers.

PARTICIPATION

Figure 12.1 shows the number of participants in Group Assessments (AC-G) and in Individual Assessments (AC-I) over the years. (The number of assessments for first level supervisors in AC-G-S and AC-I-S is not shown.) The AC-Is were introduced in the 1980s, as more and more senior managers were selected from outside, and an AC-I was the preferred solution for these selections from outside. Later, especially after 2000, AC-Is were used as an alternative for group assessments mainly owing to reasons of flexibility, as they could be organized at short notice.

From 2002 onwards the AC-Is have also been used to assess the potential of candidates on a so-called "specialist track." Unlike the candidates on the traditional "management track," these candidates were selected and assessed for senior specialist jobs such as senior IT specialists or senior product developers in private banking. Some of the exercises differed from the management track assessment.

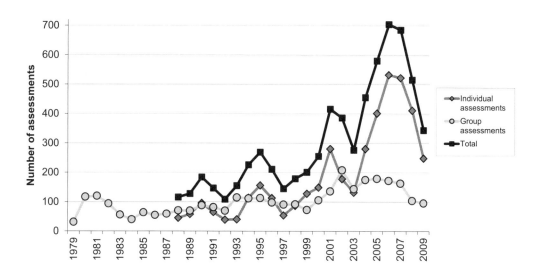

Figure 12.1 Number of participants attending the assessment programs

AC-Gs have mainly been used in the Swiss part of Credit Suisse. AC-Is have seen in recent years a substantial, but not a total, reach to banking units in other countries, especially in Europe and in Asia. One reason for the minor international use of the behavioral assessment approach is that Credit Suisse in other regions has not had the dominant market position as in Switzerland. Hence, the key HR challenges were attraction and retention, and not selection. Another reason is that pure interview assessments are still the preferred method to inform hiring decisions at a more senior level, especially in the mainly America-based investment banking business. For developmental purposes the most frequently used assessment approach across the bank has always been 360° feedback. The business areas in Credit Suisse that have continuously used assessments for selection and development have a scope of 15,000 to 20,000 employees. All assessments are conducted in German, English, French or Italian, depending on the candidate's native language. The cross-cultural compatibility within the broader Credits Suisse corporate culture is assured through careful translations, culturally non-sensitive contents in exercises and at least one native speaking assessor. The curve in Figure 12.1 shows a rather constant line for AC-Gs, whereas the number of IAs is more volatile. The reasons for this volatility are the lows in business activity of Credit Suisse, due to the global financial crises in 2001 and 2007, which led to a reduction in external recruitment. The downturn in 1995 can be explained by a merger with another Swiss bank, temporarily reducing the need for talent from outside. The downturn beginning in 2007 was particularly sharp, because the IT Division, comprising about 6,000 employees in Switzerland, decided to replace AC-G with a rigorous promotion process. That process entailed a committee of independent line managers deciding on the promotability of candidates. Another reason for the downturn was a change in the charging practice for assessments. Whilst all assessments in former years were funded out of a central budget, assessments for external candidates are now directly charged to the commissioning manager's own budget.

The Emerging Human Capital Management in Credit Suisse

Beginning in the 1990s, Credit Suisse made attempts to establish a stable process for management development and to reposition assessments according to this overall process. Today Credit Suisse has several years of experience with its state-of-the-art HCM practice, and it integrates all relevant data, instruments and actions on human capital, so that they are strategically aligned and well accepted by line management from a supervisory level up to the board of directors. Table 12.2 gives an overview of the timeline with the major steps in building a Human Capital Management in Credit Suisse, linked to the features and positioning of assessments.

Table 12.2   Timeline of major steps in building an HCM

	Organization and industry context	Major emphasis in human capital development	Features and positioning of assessments
Late 1970s	Crisis in management	Title promotions	Group Assessment (AC-G) as audit for management bench
1980s	Growing complexity of organizational structure. Employer-driven recruiting and selection	Leadership development programs (off-the-job)	Additional Individual Assessments (AC-I) to inform hiring decisions
1990s		Management Development Review (MDR) Meetings	Additional AC-G-S/AC-I-S for supervisory role
2000	'War for Talent'. Changes in strategy and organizational structure	Talent Development Process (TDP) with new Competency Model and Career Tracks	Separate AC-G and AC-I for Management and Specialist Track. Competency Model as basis for AC-dimensions. Assessment as part of Learning and Development Services
2005	Human Capital as business strategy issue	New HCM practice, integrating and acting upon measurements of Performance, Potential, Engagement and Engagement Drivers	AC informs Potential rating
2008	New HR structure and systems		Outsourcing of AC service

The hierarchical structure of a classical bank in the late 1970s was built on corporate titles. Being a member of the directorate or not was the big change in a banking career, which also changed the remuneration scheme. Therefore promoting the right employees to directors was the central theme of management development at that time. With the introduction of ACs, the promotion decisions to directors became more controlled and transparent. The AC dimensions formally specified the leadership criteria for becoming a director. Nominating candidates for an AC became a partially formal process, stirring talent discussions in management teams and replacing rather intuitive and singular decisions. HR was the administrator of candidate lists and reported the success rates in ACs back to the management teams. The independent second opinion of an AC-report was the decisive element of a promotion.

After analyzing the AC results from the early years, it soon became evident that the selection of candidates and their preparation for a director-level appointment could and should be improved. Leadership development, including formal off-the-job programs, was then the emerging topic of management development. Having a high success rate in the ACs was an important people development criterion for executive managers. Later (in the 1990s) some units started to establish so called "Management Development Review (MDR)" meetings, where the investments in the development of selected employees were addressed, not only for the director level but also on lower levels. Managers with experience as AC assessors were often the leading force behind such MDR-meetings where AC specialists had a seat at the table.

TALENT DEVELOPMENT PROCESS

Around the year 2000 the hierarchical structure of the bank became even more complex. Functional segmentation of the workforce and its link to the compensation system began to replace the traditional focus on job titles. A rather sophisticated but also complex Talent Development Process (TDP) was established for the whole organization, driven mainly by HR. This process defined the segmentation into functionally clear-cut hierarchical levels and three horizontal tracks (management, specialists, and client relationship management). The transition criteria and the training offerings from level to level in the three tracks were specified. A competency model was developed with a view to the overall strategy, extending and rewriting the AC dimensions. This model served as a "Talent Language" in various topic areas like 360°, development seminars and performance appraisals. The AC was positioned as an important source of information, but was no longer the sole criterion for evaluating the senior level of management or specialists. The TDP meetings replaced the MDR-meetings, where managers discussed and decided upon their talent. The TDP fostered a much higher and broader awareness of Talent Management issues. The basic investments and decisions in talent were more structured and transparent, in line with the growing focus on the "War for Talent."

HUMAN CAPITAL MANAGEMENT

Somehow stimulated by the positive experiences with TDP but also trying to remove its deficiencies, namely its formal complexity, its one-sided focus on succession lists, and its failure to integrate all talent-related practices, such as results of employee surveys, a new Human Capital Management practice replaced the TDP in 2005. The current Credit Suisse HCM is based on four basic measurements of human capital:

- Performance. A combined rating of the contribution of an employee based on the "what" (for example, business objectives achieved) and the "how" (for example, achieved behavioral objectives along a new streamlined competency model).
- Potential. The probability of being successful in a position on the next higher level within a time frame of about 2 years. Three main elements are considered in the potential rating: the motivation to assume more responsibility, willingness to learn, and competencies (functional, interpersonal, and intellectual).
- Engagement. An index calculated from survey answers about the employees' intention to stay in the company, to talk positively about the company and the willingness to go the extra mile ("say-stay-serve").
- Engagement-Drivers. The positive perception of employees of drivers of their engagement, such as career opportunities, pay, developmental support and feedback by the direct manager, and so forth.

These globally standard measures are assessed in three key people processes. The first process is a unified Performance Management with yearly objective settings and appraisals leading to calibrated performance ratings, which flow into compensation decisions and the HCP-Grid (see below). Second, a Human Capital Portfolio (HCP) meeting is held, where all employees at a specified level are positioned in a grid representing performance and potential. Potential is estimated by the direct manager and calibrated by their peers in a management team. The HCP grid of every organizational unit gets discussed, analyzed and compared to the strategic needs of the business in an annual (or more frequent, if necessary) meeting at more senior levels, up to the level of the CEO. These HCP meetings also decide on all relevant investments in human capital, such as training, recruiting initiatives, and nominations for successions and promotions.

The third people-process is an annual fully-fledged Employee Engagement Survey with top management attention and subsequent action meetings, where the results are analyzed on all levels and concerted actions are initiated. The results of the Engagement Survey are also an element in the analysis of the Human Capital Portfolios.

All three people-processes are primarily business processes with which the line managers of organizational units evaluate, manage and improve their human capital. HR's role is in designing and facilitating these processes and in acting as partners/coaches to the line managers' decision-making.

The AC is now positioned as an instrument to inform the potential-rating for a future senior level position. The AC provides an independent second opinion on some of the competencies of the Credit Suisse competency model, which are crucial for the rating of potential, besides functional skills and motivation.

Where and How Do ACs Help Build a Talent for Talent?

ACs play at least two major roles in Credit Suisse's overall HCM system. They clarify organizational competencies and develop managerial skills in assessors.

AC DIMENSIONS AND COMPETENCY MODELS

The "old" AC dimensions and especially their use by line managers in their role as assessors in ACs helped Credit Suisse to get to grips with competencies as one cornerstone of modern strategy-aligned talent management. Competency models, as clusters of skills, knowledge, and motivation in order to reliably classify job-relevant behavior, can unify and integrate a company's talent management instruments like interview-guides, 360° feedback tools, performance evaluations and so on. Their deeper impact is in providing a language for talking about strategy-oriented and productive behavior and motivation of employees. Line managers speak the business and economic language very proficiently but when it comes to the "soft" but very important behavior they start to stutter or they use simplifying buzzwords. Observing and describing behavior, so that others understand what is meant is a skill, is not easy to learn and practice. It is not only the words and expressions but also working with a structure and a framework for classifying behavior. Modern competency models are not basically different from classical AC dimensions, but broad competencies sometimes can be made more concrete with behavioral dimensions. At least a central part of a competency model consists of well-known clusters of dimensions such as Leadership or Problem-solving. Other competencies describe in more detail the functional skills necessary for certain jobs, and are used for managing the skills-profile of employees, for example in IT.

In the following we refer more to the behavioral part of competency models. Introducing competency models into a company is quite an effort and requires change management and a substantial learning effort. It is not uncommon that such models are introduced via new technology, such as new Talent Management applications or specific selection/development instruments. But what matters more is the correct understanding and skillful use of this new language of competencies and dimensions by management and employees. ACs are an ideal training ground for line managers to learn this language, to use it skillfully when writing reports and when talking with their fellow assessors. Long before competency models were paramount in talent management, line managers with AC experience often mentioned that they use the language of AC dimensions in all sorts of professional (for example in performance evaluations) and even in informal descriptions of behavior.

This intense use of the competency language in and outside the AC itself helps to improve the understanding of the competency model. It becomes a living language that evolves in quality and precision. The AC specialists develop a fine understanding of what are the success factors of easy-to-use and well-structured competency models or dimensions. Aspects like "behavioral," "discriminating" and "comprehensive" become practical. Therefore AC specialists and experienced assessors are a valuable source of know-how when designing, introducing and maintaining a company-wide competency model.

The integration of AC-specific dimensions and competencies in Credit Suisse was not an easy one. Assessors were partly reluctant to change some of the terminology. The usual competency language is often more functional than behavioral and less effort is invested in discriminating sharply the various well-sounding competency labels and key-words. The collaboration of competency model experts and AC specialists was very fruitful in coming up with a usable and widely accepted Credit Suisse competency model, applicable overall as well as specifically for ACs by translating broad business concepts into human characteristics and observable behavior.

The advantages of integrating the language of AC-dimensions and competencies are:

- a more obvious link to the organization's strategy and mission, by providing a broader scope in the transition from management/leadership dimensions to a comprehensive set of defined skills, behaviors and values;
- the opening up of the AC-language to other evaluation- and development-instruments or target groups, and the opportunity for more line managers to practice this basic language when talking about human capital and explaining to their employees what they expect from them.

We are convinced that without the leveraging of a long experience, especially of line managers but also of AC-specialists, both of whom are familiar with the AC dimensions, the introduction and use of a modern competency model would have been far more difficult and less effective.

AC SPECIALISTS BECOME HCM EXPERTS

The in-house specialists for building up and running a professional AC became an invaluable source of psychological know-how, practical expertise and reputation for defining and evaluating human capital, as well as for designing/adapting new instruments and processes which are usable and accepted by line management.

Although it is not uncommon that trained psychologists run ACs, it is less probable that internal psychological experts are involved in building up a talent management solution. Having such psychologists in-house, who in addition have a close contact to management (in the form of assessors and recipients of AC-reports) is an invaluable talent that can be leveraged. Due to the role of ACs as an independent second opinion, the AC specialists always had a high professional reputation. They also understood the world and the needs of line managers when dealing with talent in depth, owing to the long hours and even days of collaboration in ACs. In Credit Suisse, the AC specialists invested quite some time and resources to involve the line manager assessors in designing exercises, in interpreting yearly analytics about ACs (AC Review Day) and in finding ways to improve the impact of ACs. Thus, the AC specialists evolved in some degree to overall specialists in talent management. Intense and very personal discussions in feedback sessions with candidates as well as line managers extended this specialty to questions of how and where best to invest in human capital. The contacts and active contributions of the AC specialists in international professional circles added a key benchmarking capability and provided innovative ideas.

Despite the fact that in the early days of ACs in Credit Suisse the AC team was rather independent, and became isolated from the operational HR community, they still easily managed to get a seat at the table when new HCM processes were designed and introduced. For some experienced AC specialists, a move to HCM specialist was a welcome career transition, where they leveraged for instance their close contacts with line managers and continued to be knowledgeable supporters of assessments (see Thornton and Birri in this volume, Chapter 21).

SKILLS OF ASSESSORS IN MANAGING HUMAN CAPITAL

The hundreds of line managers trained and deployed as observers in ACs are not only fluent in the language of competencies, they have also had the following "on-the-AC-job" learning experiences that improve their skills in managing human capital:

- Distinguishing clearly between performance in the current job and potential for a future job. This is something which normally line managers still struggle with, especially when they have to make this distinction for their own subordinates.
- Understanding and avoiding evaluation errors (for example halo-effect, interpret instead of observe).
- Collecting and integrating behavioral information from different sources in a disciplined way before making a judgment in terms of a competency rating.
- Giving constructive feedback to employees, concentrating on observable behavior, also outside the AC environment.
- Learning how to explain, defend, integrate and summarize behavioral data in management meetings, like the integration sessions in ACs. This skill is invaluable, for example, in HCP meetings as described above.
- Becoming rather humble and considerate with respect to evaluating the individual competencies and the potential of employees. Becoming less susceptible to any sort

of easy way out in evaluating human capital, for example, by fancy simple new tools or questionnaires.

All these acquired skills can also be leveraged when the AC assessors get involved (as line managers) in designing and implementing new HCM processes and practices. In Credit Suisse it was obvious that the AC experienced line managers not only positively influenced the quality of HCM decisions but often were the main drivers for new and better ways to systematically evaluate, manage and develop human capital. The experience as an assessor is an investment in the human capital of these assessors and the return on investment manifests in improved people leadership behavior and as a talent for designing and implementing effective organization-wide HCM practices, for example, sustainable assessments (see Thornton and Birri in this volume, Chapter 21).

INCREASING THE BOTTOM-UP PRESSURE FOR HCM

Getting the support and the involvement of the CEO in building up a profound and integrated HCM practice is often mentioned as a success factor for HCM, and we agree with this view. Furthermore, we would like to add that ultimately it is the senior management who will make or break the optimal use of human capital. Phasing in an HCM practice from top to bottom is not a bad idea, but it takes some time and there is some danger that the quality of the process declines as you go down through the levels. In organizations like Credit Suisse, where there is an AC history with most senior managers (at least from a substantial part of the company) having gone through an AC as candidates and some of them later becoming assessors, you build up a "pull-capacity" for HCM, that makes its implementation faster, profounder and more effective. In units where there has been systematic use of ACs, there has been almost 100 percent adoption of HCP within its first 2 years of introduction, which has meant that all employees got potential ratings and were subject to discussions and decisions in HCP meetings.

The Benefits of Integrating ACs into HCM

Integrating ACs into a thorough HCM strategy and practice within Credit Suisse has had many payoffs.

BETTER UNDERSTANDING OF THE EFFECTS OF AC ATTENDANCE ON ENGAGEMENT

One advantage of systematic HCM processes lies in the availability of more and standardized data on individual employees. For instance, in Credit Suisse there are data from several years on employees' estimated potential, their performance, their learning/ training history before and after they attend an AC, and their engagement. This opens some interesting opportunities for analyzing the candidates' paths before and after an AC in order to improve pre-selection as well as the use of an AC for making career decisions. For example, the data of the yearly engagement survey can be used to study the mid to long-term influence of the AC result on engagement.

Candidates' reactions to selection methods have been reported in various research papers (for example, Anderson and Goltsi 2006). Discouragement or even quitting the job ("loser syndrome") after a negative result is often used as an argument against the use of ACs. Engagement data, which was collected yearly (2005–2009), independently of the AC attendance, provides a new way of analyzing the relationship between AC results and job-related motivational attitudes before and in the years after the AC took place. Several studies have shown a link between engagement and productivity (for example, Harter, Schmidt, and Hayes 2002) and this approach indirectly sheds light on the utility value of ACs. Figure 12.2 shows some results from such a study in Credit Suisse.

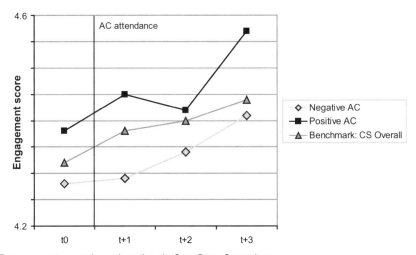

Y-axis: Engagement score based on the six Say-Stay-Serve items
X-axis: t0=6 months before AC, t+1=6 months after AC, t+2=12 months after AC, t+3=18 months after AC
AC-result: positive=majority of strengths, negative=majority of weaknesses
N (AC-G and AC-I): t0=1156, t+1=911, t+2=615, t+3=388. E.g. a t0-AC can be in 2004 or up to 2008, in the latter case with only one t+1 engagement result.

Figure 12.2 Engagement and AC result

Figure 12.2 tells us that in Credit Suisse there is no indication of discouragement or negative psychological effect after a negative AC result. Although none of the differences are statistically significant, there is some indication that candidates with a negative AC result tend to have a lower engagement beforehand (see also Anderson and Goltsi 2006).

Such results are easier to communicate to management and HR than scientific psychological studies on such effects because managers already understand what is meant by engagement and the effect is benchmarked against a Credit Suisse overall engagement score. What is important here are not only the concrete numbers (reported here without going into details), but also the practical and readily available analysis of the effects of ACs, due to the ACs being integrated into a systematic HCM strategy.

NEW WAYS OF LOOKING AT THE RETURN ON INVESTMENT IN ACs

A systematic, standardized and integrated HCM practice (as described above) promises several advantages to the business. Through streamlined processes, it will be more efficient overall. Its HR practices will be more effective; for example, performance ratings can be used directly in compensation and promotion decisions. It will also generate systematic data about the investments in human capital per organizational unit, which will open new important ways for evaluating the impact of these investments on employee engagement, customer satisfaction and especially on business performance. Quantifying the return on investment in terms of business performance per HCM practice and comparing the practices along with their return will contribute greatly to better investment decisions by the managers of organizational units. ACs are one of these practices and investments. What is their return on investment? How does it compare to other investments? How and where will a return on investment show up? These are important questions which so far have hardly been answered by traditional validation studies. The answers will not replace but rather supplement studies of prognostic validity.

HC ANALYTICS AND DASHBOARD

In recent years, a small HC analytics team has been set up in Credit Suisse. Its first priorities were to look in more detail at the relationship between employee engagement and business performance. It also tried to define and collect the necessary data in order to calculate and benchmark a set of informative and relevant HCM indicators, such as the Talent Rate, which is the percentage of employees in an organizational unit with a high performance and potential rating.

The strong link between employee engagement and bottom line business performance (Hewitt 2004; Towers-Perrin 2003) could be replicated in Credit Suisse across 58 private banking units totaling over 5,300 employees. The correlation was around $r = .55$ indicating that about one-third of the business achievement of these units is directly related to engagement.

Stimulated by such results, the HC analytics team moved on to design and test a statistically more powerful and more comprehensive framework of a causal-chain between HCM-indicators, engagement and business achievements (Winkler 2009). Such a framework should feed a HC dashboard for managers of organizational units on an annual basis, giving them proven and easy to understand indications on where they stand in comparison to their peers, and on where and how to invest. This framework and its dashboard have been used so far within private banking for some years. Longitudinal statistical analysis provides strong support for a causal link between engagement and business performance, and not vice versa. Table 12.3 gives an exemplary overview on the impact of defined HCM indicators that was found in one area of private banking in 2008. Some of the HCM indicators are "hard" numbers (for example, Talent Rate) and some are measured through perceptions in the employee survey. There are a number of indicators which had no measurable impact on engagement or business performance metrics (for example, use of 360° feedback) or showed almost no variance across the sub-units (for example, completion rate of Performance Reviews) and are therefore not included in the table. The findings with respect to AC results and number of ACs as indicators are mixed.

Based on path-analysis (an advanced method of multiple-hierarchical regression analysis) "what if" scenarios can be modeled. Such scenarios give line managers a hint on what would change in their unit's employee engagement and business achievement if they could manage to increase one or several HCM indicators. Results of such analysis are shown in Table 12.3. Put in words, the figures mean for example that an increase of 10 percent in the percentage of managers with a positive AC result in a business unit would increase the business achievement of this unit by 5 percent but leave its employee engagement unchanged. The indicator which measures AC attendance ("Number of AC reports" on whatever level (AC-G/AC-I as well as AC-G-S/AC-I-S) and independent of the assessment result) has an even stronger impact on business achievement (11 percent). What could this imply? It seems that achieving a positive result in the AC is important but attending the AC with its learning or developmental impact on employees is even more valuable. Knowing one's strengths and weaknesses, working on them and finding the appropriate job-position in an organization seems to have an even greater return on investment. The most powerful lever for business achievement seems to be the percentage of employees with both a high performance and a high potential rating ("Talent Rate") and the employees' perception on how well they collaborate ("Perception of Collaboration"). The magnitude of the two AC based indicators ("Number of AC reports" and "Managers with positive AC-result") seems to be moderate, but in comparison to other indicators like the percentage of managers with a high performance rating ("Top performing managers") or the percentage of employees having participated in specific functional trainings ("Employees participating in a job-specific Training"), they are still substantial. Especially if one keeps in mind that an AC is a one time investment, and its return continues for many years to come.

Table 12.3   The impact of a 10 percent increase in HCM indicators on engagement and business achievement

Subject	HCM indicator	Impact on	
		Engagement	Business achievement
Management quality	Top performing managers	1 percent	2 percent
	Number of AC reports	4 percent	11 percent
	Managers with positive AC-G/AC-I result	0 percent	5 percent
Perception of leadership	Perception of direct manager	10 percent	3 percent
	Perception of recognition	8 percent	12 percent
	Perception of collaboration	18 percent	22 percent
Talent management	Talent rate (high performance and potential)	10 percent	23 percent
	Perception of career opportunities	17 percent	14 percent
	Perception of learning and development	9 percent	3 percent
Functional training	Employees participating in a job-specific training	0 percent	6 percent

Relationship between HCM Indicator and Impact: An estimated 10 percent increase/decrease in the respective HCM indicator would increase/decrease Engagement or Business Achievement by the indicated percentage.

AC and Business Results

Further AC-centric analytics, not primarily for the dashboard purpose but for a better scientific insight into the impact of ACs, underpin the value of AC approved line managers for business performance.

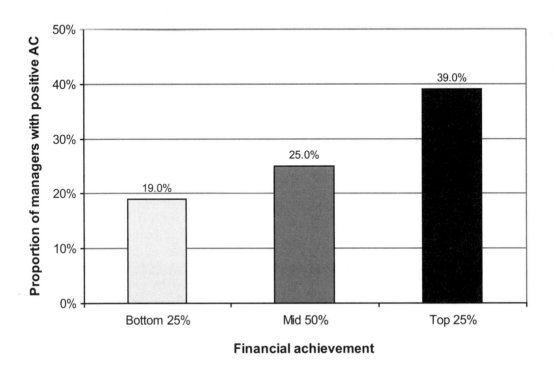

Figure 12.3 AC approved management and financial achievement

Figure 12.3 shows that business units with a higher proportion of managers with a positive assessment result (AC-G or AC-I) deliver significantly better financial results. This evaluation is based on a correlation analysis with data from 34 market areas in private banking with around 700 employees, and 127 managers.

What in this context is especially important and promising is the fact of being able to evaluate, quantify, and compare the return on investment in ACs in business terms which are understood and used by line managers for their decisions on human capital. Such analytics only become possible and relevant when ACs are clearly positioned and used as one well-defined practice along with others in an overall integrated HCM practice (see also Thornton and Birri in this volume, Chapter 21). Of course, some data collection and number crunching effort is required. But compared to the value added by fact-based discussions about AC impact, this effort is likely to pay off.

IMPROVED POSITIONING AND USE OF ACs

Credit Suisse has been using ACs extensively for evaluating the potential for a next higher position, either managerial or functional. Nonetheless the notion of "potential" has not been defined in clear terms before the implementation of HCP. Potential was rather instrumentally defined as successfully passing an AC. This led to repeated discussions and problems, because this definition of potential was related too much to believing in ACs or not. Line managers had to delegate the responsibility for a significant investment decision in human capital to a mere instrument, namely the AC.

A new clear definition of potential was a main part of designing the HCP process. Based on the sparse literature on what constitutes potential and on looking at other companies, we came up with a pragmatic definition, which was well accepted by line management and has not been challenged since then. Potential is defined as: "Current estimated potential to assume more responsibility within the next two years." Potential is rated on a four-point scale, where 1 = Employee is overly stretched in current job to 4 = has potential to be successful on the next higher level. The components which are relevant for an estimation of potential are the motivation to assume more responsibility, willingness to learn and competencies (functional, interpersonal, and intellectual).

The AC is now a way to provide an independent and detailed second opinion on interpersonal and intellectual competencies, necessary for a senior management or specialist level. It also gives some indication on motivation and willingness to learn. But these and the functional competencies have to be judged primarily by the direct manager and his peers in the HCP meeting. ACs on higher or lower levels (as they are sometimes used for special purposes) would contribute in the same way to the judgment of potential on these levels.

One might argue that this definition of potential could and should have been established and used earlier, for example when starting with ACs. In Credit Suisse the development of an integrated HCM practice was the driver for a pragmatic definition of potential, which is something we have also observed in other companies. Anyway, HCM has provided a framework within which to better position ACs. Line managers can now more flexibly and more accurately decide on, if and how to use ACs. The AC, on the other hand, can now focus its contribution on evaluating those competencies, which are mainly behavioral and assessable in AC exercises. This in return makes an AC report easier for line managers to interpret in the context of business decisions.

Summary and Conclusions

The history of ACs in Credit Suisse tells us that the journey from a high quality but rather isolated instrument for auditing leadership to one of several instruments in an integrated management of a company's overall human capital is attainable, and offers many positive benefits to both management and AC specialists.

The in-depth and practical use of behavioral statements in AC dimensions by line managers in their role as assessors facilitates the implementation of competency models as one cornerstone of a modern, strategically aligned talent management program. In-house AC specialists, who in addition to their methodological skills, have close contact with management as assessors and recipients of AC reports, acquire invaluable talent that can be leveraged when designing and implementing HCM instruments and processes. Training and deploying executive line managers as assessors is an investment in the human capital of these assessors. The return on investment is manifested in improved people leadership behavior, as well as in a talent for pushing, implementing, and executing effective organization wide HCM practices.

At the same time, ACs can benefit from being clearly positioned in an overall HCM process. For instance, a systematic HCM process provides standardized periodic data on individual employees, which can be used to analyze in detail the effects of an AC on an employee's engagement and career path. This information can help optimize the design and use of ACs. Quantifying the return on investment for a HCM practice in terms of business performance, and then comparing practices in terms of their return is one of the outcomes of systematic HCM. Thus, promising new types of business centric validation data help to more clearly evaluate the return on investment in ACs as one such HCM practice. The clear and pragmatic definition of potential in addition to performance, engagement, and other metrics is a basic part of consistent HCM. Such a definition of potential, which is also being used in other HCM practices such as succession plans, clarifies the position and purpose of ACs.

Overall we are convinced that companies with a prominent AC culture like the one described in this chapter, with business managers as assessors, are better equipped on their journey to mature business centric HCM. An AC culture provides a crucial talent for talent which should and can be leveraged, while in return a systematic HCM creates opportunities for an even more professional design and use of ACs. AC professionals may be stimulated by promising opportunities when ACs are integrated into overall HCM. AC professionals may therefore be skilled drivers on the way to an integrated HCM in their organization.

References

Anderson, N. and Goltsi, V. 2006. Negative psychological effects of selection methods: Construct formulation and an empirical investigation into an assessment center. *International Journal of Selection and Assessment*, 14, 236–247.

Harter J.K., Schmidt F.L. and Hayes T.L. 2002. A business-unit-level relationship of employee satisfaction, employee engagement, and business outcomes: A meta-analysis. *Journal of Applied Psychology*, 87, 268–279.

Hewitt. 2004. *Employee Engagement at Double-digit Growth Companies*. Hewitt Research Brief.

Ringo T., DeMarco M. and Lesser E. 2008. *Integrated Talent Management*. IBM Institute for Business Value Study.

Towers-Perrin. 2003. *Understanding What Drives Employee Engagement*. Towers Perrin Talent Report.

Winkler, S. 2009. *Human Capital Analytics. An Investigation of Success Factors, Methods, and Basic Assumptions*. Ph.D. Thesis, Zürich: University of Zürich, Applied Pschology.

13 The Challenges Associated with a Large AC in Government: A South African Case Study

ANNE BUCKETT

With the introduction of democracy in South Africa in the early 1990s, the organizational landscape required a dramatic shift, both in the private and public sectors. One of the key influencing factors that would facilitate a smooth transition to democracy relied on the ability to empower, promote and enhance the skills, competencies, and capabilities of previously disadvantaged groups so that they could fully participate in, and contribute to, a growing South Africa (Department of Trade and Industry 2006; South Africa Government Information 1998; South Africa Information 2009).

In particular, the South African government, relying heavily on the public service for support, had the challenge of not only rapidly ensuring representation of designated groups across all levels within government but also the very real task of delivering on ambitious and important strategic government objectives (South Africa Government Information 1997; South Africa Government Information 1998).

This chapter describes the practical application of the assessment centre (AC) within a government department with the aim of identifying skills gaps of managerial staff to facilitate learning and development aligned to department and government objectives. Due to the sensitive and confidential nature of the project the client organization unfortunately cannot be named or its identity revealed in this chapter.

The objectives of the project were to firstly, determine the development needs of managerial staff; secondly, to provide personal development feedback for each participating staff member; and thirdly, to contribute to the compilation of a workplace skills plan for the organization through the provision of final skills assessment reports.

Key Organizational and Design Challenges

The client organization listed certain criteria that needed to be adhered to in the delivery of the project. These included utilizing a diverse and representative pool of expert assessors, customized versus off-the-shelf exercises, and exclusion of any psychometrics (for example ability tests, personality questionnaires) in the process. The white paper on affirmative action (South Africa Government Information 1998: 16) stated that public service must 'seek to abolish or amend rules and regulations which unnecessarily restrict affirmative action activities and initiatives.' Due to past socio-economic injustices, sub-standard and limited access to proper education, and a policy of job reservation, psychometrics and similar assessments were historically considered elitist and were viewed as one of the many barriers to entry into the workplace (Department of Trade and Industry 2006). With the promulgation of the Employment Equity Act (No. 55 of 1998) the scepticism associated with psychometrics was specifically addressed and subsequently regulated (Department of Labour 1998). Additional information about the history of South Africa and applications for ACs there can be found in Chapter 6 by Meiring and Chapter 23 by Krause, this volume.

Other challenges included the requirements to customize a range of simulations across senior management, middle management, and supervisory levels; to select and train a large pool of diverse, representative and highly skilled expert assessors; to be delivered within tight timeframes and specific budget parameters; and to be administered efficiently and easily to large groups of participants based in various cities and towns across South Africa.

To ensure that the project requirements were met, a project management approach was adopted. The guiding principles included working jointly with the client to ensure success through consultation and feedback. The project was managed with regular steering-committee meetings to track and monitor progress and to address issues and concerns in a timely manner. Another guiding principle included a skills transfer component whereby designated internal staff would benefit from learning and developing skills by actively participating in the project either by facilitating job profiling sessions, assisting with test administration, or acting as a role player during the AC.

The AC designers had approximately 18 months to design a full range of simulations across managerial levels. The design process included trialling, refining, reviewing, piloting, and stakeholder sign-off prior to the official launch of the skills audit project.

Assessment Centre Methodology

Due to the tight project constraints listed above, an AC approach was adopted whereby a set number of competencies were measured across a range of simulation exercises by multiple assessors. Although job analyses were conducted for each job in the organization as part of a previous business process reengineering (BPR) project, this information was not used to inform the final competency model for each managerial level. The reason for this is that the South African government had an established competency framework for senior management and middle management and this was used exclusively for recruitment, selection, development, promotion and performance appraisal. Although the client organization had the leeway to conduct their own AC they still needed to do this within the existing competency framework. The supervisor competency model was not formalized in the same manner and therefore the core design team made an intuitive deduction of the competency model for this level.

COMPETENCIES

Although job profiling took place across the entire organization this information was used to inform the BPR project rather than the AC design. As one would expect, this in itself posed a major challenge to the design team. The key challenge was in the scoring of the behavioural indicators and this will be discussed in more detail later on in the chapter.

The senior management competency model consisted of 11 competencies. The AC for senior management was based on nine of the most relevant competencies. The competencies measured in the AC were Strategic Capability and Leadership, Programme and Project Management, Financial Management (a highly technical competency included upon request from the client), Change Management, Service Delivery Innovation, Problem-solving and Analysis, People Management and Empowerment, Customer Orientation and Customer Focus, and Communication. Two competencies were excluded from the list as being too difficult to measure in the AC: Knowledge Management which was defined as knowledge of internal systems and processes, and Honesty and Integrity which we felt would not necessarily be fairly observed across such diverse groups and cultures in the organization.

Fifteen competencies were defined as part of the established competency model for middle managers and the AC included nine of these competencies for assessment purposes: Applied Strategic Thinking, Problem-solving and Decision-making, Developing Others, Impact and Influence, Customer Focus and Responsiveness, Managing Interpersonal Conflict and Resolving Problems, Networking and Building Bonds, Planning and Organizing, and Team Leadership.

Competencies that were defined as functional in nature, rather than behavioural, were excluded from the AC: Applying Technology, Budgeting and Financial Management, Communication and Information Management, Continuous Improvement, Diversity Management, and Project Management. Upon inspection, these competencies were either too technical or too difficult to measure in a behaviourally based AC.

Anecdotal information provided by the organization indicated that a large gap in competence existed between middle management and supervisors. This information was considered when compiling the competencies for the supervisor AC. The AC for supervisors included eight competencies and was linked in a meaningful way to the middle management level: Team Management, Customer Service Orientation, Communication, Interpersonal Interaction, Change Orientation, Self Management, Planning and Organizing, and Problem Analysis and Decision-making.

DESIGN OF CUSTOMIZED SIMULATION EXERCISES

The process used to arrive at a robust, customized range of simulations was lengthy and extensive. To build up a database of relevant samples, the chief AC designer spent six months gathering information about the organization, its environment and the most pressing issues faced by the various managerial levels within the organization. This included spending actual time in the organization, having discussions with stakeholders about key organizational issues and challenges, making an extensive investigation of the client organization website to become familiar with the various directorates and their responsibilities and following reports in the media. Once the database was compiled the chief AC designer was able to categorize job-relevant samples in terms of the skills required, the level of management and relevance to the context and competencies being measured. At the end of the 6-month period the chief AC designer had completed a range of simulations for senior management, middle management and supervisors.

Senior management exercises

The customized AC exercises focused on the creation of a new division in the client organization. The fictitious division was created as an extension to the existing organizational structure of the client organization. The division had representation in four provinces: Gauteng, Eastern Cape, Western Cape and KwaZulu Natal. The duration of the senior management assessment centre was one day. The first draft of simulations for senior management consisted of a strategic report, presentation, structured interview, group exercise, and the financial management technical test.

Middle management exercises

The middle management level was divided into two groups. The first group consisted of staff who directly managed people and the second group consisted of professionals and specialists who did not manage people. The same fictitious division created for senior managers was used in this AC and exercises were pitched at the appropriate level for middle managers. The duration of the AC was half a day. The AC consisted of an in-basket, role play, and a structured interview for the managerial group, and a case study, role play, and structured interview for the professional group.

Supervisor exercises

Following the same theme and process listed above, the supervisory level AC consisted of an in-basket, role play, and structured interview for the purely supervisory group, and a project exercise, role play, and structured interview for the purely professional group. The same fictitious organizational scenario provided for senior and middle managers was presented to participants at the supervisory level, but the exercises were reflective of the nature and complexity of this level. The duration of the AC was half a day.

FEEDBACK ON THE AC EXERCISES

After a six-month design period, the AC exercises were available for critical review and comment. The first round of assessor training was scheduled. The aim of the training was to critically review the AC exercises and ensure that the assessors were properly trained in the observation and scoring of the exercises. At the first round of assessor training the biggest problems to emerge pertained to the prescribed competency model and associated behavioural indicators. If you recall our earlier discussion, the client organization had to use the approved government competency model for any type of staff measurement, including recruitment, selection, or development. However, when it came to scoring the first version of the simulation exercises, it was found that the behavioural indicators were difficult to observe physically and, hence, to interpret practically and reliably.

In addition, the initial rating scale was not optimal. It consisted of a five-point Likert scale with positive and negative behavioural indicators based on the existing competency model. Assessors also provided detailed feedback on the content of the exercises in relation to the ease of observation and evaluation. After the completion of the training course, the chief AC designer appointed a core design team to assist with the next phase in the design process. This would include making changes to the simulation exercises arising from assessor feedback and focusing on creating a workable rating scale with refined behavioural indicators. Also, a fresh set of eyes was needed to ensure continued objectivity and fairness.

Identification and Application of Design Fixes

The first round of assessor training provided the core AC design team with additional useful information in order to further refine and enhance the quality of the assessment battery. Based on this input, plus a review of existing literature and research in the AC domain, the core design team identified five design fixes to apply in the next phase of the AC design process.

REDUCED NUMBER OF DIMENSIONS

Lance (2008) and Lievens and Conway (2001) suggested that reducing the number of dimensions measured in an AC leads to positive effects on the quality of assessor ratings. Indeed, work by Gaugler and Thornton (1989) confirmed that assessor's cognitive load was reduced with fewer dimensions. To this end, the core AC design team ensured that each simulation exercise measured no more than five competencies.

STRUCTURED SCORING SCALES

To ease the scoring process for assessors, especially in view of the fact that assessors were observing groups of up to 16 participants per day, highly structured rating scales were developed. Reilly, Henry and Smither (1990), Harris, Becker and Smith (1993), Hennessy, Mabey and Warr (1998), and Robie, Obsurn, Morris, Etchegaray and Adams (2000) reported positive results when using some form of structured rating scale or behavioural checklist. The core design team therefore combined elements of checklists, clearly defined behavioural indicators, and a number of 'on target' examples in the next version of the AC exercises.

TYPE OF ASSESSOR

As the project was developmental in nature and pertained to all levels of management in the client organization, expert assessors were used. Research supported the fact that expert assessors were able to yield accurate judgements of participant behaviour (Lance 2008; Damitz, Manzey, Kleinmann and Severin 2003; Melchers and König 2008; Jones and Klimoski 2008; Kolk, Born, Van Der Flier and Olman 2002). However, the big challenge was to manage the diverse types of expert assessors in the pool: Industrial, Clinical,

Counselling, Research and Educational Psychologists. To meet this challenge, a strict set of criteria was employed when allocating assessors to various management levels.

Assessors were divided into one of three categories based on their professional registration and years of AC experience. The categories are briefly described below:

- Category 1: Registration as an industrial psychologist with in-depth experience and specialization in ACs. This category of assessors would therefore be allocated to senior management, middle management, and supervisor assessments and they were given first priority for scheduling and used extensively.
- Category 2: Registration in another category of psychology with proven and extensive commensurate corporate experience in ACs. This category of assessors would be allocated to middle management and supervisor assessments and they were used to complement the schedule.
- Category 3: Registration in another category of psychology with little or no experience in corporate ACs, and subject to compulsory training in the assessment tools of the project and supervision by the AC team leader fulfilling the role of supervising psychologist. This category of assessors would be allocated to supervisor assessments and were used as additional, supporting resources.

The guidelines for determining selection criteria were based on the conditions stipulated as part of the skills audit tender process and subsequent contract. Issues of risk to the client and individual assessor, ethics, and fiduciary and legal requirements were considered in the utilization of all assessors. Therefore, practice guidelines of the Health Professions Council of South Africa (HPCSA) regarding ethics associated with working out of scope of practice were referenced (HPCSA 2008). The HPCSA is the governing body for all healthcare and medical practitioners in South Africa, including psychologists.

As an additional check and balance, the first round of submitted reports for each assessor were thoroughly scrutinized and quality assured by the AC team leader. Detailed telephonic and written feedback was provided to each assessor and the AC team leader monitored the performance and quality of assessors work carefully throughout the project. Thereafter, a quality review was done on approximately 10 per cent of the remaining reports for quality purposes.

MAKING COMPETENCIES APPARENT TO PARTICIPANTS

There are mixed views among researchers about making competencies apparent to participants. Kleinmann, Kuptsch and Köller (1996) and Sackett and Tuzinski (2001) stated that participants will better meet the behavioural requirements of the exercises if they know what they were being measured against. However, Lievens (1998) and Thornton and Gibbons (2009) cautioned that participants could fake behaviours rather than genuinely display natural behaviour if they are aware of the competencies beforehand. As the project was developmental in nature, the core AC design team wanted to afford each participant the best opportunity to display the required behaviours in the AC. Therefore, at the end of the instructions for each simulation exercise the competencies being measured were clearly listed.

FRAME-OF-REFERENCE TRAINING

It is a well accepted best practice principle that assessor training is included as part of the AC process (International Task Force on Assessment Center Guidelines 2009; Assessment Centre Study Group 2007). Frame-of-reference (FOR) training has been widely reported in the performance appraisal domain (Day and Sulsky 1995; Woehr 1994; Schleicher and Day 1998). Schleicher, Day, Mayes and Riggio (2002) studied the effect of FOR training on AC ratings and found that this technique improved reliability and accuracy of overall ratings. Lievens (1998) reviewed 21 studies which applied design fixes to the AC in an effort to improve construct validity. The findings confirmed that assessor training, in conjunction with other applied design fixes, increased the probability of better construct measurement. In this context, the quality of assessor training, rather than the length of assessor training leads to increased validity gains.

Two rounds of assessor training took place for the project. The first round of assessor training was conducted primarily to test the strength of the first draft of AC exercises and lasted for four days. A group of 25 psychologists attended the training. The pool of assessors consisted of Industrial, Clinical, Counselling, Research and Educational Psychologists with various levels of exposure to and experience in ACs. Prior to the training each assessor received pre-course work in the form of the draft simulation exercises. They were required to complete the written exercises as if they were actual participants and familiarize themselves with the remaining exercises.

Assessor training included classic behavioural training (for example, the principles of observing, recording, classifying and evaluating), FOR training to contextualize the project and align schemata, and information about the organization, the purpose of the AC, and explanation of the competencies. There was a large practical component.

At the end of the training each assessor had completed every role play as a participant, assessor and role player. The written exercises were scored individually and then later in the group in order to ensure alignment to and understanding of the rating scale. The assessors had to produce an integrated participant report after the course which was scored by the AC team leader.

The second round of training took place one year later after extensive refinement of the AC exercises, the competencies, and specifically the behavioural indicators. This training essentially consisted of the same components as the first round of assessor training but was condensed into two days. The focus was specifically on aligning the assessors' schemata in terms of the behavioural requirements of the exercises. Again, the training was based almost exclusively on practical work to ensure consistency across the different assessors and to ensure a clear understanding of the competency requirements.

Other Design Features

Due to the large volumes of participants assessed over an extended and fairly tight timeframe, it was necessary to incorporate additional features to enhance and standardize the process.

AUTOMATED REPORTING

The report was converted into a software template. The software was coded by an IT developer and the content for the template was provided by the chief AC designer. The template consisted of four sections. Section 1 consisted of a contextual, narrative, integrated paragraph for each simulation exercise and provided a 'personal touch' to the report. Section 2 consisted of the assessment matrix. Section 3 captured the scores obtained for each behavioural indicator measured across the different competencies and exercises in the structured rating forms. This information was included so that participants were able to pinpoint development needs on a practical (behavioural) level. Section 4 was an automatically generated list of possible development courses based on the information captured in section 2. This was pre-populated in the software template.

MODEL ANSWERS

To increase assessor accuracy, a set of 'on target' model answers was created for the in-basket, case study and project exercises across the different managerial levels. In some of the role-play exercises a checklist of minimum behaviour required was listed on the first page of the assessor report form to minimize some of the assessors' cognitive load.

AC Implementation

Once the design of the AC exercises was completed, the final battery was presented to the project steering committee for approval and sign off. Thereafter three pilot sessions were conducted on a cross-section of senior managers, middle managers and supervisors. The pilot sessions aimed to bring to light any further issues pertaining to exercise relevance, instructions and timing before the scheduled implementation date. After each pilot session the group was debriefed by an assessor and issues were noted. After all the pilot sessions were completed the participating assessors went through the group feedback and discussed the impact on the exercises with the chief AC designer. Admittedly, by this stage, changes were minor.

A 6-month timeline was proposed to assess roughly 1,700 participants. The AC started with senior managers. In total, 72 senior managers were assessed at key locations around South Africa. The senior manager AC was one day in length and five participants were assessed. Five assessors were involved in each AC, employing a ratio of one assessor for each participant. Each assessor observed one participant and assessed all competencies within a specific exercise, thereby following the within-exercise rating method. Assessors had a debriefing session after the group exercise and a final debriefing and calibration session took place at the end of the AC.

A total of 705 middle managers (576 managers and 129 professionals) were assessed. Groups of 16 to 20 participants were assessed in one day and ACs were scheduled for each day of the working week. Each middle management AC was half a day in duration; therefore eight to ten participants were assessed in both the morning and afternoon. A ratio of one assessor to two participants was employed. Therefore each assessor was responsible for collating and integrating two sets of AC results from the morning session and two sets of AC results from the afternoon session. Due to the volumes of participants assessed, formal debriefing and calibration sessions were not scheduled. However, the largest majority of the work required assessors to stay over in nearby accommodation and informal debriefing occurred naturally in the evenings. Furthermore, strange results and anomalies in participant data were escalated to the AC team leader and all issues were resolved prior to the report being completed on the software template.

The same approach was employed for the supervisors. Each supervisor AC was half a day in length and a total of 908 supervisors (368 managers and 540 professionals) were assessed. In general, assessors were scheduled for two weeks at a time. In the first week assessors participated in the AC and during the second week they completed the reports. Deadlines were strictly enforced and managed. At the end of the entire process all the reports were automatically generated from the software programme. Feedback sessions were scheduled for one hour with each participant as part of a development discussion.

Results

Descriptive statistics for the final competency scores are presented in Tables 13.1, 13.2 and 13.3. The final overall competency scores were obtained by first, multiplying the assessor's rating times a weight given for that competency in that exercise; second, adding up the weighted competency ratings in each of the relevant exercises; and then finally dividing the total score by the number of applicable exercises. The final scores are interpreted on a four-point scale. Descriptive statistics were calculated to provide the organization with group trends and to highlight development areas. For this project the top two to three development areas were highlighted across the various managerial levels. The means across all five categories range from 1.67 to 2.78 with an average of 2.12 (overall average). Performance on the competencies tended towards the mean for most of the competencies, although moderate variability across the competencies with the four-point scale was obtained.

Table 13.1 Senior manager overall competency scores

	Senior managers (N=72)	
	Mean	Standard deviation
Change Management	2.11	0.742
Client Orientation and Customer Focus	2.69	0.547
Communication	2.64	0.589
Financial Management	2.00	0.671
People Management and Empowerment	2.04	0.721
Problem-Solving and Analysis	2.08	0.622
Programme and Project Management	2.31	0.620
Service Delivery Innovation	1.93	0.718
Strategic Capability and Leadership	2.29	0.615

The strongest competencies in the senior manager group were Client Orientation and Customer Focus and Communication. Service Delivery Innovation, Financial Management and People Management and Empowerment were identified as the three competencies requiring the most development for senior managers. In particular, the competency of Financial Management emerging as a development need was confirmed by national audit findings (Auditor-General of South Africa 2011).

Table 13.2   Managerial and professional overall competency scores

	Managerial (N = 576)		Professional (N = 129)	
	Mean	Standard deviation	Mean	Standard deviation
Managing Interpersonal Conflict and Resolving Problems	2.10	0.565	2.67	0.574
Customer Focus and Responsiveness	2.66	0.661	1.82	0.601
Developing Others	2.60	0.674	2.11	0.787
Impact and Influence	2.38	0.672	2.24	0.642
Networking and Building Bonds	2.57	0.691	2.59	0.7
Planning and Organizing	1.87	0.599	2.05	0.561
Problem-Solving and Decision-Making	1.98	0.592	2.19	0.648
Applied Strategic Thinking	1.74	0.578	2.11	0.64
Team Leadership	1.72	0.597	2.18	0.802

The strongest competencies for the middle management (managerial) group were Customer Focus and Responsiveness, Developing Others and Networking and Building Bonds. The top two competencies for the middle management (professional) group were Managing Interpersonal Conflict and Resolving Problems and Networking and Building Bonds. The three competencies requiring the most development in the former group were Team Leadership, Applied Strategic Thinking and Planning and Organizing. The competencies requiring the most development in the latter group were Customer Focus and Responsiveness, Planning and Organizing, Developing Others and Applied Strategic Thinking. Planning and Organizing and Applied Strategic Thinking emerged as the main competencies requiring development for the combined middle management group.

Table 13.3 Supervisors and professional overall competency scores

	Supervisors (N = 368)		Professional (N = 540)	
	Mean	Standard deviation	Mean	Standard deviation
Change Orientation	1.95	0.709	1.79	0.702
Communication	2.26	0.637	2.09	0.566
Customer Service Orientation	1.81	0.711	2.01	0.661
Interpersonal Interaction	1.94	0.622	1.83	0.609
Planning and Organizing	1.58	0.662	1.77	0.740
Problem Analysis and Decision-Making	1.67	0.606	1.83	0.611
Self Management	2.78	0.594	2.72	0.624
Team Management	1.77	0.568	1.89	0.682

The strongest competency for both the supervisors and professionals in the supervisor group was Self-Management. Planning and Organizing and Problem Analysis and Decision-Making emerged as key development areas for the combined supervisor and professional groups at this level. The supervisor group as a whole indicated a greater need for development overall and this was supported by anecdotal evidence provided by the organization suggesting a greater gap in competence between supervisor and middle management levels.

Upon completion of the project we wanted to determine whether our design fixes had enhanced the overall construct validity of the AC. As a first step, inter-correlations between the scores on the various competencies as measured by the various exercises were calculated using the combined results for the three managerial groups. Non-parametric correlations, specifically Spearman's Rho, were used. Correlations between scores on the same trait measured by different methods ranged from 0.092 to 0.922 with an average of 0.261. Correlations between scores on different traits measured by the same method ranged from 0.011 to 0.702 with an average of 0.436. Correlations between scores on different traits measured by different methods ranged from –0.030 to 0.922 with an average of 0.214.

If the AC exercises did measure discrete competencies then one would expect a higher correlation coefficient for the same trait measured across different methods than for different traits measured in the same method; that pattern is not present with our results. In fact, the correlation coefficient obtained from the same trait assessed by different methods yielded only a marginally higher correlation coefficient than the correlation of different traits measured by different methods. This result confirms the dominance of an exercise effect over a competency effect. Little evidence was found for discriminant validity among the competencies or convergent validity for a given competency measured in different exercises. Therefore, despite the implemented design fixes, there was no significant improvement in the internal construct validity evidenced by the ratings from this AC.

A principal axis factor analysis, followed by a direct oblimin rotation with Kaiser normalization was performed on the ratings to group competencies together or to identify possible method variance, the results of which are given in Table 13.4 below.

Table 13.4 Rotated factor matrix of scores for senior managers

	Factor				
	1	**2**	**3**	**4**	**5**
Programme and Project Management Report	.835				
Service Delivery Innovation Report	.751				
Strategic Capability and Leadership Report	.738		.207		
Problem-solving and Analysis Report	.657				
Communication Report	.634				
Strategic Capability and Leadership Group		−.866			
Problem-solving and Analysis Group		−.866			
Communication Group		−.832			
People Management and Empowerment Group		−.794			
People Management and Empowerment Interview			.774		
Change Management Interview			.757		
Service Delivery Innovation Interview			.726		.210
Client Orientation and Customer Focus Interview			.657		
Financial Management Financial Exercise				.679	
Financial Management Presentation		−.241		.581	
Client Orientation and Customer Focus Presentation					−.668
Programme and Project Management Presentation				.204	−.532
Change Management Presentation					−.505

Five factors were obtained including a separate factor for the financial management competency. All the ratings from the strategic report loaded onto the first factor. The group exercise ratings loaded onto the second factor. The interview ratings loaded onto the third factor. Financial management presented as a separate cluster which included the ratings from the financial exercise and the presentation. With the exception of the financial management presentation exercise ratings, all the presentation ratings loaded onto the fifth factor. It is interesting to note that the competency of financial management emerged as a separate factor while this was not the case with any other competencies. One possible explanation is that the financial management competency was highly technical in nature. The subsequent design of exercises resulted in structured model answers (right and wrong) and the assessors had little room to exercise their own judgement for financial management.

The factor analyses for the middle managers and supervisors showed the same pattern. In these factor analyses three factors were obtained. Without exception, the factors corresponded with the exercises demonstrating a clear exercise effect.

Lessons Learned

Despite the strong presence of exercise effects, the author still felt that the application of design fixes led to an increase in the quality and accuracy of assessor scores. In a project of this magnitude every effort was made to structure the process in order to reduce the cognitive load for the assessors and to maintain a high standard of quality. Without the structure, I do not believe that we would have succeeded. If we had to do it again, would we change anything? Probably not; we would still ensure that the latest research on AC design was included in our process. The addition of running the AC according to project management principles also contributed to the project staying within its timeframes.

In summary, several lessons were learned from the project:

1. The AC method contributed to the national effort to utilize human resources in an accurate and fair way. The AC method provided a framework and process of assessing and developing human talent that may not have been possible to measure optimally in another way.

2. AC practitioners can make important contributions in high-level programmes. This project was implemented with the support and backing of well established consulting firms. Demonstrated skill in ACs and being visible in the industry allowed the author to make a contribution to this project. Going forward, AC practitioners need to continue to establish themselves as credible partners in the measurement and development of human talent. One way to do this would be to contribute to further research in the AC field, especially in South Africa, as this is currently an area lacking dedicated focus. The same may be true in other, developing countries with less developed talent management programmes.

3. In culturally diverse settings, assessors need to be trained to provide sensitive evaluations of different groups, and AC practitioners are well positioned to do so. This component was challenging for the duration of the project. It is suggested that future projects, specifically those taking place in culturally diverse environments need to build in diversity training as part of assessor training in order to enhance sensitivity to different groups of people. In addition, we need to create interest in and awareness of AC methodology. In South Africa, the author would suggest that experienced AC practitioners need to play a more active role in engaging potential future AC practitioners at entry levels, such as students.

4. Task-based assessment, rather than competency-based assessment, may be indicated with certain types of simulations in this type of AC. The fact that the simulations were highly customized to the client organization may have indicated task-based assessment rather than competency-based assessment. Further research into this area would be warranted in order to confirm this position and measure its effect on construct validity. Task-based ACs are discussed in Chapter 3.

5. More extensive assessor training may be needed to eliminate variable performance of assessors with different levels of skill, experience, and quality. Whilst every effort

was made to enhance the quality of the process and tools by creating structure, providing training and building in quality controls along the way, this area still remained a challenge. A practical lesson would be to run more intensive assessor-training prior to a project of this magnitude, perhaps even going so far as to get those with less experience working on other ACs more regularly under the supervision of an experienced assessor in the build up to larger scale AC projects. An example of extensive assessor training is described in Chapter 2.

6. The real effect of cognitive overload due to volume of candidates may be unavoidable. Despite the design fixes being applied, the fact remained that the assessors had to assess up to 100 participants in a very short period of time. The process accommodated for cognitive overload in terms of the tools and simulations used and the AC process, but not in terms of the number of participants assessed. Assessors were clearly fatigued by the end of the project, due to its magnitude. Naturally, this had a very real implication in terms of sustained and consistent quality of assessor performance. A practical lesson would be to employ more assessors for future projects of this size.

Conclusion

In conclusion, the AC method provided valuable information to target development areas of participants in an objective and measurable way. The efficient and effective way the process was managed contributed to the success of the project. Furthermore, the utilization of AC design fixes as recommended in literature was one of the important differentiators contributing to the success of the project. Key development areas were highlighted and the result was an integrated and focused effort by the organization to facilitate and promote staff growth and development.

References

Assessment Centre Study Group. 2007. Guidelines for assessment and development centres in South Africa. Author.

Auditor-General of South Africa. 2011. General report on the National Audit Outcomes for 2009–10 [RP01/2011] [Online: Auditor-General of South Africa]. Available at: http://www.agsa.co.za/Portals/1/Reports/2011 per cent20reports/PMFA per cent202009–10 per cent20national per cent20general per cent20report.pdf [accessed: 7 March 2011].

Damitz, M., Manzey, D., Kleinmann, M. and Severin, K. 2003. Assessment center for pilot selection: construct and criterion validity and the impact of assessor type. *Applied Psychology: An International Review*, 52, 193–212.

Day, D.V. and Sulsky, L.M. 1995. Effects of frame-of-reference training and information configuration on memory organization and rating accuracy. *Journal of Applied Psychology*, 80, 158–167.

Department of Labour. 1998. Employment Equity Act. [Online: Department of Labour]. Available at: http://www.labour.gov.za/downloads/legislation/acts/employment-equity/Actpercent20-per cent20Employment per cent20Equity.pdf [accessed: 7 March 2011].

Department of Trade and Industry. 2006. South Africa's Economic Transformation: A. Strategy for Broad-Based Black Economic Empowerment. [Online: Department Trade and Industry]. Available at: http://www.dti.gov.za/bee/complete.pdf [accessed: 7 March 2011].

Gaugler, B.B. and Thornton, G.C. III. 1989. Number of assessment center dimensions as a determinant of assessor accuracy. *Journal of Applied Psychology*, 74, 611–618.

Harris, M.M., Becker, A.S. and Smith, D.E. 1993. Does the assessment center method affect the cross-situational consistency of ratings? *Journal of Applied Psychology*, 78, 675–678.

Hennessy, J., Mabey, B. and Warr, P. 1998. Assessment centre observation procedures: an experimental comparison of traditional, checklist and coding methods. *International Journal of Selection and Assessment*, 6, 222–231.

HPCSA. 2000. 12 December. Scope of profession. [Online: Health Professions Council of South Africa]. Available at: www.hpcsa.co.za/downloads/regulations/scope_of_practice_psychology_april_2010.pdf. [accessed: 7 March 2011].

International Task Force on Assessment Center Guidelines. 2009. Guidelines and ethical considerations for assessment center operations. *International Journal of Selection and Assessment*, 17, 243–254.

Jones, R.G. and Klimoski, R.J. 2008. Narrow standards for efficacy and the research playground: why either-or conclusions do not help. *Industrial and Organizational Psychology*, 1, 137–139.

Kleinmann, M., Kuptsch, C. and Köller, O. 1996. Transparency: A necessary requirement for the construct-related validity of assessment centres. *Applied Psychology: An International Review*, 45, 67–84.

Kolk, N.J., Born, M.P., Van Der Flier, H. and Olman, J.M. 2002. Assessment center procedures: cognitive load during the observation phase. *International Journal of Selection and Assessment*, 10, 271–277.

Lance, C.E. 2008. Why assessment centers do not work the way they are supposed to. *Industrial and Organizational Psychology: Perspectives on Science and Practice*, 1, 84–97.

Lievens, F. and Conway, J.M. 2001. Dimension and exercise variance in assessment center scores: a large-scale evaluation of multitrait-multimethod studies. *Journal of Applied Psychology*, 86, 1202–1222.

Lievens, F. 1998. Factors which improve the construct validity of assessment centers: a review. *International Journal of Selection and Assessment*, 6, 141–152.

Melchers, K.G. and König, C.J. 2008. It is not yet time to dismiss dimensions in assessment centers. *Industrial and Organizational Psychology*, 1, 125–127.

Reilly, R.R., Henry, S. and Smither, J.W. 1990. An examination of the effects of using behavior checklists on the construct validity of assessment center dimensions. *Personnel Psychology*, 43, 71–84.

Robie, C., Obsurn, H.G., Morris, M.A., Etchegaray, J.M. and Adams, K.A. 2000. Effects of the rating process on the construct validity of assessment center dimension evaluations. *Human Performance*, 13, 355–370.

Sackett, P.R. and Tuzinski, K.A. 2001. The role of dimensions and exercises in assessment center judgments. In *How People Evaluate Others in Organizations*, edited by M. London. Mahwah, NJ: Lawrence Erlbaum, 111–129.

South African Government Information. 1997. 1 October. Transforming Public Service Delivery White Paper: Draft. [Online: South African Government Information]. Available at: www.info.gov.za/documents/white papers/1997 [accessed: 7 March 2011].

South African Government Information. 1998. 23 April. Affirmative Action in the Public Service White Paper. [Online: South African Government Information]. Available at: www.info.gov.za/documents/white papers/1998 [accessed: 7 March 2011].

South Africa Information. 2009. Black economic empowerment. [Online 4 May 2009]. Available at: www.southafrica.info/business/trends/empowerment/bee/htm. [accessed: 7 March 2011].

Schleicher, D.J. and Day, D.V. 1998. A cognitive evaluation of frame-of-reference training: Content and process issues. *Organizational Behaviour and Human Decision Processes*, 73, 76–101.

Schleicher, D.J., Day, D.V., Mayes, B.T. and Riggio, R.E. 2002. A new frame for frame- of-reference training: enhancing the construct validity of assessment centers. *Journal of Applied Psychology*, 87, 735–746.

Thornton, G.C. III and Gibbons, A.M. 2009. Validity of assessment centers for personnel selection. *Human Resource Management Review*, 19, 169–187.

Woehr, D.J. 1994. Understanding frame-of-reference training: The impact of training on the recall of performance information. *Journal of Applied Psychology*, 79, 525–534.

14 Using Assessment Centres to Facilitate Collaborative, Quasi-Standardized, Industry-Wide Selection: Lessons Learned from Medical Specialty Placement in England and Wales

DEBORAH E. RUPP AND ROSALIND H. SEARLE

Assessment Centres (ACs) have a long history as a behavioural, high-fidelity method for aiding personnel selection. However, the lion's share of this research has discussed the method as a tool used by individual organizations for selecting candidates into targeted jobs. This chapter proposes an application of the assessment centre method at a higher level of analysis. That is, we discuss how professional bodies might assist organizations in collaborating with each other in order to match individuals with jobs more efficiently and effectively. The practice model we propose is applicable to jobs that are well defined and do not differ substantially from organization to organization, such as jobs within the medical field, academic jobs, and more 'standardized' professions, such as accounting.

The impetus for us articulating this approach has been our observation of a number of cases where universities, professional associations, and organizations have used assessment centres as a quasi-standardized mass testing tool for placing a large number of applicants into a large number of jobs in a short period. Whereas the programmes we have seen take important steps forward in fostering collaborative assessment and the optimal matching of people and positions, we have also observed a number of inefficiencies inherent to these processes, which serve to limit the utility gains such collaborative programmes might enjoy. In the pages that follow, we describe ways in which collaborative assessment might be carried out. Then we present a case study of a profession that is attempting such an approach. We then leverage both the successes and challenges illustrated in the case study to develop recommendations for both research and practice.

Defining Collaborative Assessment

In order to define and illustrate the complexity of an industry-wide collaborative AC programme, we foreshadow a case (which we describe in more detail later in the chapter) involving the placement of medical doctors into specialty training positions in England and Wales. This programme requires the collaboration of a number of government, university, and professional bodies. In England and Wales, hospitals are state-owned and regulated by the National Health Service (NHS). However, the training and licensing of doctors is governed by the General Medical Council (GMC), a state-mandated independent professional body charged with the development and enforcement of professional standards. Royal colleges represent each specialty area, such as surgery, paediatrics and so on, which work together with civil servants from the Department of Health to deliver the training in specific geographic regions. The royal colleges are responsible for identifying the training criteria (performance dimensions) for each of the specialty areas, and each set of criteria must be approved by the GMC, with training delivered via hands-on experience within hospital settings.

Once a year, available training positions are identified for each specialty. The number of positions can vary greatly between specialties; for example, in 2009 there were 10 openings in neurosurgery and 2,600 in general practice (GPs). Once the full listing has been assembled, graduates apply for positions via online systems. The application process closes in December each year, with each specialty receiving thousands of applications; for instance, in 2009 surgery received 2,000 and general practice received 10,000. Shortlisted candidates are invited for assessment (via assessment centres) beginning in January. Assessment centres are carried out beginning in February and March. Scores are then computed and offers made, with candidates given 48 hours to decide. All graduates begin their new posts in August.

Readers might be tempted to think that these sorts of assessment contexts differ little from large scale civil-service assessments, which have been around for centuries (Searle 2003). However, we argue that in contemporary society, as the lines between the public and private sectors become more and more blurred, and as relations between professional associations, governments, regulatory bodies, and other stakeholder groups become more and more complex, traditional, bureaucratic models of mass-assessment are less applicable to contexts such as these. Such contemporary arrangements require multi-stakeholder dialogue and alignment (Scott 2004) that, to date, assessment centre scholars have not fully considered. In these cases (and they need not be limited to the public sector), industry standards, agencies responsible for testing, and units carrying out placement decisions may be separate from one another and, importantly, may reside external to the organization taking on new hires. Further, in systems such as these, the organizations function independently and may often compete for candidates. In such situations, there is less of an inclination to pool resources owing to the belief that there is a fixed pool of top applicants.

Although it is certainly logical for firms to resist collaboration owing to competition, we posit that such resistance comes at a great cost to both employers and applicants.

In professions where the tasks and requisite Knowledge, Skills and Abilities (KSAs) are essentially the same, and hiring decisions are made in cycles, for example one mass placement per year, non-collaborative placement systems could introduce mass inefficiencies and measurement error. That is, when placement efforts are non-collaborative, candidates may find themselves being assessed over and over on the same dimensions, using the similar testing formats. In doing so, practice and pre-knowledge may bias scores (Hausknecht, Trevor and Farr 2002; Kulik, Bangert-Drowns and Kulik 1984; Sackett, Borneman and Connelly 2008). Such contexts also threaten test security. If the jobs, KSAs, and testing formats are the same across organizations, test coaching becomes quite easy, and one programme's test material may be compromised simply by virtue of exposure to another organization's selection process. Indeed, the testing literature reveals that scores can be dramatically altered by virtue of only a small number of items being compromised (Do 2010; Do, Brummel, Chuah and Drasgow 2006; Stocking, Ward, and Potenza 1998).

A Model for Collaborative, Industry-wide AC Programmes

In presenting a framework for collaborative, industry-wide AC programmes, we note from the onset that this is an idealized model, developed to serve the purpose of catalyzing dialogue within both the scholarly and practitioner domains about assessment centres applied to more complex, multi-organization systems (Magee and de Weck 2004).

PREREQUISITES

We first posit that there are some required characteristics for any collaborative, industry-wide assessment programme, without which such an approach would be inappropriate. As we noted at the start of this chapter, we feel that collaborative industry-wide ACs are only appropriate for professions with very well-defined jobs; that is, similar tasks and KSAs across organizations. Further, we predict that collaborative AC programmes are most optimal when there are a very large number of applicants whose base KSAs have already been verified; for example, graduates with medical degrees applying for postgraduate training. Such conditions create less competition between organizations for 'top talent,' allowing the focus to shift to the matching of applicant interests and preferences with individual organizational needs. Another prerequisite of industry-wide assessment programmes is the involvement of at least one independent body as a stakeholder in the process, who is empowered to represent and potentially enforce the professional standards inherent to the industry.

COMPONENTS

We would expect an industry-wide collaborative AC programme to have all of the general components of a single-organization AC programme (International Taskforce 2009), including assessment of job-relevant, behavioural dimensions or competencies; assessment of each dimension across multiple assessment components; at least one behavioural simulation exercise; multiple, well-trained assessors; the use of a standardized scoring rubric, such as behaviourally anchored rating scales or behavioural checklists;

and a systematic process for integrating dimension ratings across assessment components, such as a statistical aggregation, a consensus discussion among the assessors, or a hybrid method.

In addition to these 'standard' components, a collaborative assessment programme would include some further nuanced features. For example, apart from a single core set of dimensions relevant for similar jobs across organizations, collaborative programmes should also conduct verification studies at the local level to determine specifically the relative importance of the dimensions, as well as weighting schemes for deriving overall assessment ratings. Having organization-specific competency models that stem from an industry-wide and industry verified 'menu' of performance dimensions will assist in facilitating subsequent matching of applicants to jobs.

A second component that we argue is especially important to the success of industry-wide collaborative AC programmes is the systematic collection of applicant interest and preference data. In mass, industry-wide placement programmes such as these, positions, although somewhat homogeneous in terms of general tasks, may vary on certain characteristics that correspond in important ways with applicants' vocational interests (Low, Yoon, Roberts and Rounds 2005). Further, such massive programmes often place individuals in positions that span large geographic areas. Collecting reliable and valid data on interests and preferences would allow collaborative placement programmes to efficiently match candidates based not only on their specific skill profile (bearing in mind that various organizations may differentially weight the dimensions), but also on the needs and interests of the candidates. This increases the likelihood that offers will be accepted in the first round, and new hires will be satisfied with, remain in, and be competent in their new posts, consequently increasing the efficiency of the placement process.

A final component that we feel is critical to the success of collaborative AC programmes is the identification and utilization of all stakeholder groups influenced and impacted by the placement of individuals into the industry. Such groups might include professional associations, legal bodies such as the government, the public through the press and non-governmental organizations, labour unions, consumers/clients and, of course, the individual organizations collaborating in the process. All stakeholder groups should be represented in all stages of the development, validation, implementation, administration, and evaluation of the AC programme. It is also necessary that the assessors used in such programmes are representative of these stakeholder groups.

PROCESS

Figure 14.1 illustrates a proposed process for designing, developing, and validating industry-wide collaborative AC programmes. As is shown, we suggest the process begins with the identification of all relevant stakeholder groups. Armed with the stakeholder directory, collaborative AC developers can map the infrastructure of the programme and identify which parties are responsible for what components of the process. These might include identifying dimensions, training assessors, administering the AC, and managing aspects such as assessee data, the applicant flow process, communication protocol, public relations, final decision-making, and evaluation. Of course, this infrastructure should be developed via multi-stakeholder dialogue, with the goal of engendering buy-in of all groups throughout the entire process. At that point, the appropriate predetermined parties should verify industry-wide dimensions/competencies using methods articulated by various professional standards (AERA, APA, ACME 1999; International Taskforce 2009; SIOP 2003). Organizational-level verification should then be carried out, with the goal of determining differential weighting schemes for each organization.

Parallel to this, a process needs to be developed for identifying and measuring applicant interests and preferences, and for linking them with specific jobs and organizations. At the same time, an information system should be developed that will serve as the platform for applicant data intake, pre-assessment, such as interests and preferences, shortlisting, communication, assessment data collection and, potentially, integration and scoring. Such a system requires multiple levels of access and security, and should be accessible as appropriate to all relevant stakeholder groups.

Of course a very big step involves the identification of and/or development of assessment content, such as behavioural simulation exercises, situational judgement tests, structured interviews, personality and ability tests, and so on. This also includes the training and certification of assessors. Owing to space limitations, we refer readers to other texts that outline in detail the steps in these processes, as they are general to all AC contexts (Thornton and Mueller-Hanson 2004; Thornton and Rupp 2006). What is unique to the industry-wide collaborative AC context is that, prior to roll-out, it is necessary to carry out a multi-stakeholder review, potentially allowing for a comment period. Depending on the context, this step might also involve the issuing of press releases, the holding of town hall meetings, and various other public announcements.

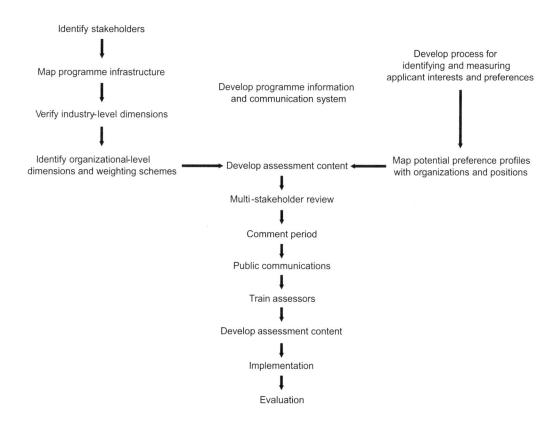

Figure 14.1 A model for collaborative, industry-wide AC programmes

Case Study: Post-Graduate Medical Placement in England and Wales

In defining industry-wide collaborative AC programmes, we provide the example of England and Wales' process for placing medical school graduates into specialty training programmes. The need for such a collaborative programme came about owing to several factors faced by the industry over the last decade (Patterson, Ferguson, Lane, Farrell, Martlew and Wells 2000). That is, whereas the cost of selection programmes was viewed as exceedingly high, common predictors used in these systems, such as previous academic attainment and interviews, were showing unacceptable levels of criterion-related validity (Blencowe, Bloor, Sheffield and Hollowood 2009; Ferguson, James and Madeley 2002; McManus, Powis, Wakeford, Ferguson, James and Richards 2005). This led to increases in government pressure on medical industry selection programmes to show both evidence of effectiveness, as well as economic utility. At the same time, some specialty areas were showing some success with the use of AC methods, which garnered the attention of the industry (Patterson et al. 2000).

These factors culminated in a decision to create a more collaborative system for placing candidates into specialty training programmes. Consequently, the 'Modernizing Medical Careers' (MMC) programme represented a joint venture between the Department of Health, the National Health Service, the General Medical Council, and the royal medical colleges. The purpose of the programme was to propose a model for widespread adoption, which utilized 'selection centres' – multistage, multi-method assessment programmes designed to successively reduce large applicant pools and make valid placement decisions (Patterson, Baron, Carr, Plint and Lane 2009).

From the outset, the goals of this programme were aligned closely with the practice model we have outlined above. That is, the industry sought to develop a programme information and communication system, sought to use an integrated competency (dimension)-based approach, and set the goal of coordinating position postings in order to streamline the placement process industry-wide. However, as we will describe below, there have been many pitfalls along the way, as well as areas of weak collaboration, which to date have threatened the success of this collaborative programme. We will describe the major issues faced by the programme as a way of more clearly articulating the special challenges and opportunities these sorts of programmes present.

PROGRAMME INFORMATION AND COMMUNICATION SYSTEM

One innovation produced by the MMC was a £6.3 million online centralized application system, the Medical Training Application Service (MTAS). This system was designed to manage more effectively both recruitment and selection, as well as to ensure that all training places were filled. Despite these advances, a number of problems ensued immediately following the roll-out of the system. For example, higher than anticipated volumes of users caused the system to crash frequently; programming errors caused applications to be lost; and miscalculations in the shortlisting procedures led confidential applicant data to be made public. Because of the security breaches themselves, as well as the significant criticism from both the media and the medical profession as a whole, MTAS was abandoned soon after roll-out, and the debacle led to the resignation of a number of senior staff members. Currently, each of the specialties uses different systems for applicant intake and data processing.

ASSESSORS

Three categories of assessors are involved in the selection process. Within specialty, consultant level doctors, representing the specialty of interest, comprise the largest group. They are selected on the basis of their skill, often through delivery or organization of postgraduate training. Otherwise these senior practitioners are involved with the relevant royal college's curriculum and training committees. A second group of voluntary assessors are from outside the medical community. These lay assessors are appointed by the Department of Health to ensure the fairness of selection procedures. Within a specialty, industrial/organizational (I/O) psychologists might also play a role in assessment. This is particularly the case for programmes utilizing standardized assessment such as the national computer-based situational judgement test, which is used for General Practice. Assessors usually attend a training session which varies in length from half a day to 2 full days. Typically, training includes an overview of the process, as well as sessions on equality and diversity. Assessors may also sit in and observe experienced assessors as part of their training.

DIMENSIONS

Consistent with both our proposed practice model and the international AC standards (International Taskforce 2009), the MMC programme always had a goal to use a competency (dimension)-based approach, incorporating both industry-wide as well as specialty-specific dimensions, and for each specialty, to assess each dimension across multiple behavioural simulation exercises. Unfortunately, this has not exactly come to pass. Instead, specialty areas have, either alone or with the aid of consultants, identified their own dimensions, as debate remains regarding these individualized dimension sets (Tooke 2008). This practice is inconsistent with research that has shown that there does seem to be convergence on a core set of dimensions across the medical specialties (see Patterson, Ferguson, Norfolk and Lane 2005; Patterson et al. 2008; Randall, Davies, Patterson Farrell 2006). Such dimensions include Communication, Planning and Organizing, Empathy, Professional Integrity, and Coping with Pressure. Despite this fact, and despite the original programme goals set by the MMC, to date there has been little effort to reach consensus on consolidated and specialized sets of dimensions that could then be used to more efficiently carry out a collaborative placement process. Instead, each specialty operates in isolation, using slightly different, un-calibrated dimensions, leading to fragmentation and loss of efficiency gains that a collaborative programme might provide.

Further, because placement into specialty training is the middle stage of three-stage career progression (medical school, specialty training, permanent position), it is necessary to identify the appropriate proficiency level for each dimension to ensure that they (a) have not already been verified by virtue of having passed the previous stage, such as a suturing exam in undergraduate training – that is, not 'undershot'; and (b) are those that will be predictive of success in specialty training as opposed to later career stages – that is, not 'overshot'. Also, although this is a selection programme, candidates are being selected for additional training, and as such, they should not be assessed on dimensions targeted for development in the course of the training. Thus, programmes such as these have the challenge of identifying more stable abilities, or already acquired skills that are predictive of success and which have not already been verified in previous stages.

EXERCISES

The lack of collaboration across the specialties also leads to fragmentation regarding the content of the assessment centre exercises. As mentioned above, despite initial collaborative goals for a consolidated placement system, what has unfolded are centrally listed yet separately developed and managed ACs for each of the specialty areas. Each selection process has decided on a number of dimensions and mapped them onto a set of exercises, but this has been further complicated by two issues.

Firstly, as mentioned above, many of the dimensions relevant for success in specialty training are common across specialty areas, and thus so is the content of the exercises used to assess them. Common exercises include:

- role play scenarios where the candidates provide feedback to 'patient' role players;
- role plays requiring communication with other professional groups;
- dynamic case diagnosis exercises within which candidates talk through their diagnosis and treatment plans; in these exercises, candidates receive results from the tests they order in the simulation;
- presentation exercises, which take the form of either prepared presentations or no-notice case study analyses;
- specialty clinical-knowledge assessments via either written assessment or computer-based multiple choice tests;
- technical simulations requiring candidates to suture, perform laparoscopic surgery, and similar.

Secondly, many of the specialty areas have used the same consulting firm to conduct job analyses and develop exercises, leading to some stark similarities in programme content. In addition, exercise performance, as opposed to dimension performance, dominates the selection process, with an emphasis on exercises, aggregating these scores to form the overall assessment rating.

Whereas a common set of dimensions and exercises may be quite useful for a completely collaborative assessment centre programme (that is, efforts could be focused on developing parallel versions of exercises rather than unique exercises across each specialty area (see Brummel, Rupp and Spain 2009)), when assessment itself is not collaborative, overlap such as that faced by the MMC programme can actually be quite detrimental. That is, for the MMC, only the listing of available positions and the application system are completely collaborative. Whereas the NHS and the GMC oversee each royal college (overseeing each specialty area), the specialty areas do not collaborate with one another. The net result is an enormous amount of repetitive exercise content. Furthermore, graduates often apply to a number of positions, within and also across specialty areas. As assessment itself is not centralized, candidates are therefore forced to go through a large number of highly similar assessment centres in a very short period of time.

Such a situation poses risks to the security and integrity of the assessment programme and ultimately threatens its ability to make valid placement decisions.

An unforeseen consequence of the current training selection process is repetitive participation in similar ACs which may have unintended *coaching and practice effects on applicants' performance*. Indeed, repetitive practice of similar test content is a large part of formal coaching programmes (Cullen, Sackett and Lievens 2006; Maurer, Solamon, Andrews and Troxtel 2001; Powers 1981). This issue is germane to the extent that coaching impacts assessment scores. Research demonstrates that practice clearly boosts performance (Lievens, Buyse, and Sackett 2005a; Raymond, Neustel and Anderson 2007) but the impact is due to memory of content rather than an increase in knowledge or skill (Lievens, Reeve and Heggestad 2007). This is consistent with the findings of Hausknecht et al. (2002), who found repeat assessments tended to raise scores yet lower validity coefficients (see also Griffin, Harding, Wilson and Yeomans 2008), illustrating the contaminating effect of unintended coaching through repetitive experiences of the assessment process, such as that present in the British medical case. Adding to this concern, research shows that the impact of re-exposure varies with different ability levels; those with the strongest improvements are those higher in ability (Kulik et al. 1984; Raymond et al. 2007; Lievens, Buyse and Sackett 2005b). The assessment cohorts in our British medical case are indeed high ability in that they have been admitted to and completed medical school. This would suggest that retesting effects could be considerably marked for these individuals.

Informal coaching effects have also been documented via the sharing of assessment content between applicants. In observing the assessment centres described above, we have noted instances where such informal coaching is clearly occurring. For example, we have observed candidates giving a very clear response to a case study based on a version of the exercise utilized in the preceding running, or observing candidates contacting friends shortly after a centre and discussing detailed content information. Although one might expect that in a high-stakes context such as this, competition between applicants would keep such coaching to a minimum, the large number of applicants and vacancies seems not to inhibit collaboration. Indeed, this raises the question of test security, especially considering the research showing that scores can be dramatically altered by virtue of only a small number of items being compromised (Do 2010; Do et al. 2006; Stocking et al. 1998).

OVERALL PROGRAMME SUCCESS

Whereas the application of quasi-collaborative AC programmes for postgraduate specialty training placement has slowly become more accepted in the UK (Blencowe et al. 2009), there are a number of issues that remain controversial and receive scepticism from within the medical profession. Further, many continue to question the reliability and validity of the assessments used to identify candidates for these highly prestigious posts (Grant 2007; Jackson and Gibbin 2006; Jefferis 2007; Kumar and Grant 2010). It should be noted that similar discontent can be found in other countries that have altered the format of medical selection (Groves, Gordon and Ryan 2007). We feel that the controversies are not a result of the collaborative model per se, but rather are symptomatic of a failure in this case to adequately utilize collaborative processes to their full potential, as well as to engage and garner support for these developments across all relevant stakeholder groups.

One component of our proposed model, which we find absent from the English and Welsh medical specialty training placement scenario, is the inclusion of applicants' interests and preferences within the placement process. Indeed, there is only limited use of such a process in the current programme since the specialty areas are carrying out assessment and placement in isolation. However, if these functions were made completely collaborative, efficiencies could be gained by an organized effort to match people and positions in a more systematic way. Gale and Grant (2002) discuss ways this might be attained (see also Kumar and Grant 2010). The person-environment fit literature, for example Kristof-Brown, Zimmerman and Johnson (2005), also provides insights as to how programmes might match candidates' personalities and geographic preferences with locations and cultures of specialty training posts.

In contrast, the MMC programme reveals considerable collusion between candidates exchanging details of the exercises to friends and online sites, whereas collaboration across the specialties remains limited. Some specialty areas operate sophisticated centralized processes, while others are more piecemeal and geographically focused. The net effect is a duplication of both candidate and assessor effort. In addition, the structure of the selection process reinforces candidates submitting multiple, non-centralized applications to many specialties in order to maximize their probability of obtaining placement. This over-exposes them to assessment content over a very truncated period of time, threatening both test security and programme validity. Although these issues may seem ominous, we believe it is important to illustrate the realities and complexities of carrying out a collaborative assessment programme. With complexity comes challenge, and we see the stakeholders in this case fighting hard against the obstacles and road blocks they have met as their programme has evolved. Our goal now is to integrate our theoretical model and the realities of the case we have presented, into recommendations for research and practice interested in carrying out collaborative, industry-wide assessment.

Recommendations

The recommendations we provide here are meant to compliment our description of industry-wide collaborative AC programmes.

First, we recommend that in the development phase, the multi-stakeholder team develop a strategic plan for upholding test security. This would not only involve the protection of assessment content, but would also include the security of data and information housed on a central system and potentially transmitted over the Internet (Reynolds and Rupp 2010). There are a number of professional guidelines for such practices, including the American Psychological Association Taskforce Report on Internet-Based Testing (Naglieri et al. 2004) and the International Test Commission Guidelines for Internet-Based Testing (2005). These guidelines offer recommendations for carrying out identity confirmations; disabling functions that allow saving, printing, and so on; and using multi-server configurations, such that the Internet, test applications, data, scoring and reporting applications, and back-ups are stored on separate servers, with the more sensitive information residing behind a secure firewall. The development team should also be aware of legal requirements that would impact their security plan. For example, the EU Data Protection and US Safe Harbor programmes provide rules and guidelines for protecting personal and sensitive data. These include protocols for giving applicants notice, access and choice regarding the use of their data and its onward transfer, guidance on ensuring the security and integrity of data, and rules about the enforcement of a system for complaints and recourse. In the US, there is further legislation regarding the definition of an Internet applicant. Industry-wide collaborative assessment programmes using a centralized information and communication system should map their process against this definition and ensure that the data collected and retained are in compliance with legal requirements.

Second, we reiterate the importance of having a diverse set of assessors representing all pertinent stakeholder groups as an ongoing mechanism for reinforcing industry-wide buy-in. At one level, just having these diverse perspectives 'at the table' for training, refresher training, update meetings, and the like, will serve as an informal change intervention, in that such a process creates a venue for regular, ongoing, multi-stakeholder dialogue. However, we recommend that collaborative assessment programmes more fully formalize stakeholder participation, explicitly building in opportunities throughout the programme; for example integration/consensus discussions during the assessment centre process to build awareness and understanding, and to collectively engage in continuous process improvement.

Third, we recommend complete collaboration both in the development of system-wide and local competency models (including the weighting of dimensions), as well as in the development and implementation of the assessments themselves. We predict that efficiency will be optimized in situations where there is centralized management of dimensions, as well as the centralized delivery and scoring of assessment content. Such a system allows for:

- more control over test security;
- pooled resources for ensuring both the validity of the dimensions as well as the psychometric rigour of the assessment components;
- a reduction in coaching and practice effects introducing error into assessment scores;
- the incorporation of applicant interest and preference data in order to integrate 'best fit' judgements into placement decisions.

Not only would these recommendations be expected to dramatically reduce the resources used to administer the system, but also lead to better placement, higher acceptance rates among first offers and lowered turnover due to increased satisfaction among those placed.

Finally, to maintain the integrity and security of the programme over time, we recommend that large-scale, industry-wide assessment programmes place systematic effort into creating multiple, parallel versions of all assessments used in the programme. Whereas the creation of parallel versions of 'paper-and-pencil' types of tests (for example, personality, cognitive ability, and some knowledge tests) is fairly straightforward and well defined in the literature (O'Brien 1989; Rottinghaus, Betz and Borgen 2003; van der Linden and Adema 1998), there is less guidance on equating test forms within the behavioural assessment domain. We direct readers to recent research providing guidance for establishing parallel tests for biodata, situational judgement tests and in-basket exercises (Clause, Mullins, Nee, Pulakos and Schmitt 1998; Lievens and Anseel 2008; Lievens and Sackett 2007; Oswald, Friede, Schmitt, Kim and Ramsey 2005). For establishing alternate forms of behavioural simulation exercises such as those often used in assessment centres, Brummel et al. (2009) recommend constructing detailed simulation specifications from which alternate simulation forms can be constructed. Alternate forms can then be equated by comparing population means and standard deviations of dimensions scores, examining possible sources of variance beyond item difficulty, determining the psychometric relationship between test forms, estimating the test equating functions for each of the dimensions and using these equating functions to adjust assessee scores.

Conclusion

Our goal in this chapter was to create a vision for twenty-first century industry-wide assessment centre operations that require intense collaboration of stakeholders existing within complex inter-organizational systems. We believe that the case study describing the attempt to create a system to place medical doctors into specialty training positions highlights the complexity and challenges involved in developing and implementing such systems. We hope that our model, the case presented, and our subsequent recommendations will spawn additional research and writing among practitioners on this important topic.

References

American Educational Research Association, American Psychological Association, and American Council on Measurement in Education. 1999. *Standards for Educational and Psychological Tests*. Washington, D.C.: American Psychological Association.

Blencowe, N., Bloor, J., Sheffield, J. and Hollowood, A. 2009. From nepotism to speed-dating: selection of specialty trainees in surgery. *Bulletin of The Royal College of Surgeons of England*, 91, 108–110.

Brummel, B., Rupp, D.E. and Spain, S. 2009. Constructing parallel simulation exercises for assessment centers and other forms of behavioral assessment. *Personnel Psychology*, 62, 135–170.

Clause, C.S., Mullins, M.E., Nee, M.T., Pulakos, E. and Schmitt, N. 1998. Parallel test form development: a procedure for alternative predictors and an example. *Personnel Psychology*, 51, 193–208.

Cullen, M.J., Sackett, P.R. and Lievens, F. 2006. Threats to the operational use of situational judgment tests in the college admission process. *International Journal of Selection and Assessment*, 14, 142–155.

Do, B.R. 2010. *Item Sharing on Assessment of Cognitive Constructs*. Unpublished doctoral dissertation, University of Illinois.

Do, B.R., Brummel, B.J., Chuah, S.C. and Drasgow, F. 2006. *Item Preknowledge on Test Performance and Item Confidence*. Paper presented at the annual conference of the Society for Industrial and Organizational Psychology, Dallas, TX.

Ferguson, E., James, D. and Madeley, L. 2002. Factors associated with success in medical school: Systematic review of the literature. *British Medical Journal*, 324, 952–957.

Gale, R. and Grant J. 2002. Sci45: the development of a specialty choice inventory. *Medical Education*, 659–666.

Grant, J. 2007. Changing postgraduate medical education: a commentary from the United Kingdom. *Medical Journal of Australia*, 186, 9–13.

Griffin, B., Harding, D., Wilson, I. and Yeomans, N. 2008. Does practice make perfect? The effect of coaching and retesting on selection tests used for admission to an Australian medical school. *Medical Journal of Australia*, 189, 270–273.

Groves, M., Gordon, J. and Ryan, G. 2007. Entry tests for graduate medical programs: is it time to re-think? *Medical Journal of Australia*, 186, 120–123.

Hausknecht, J.P., Trevor, C.O. and Farr, J.L. 2002. Retaking ability tests in a selection setting: implications for practice effects, training performance, and turnover. *Journal of Applied Psychology*, 87, 243–254.

International Task Force on Assessment Center Guidelines. 2009. Guidelines and ethical considerations for assessment center operations. *International Journal of Selection and Assessment*, 17, 243–254.

International Test Commission. 2005. International Guidelines on Computer-Based and Internet delivered Testing, Version 2005. Author.

Jackson, C.R. and Gibbin, K.P. 2006. 'Per ardua … ' Training tomorrow's surgeons using inter alia lessons from aviation. *Journal of Royal Society of Medicine*, 99, 554–558.

Jefferis, T. 2007. Selection for specialist training: what can we learn from other countries? *British Medical Journal*, 334, 1302–1304.

Kristof-Brown, A., Zimmerman, R. and Johnson, E. 2005. Consequences of individuals' fit at work: A meta-analysis of person-job, person-organization, person-group, and person-supervisor fit. *Personnel Psychology*, 87, 985–993.

Kulik, J.A., Bangert-Drowns, R.L. and Kulik, C.L.C. 1984. Effectiveness of coaching for aptitude tests. *Psychological Bulletin*, 95, 179–188.

Kumar, N. and Grant, J. 2010. Are the new junior doctor selection processes value for money? *BMJ Careers*. Publication date: 16 Jun 2010. Accessed 21 June. URL: http://careers.bmj.com.libezproxy.open.ac.uk/careers/advice/view-article.html?id=20001122.

Lievens, F. and Anseel F. 2008. Creating alternate in-basket forms through cloning: Some preliminary results. *International Journal of Selection and Assessment*, 15, 428–433.

Lievens, F., Buyse, T. and Sackett, P. 2005a. The operational validity of a video-based situational judgment test for medical college admissions: Illustrating the importance of matching predictor and criterion construct domains. *Journal of Applied Psychology*, 90, 442–452.

Lievens, F., Buyse, T. and Sackett, P. 2005b. Retest effects in operational selection settings: Development and test of a framework. *Personnel Psychology*, 58, 981–1007.

Lievens, F., Reeve, C. and Heggestad, E. 2007. An examination of psychometric bias due to retesting on cognitive ability tests in selection settings. *Journal of Applied Psychology*, 92, 1672–1682.

Lievens, F. and Sackett, P.R. 2007. Situational judgment tests in high-stakes settings: Issues and strategies with generating alternate forms. *Journal of Applied Psychology*, 92, 1043–1055.

Low, K.S.D., Yoon, M., Roberts, B.W. and Rounds, J. 2005. The stability of interests from early adolescence to middle adulthood: A quantitative review of longitudinal studies. *Psychological Bulletin*, 131, 713–737.

Magee, Chris L. and Olivier L. de Weck (2004) 'Complex System Classification,' Fourteenth Annual International Symposium of the International Council On Systems Engineering (INCOSE), 20–24 June.

Maurer, T.J., Solamon, J.M., Andrews, K.D. and Troxtel, D.D. 2001. Interviewee coaching, preparation strategies, and response strategies in relation to performance in situational employment interviews: An extension of Maurer, Solamon, and Troxtel 1998. *Journal of Applied Psychology*, 86, 709–717.

McManus, I., Powis, D., Wakeford, R., Ferguson, E., James, D. and Richards, P. 2005. Intellectual aptitude tests and A levels for selecting UK school leaver entrants for medical school. *British Medical Journal*, 331, 555–559.

Naglieri, J.A., Drasgow, F., Schmit, M., Handler, L., Prifitera, A., Margolis, A. and Velasquez, R. 2004. Psychological testing on the internet: New problems, old issues. *American Psychologist*, 59, 150–162.

O'Brien, M.L. 1989. Psychometric issues relevant to selecting items and assembling parallel forms of language proficiency instruments. *Educational and Psychological Measurement*, 49, 347–353.

Oswald, F.L., Friede, A.J., Schmitt, N., Kim, B.K. and Ramsey, L.J. 2005. Extending a practical method for developing alternate test forms using independent sets of items. *Organizational Research Methods*, 8, 149–164.

Patterson, F., Baron, H., Carr, V., Plint, S. and Lane, P. 2009. Evaluation of three short-listing methodologies for selection into postgraduate training in general practice. *Medical Education*, 43, 50–57.

Patterson, F., Ferguson, E., Lane, P., Farrell, K., Martlew, J. and Wells, A. 2000. A competency model for General Practice: Implications for selection and development. *The British Journal of General Practice*, 50, 188–193.

Patterson, F., Ferguson, E., Norfolk, T. and Lane, P. 2005. A new selection system to recruit GP registrars: Preliminary findings from a validation study. *British Medical Journal*, 330, 711–714.

Patterson, F., Lane, P. and Carr, V. 2008. Selection methods for medicine: Core concepts and future issues. In *Medical Education and Training*, edited by Y. Carter and N. Jackson. Oxford: Oxford University Press, 143–169.

Powers, D. 1981. Students' use of and reactions to alternative methods of preparing for the SAT. *Measurement and Evaluation in Guidance*, 14, 118–126.

Randall, R., Davies, H., Patterson, F. and Farrell, K. 2006. Selecting doctors for postgraduate training in paediatrics using a competency based assessment centre. *Archives of Disease in Childhood*, 91, 444–448.

Raymond, M.R., Neustel, S. and Anderson, D. 2007. Retest effects on identical and parallel forms in certification and licensure testing. *Personnel Psychology*, 60, 367–396.

Reynolds, D.H. and Rupp, D.E. 2010. Advances in technology-facilitated assessment. In *Handbook of Workplace Assessment: Evidence-Based Practices for Selecting and Developing Organizational Talent*, edited by J.C. Scott and D.H. Reynolds. San Francisco, CA: Jossey-Bass, 609–641.

Rottinghaus, P.J., Betz, N.E. and Borgen, F.H. 2003. Validity of parallel measures of vocational interests and confidence. *Journal of Career Assessment*, 11, 355–378.

Sackett, P.R., Borneman, M.J. and Connelly, B.S. 2008. High stakes testing in higher education and employment: Appraising the evidence for validity and fairness. *American Psychologist*, 63, 215–227.

Scott, C. 2004. Regulation in the age of governance: the rise of the post-regulatory state. In *The Politics of Regulation: Institutions and Regulatory Reforms for the Age of Governance*, edited by J. Jordana and D.D. Levi-Faur. Cheltenham: Edward Elgar, 145–174.

Searle, R. 2003. *Selection and Recruitment: A Critical Text*: Palgrave: Macmillan.

Society for Industrial and Organizational Psychology. 2003. *Principles for the validation and use of personnel selection procedures* (4th edition). Bowling Green, OH.

Stocking, M.L., Ward, W.C. and Potenza, M.T. 1998. Simulating the use of disclosed items in computerized adaptive testing. *Journal of Educational Measurement*, 35, 48–68.

Thornton, G.C. III and Mueller-Hanson, R.A. 2004. *Developing Organizational Simulations: A Guide for Practitioners and Students*. Mahwah, NJ: Lawrence Erlbaum.

Thornton, G.C. III and Rupp, D.R. 2006. *Assessment Centers in Human Resource Management: Strategies for Prediction, Diagnosis, and Development*. Mahwah, NJ: Lawrence Erlbaum.

Tooke, J. 2008. *Aspiring to Excellence: Final Report of the Independent Inquiry Into Modernizing Medical Careers*. London: MMC Inquiry.

Van der Linden, W.J. and Adema, J.J. 1998. Simultaneous assembly of multiple test forms. *Journal of Educational Measurement*, 35, 185–198.

15 Certifying Competencies of HR Managers with the Assessment Centre Method: Quality Assurance that HR Contributes to Corporate Objectives

R.K. PREMARAJAN

The objective of this chapter is to describe a national-level certification drive for human resource (HR) professionals in India based on the HR Compass, which is a competency model that captures the technical as well as behavioural competencies required for HR professionals in the country. The chapter first traces the background of the intervention and then goes on to detail the actual process of competency-mapping using many methods including the assessment centre approach. In order to develop a robust certification process, the competencies are assessed not only by a subject-knowledge test, but also a more detailed simulation-based assessment centre. The assessment centre approach also provides a detailed behavioural-based feedback report to participants who use the feedback to engage in developmental activities. The intervention is premised on the literature that through proper assessment and development, a well-chosen HR competency model can effectively guide the HR organization to contribute successfully to business. The chapter also identifies the challenges faced so far, and outlines the way forward in implementing this large scale intervention.

Background

People who excel at their jobs demonstrate behaviours that distinguish them from their peers. The underlying qualities of people that direct these behaviours are competencies. The HR competencies, in other words, differentiate outstanding performers from average performers in the HR function. Whilst the deeper levels of competencies, namely attitudes and traits, direct the underlying nature of people's performance, it would often be misguided without the necessary tools and techniques to deliver top level performance. It is therefore equally important to consider the professional knowledge and skills along with the necessary attitudes and traits to arrive at the entire gamut of critical competencies relevant for HR professionals. In other words, the HR expert role serves as a foundation for all other roles and competencies. The combination of technical expertise and other behavioural competencies results in superior performance. Finally competencies can offer the HR professionals an opportunity to define excellence, and, even more importantly, to demonstrate the value they bring to their organizations.

Over the last decade, there has been a drastic increase in employment in organized and semi-organized sectors in India. These conditions have led many organizations to craft strategies to find and retain good workers. The approaches range from web-based recruiting drives to luring Indian expats from the West, funding sector specific management programmes at universities, through to plans for the creation of in-house management institutes.

While the country's elite universities rival schools anywhere in the world, they graduate fewer than 100,000 students annually. The rest of the 14 million people who finish high school each year must choose between lower-level universities and vocational training schools, which haven't adapted to the requirements of India's changing economy (*Bloomberg Business Week* 2005).

The talent shortage scenario is no different for HR professionals. It is accepted that the last few years have been, and the next few years will remain, the most exciting time for HR in India. There is a phenomenal growth of industry and new sectors such as insurance, retail, telecom, IT/ITeS [Information Technology/Informational Technology enabled Services] have emerged, all of which are people-intensive. Even in the expanding manufacturing sector, organizational change and restructuring, along with mergers and acquisitions, have become fairly regular, which raises critical people issues that need to be tackled.

If we look at the employment potential across industry sectors, it is huge. According to Nasscom, IT/ITeS was to add more than 1 million white collar jobs in 2008; and an All India Management Association (AIMA) 2003 report projected that tourism and IT/ITeS would generate 20–72 million jobs by 2020.

Most of this employment-generation is happening in people-intensive sectors. This has led to a dramatic increase in the requirements for Human Resource Professionals. While it is true that the global economic downturn may considerably affect this projection, highly conservative estimates forecast a demand for at least 5 million new jobs in the next 5 years. To meet this demand, it is self-evident that there will also be a requirement for additional HR professionals, and even if one were to go by the not-so-healthy ratio of 1 HR professional for every 500 employees, we will need at least 10,000 HR professionals for this period.

So one of the challenges for the education sector will be to keep pace with the demand for HR professionals, both in terms of quality and quantity and how much of this demand will be met by the few institutes in the country which produce quality HR professionals. The truth is that specialized HR MBAs would not be able to meet even a fifth of this requirement if we were to consider the total output of the top business schools with specialized HR programmes, and even from among this pool, about 20 per cent join HR consulting firms. While this projection paints a dismal supply and demand situation at the entry level, the story is no different at other levels. While a few large organizations have focused on improving the capabilities of their HR departments, most of the organizations haven't yet made any significant efforts in this direction. Compounding this problem is the fact that many HR professionals have traditionally grown within the organization from Personnel or Administration roles without any formal HR qualifications. Therefore, there is a desperate need to address and improve the overall Human Resource competencies of HR professionals in most organizations.

The gap in the availability of quality HR professionals is apparent at the entry level as well as among the experienced. Thus, it is not difficult to realize the need for scaling up the availability of quality HR professionals through alternate routes. What we will need to consider are new models for developing HR professionals as a joint industry-academia effort.

Against this backdrop, the Confederation of Indian Industry (CII) together with the National HRD Network (NHRD) partnered XLRI Jamshedpur, a leading business school in the country, to develop a National HR Competency Certification drive known as HR Compass.

The specific objective of HR Compass is to raise the quality standards of the HR profession in the country by developing the large number of existing HR professionals, as well as by partnering hundreds of second-rung business schools to enhance the quality of curriculum and training. The quality HR professionals would go a long way in realizing the new role of HR as business partners to contribute to business. The overarching vision of this association is to raise the standard of the HR profession along the lines of the work by the Management Charter Initiative (MCI) or the National Council for Vocational Qualification (NCVQ) in the UK and the American Society for Training and Development (ASTD), or the Society for Human Resource Management (SHRM) with the help of the University of Michigan in the USA.

Contribution to Business

Traditionally, the HR function has been viewed as administrative, focusing on the level of the individual employee, the individual job, and the individual practice (Becker, Huselid, and Ulrich 2001), with the basic premise that improvements in individual employee performance will automatically enhance organizational performance. In the 1990s an emphasis on strategy and the importance of HR systems began to emerge. Both researchers and practitioners began to recognize the impact of aligning HR practices with organizational strategy. HR has now emerged as a business partner in which individual HR functions, such as recruitment, selection, training, compensation, and performance appraisal, are closely aligned with each other and also with the overall strategy of the organization.

It has also been confirmed that to effectively shift to the new paradigm, the HR professionals need to possess the critical competencies beyond the functional knowledge. While the functional knowledge (functional technical competencies) are important to delivering successful performance, translating this functional knowledge to effective outcomes for the organization would be a function of the right kind of behavioural competencies which would be the key differentiating factors that impact performance.

This is further corroborated by a 16-year long study involving thousands of HR professionals and over 28,000 line managers and peers, undertaken by the University of Michigan's Business School (Ulrich and Brockbank 2005).

The results of this study highlighted the type and nature of the competencies of HR professionals that have the most influence on company performance. It was found that Strategy-Related Competencies (change management, customer orientation, and strategic decision-making, and so on) accounted for 43 per cent of impact on business performance. The second cluster, Personal Credibility (result orientation, relationship management, influencing communication, and so on) accounted for 23 per cent of impact on business performance. The third cluster, HR Delivery (staffing, training and development, organization design, HR measurement, Legal Compliance, Performance Management) accounted for 18 per cent. However, what is pertinent to observe here is the finding that HR delivery was not a key differentiation factor across low-performing companies and high-performing companies, and they are in that sense threshold competencies. Lastly, the Business Knowledge cluster (Knowledge of the value chain labour knowledge), and HR Technology cluster accounted for 11 per cent and 5 per cent respectively.

Similar results were replicated in the 5th study on HR competency conducted by the University of Michigan and RBL Institute in 2007. Further in the context of Asia, the study by Long and Ismail (2008) also supported the relationship between HR competencies and business performance. Thus it is obvious that to effectively contribute to business, HR personnel needs to ensure that relevant competencies are adequately developed in them. The HR Compass, if fully implemented, will go a long way in enhancing the contribution of HR to business.

HR Competency Model

The National Committee on HR of the Confederation of Indian Industry (CII) had identified 'HR Competency Development' as one of the key initiatives to be taken up in 2002. After considerable discussion, the members of the Committee were unanimous in recognizing that there has not been enough work done in the country in the area of identifying and developing the key competencies required for successful practice of a Human Resources Management portfolio. CII felt that HR competencies assumed greater significance as many chief executives attempted to implement their agenda relating to leadership development and other similar people-development initiatives, which naturally require high quality HR interventions and participation. HR Managers, thus, are key stakeholders and partners in the process of building effective institutions through leadership development. Thus, the competence of HR professionals is directly related to the effective implementation of many of the chief executives' plans and programmes for realizing the competitive advantage through people strategies.

As a sequel to the above, the HR Committee of the CII decided to work on developing and rolling out a robust and generic HR Competency Model that can be recommended for implementation across the various industry segments in India.

BUILDING THE COMPETENCY MODEL

The National Committee on HR assigned the task of preparing an approach and developing the HR Competency Model to a group of five senior HR professionals representing the different industry segments. The team met at regular intervals and deliberated on the subject. It discussed various competency models after review of the relevant literature.

The committee also pooled organizational experiences in the areas of identifying and implementing Competency-based HR practices by way of interacting with both academics and practitioners in the field. The committee established an approach to building the HR Competency Model that will be useful to a wide variety of industries cutting across different lines of business, organizational sizes, and sectors. The process helped to prepare a draft set of competencies for further consideration together with suggested levels for measurement. The approach adopted by the team involved the following steps:

1. Evolve competency clusters and levels based on the available experience base.
2. Use a 'concentric circle' approach to spread out the involvement of more HR professionals, academia, and line managers besides CEOs of various organizations. This approach helped to validate and verify the relevance and importance of the competency clusters proposed as well the granularity of the levels for measurement.
3. Present to the National HR Committee periodically to keep them informed of progress and obtain further inputs and endorsements for the direction and depth in which the team was proceeding.
4. Identify and incorporate in the proposed HR Competency Model further related aspects, such as measurement criteria, roll-out plan, and suggestions for piloting the process in a few companies. The certification process will prescribe the CII approach to measuring the competence of HR professionals along with the finalized Competency Model.

MILESTONES

The committee identified a preliminary set of 19 competencies as relevant for HR professionals. These competencies fell under three headings: Business related, HR technology related, and HR role-related.

Four ascending levels of proficiencies were identified as (a) Beginner, (b) Competent, (c) Advanced and (d) Expert. Definitions of each of the competencies at each of the four levels described above were arrived at through behavioural statements.

The periodical reviews by the National Committee contributed enormously at each stage to the enhancement and development of the Model. For example, the following strategic decisions were made: the model would be generic enough to apply across industries; it would clarify the distinctive competitive advantage its implementation would provide to a company; it would be designed to suit the requirements of Indian industry at large; and a clear-cut assessment mechanism would be developed.

DEVELOPMENT AND DEPLOYMENT

As Version 1.0 of the Model was getting reviewed and fine-tuned, it was decided to partner National HRD Network (NHRD) at the national level for the deployment and delivery of the Model across the country. NHRD has the appropriate expertise to provide the requisite professional rigour and reach across the HR professional bodies in the country. It was also decided to partner XLRI Jamshedpur to provide expertise in the area of the competency mapping process. Soon after the launch, as the first phase of deployment, CII and NHRD conducted a series of Workshops and Training Programmes to take this forward.

THE MODEL

The model captures the range of competencies required to fulfil the multiple roles of HR. These have been classified in terms of two dimensions, one being Technical vs Behavioural and the other being Functional vs Generic, thus creating a 2 × 2 matrix as shown in Table 15.1. The figures in parenthesis indicate the number of competencies under each type.

Table 15.1   HR competency model

	Generic	**Functional**
Behavioural	Generic Behavioural (3)	Functional Behavioural (3)
Technical	Generic Technical (2)	Functional Technical (9)

The model therefore categorizes the competencies according to these four typologies.

Functional technical competencies

These refer to the HR specific functional knowledge and skills critical for delivering results and include Recruitment and Selection, Performance Management, Training and Development, Talent Management, Compensation and Benefit, Managing Culture, Design and Change, Employee Relations and Labour Laws, Building HR Strategy, and International HRM.

Functional behavioural competencies

These refer to the behavioural competencies, more critical for HR professionals compared to the other functions and include Service Orientation, Personal Credibility, and Execution Excellence.

Generic technical competencies

These refer to the generic competencies that are technical in nature but increasingly critical for HR to fulfil the business partner role and they include Business Knowledge and Financial Perspective.

Generic behavioural competencies

Finally, these refer to the overarching behavioural competencies that are essential for any function, more so at senior levels and they include Strategic Thinking and Alignment, Change Orientation, and Networking Management.

PROFICIENCY LEVEL

The HR professionals will be evaluated in terms of 3 levels of hierarchy, and/or scope of activities. These will be operational expert, middle-level or unit-level expert, and senior-level or corporate-level expert. In addition, it is also proposed to have a role of HR specialist. Thus to capture the differing nature of these roles and the commensurate responsibility, each of these competencies is fleshed out with behavioural anchors reflecting the scales which measure the varying degrees of a given competency that an HR professional occupying a particular role is required to display. Behavioural anchors describe observable and specific behaviours that leave little room for interpretation or assumptions. These behaviours can be measured to determine whether or not an employee meets a defined competency.

Competency Assessment: The Approach

The following assumptions have been the bases to arrive at the approach to competency assessment. These have been largely based on McClelland (1978), Boyatzis (1982), Spencer and Spencer (1992) and Ulrich (1999).

ASSUMPTION 1

While the functional technical competencies are important to deliver successful performance, translating this functional knowledge to effective outcomes for the organization would be a function of the right kinds of behavioural competencies which would be the key differentiating factors that impact performance.

ASSUMPTION 2

Functional knowledge is the tip (using the iceberg metaphor) and hence is, relatively speaking, easily observed and measured. Thus the measurement devices to assess functional technical competencies could be relatively straight forward. This could include achievement tests (that is, tests to assess the knowledge level in an area) where there are right or wrong answers.

ASSUMPTION 3

The behavioural competencies are the underlying characteristics and hence literally and figuratively are less observable and measurable. Thus the measurement devices to assess behavioural competencies have to be more carefully designed. This could include simulations, behavioural interviews, and so forth.

ASSUMPTION 4

Since the potential pool of HR professionals going through the assessment will be very large, it would be difficult to do an in-depth assessment of critical competencies if all were to be put through the same process. Conducting Achievement Tests (online or offline) is relatively simple while conducting simulation-based assessment would require trained assessors and will be a more complex, time-consuming and costly process.

ASSUMPTION 5

If the right kind of behavioural competencies are there, the target will find it easy to pick up the HR Functional Technical competencies, provided they are made literate on the competency details.

Based on these assumptions, the Exercise-Competency matrix shown in Table 15.2 has been created.

Table 15.2 Exercise-competency matrix

Exercise Competency	AT	GDM	In-Tray I (FT)	Case I (FT)	Role Play	In-Tray II	Case II	CBI
Recruitment and Selection	✓							✓
Performance Management	✓		✓					
Training and Development	✓							✓
Talent Management	✓		✓					
Compensation and Benefit	✓							✓
Managing Culture, Design and Change	✓			✓				
ER and Labour Laws	✓			✓				
Building HR Strategy	✓		✓					
International HRM	✓			✓				
Service Orientation		✓			✓			
Personal Credibility								
Execution Excellence					✓			✓
Strategic Thinking and Alignment						✓		✓
Change Orientation		✓				✓		
Networking Management							✓	✓
Business Knowledge								✓
Financial Perspective	✓					✓	✓	

AT = Achievement Test, GDM = Group Decision-making, CBI = Competency Based Interview, FT = Functional Test.

Assessment Methodology

Therefore it makes sense to ensure that the process is done in two stages. The first stage would be a series of achievement tests to assess the Functional Technical Competencies. This could be done online or offline. Each one of the assessees will be provided with a feedback sheet with the details of their performance and functional technical competency areas that they are good at and those areas that they need to develop further.

Those who achieve a minimum score (40 per cent) in stage one would be eligible for the second stage, where the most critical competencies would be assessed using simulations and behavioural interviews by trained assessors using assessment centre methodology.

No assessee will be declared as passed or failed, but their performance on the rating scale in each competency will be recorded in the transcript. If somebody wants to improve his or her performance in the certification process, it would be allowed after a gap of 18 months.

Oral and Written Feedback

Every participant in the assessment centre process will be given a brief oral feedback at the end of the exercises. A detailed written feedback with developmental suggestions will be provided within a month of the assessment centre. The feedback process will be the responsibility of the assessors themselves.

Assessor Training

To run the national level process like it is envisaged here, it is important to have a significant number of trained assessors. Because assessment centre ratings are obviously inherently judgemental in nature, training assessors is an important element in the development and design of assessment centres (Woehr and Arthur 2003). Thus, the *type* of training is also an important variable (Woehr and Huffcutt 1994). It has been concluded that, irrespective of the training approach used, assessment centres that have more extensive rater-training are more likely to result in ratings that display convergent/ discriminant validity.

The assessor training lasted for a total of 4 days. The first schedule for 3 days included the following: familiarization with the HR Competency Model, familiarization with the Behavioural Assessment Process (Observe, Record, Classify and Evaluate), and familiarization with the assessment tools (In basket, Case Analysis and Presentation, Group Decision-making Exercise, Fact-Finding Exercise. These will be generic tools and not the actual tools), Using Psychometric Tests for Competency Assessment, Designing and conducting the Behavioural Interviewing. On the last day the participants run a mini-assessment centre and prepare a developmental report. Those assessors who will be involved in an assessment centre will be given a 1-day refresher programme with specific reference to the actual tools for the centre.

While there is consensus in the literature that frame-of-reference (FOR) is a highly effective approach to rater training (Lievens 2001), and keeping in mind the suggestion by Thornton and Rupp (2006), we have deployed both behaviour-driven as well as schema-driven approaches to training assessors. This is important as the entire assessment is based on a detailed competency framework. At the same time the purpose is not only certification but also the development of professionals. What is important for the participants is also an opportunity to develop these competencies. To facilitate the development, feedback report with behavioural evidence is critical. The behaviour-driven approach, therefore, is an added advantage for the assessors to facilitate such a feedback report.

Using this approach a total of about 100 assessors have been trained. The assessors were identified by the National Committee members. They kept in mind characteristics like reputation for being objective, commitment to the process of assessment, high energy levels, and at least about 10 years of experience. While there was no formal assessment done to establish their suitability, an informal evaluation has been adopted to actively seek the trained assessors for further activities. The trainer's observation was one of the key inputs in this. About seven assessor training programmes have been conducted so far.

Development and Validation of Tools

At the end of assessor training, the trainees were invited to volunteer for taking the HR Compass forward, both in terms of being assessors as well as designers of exercises. As part of the collaborative approach, at least a dozen assessors volunteered for the process. They were able to design the various exercises under the guidance of the academic partner. These exercises included an In-basket, Case Analysis, and Group Decision-making Exercise, and so forth. While the majority of the exercises were designed by the academic partner, the involvement of senior HR practitioners went a long way in identifying the critical incidents relevant to the profession. It took several iterations before an exercise was considered for use. All exercises were administered to pilot samples from industry, as part of the validation process.

Competency Literacy

One of the important aspects of competency development is to achieve a level of competency literacy, which is about ensuring that the target group is made familiar with the 'why' and 'what' of each competency. Towards this end, the NHRD Network is currently in the process of covering as many HR professionals as possible to provide literacy on the competencies. NHRD has already conducted about 30 1-day modules on various competencies across the major cities of the country. In addition, the details of the model have also been put on the website of NHRD.

The Job Ahead

So far two pilot tests of the HR Compass Assessment have been conducted and qualitative validation done with managers. More than two dozen participants have undergone the assessment. Based on the feedback, modifications have been incorporated within the assessment mechanism. A major drive is currently under way to build the necessary level of competency literacy by means of a series of 1-day modules that NHRD is conducting. While smaller pilots are happening in pockets across the country, the intervention will be ready for a large roll-out sometime in June 2011. We are in the process of certifying another 100 assessors to run the process as the number of participants targeted would easily run into several thousands. Creating validated instruments to replace the existing ones, and a question bank of functional test items are other challenges that we anticipate having to tackle.

Conclusion

The HR Compass initiative brings together the collective effort of an industry association, a network of HR professionals, and academia with an overarching vision of establishing a national standard for the HR profession in India. The initiative aims to develop quality HR professionals through assessment and certification of their competencies using multiple tools, including assessment centre methodology. Appropriate opportunities for developing these competencies are also being proposed. Success with such an intervention, once it achieves critical mass, would definitely create HR organizations with the right competency profile, helping them to effectively play the role of strategic partner and enhancing their contribution to business.

References

Becker, B.E., Huselid, M.A. and Ulrich, D. 2001. Making HR a strategic asset. *Financial Times*, November, 2001.

Bloomberg Business Week – Online version. 2005. India: Desperately seeking talent. [Accessed: 7 November 2005].

Boyatzis, R.E. 1982. *The Competent Manager: A Model for Effective Performance*. New York: Wiley.

Lievens, F. 2001. Assessors and use of assessment center dimensions: A fresh look at a troubling issue. *Journal of Organizational Behaviour*, 22, 203–221.

Long, C.S. and Ismail, W.K.W. 2008. Understanding the relationship of HR competencies and roles of Malaysian human resource professionals. *European Journal of Social Sciences*, 7, 88–103.

McClelland, D.C. 1973. Testing for competence rather than for intelligence. *American Psychologist*, 1–14

Spencer, S.M. and Spencer, L.M. 1993. *Competence at Work: Models for Superior Performance*. New York: Wiley.

Thornton, G.C. III and Rupp, D.E. 2006. *Assessment Centers in Human Resource Management: Strategies for Prediction, Diagnosis, and Development*. Mahwah, NJ: Erlbaum.

Ulrich, D. 1997. *The Human Resource Champions: The Next Agenda for Adding Value and Delivering Results*. New York, NY: McGraw Hill.

Ulrich, D. 1999. *Delivering Results: A New Mandate for Human Resource Professionals*. Boston, MA: Harvard Business School Press.

Ulrich, D. and Brockbank, W. 2005. *HR Value Proposition*, Boston, MA: Harvard Business School Press.

Woehr, D.J. and Huffcutt, A.I. 1994. Rater training for performance appraisal: A meta-analytic review. *Journal of Occupational and Organizational Psychology*, 6, 189–205.

Woehr, D.J. and Arthur, W. 2003. The construct-related validity of assessment center ratings: A review and meta-analysis of the role of methodological factors. *Journal of Management*, 29, 231–258.

16 Pioneering Assessment Centers within Local Government in Sweden: Gothenburg's Search for Better Leaders

EVA BERGVALL

The creation of an assessment center (AC) in Gothenburg started with a discussion in 2000 about what kind of leaders the city has. Are they good or bad? Are they any different from leaders in other organizations or in the private sector? Leaders in the public sector have traditionally been appointed only on the basis of their work experience and interviews were the only tool used for selection. It is now generally agreed that this form of selection is not sufficient. Assessment centers were discussed but not used.

When AT&T started their Assessment Center in the 1950s (Thornton and Rupp 2006) it eventually influenced the Swedish telephone utility company. At that time the company was state-owned but there was a strong desire for modernization. They started their assessment center around 1980. This was the first assessment center in Sweden. A few other organizations were also using what they called assessment centers but the practice was neither widespread nor frequent.

When we in the city of Gothenburg began to discuss using tools for assessment and development, the assessment center concept was suggested by consultants. The idea was very popular since its exercises were seen as more acceptable with better face validity than different types of tests, a view supported by research (Schmidt and Hunter 1998). In addition, there was considerable evidence the AC method predicted managerial success (Gaugler et al. 1987; Hardison and Sackett 2004). This was the beginning of the development of what we have today.

Local Government in Sweden

In Sweden, cities are run by politicians who are democratically elected every four years in local elections held at the same time as the general election. The cities thus do not necessarily have the same political majority as the country as a whole.

Most civil servants are appointed. The executive board appoints the chief executive, who then appoints the organization's managers. This means that the civil servants continue in their appointments even if the political majority changes.

THE CITY OF GOTHENBURG AND ITS AGENCIES AND MANAGERS

The city of Gothenburg is the second largest city in Sweden. The city has around 500,000 inhabitants and, with 48,000 employees, is the biggest single employer in the region and one of the 10 biggest employers in Sweden. There are around 40 different agencies and 30 companies that are owned by the city, which numbers some 2,000 managers.

Figure 16.1 shows the structure of the Gothenburg City Council and the variety of work that it is responsible for.

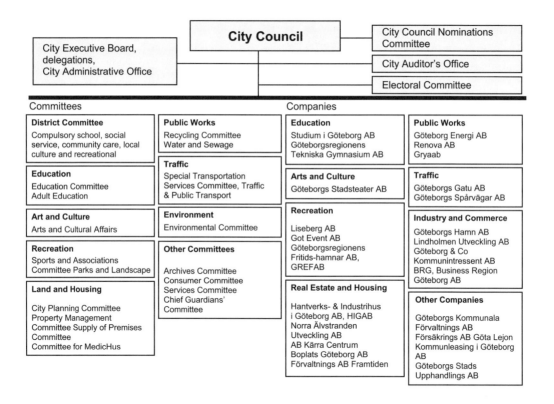

Figure 16.1 Structure of Gothenburg City Council

The Processes of Creating the Competencies

In discussions about leadership the question of "who is the best leader" always creates a lot of debate. This leads on naturally to the discussion of competencies. The hard part is to be more specific and to talk about behaviors instead of "personality" or, worse still, general descriptions based on personal impressions. Since many people in the organization have an opinion about what leader they would like to see, we began by letting as many of them as possible express their opinion. To conduct some of this work we engaged an external consultant to ensure that we did not influence people's view, as we were afraid that if *we* asked, we would only get answers that were considered "politically correct" in Gothenburg.

We began by interviewing the executive leaders, who described what they actually do as leaders. They described their day at work and provided us with critical incidents in which they explained how they had acted in those instances. As the interviews were individual, they were able to focus on their own behaviors and not on what should generally be done. We had been given informal "ratings" by the chief executive so we were able to compare stated behaviors with those considered "good" within the organization and with the less competent behaviors that emerged during the interviews.

The next step was to obtain descriptions from other groups of leaders. This was done by inviting them to attend focus groups. These focus groups were usually quite small, numbering 10–12 people and they provided a range of behavioral descriptions which were then rated in terms of their importance to the role of a leader. The groups comprised people from different parts of the organization. We had groups of leaders but also groups of other employees, such as trainees and people with a long history of working for the city. We also had people from the unions. The diversity of the groups ensured that we mirrored many aspects of leadership and also that we spread knowledge of our work within the organization.

Using all of the data we obtained from individuals and groups, we were able to construct the first draft of a document, called Leaderships Competencies in the city of Gothenburg. This first draft was communicated to all our agencies and companies.

When drawing up the competencies we also tried to take psychological theory into consideration and this meant it would be easier to describe and validate competencies in the future. Our main reference was the Big Five theory (Digman 1997) but we also looked at Ekvall and Arvonen (1991).

Between beginning the work and March 2003, our efforts had taken almost 2 years. By that time the competencies were very well known and it was only natural that they should be used in the assessment center.

The Formation of the Center for Leadership Assessment and Development

The Center for Leadership Assessment and Development (CLU) was the agency that was set up to work on leader selection and development. It was organized as a group within the HR division of the City's Central Administration and it was financed by fees. In the beginning, there were only a few participants and most centers were really Development Centers (DCs) with a developmental purpose. Growth was rapid and by 2004 assessment centers (ACs) were much more common, and by December 2009 the CLU had conducted over 2,000 assessments.

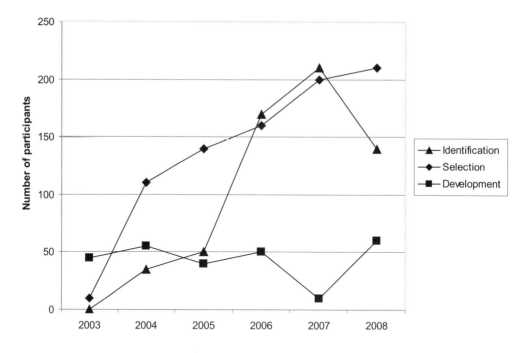

Figure 16.2 Growth of the assessment activity of the CLU 2003–2008

Development Centers are constant in numbers and the use of Assessment Centers for selection and identification is growing.

The Gothenburg Model

In this section we describe our approach to this project within Gothenburg.

SCIENTIFIC SETUP AND INVOLVEMENT OF THE WHOLE ORGANIZATION

When we began creating all the activities that are now in place, the aim was to create tools to identify, recruit and develop leaders at all levels in a structured and transparent manner. The AC was the first tool, and an important one that could actually fulfill all of these aims. It was also important that the quality of the tools should be very good and this meant that the scientific value of the methods had to be evaluated. We had planned to conduct studies from the very beginning. We contracted scientists to conduct reliability and validity studies at a very early stage. For the organization it was naturally important that the tool was cost-effective and that it could be used at different levels within the city of Gothenburg.

THE ASSESSMENT CENTER, CLU

Since it was obvious that we were going to be conducting a great many assessments, the idea of having our own premises seemed appropriate. Naturally, the history of the

Assessment Center name ensured that this idea wasn't so far-fetched. The first ACs were conducted in a hotel and others at the city's offices. The problems with both these locations were obvious. The hotel was expensive and was not really an office environment. The office we used ourselves was full of papers and people, which created unwelcome distractions.

After a year of conducting ACs we found a place that was close to perfect. It was located at the Ullevi arena, close to the city center, with perfect transport and parking facilities. The place is normally rather deserted (except during sports matches and other events and these usually take place in the late evening or at weekends.) The premises had originally been offices. They had been created by a well-known architect and, after some very minor renovation, looked very good. On one side there were 8 smallish rooms where we set up offices with computers for the candidates. There were bigger rooms on the opposite side where we furnished a special room for the assessors with computers for immediate registration of observations and for drawing up the reports. There was also space for serving lunch, so that we would not lose the candidates during breaks, and office space for the staff.

We called the center CLU (Center för Ledarutveckling) to distinguish it from the method, something that has not always been easy over the years.

PERSONNEL

The center began in 2002 with the hiring of a project leader to work with selection and development of leaders at the city of Gothenburg. When we moved in to Ullevi in 2003, a secretary was hired for administrative tasks. In 2004, two more full-time employees were hired and five people work full-time at the CLU today.

The Competencies

The work of creating competencies resulted in the following competencies and their descriptions:

- *Influence Others*. Assesses whether candidates are clear and adequate communicators, and whether they have the ability to quickly get their messages across and gain support for their thoughts and ideas. There is also an evaluation of whether the individual can make convincing arguments, contribute with enthusiasm and energy, and encourage good performance (team spirit, increased motivation).
- *Sensitivity to Others*. Assesses whether candidates have the ability to be sensitive and flexible in their interactions with others, as well as show respect, consideration, and concern for others, and whether they like working with others and have the ability to inspire team spirit.
- *Social Assuredness*. Assesses whether the candidate is easily approachable, if he or she is comfortable in meeting others and can act convincingly, confidently, and independently in both informal and formal situations.
- *Change Orientation*. Assesses the candidate's ability to envision potential changes and how he or she is able to advance the situation.

- *Goal and Results Orientation.* Assesses the candidate's ability to make plans and set goals, in both the short and the long-term; he or she should be a driving force and specify how the goals will be reached and how the results will be followed up.
- *Analytical Ability.* Assesses the candidate's ability to break problems down into smaller units and to differentiate between main causes and secondary causes; he or she should be able to identify and analyze the root of the problem and reach the appropriate conclusions.
- *Comprehensive View.* Assesses the candidate's ability to get a good overview of the situation and hold a strong general interest; he or she should get a sense of the complexity of an issue by taking different perspectives and sources of information into account. The ability to see one's activities as part of a greater context is also evaluated.

To measure the competencies in the exercises we developed what we call 1–3–5 Behavioral Anchor Rating Scales (BARS). For every competency being assessed in an exercise, a set of behavioral descriptors were constructed to illustrate how the competency might be displayed in that particular exercise. An example of this is given in Table 16.1.

Table 16.1 Part of the BARS for Sensitivity to Others for a role play with a co-worker

1	3	5
Does not ask for a description of what has happened	Does listen to a description of what has happened	Is clearly asking for a description of what has happened

The 1–3–5 BARS system was very helpful to the assessors and the descriptions could also sometimes be used to illustrate the behaviors in the written reports. Over the first few years the 1–3–5 BARS system was constantly improved to provide better examples and more accurate descriptions of the behaviors linked to the competencies.

Exercises

When we began discussing the use of an AC as a selection and development method we were thinking in terms of ready-made exercises. We also used these exercises in our first centers. These exercises did not work very well for several reasons. The realities described were taken from the business world and the public sector has different terminology and contexts. Most of the roles were male and we have to give everyone equal opportunities. The situations described were not the most important ones in our work environment; other matters are more important and more frequent. For this reason we decided to construct tailored exercises based on a public sector environment. In this work we used consultants with previous experience of assessment centers in Sweden and they have continued to support us with assessor training and conducting some coaching for further development.

We produced two sets of exercises: one for what we call Strategic leaders and one for Operational leaders. Strategic leaders are executives or top managers who have other leaders as their subordinates. Operational leaders, as the term implies, are in charge of the city's operations and have subordinates to carry out the work.

We have also been able to include the use of some computer-based exercises which provide greater realism, particularly as we have been able to put them in a local government setting.

The general setting in all of the exercises is a city of reasonable size somewhere in Sweden and depicts a day at work where the candidate has the same role throughout the whole day. It is a one-day center.

We describe below some of the exercises we have used for both Strategic leaders and Operational leaders.

STRATEGIC LEADERS

We used four different exercises when assessing strategic leaders as indicated below.

In-basket

The In-basket is a planning exercise where the candidate has around 20 topics to deal with, some of which are linked. The in-basket of today is of course an Inbox on the computer and most of the topics come by email. We started out with all of the mail in a paper-based format, but today we have a special set-up with a real email system and all the information on the computer as different web pages. We now use almost no paper in the exercise and the scoring is easy, since we have all the answers in a log.

Role play

The work with the In-basket on the computer is interrupted by a role play, in which a citizen has made an appointment to lodge a complaint.

Presentation

The candidate has to present and value two different proposals that are up for political decision and present them for the chair of the board.

Group exercise

The group exercise is designed for six participants. It is a combination of a presentation for the rest of the group and evaluation and decision-making by the group. The group exercise is not used in recruitment since we found that there was too much influence from other group members to provide a fair and standardized assessment of each candidate.

OPERATIONAL LEADERS

We used five different exercises to assess operational leaders and these are described below.

Planning exercise

The candidate acts as a manager for a group of 20 staff and he/she has to schedule the work for a coming holiday. The manager's subordinates have different expectations and needs and there are a number of customers with special demands.

Role play 1

The planning exercise is interrupted by a complaining customer who has very special demands for the future.

Presentation

The candidate has to present and value several different suggestions for how operations can be improved and the amount of money for the changes is limited. The candidate needs to present a proposal to his/her manager.

Role play 2

The candidate has a subordinate who is competent in doing his work, but who is sometimes awkward when cooperating with other people. A customer has complained about his work and the candidate needs to talk to him about improving his behavior and this requires some further planning.

Group exercise

The same group exercise is used for both the strategic and operational centers, which allows us to mix participants if necessary, to ensure we have a sufficient number of people attending the development center.

Assessors

Most assessors are managers on different levels at the city of Gothenburg. The number of assessors has grown and today there are some 30 who regularly participate in the assessments. The use of internal assessors guarantees the continuous involvement of different parts of the organization.

Assessors are currently selected on the basis of an assessment, which if adequate, results in that manager being invited to become an assessor. This is very fortunate because it means that we can have assessors with very different backgrounds and from different agencies and companies in the city. We also get very good assessors, since we can ensure they demonstrate the required standard at an assessment center.

TRAINING OF THE ASSESSORS

Initially, assessors are trained in the exercises they are going to be working with. Before they conduct their first assessment on their own, they double up with one of the more experienced assessors.

To continue as an assessor, they have to conduct at least eight days of assessment a year. The assessors also have to take part in refresher training twice a year. At least once a year some form of social event is arranged for the assessors.

Evaluating the Assessment Centers

In this section, four empirical studies are reported which provide evidence of the validity of the ratings from these ACs. The first study compares the costs of assessment and development programs run by internal staff members vs external consultants. The second study examines the relationship of AC ratings and a measure of general mental ability (GMA). The third study examines the relationship of AC ratings with a test of both personality and general mental ability. Finally, a predictive validity study in which AC ratings are correlated with job performance ratings by immediate supervisors and subordinates some time after the AC program is reported.

THE ADVANTAGE OF HAVING ONE'S OWN AC

The Assessment Center Method is often described as a very expensive assessment method. So in 2006 when the center had been in operation for around three years, we decided to ask a student in Stockholm University's Executive MBA (Erlandsson 2006) program to carry out a study as a project on the program's Project Analysis and Risk Management course. Our tailor-made center, run internally by the organization, was compared with other ways of conducting assessments in connection with recruitment and development. A cost-benefit analysis was conducted which made comparisons with:

- assessment centers run by consultants;
- traditional leadership development and selection carried out by the HR department in different parts of the organization;
- traditional models for leadership development and recruitment selection purchased from consultants.

The research was undertaken using data from the CLU with all internal costs and data from consultants taken from different offers submitted over the same period. The study did not calculate the benefits of better and safer recruitment or improved leadership. An analysis of Strengths, Weaknesses, Opportunities and Threats for external consultants and the CLU revealed that the CLU had more positive factors than the use of consultants.

Results

Figure 16.3 clearly shows that having an assessment center of one's own is less expensive for the city than purchasing services from consultants. The figures are based on conducting just over 200 assessments a year.

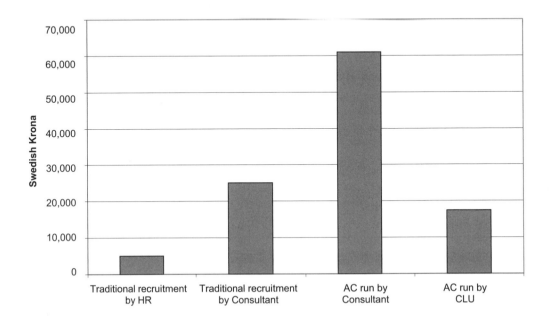

Figure 16.3 Cost comparison of the different resource models to run the ACs

The number showing how many participants are needed for it to be less expensive to run your own center was calculated, taking into consideration the total costs for running centers over a five-year period. The development cost for having one's own center was also included. The break-even point was a total of 194 traditional assessments by consultants or a total of 160 assessment centers run by consultants for an internal assessment center to be less expensive. Over the five-year period the CLU has conducted around 800 recruitment assessments, far in excess of both break-even points.

Comparisons of AC Results and General Mental Ability

BASIQ GENERAL MENTAL ABILITY TEST

The level of General Mental Ability (GMA) was measured with the BasIQ test developed for the Swedish market (Mårdberg, Sjöberg, and Henrysson-Eidvall 2000). The sample was 100 participants in our AC. One of the competencies is Analytical Ability and we expected that BasIQ would be positively correlated with this competency as assessed in the In-basket and Planning exercises. The correlations were both positive, that is, 0.59 and 0.45 respectively with BasIQ.

COMPARISONS OF AC RESULTS WITH GMA AND PERSONALITY

The objective of the second study was to examine the construct validity of the AC. The construct validity of ACs has been questioned (Sackett and Dreher 1982), so it was important to understand the meaning of scores in this program. The study focused on investigating the construct validity of the competencies and the overall AC score (Overall Assessment Rating-OAR) which was the aggregated evaluation score for each of our seven competencies. The hypothesis was that the AC measures a combination of the psychological constructs of personality and ability. There was reason to believe both ability (Schmidt and Hunter 1998) and personality (Barrick and Mount 2003; Hogan and Holland 2003) would be related to managerial performance. The study sample consisted of 90 candidates of whom 57 were women and 33 were men and their ages varied between 29 and 63.

The results from the AC were correlated with the Predicting Job Performance (PJP) test (Assessio International in press, Sjöberg, Sjöberg and Forssén 2006). The PJP is a psychological test that measures personality in terms of four different factors, as well as the GMA. The personality factors are:

- *Stability.* This personality factor relates to how emotionally stable and well-adjusted a person is.
- *Extraversion.* This personality factor is concerned with how sociable a person is, as opposed to being reserved and perhaps shy.
- *Conscientiousness.* This personality factor relates to what extent a person likes to actively plan, has a strong will, and is decisive.
- *Agreeableness.* This personality factor is largely concerned with what "style" a person has in his or her relationships with others.

The ability factor within the PJP measures general mental ability and consists of three parts: Analogies, Number series, and Logical series.

Results

Table 16.2 shows the correlations of PJP scores with AC competency ratings. Of the individual factors in the PJP, it is, as expected, Ability which has the strongest relationship with the Analytical Ability (F) competency ($r = .63$). The next strongest relationship is exhibited between a combination of four PJP factors and the Influence Others (A) competency ($R = .44$). The individual PJP scales contributing to that multiple correlation are Stability ($r = .32$), Extraversion ($r = .29$), Agreeableness ($r = .22$), and Ability ($r = .23$). The following PJP scales combine to correlate with Social Assuredness ($r = .41$): Extraversion ($r = .39$) and Stability ($r = .22$). Lastly, the Comprehensive View (G) competency was found to be significantly related to the factor of Extraversion ($r = .32$) in the PJP.

Table 16.2 Correlations between the five PJP Factors and the AC Competencies

PJP	A	B	C	D	E	F	G
1. Stability	.32*	.07	.22*	.16	.21*	.11	.20
2. Extroversion	.29*	.15	.39*	.22*	.18	.17	.32*
3. Conscientiousness	.11	-.04	.12	.14	.19	.09	.09
4. Agreeableness	.22*	.05	.17	.03	.12	.03	.01
5. GMA	.23*	.19	.09	.13	.08	.63*	.01
Multiple R	.44*	.26	.41*	.27	.27	.64*	.39*
R squared	.19*	.07	.17*	.07	.07	.41*	.15*

N = 90. * p<.05

A = Influence Others, B = Sensitivity to Others, C = Social Assuredness, D = Change Orientation, E = Goal and Results Orientation, F = Analytical Ability, and G = Comprehensive View.

The Overall Assessment Rating (OAR) scores were regressed on the five factors of the PJP. Table 16.3 shows both the bivarate correlation(r) and the beta weight (β) of the PJP scores with the OAR scores. Here it is evident that the PJP factors Stability ($r = .28$), Extroversion ($r = .37$), and Ability ($r = .34$) are related to the OAR. This suggests that participants who are awarded high scores by the assessors show a stable, extraverted personality and score higher in GMA than other AC participants.

Table 16.3 Correlations and regression analysis with OAR as the dependent variable

PJP	r	β
1. Stability	.28*	.17
2. Extroversion	.37*	.26*
3. Conscientiousness	.15	.00
4. Agreeableness	.14	.01
5. GMA	.34*	.33*
Multiple R		.50*
R squared		.25*

N = 90. * p<.05

When the relationships among the factors are taken into consideration in a regression analysis, it was found that the factors Extraversion and Ability explain approximately 25 percent of the total variance in OAR. This confirms earlier analysis (Collins et al. 2003) in which a combination of extraversion and general ability was found to adequately capture the constructs measured in a traditional AC in the aggregated OAR score. It is now also possible to generalize this result to the AC of the CLU.

The study also shows that further work needs to be done on the exercises in order to capture Conscientiousness and Agreeableness.

Prediction of Performance Ratings by Immediate Supervisors and Subordinates

A predictive validity study was conducted (Mårdberg 2008) to relate the results obtained in the ACs to follow-up data collected from immediate managers and subordinates of the managers, who at the time of the follow-up process were in management positions in the city of Gothenburg. The study provides an indication of the predictive validity of the ACs expressed as validity coefficients. The collated data from the two centers were studied. Three hundred and twenty-eight (N = 328) candidates participated in the operational centers. Of these, 118 (36.0 percent) were men and 210 (64.0 percent) women. The age range was 26 to 62 and the mean age and distribution of age were M = 45.8 and SD = 7.9.

One hundred and fifty-eight (N = 158) candidates participated in the strategic centers. Of these, 80 (50.6 percent) were men and 78 (49.4 percent) women. The age range was 31 to 61 and the mean age and distribution of age were M = 48.1 and SD = 7.2. This gave us a combined sample of 486 candidates, who had completed assessments using a range of exercises and a GMA.

The criterion came from two forms, completed by managers and subordinates, with statements in areas which are important for carrying out the tasks related to the job. Factor analyses were used to establish competence factors, that is, criteria for analyzing the centers' predictive ability. Middle managers and executives were assessed using the forms designed for assessment by immediate managers. In addition, managers were assessed by subordinates using the second form. Each form comprised eight factors.

RESULTS

Analyses of the AC ratings showed that the reliability of the assessments was good, which is a precondition of good predictions of success in management roles. Detailed studies of correlations between background data, general mental ability, and assessments of the exercises gave two fundamental results. The highest correlations were between ratings on behavioral dimensions and general mental ability and educational level. No indication of discrimination on the basis of gender or other background variables was revealed.

The predictive validity of the AC ratings for managers' performance and functions as middle managers or executives was analyzed using step-wise regression analysis. The most important results showed high correlations between the AC ratings and the follow-up data. The multiple correlation coefficients, which are the maximum correlations between the predictive variables (AC ratings) and the follow-up factors, were estimated by traditional regression analysis and are shown in Table 16.4 below.

Table 16.4 Correlations of managers' assessments of follow-up criteria with AC ratings

Criterion	Validity coefficient	Center
Strategic approach	R = 0.42	Operational
Inspires Confidence	R = 0.49	Strategic
Strategic approach	R = 0.51	Strategic
Effective reporting	R = 0.58 adj.= 0.52	Strategic
Economic responsibility	R = 0.48	Strategic
Aware of the organizational rules	R = 0.47	Strategic

Inspires Confidence is a communication factor; the others are task-oriented.

The AC's prediction of the factors generated by subordinates' assessments for the follow-up criteria are shown in Table 16.5

Table 16.5 Correlations of subordinates' assessments of follow-up criteria with AC ratings

Criterion	Validity coefficient	Center
Shows good judgment	R = 0.49	Operational
Deals with conflicts	R = 0.59	Strategic
Supports subordinates	R = 0.62	Strategic

Shows Good Judgment is a personal factor; the other two are communication factors.

Data from the strategic centers yielded seven of the nine highest validity coefficients. This may indicate that the operational centers are assessing fewer of the competency areas identified by the follow-up factors.

The managers' top-down perspective is shown by the emphasis given to the task-oriented factors of strategic approach and central management questions. The well-predicted subordinate factors are notable for good judgment and the communication areas dealing with conflicts and good relations with subordinates.

Conclusions

The strength of the AC is that the wide spectrum of factors which create the picture of the requirements regarding managers at work can be broadly predicted from the results produced by the AC. This should be seen as a natural and desirable picture of the complex process involved in recruiting effective managers to a major municipality and its satellite municipalities.

A key conclusion from these results is that the AC in the city of Gothenburg maintains a very high level of quality, that exercises and tasks generate valuable predictions and that the assessors are well-trained. The centers make a constructive and effective contribution to the identification of the managers of the future.

In respect of these aspects, research has shown that centers with a set-up like the one under discussion here, are at the cutting edge in the use of ability factors, which alongside job-samples should be at the top of the scale as regards predictive validity in meta-studies. The reason for this is that ACs are structured to deal with both. Exercises and tasks require a high intellectual level as well as appropriate education. In addition, simulations of critical tasks are used as a type of job-sample. This was shown in this study of predictive validity.

The Growth in Use of the AC and Further Development

Today the AC is used as a regular part of the recruitment process at the city of Gothenburg. Approximately half of the total number of recruitment campaigns made use of an AC in the process. The focus on competencies and behaviors has made many people in the organization aware of aspects of good leadership. It has influenced job analysis in connection with recruitment and also made leaders more aware of competencies when they conduct interviews.

Use of ACs in the selection of managers has generated the same professional approach that advanced systems for finance, technology and supervision give in their respective areas. A number of areas within the organization have been involved in the design, operation and monitoring of the ACs. This means that the organization will be permeated by human resource issues. Both the quality of management selection and development, and the commitment to managerial issues at various levels and operations in the organization, which is encouraged through the use of ACs, in all likelihood heavily outweigh the cost of the resources the system requires.

The cost of using ACs proved to be lower than we feared would be the case, owing largely to adopting a model in which we managed the process internally, supported by internal assessors. The difficulty is to maintain a very high standard of competence in the personnel working with the AC and in this regard it is very important that research continues.

The leadership task is changing all the time and that will necessarily influence the exercises that are used, so they will also have to change. The same is true of the competencies. The possibility of using the computer in more exercises will enable both of these changes. The computer has also become a much more important tool for leaders. These changes will in turn change what is done in the AC. Having a system that is a part of the organization will make this easier, as long as there are people with the necessary know-how.

The ACs used here, have reinforced the view that the AC has good reliability and sufficient validity, which means that it is a tool that the organization can trust. This of course has also increased the use of the tool.

In an AC you are trying to predict the quality of work in the future. Of course, more studies will need to be undertaken to maintain the quality of the system as it is today, but also to enable us to make the necessary changes that will ensure it meets the demands of the future.

References

Assessio International (in press). *Predicting Job Performance (PJP): Manual*. Psykologiförlaget, Stockholm, Author.

Barrick, M.R. and Mount, M.K. 2003. Impact of meta-analysis on understanding personality and performance relations. In *The Impact of Validity Generalization Methods on Personnel Selection*, edited by K. Murphy. Mahwah. NJ: Erlbaum, 197–222.

Collins, J.M., Schmidt, F.L., Sanchez, K.M., McDaniel, M.A. and Le, H. 2003. Can basic individual differences shed light on the construct meaning of assessment center evaluations? *International Journal of Selection and Assessment*, 11, 17–29.

Digman, J.M. 1997. Higher-order factors of the Big Five. *Journal of Personality and Social Psychology*, 73, 1246–1256.

Ekvall, G. and Arvonen, J. 1991. Change-centered leadership: An extension of the two-dimensional model. *Scandinavian Journal of Management*, 7, 17–26.

Erlandsson, A. 2006. Ekonomisk bedömning av AC. Unpublished report.

Gaugler, B.B., Rosenthal, D.B., Thornton, G.C. III and Bentson, C. 1987. Meta-analysis of assessment center validity. *Journal of Applied Psychology*, 72, 493–511.

Hardison, C.M. and Sackett, P.R. 2004. *Assessment center criterion related validity: A meta-analytic update*. Paper presented at the 19th Annual Society for Industrial and Organizational Psychology (SIOP) Meeting, Chicago, IL.

Hogan. J. and Holland. B. 2003. Using theory to evaluate personality and job-performance relations: A socioanalytic perspective. *Journal of Applied Psychology*, 88, 100–112.

Mårdberg, B. 2008. Kvalitetssäkring av Göteborgs stads Assessment Center för Urval av operative och strategiska chefer. Unpublished report.

Mårdberg, B., Sjöberg, A. and Henrysson-Eidvall. S. 2000. *BasIQ – begåvningstest*. Stockholm: Psykologiförlaget AB.

Sackett, P.R. and Dreher, G.F. 1982. Constructs and assessment center ratings: Some troubling empirical findings. *Journal of Applied Psychology*, 6, 401–410.

Schmidt, F.L. and Hunter, J.E. 1998. The validity and utility of selection methods in personnel psychology: Practical and theoretical implications of 85 years of research findings. *Psychological Bulletin*, 124, 262–274.

Sjöberg, A.R., Sjöberg, S., and Forssén, K. 2006. *Predicting Job Performance. Manual*. Stockholm: Assessio AB.

Thornton, G.C. III and Rupp, D.E. 2006. *Assessment Centers in Human Resource Management: Strategies for Prediction, Diagnosis, and Development*. Mahwah, NJ: Lawrence Erlbaum Associates.

17 In Pursuit of a Diversification Strategy: Using an Assessment Centre to Identify Global Talent

NATALIE LIVINGS AND WILL MITCHELL

Overview – What Made this Leadership Project Different?

The purpose of this chapter is to describe how a global organization developed a talent management solution to help stimulate cultural change. This was in order to implement an innovation strategy (the Innovation Intent) from 2007 to 2025. The client brief had a number of challenging requirements, making it a leading-edge assessment centre assignment which we describe in this case study:

- The global client required a process to identify individuals with high potential in three particular categories: leaders, innovators and specialists.
- There was a desire to measure and understand the level of Learning Agility displayed by an individual. The assessment centre included some chaotic and ambiguous challenges, which required a high level of adaptability for success.
- Successful individuals need to be culturally adaptable and draw rapidly on experience to increase their level of effectiveness. Therefore the assessment centre also required the ability to work with people from a diverse range of cultural backgrounds.

This combination of requirements provided a challenging brief, which necessitated a degree of scoping and close client partnership, in order to design and deliver a robust solution that could be applied worldwide.

Grundfos: A Global Leader in Pumps

The Grundfos Group is globally renowned for its high-quality pumps, producing 16 million units annually. It is a global market leader, covering around 50 per cent of the world market. Grundfos was founded in 1945 by Poul Due Jenson and has grown during the last 60 years as a privately owned business with a reputation for excellence and design (Ballisager 2000). This has enabled the business to take a long-term view, protected from the demands of shorter-term investors in stock markets. Based in Denmark, they now have offices in 41 countries worldwide with over 18,000 employees.

At the heart of the founder's principles has been an altruistic focus to make people's lives easier and to actively contribute to a better global environment. Grundfos have supported climate change research and have emphasized the potential impact of water supply decline around increasingly high population areas such as central China.

Values and Culture

The Grundfos values are defined around being responsible, thinking ahead and innovating: 'Be – Think – Innovate.' The historical culture within Grundfos has been collaborative and consensual, aligned with their Scandinavian roots. However, the strong technical focus of high quality in combination with a cautious and risk-averse culture presents a potential danger to the future success of this global leader. Tougher competition is emerging in local markets and the business needs to respond more quickly in developing new products.

Innovation Intent 2025

Whilst the current emphasis of Grundfos has been on pump technology, there is now a strategic intent to broaden and diversify the range of services, for example pioneering sustainable technologies such as using solar and wind power. This will require a shift in mindset towards a more dynamic and proactive culture with leaders, innovators and specialists who can forge the agenda in their respective markets. As the organization diversifies into new product areas and markets, successful employees will need to have a high degree of Learning Agility in order to understand the needs of consumers and employees from Lagos to London.

If Grundfos fails to make these cultural shifts, it risks falling behind those competitors who understand and react to the needs of consumers in a world of scarcer water resource and climate challenges.

Vision for a Talent Strategy

Grundfos recognized that as a company it needed to develop a more dynamic organizational culture in order to be able to meet its Innovation Intent. To achieve this would require a journey of culture change, inspired and championed by key talents of the future. These 'talents' would need to be identified from within the Grundfos global network and then nurtured to reach their full potential.

The first steps of the journey were described in the Group Strategy 2008–2012, which stated that:

With the Innovation Intent, the level of ambition for the future is higher than ever. Also considering the challenges of globalization and demographic change, the ambition forces us to rethink our processes to get talented and highly motivated people onboard the Grundfos team. We must change approach by building on excellence and visibly point out the talents. We must be willing to differentiate towards the best when it comes to special tasks, visibility and challenges in their daily work, but also with regard development and compensation and incentive programs.

Grundfos chose to build a brand new concept for Talent Management – and they named it 'Talent Engine Version 1', anticipating that as they progressed, they would learn, and then develop the concept further into new versions. This Talent Engine was to measure potential and build on excellence, transparency and differentiated career paths.

CO-CREATION – GLOBAL WORKSHOP

The Grundfos 'People & Strategy' Division gathered together 40 diverse people from around the world, such as general managers, business development directors, HR managers, sales directors and so on. They came from countries such as Korea, Australia, and USA and across Europe. The choice of participants was based on only two key criteria: they should be enthusiastic about the purpose, and they should be strong drivers of the Talent Engine in their local environment. They worked collaboratively for three days at Copenhagen Business School to develop the new concept and framework for Talent Management in Grundfos, and on the fourth day they presented their recommendations to the Board.

Differentiating employees based on potential, rather than purely on past performance and experience, was deemed important and represented a major cultural shift for Grundfos. During the generation of the 'Talent Engine' concept, a critical and guiding factor for Grundfos was the importance of creating a fair and defensible process that would have acceptance and buy-in from all participants (face validity). Grundfos were clear that they wanted to afford participants a stretching, yet energizing experience, so that all participants would emerge with learning for the future and a positive experience.

The assessment part of the process would need to be based on far more than the individual's previous experience and line manager performance ratings; it would need to be focused on high-potential behaviours. There was also the need for participants to be able to display these behaviours in stretching, uncertain, changeable, but realistic situations that might be experienced at more senior levels. The outcome would be that high-potential individuals would become known as 'global talents'.

Unlike the majority of high-potential programmes implemented by large organizations, Grundfos were not only interested in identifying the leaders of the future, but also acknowledged the need for different types of talent. Thus three talent pools were envisioned: leaders, specialists and innovators.

This Talent Engine v1 went live in February 2009 when approximately 100 of Grundfos' top managers received a 'golden envelope' containing guidance and instructions for the nomination of 'talents' in their own business unit. The result was a list of 135 talents from all over the world.

A Talent Driving Community (TDC) was formed to become the owner of the future development of the Talent Engine V1. The TDC consists of four advisory boards – each of these boards drives improvements and add-ons to the existing components of the Talent Engine.

- The Strategic Board ensures that the Talent Strategy is aligned with business strategic needs.
- The Nomination and Talent Centre Board ensures that the Assessment or 'Talent' Centre process, approach and tools allow the identification and qualification of global talents that the business calls for.
- The Greenhouse Board ensures that development opportunities open to global talents post-Centre are attractive and competitive, so as to secure a high level of engagement and performance.
- Lastly, the Matchmaking Board ensures that the process and tools in place support the fast allocation of global talents to strategic assignments and critical roles across the organization.

SUPPLIER ENGAGEMENT AND RESEARCH

In terms of securing a provider for the Talent Centre, that Grundfos could work effectively with in partnership, Marjanne Grønhøj (People & Strategy Partner, Grundfos) said: 'We were looking for a partner who had to be very innovative, as our talent programme goes way further than traditional talent management programmes, and very professional, as they had to ensure a strong link to the Grundfos company values.' A&DC were engaged to partner with Grundfos in April 2009 to make the Talent Engine vision a reality.

In order to design and deliver an objective, fair and consistent Talent Centre, it was necessary to establish the competencies for high-potential employees that Grundfos defined as 'global talents'. During the co-creation workshop, Grundfos had already identified these competencies, so only a limited amount of research was required to clarify and confirm these. Fourteen scoping interviews were conducted by telephone (for logistical reasons) with senior managers from different Grundfos companies around the world. This enabled a model to be created, which showed which of the ten competencies mapped onto which talent pool. Three competencies were found to be core requirements for all global talents: Communicating Effectively, Business Acumen and Delivering Outstanding Results, whilst other competencies differentiated a certain talent pool. For example Innovators were differentiated by their Creativity, but this competency was not necessary for Leaders or Specialists.

Design of the Talent Centre Approach

Following the diagnostic phase, a customized and themed Talent Centre was designed, based on 'Day in the Life' principles (Povah and Povah 2009). This would provide comprehensive and reliable information on each individual being assessed, which could be used to aid their future development. The components of the Centre were chosen to provide a holistic view of each participant; including their ability, personality and motivation or fit (Boyatzis 1982). To this end a range of tools were designed and procured, including business simulation exercises, an online personality measure and documents to aid self-reflection. The business simulation exercises ensured coverage of the typical ways in which people work; that is, alone, one-to-one and in groups (Ballantyne and Povah 2004). These included a written analysis exercise, a presentation exercise, a group discussion, and a 'crisis management' exercise. These elements of the Centre were linked and set in a parallel organization to Grundfos; a renewable energy company with similarities in terms of company vision, values and culture. A Background Document set the scene and included information such as company overview; mission, vision and values; organizational structure; and financial and performance data.

A participant's scoring matrix included their scores on the business simulation exercises, the 'Talent Q Dimensions' personality measure and the self-reflection documents. This mix of information helped the assessor team to understand which of the three talent pools (leaders, specialists, innovators) the participant would best fit in to. Whether they were to be rated as a 'global' talent depended on the scores they achieved on the various competencies, with the scores on the three core competencies being most important. Figure 17.1 shows the structure of the two-and-a-half-day Centre.

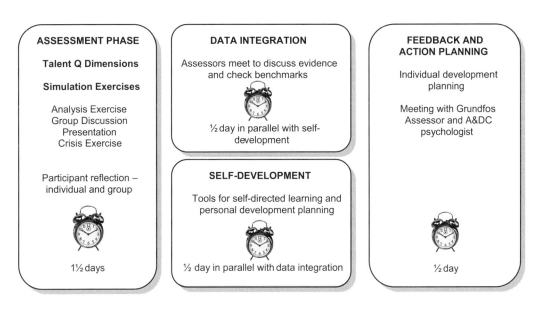

Figure 17.1 Structure of the Grundfos talent centre

During the first day and a half, participants took part in various ice-breaker exercises, then an introductory session, which included a welcome from the CEO, or a member of Group Management, and then the simulation exercises. There was also time allocated for self-reflection, and templates were provided to enable participants to structure their thoughts. On the afternoon of the second day, participants were involved in a Self-Development Module (SDM), whilst the assessors completed their marking, and met to discuss and rate participants against the benchmark for a global talent. The SDM involved a number of elements such as reflecting on their key motivators/drivers, preparing them to receive their feedback and helping them to consider their long-term career planning. In addition, consistent with one of the Grundfos values, 'Focus on People', a fitness instructor led a session on health and nutrition, which was followed by an hour of fitness, either by participating in circuit training or volleyball. This unusual intervention in an AC had the added benefit of re-energizing the participants half way through the Centre. On the morning of day three participants engaged in three activities; they received behavioural and psychometric feedback (face-to-face and written) and started to create their individual personal development plan. They discussed feedback on their performance on the Talent Centre business simulation exercises provided by one of the assessors, and they also had a discussion regarding their results on the personality measure with one of the consultant psychologists.

The output of the Talent Centre was to be a motivational and focused development plan for *all* participants, regardless of the level on which they would continue their development journey in the future – regionally or globally. This development plan then feeds into an individual's 'Talent Development Plan', which is reviewed and discussed at regular intervals with their manager in order to track what developmental actions have been taken.

Key Design Features

There are a number of best-practice AC design methodologies that we challenged to make this project different from the norm, and we outline these below.

SPECIFICITY

Conventional ACs tend to be quite specific with a focus on one job-related set of competencies, so typical assignments in talent management are to design and deliver centres for just one type of role (for example sales), usually set at one level, such as graduate, functional head or country manager.

For Grundfos the 135 talents that were nominated and then assessed were staff covering three broad levels – from employees such as finance assistants or sales representatives through to middle and senior managers, such as sales directors or plant managers. This nuance had to be considered in the design; how to design a centre that would be fair for all individuals regardless of their function, experience, seniority and longevity within the company. Care was taken to ensure that the subject matter of the exercises would not be too complex for individuals from certain non-engineering or non-technical backgrounds. Each of the simulation exercises on the first day was also designed to encourage different types of talent to shine. For example the requirements of the presentation exercise might favour leaders, the group discussion required creativity from innovators, and the analysis exercise might favour specialists.

STABILITY

In terms of stability, AC participants often respond to a brief that is given at the beginning of an exercise, and the information remains static throughout. However, this represents a relatively stable context which may not truly reflect reality. To create some unpredictability and pressure throughout the Grundfos Talent Centre various interruptions brought additional information to the participants during the exercises, such as budgetary changes.

POSITIVE PSYCHOLOGY

The AC was designed in such a way as to expose the participants to some of the principles of positive psychology throughout the centre. In an energizing ice-breaker session before the simulation exercises commenced on day one, participants stood in the centre of the room and shared stories with a partner based on prompts such as; 'I feel most energized when I am …', 'One thing I do well is …' and 'I am proud of myself for …'. This generated a great deal of energy in the room, relaxed participants and helped to put them in a positive frame of mind. In the Self-Development Module on day two, participants were introduced to some concepts related to positive psychology such as that learning from successes is more powerful than learning from mistakes and they were encouraged to consider this within their personal development planning.

CHAOTIC AND STRETCHING ENVIRONMENT

The requirement for a chaotic environment was critical to the success of the Talent Centre and an innovative approach was required beyond the conventional use of discreet exercises. The aim was to create a pressurized and highly realistic situation where all participants would become absorbed for a period of time, but could still be assessed feasibly. One of the simulations created was a 'crisis exercise', as illustrated in Figure 17.2 on the next page. Participants faced a number of linked scenarios requiring interaction with technical experts, the media, presentations to the board and a number of group discussions throughout the four-hour exercise. The various parts of the exercise were designed carefully to give an opportunity for each type of talent (specialist, leader, or innovator) to contribute. In order to try to make this exercise fair and objective certain 'rules' were introduced; for example in the 'Fact Find' meeting with the technical expert, participants were paired and had to ask questions in turn, and in the Board presentation all participants were asked to contribute to the delivery of the presentation, as well as the question session.

The dynamic environment of a crisis exercise has the potential for certain participants to dominate; for example during the media panel interview and the Board presentation, some participants could feel less confident about contributing than others. Consequently, we designed a range of questions balanced across competencies and shared around all participants to ensure complete fairness in the process, with each participant having an opportunity to respond on their own to a particular question. Other participants could contribute if the person targeted for a question had nothing further to add. This created a slightly artificial environment and structure to the task, but created an unbiased platform for the assessment.

LEARNING AGILITY

Grundfos had identified that it needs adaptable and 'learning agile' leaders, innovators and specialists as the requirements of the market evolve specifically around climate change, government legislation and technology. The body of evidence around learning agility is limited, as it is a relatively new concept. It was used by Lombardo and Eichinger (2000), who researched Learning Quotient (LQ) across ten companies.

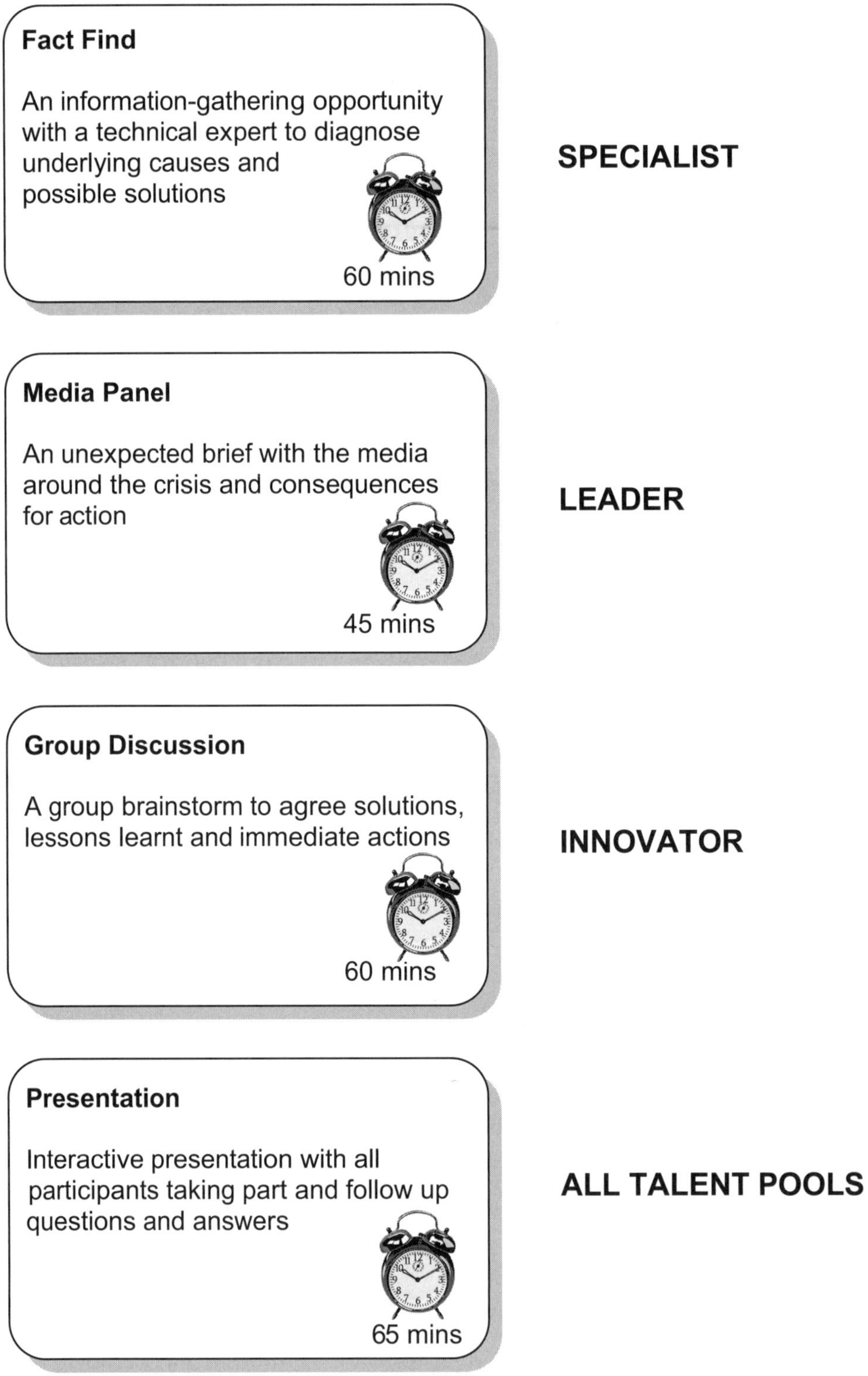

Fact Find

An information-gathering opportunity with a technical expert to diagnose underlying causes and possible solutions

60 mins

SPECIALIST

Media Panel

An unexpected brief with the media around the crisis and consequences for action

45 mins

LEADER

Group Discussion

A group brainstorm to agree solutions, lessons learnt and immediate actions

60 mins

INNOVATOR

Presentation

Interactive presentation with all participants taking part and follow up questions and answers

65 mins

ALL TALENT POOLS

Figure 17.2 The crisis exercise

Lombardo found that those individuals who demonstrated higher levels of LQ did six things particularly well:

1. Overcame complexity and ambiguity, linking new connections to solve challenging obstacles.
2. Demonstrated comprehensive self-awareness.
3. Took risks by experimenting with new approaches and took the responsibility for introducing new and innovative approaches.
4. Motivated others to deliver results in ambiguous, novel situations.
5. Demonstrated creativity and curiosity in new situations.
6. Proactively grasped opportunities, showed openness to change, flexibility and adaptability to their environment.

Other researchers such as Spreitzer, McCall and Mahoney (1997) have also found similar constructs. There is also a potential link to resilience regarding the ability to accept experiences outside one's comfort zone. Those with higher LQ try new experiences and make sense of them, rather than stay within a safe behavioural zone. Joiner and Josephs (2006) also looked at the development of learning agility through greater mindfulness and active reflection to focus attention to the current moment.

Measurement of learning agility is difficult to achieve as it is a thinking (cognitive) element which is hard to observe. However, there are a number of possible approaches that might be applicable within an AC context. One example is giving real-time feedback about performance after each exercise, and measuring change in the next exercise. Another option is to ask participants to undertake structured individual reflection, for example by recording what they did well and not so well and then identifying what they might seek to do differently next time. In this way, participants would have the chance to demonstrate learning agility when tackling the next exercise on the event. The reflection information could also be used by an Assessor to probe further. A third option is to conduct exploratory interviews with participants to determine whether, and to what degree, they are inclined to learn from experiences. These could include the use of psychometric measures to examine the talent's inclination to learn from different types of experiences and asking forward looking questions to understand how they would utilize this information in other situations.

The options were discussed with Grundfos and initially there was a preference for 'real-time' feedback which would provide an ideal opportunity to see behaviour change over time. This would have been a best case approach for learning agility but required a highly consistent approach from all assessors and also challenged the timing, resource and budget constraints of the project. We felt that these risks were too high and a more reliable approach was to allow each of the participants to have a number of opportunities during the AC to take 'time-out' in order to reflect on the exercise just completed. This is already established best practice in conventional Assessment Centres using self-report forms (Ballantyne and Povah 2004), but our approach went further in helping individuals develop deeper self-awareness through more structured questions. Participants were given time throughout the Centre to reflect on their performance, both individually and also in the group they belonged to for the group discussion exercise. They were put in the same group the next day for the crisis exercise, thereby giving them an opportunity to demonstrate some learning agility by effecting some changes.

Cultural Implications

As organizations become more global, people have appreciated that behaviour expectations are widely different across cultures and there is no perfect model of best practice behaviour. This provides a major challenge to any global assessment or development process as behavioural competencies are typically universal and cross-cultural in scope. While some global organizations have imposed their models internationally, this has clear risks if not managed sensitively. The question which Grundfos, and indeed any organization developing a global AC might ask is: 'Can I be confident that high-potential employees in different countries and continents are able to demonstrate a number of core behaviours and characteristics for effectiveness?'

There has been considerable research around cultural differences which started with Geert Hofstede (1980) with his seminal work across 40 countries in IBM during the late 1960s covering 100,000 employees. He developed a model with five dimensions to differentiate cultures:

1. Power Distance Index (PDI) focuses on the degree of equality, or inequality, between people in the country's society.
2. Individualism (IDV) focuses on the degree the society reinforces individual or collective, achievement and interpersonal relationships.
3. Masculinity (MAS) focuses on the degree the society reinforces, or does not reinforce, the traditional masculine work role model of male achievement, control, and power.
4. Uncertainty Avoidance Index (UAI) focuses on the level of tolerance for uncertainty and ambiguity within the society – that is, unstructured situations.
5. Long-Term Orientation (LTO) focuses on the degree the society embraces, or does not embrace long-term devotion to traditional, forward thinking values.

This was followed by Fons Trompenaars (1997) whose research also suggested five orientations around people relationships. One of these dimensions was individualism versus collectivism which aligns with Hofstede's earlier work. Later research by Chawla and Cronshaw (2002) explored this dimension further, looking at cross-cultural differences in AC design for leadership development. Specific universal leadership competencies were researched which are consistent across all cultures but the research was inconclusive.

However, a number of best-practice recommendations were integrated into the design of the Grundfos Talent Centre to ensure cross-cultural validity of their global leadership assessment process:

- As part of the job analysis phase, a number of senior leaders across culturally diverse countries were interviewed when refining the competencies to be assessed within the Talent Centre.
- The Talent Centre used a balance of culturally diverse assessors who could debate behavioural differences during the 'wash-up' phase, and give advice to assessors who were discussing feedback for a participant from a different culture. This was usually more pertinent where the participant had not scored well on certain competencies, and might require some feedback on how to interact better with people from other nationalities and cultures.

- Group exercises were structured to encourage all cultures to participate fully, and behavioural indicators recognized the importance of inclusivity, particularly during the crisis exercise discussions which had the potential to become emotive.

During the Talent Centres, there were was a truly global balance with attendees from Asia to the Americas as well as Europeans. There was some concern around cultural fairness given differences shown in studies of ACs held in specific regions with similar ethnic groups of talents, for example Chawla and Cronshaw (2002).

However, the principal goal of Talent Engine V1 was to identify talents who were able to work globally and to adapt to different contexts and cultures, therefore the planning of the ACs incorporated a mix of nationalities from talents and assessors.

Implementation of the Talent Centres

Once the Talent Centre simulations and supporting documentation such as the timetables had been designed and signed off by the appropriate stakeholders, the Assessor Training course materials were finalized. A two-day training course was run for sixteen senior Grundfos staff. The course included familiarizing these HR and line manager volunteers with the classic 'ORCE' process for marking exercises (Observe, Record, Classify, Evaluate), enabling them to practise marking each of the exercises, and benchmarking the level of performance that would be expected against each competency, for each job level. The Assessor Training also included input and discussion around diversity awareness, given that assessors and participants would be of various nationalities/cultures, and English would often not be their first language.

Most of the Grundfos assessors were non-native English speakers. Although they were quite fluent, it took some of them longer to evaluate participants' performance than native English speakers. This increased the amount of time required by the assessors to mark and the centre managers to quality check and amend, despite having provided pre-written electronic indicators, which assessors could edit, add and delete as appropriate, to help them when completing their write-ups. Further work is still being undertaken to improve the marking process to make it as efficient as possible, whilst still retaining the necessary rigour, objectivity and fairness.

After an initial pilot Talent Centre, which involved fourteen talents, eight assessors and four external centre management staff, some refinements were made to the content of materials and the process. Feedback was very positive from all involved. Before the pilot there was some concern that those qualified as 'talents', rather than 'global talents' would feel demotivated and frustrated. However, all participants emerged from the two and a half-day process positive and energized. They particularly valued the experience to network with their peers, and with the more senior assessors, and welcomed the very thorough, evidence-based individual feedback that they received. The assessors, who were general managers and high-level managers, also left the event feeling inspired and energized. They had developed themselves through the process of assessing others and had gained insights into how they could go back to their regions and create their own local talent development processes as a pipeline for this global initiative.

Detailed feedback was captured on an ongoing basis, following each centre. This was both in a plenary debrief and through questionnaires, from the assessors, talents and centre management team. Improvements were made periodically to the centre materials and process. For example, it was generally found that if a participant's level of English language ability was not fluent enough then they struggled throughout the process, and scored low on the competencies across the exercises. Typically they would not contribute much to the group discussions as they were still processing information whilst others were moving onto the next topic. It was therefore decided to use the IETLS test (an international standardized test of English language proficiency) as a pre-filter. This ensures that participants only attend the Centre once their business English is fluent enough, as this is the common language throughout all Grundfos companies. Other aspects of the nomination process have also been improved, to ensure that the right individuals are nominated and attend the Talent Centres. This entailed increased communication to, and involvement of, Grundfos business leaders around the world, so that they understood what a talent looks like, and how to groom and prepare them for attendance at the Centre.

There were also some goals that weren't achieved. One was to facilitate a level of self-sufficiency within Grundfos after the initial series of Centres. However, it became clear to the client that the involvement of external consultants added value to the centre management and administration of the Talent Centres, which was a role that their in-house staff either didn't have the time or the expertise to fulfil. Another goal had been to hold a Talent Centre in the US and one in Asia; however, the logistical scale of the centres made this difficult. During 2009/10 the 10 Talent Centres were all based in the Danish headquarters where there was already a purpose-built training academy with on-site accommodation, which is essential for assessors working long hours. However, there are plans to hold centres in the US and China in the future.

It is also intended to conduct a complete revision of the process and materials for Talent Engine version 2, in order to check alignment with strategy, refresh the design and protect against 'leakage' of content to a wider audience. This will also take into account a statistical evaluation of the results from version 1.

Development Post-Talent Centre

Following the Talent Centre, individuals rated as global talents enter the 'Greenhouse'. This is a virtual institution providing a variety of development offerings, which can be tailored to the individual depending on their Talent Development Plan, and agreed with their line manager and HR contact. Some examples of features of the Greenhouse are:

- MatchMaking – matching global talents with strategic assignments. These are diverse projects created by Regional Directors, Business Directors or Senior Vice Presidents. This is an important initiative for Grundfos, as they can develop and challenge talents, whilst at the same time also making an immediate and concrete business difference.
- Masterclasses – are focused learning opportunities targeting specific development needs that were identified at the Talent Centres, for example Developing Others. This is an agile concept as it captures the needs of a small group of people and offers targeted development in the short-term.
- The Greenhouse Community – is a virtual network, where the global talents can connect with each other, the assessors and key stakeholders from top management.

They can see each others' profiles, ask questions, conduct polls, and exchange ideas, knowledge and experience. Group Management can check the community whenever they are travelling, in order to make sure they meet the global talents at their intended destination.

- Dedicated HR contact – each talent has a dedicated contact, who helps to facilitate and support the development process for the individual talent, ensuring that the talent does not get 'lost' in the process.

A danger still exists that those talents not evaluated as 'global' may become demotivated once back in their homeland. Some regional companies have created 'Green Tents' in order to mirror the elements of the Greenhouse, but on a regional or local basis, to try to combat this.

Evaluation

The Grundfos Talent Centres were very well received by most participants and there was much positive feedback to the programme team around the value and impact of the Talent Engine approach. For example the client Marjanne Grønhøj (People & Strategy Partner, Grundfos) was pleased with the 'innovative and pioneering concept … a valuable programme of very high quality to Grundfos'.

This is a basic 'reaction' type of evaluation which fulfils level 1 of Kirkpatrick's evaluation model (Kirkpatrick, 1996); however, what really matters for any talent management intervention is long-term change in behaviour of individuals and the improvement in performance metrics across the business. This is harder to measure. Investing time for this more sophisticated evaluation research at the end of a talent management initiative has historically been supported by senior stakeholders, at least in principle. However, when it comes to actually making a financial commitment to undertake research, there is often a desire to opt for the simplest and cheapest approach which is less likely to provide the real evidence needed by stakeholders.

In reality, evaluation has become an essential element of the design process now that there is increasing focus on human capital reporting across organizations with the valuation of a business based more upon intellectual capital rather than physical capital. The Chartered Institute of Personnel and Development (CIPD) in the UK has conducted a recent study on human capital reporting (Baron 2007) and emphasized the importance of integrating evaluation at the outset of development programmes. Often, the critical need is commitment to evaluation as an integral part of the planning process so that benchmark metrics can be identified before the intervention takes place. The key outcomes can then be measured before and after the process and linked to the bottom-line through statistical analysis. This provides a compelling basis for investment in your people.

Grundfos undertakes regular employee engagement surveys to look at attitudes towards leadership effectiveness, communication, development and engagement on an annual basis and we have looked at a range of methodologies with them to explore behaviour change. This is most powerful if it is linked to outcome metrics around quality and performance and ultimately financial metrics. Grundfos experienced tough economic conditions over 2009/10 in common with the global economy and therefore the planned linkage research around attitudinal measures to employee engagement and performance metrics was deferred. However, owing to Grundfos' ownership, they do not have to answer to shareholders, and have the enviable position of being able to develop their staff without having to prove a return on investment.

Summary

Grundfos needed to identify high-potential 'talents' with a range of signature strengths (innovators, specialists and leaders). Therefore, any solution needed to challenge conventional AC wisdom, as it needed to assess each of these talents at one single event. This required a universal approach assessing a broad range of competencies across a wide range of functional roles such as sales, marketing, production and design. A fair and defensible process was designed so that all participants fully accepted the findings from the Talent Centre.

Grundfos identified 'learning agility' as a key characteristic that successful global talents would need in order to operate across cultures and learn quickly from experience. Sternberg et al. (1995) found that this 'learning intelligence' is far more predictive of organizational success at senior levels than basic IQ. Information and tasks were introduced during exercises, in order to create some unpredictability and pressure, reflecting contemporary and realistic challenges of the fast-paced business world. This was achieved whilst balancing the need for consistency and reliability of behavioural measurement by assessors throughout the event. In addition, opportunities were included after simulations for participants to reflect on how they had performed and where they could improve their performance in the future, both individually and as a team.

Grundfos is a global, English-speaking organization, which means that successful individuals need to be fluent in English, culturally adaptable and able to work with people from a diverse range of cultural backgrounds. The design of the Talent Centres reflected this.

References

Ballantyne, I. and Povah, N. 2004. *Assessment and Development Centres* (2nd edition). Aldershot: Gower.

Ballisager, O. 2000. *Grundfos – More than Pumps*. Denmark: Wiley.

Baron, A. 2007. *Human Capital Management: Achieving Added Value through People*. London: Kogan Page.

Boyatzis, R. 1982. *The Competent Manager: a Model for Effective Performance*. New York: Wiley.

Chawla, A. and Cronshaw S. 2002. The science and practice of cross-cultural leadership evaluation. University of Guelph PhD paper.

Hofstede, G. 1980. *Culture's Consequences: International Differences in Work-related Values*. Newbury Park, CA: Sage.

Joiner, W.B. and Josephs, S.A. 2006. *Leadership Agility: Five Levels of Mastery for Anticipating and Initiating Change*. US: Jossey-Bass.

Kirkpatrick, D.L. 1996. Evaluation. In *The ASTD Training and Development Handbook: A Guide to Human Resource Development* (4th Edition), edited by R.L. Craig. New York: McGraw Hill, 294–312.

Lombardo, M.M. and Eichinger, R.W. 2000. High potentials as high learners. *Human Resource Management*, 39, 321–329.

Povah, N. and Povah, L. 2009. *Succeeding at Assessment Centres for Dummies*. Chichester: John Wiley & Sons.

Spreitzer, G.M., McCall, M.W., and Mahoney, J.D. 1997. Early identification of international executive potential. *Journal of Applied Psychology*, 82, 6–29.

Sternberg, R.J., Wagner, R.K., Williams, W.M., and Horvath, J.A. 1995. Testing common sense. *American Psychologist*, 50, 912–927.

Trompenaars, A. 1997. *Riding the Waves of Culture: Understanding Cultural Diversity in Global Business*. New York: Irwin.

18 *Integrating a Developmental Assessment Centre with other Human Resource Interventions*

SANDRA BETTI AND SATIKO MONOBE

The success of a company is related to the quality of the personnel and the leadership of the company. This chapter describes the evolution and application of a system of human resource development guided by the objective of improving the qualifications of personnel at all levels. The system is based on principles of learning and self-development, drawing strength from a culture of coaching (Crane 2002) and constructive feedback processes (Bee and Bee 1996). In all of its stages, the system emphasizes the importance of learning, behavioural change, and the necessity to diagnose the factors that may be affecting a person's performance and/or development.

The system seeks to develop high performance teams. It seeks to assist people in realizing their *potential*, improving their *performance* and accelerating their *learning curve*, so that they may be successful not only as professionals, but in every area of their lives.

As a part of this system, the Development and Assessment Centre (DAC) presents a snapshot of each participant's capabilities. The snapshot shows each person's profile and competencies (Rosier 1996), and the results achieved in the DAC. This becomes a tool to guide the participant in his/her self-development, as well as a tool for the organization to make strategic and operational decisions about career management, human resource allocation, and employee development.

This chapter describes the development of this system in Brazil and other countries and provides a description of its key elements as well as four case studies. The chapter ends with a summary of some of the lessons learned over the past 20 years assessing over 78,000 personnel in several large organizations in Brazil and other countries.

Development of the Integrated System

The authors' work with DACs started in 1979, within the HR department of one of the biggest banks in Brazil, Banco Itaú. The bank had identified the need to develop a new method with which to assess managers in the commercial department. It also wanted to develop a reliable set of criteria for choosing regional superintendents from a group of over 1,000 bank managers. To achieve this they needed to understand the candidates from a broader perspective than just through psychological testing and case histories. It was decided to broaden the range of tools to include competency-based interviews and behavioural techniques, such as group interviews, games, and simulations, which until then had been restricted to the training and development department. The goal was to verify people's competencies in action, in groups of 20 participants and 5 assessors. (Bank directors sometimes also participated as observers.) Once the system was implemented the people with the most talent, capable of delivering the best results for the company, quickly stood out. The Bank monitored the careers of many of the people and consequently the assessment decisions were validated. Most people were successful in their new roles, which was an indication that the approach assessed human potential relatively accurately.

The system evolved while the authors were working with the Banco Nacional at the end of the 1980s. The DAC gauged potential, but there was still something missing, as talented people did not consistently bring good results to the company. The answer came in the form of George Odiorne's (1984) matrix model. In the banking industry in Brazil, it was common to use this model (as shown in Figure 18.1), in which an individual can be categorized in relation to their performance and potential. A brief description of each category follows.

a) *High-Flyers* have high potential and high performance. They show a high level of competency, reliability, productivity, and leadership. They also demonstrate strong communication skills, commercial aggressiveness, confidence, flexibility, creativity, and ambition. As high-level professionals, they also demand challenging positions that can compensate them with recognition and growth opportunities.

b) *Backbones* have low potential and high performance. They are competent, committed, faithful, stable, reliable, and responsible professionals. Backbones are very good at current positions, but have difficulty in remaining competent in positions of a greater scope, or that require a higher level of complexity or abstraction, as they are on the threshold of competence.

c) *Trainees* have high potential and low performance. They have excellent potential to migrate to being High-Flyers, but are still immature and need to go through an intense training or integration programme in a new area/company.

d) *Problem 1s* have high potential and low performance. They have excellent potential, but for some reason they do not bring results and achievement. They show a lack of motivation, productivity and commitment. They can improve their performance through deep diagnosis, feedback and specific corrective actions.

e) *Problem 2s* have low potential and low performance. They have limited overall potential. Nevertheless, they are able to become competent maintainers as long as the company provides a full problem diagnosis, corrective/constructive feedback, and a plan of action for performance recovery and implementation of corrective actions.

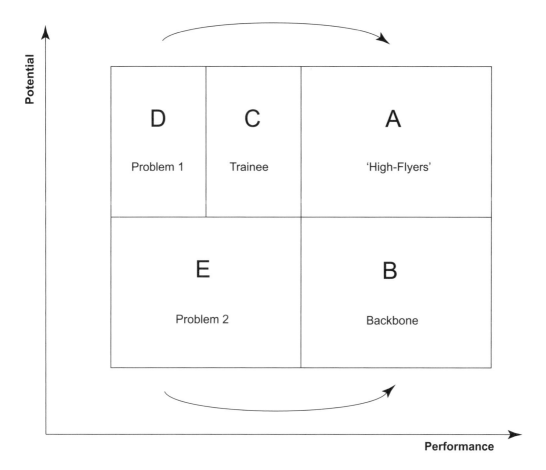

Figure 18.1 Odiorne's performance-potential matrix

The bank decided to use this model and a committee of managers assessed each member of their team, using perception as their sole methodology. Next the participants were ranked and each person was plotted on the matrix.

In 1991, the authors of this chapter did an HR mapping project for BRB – Banco Regional de Brasília. The goal was to assess 1,200 people over the course of 4 months. It was decided at that point that the two methods should be combined: (a) potential would be assessed in workshops consisting of 20 participants and 5 assessors in group interviews, games and simulations; and (b) performance information was obtained from a committee made up of managers. The potential and performance information was used to map individuals into the matrix for that purpose. Since then, this format has been used in companies from several different segments all over Brazil, Latin America, and other countries, as described in the four case studies which follow.

Method to Assess Potential

The method to assess potential looks at peoples' capacity to learn and perform functions at different levels of responsibility and complexity; their ability to develop new skills; and their values, characteristics, interests, accomplishments and knowledge from the following perspectives: personal, interpersonal, technical and managerial. The workshops to assess potential include games and simulations (Nadler 1984) which are group tasks of complex design (consisting of internal and external variables), in which critical decision-making points and role playing exercises are built in. Why is so much emphasis placed on games? According to Plato, 'You can discover more about a person during one game than in a year of conversation.' During games people tend to disarm themselves; they forget to play the 'ideal person' role, and become more spontaneous. It is easy to identify those who take risks; those who buckle under pressure; those who cooperate; those who show leadership, systemic vision and strategic planning; as well as those who can readily take decisions or work well in teams.

The process used to assess individuals is shown in Figure 18.2 and is explained in the sections below.

COMPETENCY CLUSTER VALIDATION

The process begins with a meeting with the main executives of the company, during which the company's strategic plans are discussed as they relate to HR and the profiles the company will need in the coming years. The main objective of this phase, which lasts between six to eight hours, is to get the group to talk, understand the process and reach consensus about which competencies they need for organizational success.

PROJECT COMMUNICATION

This stage involves disclosing, raising awareness and answering questions regarding the scope and objectives of the project. The internal communication process seeks to raise awareness in both the participants and the assessors. A presentation about self-development, which lasts two hours on average, is also part of this stage. The presentation serves to explain the reasons for the DAC and explains HR's role in strategic management, leading to better results overall, increased competitiveness, and the creation of high-performing teams. The presentation also highlights the opportunities for employees to accelerate their self-development and increase their employability, by providing them with professional coaching and feedback from the organization, which in turn increases their chance of achieving personal and professional success.

WORKSHOPS TO MEASURE POTENTIAL

In the next stage, workshops to measure potential are conducted. A two-day workshop is held, consisting of a combination of techniques and procedures such as competency interviews, career questionnaires, simulations, games, and group interviews. In each workshop there are twenty participants and five assessors who observe the participants. This stage has the essential features of the traditional assessment centre method.

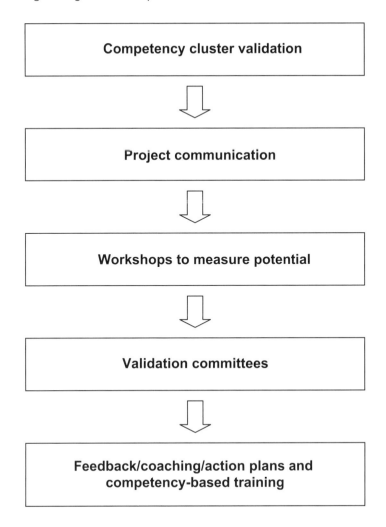

Figure 18.2 Stages in the assessment process

VALIDATION COMMITTEES

The information obtained in the workshop is then validated by a group of managers who compare it with information about the participant's on-the-job results, processes, and level of commitment provided by a group of managers. This stage verifies the assessment data, tests the accuracy of observations, validates hypotheses, and provides diagnoses. The committees can be 90° (only managers), 180° (managers and team members) or 360° (managers, team members, co-workers, internal clients and even, on occasion, external clients).

This stage culminates in the creation of rankings and individual reports for each participant, highlighting strengths and development needs, which serve as the basis of feedback.

FEEDBACK, COACHING, ACTION PLANS AND COMPETENCY-BASED TRAINING

Each person receives feedback in the presence of their manager and the HR consultant so that content can be discussed, doubts cleared and action plans designed. Seminars (usually in 8 hour blocks) to work on the main behavioural competencies (most notably Leadership, Teamwork, Creativity, Negotiation, and so forth) are set up.

Case Studies

In this section, four case studies are used to illustrate the impact and results obtained using the DAC method within this particular process. These case studies are based on interviews with executives from diverse areas, in which information on objectives, benefits, criticisms, doubts, and contributions to the employees' level of qualification and the organization's strategy was provided. See Appendix for a list of executives interviewed.

CASE STUDY 1: EMBRACO

Embraco is a multinational company of Brazilian origin, now part of Whirlpool. It is a world leader in the manufacture of hermetic compressors. Besides their main factory in the south of Brazil they have factories in China, Italy, Slovakia, and the USA. A total of 290 assessments have been conducted in these countries over the course of seven years.

Embraco had been running its own talent pool programme for ten years, using internal analysis to guide the company's investments in people, identifying highly skilled professionals as well as high-potentials. But there were doubts about the company's ability to fully assess its own employees' skills and their potential, since year after year people had similar assessments and steadfastly retained their organizational positions. The doubt was whether they were being properly assessed for potential. In 2003, a third-party assessment was sought to better develop a global pool of 90 key-executives by mapping current employees. The new assessment had to match the company's values, preserve their ongoing internal evaluations, and provide an unbiased capacity for multinational assessment, and differentiate performance from potential. The first big improvement sought by the DAC was to establish a standard benchmark against which to compare people. Initially it focused primarily on personal development. A key goal was to overcome any mislabelling of the employees by the company. A few people had adverse reactions, despite the awareness campaign that was run to explain the benefits of a new assessment system, which was meant to overcome possible biases in the previous system.

The potential for personal growth was highly stressed, for the DAC could easily be wrongly perceived as a means to remove those who were burnt-out. The opposite was actually true: personal development was encouraged through the DAC. Lastly, the DAC would be repeated every three years to create benchmarks for the company's people development strategies, and to show the system's evolution.

Personal growth

Something noteworthy for a company composed mainly of engineers, stereotypically wary of interpersonal relationships, has been the thriving of newly identified leaders.

In this regard, the DAC data helped people understand not only the essence of their personality, but also their current psychological state, improving their self-awareness as both private and public individuals.

Organizational growth

The DAC is considered a 'parting of the seas' at Embraco, for it developed many new leaders. In time, feedback became common practice, reaching even the highest VP levels, and HR management evolved from a guessing game into a more objective and helpful assessment. The company began applying the DAC on all key-employment processes, even developing a DAC using Skype to successfully assess a Swedish executive. Every 3 years, the DAC is conducted at each factory to pool the 90 global key executives, helping to identify across borders the group's strengths, weaknesses, and the issues developing overseas.

Global impact

In 2005, after careful analysis of the DAC data, a customized MBA programme was formed together with leading universities in China, Slovakia, Italy, the USA, and Brazil. The educational programme was based on Embraco's organizational competencies and focused on behavioural change. The programme was highly successful and consequently the experience was repeated in Brazil and China.

A major obstacle to people management is in grasping how people's internal motivation is influenced by different cultures. For example, giving feedback wasn't a common activity in some factories, mainly owing to cultural influences. Specifically, Italians have a highly hierarchical tradition that precludes feedback and the recent past of autocratic regimes in China and Slovakia work to inhibit confrontation between employers and employees.

Despite less than complete commitment from management, the international experience was successful. And, though maybe circumstantial because of the youthfulness of its team, Slovakia broke all expectations; amazingly even surpassing Italy's more knowledgeable management team. Certainly the DAC played a key role in this, aided as well by the presence of some Brazilian expats who helped their foreign colleagues to loosen up during the process. With this organizational impact the DAC transcended the status of a mere talent pool. In 2003 there were only Brazilians holding the key positions at Embraco's factory in Slovakia. Seven years later, local talent had taken up the majority of those positions and were able to not only bear their predecessors workload, but also take on new responsibilities. The changes imparted by the DAC also helped Embraco to raise the bar in Slovakia's local market, where it is admired for its supportive stance towards personal development.

CASE STUDY 2: BRASKEM

Braskem is a large Brazilian petrochemical company and one of the three biggest industrial conglomerates in the country. Its rapid progress was characterized by multiple acquisitions. The company itself was the result of the merger of six companies in 2002. As Braskem was being consolidated, several key positions, right up to the president's position, were filled by people hired from outside Braskem. Between the company's second and fourth years, all the new positions, from the managerial level upwards, were filled by employees. Consequently, 1,430 assessments in four other merger processes were conducted, using DACs at leadership and managerial levels.

Consolidation

After its consolidation, Braskem started to buy other companies. They used DACs to facilitate the integration between the new assets. The company wanted an objective third-party assessment, which reviewed the potential, backgrounds and expectations of the new employees. This would help in the strategic decision-making process, especially for those concerned with personnel allocation in overlapping positions. The DAC was considered from the start to be a tool for development, not a mechanism for transferring people. It was perceived as a gift to employees. Whether or not the employee stayed in the company, he or she could use the DAC to gain self-knowledge to make better life decisions. Specific exercises were developed to assess competencies, values and characteristics that were of interest to Braskem.

Acquisition tension

The DAC brought agility to the merger process, which had rapid integration as a top priority. Usually by the time an acquisition was announced employees had already been living in an anxious state for months. This state naturally unsettled them, paralyzing their good intentions and lowering their level of motivation. Mergers require quick decision-making, not only so that money and talent isn't lost, but also so that clients don't become alienated, with concerns about future levels of service; whether prices will remain constant; and whether they will have access to technical assistance if they need it.

At Braskem it was a situation ripe for causing anxiety: the organization was in a vulnerable situation and the employees were forced to face the real possibility of losing their job. The prospect of participating in a DAC also increased the tension felt by the employees. Good communication was essential to help diffuse the tension. Communication efforts focused on explaining the methodology to be applied. So that employees didn't succumb to the vulnerabilities and insecurities inherent within the merger process, the company emphasized its commitment to meritocracy and to not labelling people as a result of the DAC process. This approach helped to put people at ease, thus allowing them to loosen up and actually enjoy the experience. People who had lost sleep worrying about the DAC ended up embracing the process, as they noticed how serious and helpful a third-party perspective was, especially when using a well-tested methodology.

The DAC also played an important role in increasing the HR department's knowledge of the employees. This helped in making decisions about overlaps and clarifying options for employee placement. It also updated the acquiring company with information regarding specific people, from their interests and expectations to their academic transcripts and previous work experience. In cases where the acquired company already had an assessment process in place, those records were examined. This helped to very quickly decrease the knowledge gap regarding the employee.

Mergers

With such information on hand, Braskem's acquisition decisions were made more quickly and with more transparency. The first company to be incorporated into Braskem was Politeno and one month after the acquisition, external consultants were retained to assess 200 new engineers, technicians and administrators. The consensus meeting happened at night, after each DAC. At the end, the company executives had all the information they needed about the profile, potential, competencies and performance of the newly incorporated group. This helped validate reallocation decisions.

The second merger, with a company called Ipiranga, was more complicated. Ipiranga had been a big competitor who had fought a long battle not to be bought out. Its employees felt a high degree of attachment to the industry and they were suspicious of their new owners. In their case, a positive feedback system was used to maintain their enthusiasm and motivation. Leaders were encouraged to take ownership of their assessment reports and give their own feedback. Surprisingly, the feedback was quickly accepted. Apparently the fact that the reports were validated by the team leaders made the process more legitimate in their eyes.

In the third acquisition, Copesul, success stories from the Ipiranga experience were used to show that it was possible to survive the DAC and emerge stronger as a result of it. The outcome of the DAC was an extremely valuable map that identified the high-potentials, the high-performers and the high-value people. The high-value people were those that served as living memories of factory plants and other important historical information. Identifying the high-value employees was simple: ten out of ten employees spoke of them. Amongst this group were those who did not want to be part of a big company and who ended up going to work for other companies. Other high-potentials decided to stay with Braskem for the learning challenge. The decision to willingly participate in the DAC was a strong indication of the employee's acceptance of the Braskem business model. Those who resisted the company's model for development often resisted everything else as well.

Beyond the DAC were the company's plans to retain good employees. A diverse group of leaders were brought to Braskem. Their philosophies were assimilated into the culture of the company and vice versa. Braskem was transferring culture, coaxing people out of their comfort zone, putting them in an environment where they were forced to use technical competencies that they didn't even know they had. The company's success relied on the proper allocation of human capital. Upon arriving at Braskem, people had to hit the ground running. There was no stability; the diversity of the personnel was vast and the common link was a commitment to make the company grow.

The role of the leader at Braskem was to become acquainted with the information collected at the DAC and, with help from the HR department, guide the employee in the individual development programme. This is a highly individualized process, one that seeks to guide people's careers not only in regard to formal education, but also in regard to on-the-job activities. Afterwards the information collected at the DAC was also cross-referenced with information from the succession plan, to map out employees' potential and maturity for assuming a key function and the timeframe for that to happen. Thus, the assessments helped in the development of those who stayed on at the company.

Reallocations tend to have a success rate of approximately 50 per cent. A significant factor in determining whether or not a person will succeed depends on where that person is allocated. By identifying loyal and talented people the DAC had a success rate of between 85 per cent and 90 per cent. In fact, some of the people coming from the acquired company are considered the company's future leaders. This has only made Braskem better off. The company was born of a merger and has grown through more mergers. Had it not known how to bring out the best in its people, the merger strategy would probably have failed.

A better team

A remarkable thing at Braskem is the multilateral decision-making process, in which the most talented people are compared to each other, regardless of whether they are from the acquired company or from the acquiring company. Transparency is fundamental in the process. Decisions had to be made quickly and fairly to do justice to a company with the intention of becoming the fifth largest petrochemical company in the world. The various mergers led to a mindset of growth, creating a working environment where employees are constantly stimulated to move beyond their comfort zone. The bar was raised even more by prospecting only the very best talent outside the company. This growth model, which stimulated people to challenge themselves and seek qualifications, ended up creating a natural selection process, in which those that didn't rise to the occasion weeded themselves out.

CASE STUDY 3: GLOBOSAT

Globosat is the leading Brazilian paid-TV company. It goes back 20 years, employs over 1,000 people, and broadcasts over two dozen TV channels. It is the biggest paid TV broadcaster in all of Latin America. It broadcasts to the USA as well. The particularities of the employee body, which includes journalists, TV producers and editors, all of whom are spread out in 12 different areas of the company, presented a big challenge to the DAC in the 520 assessments conducted over the course of 6 years.

Beginning

Globosat commenced economic activities in 1991. Until 1993 it was responsible for both programming and distribution operations. Then it underwent a strategic repositioning which led to these two operations being separated. Globosat was left with only the programming and production operation. The company grew over the years, until about 2000 when it finally overcame what had been persistently negative operating results. This was credited to the management team, who focused their entire energy on achieving a turnaround. The company decided it needed to know its employees better, so that it could not only attract new talent, but also retain the best people by better allocating them within the company. The consensus was that managers should encourage practices such as feedback sessions, with an eye to developing the organization as a whole. Despite dealing with creativity, the company was viewed as business first and foremost, and there was no culture of managing and developing talent. A new approach, which contrasted starkly with the company's established pragmatic style, was implemented.

IT department/change

The DAC process started in 2004 in the IT department, an area that accounted for the reliability of access to information. It was a department whose importance had been disregarded, dismissed as being full of shy analysts and programmers, all of whom were relegated to a dozen or so cubicles. Because of the company's restructuring process, they needed the IT professionals to reposition themselves as drivers of change and creators of new solutions. Upper management was keeping a close eye on the restructuring so that it could assess the potential impact of the DAC activities on the organizational culture. The result was much better than expected. The process of identifying talent and qualifying employees ended up being replicated in other areas with a lot of success. Today it is used in most of the company's departments.

Approval

From the start there was a certain amount of fear on the part of the employees, as well as disbelief and suspicion from middle management. The fear came from having a centralizing corporate culture that only embraced the DAC after observing its success in the IT department. The HR department was next. Other departments saw how it could improve their prospects as well and ended up signing up for it too. They actually even came to see it as a fun activity and this was reflected in positive word-of-mouth comments about the effectiveness of the DAC. This was both critical and rewarding for the HR department, which was able to build on this growing momentum. When the results started to come in, managers started to seek out the HR department to help them implement the method in their own departments. It was a process of gradual awakening. This stage also served to slowly build confidence, since the fear of new things is easily transmitted from a manager to his team. Approval became more widespread as people reaped the benefits of increased self-knowledge. The commercial director's participation in an assessment process generated surprise at first, then approval. Especially with a small HR team, it is very helpful when the leader sets the example.

Changes

Starting in 2006, a DAC has been conducted every year for new employees, thus working to ensure consistency in the results achieved and uniformity in the group over the years. At the same time, great care has been taken to maintain the enthusiasm among the older employees. Activities like paintball games and negotiation workshops are used for this purpose, as well as for the purpose of filling in the development needs identified in the mapping, so long as a qualified leader is guiding the activity, with assistance from HR. When low-performing, high-potential employees are identified, the reasons are always analyzed, as was the case with trainees, a group with very young people, or as was the case with people who couldn't adapt to their leader's style.

Dismissals

Dismissals are complicated in Brazil owing to the multiple social relationships people create at work. This is even more the case in conservative organizations. The complication is derived from the paternalistic culture inherited in Brazil from its Portuguese origins, in which a lot of value is placed on trust, as in 'I have to trust the person who watches my territory. He may not be good at his job, but he has to be trustworthy.' This is very different from the Anglo-Saxon culture, in which what matters most is performance, not loyalty, in many companies. People who are resistant to change and who demonstrate low potential and low performance end up being dismissed, but always with the care of not having their dismissal connected to the DAC and only after two or three years of repeated attempts to motivate them. It has even been known for informal meetings to take place, in which people are advised to change their behaviour. The 'bad apples' make up less than 30 per cent of the teams. Among the other 70 per cent there are usually 'eagles' and guardians. Wisdom is necessary to find the right balance and to give space in which things can take their due course.

HR gains strength

Everyone perceives things in his or her own way and there is no right or wrong perception of something. To decrease the noise that sometimes is created in assessments, various techniques are combined to assess potential and performance, and at the same time work on participants' strengths and development needs. At Globosat this approach was particularly useful: it produced a big picture view rather than many individual pictures. For a company that still today resists external consultants, the results from the DAC, which came from the ground up, helped break some of that resistance.

HR did not impose anything on those who, from the start, did not believe in the DAC. It simply delivered impressive results. The HR department went from being perceived as an unimportant department to being a true partner in the business, as well as a source of internal consultancy. It is a winning combination, but one that was a long time in coming.

Evolution/return on investment (ROI)

Despite initial resistance, the teams did become more united, improving the overall performance of the company. The increased qualifications of employees also translated into better service. HR started as an unimportant department, whose importance had been dismissed, due in part to its inability to deal with the amount of work being handed over, but became a corporate structure in continuous evolution and which seeks to reward good results. Assessments are a reality; however, the company still has not reached a point where the organizational indicators have evolved sufficiently. They are trying, but they are seeking something that may not be possible to quantify exactly. ROI is a more complicated subject, especially when assessing behaviour. Nowadays the company's evolution is noticeable to a team whose members know each other individually as well as professionally, which rises to expectations with less complaint, within budget and with a good relationship between departments. As the company grows we have observed that people are being promoted within the company and, of course, very importantly, the company is profitable. Starting from a position of weakness, the company is nowadays the second-best performing in the group to which it belongs. Of course there are other contributing factors, but this is a very good indication of the effectiveness of the DAC.

CASE STUDY 4: BRADESCO

Bradesco bank is a traditional Brazilian retail bank, with thousands of branches spread across Brazil. In 2009, the year when it achieved its best economic result so far – R$8.12 billion – it was the highest-grossing company in the country. It is one of the biggest banks in sheer volume compared to all national banks. Bradesco is also one of the most profitable among Latin and North American banks. It is also considered, year after year, one of the best companies to work for in Brazil. The bank invests R$90 million per year in personnel development. DACs for managers are run at all levels, with an average of 5 to 10 groups assessed per month, totalling more than 16,000 assessments over the course of the past 15 years.

Investing in employees

Since the bank's inception in 1943, one of the most critical tasks of a Bradesco manager has been to train employees, taking them from simply being a new hire to becoming a potential bank manager in another branch, which in turn allows for the growth and expansion of the bank. The person behind the philosophy of investing in employees is the founder of the bank, Amador Aguiar. This philosophy has proved itself to be on track over the course of the past 50 years, a period in which Bradesco rose to and remained in a leadership position in the rankings of national banks.

Investing in employees is not easy. It demands work, but it is a great competitive advantage: it creates a sense of loyalty and dedication in the employee, as well as an elevated state of motivation. Bradesco hires from outside the company only for entry-level positions. Employees start off as clerks and are stimulated to progress through the ranks, having the possibility of eventually reaching the top, as did many of the current directors.

The philosophy of investing in employees brings with it the need for the company to know its employees soon after they are hired. That way they don't waste time in preparing a disinterested person for a managerial position, which takes up to 8 years for a person to reach. Should the employee give up the job, the organization loses everything invested in that person and has to face the difficult job of starting over.

The referral system works well in smaller organizations, but, with the bank's growing size they decided to create a training department in 1992, using teachers from the Bradesco Foundation. They faced difficulties in the training sessions due to lack of uniformity among employees. There was also the perception, shared by the president as well, that people stayed too long in the same position.

A new approach

Bradesco needed a complete revamping of its internal placement process. A more technical DAC needed to be carried out, since internal assessments were already in place in which employees had to take an exam in order to be promoted. The different strategic areas of the organization had already come to a consensus on the necessary corporate competencies. The first assessment project to identify high-potential employees began in the mid-1990s with the most sensitive positions, namely middle-managers who were about to assume senior management positions. The results soon appeared: managers with high potential were identified. Consequently the task of training employees became easier, since the group became more uniform and the return became more straightforward.

In the beginning some people resented the loss of power to nominate their favourites for a position. Thus initial resistance was high but has been decreasing ever since. The economic and political scenario also contributed to management's maturity, that is, the banking consumer-protection code and SA8000, a norm/certification that demands corporate responsibility in issues of management and governance.

Mergers

Another key point for the DAC to meet with internal approval was the mobilization of talented people from the banks that were incorporated into Bradesco after the merger process. Between 1998 and 2006, more than 30,000 employees from different levels and corporate cultures joined the bank. In time, some of them came to occupy high-level positions within the bank. Additionally, many of the banks that were incorporated already had DAC practices in place. This fact made HR's job more dynamic, since until then they had performed mostly operational work, such as benefits, payroll, admissions, dismissals and recruitment.

Approval

Initially few people believed it would be possible to run an efficient DAC in a bank with 90,000 employees. Little by little, the assessment model won departments over. Nowadays the DAC is constantly being used to validate high-level promotions and to relocate branch managers, resulting in about 40 assessments per week. Nowadays, if a person does not pass the first assessment, he or she is not promoted, but is nominated to develop the appropriate competencies. Dismissals only happen when all the possibilities have been exhausted and there has been no improvement in the person's competencies.

Until 2008 some doubts still lingered. At this point a quantitative analysis was performed on the people who had been promoted against the advice of the DAC. It turned out that those people had been largely unsuccessful in their new positions. This result finally won over the remaining critics of the DAC.

In 2009 the organization's managers were inserted into the DAC process. Now Bradesco has a new process, called the Advanced Development Programme, which encompasses the DAC and incentives for international exposure and academic or work experience abroad. The DAC maps out the competencies, performance and potential of the 204 key executives in the organization, most of whom have been in the organization for an average of 20 years. The intention is to qualify bank employees to take a qualitative leap going into the future. This process was underway in 2010 when this chapter was written.

Conclusion

This chapter and the case studies reported within it serve to illustrate the progress that has been made in Brazil over the past 20 years, with regard to the growing acceptance of the DAC method. During this time it has established itself as a tool for self-development and for obtaining high-performance teams and establishing a legitimate win-win proposition for both the organization and the employee. By expanding the scope of the system from a one-sided assessment to a multifaceted development tool, the results significantly exceeded the original expectation for the DAC. In the authors' view, the learning curve is accelerating, pointing towards a state of individual and organizational maturity in which all the stakeholders will benefit more readily from the DAC process. These experiences also show that people were more alike across cultures than one might initially think.

References

Bee, R. and Bee, F. 1996. *Constructive Feedback*. London: Institute of Personnel and Development.
Crane, T.G. 2002. *The Heart Of Coaching*, San Diego, CA: FTA Press.
Nadler, L. 1984. *The Handbook of Human Resource Management*. New York, NY: Wiley.
Odiorne, G.S. 1984. *Strategic Management of Human Resources*. San Francisco, CA: Jossey-Bass.
Rosier, R. Jr. 1996. *Competency Model Handbook*, Volumes 1–4. Brussels: Linkage, Inc.

Appendix: Interviewees

EMBRACO: WWW.EMBRACO.COM.BR

Silvio Fernandes D´Aquino – Corporate Lean Director
Roberto Holthausen de Campos – Business and MKT VP
Lainor Driessen- Operations, Quality, Health, Safety and Environment VP
Carlos Lienstadt – HR Director
Márcio Schissadti – Engineering Resources Director
Gerson Heusy – IT Support and Services Senior Manager
Carlos Rosa – Brazil HR Senior Manager
Mônica Pietschnann – Brazil HR Development and Recruitment Leader
Mônica Granthan – Corporate HR Consultant
Eliane D. Beje – HR Specialist

BRASKEM: WWW.BRASKEM.COM.BR

Luiz de Mendonça- Senior VP Braskem
Eliana Cristina Granato – Manager of People and Organization
Andrea Barradas – Director of People and Organization
Camila Dantas – Manager of Education and Careers

GLOBOSAT: WWW.GLOBOSAT.COM.BR

Leila Felício- HR Director
Pedro Garcia – SportTV Business Director and General Director of *Premiere* channels.
Alberto Pinheiro Mascarenhas – IT Manager
Érica Torres Placa – HR Coordinator
Fabile Migone – HR Development Coordinator

BRADESCO: WWW.BRADESCO.COM.BR

Milton Matsumoto – Executive Director
José Luis Rodrigues Bueno – Human Resources Director
Julio Alves Marques – Director of Ombudsman Department
Glaucimar Peticov – Executive Superintendent for Training
Sergio Nonato Rodrigues – Executive Superintendent for HR
Aparecida de Fátima Russini – Executive HR Manager
Maria Lúcia Perosa – Executive HR Manager
Roseli Chagas – Executive HR Manager

19 *The Evolution of an Assessment Center Program in a Pharmaceutical Sales Organization over a 15-Year Period*

DAVID C. PURDY

The purpose of this chapter is to describe the design, implementation, and evolution of an assessment/development center program in a pharmaceutical sales organization. The participants include high-potential sales representatives being prepared for front-line sales manager positions, as well as current managers being prepared for manager of manager positions. The case study describes the practical aspects of using assessment centers to accomplish various talent management objectives in commercial environments, including identifying and developing emerging leaders, determining their training needs, and planning for leadership succession. Reasons why the programs evolved over time are presented, along with lessons learned in this process.

Initiation and Implementation of an Assessment Center for Future Sales Leaders

Following the merger of two pharmaceutical companies in 1995, the senior leadership committee of the newly merged company decided to establish a new assessment center (AC) to replace the program that one of the legacy companies had previously conducted. The original program had relied heavily on internal resources (regional sales directors), and the senior leadership team wanted the new program to be conducted entirely by external, professional assessors. They believed that given the recent merger and rapid changes in the industry, it was essential that directors stay focused on the sales management function rather than on the time-consuming requirements of being AC observers. They also wanted to ensure that the new program was as objective and legally defensible as possible. Concerns had been raised that the previous program was too "opinion based," given that the major component of that process was an in-depth behavioral interview focused on leadership and achievement motivation. The new senior leadership team wanted to put a much greater emphasis on objective behavioral observations drawn from a wide variety of management simulation exercises, reflecting the increasing demands of the front-line sales manager job. Having just attended the 1995 International Congress on Assessment Center Methods, the training director had learned of new AC practices, as well as the *Guidelines and Ethical Considerations for Assessment Center Operations* (1989 version), which specifically delineated proper observation techniques (recording, evaluating, and aggregating information), and he was determined to improve the company's approach to conducting ACs.

The focus was to be on identification of management potential among current sales representatives who had expressed an interest in moving into a district sales manager role and whose sales managers had supported their aspirations. At the time, this was the most common use of ACs, with a contemporary survey (Gaugler, Bentson and Pohley 1990; later published in Spychalski, Quiñones, Gaugler and Pohley 1997) showing that over 68 percent of users were positioning their assessment centers for promotion and early identification of management talent. After a series of presentations, meetings, and conference calls with the senior leadership team, approval was given to conduct a pilot program that would incorporate the specific features desired by the company.

KEY FEATURES OF THE PILOT PROGRAM

- Eight participants (current sales representatives); four external, professional assessors.
- Competencies (based on a job analysis of the district sales manager position): Influencing, Problem Analysis, Decision-making, Planning and Organizing, Delegation, Management Control, Sensitivity, Stress Tolerance, Oral Communication, Written Communication.
- High-fidelity management simulation exercises based on real life challenges faced by pharmaceutical sales managers (and incorporating the newly-issued laptop computers used by sales representatives and managers in the field): Budgetary decision-group exercise, Promotional decision-group exercise, Curbstone conference exercise, Coaching and counseling exercise, Analytical exercise, Inbox.
- Provision of an overall promotional readiness evaluation.
- Scheduling of telephone feedback conferences within a month of the session (with participants' district sales managers included in the discussions).

REACTIONS TO THE PILOT PROGRAM

Most participants provided positive feedback on the AC, reporting that it was a high-impact learning experience, a challenging opportunity to try on the district sales manager role, and a good forum in which to receive objective feedback. While many managers seemed pleased with the new program (for example, remarking on the thoroughness of the reports and the detailed behavioral observations), some managers expressed the concern that they were not directly involved in the center and that the external assessors might not understand the company's corporate culture. During and after the feedback calls, they raised questions about the new exercises, the assessors, and the rating system.

Based on these questions, it became clear that the managers needed a better understanding of the exercise content, the qualifications of the assessors, and the rationale behind the rating system. Some managers suggested that the exercises be cast completely within the client company, but it was successfully argued that such company-specific exercises may in fact penalize those without certain experiences (a concern raised by Thornton and Rupp, 2006: pp. 121–122). In response to these comments, the training department prepared a detailed written explanation of the new program (including a full description of the simulations, with an emphasis on the job-specific and industry-specific nature of the exercises) and distributed it to senior sales management. This served to clarify the purpose of the AC, the reason for using professional assessors, and guidelines on how to use the written report for developmental purposes. The memo also included an evaluation survey to assess the ability of this process to provide timely and accurate feedback. A key learning from this experience was that an organizational policy statement should have been offered prior to conducting the first program, an approach recommended in the *Guidelines and Ethical Considerations for Assessment Center Operations* (International Taskforce 2009).

Based on the written feedback from the pilot program participants and their managers, the decision was made to continue with the program and schedule a series of sessions over the remainder of the year. In addition, several changes were made to the program:

• A detailed *Manager's Handbook for Career Planning* was designed to help the district sales managers support the developmental planning work of their sales representatives. The handbook included a comprehensive list of developmental activities and learning strategies, including skill practice opportunities within the territory and district, coaching tips, books, audio/video resources, and seminars. In addition, the handbook included guidelines on how to support and encourage the sales representatives as they worked to develop their management skills. As pointed out by Ballantyne and Povah (2004: p. 158), "line manager support is clearly a key aspect of making post-center development happen." The participants' managers were encouraged to provide continued support of the sales representatives' development and to set deadlines for the attainment of developmental objectives, similar to the suggestions provided by Thornton and Cleveland (1990).

• A *Career Planning Guide* was also produced to help participants establish a step-by-step developmental planning process to follow after the assessment center. The guide included short tutorials on each of the competencies, as well as a self-assessment (with 20 evaluation statements for each of the 10 competencies) and planning forms (with a list of developmental action steps and target dates for completion) to help the sales representatives build a personal development plan. The forms made provision for input from the participant's manager and director. A six-month development plan review was also included.

• Separate conferences were scheduled with the participants' regional sales directors to discuss the results of the feedback conferences. This enabled the feedback givers to discuss the degree of buy-in or push-back demonstrated by the participants during their conference. Special challenges were discussed and possible support strategies were considered.

• Welcome dinners were added to the agenda for the arrival evening, giving the participants the chance to learn more about the content and objectives of the program. During the dinner, a training manager from the client company provided a brief overview of the process and responded to questions from the participants. This served to reduce any pre-program anxiety.

During the 12 months following the pilot, 79 sales representatives attended the program.

REACTIONS OF MANAGERS – ONE YEAR LATER

A managers' meeting was held to address questions that had been raised during the first year of conducting the AC programs. Based on input from the district sales managers and the regional sales directors, the following changes were proposed by the training department and the external consultant, and accepted by the senior management team:

- Recast the rating categories to match the internal performance evaluation criteria: exceeds expectations; meets expectations; or needs improvement.
- Add an inbox interview session after the exercise to provide the assessors with a more comprehensive understanding of the participant's thought process and decision-making rationale.
- Add an exercise/dimension matrix to the reports, showing ratings on each competency by exercise, and including the relative weighting of each rating. These weightings were determined via a survey of current district sales managers and regional sales directors who were requested to allocate 100 points among the 10 competencies, based on the relative importance of each to success as a pharmaceutical first-line sales manager within this company. As a result, each competency was given a weighting on a one to four-point basis.
- Reword the overall evaluation categories:
  - promotable with minimal development;
  - promotable with some additional development;
  - promotable with extensive development;
  - not promotable at this time.
- Assign one external feedback giver to each region, allowing the regional sales directors to establish a working relationship with that person and to tailor the developmental planning process to the needs and opportunities available in each region.
- Schedule a pre-feedback strategy session between the external feedback giver and the regional sales director to discuss a plan for the feedback conference, including an exploration of potential learning opportunities within the context of the participant's current role.
- Use the term Career Development Center (CDC) instead of assessment center.
- Encourage regional sales directors to attend a Career Development Center session at some point during the coming year in order to become more familiar with the exercise content, the external assessor team, and the program methodology. The expectation was that these line managers would be in a better position to provide ongoing developmental support to participants if they understood the program more completely. Ferguson (1991) emphasized the benefit of having line managers involved before the center, through nomination and preparation, and after the center, through some type of ownership of the developmental action plan along with the participant.

- Provide guidelines to district sales managers to help them in their efforts to support the development of their sales representatives. These included recommended on-the-job coaching tips, as well as monitoring and follow-up techniques to help keep the plan alive.
- Make video recordings of all group and one-on-one exercises so that the district sales managers could review them with the participants after the CDC and provide further coaching and development.
- Arrange for external assessors and role players to spend a day in the field with a sales representative and an administrative day with a district sales manager in order to expand their understanding of the nature of the job and the demands of the position. In addition, several assessors attended managers' meetings.

Development of a Dual-Track Program

As the client company continued to expand, there were increasing openings for entry-level positions in the marketing department, namely associate product manager and product manager. The CDC program was redesigned to include both district sales manager and product manager simulations, resulting in the following combination of exercises:

- *Sales management exercises:* Budgetary decision group exercise, Curbstone conference exercise, Counseling exercise, and Inbox exercise.
- *Marketing management exercises:* Marketing case-study exercise, Group presentation exercise (based on the Marketing case-study exercise).

In each participant's report, a separate analysis was provided for the sales management and the marketing management components. Overall promotional readiness ratings were also given for each area. As a result, some participants were deemed more ready to move into district sales manager roles than into product manager roles, or vice versa. Participants sometimes discovered during the CDC that they enjoyed one functional area much more than the other, which enabled them to determine whether to pursue the sales management or the marketing management track. However, this dual-track program was discontinued after several sessions, as most participants stated that they were more interested in district sales manager roles than product manager roles.

Launch of an Advanced-Level CDC

Given the success of the CDC at the point of moving from sales representative to manager, the company decided to expand the program to the next level up, for managers being developed for the regional sales director position. As the company continued to expand its sales force, to support the launch of several new "blockbuster" products, new regional sales directors needed to be identified and developed. The company's preference was to promote from within as much as possible, so the training department was charged with creating a new program for this purpose. Work was undertaken to design a set of robust new director-level simulations. Based on input from senior sales management regarding typical challenges faced by regional sales directors, the following exercises were designed:

- *Leaderless group discussion.* Three case studies representing actual management problems facing the company are presented to the group of participants. Acting as members of an advisory panel, they are asked to determine the two most important issues, discuss them in depth, and submit their recommendations to senior management.
- *Management dialogue.* The participant plays the role of a recently promoted regional sales director who is meeting with a district sales manager whose district has recently slipped to a relatively low standing within the region. The participant must uncover the reasons behind this trend and develop a plan of action to address the problem in the time allotted. Following the session, the participant writes a memo to the national sales director describing the results of the meeting.
- *Realignment case study.* The participant has been appointed to a special project and charged with developing sales strategies and tactics for the company's prescription products, determining a promotional budget, and reducing expenses. Following the preparation of a written report, the participant then delivers his recommendations in an oral presentation.
- *Group presentation exercise.* The participants must work together to prepare an overall recommendation to senior management using the results from their individual analysis of the realignment case study (described above). The participants then offer their recommendations in a group oral presentation to the panel of observers, who later ask follow-up questions.
- *Inbox exercise.* As a new regional sales director with a pharmaceutical company, the participant is expected to work through an inbox containing 40 messages. Among the various messages are items related to an upcoming regional meeting, hiring issues, and a possible case of sexual harassment.
- *Strategic presentation exercise.* The participants are part of a national task force studying various issues affecting the company. Each participant is asked to select a topic and prepare a 15-minute presentation to the other participants and the team of observers. The audience is encouraged to ask questions during the question-and-answer period following each presentation.

These advanced-level CDC programs were conducted with participants who were currently in the roles of district sales manager, training manager, and marketing manager, all of whom were aspiring to regional sales director positions. Sales vice presidents took part in two of the exercises (strategic presentation and group presentation), and they asked challenging questions of the participants after their presentations, often following up with specific probes about long-term effects, return on investment, and potential unintended consequences of their recommendations.

Initially, this program measured the same competencies as those used in the district sales-manager-level program. However, the client later launched an internal competency modeling study and identified a set of competencies specific to the regional sales director position. This model was incorporated into later sessions of the program. These included: Leadership, Strategic Focus, Judgment and Decision-making, Building Talent, Communicating With Impact, Interpersonal Savvy, Building Effective Teams, Written Communication, and Work Management.

Design of a Management Development Lab

Another merger occurred in 1999, and during the following year, the company continued to expand its sales force, and it became clear that a more comprehensive management development program was needed. In an effort to pre-qualify possible participants in the management development program (of which the Career Development Center was a major component), the concept of a Management Development Lab (MDL) was introduced. The program was designed for sales representatives who had expressed an interest in pursuing opportunities in first-line sales management. The MDL was intended to provide exposure to key job activities within the district sales manager position, as well as introductory training in the competencies related to successful performance in this position. Using the concept of a Developmental Assessment Center (Thornton and Rupp, 2006), the MDL was built as "a collection of workplace simulation exercises ... that provide individuals with practice, feedback, and developmental coaching on a set of developable behavioral dimensions, found to be critical for their professional success" (p. 58).

A design team comprising staff from the client and the external provider produced three simulation exercises (group discussion, coaching exercise, and inbox exercise) that could be conducted at regional locations, using regional sales directors as the facilitators. After an initial pilot program, the decision was made to shorten the program and simplify the process, as the original version was too time-consuming to conduct. Following a redesign, the external provider conducted training sessions to provide the facilitators with skills in observing behavior, giving behavior-based feedback, and designing specific development plans. In addition, district sales managers were trained to be role players, and regional administrative coordinators were trained to facilitate the electronic inbox exercise. These MDL programs were then conducted internally by the client company at regional locations. The MDL participants who were deemed ready now moved on to the Career Development Center (CDC) within a 4–12-month time period. Those needing further development were given time to complete a development plan before being considered for the next step of attending the CDC. Follow-up research showed that adding the MDL program to the overall management development process greatly reduced the percentage of CDC participants falling into the lowest two overall rating categories (from 24 percent to 5 percent of participants) and increased the percentage in the top category (from 21 percent to 38 percent of participants).

After seven years of conducting this internal MDL program, the client company decided to discontinue it, based on the heavy time and staffing requirements. Realizing that nearly all high-potential sales representatives would benefit from introductory leadership training, the company instituted a series of region-based workshops, focusing on basic management skill sets.

Ongoing Evolution of the Program

Since its early inception the Career Development Center program has evolved in a number of ways.

SHIFTING THE FOCUS FROM ASSESSMENT TO DEVELOPMENT

Following another merger/acquisition, the prevailing philosophy of the company shifted towards an emphasis on development of management talent rather than assessment. Survey data at that time showed that 69 percent of companies using assessment centers focused on development (Kudisch et al. 1998). Despite the name of the program, the Career Development Center was viewed more as an evaluation of readiness for management than an opportunity to learn about leadership functions and effective management practices. The external provider was charged with adjusting the program to reflect this new emphasis on experiential learning and development. As noted by Thornton and Rupp (2006, p. 48), adult-learning research has contributed insights for designing effective developmental assessment centers, including the importance of having "an opportunity to be actively involved in the learning process," "supportive conditions for learning," and "credible people to support success." In the past, many participants had demonstrated more of a "performance orientation (concern for doing well or garnering positive evaluations)" rather than a "mastery orientation (concern for learning)" (Ford, Kraiger and Merritt 2010). The new program objective was to emphasize skill-building instead of achieving a high score. Several changes to the program were therefore recommended to place a greater emphasis on learning and development:

- *Video Review Sessions*. On the first day of the program, video recordings of each coaching and counseling exercise were made, and then at the end of the second day, an external facilitator reviewed one of the recordings with the participant in a private session. At various intervals, they paused the playback to discuss observed behaviors, both effective and ineffective. This new feature was very well received by the participants.
- *Development Discussions*. The external facilitators also conducted an in-depth discussion with each participant, exploring their thoughts regarding ongoing development, including their preferred learning style, which included: self-directed strategies, such as reading books, listening to audio or online programs; classroom learning, such as academic coursework, seminars, or workshops; on-the-job learning; and so on. This discussion was based on a background review form that participants completed as pre-work, prior to attending the CDC. As a result of these discussions, the assessor teams were better able to offer customized developmental strategies to each participant.
- *Feedback Conferences*. During the hour-long telephone feedback conferences, which were conducted two to three weeks after the CDC, the assessors focused more on "where to go from here" than "what you did during the program." Both the participant's immediate manager and second-line manager joined the feedback conference and took part in helping to design a six to twenty-four month developmental plan of action. This plan was to be in writing, with progress reports built in at three-month intervals. These changes were instituted in order to gain greater support for developmental action planning and to increase the likelihood of improving management skills post-CDC.

DESIRE FOR GREATER INVOLVEMENT BY THE COMPANY'S LINE MANAGEMENT

For several years, there had been discussion among senior leaders that perhaps the program should be conducted internally using regional sales directors as the assessors, instead of using external assessors. After considerable discussion, it was determined that the external provider would continue to conduct the program but would incorporate regional sales directors in the observation process. The belief was that the addition of internal assessors would enhance the credibility of the program results and provide the directors with a better understanding of the process. In addition, it was meant to reinforce their role as active supporters of ongoing leadership development. Under the new model, the programs were conducted at the client's training center, and each external assessor was paired with a regional sales director, or an assistant vice president, at the advanced-level sessions. Together they observed exercises and collaborated on the key findings to include in the analysis. While the internal observers did not provide competency ratings, they did complete basic observation forms that allowed for chronological capturing of behaviors. The external assessors completed the exercise rating forms, which included behaviorally anchored rating scales. At the end of the two-day observation process, the internal observers returned to their jobs, and the external assessor team completed the process, including the assessor integration meeting, the report writing, and the delivery of feedback.

ONGOING MODIFICATIONS TO EXERCISES

In response to major changes within the pharmaceutical industry, the external provider continued to revise the exercises to reflect changes in the role of the district sales manager. By the mid 2000s, it was becoming increasingly difficult for sales representatives to see physicians. In addition, new guidelines were introduced by the Pharmaceutical Research and Manufacturers of America (PhRMA) that restricted the marketing activities of sales representatives. District managers were challenged with maintaining sales goals and keeping their sales teams motivated under much more challenging conditions. Sales force expansions subsided, and the opportunities to advance into management positions diminished. In response, the client company adopted new coaching models and competency models, and these changes were incorporated into the content of the simulations. Recognizing that participants sometimes shared the details of the exercises with future program participants, the exercises were continually rotated to mitigate the impact of such coaching.

VALIDATION RESEARCH

Given the large number of participants in the assessment/development centers over many years, it was decided to conduct a validation study to determine whether there was a correlation between a participant's performance in the assessment/development center and his/her performance as a district sales manager. Regional sales directors completed a survey that involved rating their district sales managers on ten job performance factors. Various linear correlations were calculated to assess the degree to which the overall weighted scores from the assessment/development centers were related to on-the-job performance ratings. Results showed a strong positive correlation between the two variables, (r = .377, p. < .01). The study demonstrated that there is a significant accuracy by which the assessment/development center results relate to subsequent on-the-job performance ratings.

RENEWED FOCUS ON ASSESSMENT

Recognizing the predictive validity of the assessment center process, the company decided to place a greater emphasis on the results as a means of identifying those who were ready to assume a management role. The study made clear that many of the lower-performing district sales managers had been rated in the AC as needing significant development. As a result, the overall evaluation scores were given greater credence and the readiness-level cut-off scores were made more stringent, particularly as the company was going through a period of "top-grading" and making an effort at every level to hire and promote the best. The program was renamed the District Sales Manager Assessment (DSMA). Likewise, the advanced-level program was renamed the Regional Sales Director Assessment (RSDA). Once again, the program was referred to as an assessment center, and the chronological sequence depicting the evolution of the program is shown in Table 19.1.

Program Status – 15 Years Later

After 15 years of conducting the assessment/development center program, over 1,200 participants have taken part in the sessions, and many of them have subsequently been promoted to manager, director, and senior executive positions. The program started out being sponsored by the training department and later came under the ownership of the human resources department, enabling more comprehensive support. Many lessons have been learned, but the following are worth highlighting:

- Exercises need to be regularly updated to reflect the evolving role of the position(s) being assessed.
- Management needs to be involved at all levels for ongoing program and participant support.
- The purpose and use of the program must be explained and communicated to all parties, both participants and users of the results, on an ongoing basis, and not just periodically.
- Providing feedback via video has been one of the most successful additions to the program. Participants appreciated the immediate feedback and often commented that they observed behaviors that they never realized they were displaying.
- Involving participants' managers and directors in the feedback conference has ensured a better understanding of the results and improved the buy-in of the developmental recommendations.
- Requiring assessment center participants to complete a written career development plan in conjunction with their managers increases the likelihood that action will be taken. Incorporating the training department in longer-term follow up also helps to keep the plan alive.
- Effective assessors need to possess a unique combination of traits and capabilities. First of all, they must be observant of human behavior, aware of effective management

Table 19.1   Evolution of the assessment method

Approximate time period: dates	Name of program	Major purpose	Organizational, business challenge	Reason for change	Key features
1995–1998	Assessment Center, then Career Development Center (CDC)	Identification of leadership potential; assessment for promotion from sales to manager	Merger; sales force expansion	Earlier program relied on internal assessors (time, expertise issues) and focused on in-depth behavioral interviews	Professional (external) assessors; real-life management simulations; interactive feedback conferences
1999	Dual-Track Program	Placement into district sales manager or product manager development tracks	Expansion of positions in marketing (as well as sales management)	Need to identify potential for marketing management as well as sales management	Combination of sales management and marketing management simulations
1999	Advanced Level CDC	Promotion to regional sales director	Sales force expansion	Desire to promote new directors from within the company	New regional sales director-level simulations and competencies
2000–2007	Management Development Lab (MDL)	Pre-qualify candidates for management development	Merger; continued sales force expansion	Provide initial exposure to management; develop pipeline of potential managers	Internally conducted on regional basis; expanded developmental training
2004–2007	Revision of CDC	Shift from assessment to development focus	Merger	Philosophy shifted after merger, with a greater emphasis on development	Video review; development discussion; involvement of managers in feedback conferences
2007–present	District Sales Manager Assessment (DSMA)	Return to focus on assessment	New pressures on pharma industry	Period of top grading; effort to promote the best from within	Professional assessors along with directors
2007–present	Regional Sales Director Assessment (RSDA)	Return to focus on assessment	New pressures on pharma industry	Period of top grading; effort to promote the best from within	Professional assessors along with vice presidents

practices, and clear in their communications. In addition, they must be supportive facilitators, gracious hosts, and wise counselors.

Areas for further research have also emerged, including the following:

- Since the addition of internal assessors to the assessment center, how much more (or less) predictive of future success are the overall scores?
- To what extent have competency ratings and overall scores improved over the years, given the additional training and development offered to emerging managers? More specifically, what is the relationship between completing the post-assessment center career development plan and competency improvement?
- What would a validation study reveal about the predictive ability of the Regional Sales Director Assessment (RSDA) results?
- Which competencies and simulations explain a greater degree of the variance in subsequent on-the-job management performance?

Over the years, the program has been widely supported across the organization, and it continues to evolve as the industry changes in response to economic and political forces. Despite modifications to competency models and exercise content, the process is still grounded in the fundamental principles of careful behavioral observation and effective leadership practice. The sustainability of the program can be attributed to ongoing adaptations to organizational needs and avoidance of the "failure factors" as described by Thornton and Birri in Chapter 21 of this book.

References

Ballantyne, I. and Povah, N. 2004. *Assessment and Development Centres* (2nd Edition). Aldershot: Gower.

Ferguson, J. 1991. When is an assessment centre a development centre? *Guidance and Assessment Review*, 7, 1–3.

Ford, J.K., Kraiger, K. and Merritt, S.M. 2010. An updated review of the multidimensionality of training outcomes: New directions for training evaluation research. In *Learning, Training, and Development in Organizations*, edited by S.W. Kozlowski and E. Salas. New York, NY: Routledge, 135–165.

Gaugler, B.B., Bentson, C. and Pohley, K. 1990. *A Survey of assessment center practices in organizations*. Unpublished manuscript.

International Task Force on AC Guidelines 2009. Guidelines and Ethical Considerations for Assessment Centre Operations. *International Journal of Selection and Assessment*, 17, 243–253.

Kudisch, J.D., Rotolo, C.T., Avis, J.M., Fallon, J.D., Roberts, F.E., Rollier, T.J. and Thibodeaux, H.F. III. 1998. *A preliminary look at assessment center practices worldwide: What's hot and what's not*. Paper presented at the 26th annual meeting of the International Congress on Assessment Center Methods, Pittsburgh, PA.

Spychalski, A.C., Quiñones, M.A., Gaugler, B.B., and Pohley, K. 1997. A survey of assessment center practices in organizations in the United States. *Personnel Psychology*, 50, 71–90.

Thornton, G.C. III, and Cleveland, J.N. 1990. Developing managerial talent through simulation. *American Psychologist*, 45, 190–199.

Thornton, G.C. III, and Rupp, D.E., 2003. Simulations and assessment centers. In *Comprehensive Handbook of Psychological Assessment, vol. 4: Industrial and Organizational Assessment*, edited by J.C. Thomas and M. Hersen. New York: Wiley, 318–344.

Thornton, G.C. III, and Rupp, D.E. 2006. *Assessment Centers in Human Resource Management: Strategies for Prediction, Diagnosis, and Development*. Mahwah, NJ: Lawrence Erlbaum.

20 Influencing Decisions About Assessment and Development Centres for Talent Management

SEÁN BOYLE

One might suppose that decisions about employing assessment centres and development centres (AC/DCs) as a tool for talent management would be routine ones, given their substantial research bases and compelling evidence of validity and effectiveness (Arthur et al. 2003; Jones and Whitmore 1995; Meriac et al. 2008). But decision-making in organizations is seldom based on hard evidence alone, and the processes by which organizations decide to implement AC/DCs and integrate them into their talent management strategy are not readily amenable to systematic research. Power and personality may well be more important than research and rational argument in determining what actually happens in organizations (Miller Hickson and Wilson 1996). Nevertheless, changing organizational demands mean that decisions to implement, adapt, extend or even abandon the use of AC/DCs are often required.

Furthermore, as this volume demonstrates (see Birri and Melcher Chapter 12; Thornton and Birri Chapter 21, this volume) the success of an AC/DC programme depends not only on its technical soundness and efficient administration, but also on the extent to which it supports the organization's talent management and broader business strategies, and is seen to do so. Therefore AC/DC designers and process owners – whether internal staffers or external consultants – have a significant role to play in influencing thinking about the talent management strategy and in translating it into practical, successful interventions. This entails consideration of issues such as confirming the appropriateness of AC/DCs, securing the understanding and support of decision-makers and stakeholders, positioning assessment and development centres within the organization's repertoire of tools, ensuring organizations make sound decisions about the deployment of AC/DCs, and maximizing the benefits for the organization.

To undertake a preliminary exploration of these topics I convened an expert panel of 10 experienced AC/DC practitioners,[1] both in-company experts and external consultants,

1   I am grateful to the panel members for their insights and contributions. They include Max Ashmore, HR Development Director, Louis Vuitton Malletier, Paris; Stuart Duff, Partner and Head of Development, Pearn Kandola,

and interviewed them individually about their experience of implementing AC/DCs. Four of the panel members are internal senior talent management professionals with ownership for AC/DC processes in their organizations – two global professional service firms and two world leading brands in their respective markets. For the purposes of this chapter they are referred to as 'talent managers'. The remaining six were consulting business psychologists, specialists in the design and delivery of AC/DCs with over a century of collective experience in working with a wide variety of blue-chip businesses and public services organizations.

An obvious limitation of this approach is the absence of a 'control group' of equally knowledgeable and experienced professionals who choose not to recommend or implement AC/DCs, therefore it cannot claim to be a scientific or even a representative survey. Nevertheless, what follows is a distillation of themes, experiences and perceptions shared by expert practitioners which hopefully throws some light on the otherwise under-researched topic of how organizations make AC/DCs an effective part of their talent management strategy. Unless otherwise attributed to a published source, or a direct quotation, the comments following represent my attempt to capture the consensus of opinion as expressed by the individual panel members.

It seems appropriate to view the process of adopting and implementing AC/DCs as an organizational development (OD) intervention since it requires comprehensive and coordinated communication, influencing and process management to bring about change in the organization's capabilities to leverage its talent and human capital. The general OD model of planned change, with its phases of entering and contracting, diagnosis, intervention and evaluation (Cummings and Worley 2009) captures key features of implementing a typical AC/DC programme. For present purposes, in restricting our focus to the factors influencing how AC/DCs are deployed, the key objective of the contracting and diagnostic phases is to ensure alignment with the organization's strategic direction; the critical factor in the intervention phase is getting buy-in from stakeholders; and the outcome of the evaluation phase will be heavily influenced by the extent to which the programme achieves organizational fit. As with many OD interventions, these should be thought of as iterative processes, not as neat, discrete sequential steps.

Ensuring Alignment with the Organization's Strategic Direction

The panel members were unanimous in the view that transparent strategic alignment is a significant influence on organizational acceptance of an AC/DC programme. To be judged a success, an intervention has to be seen to be consistent with the organization's strategy and has to support it operationally (Holbeche 2009). Critical requirements for alignment are that AC/DCs are addressing key drivers of the talent management strategy; that the design methods accurately capture the behavioural correlates of the strategy; that the AC/DC programme is closely integrated with other talent management initiatives; and that the talent manager/

Oxford; Johanna Fullerton, Director, Seven – Psychology at Work, Dublin; Corinna Gillies, formerly Senior Manager Leadership Development, KPMG, London; Andrew Hill, Director of Talent Management, DBM, London; Jörg Iten, Director, Iten and Müller, Zürich; Kathrin Menges, Head of Global HR, Henkel KGaA, Düsseldorf; Michael Pearn, Occupational Psychologist, Dublin; Ceri Roderick, former Partner and Head of Assessment, Pearn Kandola, Oxford; Tina Two, UK Director of HR and Development, K&L Gates, London.

process owner has the credibility and trust of the top team to make operational decisions in support of the strategy.

STRATEGIC DRIVERS

A perceived benefit of the process is that the information it can generate is useful for so many strategically important purposes. When asked what issues prompted organizations to consider using AC/DCs the reasons most often mentioned by panel members correspond to the dominant concerns of talent management – selecting talented job applicants, identifying potential among existing staff, diagnosing development needs and generating reliable information for succession planning (Millar 2007, American Society for Training and Development 2009). A frequently mentioned driver in meeting the organization's strategic objectives for talent management is the need for more objective, consistent and trustworthy data about the capabilities and potential of the talent pool:

> *Even though we have robust data on individuals' current performance, it is the evaluation of potential for future responsibilities and challenges that we need in order to address the strategic goals.*

This is sometimes accompanied by a lack of faith in the existing performance management systems, or a need to counterbalance a dominant subjective decision-making style in the organization's culture:

> *The culture here is very people-driven, but subjective. Managers will describe people as 'great' or 'awful' but when challenged they can't articulate it. We are not good at delivering constructive feedback, and we need concrete, factual evidence. The development centre can provide this, and the managers can learn the skills they need.*

From a risk perspective, effective management of succession planning features prominently among senior executives' mission-critical priorities. Retaining and motivating top talent by demonstrating commitment to their development is also a driver:

> *One of the issues that prompted the development of the talent programme was that we were losing key people; and at exit interviews they were saying they didn't realize they were wanted. Now, the programme provides a pipeline of highly motivated people who feel valued, and therefore aren't looking elsewhere for opportunities.*

Additionally, mergers or restructuring often provide an impetus for organizations to undertake more-or-less formal reviews of their talent management activities against best practice standards, or to benchmark themselves against competitors and sector leaders.

CAPTURING THE BEHAVIOURAL CORRELATES OF THE STRATEGY

The rigorous design methodology used to develop AC/DCs was an attractive feature for the talent managers on the panel. Whether this took the form of a complete competency definition exercise and development of bespoke simulations, or a more limited analysis and review of an existing competency framework, with customization of existing exercises and whether it was conducted in-house or with the help of external consultants, it promised the possibility of designing a programme based on a diagnosis of the organization's strategy, and of translating it into behavioural terms.

> *My client was introducing a new talent management process and needed the tools to get a base line measure of key skills needed to deliver the strategy and make meaningful comparisons between people, and across different divisions and geographies. For them, the perceived advantages were concerned with accuracy, objectivity, creating a level playing field. They wanted to identify the best people by comparing them against a standard, not just rely on their own managers' say-so.*

This process of operationalizing the strategy is regarded as an effective way of educating staff by illustrating how individual behaviour contributes to the strategic objectives. Even though some consultants found that some clients were dissuaded from using AC/DCs by the high development costs and time required, the talent managers felt that the more tailored the programme was to their specific requirements and culture, the easier it was to convince key players of its overall strategic value.

INTEGRATING AC/DCs WITHIN TALENT MANAGEMENT

Thornton and Birri (see Chapter 21) point out that even a well designed AC/DC will achieve success only if it is fully integrated into the talent management system of the organization. Talent managers and consultants agree that AC/DCs should be an integrated component of the organization's talent management activity, and not a stand-alone initiative. In particular, how people get to participate on the programme, and where the AC/DC stands in relation to career progression and performance management procedures requires clarification. Highlighting the continuities and links between elements, and using a common language of competencies can ensure that the talent management strategy operates in a consistent fashion. Furthermore, they felt that it was pointless to introduce a sophisticated process such as an AC/DC if the basic talent management processes were not already in place. A certain level of competence in performance assessment was seen by some as a necessary precondition, as was access to a sufficient range of training and development resources to meet the diagnosed development needs.

Many other techniques and interventions overlap or compete with AC/DCs to address the same or similar objectives, including individual assessments, 360° feedback, one-to-one coaching, and psychometric assessment, as well as more conventional approaches such as performance reviews, counselling interviews and mainstream training and development initiatives. For the talent manager, matching the appropriate techniques with the varied organizational demands, or making choices between them, are key tasks. In choosing processes and initiatives to deliver the strategy there is no single 'decision model' shared by all the panel members, but most would include questions and tests such as what available tools best meet the requirements of the talent management strategy; what 'infrastructure' is necessary to enable the tools to be used effectively; and what human, financial, temporal and logistical resources are required.

For experienced practitioners, AC/DCs are the tool of choice, in that they are viewed as by far the most robust and valid method for many applications. But the final choice is often dictated by more practical considerations such as cost, timescales, resource availability and acceptability to candidates.

Given the experience and preferences of the panel members, it is not surprising that AC/DCs feature prominently on the list of tools for consideration. Nevertheless, they were clear that they were not in the business of making the problem fit an available solution. The decision to proceed with an AC/DC is carefully evaluated to assess its contribution to the overall talent management strategy, and regularly reviewed even in the case of long-running programmes. And even where they are specifically commissioned to design an AC/DC process, external consultants see it as their responsibility to challenge the client's diagnosis and to test the suitability and feasibility of an AC/DC in the client's particular circumstances.

BEING TRUSTED WITH DECISIONS

Although the strategic priorities for talent management are usually articulated at executive level, this does not mean that talent managers or external consultants need to engage in top-level strategy *formulation* discussions in order to make decisions about what tools to use – in practice, this was seldom the case. In the panel members' experience the proposal to employ AC/DCs is invariably an operational one, based on an assessment of what initiatives are needed to fulfil the strategic goals. Subject to budget approval, decisions concerning the choice of tools and techniques to address them generally fall within the remit of talent management professionals (who may or may not have been involved in formulating the strategy) either based on their own assessment of what is needed or with the support of external specialists:

> Senior management don't normally request a specific tool. They are looking for additional elements to support their decisions, but they leave it up to HR to provide it.

However, earning the legitimacy and trust to take such decisions requires patient and subtle diplomacy to ensure the talent management agenda is taken seriously by the organization's leaders. For the talent managers in this sample at least, the mechanisms for aligning the talent management strategy and its constituent initiatives and activities to the broader business strategy relied heavily on communication, experience and intuition. Even where formal procedures existed, 'taking soundings' and 'being aware of the issues and the way the business is heading', mediated by networking and good relationships across the organization, are critical in this respect, both to understand the business issues and to appreciate what initiatives or solutions would be feasible and politically acceptable. If talent managers can demonstrate by their track record that they understand the business and can deliver practical solutions to real business concerns, their judgement of the need for and value of initiatives such as AC/DCs is more likely to be accepted by the organization's leaders.

Getting Buy-In

The proposal to implement an AC/DC programme usually originates within the talent management function in response to business needs expressed in the ongoing dialogue between talent managers and the rest of the organization, but its widespread adoption depends on securing the active support of those affected by the programme. Unless key decision-makers, prospective participants and their managers buy into it, the programme is likely to be seen as 'just another HR activity' that will not realize the intended benefits or meet the organization's strategic goals. The necessary commitment of time and energy to deliver the programme and follow up on the outcomes is unlikely to be forthcoming unless those involved feel that it is delivering value both to individuals and to the organization as a whole.

To achieve buy-in, as well as demonstrating personal conviction and commitment, the talent manager needs to develop an extensive network of supportive relationships, ideally including a top-level champion, together with stakeholder groups such as potential assessors/observers and prospective participants. Exploiting the expertise of external consultants, and drawing on research findings can also provide both scientific/technical and process skills to win support.

BUILDING PERSONAL CONVICTION

As one talent manager put it, 'in seeking buy-in, you have to be convinced to be convincing', and for many it is the personal experience of AC/DCs that generates the conviction and drive needed to attract support and engagement for the process. Even though most talent managers will have learned about AC/DCs in their formal professional education, and for many the research evidence is compelling at an intellectual level, the power and potential of the process is fully appreciated only when it comes to life. Thus for some, earlier experience in a support role, in a previous organization, or even as a participant, was critical in forming an understanding of the value of the method. Others, before seeking top management commitment or announcing the process to the wider organization, undertook a pilot event to understand better how it might work in their business. Describing how DCs were introduced to the business, one talent manager recounted:

> I knew I had to have an influencing strategy. To bring the proposal to the Executive Committee, I would have to be able to give examples and field any question they would throw at me. After a few pilot events, I felt I could do that; I understood and believed in the process. I could see how it would work for us, and I could convince them.

CREATING SUPPORTIVE RELATIONSHIPS

The quality of certain relationships can make or mar the programme. The talent manager's credibility with senior management has already been mentioned, but the support of a 'champion' can also be decisive. Strong relationships are also needed between the talent manager and those directly affected by the programme, such as the prospective participants and their managers; and between the talent manager and the external consultancy support.

The role of the champion

Where talent managers have high credibility based on a solid track record of delivering business solutions, they may not need much additional support to win commitment for their proposals. But most found it invaluable to have a champion for the process, as did the external consultants: 'I can't think where it has worked without one'; 'It's a given, otherwise there is no one there to look after it'; 'That's what makes it fly or fall.' Ideally, the champion is a high profile opinion leader within the organization, typically an executive board member or partner, someone who believes passionately in the value of the programme and is prepared to be its public face, and who has the credibility and clout to get issues on the agenda, open doors, overcome obstacles and make things happen. In some cases, the champion, the process owner and the talent manager are one and the same person, but especially in larger organizations the level of involvement needed to manage the detail of the process on a daily basis precludes the most senior people from combining these roles. Furthermore, it is often an advantage to have a champion who is not part of the HR function, but is seen instead to embody the interests of the whole organization.

Talent managers are usually aware from their interactions across the organization who are the likely candidates for champion, and what degree of lobbying and influencing is needed to win their support. It will often be someone who has already shown an interest in development issues, and who supports change and improvement initiatives. As well as providing public support, the champion is often a valuable mentor and confidante of the process owner who can offer advice on how to influence other interest groups within the organization.

Engaging management

Convincing senior managers that the programme will deliver meaningful benefits to them and securing their active involvement in its design and delivery are key challenges for the internal talent manager. The groundwork must be prepared and the organization's leadership need to have confidence that the talent manager understands its issues and can deliver.

> *There will be implementers, budget holders, approvers, and those who set the strategic direction of the firm. How much time depends on the interests of those involved. But at least annually, there will be a discussion between (the talent manager) and the head of the business about where the firm is going, where are the gaps, what likely future gaps, where do you want us to direct resource to build skill in those areas, and AC/DCs would form part of that.*

Even if the talent manager has a clear idea of the purpose of the AC/DC and how it will work in practice, it is unlikely that all executives whose approval is required will be similarly well-informed, and a good deal of lobbying and communication by the talent manager is usually needed to dispel misunderstandings and manage expectations, most often by means of informal, face-to-face discussions.

Some panel members found that a worthwhile way to generate discussion around critical issues about the operation of the programme and to uncover concerns and handle objections was to get senior managers to agree on a policy statement that would spell out clearly the aims of the programme, who was to be involved and how they would gain access, what decisions might be made on the basis of observations, what happens to the data and so on. Such a policy statement is, of course, a valuable document in its own right (International Task Force on Assessment Center Guidelines 2009).

Securing executive level approval and resources is, however, only the first skirmish of a long campaign. Creating an organizational mindset that values talent development is a long-term process, and for the talent managers on the panel it is the necessary foundation on which initiatives such as AC/DCs can be built. This requires regular discussions with managers throughout the organization about how they assess and develop their people to prepare them for bigger tasks and challenges, and educating them about what can be achieved. The benefits of doing so were clear to this talent manager:

> It's such a strong successful part of our infrastructure for such a long time, that there is not a lot of persuasion required; all I have to do is make sure that what I am designing is valid and robust and meets the needs of the business; the name 'development centre' carries a lot of weight here.

Especially where an AC/DC programme is being produced from scratch, involving line managers in all phases of programme design is necessary to ensure that the programme meets their requirements and reflects organizational reality. Even if only a small group of line managers can be involved, it adds greatly to the credibility and perceived relevance of the programme if it is seen to be the product of those at the 'sharp end', rather than solely an HR or consultant-led initiative, or an off-the-shelf solution.

Sometimes the managers can be involved through a formally constituted project management team that oversees the development of the programme, but in other instances, it can be an informal arrangement. It is more important that they are the managers of the target participant group, and that they have the reputation of having their fingers on the pulse of the organization, and are role models for the participants. If external consultants are employed to design the programme, they can facilitate the managers' involvement in activities such as competency definition, providing the raw material and ideas for simulation exercises and acting as 'guinea pigs' for initial exercise trials. From this group also, the initial panel of AC/DC observers is often drawn. This cadre of managers as they begin to see the process taking shape can become important allies of the talent manager in winning their colleagues' support.

The participant perspective

The target participants have much to gain from an AC/DC programme, but panel members were all aware of the risks to motivation and self-esteem (see Fletcher, Chapter 8 in this volume) and from past experience of HR initiatives, they may regard the programme with enthusiasm or apprehension and suspicion. Winning their support is therefore a high priority for the talent manager. As soon as people become aware of the impending programme, any gaps or voids in communication will be filled by rumour or half-truths, so a quick and comprehensive communication strategy needs to be in place from an early stage of the planning.

There is a common core of information that all prospective participants seek. This includes a clear statement of the purpose of the AC/DC, what it is, why the organization is implementing it and what outcomes it hopes to achieve; how it fits with the broader development strategy of the organization and with specific initiatives; what is the target group, how is it identified and defined; whether participation is mandatory or voluntary; how are participants nominated, by whom and by what criteria; who are the observers and what qualifies them for the role; what information is collected during the AC/DC, what happens to it; what formal reports are produced, who has access to them for what purposes, how long are they regarded as valid and how long retained by the organization; what recommendations or decisions are made, how are they integrated with other data on participants; and what benefits can the participants expect to obtain from their involvement. In the experience of the panel members, clear and full disclosure on these points, together with an openness to prospective participants' concerns and readiness to take them on board, elicits a positive response in most cases. Conversely, anything less than transparency about the purposes of the AC/DC creates suspicion, particularly if participants have had negative experiences in the past, typically 'we were told it was only for our own development, but in practice it was used to make promotion decisions'.

Additional briefing will be needed following major transitions such as mergers, restructuring or downsizing since there is often a need to redefine the organizational culture, speed up the formation of work teams or promote engagement. Identifying and retaining high potential talent in these circumstances is essential, with AC/DCs forming part of the strategy, but the communication process needs to be handled sensitively to convey to the participants that they are valued and are seen to have a future in the firm, without demoralizing and devaluing the contributions of those not invited to participate.

USING EXTERNAL CONSULTANTS EFFECTIVELY

The nature of the relationship between internal talent managers who own the AC/DC process and external consultants varies greatly, ranging from the purely transactional, where the consultant is an 'extra pair of hands' working on the design and delivery of the programme as directed by the process owner, or the provider of 'off-the-shelf' solutions, to the genuinely collaborative, where the AC/DC programme is a seamless blend of technical know-how and organizational savvy. Although the external consultant will usually bring a higher level of specialist knowledge, what is particularly valued by the process owner is the consultant's broader perspective and market insight that comes from working with a wide range of organizations. Even where the AC/DC programme operates at quite high levels in the organization, the interface with the rest of the organization is typically managed by the process owner, with the external consultant often supplying invaluable but usually invisible support.

The talent managers were quite consistent in what they expect from the consultants they engage to support them. In addition to a high level of professional expertise and innovative thinking in AC/DCs, what the client values in the external consultant is the ability to grasp quickly the essence of the organization and its concerns and to deliver solutions that drive the strategy, They want consultants they can work with productively, and who base their solutions on the client's agenda, not their own. Some verbatim comments illustrate their expectations:

> *I am looking for expertise, they have to convince me they are really good in doing this; I'm not looking for people who say they can do everything, because you can't be good at everything. I like consultants with a proven track record and good contact with other relevant companies of a similar size and global set-up. They need to be open, to listen and understand, to try to solve my problem rather than trying to sell their ideas and products and telling me I need to go a different way (though I can be convinced).*

> *Firstly I am looking for consultants who understand the environment that it has to fit – you can't put in a product that is the wrong shape and expect it to be accepted. You need people who can design it so that things can be tested and retested, and that conforms to good practice. They have to have knowledge, experience and understanding of the firm. It should be something bespoke for the firm, not 'off-the-peg'. After that, it's who can I work with, who do I like?*
>
> *I want experience, knowledge, expertise, impact. If they were going to talk to my boss, would I feel relaxed or nervous? If I'm honest, clients are looking for like minded people – is the chemistry right, do I like them, are they picking up on my cues, the specific words I am using, can they detect the culture?*

Consultants for their part need to be ready and able to help clients elaborate and refine their approach where required. In their view, clients who encourage and value challenges to their thinking get the best out of their consultants; although the strategy may be a given, the creative interplay between client and consultant often results in better solutions.

USING RESEARCH FINDINGS

The extensive research base underpinning AC/DCs represents a valuable resource for influencing organizational decision-making and provides a good deal of reassurance to stakeholders that the AC/DC process is sufficiently robust, fair, accurate and cost-effective. Although it was rare for panel members to base their arguments solely on academic research, it was important for them to know that should questions arise, they would be able to find answers to them. When speaking to business leaders, both external consultants and internal talent managers draw on research evidence that addresses the business benefits, for example utility, return on investment, and improved decision-making. The talent managers, who as process owners are usually knowledgeable about and interested in the broad research issues, expect the consultant to be up to date, to be an intellectual sparring partner who can proactively and selectively present the latest research to advise on adjustments and improvements that will maximize the benefits of the AC/DC process, but these discussions seldom involve the wider business stakeholders.

For the external consultants, it was common practice for them to provide prospective clients with a small amount of research evidence initially, and to gauge from the client's response whether more was needed. The research base is also critical in forming their conceptions of best practice and guiding the design of AC/DCs, but it also reinforces their professional and scientific self-image since it confirms that their area of practice is well founded and clearly differentiated from temporary fads and fashions. However, a number of the consultants mentioned that they rely less on research-based arguments than they did in the past, in part due to the fact that clients are better informed and there is less need to convince them of the benefits, and partly because the consultants themselves are more experienced in speaking the language of business and judging what will carry weight with their audience.

Achieving Organizational Fit and Maintaining Support

Once the AC/DC programme is up and running, policy and procedural decisions about its operation influence the extent to which it becomes part of the fabric of the organization.

Integration with other talent management initiatives has already been discussed, but other factors are also important determinants of organizational fit. The role of managers as assessors/observers can make visible the organization's commitment, while the calibre of consultant and the way ethical issues are handled can influence the perceived credibility of the process. The participants' experience of the programme, and the follow-up provided are key elements in sustaining the programme for the long-term. Finally, in a changing business climate, AC/DC programmes need to adapt to new circumstances and outlooks.

EMPLOYING MANAGERS AS ASSESSORS/OBSERVERS

Despite the findings that psychologists make better assessors than managers (Gaugler et al. 1987; Sagie and Magnezy 1997), in some respects there are considerable advantages to be gained by using managers as observers in combination with external consultants, in order to generate understanding of and commitment to the process. Where these are senior people and opinion leaders, they can be very influential in disseminating knowledge to the rest of the organization and in winning support for the process. However, it is becoming increasingly difficult for senior managers to find the time to be full assessors, and some panel members have found ways to involve them in the process but with a reduced role or time commitment.

For example, consultant-assessed activities can be grouped together on the first day, so that the organization's assessors are not needed on that day. Some panel members have implemented, and all are considering, some degree of technology-facilitated assessment (Reynolds and Rupp 2010) so that some exercises can be assessed remotely or automatically, or the integration meeting conducted by videoconferencing. In the course of recasting an existing programme in a more developmental direction, one talent manager found that by making the participants responsible for collating and managing their own feedback and rebalancing the managers' role towards that of coach and role model (with consultants doing the assessing) her previous concerns about the objectivity of managers' assessments were removed while the benefits of their presence and contributions were maintained.

CALIBRE OF CONSULTANTS

The calibre and composition of the team fielded by the external consultant also contributes to the ongoing acceptance of the process. The consultant members of the panel were acutely aware of the talent managers' sensitivities about the consultant team. Sometimes it was simply a matter of appearance: is the style of dress and behaviour appropriate for the organization? On other occasions it was age: Would a 50-something manager accept the judgement and feedback of a consultant young enough to be a son or daughter; or conversely in a graduate recruitment context was it projecting the right progressive, dynamic image, to have an assessor panel of grey heads, however wise-looking? Sometimes the expectation was that the organization's diversity agenda should be reflected in the assessor team.

More often, it is quality and credibility that are at issue. According to a consultant:

Internal HR people get very nervous about who they put in front of senior people. They want to know that the people in my team know their stuff, are organizationally savvy, and won't get into trouble. As the consultants will be dealing with very smart people, they need to be able to talk about the business context, not just the psychology. It only takes one senior manager to meet one consultant they don't rate for the whole project to be in the water.

INTEGRITY AND ETHICAL CONCERNS

Provided basic principles (such as those set out in the International Task Force on Assessment Center Guidelines 2009) are adhered to, AC/DCs do not present many ethical problems to the stakeholders. The principal issue, mentioned by all panel members, concerns the use of information obtained in the course of the AC/DC. Confidentiality was seen as essential to winning the confidence of stakeholders and maintaining trust in the process. Although details varied according to specific applications and organizational norms, it was deemed crucial to communicate and implement a clear policy on what use is made of information, how it influences decisions about individuals' career progression, how it is handled and stored, who has access to it, for how long it remains valid, and so on.

Allied to this is the need to use the information, in feedback and elsewhere, in a way that respects the individual's dignity and self-worth. The confidentiality and security of exercise materials and processes also need to be managed both for reasons of cost and validity. While there is merit in Sackett's (1987) assertion that in a well-developed behavioural exercise, true score variance will not be significantly affected by basic advance 'knowledge' of its contents, nevertheless access to information about exercises and processes needs to be managed systematically to avoid any perceptions that some participants might have an unfair advantage.

While most of the panel members could imagine situations in which AC/DCs could be used in ethically dubious ways, they had very few actual examples of such practice. The consultants often had to adopt an educative role, explaining why particular checks and balances were needed, but this was usually accepted, and they experienced little resistance to standards of good practice when this was explained and justified.

A more serious risk to the integrity of AC/DCs is the gradual erosion of standards and principles that can take place over time and so can subvert their purpose and jeopardize support. Talent managers need to be continually aware of such risks. There is no surer way of destroying the credibility of an AC/DC process than to use it, or allow it to be used, for a different purpose from its declared aim. This is particularly the case where the declared aim of the programme is purely developmental, but where outputs are used, surreptitiously or otherwise, to support placement, promotion or deselection decisions. And in situations where the AC/DC does have a formal role to play in succession planning and promotion, there are risks that the AC/DC programme could come to be seen as an alternative way of conveying 'difficult' messages to people. Where the performance management system is ineffective, managers who are unwilling or unable to address performance issues may be tempted to nominate underperformers to attend the AC/DC where they will 'get the message' that further progression is unlikely.

SUSTAINABILITY

In the words of one of the consultants, the most significant questions asked of consultants when formally pitching to provide AC/DCs are: 'What happens afterwards? How can you ensure sustainability to make it work and generate the benefits?' The critical factor, in his view and echoed by others, is what happens beforehand. If attendance at an AC/DC is isolated from the participant's everyday working life, with little preparation or involvement on the part of the participant's manager there will be little long-term benefit. But forging relationships and clarifying expectations with the participants and their managers before the event creates a better chance of sustaining the momentum and getting actions on development plans afterwards.

While recognizing that participant reactions are of limited value as a programme evaluation measure, they are an indication of cultural fit and they are critical as a means of maintaining support. 'The participant response tells you very quickly what works and what doesn't in this environment, and it can have a huge impact in securing the budget for the future of the programme' said one consultant. 'Negative reactions get reported back to the sponsor very quickly, and reflect badly on the programme' according to another. The participants' expectations and experience of the programme also need to be managed carefully.

> The process generates powerful, tough feedback. We were not used to that here. The challenge is to ensure that participants do not feel really demoralized and left to their own devices. You have to tread very carefully that it doesn't backfire, because if we have bad experiences here, it will travel like wildfire. You would soon hear comments like 'I wouldn't send anyone on that programme, they come back fragile.' It takes a lot of hand-holding.

FUTURE PROOFING

Being able to demonstrate continuing relevance to organizational issues and concerns is a critical requirement for maintaining support. Though some would say that the 'look and feel' of an AC/DC is a superficial feature that has little effect on its validity, the panel members believed that it contributes to stakeholders' confidence in the process and their perceptions of its value. They were confident for the future of AC/DCs, since the basic model is sound and the fundamental concerns that the AC/DC process is designed to address will continue to be relevant to organizations, but just as it has evolved to meet the changing needs of organizations over the past half-century, it must retain the flexibility to do so in the future. If it is seen to represent outmoded ways of working or concerned with issues that no longer exercise the minds of business leaders, however superficial these views might be, organizational support will melt away. Both talent managers and consultants see it as their responsibility to keep abreast of, and if possible to anticipate, changing business concerns, explore their implications for the human qualities needed to lead and manage organizations and integrate these insights into the design and delivery of AC/DCs.

Among the challenges to be addressed are the effects of globalization both on the structure and function of businesses and on the talent market, the impact of technology on ways of working, and differing generational attitudes and expectations, to name but a few. Globally operating companies, for example, have to contend with tensions between organizational versus regional cultures and values: should the organization assert a unitary company culture or strive to value difference and adapt to local circumstances? Are existing competency models interpreted similarly in different locations and how well do they capture the need for qualities such as intercultural sensitivity? Is it really possible (or desirable) to deliver a global AC/DC programme consistently? Where talent flows swiftly and globally, how accurately can potential be spotted and developed? The contributions in Part 3 of this volume address these topics in depth and provide insights into how they are dealt with.

Just as working patterns have been revolutionized by information technology, most AC/DC designers now make use of technology both to create more realistic scenarios and simulations that mirror new ways of working, to streamline the assessment process itself, and to provide real time developmental input (Reynolds and Rupp 2010). Most clients now expect, and most consultants can provide sophisticated IT platforms to deliver AC/DC content and to manage the process. And as a 'sales' aid, an IT-enabled process can be used to demonstrate the AC/DC to prospective clients and internally to prepare and engage participants in a way that paper based approaches never could.

The IT revolution has facilitated to some extent the entry of the 'Y' or 'trophy' generation (Alsop 2008) into the workforce. Even if Generation Y is an oversimplified stereotype with no empirical justification (Pralong 2010), some panel members say they have already detected a shift in expectations and attitudes among the target population for fast-track programmes: a strong sense of entitlement with self-esteem to match, a desire for frequent feedback, as long as it is positive, and an instrumental view of their contractual relationships. If, as some see it, the traditional model of AC/DCs embody a set of assumptions about working life and values that are challenged by the Y generation, there is a risk that AC/DCs will detect only the negative features of this trend, and that the positives, such as the initiative and vision, the desire for empowerment and responsibility, the flexibility and change orientation, will be overlooked.

The traditional spatial and temporal boundaries of AC/DCs are no longer fixed – it is entirely feasible to construct a 'virtual' AC/DC, where participants need never leave their desks, or can take part at a time of their own choosing from anywhere with an Internet connection, and receive feedback and coaching from remote observers. The panel members see obvious attractions in this approach for selection based assessment centres, but the advantages of virtual reality for internal development have to be balanced by the need to maintain the essential human contact and interaction that has been the hallmark of AC/DCs and the basis of management and leadership.

Conclusions

If there is a lesson to be learned from this impressionistic review, it is that when organizations experience well developed, expertly managed AC/DCs they are valued as powerful, worthwhile and flexible tools for managing and developing talent. Influencing organizations' decisions about whether or how to run an AC/DC programme is then, in one sense, pushing at an open door. The challenges to be overcome are seldom those of resistance, hostility or disbelief. The influencing tactics to be employed do not require subterfuge or manipulation. As a given, a high level of technical expertise in AC/DC methodology and professional wisdom are needed to convince. But in addition, exerting influence is often a case of working with the grain of the organization, tuning in to its goals, challenges and way of doing things, utilizing its channels of power and communication and balancing competing interests and priorities. Above all, transparent communication of aims, processes and outcomes, together with active involvement of stakeholders are essential components of any effort to win support.

References

Alsop, R. 2008. *The Trophy Kids Grow Up: How the Millennial Generation is Shaking Up the Workplace*. San Francisco: Jossey-Bass.

American Society for Training and Development 2009. *Talent Management Practices and Opportunities*. Alexandria VA: ASTD Press.

Arthur, W. Jr., Day, E.A., McNelly, T.L. and Edens, P.S. 2003. A meta-analysis of the criterion-related validity of assessment center dimensions. *Personnel Psychology*, 56, 125–154.

Cummings, T.G. and Worley, C.G. 2009. *Organizational Development and Change* (9th Edition). Mason, OH: South-Western Cengage Learning.

Gaugler, B.B., Rosenthal, D.B., Thornton, G.C. and Bentson, C. 1987. Meta-analysis of assessment center validity. *Journal of Applied Psychology*, 72, 493–511.

Holbeche, L. 2009. *Aligning Human Resources and Business Strategy* (2nd Edition). Oxford: Butterworth-Heinemann.

International Task Force on Assessment Center Guidelines. 2009. Guidelines and ethical considerations for assessment center operations. *International Journal of Selection and Assessment*, 17, 243–254.

Jones, R.G. and Whitmore, M.D. 1995. Evaluating developmental assessment centers as interventions. *Personnel Psychology*, 48, 377–388.

Meriac, J.P., Hoffman, B.J., Woehr, D.J. and Fleisher, M.S. 2008. Further evidence for the validity of assessment center dimensions: A meta-analysis of the incremental criterion-related validity of dimension ratings. *Journal of Applied Psychology*, 93, 1042–1052.

Millar, B. 2007. *Building an Integrated Talent Management Strategy – a Briefing Paper*. London: Economist Intelligence Unit.

Miller, S.J., Hickson, D.J. and Wilson, D.C. 1996. Decision making in organizations. In *Handbook of Organization Studies*, edited by C. Hardy, S.R. Clegg and W. Nord. London: Sage.

Pralong, J. 2010. L'image du travail selon la génération Y. *Revue internationale de Psychosociologie*, 16, 109–134.

Reynolds, D.H and Rupp, D.E. 2010 Advances in technology-facilitated assessment. In *Handbook of Workplace Assessment: Evidence-based Practices for Selecting and Developing Organizational Talent*, edited by J.C. Scott, D.H. Reynolds. San Francisco: Pfeiffer, 609–641.

Sackett, P.R. 1987. Assessment centers and content validity: some neglected issues. *Personnel Psychology*, 40, 13–25.

Sagie, A. and Magnezy, R. 1997. Assessor type, number of distinguishable dimension categories, and assessment centre construct validity. *Journal of Occupational and Organizational Psychology*, 70, 103–108.

21 Failure and Success Factors in Assessment Centers: Attaining Sustainability

GEORGE C. THORNTON III AND RAIMUND BIRRI

The history of applications of assessment centers (AC) is sprinkled with miserable failures and glorious success stories. The purpose of this chapter is to present 10 factors leading to failure of ACs and 10 factors leading to sustainability of ACs. We draw on our own experiences, experiences related to us by others, situations where we have been invited to intervene at a later date, and court rulings on ACs challenged in employment discrimination litigation in the United States. We begin by relating the failure factors. If the development or implementation of the AC suffers from one or more of the flaws, it will very likely fail. At the very least, organizations must avoid the failure factors. But avoiding failure factors may not be enough to lead to longevity of an AC. Avoiding the negatives creates a situation that may be thought of as necessary but not sufficient conditions to sustain an AC over time. The list of success factors may be thought of as important conditions to maintain an AC over time.

Factors Leading to Failure of Assessment Centers

We start with the failure factors that are almost certain to mark the AC for an early death. While it might seem that no one would commit these errors, they are all drawn from real experiences. To avoid embarrassment to ourselves or others, we do not name the designers or organizations.

ASSESSING THE WRONG DIMENSIONS

An AC is doomed to fail if the designers neglect to identify dimensions or competencies that are central to the purpose of the AC and the corporate strategy for talent management. The worst case is when a highly marketed competency list is adopted by an organization without studying the job to which the AC will apply. The development of each AC should begin with a careful study of the target job in the target organization (International Task Force 2009). The organization needs to specify how the job is being done successfully now or how it wants the job to be done in the future. An organization may have a thorough job analysis or competency model, but that may not be enough. Competency models may be expressed in quite abstract terms which may not be amenable to assessment unless they are operationalized into measurable dimensions. If the purpose of the AC is development, the dimensions should be restricted to those that can be developed in the context of the AC method (Rupp, Snyder, Gibbons and Thornton 2006).

USING SEEMINGLY IRRELEVANT ASSESSMENT TECHNIQUES

Face validity is important. If the tests, questionnaires, and simulation exercises do not appear to be relevant, stakeholders have a ready basis for complaints if problems arise. Even though the scientific research literature may support the validity of tests of intelligence and certain personality characteristics for predicting managerial success (Thornton, Hollenbeck and Johnson 2010), methods of measuring these characteristics may be difficult to defend, especially in high-stakes selection and promotion applications. Depending on the purpose of the AC, simulation exercises can have various levels of different aspects of fidelity (Thornton and Kedharnath, in press). Moderate levels of fidelity may be appropriate for an AC designed to help identify individuals with long range potential to move into any number of future positions that may not even be known by the organization. In such applications, the content of problems embedded in the simulated positions need not be representative of any job which currently exists. On the other hand, a developmental AC used to train marketing managers to be more effective in specific newly appointed positions may call for simulations that have tasks and content that is nearly identical to the job.

What is common in these applications is that the exercises should have face validity to the participants, so they engage in the activities with high motivation, and to other stakeholders so they embrace the findings. This means that the labels of the dimensions should be in the natural language of the managers (Thornton and Rupp in press). In addition, the definitions of the dimensions should clarify the behavior that is representative of on-the-job behaviors. The definition and behavioral examples from relevant exercises create face validity for persons being assessed, assessors, and other stakeholders in the organization.

USING ASSESSORS WHO LACK CREDIBILITY OR SKILL

Over the years, many different types of assessors have been used (Thornton and Rupp 2006): managers in the target job or one or two levels up; human resource managers; consultants with backgrounds in industrial and organizational, clinical, and counseling psychology; persons trained to score individual exercises (for example, "in basket specialists"). Each of these types may or may not have credibility in a given organization. For example, in some organizations, middle-level managers are the most credible assessors, but in promotional ACs in police and fire departments in the United States, middle-level managers in the host organization may not be acceptable due to suspicion of bias for or against certain candidates.

Part of the process of establishing credibility is adequate assessor training. A program may fail because assessors are not trained in the processes of behavioral observation, classification, and evaluation. Failure may ensue if the integration process is not handled properly so as to avoid the domination by certain assessors (Dewberry, Chapter 7 in this volume).

NOT MAINTAINING SECURITY OF ASSESSMENT MATERIALS

An AC in a high-stakes selection or promotion program will fail if the detailed content of the simulation exercises is made known to candidates. The distribution of such "insider" information is likely to be uneven, and some candidates will have legitimate complaints. This concern presents a dilemma because designers wish to be able to pre-test the exercises to ensure they are relevant to the job and do not contain any biased or inappropriate content. Attempts to get judgments from subject matter experts (SMEs) about the representativeness of the content before administration in actual promotional testing provide opportunities for actual or perceived leakage. Organizations should err on the side of seeking input only from SMEs who are highly trusted.

ALLOWING VARIATIONS IN ADMINISTRATION

Failure to follow standardized procedures opens the AC process to criticisms of favoritism and even legal liability (Thornton, Wilson, Johnson and Rogers 2009). A hallmark quality of sound testing is the standardization of instructions, setting, time limits, materials available, and so forth. There are times when the sequence of activities may be altered to accommodate resource constraints such as the number of assessors, role players, or available rooms. With stand-alone exercises that are not linked together as one might find in a "day of the life" assemblage of exercises, variation in the sequence of exercises should not be problematic. We are aware of a situation where the AC was run in a large building scheduled for demolition. A door was missing on one conference room where an exercise was being administered. Some candidates scheduled to participate later in the exercise allegedly overheard conversations in that room, and thus had unfair opportunities to prepare. There may be situations that call for variations in administration for individuals with documented disabilities. The organization may be required to provide reasonable accommodations in testing for disabled individuals in the form of additional time, a reader, or a signer. In such situations, the organization may wish to state a general policy regarding legitimate accommodations in program descriptions to avert criticisms from non-disabled participants.

PRODUCING AN OVERLY BURDENSOME PROGRAM

An AC program that exceeds the organization's resources of space, staff, cost, and so forth will soon disappear, if the organization has not established its economic utility. There is no question ACs are expensive; certainly in comparison with other methods such as cognitive ability tests and personality questionnaires. Whereas tests and questionnaires may cost little more than $10 to $25 per person, ACs may cost several hundred dollars per person. Studies have shown that the economic utility of an AC will justify the added expense when certain conditions are met, for example, when the validity of an AC is larger than the validity of an alternative method or the AC adds appreciable validity beyond the alternative (Thornton and Potemra 2010).

Aside from the pure economic cost, an assessment center can place a heavy burden on human resource managers to design and administer the program, and on managers to serve as assessors. One short-lived program set out to assess nearly 20 dimensions. Assessors were burdened to document relevant observations, struggled to differentiate among similar dimensions, took extensive time to write up reports after each exercise, took an inordinate time to complete the integration discussion, and spent excessive time to write and deliver feedback reports. Some programs fail due to additional costs incurred when expectations are raised among internal candidates that something will be done to follow assessment with some form of training or other developmental experience. Still others have failed when the organization has not made good on promises for subsequent development.

FAILING TO DOCUMENT EFFECTIVENESS

Challenges to an AC over time are almost inevitable. Objections may come from internal or external sources. Some assessees may disagree with the results; some middle managers may see the assessments as an infringement on their prerogatives to promote whom they want. Agents of government watch-dog groups such as the Equal Employment Opportunity Commission in the United States may challenge the validity, fairness, and legality of the AC. If the organization does not have contemporaneous documentation of the steps in developing, administering, and evaluating the AC, it is difficult to marshal supportive arguments. Judges in employment discrimination litigation in the United States are particularly suspicious of reports that are written only at the time of challenges some time after design and administration (Thornton, Eurich and Johnson 2009). The threat of formal legal challenge in the absence of adequate documentation of value has led to discontinuation of ACs.

FAILING TO CONSIDER CULTURAL CONSIDERATIONS

Cultural conditions may differ from division to division within a single company, from company to company within an industry, from one region of a country to another, and from one country to another country. Failure to accommodate cultural preferences may doom an AC. Within the United States some sections of the country are more formal and regimented, whereas others are more relaxed. The same exercises that call for individuals to demonstrate their individual superiority over others may be quite acceptable in the US and other countries that value individual merit, but may be rejected in countries that put more value on collective actions and recognition.

While there are several required elements of the AC method (International Task Force 2009), each can be designed somewhat differently. Failure to word definitions of dimensions in the language of the host setting, to eliminate wording in exercises that may be offensive, or to provide feedback that is sensitive to cultural norms have doomed ACs in cross cultural settings.

VIOLATING PROFESSIONAL AND LEGAL REGULATIONS

An unfortunately common occurrence is the use of results of an ostensible developmental AC to make promotion or layoff decisions. In one AC where it was announced that the purpose was to provide individuals with feedback on developmental needs and help with developmental planning, the organization experienced a severe decline in business and had to lay off supervisors. Top executives insisted on using the assessment results to identify the weakest supervisors. The program became labeled "the assassination center" and was immediately discontinued. Other professional violations include failure to provide participants with informed consent to gather certain information, and failure to maintain security of individuals' assessment results (International Task Force 2009).

AC procedures that do not comply with applicable city ordinances, state regulations, and federal laws are doomed to failure. Cities may mandate that personnel practices follow certain regulations; obviously ACs must comply. In the United States, violation of statutes dealing with equal employment opportunities must be observed. In Europe, organizations must not violate laws that restrict the transfer of certain personnel records, including AC results, across country borders. A summary of employment discrimination laws in several countries is found in Myors and others (2008).

FAILING TO FOLLOW AC GUIDELINES

Applications of the AC method are guided by sets of standards promulgated by various professional groups around the world. The guidelines provided by the International Task Force (2009) have legitimatized the method for over 25 years. More recently, groups in Germany, Indonesia, the UK, and South Africa have written similar guidelines that apply to each specific country. While these documents may not be legally binding, and there may be no formal enforcement mechanisms, these guidelines are used by stakeholders who scrutinize AC operations. We are aware of instances where an employee union was successful in getting an AC dropped because it did not comply with the guidelines.

Factors Leading to Sustainable Assessment Centers

We now turn to a very different set of considerations for the maintenance of ACs. It goes without saying that the developer should avoid making the mistakes implied by the factors leading to failure. But, we have observed that just because the organization chooses the right dimensions, uses exercises with face validity, and so forth, that does not mean the AC will survive over time. Other factors lead to sustainability over the long haul. We now describe 10 factors that we have observed are part of the conduct and context of the AC which lead to long life.

GETTING THE RIGHT PEOPLE ON THE BUS

Collins' (2001) research identified a fundamental factor for organizational success: leaders of companies that go from good to great start not with "where" but with "who." They start by getting the right people on the bus, the wrong people off the bus, and the right people in the right seats. ACs are primarily a people business. Their output, reputation and credibility depend above all on the quality of the people involved as AC specialists and as assessors. Choosing the wrong type of assessors or not training and preparing them adequately for their job will lead to failure. The AC specialists involved and especially their manager must also be selected and reviewed carefully. Starting an AC initiative should focus on identifying and selecting the best specialists and leader before deciding and shaping organizational and technical options. Maintaining and developing high performance in people is one of the fundamental management tasks of running an AC initiative. It is obvious that quality means psychological and methodological knowhow in assessment. In addition, experience with the job level to be assessed and personal credibility in the view of the assessees and top management is relevant as well. It would be highly desirable if senior members of an assessment team had successfully passed the AC they are working on. It also helps if the leader of the AC initiative has multiple connections throughout the organization. Even if the right types of assessors are chosen, a constant and careful review of the quality and credibility of each assessor is needed, with subsequent action if an assessor does not meet the highest standards. The same is true with the AC specialists. Any questions about ethical integrity have to be acted upon immediately. Periodic review sessions of specialists and assessors are a must in an AC team.

PRODUCING INDEPENDENT AND STRAIGHT-FORWARD "SECOND OPINIONS"

Accurate decisions about people are a basic and powerful means of managing an organization. They are also difficult decisions because hard data and foolproof criteria are seldom available, personal relationships are at stake, and organizational politics have to be taken into consideration. AC reports with independent assessments of interpersonal and conceptual skills have the potential of influencing people decisions. They can improve people decisions but they also enter the power game of such decisions. Managing the positioning and the contribution of AC reports is not only a question of the validity of AC reports but also a fine understanding of the power game. Positioning ACs as independent second opinions, where the responsible line manager has the right and power for the final decision, keeps ACs out of many hazardous situations. This also ensures that ACs do not get overburdened with responsibilities which they can never fulfill. In addition to the independence of the AC rating, its standardization across the company gives individual decision-makers a welcomed benchmarking for their judgments about people. ACs should act like independent rating agencies, whose ratings are understood, comparable, and serve as additional second opinion for individual business decisions. The independence can be assured by using assessors who have no stake in the candidates' careers and by making the AC report an official product of the team of assessors.

The importance of both conceptual and interpersonal behavior and skills to successful business careers is undisputable. Research (Schmidt and Hunter 1998), as well as personal experiences of senior leaders, indicates that conceptual skills (for example, Reasoning Ability, Problem-Solving, Planning/Organizing) are at least as important as interpersonal behavior (for example, Communication, Persuasiveness). The AC method is very valid for assessing dimensions related to both sets of skills by using a variety of situational exercises. In addition to psychometric tests and questionnaires, ACs can in some detail describe the strengths and weaknesses of a candidate, thus adding information on how to best deploy a candidate or how to leverage the strengths and minimize the impact of weaknesses. ACs which provide in-depth diagnoses of conceptual, as well as interpersonal skills, are a powerful force to guide decision-makers in people decisions over the long run.

MAKING IT A LEADERSHIP TRAINING EXPERIENCE FOR ASSESSORS

The economic utility of ACs is determined by selection rates, costs, and validity coefficients (Cascio 1982). Many experienced assessors mention an additional type of utility in the form of leadership training for the assessors. This training consists of skillfully using the competency language (Birri and Melcher, Chapter 12); presenting, arguing for and defending behavioral observations in integration sessions; giving open behavioral feedback; networking among assessors from different divisions; and so forth. The design and the administration of ACs can and should foster this type of utility by:

- giving assessors the chance for consecutive assignments in order to broaden the experience;
- involving assessors in all phases of assessment, for example, writing the reports and giving initial feedback and not just observing and evaluating behaviors;
- conducting integration sessions;
- allowing enough time for networking.

When executive managers ask to serve as assessors, despite their tight schedule and overburdened day-to-day activity, you have reached the level where an AC is a much appreciated learning experience. This is not just a matter of increased utility but it also creates a sustainable personal relationship among executive managers and the AC specialists. Learning happens if there is a certain amount of discretion and room for mistakes. The AC specialists' tricky task is therefore to create this type of learning atmosphere and at the same time make sure that mistakes get corrected and that assessors improve.

PRODUCING A VISIBLE PRODUCT WITH DIAGNOSTIC QUALITY

If you do not document the effectiveness of an AC process in an organization you are doomed for failure, especially if you get involved in a legal case in the US. Such visibility is important to not only external compliance agencies but also to internal stakeholders of the AC. Equally important for the long range viability of an AC, executives, managers, and assessors are more supportive if they are regularly informed and involved in the process and its further development. Actions that may give the AC process more visibility include:

- regular validity studies of different types;
- yearly review sessions with the group of assessors;
- always asking the assessors and the managers requesting assessment services for feedback about the process and the result, and then acting upon this feedback;
- involving assessors in designing and testing simulations;
- yearly short reports about the AC for top management, including statistics, trends, costs, new developments, and so forth;
- using and analyzing statistical and judgmental ("clinical") integration of findings in simulations.

It is the task of AC specialists and its manager to devote regular efforts to this communication and marketing task.

MAKING THE AC A CENTRAL PART OF THE HUMAN CAPITAL MANAGEMENT PROCESS

Human capital management (HCM), or talent management, has become one of the decisive business processes for reaching a competitive business advantage. Simple, as well as valid and consistent, measurements of key indicators like potential and performance are often mentioned success factors for HCM (Effron and Ort 2010; Fitz-Enz 2010). From the perspective of line managers and participants, if ACs are clearly positioned relative to other assessment techniques (for example, multi-rater feedback systems), they contribute to measuring potential and competencies in a standardized and consistent way. Competency models are a cornerstone of talent management. Such models are the groundwork for the behavioral definition of dimensions. ACs then are a perfect training ground for line managers (for example, serving as assessors) and candidates to learn to use dimensions as a common language for business related behavior. On the other hand, ACs can take advantage of being a clearly defined part of a human capital management process. This symbiosis (see Birri and Melcher, Chapter 12 in this volume) protects ACs from various threats, such as cost-cuttings, new HR fads, and seemingly competitive instruments like multi-source ratings systems and online tools.

MAKING IT A SELF-SPONSORED PROGRAM, NOT A GREAT MAN INITIATIVE

The support of the CEO is no doubt a powerful and necessary prerequisite for introducing ACs in a company. However, once the AC process is established, this support alone will not be sufficient for sustainability. The CEO may change or his/her priorities may shift to other issues. Sustainably managing an AC service requires a careful consideration of its numerous clients, suppliers and stakeholders. Treating and respecting these people as partners and not as entities that need to be enlightened about the method and results insures continuous support on the long run from an impressive start to endurance and sustainability. Building such long-lasting quality relationships with the partners depends in large part on the continuity and stability of the AC team. Significant personnel or basic procedural changes in the AC service need to be executed in the broader context of all partners.

The context is especially vital if parts or all of the AC services are outsourced. The outsourcer should clearly state what is expected in terms of service-quality and how and when the services will be evaluated. A senior relationship-manager (accompanied by a technical AC-specialist) with excellent contacts to line-managers (recipients of the AC-reports) should be in charge for building-up and maintaining a constructive partnership with the service-provider. The value added by the service-provider should not only be based on lower and more flexible costs but also and mainly on providing additional and broader expertise thanks to serving different clients/companies and following tightly the scientific progress of the field.

KNOWING AND LEVERAGING WHAT HAPPENS AFTER AN AC

AC reports influence people decisions and provide valuable insights into development needs and development opportunities. But, AC results on their own are not sufficient for positive effects: they have to be accepted as valid by the recipients (that is, management and candidates); they need to be understood and interpreted correctly; and the insights have to be transformed into appropriate decisions and action plans that are pursued in the future. Even though an overwhelming number of the scientific studies about ACs focus on the assessment process in its narrow sense, an AC service that ends with delivering scientifically proven valid AC reports falls short of its full utility. What comes after the AC is at least as important as the AC itself for assuring the value added of a costly AC. The quality of feedback sessions, the reaction and attitude of candidates and their management, the way the reports are used, and the impact of actions taken need to be studied systematically (Byham 2005, Odermatt 2006) and understood in detail in order to influence and maximize the use of the AC reports. Asking participants long after the AC on how their AC report influenced their career often provides surprising insights which help to optimize feedback sessions and to understand the factors that lead to a sustainable impact (Birri and Naef 2006) or avoid a deep rooted and long lasting aversion to ACs.

USING MODERN HUMAN CAPITAL METRICS TO DEMONSTRATE THE VALUE OF THE AC

An important part of the HR function is to manage the risk of legal challenges of discrimination or unfair treatment. Management is dependent on and thankful for this protection against legal troubles. Failing to document effectiveness is a factor that leads to failure of ACs. In addition to avoiding legal troubles, management increasingly wants to know more about the return on investment (ROI) of ACs, compared to other investments in their human capital. Traditional evaluation studies of ACs like prognostic validity coefficients can prove the effectiveness of the instrument overall. But they tell us little about the impact on business performance in an organizational unit, compared to the impact of, for example, a 360° feedback program or a training initiative. In addition, correlation coefficients are not the language which managers use to talk about their investment returns. Modern human capital metrics (Fitz-Enz 2010) are more geared toward the needs of managers, consist mainly of leading indicators and not just describing what happened in the past, and look at the portfolio of investments instead of just a single investment. Birri and Melcher (Chapter 12) show an example of human capital metrics in relation to AC operations. Such metrics can help to close any gaps between AC specialists and managers, enhance the case for ACs, and lead to a more refined usage. All this will contribute to the sustainability of an AC initiative.

REVISING THE AC IN RESPONSE TO ADVANCES IN RELEVANT PROFESSIONS AND EXPERIENCE

Human resource management (HRM) and industrial/organizational psychology are dynamic fields. Advances in theory, research, and practice are continually offering opportunities to improve AC programs. While the essential elements of the AC method remain stable, AC specialists can use new methods of understanding work requirements, presenting assessment stimuli, training assessors, capturing behavioral responses, managing integration of data, and preparing and delivering assessment reports.

In addition, the experience of conducting ACs in an organization provides a rich source of information that can lead to program improvements. Feedback from candidates, assessors, and consumers of AC results should be heeded. Statistical analyses of assessment results provide evidence of inter-rater agreement, demographic comparisons, relationships with criterion measures, and human capital metrics. Use of these external and internal sources of information to continuously improve AC operations demonstrate responsiveness to various stakeholders and contribute to sustainability.

THERE IS NO SILVER BULLET

One mistake alone can lead to failure of an AC initiative. On the other hand there is no single effort, trick, or measure that guarantees success and sustainability. While avoiding factors for failure is more of a methodological, technical, and administrative skill, the application of factors leading to sustainability is a set of management, leadership, and organizational development tasks. Managing an AC initiative is like managing some other service or product of an organization. Managing means shaping and balancing of efforts like R&D or marketing as well as involving various customers and stakeholders. Leading an AC initiative through an internal AC team or a well thought-out relationship with an external provider, means having a clear vision of its purpose and driving it constantly forward.

Applying the preceding factors for sustainability must be based on a thorough analysis of the strengths and weaknesses as well as challenges and threats of an AC initiative in a specific organization. The result of such an analysis must be a focused and balanced set of actions and objectives along with other factors for sustainability. Environmental as well as technical changes have to be constantly monitored and incorporated. Focusing and relying on just one of these factors for sustainability might help in the short run, but will soon wear out. The interplay among these factors is as important as their individual implementation. The list of such factors is also not exhaustive; the specific situation of an AC initiative in a particular organization might involve additional factors.

Summary

A comparison with Herzberg's (1966) theory of motivation may be apt. He posits that meeting hygiene needs (for example, providing a safe workplace) may eliminate dissatisfaction but not result in hard work or satisfaction. By contrast, effort on the job and satisfaction come only by fulfilling the motivator needs (for example, providing meaningful work and recognition). Analogously, avoiding the failure factors will avert an early demise of an AC, but sustainability comes only with execution of the success factors. Developing, implementing, and validating an assessment center certainly requires technical expertise. At the very least, to avoid failure, the AC practitioner must conduct thorough job analysis and competency modeling, design psychometrically sound assessment methods, and implement standardized and practical assessment procedures. To ensure that the AC method maintains a sustainable existence in the organization, other more complex steps must be taken. The AC must be an integral part of the complex organizational talent management system and produce information that contributes to accomplishment of the organization's corporate strategy.

References

Birri, R. and Naef, B. 2006. *Wirkung und Nutzen des AC-Feedbacks im Entwicklungsverlauf von Nachwuchs-Führungskräften [Impact and Usefulness of Assessment Center Feedback for the Development of Junior Managers]*. Wirtschaftspsychologie, Heft 4, 58–67.

Byham, T.M. 2005. *Factors affecting the acceptance and application of development feedback from an executive assessment program*. Unpublished Dissertation. University of Akron.

Cascio, W.F. 1982. *Costing Human Resources*. Boston, MA: Kent.

Collins, J. 2001. *Good to Great. Why Some Companies Make the Leap ... And Others Don't*. New York, NY: HarperCollins Publishers Inc.

Effron, M. and Ort, M. 2010. *One Page Talent Management*. Boston: Harvard Business Press.

Fitz-Enz, J. 2010. *The New HR Analytics: Predicting the Economic Value of Your Company's Human Capital Investments*. New York, NY: AMACON Books.

International Task Force on Assessment Center Guidelines. 2009. Guidelines and ethical considerations for assessment center operations. *International Journal of Selection and Assessment*, 17, 243–254.

Myors, B. et al. 2008. International perspectives on the legal environment of selection. *Industrial and Organizational Psychology*, 1, 206–246.

Odermatt, A. 2006. *Vom Feedback zur Entwicklung [From Feedback to Development]*. Lizentiatsarbeit. Universität Fribourg.

Rupp, D.E., Snyder, L.A., Gibbons, A.M. and Thornton, G.C. III. 2006. What should developmental assessment centers be developing? *The Psychologist Manager Journal*, 9, 75–98.

Schmidt, F. and Hunter, J. 1998. The validity and utility of selection methods in personnel psychology: Practical and theoretical implications of 85 years of research findings. *Psychological Bulletin*, 124, 262–274.

Thornton, G.C. III, Eurich, T.L. and Johnson, R.M. 2009. Industrial/organizational psychologists as expert witnesses in employment discrimination litigation: Descriptions and prescriptions. *The Psychologist Manager*, 12, 187–203.

Thornton, G.C. III, Hollenbeck, J.P., and Johnson, S.K. 2010. Selecting leaders: Executives and high potentials. In *Handbook of Employee Selection*, edited by J.L. Farr and N.T. Tippins. New York: Routledge, 823–840.

Thornton, G.C. III and Kedharnath, U. (in press). Work sample tests. In *Handbook of Testing and Assessment in Psychology*, edited by K.F. Geisinger. Washington, D.C.: American Psychological Association.

Thornton, G.C. III and Mueller-Hanson, R.A. 2004. *Developing Organizational Simulations: A Guide for Practitioners and Students*. Mahwah, NJ: Lawrence Erlbaum.

Thornton, G.C. III and Potemra, M. 2010. Utility of assessment center for promotion of police sergeants. *Public Personnel Management*, 39, 59–69.

Thornton, G.C. III and Rupp, D. (in press). Research into dimension-based assessment centers. In *The Psychology of Assessment Centers*, edited by D. Jackson, C. Lance and B. Hoffman. New York: Routledge.

Thornton, G.C. III and Rupp, D.R. 2006. *Assessment Centers in Human Resource Management: Strategies for Prediction, Diagnosis, and Development*. Mahwah, NJ: Lawrence Erlbaum.

Thornton, G.C. III, Wilson, C.L., Johnson, R.M. and Rogers, D.A. 2009. Managing assessment center practices in the context of employment discrimination litigation, *The Psychologist Manager*, 12, 175–186.

International Issues and Implications

22 A Review of Recent International Surveys into Assessment Centre Practices

NIGEL POVAH

The purpose of this chapter is to summarize the key findings arising from some of the recent international surveys that have been conducted into assessment centre practices. The assessment centre (AC) method has grown steadily in popularity over the years and we are now witnessing its wider global use. However, with such exposure comes a greater risk of inconsistency and failure to adhere to the standards exemplified by good practice. With assessment centre usage originally being concentrated in the US, followed by Europe (principally the UK, Germany and the Netherlands) and South Africa, it wasn't too difficult to monitor and influence best practice. Today ACs are conducted in every corner of the globe and whilst there are still many examples of best practice, there is also a greater need than ever to advocate those standards that have made the AC the successful tool that it is. This chapter will therefore attempt to highlight those instances where questionable practices risk violating the well established standards of best practice.

There is also a need to acknowledge that cultural differences have influenced the design of some of these ACs in different parts of the world. Indeed it is evident that certain AC features which are acceptable in some countries may not be acceptable in others and Briscoe (1997) points out that this can stimulate the design of different exercises; the choice of different dimensions; the use of assessors from both the host and home countries; the evaluation of behaviours and the nature and format of the feedback process. Recognition of these developments and the variations they have prompted, has led to a number of international surveys being conducted over the last decade and this chapter aims to provide a summary of these and will highlight some of the emerging trends. The approach will be to focus on a major global survey conducted by Assessment & Development Consultants (A&DC) in late 2007, with the results being published in early 2008 and to highlight how these compare and contrast with the findings from similar surveys.

This survey and the others referred to in this chapter, all offer a number of potential benefits to practitioners, such as:

- enabling them to evaluate their AC against best practice standards;
- identifying innovative ideas for AC design and/or implementation;
- providing evidence to justify recommendations to their clients;
- recognizing how cultural influences can have an impact on their AC;
- achieving global consistency when using an AC for Talent Management;
- considering variations in design and implementation to meet a client need.

About the Survey

HR professionals, occupational psychologists and assessment centre practitioners worldwide, were invited by email to participate in the research survey which was hosted online. The survey covered similar topics to previous surveys examining international AC practices (Spychalski et al. 1997; Kudisch et al. 2001; Krause and Gebert 2003; Krause and Thornton 2009; Eurich et al. 2009 and Thornton and Krause 2009) and comprised 44 multiple choice questions with over 350 possible response items, supplemented by a number of free text response formats. Data were gathered from a total of 443 respondents, representing 354 organizations and 22 independent consultancies, all of whom completed or partially completed the survey and provided invaluable information pertaining to the types of assessment centre methodologies that they employed within their organizations, for either selection or development purposes. These 443 respondents were based in 43 different countries covering five continents.

By comparison, Kudisch et al. (2001) summarized data from an international sample of 114 organizations; Krause and Gebert (2003) collected data from 281 German, Swiss and Austrian organizations and compared this with an earlier survey conducted by Spychalski et al. (1997) who had collected data from 215 US organizations; Krause and Thornton (2009) collected data from 97 organizations, 45 of whom were from Western Europe and 52 from North America; Eurich et al. (2009) collected data from 54 US organizations; and Thornton and Krause (2009) collected data from 144 organizations in 18 countries. Thus the survey highlighted in this chapter is the most widespread survey of its kind. Readers should note that other chapters in this book also contribute to the body of knowledge that we are accumulating about global AC practices; so the interested reader should refer to Krause's Chapter 23 for details about another survey and the remaining chapters in Part III, which describe the AC practices being employed in a number of different countries.

The majority of respondents (78 per cent) came from private sector organizations, with 19 per cent from the public sector and the remaining 3 per cent from not for profit organizations. European respondents formed the majority of the sample (48 per cent), with significant contributions from Asia (23 per cent) and Africa (14 per cent). Oceania formed 8 per cent of the sample, with North America and South America being combined to form the 'Americas', which contributed 7 per cent of the total sample. The two American continents were combined due to a small representation of respondents from both regions. The disappointingly small response from the US in particular, means that it is necessary to compare the results with other surveys which focus more strongly on the US, such as Krause and Thornton (2009) and Eurich et al. (2009), in order to draw any firm conclusions regarding US practices and how they compare with other regions around the globe.

Respondents were invited to indicate if they wished to answer the survey with reference to assessment centres (ACs) or development centres (DCs) and 280 chose to answer in relation to ACs and 132 in relation to DCs, with the remaining 31 referring to both ACs and DCs or not providing any indication. Thus any comparisons made between ACs and DCs will be based just on these 412 respondents, with 68 per cent (280) referring to ACs and 32 per cent (132) DCs. This split was also evident across all five continents with respondents focusing on ACs 55–75 per cent of the time.

However, an obvious oversight of the survey was that no definitions were provided for an AC or DC and respondents were left to interpret these as they wished, although it is reasonable to assume that in simple terms, respondents most likely regarded the purpose of an AC to be for selection and a DC for development.

Figure 22.1 shows that the survey supports the notion that assessment centres, in one form or another, are being run by organizations of varying sizes, as the majority of respondents came from organizations of either less than 50 people (32 per cent) or more than 2,500 staff (30 per cent). The high volume of small organizations may partly be distorted by small consultancy firms running ACs on behalf of their clients.

However, it is interesting to note that the size of the organization correlated with the number of ACs and DCs conducted per year, with larger organizations running significantly more ACs (r=.208, p<.01) and DCs (r=.204, p<.01) per year. Also, there was a positive correlation between organizations who run both ACs and DCs. Companies who run a high number of ACs also conduct a high number of DCs (r=.603, p<.01). The age of the organization also positively correlated to the number of ACs and DCs conducted per year (AC, r=.188, p<.01, DC=.139, p<.01). This finding suggests that larger organizations, which have been established for a longer period of time, may be more likely to adopt AC methodology, incorporating both ACs and DCs into their talent management processes.

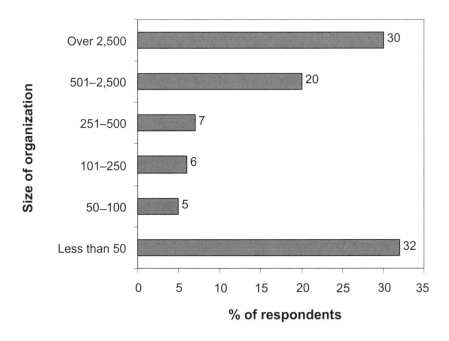

Figure 22.1 Size of organization (staff numbers)

Uses of AC Methodology

AC methodology entails using an assessment process of observing, recording, classifying and evaluating (ORCE) behaviour in accordance with well established principles, as defined by the International Task Force on Assessment Center Guidelines, of which the most recent version was published in 2009. However, this methodology can be used as the basis for running an assessment centre (AC) or a development centre (DC), which gives rise to it being used for a number of different purposes.

Across the total sample, the most popular uses of AC methodology were External Recruitment (non-Graduate) 57 per cent, Diagnose Development Needs 56 per cent, Identify High Potential 50 per cent, Graduate (College Leaver) Recruitment 49 per cent, Inform Internal Promotion 45 per cent and Succession Planning 38 per cent. This suggests a roughly equal emphasis on selection, promotion and development purposes, although it would be wrong to read too much into this, as respondents were allowed to indicate as many different uses for AC methodology as they wished, depending on the number of different types of centres they ran. Notwithstanding this caveat, the data showed a strong level of support for External Recruitment (69 per cent) in Europe, followed by Diagnose Development Needs (57 per cent) and Identify High Potential (48 per cent), whereas in the Americas it was Diagnose Development Needs (58 per cent) that jumped ahead of External Recruitment and Identify High Potential (42 per cent) which were equal second. This finding is consistent with the results of a US survey by Eurich et al. (2009), which also reported the prominence of AC usage for promotion and development, rather than selection. One possible explanation of this trend could be that the more litigious nature of the US, coupled with the desire for 'lean assessments', which strive for high quality decisions to be made in a short time period, has made HR managers more wary of using ACs in the cauldron of selection. Ironically however, these two conflicting issues may be causing them to spurn the very tool that is best equipped to give them fair, objective and valid selection outcomes.

Job Analysis

Only 55 per cent of the organizations from our sample reported using a dedicated form of job analysis in order to select the dimensions/competencies to assess on an AC. Although a further 35 per cent were adhering to part or all of an existing framework in their assessments of participants. Fortunately therefore, it seems that only 6 per cent of the organizations in our sample run ACs without measuring any specific competencies and 4 per cent 'didn't know', although this raises the concern of 'what are they measuring?'

The popularity of the job analysis techniques employed by respondents were Job Descriptions (89 per cent), Job Activity (incumbent) interviews (42 per cent), Critical Incidents (37 per cent), Questionnaires (36 per cent), Visionary interviews (36 per cent), Repertory Grid (17 per cent), Shadowing (9 per cent) and Diary Study (5 per cent). Indeed 'reviewing job descriptions' was the most popular technique on all five continents and it is no surprise that this should be the logical starting point for job analysis research. Reassuringly the least popular techniques of 'Shadowing' and 'Diary studies' were always used in conjunction with at least two other methods of investigation and this is consistent with the widely held view that no single method will suffice (Thornton and Rupp 2006).

These results weren't too dissimilar to the US findings reported by Spychalski et al. (1997) and Eurich et al. (2009) and the consistently strong message from these surveys is that most practitioners recognize the importance of conducting comprehensive job analysis prior to designing an AC, as it provides a firm foundation upon which the whole event can be built.

Dimensions/Competencies

The most popular dimensions/competencies used to assess participants within an AC were Teamwork (83 per cent), Leadership (79 per cent) and Planning and Organizing (73 per cent). However, it is interesting to note that Leadership (80 per cent) jumps ahead of Teamwork (74 per cent) for a DC, with Problem Analysis (69 per cent) coming third. This swap of the top two is not surprising, as many DCs will be for first-line managers or middle managers, therefore there will be a need to assess and/or benchmark their ability to lead people as part of their development, whereas not all ACs will be assessing people for managerial roles and their ability to work within teams is often seen as an even more important competency.

Table 22.1 provides a detailed breakdown by continent and it is clearly apparent that Planning and Organizing would have fared better, but for the surprisingly low level of support from the Asian continent, where it was ranked 17th. It is difficult to provide a clear explanation as to why this strange result occurred, but it is markedly at odds with all of the other continents. However, one possible explanation is that Asian cultures for the most part, have a lower predisposition to display 'Uncertainty avoidance' which is one of the four dimensions (the others being individualism/collectivism, masculinity/femininity and power distance) within Hofstede's widely accepted framework of cultural differences. Hofstede (1991) defines uncertainty avoidance as the extent to which members of a culture feel threatened by uncertain or unknown situations and the lower this is, the lower the need for structure and the inclination to plan and organize things.

These ten competencies cover the top six for each continent and overall they are quite similar to the six construct and criterion valid dimensions reported in two meta-analyses studies (Arthur et al. 2003; Bowler and Woehr 2006), which were Communication, Problem-solving, Organizing and Planning, Influencing Others, Consideration/awareness of others and Drive. However, it is interesting to note that these studies make no mention of either Leadership or Teamwork, although it might be argued that these are regarded as 'meta-competencies' for which the aforementioned dimensions could be claimed to be contributory factors. This view is echoed by Lievens and Thornton (2005) who question the viability of assessing broad organizational competencies such as Teamwork and Customer Service as they lack specificity and objectivity. They suggest that such competencies need to be put in operational terms and in the case of the latter this would mean classifying it into behaviours such as active listening, information seeking and oral communication.

The table also highlights some interesting variances. For example, Africa placed much lower emphasis on Persuasive Oral Communication (9th) than all other continents, who included it in their top six. This may be due to the large number of South African respondents (72 per cent) and the historical influence of apartheid where the command and control doctrine created little need or opportunity for people to display Persuasive

Oral Communication. The Americas were alone in giving Problem Analysis a very low rating (15th) whereas all other continents placed it in their top five. Asia and the Americas both de-emphasized Interpersonal Sensitivity (ranking it 13th and 12th respectively) when the others all placed it in their top seven. In the case of both of these variances it is easy to speculate about possible explanations but much harder to come up with a valid justification, so the basis of variations in the use of different competencies on ACs across the globe is still an area for further investigation.

Table 22.1 Competencies selected (top six for each continent)

	World (rank)	Africa		Asia		Europe		Oceania		Americas	
		%	Rank	%	Rank	%	Rank	%	Rank	%	Rank
Leadership	1	83	2	72	2	78	2	88	1	81	1
Teamwork	2	78	4	74	1	81	1	73	2	77	2
Problem Analysis	3	85	1	65	3	73	4	67	5	48	15
Planning and Organizing	4	82	3	41	17	77	3	61	7	65	3
Persuasive Oral Communication	5	65	9	57	6	73	5	73	3	61	6
Decisiveness	6	77	5	57	5	63	6	61	8	65	4
Interpersonal Sensitivity	7	68	6	47	13	59	7	70	4	52	12
Strategic Perspective	8	55	12	51	10	58	8	48	19	58	9
Openness to Change	9	47	16	54	7	56	10	55	9	55	10
Customer Service	10	67	8	58	4	49	18	52	15	42	19

The total number of competencies being assessed on an AC has always been an issue of debate due to the increasing difficulty of differentiating one from another as the list gets longer. Various studies and surveys (Krause and Gebert 2003; Eurich et al. 2009; Thornton and Krause 2009) confirm that around 75 per cent of organizations assess 10 or less competencies on their ACs and fortunately in recent years this number appears to have come down as research evidence (Lievens and Conway 2001; Woehr and Arthur 2003) highlights that the construct validity of the AC improves as the number of competencies decreases. Indeed over half of organizations assess three to seven competencies with six to seven being most popular and they typically assess two to five competencies per exercise.

Exercise Simulations

Table 22.2 examines the results of this survey along with two of the recent surveys conducted in the US, in order to compare the frequency of use of different exercise types around the globe, which when linked to the competencies being assessed in those different territories reveals some interesting observations. The first observation is that Interview Simulations (sometimes referred to as Role plays) and Oral Presentation exercises are generally the two most popular exercise types used around the World, with in-baskets also being consistently popular. These findings support the view put forward by Thornton and Rupp (2006), that such 'situational' exercises are the mainstay of ACs. There could be a variety of explanations as to why this might be so but Thornton and Krause (2009) suggest that it could be due to an increase in the 'people-focused' demands of the workplace and the recognition of the need to adopt more democratic and engaging styles of management.

The second observation is that Non-Assigned Role Group Discussions and Analysis Exercises (similar to what the US refers to as Case Studies) appear to be much more popular around the globe than they are in the US. There could be a number of possible reasons for these variances, but two possible explanations stand out. Firstly, there has been a growing enthusiasm in the US for online assessment, as it is less time consuming and reduces or eliminates the costs of travel, so staging a Group Discussion becomes practically more difficult to arrange. This could also explain the greater popularity of In-Baskets, which can be delivered remotely in the form of an email Inbox. Secondly, according to Table 22.1, the US is much less inclined to assess Problem Analysis than the rest of the world and even if this weren't so, it could be that cognitive ability is usually assessed by other means such as psychometric tests.

Table 22.2 Comparing US and global use of different exercise types

Exercise types	A&DC global survey (N=443) %	Thornton and Krause international survey (N=144) %	Eurich et al. US survey (N=54) %
Interview Simulations or Role Plays	67	61	76
Oral Presentation Exercises	62	79	64
Non-Assigned Role Group Discussions	57	73	15[1]
Analysis Exercises or Case Studies	57	65	38
In-Basket/In-Tray/Inbox Exercises	53	59	57
Assigned Role Group Discussions	33	28	28[1]
Scheduling or Planning Exercises	32	37	48
Fact Find Exercises	30	44	29

---

1   The Eurich sample cites a 43% frequency rating for Group discussions, of which 64% are with Assigned Roles, thus accounting for the 15% and 28% figures.

Scheduling or Planning exercises and Fact Find exercises were the two least popular exercise types, although the former was much more popular in the US than globally, perhaps because of the US preference for action, thus creating the need for a plan to support that action.

Use of Other Assessment Tools

It is quite common for most ACs to include the use of additional assessment tools, with the most popular ones being an interview and/or a personality questionnaire, both of which were used 79 per cent of the time, followed by ability tests which featured 69 per cent of the time. This pattern was consistently observed across all continents as shown in Table 22.3.

Table 22.3 Additional assessment tools most frequently used

Additional assessment tools	Africa		Asia		Europe		Oceania		Americas	
	%	Rank	%	Rank	%	Rank	%	Rank	%	Rank
Personality questionnaires	80	1	72	2	80	2	92	1	77	1
Interviews	75	2	74	1	84	1	81	2	69	2
Ability tests	71	3	63	3	73	3	81	3	46	3
360° feedback	37	4	35	4	20	4	31	4	31	4

When comparing the use of additional tools on ACs and DCs, Interviews are most frequently selected on ACs (84 per cent), with Outdoor Activities selected least often (7 per cent), as shown in Figure 22.2. For DCs, the most frequently selected tool was a Personality Questionnaire (78 per cent), and a Situational Judgement Test (SJT) was the least frequently selected tool (11 per cent), which is little surprise as it is most commonly used as a sifting tool within the selection process. Personality assessment in development and assessment (for selection) may be useful for evaluating the extent to which an individual's values and motives fit with the culture of the organization, and how these may be affecting that person's working performance at that time (for a DC), or the likelihood of them fitting in with the organization's values and culture once commencing employment (for an AC). Interviews, however, may be more common in assessment for selection because they enable the assessor to gain an understanding of the level of 'fit' that a participant may have with the organization through face-to-face interactions. The other notable difference between ACs and DCs is the greater popularity of 360 multi-rater feedback questionnaires used on DCs (44 per cent), compared with ACs (20 per cent). This is totally consistent with the fact that 360 is generally considered as useful for development but too subjective and therefore unreliable in high-stakes selection.

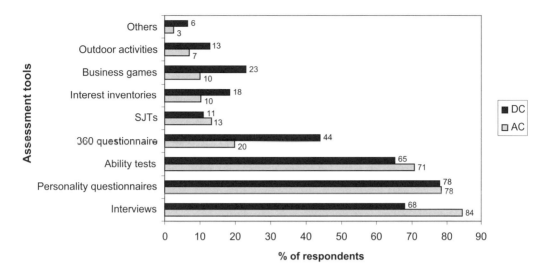

Figure 22.2 Additional assessment tools used on ACs and DCs

Assessors

More often than not, assessors are either HR staff (61 per cent; rising to 68 per cent for ACs and dropping to 48 per cent for DCs) or Line managers (53 per cent; rising to 55 per cent for ACs and dropping to 48 per cent for DCs) and this was consistent with the Thornton and Krause 2009 survey, which reported similar findings of 66 per cent and 70 per cent respectively. Table 22.4 shows that this pattern was repeated across all continents except for Oceania, which gave higher prominence to expert staff, rather than HR staff or psychologists. Conversely Africa reported the prevalent use of psychologists, which may be due to the high response rate from South Africa (43 out of the 60 African respondents), where psychologists have established their credibility as AC experts as long ago as 1981, when they formed the Assessment Centre Study Group (http://www.acsg.co.za), thus legitimizing their high level of involvement in ACs.

Table 22.4 Who acts as assessors across continents?

% using this type of assessor	Africa	Asia	Europe	Oceania	Americas
HR staff	73	64	57	50	59
Psychologists	55	18	31	7	35
External consultants	36	40	33	57	41
Line managers	45	60	54	50	41
Staff with expertise	18	20	33	43	12
Participants' colleagues	0	2	5	7	0
Participants themselves	0	2	2	7	0
Others	9	2	8	0	0

Assessors were generally one (AC = 57 per cent and DC = 59 per cent) or two (AC = 43 per cent and DC = 50 per cent) organizational levels above the participant and occasionally at the same level (AC = 33 per cent and DC = 28 per cent) or more than two levels above (AC = 34 per cent and DC = 25 per cent).

With regard to the ratio of participants to assessors, the International Task Force on Assessment Center Guidelines (2009) states:

> The maximum ratio of assessees to assessors is a function of several variables, including the type of exercises to be used, the dimensions to be evaluated, the roles of the assessors, the type of integration carried out, the amount of assessor training, the experience of the assessors, and the purpose of the assessment center.

However, a 2:1 ratio has generally come to be regarded as most appropriate as this isn't considered overly burdensome for the assessors, nor is it as resource-hungry as a 1:1 ratio. Table 22.5 reveals the ratios typically employed within each continent and it is evident that Europe and Oceania are most committed to this notional best practice standard by employing assessor to participant ratios of either, 2:1, 1:1 or 1:2 within their centres. However, it is surprising and concerning that only 50 per cent or less of the respondents from Africa, Asia and the Americas, are adopting this standard; given that it is generally recognized that the quality and accuracy of an assessor's evaluations of a participant will be lowered when there are a greater number of participants for them to assess at any one time. This suggests that in these regions, consideration should be given to increasing the number of assessors so as to reduce the demands made on each of them, thus improving the likelihood of a fair and accurate evaluation of each participant's performance.

Table 22.5 Assessor to participant ratios by continent

Assessor: participant ratio	Africa (%)	Asia (%)	Europe (%)	Oceania (%)	Americas (%)
2:1	14	19	23	7	18
1:1	21	12	21	17	18
1:2	10	18	31	34	14
Best practice total	**45**	**49**	**75**	**58**	**50**
1:3	9	11	9	14	4
1:4	7	5	4	3	14
1:5	16	10	3	7	4
Don't know	16	23	7	14	29
Other	9	2	3	3	0

Assessor Training

The survey results suggest that three-quarters of the respondents train their assessors, but disappointingly, at least 20 per cent do not. Comparisons across the continents, show some consistency (see Figure 22.3), with the Europeans being most inclined to follow best practice and the Americas the least, but as stated previously, this low response (56 per cent) may be due to the small US sample (only 8 of the 33 respondents).

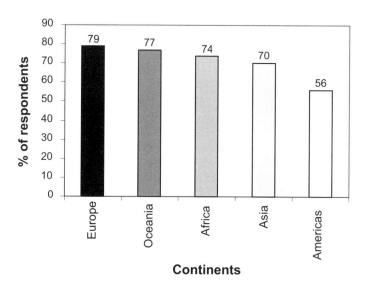

Figure 22.3 Percentage of respondents who train their assessors

Indeed other surveys focusing on the US (Krause and Gebert 2003, Eurich et al. 2009) seem to support this view, as they report at least 93 per cent of organizations within the US conduct assessor training, in which case the lower response in the Americas is more likely attributed to practices within South America which makes up 76 per cent of the Americas respondents.

DURATION

Assessor training duration varied quite considerably among respondents, with the highest proportion (29 per cent) stating that their training duration lasted between half to one day, as shown in Table 22.6.

Table 22.6   Length of assessor training across total sample

Length of assessor training	% of total sample
Less than ½ day	10
Between ½ and 1 day	29
Between 1 and 1½ days	13
Between 1½ and 2 days	19
More than 2 days	24
Other	4
Don't know	1

The International Task Force on Assessment Center Guidelines (2009) points out that the 'length and quality of training are not synonymous' and it is difficult to prescribe the most appropriate length of the training, as numerous factors will influence this, such as the number of exercises and dimensions, the expertise and experience of the assessors and the nature and complexity of the AC. Extensive experience suggests a useful rule of thumb of two days' training for each day of exercises, particularly with less experienced assessors. This view is supported by the *British Psychological Society's Best Practice Guidelines* (2003), which states that assessor training should ideally be at least two days in duration, therefore the fact that only 24 per cent of the respondents dedicated such time to the process is disappointing.

Additionally, when assessor training was compared across continents (see Table 22.7), it was interesting to find that a higher proportion of respondents from the Americas and Africa dedicated the most time to assessor training (above two days), and Asian, European and Oceania respondents most frequently stated that they dedicated between half to one day for assessor training. It is also interesting to note the bipolar nature of the data from the Americas, where 47 per cent of respondents reported that assessor training was less than one day and another 47 per cent reported that it was two or more days, with nothing in between. This presumably reflects how the assessor training requirements and circumstances tend to vary from one situation to another due to the factors mentioned above.

Table 22.7 Length of assessor training by continent

Training duration	Africa %	Asia %	Europe %	Oceania %	Americas %
Less than ½ day	5	11	10	9	27
½–1 day	14	26	31	41	20
1–1½ days	9	17	16	5	0
1½–2 days	23	17	21	18	0
More than 2 days	40	24	18	18	40
Other	0	2	1	5	7

CONTENT

It is evident that the 'Role of the Assessor' is the most frequently included component of assessor training for a majority of the survey respondents (85 per cent) who reported training their assessors (see Table 22.8). Best practice advocates that assessors should be familiar with the exercises and the competencies that they are assessing the participants on, and encouragingly both of these aspects were frequently rated as being included in the assessor training 76 per cent of the time. These findings are very similar to the results from the international survey conducted by Thornton and Krause (2009), who reported that the most popular components of assessor training were 'Knowledge of Exercises' (89 per cent), 'Method of Behavioral Observation' (78 per cent), 'Errors of Judgement' (77 per cent), 'Ability to observe, record, classify behavior' (76 per cent), 'Use of behavioral system' (71 per cent), and to a large extent these concur with the top five components listed in Table 22.8.

Table 22.8 Assessor training content across total sample

Assessor training content	%
Role of the assessor	85
Familiarity with Organizations' Competencies	76
Practise Assessing on Simulation Exercises	76
How Competencies are Displayed in Exercises	67
Behavioural Observation Techniques	67
Centre Logistics	61
Interviewing Skills	57
Feedback Skills	56
Common Rater Errors	55
Benchmarks for Effective Performance	42
Coaching Skills	21
Other	5

The main point of variance would appear to be that less prominence is given to 'Common Rater Errors' (55 per cent), compared with the 77 per cent reported by Thornton and Krause. It is difficult to offer any definitive explanation as to why this might be, although it is possible that it is of much greater concern in the US, where the threat of litigation means that organizations are keen to avoid basic rating errors which could leave them open to accusations of bias and prejudice. This view is reinforced by the Eurich et al. survey, where 'Knowledge of and sensitizing to errors of judgement' was the fourth most common factor to feature in assessor training, occurring 60 per cent of the time.

It is also worth noting that 'Feedback Skills' is incorporated into the assessor training according to 66 per cent of the DC respondents, compared with only 54 per cent of the AC respondents. Similarly 'Coaching Skills' was at 34 per cent for a DC and 15 per cent for an AC. This is not surprising, as the DC is very much the start of a process (Ballantyne and Povah 2004), in which feedback and coaching are ongoing activities, whereas the focus of an AC is whether an individual can perform competently within the target role and thus the AC is more the end of a process.

Assessment Centre Design

AC design is influenced by many factors, the most significant of which are the purpose of the centre (principally selection or development), the number of competencies and exercises that will be used as the basis of the assessment, the number of participants expected to attend, the anticipated duration of the centre, the decision-making process, and the feedback process.

DURATION OF THE CENTRE

Almost half of the respondents (45 per cent) stated that their centres lasted between half to one day, with twenty-two per cent citing one to one and a half days and thirteen per cent one and a half to 2 days. Given the different scale intervals, this isn't too dissimilar to Thornton and Krause (2009) who reported 31 per cent for 1 day and 46 per cent for 2 days. Table 22.9 shows that this trend is consistently evident across continents, although Oceania and Europe are much the strongest proponents of the ½ to 1 day duration (55 per cent and 50 per cent respectively) and the Americas are the most inclined to run centres of less than ½ day (25 per cent).

Table 22.9 Duration of centres across continents

Duration of centres	Africa %	Asia %	Europe %	Oceania %	Americas %
Less than ½ day	6	17	5	3	25
½–1 day	45	32	50	55	32
1–1½ days	17	21	25	17	25
1½–2 days	19	15	13	10	4
More than 2 days	11	10	7	10	4
Don't know	2	5	1	3	11

This latter observation is also noted by Thornton and Krause (2009), who highlight the growing pressure for 'lean assessments' (high quality decisions in a short period of time), which is a US phenomenon driven by the increasingly popular use of online assessment, a trend that is likely to catch on globally before too long. However, this is a source of some concern, as the desire for greater haste and convenience will undoubtedly lead to a compromise in the quality of the AC, which in turn risks reducing their validity and overall effectiveness.

When comparing AC and DC respondents, it is evident that 68 per cent of ACs last for no more than one day, whereas 64 per cent of DCs last for at least one day. As one might expect, there is far more variation in the duration of DCs than there is for ACs, where 56 per cent of respondents reported that their ACs lasted half to one day, as Figure 22.4 illustrates. This is because DCs usually incorporate more components within the process, such as feeding back of results and personal development sessions based on improving participants' performance, regardless of whether the purpose of the DC is to combine diagnosis and development planning or to focus entirely on development, both of which could be classed as DCs. Additionally if there were a diagnostic aspect to the DC, it would be expected that the data integration session would be longer than for an AC, as each participant would be discussed in greater depth on topics relating to their performance, as opposed to an AC data integration session which would be focused on whether the participant could perform to an effective level or not.

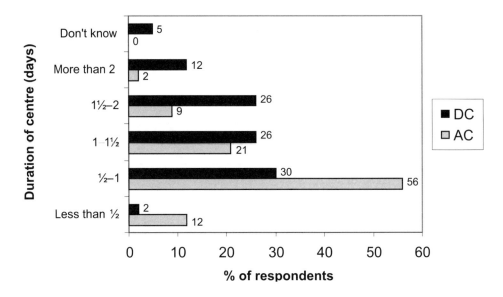

Figure 22.4 Duration of ACs versus DCs

NUMBER OF PARTICIPANTS

The highest proportion of respondents (25 per cent) stated that they assess 6 participants during one of their centres, which is a comfortably manageable size. Next most popular was less than 4 (16 per cent) and then 8 participants (15 per cent). Unsurprisingly even numbers of participants were strongly favoured over odd numbers, with 9 and 7 being least popular (only 1 per cent), the latter of which is a particularly awkward number for running group discussions (too large for a single group and too small to split into 2 groups). Generally speaking this global trend was repeated across the continents, except Oceania favoured 8 participants (28 per cent) rather than 6 (10 per cent) and the Americas preferred less than 4 participants (32 per cent) rather than 6 (11 per cent),which may be due to their enthusiasm for online assessment referred to in the previous section.

One surprising and potentially worrying observation was the number of respondents who reported centres with more than 12 participants: Oceania (17 per cent); Asia (12 per cent); Africa (11 per cent); Americas (11 per cent); Europe (9 per cent). Linking these findings to the reported Assessor–Participant ratios given in Table 22.5 reinforces the concern about the impact of cognitive load on assessors, who are required to observe large numbers of participants on large centres. Europe alone stands out as the continent which is attempting to adopt a prudent approach to best practice in this regard.

DECISION-MAKING PROCESSES

A consensus discussion was cited by 75 per cent of the respondents as the most frequently used decision-making process for determining final evaluations. This dominance was replicated across all continents, ranging from 64–81 per cent and is broadly similar to the results found by Kudisch et al. who reported 65 per cent favouring a consensus discussion, as opposed to Thornton and Krause who found only 47 per cent favoured this method.

By contrast a purely arithmetic (statistical) formula was much less popular, being favoured by 13 per cent of the total sample, with a range of 11–19 per cent across the continents.

The most popular duration of these consensus discussions ranged from 11–30 minutes for each participant and this was the case for 50–59 per cent of the respondents from each continent. Table 22.10 shows the continental differences for both ACs and DCs and it highlights that discussion times for each participant are generally shorter for ACs than DCs, which is to be expected, given that more details of a participant's performance would be discussed during a DC 'wash up' compared to an AC.

Table 22.10 Length of consensus discussions per participant for ACs and DCs

Minutes per participant	Africa (%)		Asia (%)		Europe (%)		Oceania (%)		Americas (%)	
	AC	DC	AC	DC	AC	DC	AC	DC	AC	DC
Less than 10	17	0	14	5	12	5	0	0	8	0
11–20	26	40	29	23	29	17	42	20	23	67
21–30	30	0	21	36	24	27	25	20	31	0
31–45	13	20	18	23	14	27	33	20	8	33
46–60	9	20	0	5	14	15	0	40	23	0
More than 60	4	0	14	5	3	7	0	0	8	0
Don't know	0	20	4	5	4	2	0	0	0	0

FEEDBACK PROCESSES

Over half of respondents (62 per cent) stated that they provide feedback to their participants 'sometime after the Centre', with 32 per cent suggesting that feedback is provided at the end of the day, and only 12 per cent claiming that they provide feedback after each exercise. As one would expect, the results differ between ACs and DCs, with respondents reporting that they provide feedback after the centre 68 per cent of the time for an AC and 49 per cent for a DC; at the end of the centre 27 per cent of the time for an AC and 41 per cent for a DC; and after each exercise 6 per cent of the time for an AC and 25 per cent for a DC. This reflects their different purposes resulting in the greater flexibility for the provision of feedback on a DC, compared with the AC, where feedback is most likely to be given after the event when the more significant decisions about participants have been taken. These trends were generally repeated across all continents, with one notable exception, that feedback after each exercise on an AC was occasionally undertaken in the Americas (17 per cent) and Asia (13 per cent), but not at all in Africa or Oceania and very rarely in Europe (4 per cent). It is very difficult to interpret these continental variations with any certainty, but one possible explanation is that feedback after each exercise is sometimes given so participants have an opportunity to demonstrate their ability to learn, by attempting to adapt their behaviour so as to improve their performance in subsequent exercises. Successful participants are credited with having demonstrated a competency such as Learning Agility. However, in the absence of more information, we can only suggest that this is clearly a matter for some further research.

Respondents indicated that feedback is provided orally to participants about 84 per cent of the time and this is usually provided individually (73 per cent). Written feedback is generally provided to participants 57 per cent of the time, with this being more prevalent for DCs (71 per cent) than ACs (49 per cent). This is not surprising, as the whole point of a DC is to provide participants with detailed reports and feedback regarding their performance at a centre, so that they can work on their development needs. An AC for selection purposes does not require the participant to have such detailed feedback, as their key concern is whether or not they have been selected for the role. However, feedback of some variety should always be provided to AC participants, and it is encouraging to see that many AC respondents are providing feedback in one form or another.

USE OF TECHNOLOGY

Some 60 per cent of respondents reported the use of technology within their centres (58 per cent for ACs and 64 per cent for DCs) and this is consistent with the 61 per cent reported by Eurich et al. (2009). These responses were higher than the 43 per cent reported by Thornton and Krause (2009) regarding the use of computers, but this could be due to the different nature of the questions, with the former including video cameras and audio tapes, and so on.

The use of computers by participants to complete their exercises was clearly the most popular use across all five continents as shown in Table 22.11. Next most popular were the use of computers by assessors and resource centre managers to support them with marking, report writing and data compilation.

Table 22.11 Different uses of technical equipment across continents

Technical equipment	Africa %	Asia %	Europe %	Oceania %	Americas %
Audio tapes to record exercises	17	33	2	20	14
Audio tapes to record feedback	8	13	2	10	14
Video cameras to record exercises	17	29	24	20	14
Video cameras to record feedback	17	13	16	40	29
Computers for exercise (participant)	92	67	55	50	43
Computers for results (assessor)	33	46	43	30	43
Computers for Resources Centre Managers	50	17	45	10	29
Computers to monitor validation	17	13	31	0	14
Other	8	0	12	0	14

Respondents also reported how their use of computer based assessment tools was likely to change in the future compared with how it is at present and the most significant change by far, was the anticipated growth in the use of electronic in-baskets from the current 19 per cent to 57 per cent. This predicted change is most likely due to electronic in-baskets reflecting the email working practices that most people engage in daily, thus adding to the face validity of this type of assessment tool. Furthermore, its time-based calendar and communication features, enable it to act as a central hub which can introduce other components of the AC, thus assisting with centre administration and enhancing data capture regarding a participant's performance.

EVALUATION

Best practice advocates that ACs should be evaluated to check that they are valid and fit for purpose, so it is disappointing to find that only 53 per cent of respondents reported carrying out some form of validation/evaluation. This is comparable to the 50 per cent reported by Eurich et al. (2009) and higher than the 34 per cent reported by Thornton and Krause (2009), although we cannot be sure of the levels of rigour applied by respondents within any of these surveys, due to the likely variation in the validation methodologies they applied. However, one thing is for certain; in all three surveys it is evident that evaluation was not given the emphasis it warrants and practitioners should probably make more effort to secure client agreement to support this important process.

Conclusions and Recommendations

This paper summarized some of the main findings arising from a survey undertaken by A&DC in 2008 (for access to the full report see Povah et al. 2008), which with 443 respondents from 43 countries is the most widespread survey of its kind. Analysis of the data was aided by making comparisons with other recent surveys, which helped to reinforce the findings of those surveys, thus adding to what we know about AC practices in general. However, this particular survey went further than most, by providing a more comprehensive view of the different practices seen across the globe and data were collected and analysed to identify any trends that were evident from five continents. Given the aforementioned intention of this paper, readers may wish to review the findings in conjunction with some of the topics raised in a number of the other chapters within the book, which focus on AC design and implementation in specific countries, many of which can be found in Part III.

Another benefit of such surveys is that they act as a conduit between the researcher and the practitioner, in that the findings from the survey can inform the practitioner's thinking in terms of how they design and implement their ACs. Conversely they also enable practitioners to alert researchers to the issues that are currently attracting attention with their clients and which would benefit from further research. For example, one obvious limitation of this survey was the failure to provide specific definitions that would contrast ACs from DCs and respondents weren't asked to specify the format and purpose of their DC. For example, was the DC purely diagnostic, so feedback could be provided post-DC; or was it diagnostic with feedback provided on the DC and a development plan created for post-DC implementation; or was it designed to provide diagnosis and feedback, which enabled development to take place during the DC? Obtaining this understanding would have enabled a much more valuable interpretation of the data.

On the whole there was a reasonable amount of evidence indicating that effort was being made to follow best practice, such as a sensible approach to job analysis using several different techniques, the focus on an appropriate set and number of competencies, the use of a suitable number of simulations, the selection of assessors (line managers, HR staff and psychologists), all of which are reassuring.

However, there were also some areas of concern, such as the amount of time spent on assessor training, with nearly 40 per cent of respondents admitting to spending less than 1 day and 72 per cent spending at most 2 days; the diminishing duration of ACs, particularly within the US and Asia, where some are less than half a day; the numbers of participants attending ACs coupled with the high participant-to-assessor ratios, which place an obvious cognitive burden on assessors and risk impacting the quality of the process; and the limited focus on evaluation and validation, although this may be due to a lack of client interest, rather than any negligence on the part of practitioners.

It is also evident from this survey that there is widespread global variation in AC practices as one would expect, and one of the obvious lessons to emerge from this, is that more needs to be done to achieve higher levels of consistency, particularly as organizations are keen to make judgements about their people in order to progress their Talent Management strategies. A challenge for global operations is to decide when and how much variation is appropriate to accommodate cultural differences, yet still provide standard evaluations across countries and regions. Unfortunately there isn't a 'one size fits all' solution, as it will largely depend on the nature of the challenge. For example, some organizations might wish to take an existing AC or DC into a new country, when a series of questions will arise about the transferability of the centre. These questions will probably include:

- What is the working language and will translation be necessary?
- Are the exercise simulations readily transferable without adaptation or localization?
- To what extent will cultural variations impact on participant behaviour?
- Should assessors be imported or should local assessors be used, or should they be a mix of both?
- Whatever the case, what steps will be taken to ensure assessor consistency and inter-rater reliability?

Other organizations might wish to create a centre which can be used in multiple global locations, in which case they will wish to ensure that the exercise simulations are constructed in such a way as to afford all participants a fair and equal opportunity, thus avoiding any risks of adverse impact. This might necessitate ensuring that there is a truly international design team who can ensure an adequate level of diversity awareness when creating the content of the centre. As can be seen there are many issues here and the relatively new focus on global strategies is still creating challenges for the large Multinational Corporations (MNCs), who are trying to develop new global solutions to tackle these challenges and this is therefore another area that is ripe for further research.

It is hoped that readers of this chapter have been able to gain some valuable insights, such as identifying best practice issues which might be impacting on the ACs they run, evaluating the extent to which their ACs incorporate the most appropriate 'state of the art' thinking, recognizing the extent to which cultural factors may be impacting their ACs, learning how to justify their recommendations to their clients in order to maximize the validity and robustness of their centres, and becoming a true advocate for global consistency when using ACs for Talent Management. Even if readers have only been able to benefit from some of these insights in one of these areas, it is hoped that the time invested in reviewing the contents of this chapter will prove to have been worthwhile.

References

Arthur, W., Jr., Day, E.A., McNelly, T.L. and Edens, P.S. 2003. A meta-analysis of the criterion-related validity of assessment center dimensions. *Personnel Psychology*, 56, 125–154.

Assessment Centre Study Group of South Africa. [Online]. Available at: http://www.acsg.co.za/about-us/history [accessed: 3 November 2010].

Ballantyne, I. and Povah, N. 2004. *Assessment and Development Centres* (2nd edition). Aldershot: Gower.

Bowler, M.C. and Woehr, D.J. 2006. A meta-analytic evaluation of the impact of dimension and exercise factors on assessment center ratings. *Journal of Applied Psychology*, 91, 1114–1124.

Briscoe, D.R. 1997. Assessment centers: cross-cultural and cross-national issues. *Journal of Social Behavior and Personality*, 12, 261–270.

British Psychological Society: Psychological Testing Centre. 2003. *Design, implementation and evaluation of Assessment and Development Centres. Best Practice Guidelines.* [Online]. Available at: http://www.psychtesting.org.uk/the-ptc/guidelinesandinformation.cfm [accessed: 19 April 2010].

Eurich, T.L., Krause, D.E., Cigularov, K. and Thornton, G.C. III. 2009. Assessment centers: Current practices in the United States. *Journal of Business Psychology*, 24, 387–407.

Hofstede, G. 1991. *Cultures and Organizations: Software of the Mind.* London: McGraw-Hill.

International Task Force on Assessment Center Guidelines. 2009. Guidelines and Ethical Considerations for Assessment Center Operations. *International Journal of Selection and Assessment*, 17, 243–253.

Krause, D.E. and Gebert, D. 2003. A comparison of assessment center practices in organizations in German-speaking regions and the United States. *International Journal of Selection and Assessment*, 11, 297–312.

Krause, D.E. and Thornton, G.C. III. 2009. A cross-cultural look at assessment center practices: A survey in Western Europe and North America. *Applied Psychology: An International Review*, 58, 557–585.

Kudisch, J.D. Avis, J.M., Thibodeaux, H. and Fallon, J.D. 2001, April. *A survey of assessment center practices in organizations worldwide: Maximizing innovation or business as usual?* Paper presented at the 16th annual conference of the Society for Industrial and Organizational Psychology, San Diego, CA.

Lievens, F. and Conway, J.M. 2001. Dimension and exercise variance in assessment center scores: A large-scale evaluation of multitrait-multimethod studies. *Journal of Applied Psychology*, 86, 1202–1222.

Lievens, F. and Thornton, G.C. III. 2005. Assessment centers: Recent developments in practice and research. In *Handbook of Personnel Selection*, edited by A. Evers, N. Anderson and O. Voskuijl. Malden, MA: Blackwell. 243–264.

Povah, N., Crabb, S. and McGarrigle, R. 2008. *The Global Research Report: An International Survey of Assessment Center Practices*. [Online: A&DC]. Available at: http://www.adc.uk.com/page.aspx/239/Research_Findings [accessed: 9 February 2011].

Ryan, A.M., McFarland, L., Baron, H. and Page, R. 1999. An international look at selection practices: nation and culture as explanations for variability in practice. *Personnel Psychology*, 52, 359–391.

Spychalski, A.C., Quiñones, M.A., Gaugler, B.B. and Pohley, K. 1997. A survey of assessment center practices in organizations in the United States. *Personnel Psychology*, 50, 71–90

Thornton, G.C. III and Krause, D.E. 2009. Selection versus development assessment centers: An international survey of design, execution, and evaluation. *The International Journal of Human Resource Management*, 20, 478–498.

Thornton, G.C. III and Rupp, D.R. 2006. *Assessment Centers in Human Resource Management: Strategies for Prediction, Diagnosis, and Development*. Mahwah, NJ: Lawrence Erlbaum.

Woehr, D.J. and Arthur, W. 2003. The construct-related validity of assessment center ratings: a review and meta-analysis of methodological factors. *Journal of Management*, 29, 231–258.

23 Assessment Center Practices in South Africa, Western Europe, and North America

DIANA E. KRAUSE

AC programs continue to spread to more and more countries around the world (Lievens and Thornton 2005). Thus, it is of the uppermost importance for those organizations operating on an international level to possess the relevant knowledge regarding intercultural assessment center practices. However, hardly any empirically supported findings are available concerning this topic. This is an important and relevant area of concern for organizations, not only because of the globalization of the markets, but also because research into cross-cultural issues for assessment centers is still in its infancy. This is also reflected in a recent book on ACs, where the chapter "Cross Cultural Assessment Centers" can only reveal that more research is necessary in this subject area (Thornton and Rupp 2006).

With a view to the question of intercultural AC practices, organizations are encouraged to balance the need for a culture-specific assessment center design and the parallel need for culture-unspecific standardizations of the assessment center program (Krause and Thornton 2009) to derive internationally valid performance predictions based on the assessment center results. One condition for such a balance is to learn more about the region-specific similarities and differences in current assessment center practices. This chapter presents research results from two individual studies in the field of assessment center practices (Krause and Thornton 2009; Krause, 2010b) in three regions: South Africa, Western Europe, and North America. The region-specific approach is highly important because the findings of AC applications from one region cannot be generalized to other regions or countries as the economic, social, political, and educational circumstances vary from one country to the next (Krause 2010a). Consequently, the AC practices are highly heterogeneous not only within one region or country but also between countries. For a review of international differences in personnel selection practices in general, see Ryan, McFarland, Baron and Page (1999).

Selected results from the studies mentioned above will be presented in this chapter in a practice-oriented way. The following areas of assessment center practices are considered: main objectives of the assessment center program, the job analysis techniques used, the various job requirements (dimensions) being assessed, the types of exercise simulations used, the data integration process, and the feedback process. This chapter intends to describe assessment center practices with regard to the selected areas and to generate regional recommendations for action with the aim of improving assessment center practices. With regard to the evaluation of current practices in the three regions required for this purpose, we used the following types of information: guidelines and ethical considerations for assessment center operations (Task Force on Assessment Center Operations 2009), which may be considered as the quality standards for North America, South African guidelines for AC procedures (Schlebusch and Roodt 2008, Appendix A), which may be used as the quality standards for South African assessment center practices, suggestions for cross-cultural AC applications (Task Force on Assessment Center Operations 2009), and scholarly papers that indicate aspects relevant to increase the predictive and construct validity evidence of an AC.

To identify the similarities and differences in the current AC practices in the three regions, two studies regarding the state of the art of AC programs were conducted. In both studies, the HR experts were heads of the HR department, chief department heads, divisional managers or personnel specialists.

In study one (Krause and Thornton 2009) the assessment center practices in North America (N = 52 organizations; which was split into Canada n = 5, United States n = 47) were compared to the assessment center practices in selected Western European countries (N = 45 organizations: Austria n = 3, France n = 2, Germany n = 18, Netherlands n = 1, Sweden n = 2, Switzerland n = 12, and United Kingdom n = 7). In doing so, we developed a questionnaire which contained 176 assessment center features. This questionnaire was filled out online by Human Resource experts from each organization under study.

In study two (Krause et al. 2010a), we specifically analyzed South African assessment center practices for the first time. This contrasts with the global study described by Povah in Chapter 22 of this volume, where there were 60 respondents from Africa but the analyses were conducted on a continental basis and there was no specific breakdown of the responses from the 43 South African respondents. The questionnaire used in our study included 62 assessment center features. In collaboration with SHL South Africa, South African organizations were contacted and HR experts from those organizations described their assessment center programs.

AC Programs in South Africa

The AC program was introduced into a South African insurance company (Old Mutual group) by Bill Byham in 1973. During the next few years, Old Mutual group implemented developmental centers in its offshore companies such as Zimbabwe, England, Thailand, Malaysia, and Hong Kong. One year later, the Edgars group was a pioneer in developing and running ACs in South Africa. In 1975, another South African organization, Transport Services, found out how companies in the US like AT&T and IBM identify their potential. Over the next few years, Transport Services assessed 670 managers and expanded the assessment center as a tool for selection and developmental purposes (Meiring 2008). Other South African organizations (for example, Stellenbosch Farmers Winery, Department of Post and Telecommunication Services, Naspers, South African Army, and South African Police) soon followed in the development, execution, and validation of the AC method.

We have to consider that AC practices in South Africa have changed dramatically during the last three decades. Economic, socio-cultural, and political circumstances (see Herriot and Anderson 1997; Klehe 2004; Krause 2010b) in South Africa influence past and present AC practices. For example, the primary economic sector in South Africa (manufacturing, services, mining, agriculture) was restructured after apartheid and is now well-developed in many areas so that quality-functional investment into the AC program (for example evaluation of the program) have been made. This is especially valid for a developmental AC. With respect to the South African cultural and social conditions, we have to account for the ethnic diversity of the nation's disparate groups, the different languages (such as Zulu, Xhosa, Swani, Sotho), and the religious diversity. The South African culture and social conditions influence AC practices in many ways. For example, in selecting and presenting the exercises and simulations diversity in ethnic groups, language, the composition of the observer pool, religion, and the method of delivering feedback need to be considered. Last but not least, the political system in South Africa has an impact on the use of AC programs. In the post-apartheid era a transition to democracy, and full recognition of human rights was achieved. International isolation of the country has been overcome, international investments have been made, the accessibility to the educational system for more individuals than before was carried out, and new jobs have been created. The political change also influences the use of ACs. Specific employment legislation has been enacted. Laws now regulate promotion of equality and prevention of unfair discrimination, employment equity, skills development, and occupational health and safety, all of which need to be considered in the design, execution, and evaluation of ACs (additional information about the history of South Africa and applications for ACs there can be found in Chapter 13 by Buckett and Chapter 6 by Meiring in this volume).

Main Objectives of the Assessment Centers

The aforementioned guidelines indicate that the AC should be designed to achieve a stated objective. As shown in Table 23.1, two-thirds of the South African organizations use the AC for both goals: personnel selection as well as personnel development. Only a few South African organizations state that the main objective of their AC is personnel development. These practices are comparable with the practices in Western European organizations in which nearly half of the organizations use the AC for personnel selection as well as personnel development purposes and an additional quarter of the organizations use it exclusively for personnel development goals. These findings contradict AC practices in North American organizations (see Table 23.1) in which an increasing trend towards developmental assessment centers has been observed during the last few years. Table 23.1 shows that, nearly two-thirds of the North American organizations use the AC exclusively for personnel development objectives. In a developmental center, candidates' learning and development is eminently important (Woo, Sims, Rupp and Gibbons 2009). For all three regions under study it is evident that it is less common to use the AC solely for selection purposes.

Table 23.1 Main objective of assessment center practices

	South Africa (N = 43) %	Western Europe (N = 45) %	North America (N = 52) %
Personnel selection	22	34	20
Personnel development	13	25	59
Personnel selection and development	65	41	21

Use of Job Analysis Techniques

Regardless of the purpose of the AC program, professional recommendations in South Africa, Western Europe, and North America indicate that a systematic job analysis prior to the AC should be conducted (Schlebusch and Roodt 2008, Task Force on Assessment Center Operations 2009). Actually, nearly all of the organizations report using various job analysis techniques, which is a positive sign in current AC practices in all three regions. Indeed Table 23.2 shows that the organizations in all three regions use a wide variety of such techniques, which is encouraging because no single technique will suffice (Thornton and Rupp 2006). In South Africa, the most frequently used job analysis techniques are job description and competency modeling. The wide use of competency modeling shows that job analyses are conducted in great detail very carefully. On the other hand, a method that is relatively unused in South African organizations is the critical incident technique (Flanagan 1954). This method attempts to determine "critical" behaviors related to the target position. The resulting information makes it possible to distinguish between successful and unsuccessful job candidates. For both managers and employees, the critical incident technique would be well suited for clustering the job requirements related to a specific position. Consequently, South African organizations should consider using the critical incident technique more frequently than in the past. Compared to South Africa, Western European organizations more frequently use interviews with supervisors, interviews with job incumbents, and the critical incident technique (see Table 23.2). In North American organizations, however, job description, interviews with job incumbents, and interviews with supervisors, and questionnaires completed by job incumbents are more common than other methods of job analysis (see Table 23.2).

To sum up, the absolute amount of each job analysis technique varies greatly between the regions. This finding is in line with past results on the application of job analysis methods (Krause and Gebert 2003, Krause, Meyer zu Kniendorf and Gebert 2001, Krause and Thornton 2009). With respect to an assessment centers' predictive and construct validity evidence, it is also significant which kind of job requirements (dimensions) are assessed in the programs; a question that we will discuss in the next section.

Table 23.2 Job analysis techniques

	South Africa (N = 43) %	Western Europe (N = 45) %	North America (N = 52) %
Job description	47	41	76
Interview with job incumbents	23	39	56
Questionnaire to job incumbents	16	14	41
Interview with supervisor	26	59	54
Questionnaire to supervisor	16	16	29
Critical incident technique	2	36	27
Observation of job incumbents	5	7	31
Workshop or teamwork	9	36	15
Competency modeling	44	43	20

Percentages do not add to 100 because respondents could choose more than one option.

The Various Job Requirements Being Assessed

With respect to the various job requirements (that is, "dimensions") being assessed, we used the results of two meta-analyses (Arthur, Day, McNelly and Edens 2003, Bowler and Woehr 2006). These two meta-analyses have shown that six job requirements are construct and criterion valid, namely Communication, Consideration/Awareness of Others, Drive, Influencing Others, Organization and Planning, and Problem-Solving. According to Arthur and colleagues (2003), Communication means the extent to which someone provides oral or written information, answers questions, and deals with challenges. Consideration is defined as the extent to which a person pays attention to other people's feelings and needs and the awareness of the consequences of one's own decision-making for others inside and outside the organizations. Drive includes the degree to which an individual maintains and keeps a high arousal level, the extent to which the individual sets up high goal-standards, tries everything to meet these standards, and wishes to be promoted to the next level. For example, a European professor might sit in their study in the middle of July without any air conditioning, continuing to write a book chapter although the temperature outside is 100.4 degrees Fahrenheit. Influencing Others refers to the degree to which someone convinces others to do something to reach desired results, and to the extent to which one's own behaviors are controlled by one's own beliefs instead of other people's opinions. Organizing and Planning includes the distribution of one's own resources and tasks to perform efficiently as well as the extent to which the individual anticipates future events. Problem-Solving delineates the extent to which someone collects, analyses, and processes data and information, generates different options and ideas to act, selects realistic action strategies, uses existing resources in a new way, and rethinks solutions before acting.

   With respect to the assessment of these job requirement we found that two-thirds of the South African organizations assess Communication, Organizing and Planning, Problem-Solving, and Influencing Others; at least one third of those organizations assess Consideration/Awareness of Others and Drive (see Table 23.3). In Western Europe, virtually all organizations assess Communication skills and Problem-Solving, and at least two-thirds of the organizations assess Influencing Others and Organizing and Planning. In contrast, the most popular dimensions being assessed in North America are Communication, Problem-Solving, and Organizing and Planning. The comparison of the absolute amount to which the dimensions are assessed shows that all of the dimensions are less frequently assessed in South African organizations compared to Western European and North American organizations. However, the meta-analysis by Arthur et al. (2003) has confirmed that Communication, Influencing Others, Organizing and Planning, and Problem-Solving are the best dimensional performance predictors. These job requirements accounted for 20 percent of the variance in performance. Consequently, we can conclude that the most frequently assessed dimensions in all three regions are also the ones with the most predictive validity evidence. It goes without saying that this is a positive sign in current assessment center practices. Notwithstanding, the question remains as to whether this standard repertoire of dimensions is sufficiently up-to-date with the reality of requirements in our age of globalization and internationalization. With a view to changing conditions, it might be necessary to alter requirement profiles, in a way that depicts constructs such as intercultural competence, charisma or tolerance of ambiguity, to a far greater extent.

Regardless of the nature of the job requirements, the next feature of our research was to focus on *how* these job requirements are assessed; in other words, which exercises and simulations are used in the three different regions.

Table 23.3   Job requirements being assessed

	South Africa (N = 43) %	Western Europe (N = 45) %	North America (N = 52) %
Communication	63	98	90
Consideration/Awareness of Others	33	80	49
Drive	33	70	37
Influencing Others	58	75	61
Organizing and Planning	67	73	83
Problem-Solving	67	84	90

Percentages do not add to 100 because respondents could choose more than one option.

The Types of Exercises and Simulations Used

All organizations in the three regions use a mixture of different exercises (Table 23.4). This is a positive finding because an AC's predictive validity increases if a wide variety of exercises is employed (Gaugler, Rosenthal, Thornton and Benson 1987). Yet, the mixture varies between the countries. The most frequently used exercises in South Africa are in-basket exercises, presentations and role playing, followed by group discussions.

These South African findings are in line with the most frequently used exercises in North America. In the US and Canada, in-baskets, presentations, and role playing are also widespread. In Western European countries, the most common exercises are presentations, group discussions, role playing, and case studies. The frequent use of these and not other exercises can probably be explained in terms of the AC's social acceptance. For example, organizations in many countries appear to prefer exercises that demonstrate the candidates' ability to deal with complex tasks. These kinds of exercises are presumably perceived to be more activity specific than other types of exercises. The frequent use of presentations and role playing in all three regions is consistent with Thornton and Rupp's (2006) statement that situational exercises are still the "mainstream" of AC programs. Typically, the candidates' dimension-based and exercise-based performances are integrated in the final stage of the assessment program so that a decision can be reached regarding promotion, selection, or development. To integrate these data, several different methods are used, in particular: an assessor consensus discussion, statistical aggregation, and a combination of an assessor consensus discussion and statistical aggregation.

Table 23.4 Types of exercises and simulations

	South Africa (N = 43) %	Western Europe (N = 45) %	North America (N = 52) %
In-basket	54	35	55
Presentation	51	92	58
Background interview	16	48	40
Situational interview	23	48	48
Role-playing	49	88	78
Case study	26	78	38
Fact-finding	16	20	33
Planning exercises	16	40	48
Sociometric devices	2	5	5
Group discussion	37	90	45

Percentages do not add to 100 because respondents could choose more than one option.

The Data Integration Process

As you can see in Table 23.5, the frequency of each kind of data integration process is highly similar in the three regions (for further details on the data integration process see Chapter 6 in this book). Two-thirds of the South African organizations and approximately half of the organizations in Western Europe and North America use a combination of an assessor consensus discussion and statistical aggregation. In addition, approximately one-third of the organizations in all three regions use just an assessor consensus discussion, while the least frequently used method in all three regions is pure statistical aggregation. These results contradict previous surveys (Krause and Gebert 2003; Kudisch et al. 2001; Spychalski et al. 1997) in which a much greater proportion of organizations used a consensus discussion. The trend to combine assessors' consensus information with statistical aggregation may be the outcome of two factors. Firstly, statistical integration may ensure overall ratings that are just as accurate as consensus ratings (Thornton and Rupp 2006). Secondly, there is a need for public organizations to increase the appearance of objectivity associated with statistical integration, in contrast to the seemingly subjective consensus discussion.

Table 23.5 The data integration process

	South Africa (N = 43) %	Western Europe (N = 45) %	North America (N = 52) %
Assessor consensus (OAR)	32	38	42
Statistical aggregation	7	6	8
Combination of OAR and statistical aggregation	61	56	47

The Feedback Process

Regarding the feedback process, it is obvious that the most common ways of delivering feedback in all the regions is a combination of oral and written methods (see Table 23.6). In all three regions, it is less common to provide written feedback alone. This practice can be seen in a positive way because written feedback alone could be easily misinterpreted; it could lead to frustration, confusion, and a lack of understanding and therefore could lead to negative work outcomes, including reduced organizational commitment. The frequencies in the different types of feedback are similar to those identified in earlier studies (Krause and Gebert 2003, Kudisch and colleagues 2001, Spychalski and colleagues 1997).

Compared to the positive trend in current assessment center practices to provide oral and written feedback, our two studies have also identified one negative trend. This is related to the timing of feedback. As shown in Table 23.6, it is typical in more than half of the organizations in South African and North America and in one-third of the Western European organizations to deliver feedback more than one week after the AC program. Only seven percent of the South African organizations and 25 percent of the North American organizations provide feedback immediately after the completion of the program. An exception from this trend can be seen in Western European organizations. More than half of them provide feedback directly after the candidates have finished the AC exercises and simulations. However, several studies on learning and development have shown that feedback is most effective when it is given as soon after the behavior in question as possible (for a brief summary see Thornton and Rupp 2006).

The current practices in South Africa and North America and the research results point out the practitioner-research gap once again. Only a minority of organizations in South Africa and North America consider the suggestions made by researchers. Contrariwise, in most organizations in South Africa and North America a time lag between the behaviors shown in the AC exercise simulations and the feedback is typical.

Table 23.6 The feedback process

	South Africa (N = 43) %	Western Europe (N = 45) %	North America (N = 52) %
Types of feedback			
Oral	18	28	32
Written	3	5	19
Oral and written	79	64	46
Timing of participant feedback			
Directly upon completion	7	54	25
Up to 1 week after the AC	36	15	17
More than 1 week after the AC	57	31	58
Format of the feedback			
On specific dimensions	46	65	53
On specific exercises	14	43	40
OAR (Overall assessment rating)	29	73	50

Percentages do not add to 100 because respondents could choose more than one option.

Finally, the feedback includes information about the overall assessment rating, specific dimensions, or specific exercises (see Table 23.6). In South Africa it is relatively unusual to provide feedback on ratings in each exercise compared to feedback on specific dimensions and the overall assessment rating. In contrast, in Western Europe it is very common to deliver feedback on the overall assessment rating and on the performance in specific dimensions. The feedback includes all three types of information: the candidates learn about the performance appraisal in specific exercises, specific dimensions, and the overall assessment center rating.

In the following section, we offer suggestions for ways in which HR experts can improve their ACs.

Suggestions to Improve Assessment Center Programs

Although many features in the AC program are carried out very carefully, in great detail and with a lot of methodological effort, there is still room for improvement in all three regions. In all three regions, HR experts are encouraged to think about the specific job requirements that need to be assessed and the types of exercises that should be used. From an academic viewpoint, organizations should use the job requirements and exercises with the highest validity evidence. In line with this argument, we may ask if other dimensions such as intercultural competence, charisma, or tolerance of ambiguity should also be considered in our world of globalization and internationalization. Furthermore, for cost reasons, no organization is able to use ineffective and inefficient exercises today. Organizations in all three regions are invited to review the types of exercises used and to consider if the mainstay of exercises employed is the most appropriate way of assessing their candidates.

Additionally, South African organizations are encouraged to improve their assessment center programs by providing more timely feedback. Thornton and Rupp (2006) found that the maximum learning and behavioral change occurred when feedback was delivered immediately. It is also worthwhile for South African organizations to rethink the form of the feedback. It might be beneficial to provide the overall assessment rating in addition to the feedback on specific exercises or dimensions. South African organizations should standardize their feedback procedure in terms of its content and its medium to reduce uncertainty during this final AC stage.

Moreover, Western European and North American organizations should invest more time, personnel, and money into the execution of the job analyses. Organizations could ask whether the currently used methods of job analysis are indeed the most appropriate ones. For example, more than half of the organizations in Western Europe and North America interview the supervisor of the job incumbent in order to determine the job requirements. The question remains if the assumptions of supervisors are in fact congruent with the tasks and requirements of the job incumbent or if it is rather the supervisors' implicit assumptions regarding the incumbents' job that are reproduced in the job requirement profile. Thus, it is a cause for concern that the job incumbents themselves are rarely questioned regarding their tasks.

To sum up, this chapter pointed out some important AC practices in South Africa, Western Europe, and North America. However, many things are still unclear and there is a need for intercultural research; for example regarding AC practices in other regions such as Indonesia, or Eastern Europe. Other chapters in this book describe AC practices in other countries.

References

Arthur, W. Jr., Day, E.A., McNelly, T.L. and Edens, P.S. 2003. A meta-analysis of the criterion-related validity of assessment center dimensions. *Personnel Psychology*, 56, 125–154.

Assessment Centre Study Group. 2007. *Guidelines for Assessment and Development Centres in South Africa* (4th Edition). Available from Assessment Centre Study Group (ACSG), www.acsg.co.za.

Bowler, M.C. and Woehr, D.J. 2006. A meta-analytic evaluation of the impact of dimension and exercise factors on assessment center ratings. *Journal of Applied Psychology*, 91, 1114–1124.

Flanagan, J.C. 1954. The critical incidents technique. *Psychological Bulletin*, 51, 327–358.

Gaugler, B.B., Rosenthal, D.B., Thornton, G.C. III and Benson, C. 1987. Meta-analysis of assessment center validity. *Journal of Applied Psychology*, 72, 493–511.

Herriot, P. and Anderson, N. 1997. Selecting for change: How will personnel and selection psychology survive? In *International Handbook of Selection and Assessment*, edited by N.R. Anderson and P. Herriot. London: Wiley, 1–32.

Klehe, U.C. 2004. Choosing how to choose: Institutional pressures affecting the adoption of personnel selection procedures. *International Journal of Selection and Assessment*, 12, 327–342.

Krause, D.E. 2010a. *State of the art of assessment centre practices in South Africa: Survey results, challenges, and suggestions for improvement.* Keynote address at the 30th annual Assessment Center Study Group Conferences. Stellenbosch, Western Cape March 17–19, 2010, South Africa.

Krause, D.E. 2010b. *Trends in der Internationalen Personalauswahl. Praxis der Personalpsychologie* [*Trends in International Personnel Selection*]. Göttingen: Hogrefe.

Krause, D.E. and Gebert, D. 2003. A comparison of assessment center practices in organizations in German-speaking regions and the United States. *International Journal of Selection and Assessment*, 11, 297–312.

Krause, D.E., Meyer zu Kniendorf, C. and Gebert, D. 2001. Das assessment center in der deutschsprachigen wirtschaft [The assessment center in the German economy]. *Personal – Zeitschrift für Human Resource Management*, 53, 638–642.

Krause, D.E., and Thornton, G.C. III. 2009. A cross-cultural look at assessment center practices: A survey in Western Europe and Northern America. *Applied Psychology: An International Review*, 58, 557–585.

Kudisch, J.D., Avis, J.M., Thibodeaux, H. and Fallon, J.D. 2001, April. *A survey of assessment center practices in organizations worldwide: Maximizing innovation or business as usual?* Paper presented at the 16th annual conference of the Society for Industrial and Organizational Psychology, San Diego, CA.

Lievens, F. and Thornton, G.C. III. 2005. Assessment centers: Recent developments in practice and research. In *The Blackwell Handbook of Personnel Selection*, edited by A. Evers, N. Anderson and O. Voskuijl. Malden, MA: Blackwell.

Meiring, D. 2008. Assessment Centres in South Africa. In *Assessment Centers: Unlocking the potential for growth*, edited by S. Schlebusch, and G. Roodt. Randburg: Knowres Publishing.

Ryan, A.M., McFarland, L., Baron, H. and Page, R. 1999. An international look at selection practices: nation and culture as explanations for variability in practice. *Personnel Psychology*, 52, 359–391.

Schlebusch, S., and Roodt, G. 2008. *Assessment Centers*. Johannesburg: Knowres Publishing.

Spychalski, A.C., Quiñones, M.A., Gaugler, B.B. and Pohley, K. 1997. A survey of assessment center practices in organizations in the United States. *Personnel Psychology*, 50, 71–90.

Task Force on Assessment Center Guidelines. 2009. Guidelines and ethical considerations for assessment center operations. *International Journal of Selection and Assessment*, 17, 243–254.

Thornton, G.C. III and Rupp, D.R. 2006. *Assessment Centers in Human Resource Management: Strategies for Prediction, Diagnosis, and Development*. Mahwah, NJ: Erlbaum.

Woo, S., Sims, C., Rupp, D. and Gibbons, A.M. 2009. Correction to "Development engagement within and following developmental assessment centers: Considering feedback favorability and self-assessor agreement." *Personnel Psychology*, 62, 199–200.

24 Assessment Center Adaptation and Implementation in Indonesia

VINA G. PENDIT

The assessment center (AC) method started to gain recognition outside the military organization in Indonesia in 1990 when Fajar Bastaman (1992), who at that time was the Head of the Sub Directorate of HR Development, was assigned to develop the directors' AC program while PT Telkom was under the leadership of the late Cacuk Sudarijanto. As a government-owned organization, PT Telkom had grown substantially with as many as 40,000 employees, so it was imperative that it should always be ready for the succession of its key positions in all offices across the country. The existing method for succession planning was no longer considered capable of meeting the growing needs of PT Telkom to identify potential managers. Assisted by Roger Gill, a consultant from DDI, a number of personnel from PT Telkom were trained to be administrators and assessors. Since then, the method of mapping employees' areas of strength and weakness through ACs has increasingly gained popularity. PT Telkom's AC became the benchmark for other ACs established in Indonesia. The AC served not only as a tool to discover people's areas of strength or weakness, but it also provided data which highlighted the capabilities of the organization's HR department to support various HR processes. Organizations began to draw on reports resulting from ACs for various systems of Human Resource management such as selection, development, career path planning as well as succession and promotion.

Benefits of and Concerns about Assessment Centers

The success of Assessment Centers in garnering the interest of HR practitioners in Indonesia was inseparable from the effectiveness of the methodology itself. Until then, HR practitioners in Indonesia mostly relied on psychological tests and other aptitude tests to measure one's capabilities and skills. Track record and performance achievement were also included as additional elements in assessing someone. However, the information had not been sufficient to provide a clear picture to predict one's success in the future.

On the other hand, it is possible to customize ACs to suit organizational needs, for the purpose of succession planning, predicting future success, and so on.

In addition, with its holistic approach, an AC enables an organization to understand each individual in a more comprehensive manner. The use of different assessment tools helps to achieve the aforementioned objectives and allows the organization or designer of the AC program to introduce specific tools for the organization whenever necessary. For instance, PT Telkom adopted the *Occupational Personality Questionnaire (OPQ)* as one of the tools in their AC program.

Furthermore, the AC provides another widely perceived benefit: it does not require a psychologist to be the assessor. Indeed this benefit has made ACs more appealing and enables them to overcome obstacles voiced by some AC users. It is also possible to design an AC within a business context, eliminating psychological jargon understood only by a few people. The involvement of non-psychologists in the process of AC implementation enables designers and providers of ACs to ensure that the particular program is relevant to the current situation and based upon significant daily issues within the workplace. When it was established in 1997, PT Toyota Astra Motor's Assessment Center involved line managers as assessors in addition to HR managers. With management involvement, the use of this method gained more acceptance. The AC had also turned into a learning tool for those line managers who became assessors and therefore had to understand and learn about the behaviour of new managers acquired by the company. In addition to line managers, general managers and directors who at that time were still active, as well as those who were approaching retirement, were engaged in PT Toyota Astra Motor's Assessment Center. Their seniority also helped to increase the credibility of the ACs. ACs gained popularity owing to these aforementioned benefits and in 2000 at least six institutions/organizations, as well as a number of individuals who independently provided the service to some organizations, developed into AC service providers.

This increased level of activity served to raise a number of concerns amongst this better-informed group of observers and AC providers; their concerns include:

1. Many evaluation programs which claimed to be ACs in reality only conducted a series of tests or interviews. The popularity of ACs had been used to raise the sales of testing services by providing various testing packages.
2. Many parties had questioned who should evaluate the data from an AC; that is, whether it could be a trained individual or if it had to be a psychologist.
3. The ubiquity and popularity of ACs had also raised concerns amongst some of those who had been assessed. They were apprehensive about the possibility that the data would be regarded as the only major factor in decision-making, thus presenting a one-sided view of their capabilities.

Ethical Guidelines for Assessment Center Operations in Indonesia

A number of Assessment Center practitioners, users as well as participants, who shared similar concerns gathered on September 20, 2001 in a seminar organized in Jakarta by PT Daya Dimensi Indonesia under the title "Playing Your Talent Card." Professor George Thornton III from Colorado State University, who was a member of the international task force who prepared the *Guidelines and Ethical Considerations for Assessment Center*

Operations, (International Task Force on Assessment Center Guidelines 2009) was one of the key speakers in the seminar. He was also involved in facilitating the formation of a similar task force for Indonesia and led the discussion to delineate the importance of a new set of guidelines for Indonesia in response to the doubt and controversy surrounding this method. It was agreed that the Indonesian Task Force would be the team to formulate the *Ethical Guidelines for Assessment Center Operations in Indonesia*. The Indonesian Task Force henceforth held several meetings to devise in a detailed manner steps to be taken in formulating the aforementioned guidelines.

An initial step in formulating the *Ethical Guidelines for Assessment Center Operations in Indonesia* was to review the international guidelines and attempt to adopt similar methods in Indonesia. In general, items listed in the International Guidelines were acceptable with a little addition on the history of the AC method and its extensive application in Indonesia.

The completed draft of the *Ethical Guidelines for Assessment Center Operations in Indonesia* was distributed to a number of parties who gave feedback. The first review process was facilitated by the Office of the State Ministry for Administrative Reform, AC providers, organizations that frequently sent their employees to ACs, expert staff from Lemhanas (National Institute of Defence) as well as members of the task force itself.

Quite a lot of feedback was obtained from the first review process, particularly regarding the legal enforcement of the *Ethical Guidelines for Assessment Center Operations in Indonesia*. This was a high-profile issue due to the absence of an authorized institution to supervise and conduct qualification testing of the parties involved in an AC, evaluate the validity of an AC program, and examine the qualifications of the assessors, and so forth.

The task force had agreed that the *Ethical Guidelines for Assessment Center Operations in Indonesia* should not be a statute or regulation with legal consequences but would serve as a reference document for providers, users, and participants, aimed at helping them to understand what is required to conduct a proper AC, to meet the standards of best practice, and to achieve the desired objectives.

It was agreed that the task force was not only expected to deliver the *Ethical Guidelines* but also to form an association that would oversee the implementation of ACs in Indonesia.

In 2002 the present author represented the task force for the *Ethical Guidelines for Assessment Center Operations in Indonesia* at the 30th International Assessment Center Congress in Frankfurt, Germany, to convey the draft of the *Ethical Guidelines*. This process was also facilitated by Professor Thornton, who in one particular session invited the members of the International Task Force to comment on the draft of the *Ethical Guidelines of Assessment Center Operations in Indonesia*. Invaluable feedback given at that time was that the *Ethical Guidelines* should be easy to understand and conduct by different parties involved. It is very important to use common terms and everyday language to ensure that people can use the documents as guidelines and for reference. The task force members also provided support for the enthusiasm and effort put in by the task force in Indonesia in establishing their version of the *Ethical Guidelines*. After several revisions, the *Ethical Guidelines for Assessment Center Operations in Indonesia* was officially launched on October 14, 2004 accompanied with a small seminar on Cultural Adaptation on Assessment Center Implementation delivered by Professor Thornton.

Even though the Indonesian Task Force has completed its principal task of establishing the *Ethical Guidelines*, some members have agreed to form an association that will support AC observers in guarding the implementation of the *Ethical Guidelines*. The PASSTI (Perkumpulan Assessment Center Indonesia or Indonesian Assessment Center Association) was born, with its main agenda to organize a biannual Assessment Congress started in 2005. The official office for the group is in Bandung in PT Telkom's assessment center facility. To date, PASSTI has held two national congresses on August 23–25, 2005 at Grand Aquila Hotel, Bandung and July 24–26, 2007 at Borobudur Hotel, Jakarta, and a seminar on Ethics of Assessment Center Operations at Mercure Grand Mirama Hotel, Surabaya on August 13, 2009.

Assessment Center Adaptations and Implementation in Indonesia

The existence of ACs in Indonesia, which became increasingly popular in the late 1990s, was inseparable from the situation in Indonesia at that time. The following conditions affected the existence and roles of ACs in human resource management.

POLITICAL SITUATION

On May 21, 1998 the regime of President Soeharto collapsed following a series of protests and demonstrations conducted by a number of students in the capital, Jakarta (Soeharto 1998). The momentum was marked by an official resignation speech of the president who unequivocally declared his resignation for failing to form a Reformation Committee in response to the development of the political situation and demands of the people at that time. This event marked the beginning of the reform era. The students posted a list of demands, including bureaucratic and legal reforms, corruption eradication and transparency in every aspect of life. At that time there was also pressure to conduct a general election immediately and an appeal to resolutely achieve democracy as set out in the Constitution of Indonesia (UUD 1945) pertaining to freedom of association and assembly and freedom of expression. This was manifested by the emergence of dozens of small and large-scale political parties as well as new political figures from various circles who audaciously expressed their opinions and views through articles published in magazines and newspapers, blogs on the Internet or debate forums broadcast over the radio or television. Dozens of officials as public policy-makers were presented in various talk shows to disclose their controversy-provoking policies.

Even though more than 10 years have passed, the demands for reform still reverberate. A direct presidential election (by the people and not through parliament) has been carried out. A number of new parties have emerged, become strong and managed to catch the attention of the public. Transparency has grown into something imperative in every aspect of society and some local government elections were plunged into chaos owing to a lack of transparency in their implementation. People were involved in street protests and even engaged in acts of anarchy.

Changes in the political situation were marked by the emergence of different political parties representing different interests of the people that had not been channeled. The same thing held true in the workplace, where various parties emerged and attempted to convey the aspirations of workers. A number of associations, for example unions representing the workers, started to emerge. Government and private organizations were no longer able to dismiss or counter the existence of such groups, unions or the parties within their organizations.

The flux of demands for these changes also affected the workplace. Workers increasingly demanded openness and transparency in workforce management. On the other hand, organizations should be ready to face these changes by engaging employees in open dialogue and listening to their aspirations and opinions. Mutual relationships between workers and organizations might elicit friction as well as opportunities for a more effective collaboration in attaining mutual goals.

The changing political situation has encouraged human resource managers and practitioners in many organizations to develop and implement effective ways to assess and portray employees' potential. The AC method has come to be seen as a more transparent and appropriate tool suitable to the prevailing needs at that time, since it is more applicable as a measuring tool in the workplace than various psychometric tools previously used. Communication conducted with participants preceding an AC invariably endorses this transparency. Participants learn about what they will encounter and how the results of the AC will be employed.

ECONOMIC SITUATION

When the reformation era started (1998–2000), economic conditions had not been stable. A large number of companies refrained from large-scale investments. In the workplace, the economic turmoil of the country owing to a monetary crisis sweeping across Asia at that time had forced some companies to conduct mass layoffs. Some companies closed their businesses; others drastically reduced the number of employees. The process was inevitable, yet it had to be conducted thoughtfully. Some organizations had requested assistance to conduct the AC process, aiming to develop a better employee mapping, to facilitate smooth decision-making pertaining to retaining or releasing an employee.

Another condition, namely an increasingly open world economic order, had also accounted for the rise in the need for a more comprehensive assessment method. During 1996–97 Indonesia, as a member of ASEAN countries, started to be bound by a number of trade agreements, such as AFTA (ASEAN Free Trade Area) which became fully effective in 2003. This agreement precipitated wider opportunity for free trade among ASEAN members. It is sufficient to say that the agreement could be regarded as presenting both opportunities and threats: opportunities in the sense that it provides a possibility for Indonesian products to enter foreign markets with little or no restrictions. On the other hand, this condition also posed a challenge to produce high quality products to be competitive in the free market. In terms of human resource management, qualified personnel also have great opportunities to work in other countries, while at the same time personnel from other countries have the same equal opportunities to work in Indonesia. The urge to promote the quality of personnel became more and more evident and imperative. The AC, as a method to identify one's areas of development, is essential to achieve this goal. An AC program, well designed to portray competencies needed in the future, will provide rich data on areas of competencies demonstrated by participants as well as areas to be developed.

CULTURAL SITUATION

Indonesia is a society of more than 500 ethnic groups, each with different cultures and languages. Consequently, it is quite difficult to depict the real culture of Indonesians and how it has influenced their behavior. Indonesia has experienced a long period of colonial rule, under the Dutch for more than three centuries and under Japanese occupation for three and a half years. One of the few references on the mental attitude of Indonesians was written in 1974 by Koentjaraningrat, a professor of anthropology at the University of Indonesia. He encountered challenges in depicting the different mentalities of Indonesians, given the various ethnic groups and dialects. In general, Koentjaraningrat described the first mental attitude of Indonesians as farmers and as civil servants known as *priyayi* (deemed upper class). In 1974 84 percent of people lived in rural areas and earned a living as farmers and the rest were civil servants. As farmers, people only work to meet their basic living needs so they do not have to work hard. Civil servants work to gain happiness as manifested in high status in society, power and symbols of wealth, such as luxury homes, cars and clothing. These mental traits, according to Koentjaraningrat, do not motivate them to work hard to improve their quality of life.

The second mental attitude touches on the aspect of time, which is very limited. Life orientation is determined by the current situation, especially for farmers. For the civil servants and *priyayi*, the time aspect is determined by the past, namely reminiscing about the glorious past.

The third mental attitude is the perspective toward nature. Farmers harmonize with nature, live in accordance with nature's wish, and refrain from exploiting nature. Civil servants depend on fate which could be good or bad. A good attitude is to adapt to nature and be able to manage nature without spoiling it.

According to Koentjaraningrat, in the social aspect of relationships among human beings, farmers highly regard the concept of equality. In this world, humans cannot live alone and need each other. That is why they tend to be conformist, keep a low profile and do not exert themselves. Civil servants tend to be oriented to their superiors, those who are older, senior and with high rank. They always wait for orders from their superiors. This attitude suppresses the desire to be independent, critical, and creative.

Solidarity is also another important characteristic in the society. Members of the society help each others with high solidarity based on *pars pro toto*. This reflects in the behavior of sharing and collaboration among people.

All those mental attitudes and tendencies have an impact on how a person reacts to his or her surroundings. These tendencies are evident in the behavior of AC participants in their reactions during simulations and interviews. The next section describes the reactions of typical Indonesians to some of these assessment exercises.

Impact on the Behavior of Indonesians on ACs

The AC has been defined as a standardized procedure in which multiple assessment techniques such as situational exercises and job simulations, for example business games, group discussions, reports, and presentations, are used to evaluate individual employees for various purposes. What differentiates the AC from other psychological evaluation methods is the observation of behavioral responses by participants to the stimuli provided during the process. Based on the aforementioned description of the situation in Indonesia and experiences in the process of the AC, the need for adapting the process in Indonesia is a must. The materials used in the AC have to be modified to the environmental and cultural conditions of Indonesia. These are some of the writer's experiences as an AC provider, in applying the method designed by Development Dimensions International (DDI) which has been carried out in a number of countries, including Indonesia.

The writer has observed that in a number of simulations completed by participants, the behavior is much influenced by the mental attitude and culture of Indonesians. Behaviors in the background interview, in an in-basket or in-tray, in interactive simulations (role plays) with subordinates, colleagues, and clients, and in group discussions are all subject to these influences. Adjustments in timing and methods to deal with reading limitations have to be considered.

THE BACKGROUND INTERVIEW

In the implementation of an AC, interviews have often become part of the assessment process. The interview method described here is based on the identification of competency-aligned behaviors. The methodology entails obtaining evidence of the behavior of a person related with his or her past experiences in former work places, learning institutes, or in other daily activities.

Based on the writer's experience when conducting interviews and listening to a number of recorded interviews using this method, it is often difficult to get the complete picture of a participants' behavior relying only on what is expressed when responding to the interviewer's initial questions. The interview method is designed to assess behavioral competencies by analyzing the participant's answers in the format of STAR:

- *Situation/Task* of the particular event that the interviewee was faced with;
- *Action* that was taken by the interviewee when facing the situation or task;
- *Result* that was achieved or occurred in response to the action taken by the interviewee.

Among these, the part which often became the focus of the interview was to determine in detail what the participant was actually doing. Difficulties often arose during the interview process, especially when participants answered by using the word "we" instead of "I," thus bringing into doubt whether the person had carried out the action, or whether it also involved others in its execution. For instance, when replying to a question related to the interviewee's experience in making a particular decision, an interviewee replied: "We then contacted a number of parties related with our project to make sure that they have the material that we needed before we issued specification adjustments." If the interviewer was not careful in monitoring the answer, it would be difficult to clearly understand who had actually carried out the action. Even if there was more than one person, it is not clear what role the interviewee had played in the situation. The habit of replying with the word "we" is actually related with the culture of Indonesians who often give priority to togetherness in every activity. The togetherness has also obscured the role and responsibility of the person involved in an activity. Answering like this with the word "we" is, of course, not unique to Indonesia as people in some other countries can also be reluctant to boast, but the tendency may be more pronounced here. In Indonesia, the culture of togetherness has a strong impact on individuals when prioritizing politeness and subordinating themselves is more important and valued by the society.

However, in an AC, it is very important to be familiar with the behavior of an individual, not group behavior, although other people were also involved during the event. In such a situation, it is very important for the interviewer to ask further questions to clearly know the role of the interviewee in the situation, such as who else was involved in the activity, what was his or her role in the situation, or to explain in detail the steps he or she took in that situation. An obvious consequence of the repeated use of "we" is the need for a longer interview because the interviewer has to spend more time clarifying and asking follow-up questions.

One of the ways of trying to resolve the problem is by explaining to all participants during the early stages of the AC what will happen and what is expected of them, so they can fully present themselves during the assessment. An introductory explanation is also necessary during the rapport-building process of the interview so as to emphasize the importance that participants should provide explanations about themselves and not about the other persons in the situation.

IN-BASKET OR IN-TRAY SIMULATIONS

This is the most popular simulation but the most difficult for assessors to obtain complete evidence. Why is that so? This simulation will provide maximum information only when participants are able to clearly put their thoughts, in detail, into words as a form of response for the incoming letters or memos.

The problems that frequently arise are:

- Very short replies which are immediately directed at the solution without explaining why the action was taken. For example, a memo containing information regarding a particular request should have been immediately responded to by the participants. However, they often respond briefly by expressing the action they would take without explaining why they had taken the action.
- Delegating the item to an appointed person to follow up without any explanation why and how it should be resolved.
- Postponing the decision because the participant wished to ask his or her superior for approval.

As a result, information which could be derived from the in-basket simulation is very limited due to these three problems. Despite this, at a later time, participants are quite able to explain in detail their understanding of the issues in the in-basket.

The custom of replying in a brief manner is probably due to Indonesians' habit of not expressing their thoughts in words despite the fact that it is far more effective to express one's thoughts in written form. The wish to constantly get approval from one's superior, or those with authority, is also associated with the culture of the Indonesian people, as they feel secure if they also get approval and support from other people before carrying out their tasks. Consequently, the AC has included the debrief process, a process of trying to explore with participants what they have written when responding to items in the in-basket.

The debrief process after participants complete all in-basket items can be carried out in written or verbal form. The purpose of the debrief is to obtain detailed explanations on the participants' basic thoughts on actions and decisions. In the written debrief, participants must answer a number of questions for each item in the in-basket. A verbal debrief is conducted by an assessor using a list of questions.

Besides the adjustments carried out at the AC, adaptations are also necessary in expected standard behaviors needed to earn a high rating. The in-basket is aimed at simulating behavior related to decision-making (including analysis) and delegation, especially for items that require settlement by other related parties. Standard expected behaviors need adaptation and redefinition for Indonesia, for example in assessing the competency of delegation. A participant who is generally regarded as being capable at delegation is one who is able to share appropriate responsibilities and assign decision-making authority in appropriate areas to appropriate individuals, considering positive and negative impact, organizational values or structures and enhancement of the individual's knowledge and skills.

However, when assessing Indonesians this required standard of behavior needs adjusting, as it is related to a participants' preference for assigning work to a unit or a particular person without explanation as to why the specific person or unit is carrying out a task. Given this tendency such responses are assumed to have met the criterion as "shared appropriate responsibilities" and will gain credit as a behavioral strength when the assignment is followed up with an explanation as to why the person or unit is assigned to the job.

INTERACTIVE SIMULATIONS

This is usually one of the most interesting simulations in which to observe how an Indonesian conducts such a discussion with another person. There are several things that should be noted when observing these behavioral interactions. A longer time is needed to initiate an interaction. Indonesian culture, which places importance on the value of "tepo seliro," or thoughtfulness, often makes a discussion longer and not to the point. At times, the words expressed are full of metaphors, or words with hidden meaning. It is not easy for Indonesians to express their opinion forthrightly or to the point. This is evident in a situation in which the response of "building rapport" and introductory dialog on a current situation turns into a long conversation. Building rapport can be expressed by asking about common things, such as the current working situation, traffic conditions, or personal matters, such as their health, family, number of children and their general condition. Whereas these questions may be asked by Westerners, they are probably more prevalent and take more time in Indonesia. So, a role player in Indonesia must anticipate such questions and be prepared with answers that are quite general.

Indonesians initiate a monolog rather than a dialog. Indeed it is an interesting feature of many interactive simulations that there is little or no dialog, especially when the discussion enters its substantive phase. This is obvious particularly in an interaction with a subordinate and those with lower status than the participant. Participants, especially those aged above 40, are participants who are still used to the old education method and tend to uphold hierarchy in an organization and show they are more knowledgeable and wise. Consequently, the simulation situation between a superior (the participant) and subordinate will easily turn into a one-way conversation. Here, the participant is dominant and speaks more in the form of advice and various analogies, or metaphors, to express thoughts, without trying to ask or listen to the underling (the role player). In such a situation, the role player should be able to initiate a two-way dialog without having to redirect the discussion, as it is the job of the participant to show that he or she is able to resolve the issue being discussed. In general, the role player would say words like, "What do you mean, Sir/Madam?" or "I still don't understand. What should I do?"

The relationship between body language and what is actually said must also be considered. To reach an agreement and solution is something that everyone wishes to achieve in an interactive simulation. The problem that often arises is the lack of a clear statement on an agreed position. In the same situation in Western countries, an agreement is marked by a response that is expressed directly at the end of a dialog that it has been mutually agreed. It is quite difficult to find a clear behavior indicating mutual agreement in Indonesia. The word "yes," or "okay" at the end of the conversation is often regarded as an affirmative. Body movements, such as a head bow, smile and hand shake, might appear to suggest agreement has been reached. However, this could be misleading as Indonesians always smile and bow their head to show their friendly nature, even when there is no agreement. To clarify the matter, participants and role players are required to fill out debrief questionnaires on their expectations from the interactive simulation, actions taken and the final conclusion achieved, so as to help assessors ascertain the extent of the agreement or agreements reached.

In general, based on the writer's experience, apart from the aforementioned factors, the implementation of an interactive simulation takes longer than what is required in some Western countries, where a dialog may reach agreement in 10–15 minutes. This is especially true for interactive simulations carried out at the junior to middle management level. Based on our experience, the time needed for each interaction to hold a dialog and reach agreement is 15 minutes. With an additional time of 5 minutes for preparation, the total time needed for an interactive simulation is 20 minutes. Of course, some complex interactive simulations require more time.

TIME NEEDED TO ABSORB WRITTEN MATERIAL

The education pattern in Indonesia, which tends toward being a one-way approach in providing information and instruction, has caused AC participants to be less inclined to look for learning materials and reading the materials provided to them. The lack of direct experience in reading and analyzing book contents has caused them to be slow in absorbing written material. Although the teaching method in the past 10 years has mostly adapted to the active teaching model, it has yet to have an impact on AC participants, most of whom are above the age of 30 and experienced the old teaching methods in their school days.

Current technological advancements have reduced people's reading skills. They prefer to seek information from film and television. This will further inhibit a person in absorbing written information. Participants in an AC require a relatively long period of time to grasp written materials. A higher level of concentration is needed to understand the background information of a fictitious company depicted in a "A Day in a Life" simulation. In this simulation a participant is asked to read and understand the background details of the company before being involved and able to play a role in various simulations designed as part of the daily activities of a manager or senior executive.

To overcome the situation, ACs often provide participants with pictures, tables and diagrams to facilitate the interpretation of any reading materials. The adjustments are made not only by providing different presentations on reading materials, but also by giving additional time to absorb such materials. The same is also true for other exercises that require considerable time to understand the content before tackling the task, such as in-baskets, analysis and strategic planning exercises.

Conclusions

The presence of the Assessment Center is of great importance, especially if adjustments have been made to achieve the desired target. The adjustments may include various aspects of the AC method:

1. The center must make time adjustments. Based on the explanations above, the time needed to conduct a comprehensive program is longer compared with that in Western countries; the time difference could be as much as three hours in a "day in a life" assessment program. Adjustments in implementation procedures, in which extra activities, such as briefing and/or debriefing, at the start or end of a simulation are needed to ensure that participants provide the most informative responses.
2. Simulation content and material must be adjusted. For example, in an interactive simulation, role players should be given detailed guidelines to ensure answers to questions which are often not in line with topics being discussed, especially relating with personal issues of the role players. Besides that, the background material of fictitious companies, which is a crucial part of a "Day in a life" program, should include visual aids to make it quicker and easier to absorb.
3. Assessors must understand and agree with the standard behaviors which show whether the participant has complied with, exceeded, or failed to reach the performance criteria. The assessor and assessment program initiator need to agree on the behaviors that are likely to occur and need to be included in the rating categories.
4. Include AC participants and data users as an integral part of efforts to further improve and ensure that the programs serve as a stimulant to instigate behaviors for assessment and determine the relevance of the simulations with the tasks of the participants in their daily work.

The AC method has been proven to be a valuable HR intervention to address critical unique aspects of the history, culture, and political situation in Indonesia over the past 20 years. ACs bring a needed transparency to HR functions in commercial and government organizations. ACs also help organizations, especially their top management, to make fair and objective decisions about talent by using AC data as part of their decision-making process. At the same time, participants who experienced ACs also see this process as providing a relevant insight to the contextual leadership of a particular organization and they are more receptive to the use of managerial simulations being used to predict their potential as a manager, rather than psychometric tests.

Finally, writing a local set of AC guidelines has been an effective way of gaining consensus on the proper implementation of ACs in Indonesia. Adjustments to the essential elements of the method have made ACs more effective.

References

Bastaman, F. 1992. *Application and Development of Assessment Center in Indonesia*. Presented for the 20th International Congress on Assessment Center Method, Williamsburg, Virginia, USA, 19–22 May 1992.

International Task Force on Assessment Center Guidelines. 2009. Guidelines and ethical considerations for assessment center operations. *International Journal of Selection and Assessment*, 17, 243–254.

Koentjaraningrat. 2007. *Manusia dan Kebudayaan di Indonesia* [*The People and Cultures in Indonesia*]. Jakarta: Penerbit Djambatan.

Koentjaraningrat. 1985. *Kebudayaan, Mentalitas dan Pembangunan* [*Culture, Mentality and Development*]. Jakarta: PT Gramedia.

Marzali, A. 2005. *Antropologi & Pembangunan Indonesia* [*Anthropology and Indonesia's Development*]. Jakarta: Prenada Media.

Naskah Pernyataan Berhenti President Soeharto [Resignation Statement of President Soeharto]. 21 May 1998. Arsip Nasional.

25 *Variations in Assessment Centers in South Korea's Public Service*

MYUNGJOON KIM

The assessment center (AC) method originated in the Second World War and has spread across the world over the last 50 years (Chapter 11, Thornton in this volume). It has been used as a group decision-making process for objective selection and promotion in private enterprises and government organizations, and more recently for developing individual competencies such as leadership.

Researchers and practitioners have been developing assessment centers (AC) and development centers (DC) for many purposes in different parts of the world and this raises the question of how elements of the AC method should be modified or reconstructed when it is used in new countries. At its simplest, one can say that the AC method has to be adjusted to the cultural aspects of each new country and this means it is necessary to understand the relationship between elements of the AC method and the unique features of cultural characteristics. However, conducting the necessary research is problematic. It would be difficult to obtain enough resources (such as time, money, and access to ACs in organizations) as well to exert adequate control of the variables in the AC method, to execute such a study. Therefore, it might be beneficial to focus on how the AC is actually used in other countries.

This chapter will examine the geographical and political context of South Korea, within which the ACs have been developed, and describe four recent case studies of ACs in the central and local government. It concludes with some general observations of the use of ACs for selection and development.

Unique Characteristics of South Korea

For over 5,000 years, the Korean agricultural history has greatly influenced the South Korean economy. With a clear solar term of 24 divisions of the year in the Korean peninsula, farmers could easily cultivate their lands in ways which directly led to success in farming. To be successful in farming, farmers had to be diligent; they had to repeat planting and harvesting based on the solar calendar each year. This unique characteristic naturally led Korean people to live a "quick and fast" lifestyle. This natural tendency to work at a fast pace was one major factor in the rapid growth of the South Korean economy.

Along with the agricultural system, the Korean society traditionally was divided into classes. In Korean agricultural society, farmers were highly regarded as a source of the economic base. Therefore, administrative officers who supervised the key industries in the country were considered among the top government employees, followed by farmers, technicians, merchants, and artisans. This division of classes in the past still has an effect on organizations in South Korea today. Most Korean people focus on social norms behind certain jobs instead of individual interests. Moreover, since the system of rank order is socially established from the past up to the present day, employers have great authority in selection and promotion processes.

Other than just the factors of geographical location and social class, there were two unique cultural characteristics that also helped the South Korean economy: the Korean War and "Chaebol." After the Korean War in the 1950s, people had to rebuild everything from nothing. The economic system had collapsed, and there were no resources to make enough gross national product to revive the economy. The Korean sovereign credit rating had fallen to the bottom. At that time, Korea was one of the poorest countries in the world, and the national income per head was around US$67. The Korean War divided the country into two different nations with two different regimes. Although North and South Korea share the same language and historical origin, they have been two different countries for the last 60 years. This division in the Korean peninsula led to unique government systems in both countries for decades after the Korean War, namely "military governments." With an unstable national security, military regimes were able to get involved and hold political power. In the decades from the 1950s to the 1980s, the military strongly influenced the political, economic, and organizational systems, which endorsed the fast-paced, class-based, collective culture in South Korea.

With a pro-democracy movement and modernization, the military regime made an average 9.67 percent rate of economic growth, and national sales improved up to 455 times. Of course, there are still many controversial debates about president Park Jung Hee's 18 years of dictatorship with the military government from 1961 to 1979, yet there is no doubt that it was the era in which the base of the South Korean economic system developed.

As the economy grew, the Chaebol became one of the main factors that led to rapid growth in private enterprises. A Chaebol is a South Korean conglomerate, usually owned by a single family, based on authoritarian management and centralized decision-making. A Chaebol is a special arrangement found in the South Korean economic system when compared to other countries. Unique characteristics of the political and economic systems led to the growth of the Chaebols, which in turn took a primary role in contributing to rapid economic growth of South Korea over a 20-year period.

Historical cultural characteristics may have faded in the Korean social atmosphere, yet they have not completely disappeared. Current characteristics of organizations clearly reflect the cultural uniqueness of South Korea.

Human Resource Systems in the Public Sector

Public officials in South Korea are organized into nine different grades: grade-9 public official is the lowest position and grade-1 to grade-3 public officials are the highest positions and are named Senior Executive Service officers. Grade-5 officials (called deputy directors) are the middle-level manager position. To become a grade-5 deputy director, candidates must pass the administration exam. In 2010, the administration exam selected 240 people and the diplomat exam selected 39 people. Candidates undergo very intensive competition to pass: the selection ratio is 60:1 for the administration exam, and 300:1 for the diplomat exam. The administration exam includes general content, which requires government officials to have various work experiences in the government, but the content of the exam is not specific to any one specific job or department.

As described above, South Korea is a generalist society in a collectivist culture. Furthermore, social networks based on one's birth-origin or region play an important role. These cultural tendencies have influenced the selection and promotion system. Deeply rooted geographical and political factors have influenced how this generalist society has become organized.

In the following sections, four case studies are presented which illustrate how the AC has been implemented in organizations that reflect the unique characteristics of the South Korean culture. For each case study, the job and purpose of the AC will be described, along with the key elements of the AC process such as competencies, exercises, and assessors.

Ministry of Public Administration and Security (MOPAS)

The AC for the Senior Executive Service was first introduced to the Ministry of Public Administration and Security (MOPAS) in June 2006 to enhance its evaluation system. This is part of a system that promotes section heads to become Senior Executive Service officers. The Ministry (formerly The Civil Service Commission) organized the AC method by benchmarking various foreign governments, especially SELEX's Assessment Center of Canada. Based on this information, the Ministry adopted the AC as a reliable and fair tool to select qualified candidates.

Furthermore, reflecting the results of the AC, a model for the development of senior level officials was formed to guide their education and training. In this way, the relevance of senior level public officials would be confirmed by using the AC. Through these changes, the AC method contributes to the improvement of government administration of senior level public officials, and it is expected to increase the productivity and the economic growth of the Korean government with fair promotion systems.

COMPETENCIES

Competencies for the MOPAS AC were defined during experts' meetings based on the competency modeling, job analysis, and benchmarking of previous programs. Competencies are grouped into three categories: thinking, task performance, and relationships. To allow these competencies to be easily applied to all ministries, they were generated to reflect behaviors generally expected from all senior level officials rather than any specific job. In March 2009, nine initial competencies were trimmed to six, and the simulations were reorganized into four simulations according to feedback from assessors, candidates, and experts during the first two and a half years of operation. See Table 25.1

Table 25.1   Competencies in the Ministry of Public Administration and Security AC

	Competency	Definition of competency
Thinking	Problem analysis	Identify and understand the problem through the analysis of information and investigate the key factor of the problem.
	Strategic thinking	Set up a goal and long-term vision and determine a plan to be carried out based on the order of priority.
Task performance	Goal oriented	Establish various plans to maximize the result of given tasks, and pursue efficiency and effectiveness in the process of achieving a goal.
	Managing change	Understand the directions and situations of environmental changes, and manage individuals and organization to adopt and adjust appropriately.
Relationships	Customer satisfaction	Recognize others related to the task as customers and understand their desires and try to fulfill their needs.
	Conflict management	Understand relations and conflicts among people and suggest reasonable solution in balanced perspective.

SIMULATION EXERCISES

In order for candidates to be considered for the Senior Executive Service, they are assessed in four exercises that simulate important aspects of the job. The exercises are a one to one role play, a one to two role play, an In-basket, and a leaderless group discussion. See Table 25.2.

Table 25.2   Exercises in the Ministry of Public Administration and Security AC

Exercise	Description	Time
One-to-one role play (1:1)	Interview with a reporter in order to take action on a pending issue. Presentation on a task measure, coaching subordinates, and so on.	Preparation: 30 minutes Execution: 30 minutes
One-to-two role play (1:2)	Situation that requires overlapping tasks among different departments to be resolved.	Preparation: 30 minutes Execution: 30 minutes
In-basket	Situation that requires handling multiple tasks within a certain period of time.	Preparation: 50 minutes Execution: 30 minutes
Leaderless Group discussion	Situation that requires coordination and collective agreement on common issues among departments.	Preparation: 40 minutes Execution: 50 minutes

ASSESSORS

The MOPAS has been issuing certificates to those who completed the two-day assessor training in order to develop a pool of qualified assessors. Since August 2008, 155 trained assessors have been certified: 94 are former senior level officials, such as managing section heads, who serve as internal assessors; the other 61 assessors are external assessors, including professors and practitioners with psychological backgrounds from areas such as industrial/organizational psychology, public administration, and human resources in business administration.

The assessors are mainly males over 45 years of age. This reflects the characteristics of society and the average age of the Senior Executive Service officers. In response to the strong effect of the Confucian ideas, women entered the workplace relatively later than men, and women comprise less than ten percent of the Senior Executive Service, according to statistics from 2008.

ASSESSMENT PROCEDURE

The AC is operated at various sites. Seven assessors evaluate six candidates per day. The performance of any given participant is observed by only five of the seven assessors. The other assessors attend the integration meeting and contribute to the evaluation. From June 2006 to December 2010, 2,022 candidates were assessed in 337 ACs.

RATING SCALE

The AC employs a 1–5 rating scale, and legislation would be required to change the scale. Candidates who receive an average rating of 2.5 or higher pass the assessment. Central tendency may influence the reliability and fairness of evaluations. Unlike behaviorally anchored rating scales which provide standards to judge the different levels of behavior, the rating scale only provides a list of expected positive and negative behaviors. This may cause differences among assessors.

INTEGRATION MEETING

This AC operates as a group decision-making process. All assessors, including the five assessors who observed the candidate's behavior and the two assessors who didn't officially observe the candidate, contribute to the evaluation. Thus when assessing each candidate, all seven assessors evaluate the candidate in the integration meeting even though only the assigned five assessors actually observed the exercises.

CUT-OFF RATE

Only 15–20 percent of candidates are eliminated. It seems as if the emphasis is on eliminating candidates who appear to lack the competencies of a senior level public official rather than selecting the most qualified and outstanding candidates. This tendency is due to a preference for paternalism, rather than making objective decisions in determining who is not promoted in South Korea.

VALIDITY OF THE ASSESSMENT CENTER AND CANDIDATE SATISFACTION

As the AC has continued, positive feedback from those entering the Senior Executive Service through the ACs is increasing. A survey was conducted of the candidates who had been involved in the ACs for three years (2006–2008). The result was positive: 96 percent of the subjects responded that the AC's tasks reflect the actual work in the field and situations encountered by public officials (that is, the AC had high fidelity), and 99.3 percent said that the method is both reliable and fair.

Since the government has taken a lead in managing the ACs in South Korea, other departments and local organizations are benchmarking the process. The AC method of the Senior Executive Service is used as a standard when other departments adopt and manage the AC method.

Ministry of Foreign Affairs and Trade (MOFAT)

Legislation was passed to improve the Ministry of Foreign Affairs and Trade (MOFAT) for the purpose of improving the competencies of Foreign Affairs' officials. As a part of this effort, an AC was set up to develop the competencies.

The AC for MOFAT is organized by The Office of Diplomatic Competency Assessment (ODCA) which is affiliated with The Institute of Foreign Affairs and National Security (IFANS). The ODCA is composed of a total of nine officers who are directly positioned under the chief of the IFANS. Team members include a counselor, team leader, and five secretaries; they are supervised by the chief of the ODCA. They execute the AC/DC for evaluating and promoting candidates for senior Foreign Service officers and section chiefs of MOFAT.

Duties of the MOFAT are different from those of other domestic general public organizations. To perform these duties, employees in this Ministry are expected to have special abilities and qualifications compared to those in any other public ministries, because they carry out tasks based on the culture, language, ways of thinking, systems, customs, and diplomatic understanding of the country of sojourn. For example, although there may be distinctions among different positions in the Ministry, the AC focuses on the ability to understand the values and needs of different cultures and to create a cooperative atmosphere working with officials of various countries of sojourn and international organizations.

Councilors not only have to manage or administer all the business as a middle manager in the organization but also have to guide subordinates toward productive outcomes. Thus, the AC for councilors has expectations regarding performance in these areas. Likewise, the AC for ministers evaluates competencies that one must possess as senior level public officials.

COMPETENCIES

The ODCA evaluates candidates against six competencies split into two groups. The diplomatic competency group includes Building Relationships with Foreign Countries, Negotiation Skills, and Managing Crises and Critical Situations. The diplomatic competencies are used for both middle-level management and senior-level executive ACs. The management competency group includes Strategic Thinking Skills, Performance Management, and Coordinating/Integrating Skills. The management competencies are further specified for each of two levels: for middle-level management positions, the competencies include Performance Management, Conflict Management, and Human Resource Development; for senior-level executive positions, the competencies include Strategic Thinking, Change Management, and Coordinating/Integrating Skills.

SIMULATION EXERCISES

The six competencies have been assessed by six different simulations: an In-basket exercise, a one to one role play, a one to two role play, a presentation, a leaderless group discussion, and an interview. These simulations are similar to the AC for the Ministry of Public Administration and Security (MOPAS). Some changes have been made in 2010, in terms of which competencies are assessed in the various simulations.

Assessment of councilors (middle level) and ministers (senior-level public officials) involves appropriate assessment methods according to the particular position's job characteristics and particular competencies that are measured. Table 25.3 lists simulation exercises used in the ACs for the councilor and minister candidates.

Simulations in this AC have higher fidelity compared to those of other departments. These simulations are based on special situations or specific case files of foreign businesses, rather than the general work environment of public officials. The typical content of the simulations consists of political and governmental affairs, consular representation, economy/trade, and cultural diplomacy.

Table 25.3   Assessment method according to job positions

Councilor candidates	Minister candidates
In-basket	One-to-one role play (1:1)
Presentation	One-to-two role play (1:2)
One-to-one role play (1:1)	Presentation
	Analysis exercise

ASSESSORS

In most ministries, assessors came from a diverse range of backgrounds, including professors of industrial/organizational psychology, business administration, and public administration, consulting practitioners, former ministers, and current senior-level officials. On the other hand, the assessors at MOFAT are chosen mainly from former ambassadors owing to distinct Foreign Service situations. Current departmental heads would sometimes participate in the ACs in some departments; however, the MOFAT prefers retired ambassadors as assessors. In general, the assessor pool was composed of around 100 potential assessors.

For this process, the Institute of Foreign Affairs and National Security gives retired ambassadors a title "assessment center ambassador" and manages these assessors. The retired ambassadors participating in the AC are actively involved in the construction of simulations. Retired ambassadors also help select simulation topics and provide feedback on the simulations to improve their quality.

ASSESSOR TRAINING

There is no doubt about the need for capable assessors as well as suitable simulations in order to conduct an effective AC. Thus high priority is placed on selecting and training appropriate assessors for any AC in Korea. Assessors are typically trained for 2 days to learn about the assessors' role. The government has been training assessors for ACs since 2006, when it started using ACs to promote Executive Service officers. However, the government had great difficulty in conducting this training, owing to the lack of experience of running ACs.

PROCEDURE

The AC for senior Foreign Service officer positions in MOFAT is held regularly twice a year to accommodate diplomats who work all over the world. In addition, because there is a small assembly, specifically for the MOFAT AC, assessment can take place anytime. ACs for councilors and ministers take place when there are a sufficient number of applicants. However, generally a total of 25–30 applicants are assessed per day over a 5-day period.

City of Seoul Public Official Assessment

The first AC to promote Senior Executive Service officers in 2006 influenced local governments in Korea. For many years, Seoul used written knowledge tests to make promotion decisions. But in 2007, Seoul decided to use the AC method, and it started to use ACs in 2008 to promote lower-level employees to grade-5 deputy director.

In Korea, there are three different national examinations: Foreign Service examination, Bar examination, and Civil Service examination. Among them, the Civil Service examination is a test to select candidates in order to achieve effective and rational public administration. If a candidate passes this exam, he or she will become a deputy director (classed as a grade-5 official on the 9-grade hierarchical system). However, without taking the Civil Service exam, there had to be another way to promote grade-6 officials to grade-5. There are 800 to 900 candidates each year for this promotion. Among those candidates, about 200 are promoted to a grade-5 official. About 100 out of these 200 are promoted based on their past records by superiors, and the rest of the candidates have to go through the AC.

Seoul is the capital city of South Korea with a population of over 10 million, and it has the biggest budget among all local governments. Grade-5 deputy directors of Seoul are in charge of planning and supervising major administration policies in 46 departments, each of which is composed of 5 to 10 team members. These team members work cooperatively with other departments. Thus, grade-5 deputy directors' performance and abilities can both directly and indirectly influence over 10 million Seoul citizens.

The former promotion system consisted mainly of a written examination that tested basic knowledge. The test consisted of multiple-choice questions, and people who got high scores were promoted. Candidates prepared for the test at private institutes or at libraries during office hours; sometimes they spent 6 months to 1 year preparing for the test. This type of exam has been in use for the last 50 years, not only in Seoul, but also in many other local municipalities. This raised many controversial social and ethical issues. For that reason, Seoul developed a competency-based assessment system in 2008 to diverge from the knowledge-based appraisal system. The new system prevents people from neglecting their work to prepare for the test.

Seoul redesigned the team leader's promotion system to train the Global Top Ten of talented people by promoting those who concentrate on work, generate high achievement, and possess potential competence as a section head. Introduction and implementation of the AC method in Seoul has been highly praised as a paradigm shift of the promotion method for local government public officers. The method has become a benchmark for many other local governments.

COMPETENCIES

Before implementing the AC, Seoul developed a competency model for grade-5 deputy directors. The competency model is divided into two parts, namely general competencies and assessed competencies, as shown in Table 25.4.

Table 25.4   Competency model of grade-5 deputy section head of Seoul

General competencies	Assessed competencies
• Professionalism • Public Official Ethics	• Policy Plan • Mission • Management • Mediation • Communication • Creating Teamwork

General competencies consist of Professionalism and Public Official Ethics, which are common competencies expected from all public officials; these general competencies are excluded from the AC for grade-5. The six assessed competencies are each composed of two or three sub-competencies; for example, Communication is made up of Active Listening, and Effectively Delivering an Opinion.

EXERCISES

AC exercises used for the Seoul Public Official Assessment include an In-basket, a role play, and a case study which represent the regular work of a grade-5 deputy director. Because the assessment for the grade-5 deputy director promotion is very competitive, various factors could have strong influences on the AC results. The content of exercises can give some candidates an advantage (or disadvantage) over others. Considering this problem, when designing simulations for grade-5 promotions, simulations must be set in organizations other than the city of Seoul itself. Thus the simulation exercises in the Seoul AC must pursue a public interest, have various jobs and businesses and have organized groups, teams, budgets, and so forth, similar to those of Seoul, but must not actually be from Seoul.

In addition, the simulations need to be modified after every trial for confidentiality reasons. A simulation that was used once for a promotional exam turned out to be a pre-exam form in many private educational institutes or in private lessons. Although most of the candidates are aware of the fact that private lessons for ACs are not so effective after all, there are still private lessons and educational institutes available for candidates who seek to achieve better scores.

Although the three assessment exercises were chosen because they are good methods to assess attributes required for the target jobs, they were also selected to ease the administrative burden of the Seoul AC for grade-5 deputy director. This screening process has to assess about 200 applicants at a time, and the exercises need to be completed in 3 days. Thus, assessment methods such as a written exercise that can be completed by a large group of about 200 applicants are appropriate. The use of time-intensive methods such as presentations, other individual tasks, and group discussions are relatively limited.

CANDIDATES

The grade-5 deputy director takes on many roles. To manage administrative tasks, 5–10 people are chosen as a team, who cooperatively work with other departments. They supervise the work of departmental colleagues. Although there are some variations based on their duties and initial levels, employees (grade-9) working for local governments in Korea generally take about 20–25 years to be promoted to grade-5 deputy director. Consequently, at least 65 percent of the grade-5 officials are aged about 50. Grade-5 deputy director candidates who first started off as grade-9 employees all yearn to be promoted because grade-5 is the highest level they can reach; this is an ideal level from which to retire. Driven by this desire, candidates have generally taken both the former promotion test and the current AC very seriously.

PROCEDURE

The Seoul AC for promoting candidates to grade-5 deputy director has been run twice a year since 2009. No specific unit was assigned to take charge of the AC; therefore a Task Force Team has been organized for this purpose. Owing to the specific challenge that the Seoul AC has to assess a large number of people in a short period of time, a one-week schedule is followed as shown in Table 25.5.

Table 25.5 Seoul Assessment Center schedule

Day	Candidates	Assessors	
1	All candidates complete In-basket: 120 minutes		
2		Rate In-basket and prepare for interview	
3		Rate In-basket and prepare for interview	
4	All candidates complete Case Study: 240 minutes	Rate In-basket and prepare for interview	
5	1st class completes Role Play and follow-up Interview for In-basket	Some assessors conduct Role Play and follow-up Interview for In-basket	Some assessors rate Case Study
6	2nd class completes Role Play and follow-up Interview for In-basket		
7	3rd class completes Role Play and follow-up Interview for In-basket		

As a group, all candidates complete the written exercises on the same day: the In-basket on Day 1 and the Case Study on Day 4. The assessors evaluate the In-basket and prepare for the follow-up Interview on the In-basket on Days 2, 3, and 4. On Day 4, the candidates complete the Case Study. Then on either Day 5, 6, or 7, classes of candidates complete the Role Play and answer questions in the follow-up Interview on the In-basket. Candidates are divided into three classes and assessed on the Role Play that has different content on Days 5, 6, and 7. The content of the Role Play is different from one class to another so as to maintain security. Some assessors evaluate the Role Play and In-basket Interview on Days 5, 6, and 7, while other assessors rate the Case Study.

THREE STRIKES OUT SYSTEM

In Seoul, the "three strikes out system" limits the promotion possibilities to the grade-5 deputy director to no more than three ACs. This policy addresses the concern of candidates who argue about validity of the assessment and the management of assignments. Some candidates want a second chance after they have failed. Since 2008, the AC has been conducted over four times and no lawsuit case has yet been filed.

CANDIDATE ORIENTATION

The AC for grade-5 deputy director provides a one and a half-day orientation. Candidates have anxiety over the AC, because they are taking part in something very different from what has been used for over 60 years to determine promotions. Thus, the purpose of the orientation is to explain the purpose, validity, and assessment methods, thereby reducing the candidates' nervousness. In addition, the orientation provides an opportunity for candidates to practice and become familiar with AC exercises.

ASSESSORS AND RATING CRITERION

Because the AC of Seoul evaluates a large group of people in a short period of time, many assessors are needed. The assessors are professors and practitioners with psychology backgrounds. Assessors are divided into two groups to evaluate the In-basket and the role play exercises. Retired government officers above grade-3 (above the general section head level) join each group to form groups of three and rate the case study exercises. Assessor training provides information about the purpose, the duration of assessment, rating system, and other matters. Frame of reference training (Schleicher, Day, Mayes and Riggio 2002) is carried out on the day of the assessment in order to maintain security.

Assessors use behaviorally anchored rating scales which are relatively new in Korean ACs. The standard is needed to calibrate the rating level among assessors because 50 to 60 assessors evaluate competencies of around 200 candidates. In order to standardize the rating scales, Seoul provides an assessment anchor for each competency to enhance the credibility among assessors. Thus, anchors for each sub-competency are provided in order to increase assessor reliability.

AWARENESS OF THE ASSESSMENT METHOD

Seoul introduced ACs in 2006. There was resistance to AC methods at the beginning; however, there is a growing tendency to accept the new ACs. Many candidates are still unfamiliar with the AC method and they show some dissatisfaction about this promotion process. Candidates prefer to decrease the weight of AC results in the promotion system from 100 percent to 40–60 percent or switch to a pass or fail type of examination.

Central Officials Training Institute (COTI)

The Central Officials Training Institute is a training facility that is a part of Public Administration. COTI is responsible for (a) training national public officials, (b) supporting and cooperating with education and training agencies at every grade of public officials, (c) researching, developing, and supplying education materials and techniques, and (d) providing foreign public officials educational training and international cooperation. The senior officials system was introduced in July of 2006. COTI applies a Developmental Assessment Center (DAC) program to examine an individual's competencies through simulation exercises that are composed of work conditions and problem-solving activities. Feedback leads to a detailed self-development plan. The DAC was reorganized into a participant-oriented system called participative training; it involves simulation exercises, feedback, and consultation with experts. It includes high ranking public officials, section heads, grade-5 officials, and so on. The purpose of COTI is to improve participants' developmental assessment. It specifically emphasizes the importance of feedback, cooperative education, and participative training.

COMPETENCIES

Competencies that are used in this process for high-ranking public officials and section chiefs are the same as competencies used by Public Administration. Therefore, there are no differences in the competencies for assessment centers and development centers. The competencies for grade-5 promotion participants are shown in Table 25.6.

Table 25.6   COTI grade-5 competency model

Role	Competency	Content
Policy Maker	Task Planning/ Organizing	Participants propose new policies that reflect major Issues and trends in related fields, and generate professional and detailed reports that effectively deliver core concept.
	Problem Analysis	Participants examine and prevent potential problems before passing policies and start working on the project. Moreover, they constantly check and administer the starting process, and resolve or suggest solutions to any obstacle they may encounter.
Task Performer	Information Management	Participants promptly collect and analyze data, and they diagnose the present condition based on collected data.
	Initiative in Task Performance	Participants consistently strive for a better outcome by engaging in work with strong responsibility on a given task.
Task Coordinator	Cooperation and Support	Participants are able to earn active collaboration and support whenever needed by always maintaining a cooperative relationship.
Teamwork Expeditor	Teamwork Oriented	Participants provide links among superiors and subordinates, and they stimulate teamwork promotion and voluntary cooperation for effective task performance among departments.

EXERCISES

COTI uses In-basket, role play, presentation, and group discussion exercises to assess high ranking public official participants and section head participants in order to develop and improve competencies.

PROCEDURE

On the basis of the data collected in 2010, the DAC was implemented 13 times per year (with 250 candidates) for Senior Executive Service, and 19 times per year (with 456 candidates) for section head. Groups of 12 to 15 participants participate in the group training activities. The training includes theory, simulation practice in the necessary competencies for each position, facilitator and co-participants' feedback, and written self-development plans.

In the one hour of theory training, people learn about the definition of each competency and the DAC method applied to it. They then practice in simulations and receive feedback from colleagues and facilitators. Through feedback, people identify their strengths and weaknesses, and determine ideas for competency development. Lastly, participants write self-development plans to constantly improve their competencies in the future.

FACILITATORS

Two to three facilitators participate in each DAC. Facilitators are responsible for providing information on theory, simulations, and feedback. Previous and present grade-5 section heads, professors from the central official training institute, or private experts take the role of facilitator. They must be certified in both written and simulation trainings in order to be qualified to appraise participants in the DAC program.

Facilitators need to have not only an understanding of the competencies and exercises in the program, but also the skills to observe, record, classify, and evaluate behaviors, and to give feedback to participants. However, the DAC trains so many participants at once that it is hard to provide the desired level of individually based feedback.

COMPETENCIES

The competencies are used for both assessment and training purposes because the DAC is used for practice. However, the competencies of the DAC are used in different ways from the competencies of assessment, because the purpose of training competencies for development is different from the measurement standards for competencies in assessment.

FEEDBACK

To provide feedback in the competency development program, two facilitators are included in a 20-people class. However, two facilitators cannot provide precise feedback to all 20 participants immediately, so before facilitators give feedback, each colleague provides feedback for each other first.

After the participants have completed the exercises, behavioral feedback is provided by their peers and the facilitators. Facilitators offer feedback on points that may improve participants' behavior. However, in the case of self-development plans, there is not much enduring change because no one gives any feedback if the participant does not carry out the plan in their current work once the training is over.

PARTICIPANTS' MOTIVATION

The DAC was first introduced to prepare individuals for the new promotion system (that is, the assessment center) of Senior Executive Service and section head. Therefore, participants have a stronger desire to build experiences before taking an actual AC, rather than the desire to develop their competencies. It is important to note that participants need to have motivation to develop their competencies, and facilitators have to encourage them. However, the DAC of COTI is a little behind on providing directions. Thus, it is necessary to decide whether to schedule the DAC before the AC as usual or to do it after the AC.

Conclusions

The experiences with the assessment center method in South Korea leads to some conclusions about the use of the method for selection/promotion and for development.

The short history of the method in South Korea took place mainly in the public sector. Lessons have been learned that suggest the method will be used for many more years.

SELECTION AND PROMOTION

Assessment centers were first introduced in 2006 when the government's high-ranking public official system was first implemented. However, even though the actual implementation of the system was late, the Korean government actually organized a team to prepare for ACs in 2003 and benchmarked various methods from foreign countries. Even though much was learned from others' experiences and the basic elements of the method were adopted (International Task Force on Assessment Center Guidelines 2009), adaptations were made to work in the unique features of the South Korean culture and business environment.

Because of a shortage, and even absence, of experts, it became necessary to use many employees such as administrators and assessors to not only evaluate about 300 high ranking public officials, but also to manage the ACs each year. Thus, there were trials and errors due to running the project without having well-trained experts. The lesson is that people who are responsible for any AC program need enough resources in order to perform well, such as financial, personnel, references, guidelines, and so on.

In South Korea, the AC method is widely used for promotions in the government, but the amount of actual competition in the programs may be low. The elimination rate for members of the Senior Executive Service is 15 percent, and that for section heads is about 17 percent. Such percentages may defeat the screening purpose of the AC, but this can be attributed to paternalism and nepotism: the process eliminates those low in productivity rather than selecting those high in productivity.

The government has taken the lead in using ACs in Korea. ACs are used in both the public sector and the private sector in many other countries; however, the use of ACs in Korea is largely limited to government departments and related institutes. This pattern is due to the fact that private businesses make decisions for promotion using the traditional appraisal system based on past performance rather than predicted future performance.

The competition for positions as public officials in Korea has always been fierce, and such competition is still growing today. Before ACs were introduced to the country, promotions depended on knowledge-based tests. As a result, chunks of unnecessary knowledge were acquired. Candidates' desire to make a good impression on one's superior continues to be strong.

DEVELOPMENT

Most participants in developmental assessment centers regard it as a practice tool to prepare for their promotion rather than to evaluate and develop their competencies. Their motivation tends to lie more on how they are going to earn most points in their AC which can greatly affect promotion decisions. In order to control or change this attitude and motivation, DACs should take place after promotion and selection decisions have been made.

The DAC, ideally designed for development purposes, is used for different positions and has different methods compared with ACs. They give feedback that is supposedly related to promotion and selection. However, the Korean DAC is often conducted under poor conditions with two or three facilitators for a group of 20 people. Thus, assessors cannot complete their duties of observing, documenting, categorizing, maintaining peace, and integrating. Furthermore, because colleagues and assessors are involved in the process of feedback in an open space environment, the content of feedback is somewhat limited. An effort to correct the problems listed above continues.

Assessment centers and development centers are still in their infancy in South Korea. They have some unique features in their formation and process. This does not mean it is impossible to apply these methods in the Korean culture. As many other assessment tools do, the AC/DC has an immense potential in Korea, if they can keep blending with the country's culture, language, and so forth. More research and development is crucial.

References

International Task Force on Assessment Center Guidelines. 2009. Guidelines and ethical considerations for assessment center operations. *International Journal of Selection and Assessment*, 17, 243–254.

Schleicher, D.J., Day, D.V., Mayes, B.T. and Riggio, R.E. 2002. A new frame-of-reference training: Enhancing the construct validity of assessment centers. *Journal of Applied Psychology*, 87, 735–746.

26 The Contribution of Assessment Centres to the Selection and Development of Future Leaders in the Singapore Public Service

GLENN J. NOSWORTHY AND EE-LING NG

This chapter provides a brief overview on the use of the assessment centre (AC) method in the public service of the Republic of Singapore. Singapore provides an interesting context because of its unique blend of Asian and Western cultures, its strong commitment to the merit principle, and its highly competitive educational system. While there are aspects of the setting that are unique to Singapore, we also believe that there are worthwhile lessons to be derived from our experience that will resonate with practitioners working in other settings.

We begin the chapter by offering some relevant background information on Singapore and its public service followed by brief descriptions of four ACs with which we have had some involvement. We then discuss some of the challenges that AC professionals may face in the Singapore context and close by highlighting some of the lessons we have learned along the way during our more than ten years of work in this area. Throughout the chapter we will draw upon the four 'exemplar' ACs that we have described.

Setting the Scene: Singapore and the Singapore Civil Service

Based on 2010 population data (Singapore Department of Statistics 2011), Singapore is a small nation (710 km²) with a population of almost 5 million, of which 36 per cent are foreigners employed in various sectors. It is a multi-racial and multi-religious society that has become increasingly cosmopolitan and urbanised over the years. There are four official languages: English, Mandarin, Malay and Tamil, although English is the primary medium of education and the common language used for business.

Despite its short history, Singapore has achieved a strong international standing with a reputation for political stability, effective governance, and business competitiveness. Without any natural resources, it has built its success by integrating into the global economy and this is reflected in its global mindset, pro-business stance and liberalized immigration policies. The development of the nation has been supported by a forward-looking, efficient, and capable public service.

The Singapore Public Service comprises about 124,000 officers serving in 15 Ministries and over 50 Statutory Boards. Ministries enjoy a high degree of autonomy and flexibility to manage their own human resources although they operate under the personnel policies set out by the Public Service Division (PSD), a Ministry under the Prime Minister's Office. Only the Administrative Service, the premier scheme in the civil service, and the Management Associates Programme, is centrally managed by the PSD to ensure that top talents within the Public Service are suitably nurtured and groomed for future leadership positions. All Administrative Officers and Management Associates are put through a rigorous and comprehensive selection process to ensure that only the most capable individuals, with the passion and commitment for public service, are appointed into key leadership positions. Indeed, the human resource (HR) policies of the Singapore Public Service operate on the key principles of meritocracy and performance with regard to appointment, promotions and rewards. Psychometric tools, such as cognitive ability tests, situational judgement tests, personality inventories and competency-based interviews, are therefore, well-received and accepted within the HR community because of the objectivity and value they provide within the talent management process.

Examples: Four Assessment Centres in the Singapore Public Service

In this section we describe four ACs. Within the limits of proprietary information, we describe the purpose of the AC and the key elements of dimensions assessed, exercises, and operation of the AC.

MINISTRY OF EDUCATION

As far as we are aware, the AC for the Ministry of Education represents the first public service assessment centre in Singapore with a fully customized design. The AC, which provides a key source of input for school principalship appointments, also represents one of the first fully-integrated ACs in Singapore, where all the simulation exercises are built around a single fictitious organization and the issues across exercises build one upon the other.

Launched in 1999, the AC was developed by an integrated team of Canadian and Singaporean psychologists (including both authors) led by Dr Len Slivinski, formerly a senior public servant and psychologist within the Canadian Public Service. The centre consists of the following five exercises:

- a vision presentation;
- an in-tray exercise;
- a written case analysis;

- an interactive role play;
- a taskforce exercise.

The assessors comprise primarily Senior Education Officers within the Ministry. The AC operates with a ratio of approximately four assessors to six candidates, and with at least two assessors observing a candidate for all exercises except the in-tray exercise which is scored separately by trained personnel. Assessors meet to share their observations and individual ratings, discuss evidence, and decide on the final competency ratings for each candidate.

The AC is still in operation, and over the past decade has gone through several significant content revisions and design enhancements. Some of these changes were necessary simply to address the need to keep fiction a step ahead of reality and concerns around test leakage; but other changes were made as innovative new practices were introduced to meet evolving and changing organizational needs and challenges. Indeed, The Ministry of Education AC provides many illustrative examples of the need to ensure that an AC does not remain static in its design, but continually reinvents and reshapes itself to stay relevant in meeting organizational needs. These will be further elaborated below.

MINISTRY OF FOREIGN AFFAIRS

The AC for the Ministry of Foreign Affairs (MFA) presents another interesting case of how the purpose and structure of an AC can evolve over time. This AC was initially designed to be used in a graduate recruitment process, following a selection stage consisting of a series of cognitive ability tests, a written comprehension test, and a test of writing skills.

When this AC was first developed in the year 2000, university graduates would apply to the MFA to be Foreign Service Officers (FSOs) and, based on their AC performance and a follow-up interview, they would be appointed to either the Functional or Political job tracks (the former responsible for more operational work and the latter for setting diplomatic policy). In broad terms, the AC consisted of the following exercises:

- a political analysis and presentation;
- a role-play interaction;
- a written test of administrative skills (tasks involving scheduling and budgeting);
- a group problem-solving exercise.

Assessors were a mix of government psychologists and trained MFA officers. This AC is still in operation 10 years later, though it has evolved in terms of its content, format, and purpose, changes that are described in some detail below.

PRESIDENT'S SCHOLARS ASSESSMENT CENTRE

Singapore invests heavily in the selection and development of 'scholars', young high potentials who will attend the world's best universities at public expense and who will return to eventually take up key leadership positions in the public service. The most prestigious of these scholarships is the President's Scholarship, which is offered only to those considered to be exceptional in their intellectual and leadership potential.

Candidates for the President's Scholarship are highly selected, having already successfully passed several stages of assessment:

- academic performance and extra-curricular leadership activities;
- cognitive ability tests;
- a situational judgement test;
- a structured interview;
- a panel interview.

Among the individuals offered a government scholarship through this demanding process, a select few top performers are invited to compete for the prestigious President's Scholarship. The President's Scholars Assessment Centre (PSAC) is designed to provide additional diagnostic information for the final decision-makers, who meet with the candidates at a panel interview that takes place several days after the AC.

This process poses several challenges for the AC designer. First, the candidates – recent high school graduates – do not have much life experience at this stage, so the AC exercises (and rating guidelines) have to be sensitive to this fact. Second, we are trying to develop a process that will predict performance several years hence, and at the start of a life stage during which the individual may have many life-altering experiences. Third, the PSAC must take place in no more than two days, but can involve as many as 20 candidates; this has implications for both the design and scoring process (as is discussed below).

In this case, the AC consists of a group exercise, an analysis presentation exercise around a fictitious issue that would have an impact on national policy, and two individual interactive exercises where the 'stakeholder' role is played by a professional actor and which vary in terms of the need for the candidate to be supportive versus assertive. The assessors are senior public service leaders (holding Director-level or equivalent appointments) from the Singapore Administrative Service, and each candidate is observed by four assessors across the exercises. Assessors do their individual scoring using an automated but flexible Excel-based scoring form, then meet as a group following the AC to discuss their scores and observations and to reach a consensus on each candidate. All candidates, regardless of their performance at the AC, proceed to an interview that is conducted by a selection panel comprising members of the Singapore Public Service Commission who will have already received a candidate report prepared by one of the assessors (along with other assessment and background information). It is this final panel that makes the decision as to which of the candidates will receive the President's Scholarship that year.

BEACON PROGRAMME: A DEVELOPMENT CENTRE FOR THE PUBLIC SERVICE DIVISION

The Beacon Programme is the Singapore Public Service's first development centre (DC), designed using AC methodology. The DC was designed as an early developmental intervention for entrants to the Management Associate Programme (MAP), a public-service wide talent-management scheme that was established to groom young high-potential officers for future leadership positions. The participants of the programme are typically fresh graduates and most would have only just commenced their careers in the civil service.

The Beacon Programme was designed to (1) provide initial guidance for an active and ongoing development review and feedback process throughout the management associate's career, (2) provide management associates with a better understanding of the qualities required for success in the civil service, and (3) offer a realistic job preview of demands and expectations within the Civil Service work environment.

The development centre comprises a personality assessment and four simulation exercises, namely:

- an interactive role play;
- a supervisor briefing and fact-finding exercise;
- an inbox exercise;
- a taskforce exercise.

Throughout the course of the one-day DC, participants are given the opportunity for journaling, reflection, self-assessment, peer feedback, and assessor feedback. Participants receive both oral and written feedback that highlights areas of strength and development need; no quantitative ratings are provided as there were concerns, within a highly performance-oriented work culture, that participants would give too much focus to the ratings and fail to attend to the key developmental messages.

As part of a 'leaders developing leaders' philosophy that was being introduced into the broader leadership development framework of the Public Service Division and Singapore Civil Service College, the Beacon Programme also became a means where more senior civil service leaders were equipped and inspired to act as coaches and mentors to the participants. Thus, we see here a case of where the AC method successfully supports an organization's talent-management system, and in doing so, extends beyond its original aim to produce broader organizational benefits. The theme of assessment and development centres being catalysts for organizational cultural change is further discussed below.

Challenges in the Singapore Context

We now describe challenges for the AC method in Singapore, including the lack of familiarity with the method, language issues, and potential that the content of the programme will leak to subsequent candidates.

UNFAMILIARITY WITH THE ASSESSMENT CENTRE METHOD

When the use of ACs was first being explored by the Singapore public service in the late 1990s, they were very much considered to represent a rather esoteric and even experimental approach. While it is true that some multinationals and consultancies were using ACs on the island (and, indeed, the Ministry of Defence had been using the AC methodology for officer selection as early as the 1980s), there was very little exposure to and familiarity with this method within the broader public service. This meant that a great deal more effort had to be put into building support and understanding among decision-makers. For example, several personnel from the Public Service made site visits to public service ACs in operation in the US, the UK, and Canada to gain an appreciation of the practices and challenges associated with AC design and operation. This was followed up with a visit to Singapore by a team of AC professionals who were formerly senior psychologists with the Canadian Public Service.

At that time, psychology as a discipline – and especially occupational psychology – was still largely unknown and unrecognized in Singapore. There were few individuals with training in psychology beyond the undergraduate level, and the local universities only had small psychology departments. The relative lack of exposure to occupational psychology among organisational decision-makers at that time meant that more effort and persistence was required in informing (and even educating) people about assessment practices with which they were only vaguely familiar. Over the past ten years, however, interest in all areas of psychology has flourished in Singapore as people come to see the value of the discipline in applied settings and as young people come to see it as a viable and respectable career option. As a result of an increased awareness of occupational psychology in particular, there is now a greater shared understanding across the public service of a range of selection tools (structured interviews, assessment centres, cognitive ability tests, and so forth), and discussions of these matters generally tend now to be of a much higher level than in the past.

LANGUAGE ISSUES

While the language of business and government in Singapore is English, many Singaporeans live in households where the primary means of discourse is a language other than English (typically Mandarin Chinese or a Chinese dialect, but also Malay, or Tamil). In the past, many Singaporeans also received their education in Chinese, which meant that they may have had relatively little exposure to English. The result is that some Singaporeans – typically in their 50s or older – are not especially proficient in English, and this can create a challenge for assessment processes where language proficiency is important.

This concern was sometimes expressed by decision-makers in the public service, the issue being whether long-serving, demonstrably capable managers who were not especially articulate in English would be at an unfair disadvantage in an AC. The response at the time was that 1) English is the language of communication in the public service, so any impact on AC performance would likely mirror impacts on job performance and potential, and 2) English proficiency would be reflected primarily in ratings on 'communication skills' competencies and would be kept distinct from other competencies assessed (for example, one could still be evaluated very positively on interpersonal skills even if one had relatively modest proficiency in English). This rationale was generally accepted, and the matter of English proficiency of candidates has become less of an issue over the years as the generation of Chinese-educated Singaporeans has entered retirement. Even so, AC designers in Singapore need to be especially careful that the reading level of exercise materials reflects that of the documents candidates would have to read and write in the target job/level.

CONTENT LEAKAGE

Content leakage takes place when information concerning exercise content, rating guidelines, and so forth, finds its way into the 'public domain' via disclosure by candidates (or other persons involved in the process), misplaced materials, and so on. It is an issue for any AC, but perhaps a greater risk in Singapore because of the nation's small size, its high population-density, and its highly competitive society. Of course, the issue becomes of particular concern for exercises in which the candidate is confronted with unexpected information/events or where being able to do research on a topic in advance of the AC would give the candidate some advantage. We suspect that the risk is greatest for the entry-level ACs (for example, for Ministry of Foreign Affairs) because the stakes for the candidates are so high and because the selection processes are so competitive.

Moreover, we find that students have very tight and extensive networks, especially the scholar candidates who tend to hail from a small set of the nation's top schools. While we have no evidence that content leakage has actually occurred, we have come across instances on Internet forums in which prospective candidates have requested information on AC processes (though these requests have not been responded to, at least not publicly). Nonetheless, the potential for leakage means that AC content must be 'regularly' revised in order to minimize any potential impact, and this would seem to be especially important in Singapore for the reasons given. For some assessment centres, exercises that are considered more sensitive to leakage may be modified on an annual or biannual basis.

Lessons Learned

In this section we describe some of the lessons learned from developing and implementing AC programmes. The lessons include the importance of establishing relationships to build support, gaining commitment from staff to be assessors and thus sustain the AC over time, and changing the AC to meet evolving demands in the agencies.

BUILDING SUPPORT FOR AN ASSESSMENT CENTRE

As previously noted, Singapore society represents a unique mix of Asian (primarily Chinese) and Western elements. It is also a very small nation which, lacking natural resources, has achieved great success by integrating into the global economy, building a strong talent base, and 'importing' talent where necessary. These facts have implications for how one achieves buy-in for new initiatives and practices within an organization here.

To begin with, while relationships between consultants and organizational representatives are important anywhere, they seem to be particularly important here. This may relate to the Chinese notion of *guanxi*, which refers to the role of networks and connections in social and business life. While one's qualifications and experience are still very important, the practitioner in Singapore may have to direct more effort at building relationships with key organizational decision-makers here compared with what is required in the West.

Organizational decision-makers need to have trust in the practitioner – trust in terms of both capability and commitment – and this requires dedicated effort at relationship-building on the part of the practitioner. More specifically, it is important to cultivate organizational champions who will support the AC where and when it meets resistance. This relationship-attentive approach was exemplified by Dr Len Slivinski, the former senior Canadian public servant and psychologist who led the effort to develop the AC for the Ministry of Education. Dr Slivinski made it a point to personally engage with senior people in the Ministry and elsewhere in the public service and explicitly positioned the AC as a collaborative venture in which overall ownership of the AC rested with line management rather than external professionals. This approach was instrumental in overcoming concerns and resistance to what was then seen to be a very experimental and 'untested' method of assessment (at least in the Singapore context), and it continues to contribute to the successful integration of the AC into the workings of the Ministry.

Singapore very much relies on partnerships with multinationals to help drive its economy, and many top companies have located their regional headquarters or manufacturing operations here. As a result, Singapore (and Singaporeans) has substantial exposure to international 'best practices', and there is a strong tendency to benchmark local practice against overseas practices, though with an understanding that processes need to be adapted to local organizational and cultural contexts. Therefore an important aspect of gaining support for an AC is highlighting that the method is used widely by respected international firms as well as public service organizations in other nations. That said, HR personnel in the Singapore public service are often quite sophisticated, so one also needs to provide evidence of the validity and utility of the AC method; they are also open to innovation so long as one can make a reasonable case for it. Hence, it appears that perhaps to a greater extent than elsewhere, one can reinforce buy-in through appeals to international best practices, but one cannot rely on this alone to build support for or sustain an AC.

SUSTAINING AN ASSESSMENT CENTRE

While building support and recruiting process 'champions' are critical in the early days of a new AC, other factors come into play over the longer term. One will still need to leverage on good relationships with organizational representatives and cultivate champions for the process, but once an AC has been established within the organization there are other opportunities and challenges. Birri and Melcher (Chapter 12 in this volume) discuss processes Credit Suisse used to sustain ACs over 25 years, and Thornton and Birri (Chapter 21) discuss ten factors that lead to sustainability. We have found that the greatest challenge to the sustainability of ACs in our context is the resources they require, especially in terms of the time commitment of personnel from the client organization who are typically involved as assessors and administrators. It can be difficult for staff to find the time to assist on an AC of two or more days, and so over time the AC can come to be seen as a burden with uncertain value to the organization. Paradoxically, however, these same assessors can be an important source of support for an AC.

A case in point was the Ministry of Foreign Affairs Assessment Centre. The internal assessors at MFA are mid-career Foreign Service Officers who typically rotate in and out of Singapore for three-year periods. Because these assessors are regularly leaving for overseas postings, it is not possible to build a stable assessor pool over the longer term, and there was an almost constant need to train new assessors. To reduce the 'burden' of the AC, the process was reconfigured so that there would be one internal (MFA) assessor working with two external assessors (the reverse of the earlier arrangement), and only external assessors would prepare the candidate reports. Even with these changes, however, the AC continues to pose a challenge from a staff perspective (though MFA's commitment to the process remains firm, with a full redesign of the AC completed in 2010).

Innovation – or at least the use of 'non-traditional' methods – has also helped us manage the perceived burden associated with assessment centre work. This was very much the case with the President's Scholars Assessment Centre in which as many as 20 candidates have to be assessed in a two-day period owing to process requirements and constraints on candidate availability. It was important, under such circumstances, to minimize the assessors' workload (and mental load) while maintaining rigour, so we introduced a more automated scoring process using computer-based spreadsheets. In this case, assessors rated performance using weighted behavioural indicators (using a three-point scale), and this set of indicator ratings was automatically converted into an overall competency rating out of seven, which the assessor could partially override with justification. The behavioural indicators were numerous, very specific and somewhat overlapping in content, much like the items in a questionnaire used to measure a theoretical construct. Assessors having experience with more traditional rating methods have expressed a preference for this automated approach, but the impact on reliability and validity has yet to be established. This AC represented a case where organizational exigencies rendered a more standard approach unviable, making it necessary to introduce some innovation into the process.

HOW ASSESSMENT CENTRES EVOLVE OVER TIME

The need to adapt the 'traditional' AC methodology to meet organizational requirements is, of course, not unique to the Singaporean context, but our experience in this regard might still be of interest to the reader. ACs, of course, must be 'refreshed' periodically in order to maintain alignment with organizational priorities and keep ahead of potential content leakage. However, sometimes the needs of the client organization shift in a way that has an impact on an existing AC, thus requiring changes to be made in process or format. The Ministry of Foreign Affairs AC for entry-level selection is a good example because it has had to change in two significant ways over the past few years.

The first instance concerned the measurement approach of the assessment centre, which shifted from an exercise-based scoring format to a more traditional competency-based format. This was driven by internal changes to employee classification and recruitment processes that had an impact on the information the organisation required from the assessment centre. While the exercise content remained the same, it was necessary to modify both the scoring process (to provide competency rather than exercise scores) and the reporting format.

A second major change occurred some years later when MFA decided that it wanted to pilot the use of the AC as part of its scholar selection process. While the overall AC scenario was to be retained, some changes were made to the exercise requirements, scoring process, and report format to accommodate some of the competencies and behavioural elements that are especially critical to success as a scholar. At the pilot stage, one of our concerns obviously was whether young people (who were just completing high school) would have enough life experience to effectively manage the intellectual and interpersonal demands of the AC exercises. However, the reality has been that the scholarship applicants typically outperform the university graduates on the various AC exercises, including on the rare occasions when they have participated together at the same run of the AC. This outcome was also consistent with our desire that the AC measure key competencies – analytical skills, interpersonal skills, and so forth – rather than 'crystallized' knowledge of international politics, government policy, and diplomatic protocol.

CATALYSTS FOR ORGANIZATIONAL CULTURAL CHANGE

ACs and DCs are not only affected by demands arising from organizational change, they can also be used to actually support and drive such change. For instance, in the Beacon Programme DC, although engaging external trained observers would have made the programme administratively and logistically simpler to manage (and this may have led to more rigorously and 'professionally' conducted assessments) a decision was made to train young Administrative Officers (who are typically four years senior to the Beacon participants) to be both observers and coaches for the participants. This decision reflected Public Service Division's desire to build a coaching culture within the civil service and to inculcate a sense of responsibility amongst its leaders at an early stage in their careers so that they would understand that a key aspect of their role as leaders within the public service is to develop future leaders. The observer training became a part of a milestone leadership programme that all newly appointed Administrative Officers had to attend. As one of the key training objectives of the milestone leadership programme was to equip them with people development skills (for example, providing performance feedback and coaching), the observer duties that they had to perform at the Beacon Programme became a means for them to apply and embed the learning from the milestone programme, and it became a forum for coaching/mentoring relationships to be formed between juniors and seniors. In other words, the Beacon Programme ended up being a developmental opportunity not only for the Management Associates who were the participants of the Programme, but also the junior Administrative Officers who were the observers in the Programme.

Similarly, in the AC for identifying Principalship potential at the Ministry of Education, what started out as an AC for providing information to aid in promotion decisions, became a platform for creating a shared understanding on what the Ministry viewed as good leadership. Over the more than 10 years that the assessment centre has been in operation, more than 100 internal Ministry staff at senior leadership levels have been trained as observers, and this in turn would undoubtedly have had both an indirect and direct influence on the people development capabilities of the Ministry as a whole.

Conclusion

With its commitment to the merit principle and objectivity in appointments and promotions, the Singapore public service has turned out to be fertile ground for the AC method. As a tool for diagnosis and development, the method is also gaining a foothold here. Of course, as Singapore represents a unique mix of cultures, demographics, and national values, the introduction, design and implementation of ACs has to be adapted somewhat to local settings (for example, in terms of what issues might be considered appropriate for analysis and group discussion exercises). However, we believe that there are still valuable experiences and lessons we can share from this context just as Singapore continues to learn from practices developed elsewhere.

References

Singapore Department of Statistics. 2011. http://www.singstat.gov.sg/stats/latestdata.htm/ [accessed: 10 January 2011].

27 Eating the Elephant: Tackling the Challenges of Introducing Assessment and Development Centres in East Africa

ZIA MANJI AND MADELEINE DUNFORD

To put assessment and development centre (ADC) usage into context in east Africa is to see how much the role of human resource management has changed within the past decade. Until quite recently large organizations did without a human resource function, at best relying on a Personnel Manager whose main responsibilities revolved around hiring and firing.

Organizations perceived personnel management to have the least strategic importance. Today, the importance and relevance of human resource management is widely acknowledged and this has met with a rapidly evolving professionalism around the function. As such, the calibre of managers viewing human resources as a career option has improved and human resources has an executive position on most large companies' boards.

Previously, it was not common practice to be open about talent review results, which were based on line-manager opinion, and performance feedback was rarely shared with participants. Today the paradigm shift is evident. Organizations embrace the concept of talent being a key asset and therefore worth investing in. The introduction of development centres for succession planning and talent review, the use of 360 degree programmes and open feedback of results leading to coaching programmes, is more common. Therefore, we can argue that there has been an evolution within human resource management in east Africa – a gradual process in which the appreciation of assessment and development centres has played a part. This chapter seeks to examine how the cultural shift of investing in people and particularly the use of centres came about, and what challenges were faced in introducing these practices into an emerging market, which often grapples with 'worst practice'. To undertake the examination of these changes we selected a panel of nine ADC users and interviewed them individually.

These users had varying levels of experience of ACs and DCs ranging from graduate recruitment ACs to senior management diagnostic DCs.[1]

Taking a Step Back

For many organizations, before the introduction of assessment and development centres, the challenge was to create awareness around the use of competencies, and often the role of consultants was to help design competency frameworks. Multinational organizations often had a globally defined competency framework, but the use and understanding of that tool rarely extended beyond the human resource function in their local subsidiaries.

Only recently has the concept of competencies been integrated into role profiles, performance reviews or development. For example, the development of the leadership competency framework at Kenya Commercial Bank in 2007 was seen as 'ahead of its time' but today it is a 'common language' with the understanding of competencies ingrained, thanks to years of 'communication, communication, communication and simplification to attitude, skills and knowledge (ASK)'. This challenge often meant taking a large step back to educate, define and create the frameworks as a foundation on which to build centres.

Before the introduction of assessment centres (ACs) most organizations were using unstructured interviews for selection, which they openly admit were questionable in terms of their objectivity and thoroughness. Companies still struggle with nepotistic recruitment tendencies and managers wanting to short-cut assessment processes; although some are now trying to use competency-based interviews, this advancement is hampered by the fact that few organizations have invested in the required interviewer training.

Progressive organizations were using psychometrics before the introduction of ACs, but there was a realization that making potential managers complete aptitude and personality tests not only lacked face validity but offered no holistic assessment on which to base important selection decisions. Furthermore, organizations cited examples of candidates having access to psychometric test questions before the assessment, due to lack of controls. In some cases, organizations attempted to develop AC-type exercises, which did not adhere to best practice processes. Managers gave examples of when they used to assess groups of up to 20 participants in an hour-long group discussion whilst untrained observers walked round the room.

In many ways therefore, when ACs were introduced in 2004, they were entering a market with little or no understanding of competencies and competency-based assessment.

Introducing Assessment Centres

The first step before introducing centres was to enable the newly evolved human resource practitioners to influence the change within the organizations adopting the process.

---

1   We are very grateful for the insights and feedback provided during interviews by Alban Mwendar, Group Human Resource Director of *East African Breweries (EABL)*; Jaine Mwai, Head of HR, *EABL*; Winnie Pertet, Service Delivery Manager, *EABL*; Madren Oluoch-Olunya, Talent Delivery Manager, *EABL*; Lyn Mengich, Human Resources Director, *Barclays Bank Kenya*; Jane Kabutha, Assistant General Manager – Human Resources, *Commercial Bank of Africa*; Sammy Chepkwony, Human Resources Director, *James Finlays-Homegrown*; Elizabeth Chemengen, Talent Manager, *Kenya Commercial Bank (KCB)*.

They were tasked with explaining issues to do with the validity of the process to their executives, and that recruiting more competent managers through valid assessment processes would fit with management objectives. They needed to emphasize the higher level of accuracy when using centres compared to basic aptitude tests.

Adopting these new practices was therefore 'linked to business objectives and the need to see results.' So the challenge was selling the business case of spending more on assessments, which would 'benefit the company's strategy'. Companies also stressed that the use of the 'best tools in the market' was part of their attempts to promote their employer brand.

There is no doubt that implementing these processes meant a cultural shift in recruitment, and convincing the executives to embrace a system that would be more resource hungry meant the human resource practitioners involved were faced with questions regarding validity and return on investment of the process. Sometimes senior executives, with little understanding of ACs and appreciation of competencies 'could not see the relationship between the tools and the job. But over time the tools were well received, especially when internal candidates were given feedback'.

It was generally easier for the local subsidiaries of multinationals, as they were implementing a global assessment policy and could argue that if they did not adopt such processes they ran the risk of lowering their local standards. However, there is still some scepticism that these tools can tell line managers more about a candidate than the business or social network that referred the candidate to them in the first place.

This resistance is likely to ease over time as organizations that have been using centres since their introduction are recognizing that the process not only leads to improved quality of talent, but also better retention. For example, at KCB, they have recruited 60 Management Trainees through centres since 2007 in Kenya and none of them have left the company, significantly reducing the turnover they used to experience on the programme. The implementation of ACs has changed perceptions internally about recruitment and development practices within those organizations. The introduction of ACs has also changed perceptions externally.

EXTERNAL PERCEPTIONS

One of the challenges faced by participants was a total unfamiliarity with the concept of work simulation exercises. The education system in Kenya, even though accepted by businesses as offering more and better-quality graduates than its regional neighbours, still relies on traditional book-based teaching methods and rote learning, so graduates are unlikely to have ever been exposed to concepts such as analyzing business case studies. Candidates are familiar with interviews or tests and even when they are briefed before an AC, they come expecting to be examined in some traditional way.

That lack of exposure could be seen as a bias, especially at graduate level. There was also a feeling that the 'case studies written were too removed' from the participant's 'area of specialization'. However, organizations acknowledge that they need to assess a candidate's potential beyond their area of study and use a standardized process, which highlights the need to localize exercise content as much as possible. Even small changes ensure better acceptance. This is also apparent at senior levels when the use of general management exercises is seen as too challenging, if the content is not an identical replication of a manager's current responsibilities. This points to an inability to think cross-functionally, and reflects the recent employer sentiment, that local MBA holders are not exposed enough to practical business situations.

Generally though, external perceptions of clients using centres have been very positive and graduates, even if not appointed, are happy to have gone through the process. As part of employer-branding it shows the employer is one of the leaders in managing talent. There is an appreciation that 'centres are transparent and remove biases, as the assessors change between exercises and there are different opportunities to be myself'. Other feedback received by organizations using centres includes the sentiment 'that this is an organization that takes recruitment seriously and professionally'. Candidates felt those organizations doing so were in a 'different league altogether'. On issues of transparency in recruitment, the 'complaints disappeared' and the centres have helped 'remove bias' found in interviews. So the feeling was that 'candidates that had not been through it before were very impressed and felt that the quality of the resources in the organization must be high if everyone goes through this'.

INTERNAL PERCEPTIONS

Internally, there were obvious benefits in the use of centres; 'it removed bias, introduced professionalism and it was seen as a 'foolproof' process. When line managers see a newly recruited candidate they know it is the right person'. For senior managers, ACs are generally seen as 'positive, objective and professional'. However, from internal participants going through ACs as part of a promotion process, the ACs faced resistance, with participants feeling somehow disadvantaged by the new process. A solution to this was recognizing the importance of giving feedback and handling post-centre expectations, as discussed below, in the section on development centres.

Another internal difficulty was the lack of correlation in some instances between line-manager perceptions of a candidate and centre results. Given the cultural nepotistic tendencies within the region, coupled with a tradition of informal unstructured interviews, recruitment has been open to serious bias. ACs run contrary to these processes. The situation is further extenuated when interview panels are untrained, and if their preferred candidates do not perform well at the ACs. This has led recruiting managers to question the validity of the AC process, especially if they haven't been trained as assessors and therefore lack an appreciation of the AC's thoroughness. The challenge then has been for human resources to explain the process and encourage the use of AC results to provide more focused and in-depth interviews. Additional confusion can be created if the interview rating scale is not consistent with the one used during ACs, making it harder to integrate the results. Furthermore, although organizations claim to be using competency-based interviews, in reality it is common to find these interviews being rather unstructured with a lack of behavioural indicators and post-interview evaluation. Any instances where senior managers try to 'overrule' centre results at final interview have led to assessor demotivation, with assessors questioning the point of the process if their results are not used objectively.

ACs are well known for being time-consuming, which leads to another common challenge: that although trained assessors wish to attend ACs, their line managers, if not fully 'aligned' to the process, may not give them the time required to attend. There is a sense even from some assessors, that ACs are 'not their day job' and therefore 'not linked back to their personal performance, especially when attending an AC outside their function; if it is in their function there is more support'. This highlights the need for internal education to ensure buy-in, and there is a move by companies to make AC attendance a key performance indicator for assessors.

The barriers to ensuring assessor-participation are exacerbated by ACs themselves being seen as long and intensive. Expecting assessors to complete more than three reports per day has been difficult. Therefore, management of the assessor's cognitive load is important, which can mean reducing the assessor–participant ratio to one to one. Third-party providers continue to do most of the AC administration, including participant briefings and set up, both to reduce assessor workload and to ensure participants are correctly instructed.

Culturally, east Africans have a different perspective on timekeeping. Ensuring assessors and participants arrive on time and keeping track of time during exercises is an ongoing concern. Interestingly, the culture around timekeeping is organization-specific, with punctuality being a key corporate value for some, so in those instances this issue never arises.

Organizations that have a large contingent of trained assessors and competency-based interviewers have faced less internal resistance on accepting AC attendance and results. For these organizations, there is a sense that the implementation of best practice in ACs and interviews filters through to 'forcing better practice at other levels'; this has led to a 'push to improving policy and cutting out the short cuts' in recruitment generally.

In most cases, 'those trained, want to be assessors … they find value in it themselves and they appreciate participating'. There is the recognition that assessors will have different levels of engagement and that 'it is not easy and it is not for everybody, so some struggle'; this means assessor-selection has been looked at more carefully before training, with some organizations making it more of a privileged and 'nice to belong to' group within the organization.

Centre management and timetabling complexities have led to a continued sentiment in the market that there is value in having a third-party design and manage their ACs. Advantages are recognized as management of the 'logistics'; ensuring 'fairness and objectivity, especially for internal candidates'. This ensures the 'quality of the process is maintained (and third parties) keep you updated on new developments'.

Cultural and Regional Differences

Introducing centres coincided with the region's commercial transformation, with increased investment in Kenya, and by extension east Africa, as an important emerging market. Kenya's economy was liberalized in the mid 1990s and Uganda and Tanzania have opened to foreign investment over the past decade. The sudden increase in demand for talent, the scarcity of graduates and managers in some markets, combined with the stringent work-permit regulations, means there has been an increasing war for talent in the region.

In particular, the banking and telecommunications sectors have evolved rapidly, and those organizations are competing in the same talent pool. For instance, large banks struggle to find management within the Risk and Treasury functions. In the telecommunications sector there is intense competition for engineers, which has impacted the ability for other sectors, such as the large manufacturers, to attract the same graduates. This has resulted in the rising cost of talent in these areas and, therefore companies are more determined than ever to ensure they make the right recruitment decisions.

There are distinct differences within the region's talent markets. In Kenya, there is a surplus of graduate talent, but a general recognition that the 'university explosion, with a university on each block' means you need to look ever closer at the quality of that talent, beyond the 'paper qualifications'.

This is linked to the major transformation over the last decade in higher education in east Africa. The education system is characterized by massive demand for places, rapid growth in providers, large numbers of unemployed graduates, diminishing faculty numbers and the continued brain drain of top students. As a result the quality of students graduating from local universities leaves a lot to be desired. For companies targeting graduate intakes, ACs will become an increasingly critical component of their recruitment process and talent strategy.

Following the liberalization of the education sector in east Africa in the 1980s new educational institutions, especially private universities and colleges, have mushroomed in a short time. In Ethiopia, for example, where no private institutions existed in the 1990s, there are over 60 today. In Kenya, there are 6 public universities, 14 private universities and over 250 mid-level colleges, many of which have applied to become universities (Teferra 2008). In reaction to the increasing demand for places, coupled with the intensifying private competition, public universities have started cost-sharing initiatives including parallel programmes, raising concern around equity and quality. Competition amongst private institutions which are wholly dependent on tuition fees is generally precarious and they are resource-challenged. The lack of quality assurance, and the inadequate capabilities of accrediting bodies, justifies the concern that stakeholders, including employers, have about the quality of graduates joining the workplace. The Ministry of Education in Kenya closed down five private universities between 2004 and 2006 (Mahajan 2009). Funding of public universities remains an undisputed challenge. 'Low economic growth rates, weak investment outlook, unsustainable unemployment rates, grinding poverty … will continue to constrain Africa's ability to generate meaningful revenues in the context of a "liberated" educational subsystem, which until recently was dubbed "a luxury"' (Teferra 2008).

If this is not enough of a concern, the future of the education system in east Africa should be. In 2003, the Kenyan government introduced a Free Primary Education programme that saw the enrolments in primary schools triple. The cost of private education more than doubled, now 20 times more expensive than government-funded schools, as richer families moved students out of the state system in the light of declining quality of education. In 1997, only 3.4 per cent of students were enrolled in private schools and by 2006 this had increased to 9.2 per cent (Bold et al. 2009). This, coupled with the rise in the teacher–pupil ratio, has resulted in a large performance gap between the public and private schools. A recent Annual Learning Assessment provided disturbing results with two out of three 8-year-olds unable to read this sentence: 'They play each day' (Uwezo 2010). This inequity will affect the already low enrolment-rates at public universities (only 100,000 students enrol per year in public universities in Kenya), which suffer from limited funding, poor-quality teaching and low research-output. The lack of competence at the bottom of the learning ladder will hurt the performance of students at higher education levels in the future. The ultimate dilution of the quality of graduates in the region means that companies will become more selective on their graduate programmes and require a more robust and objective means of selecting their future talent. ACs will play a role in setting standards and providing a reliable means of evaluating graduates as the education system can no longer be relied upon. This is already evident, given that the most commonly assessed dimension in Africa at ACs is problem analysis, as compared to a ranking of 5th in Europe and 15th in the Americas (Povah et al. 2008). This reinforces the fact that employers question whether local graduates can demonstrate this critical skill.

DEMONSTRATING RETURN ON INVESTMENT

As organizations increasingly see the need to use ACs, one of the challenges will be how to justify the process financially, especially with graduate applications increasing annually. The demand for more robust ACs culminates in additional exercises and test usage, including the addition of psychometric instruments. The challenge is how to measure the additional gains from an improved process and the resultant incremental costs.

Utility analysis undertaken by us in 2007 for East African Breweries (EABL) compared the financial returns of an AC combined with psychometrics undertaken in 2005 versus a selection process using only interviews in 2003. The results showed a return on investment of 49 per cent over 2 years.

Whilst Kenya suffers an oversupply of graduates, in Tanzania the opposite is true. Until recently the country, with a larger population than Kenya, has had only one university. This results in the fact that in Kenya large companies receive 8,000 graduate applications a year for their trainee programmes, whereas in Tanzania they receive fewer then 40 applicants. In Tanzania the use of English in education and business is not as prevalent when compared to Kenya and Uganda and this also impacts assessment results. Regional aptitude testing by us of 48 graduates in 2002 for a large multinational's management trainee programme produced results that showed that Tanzanian graduates' verbal ability scores in English averaged 9.25 compared to Kenyan graduates who averaged 13.44. This exercise showed the dangers of encountering adverse impact when using the same tool across the region. Another consideration is that having the largest regional economy and longer exposure to multinational working culture has led to Kenyans being 'more cosmopolitan, more exposed' than other markets.

Tanzania has a culture that emphasizes equality over competition, and this influence sometimes impacts the way Tanzanian candidates approach an AC. They rarely contradict other's points of view or fight to be heard during group discussions, being mostly collaborative: 'not forceful, more graceful' in approach. Therefore, combining Tanzanian with Kenyan candidates in such exercises is not suitable, as Kenyans, with their competitive background, tend to be less interested in formalities and protocol. In some instances this has led to some organizations lowering the benchmark for Tanzanian candidates, when using the same AC exercises across the region.

Unfortunately, the talent vacuum in Tanzania has resulted in companies using expatriate Kenyan and South African management, which has led to a backlash and tightening of work permit rules within Tanzania. A further consequence has been Tanzania's delay in embracing the East African Community, which will allow free movement of talent. However, this background is encouraging companies to invest in developing existing talent within Tanzania, which can only be beneficial in the long term.

These regional differences mean that organizations find it hard to attract and select talent of standard quality across the different markets, making diversity in their workforce a challenging goal.

In Sudan and Ethiopia, which have seen more recent foreign direct investment after the end of their political conflicts, talent is even harder to attract or assess. There is a sentiment that candidates from those countries lack basic skills, and some technical professions, such as engineering, cannot find suitably qualified candidates, given that there are no local training institutions. Therefore multinational organizations wishing to recruit Ethiopians and Sudanese adopted a strategy of sourcing talent from the diaspora as a way of 'enticing them back home', given that they had fled their countries during the conflicts. In 2009 EABL managed to source Ethiopian and Sudanese candidates who were based abroad and found that they performed better on ACs than regionally based graduates, a fact attributed to their international exposure. However, currently there are still operations in Sudan, for instance, which are fully managed by Kenyans, but local talent is being fast tracked into management.

CULTURAL NORMS

The lack of international business exposure in some of these markets has made using work simulation exercises even more problematic. Organizations often have to use lower-level exercises than the role being assessed and in bilingual markets such as Rwanda and Mauritius they have to extend the exercise timings. There are exercise types that are considered culturally alien as well. For instance, when using one-to-one simulation exercises, managers in Sudan have been known to refuse to partake, claiming such 'role playing' is 'for children', even when these exercises are being used for development purposes. The theme of not identifying with the simulations, especially where candidates viewed the one-to-one exercises as assessing their acting skills more then competencies, is repeated again in other countries. It is common that there is a fair amount of second-guessing by candidates, who sometimes even ask assessors: 'how am I supposed to behave?' or who feel it necessary to refer positively to the organization holding the centre in some way during their interactive exercises.

Multinational corporations are increasingly looking at ways of enhancing talent exchanges across subsidiaries. For example, EABL aims to exchange Tanzanian with Kenyan staff and management exchanges between Uganda and Kenya are already common within the group. Pan-African management trainee programmes in such organizations are increasingly being used to rotate talent and offer the young professionals more international exposure. ACs are being used to select talent for such international assignments.

SOCIETAL INFLUENCES

Another cultural barrier to ACs can be the hierarchical nature of society and business in the region, whereby it is quite accepted to be very traditional and directive in approach. Taking orders without question is accepted by subordinates as the norm in some organizations, meaning the one-to-one meeting simulations between managers and subordinates typically end before 30 minutes, with it unusual to see a manager engaging, empathizing with or using a coaching style with the subordinate role players.

Furthermore, assessors from within that culture might consider that authoritative style acceptable, which influences their evaluation of the candidates' leadership competencies.

Traditional beliefs around gender-specific roles can also manifest themselves in AC behaviour, with group discussion participants often appointing a female participant to be a scribe and a male participant to chair the session. This has implications on the sensitivity needed in the design of AC timetabling to ensure a gender balance if possible in group exercises.

The other consideration is to ensure that the assessors are selected from a cross-cultural pool that includes assessors from the home country to allow for better understanding and insights. To ensure consistency across the region, guides for assessors and behavioural indicators are not generally amended.

Development Centres

Development centres (DCs) have recently grown in popularity within the region, despite facing implementation challenges, due to being seen as a novel intervention for internal talent development.

Using DCs was a priority shift for many organizations, where the focus had been on attracting external talent from the market rather than 'proactively identifying succession risks and having personal development plans' for internal talent. This shift for some came about due to the 'war for talent that bought focus on talent management to cover for successions and a healthy talent pipeline, including talent mapping'. The challenge of selling the concept internally was often easier for those who were already using ACs that had provided positive returns. The exposure to DCs abroad by some senior management in multinationals has resulted in an appreciation of the impact that well-constructed DCs can offer local operations.

However, since the concept was unknown, participants often considered it an assessment rather than a development process, and this confusion continues to cause anxiety before DC-attendance. The importance of communication and policy development is repeatedly raised as a key factor in a programme's success. Participants often raise concerns about a hidden agenda and this needs to be managed through pre-assessment briefings. This also highlights for many organizations the need to communicate the separation between a participant's DC performance and their performance management results, so that centres are viewed purely from a developmental standpoint.

It is not only participant perceptions that need to be managed. Sometimes line managers felt they were not sufficiently involved in pre-DC decision-making. This has led to delays in some organizations implementing DCs, since the internal debate on who should go through the process, and for what reasons, can turn political. There is special concern on how to manage those not selected for DCs, as that can lead to 'resistance because those not nominated claim favouritism'. Typically, appraisal ratings are used for identifying who will be in the talent pool for DCs, which can themselves be open to bias. The centre selection process is considerably easier for a diagnostic DC with a developmental purpose, as a whole management strata or function is included. However, in organizations which have gained experience in using DCs, participating in the process is becoming 'aspirational'. James Finlays surveyed their DC participants and received 'excellent' feedback as 'participants can see growth, with some even being sent on INSEAD Business School training abroad' as a post-centre intervention.

Post-centre feedback and follow-through is as important as the pre-centre communication, and is another area that organizations have sometimes found difficult. This relates to whether an organization's culture is ready for the process since it depends on 'whether candidates are prepared to receive feedback, as feedback can be positive or negative and that outcome needs to be managed'. There needs to be work around 'preparing the organization's culture on giving and receiving feedback to be honest and accepting'. Who gives feedback and how that is done is therefore critical. Feedback is more likely to be well received and acted upon when DCs provide detailed reports, and verbal feedback, from someone other than a line manager who has been trained to give behavioural feedback. Social culture as well as corporate culture plays a part here, with observations from assessors highlighting that the African culture in itself does not embrace giving or receiving feedback of a negative kind, especially from one who is younger than you. This affects the reception of the feedback and can hinder the whole process.

As a DC is the start of a developmental process, a key learning by organizations has been the need for concerted effort post-centre, to reap the full benefits. Companies summed this up as 'HR and executive leadership needs full time attention for (the process) not to die'. There is a realization by organizations that have traditionally relied only on training that fulfilling development needs to be highlighted at centres; they require other more specific interventions, including work exchanges, competency specific workshops, e-learning and behavioural-change coaching. The linking of DC feedback and relevant post-centre interventions has been particularly difficult in a business environment where such offerings were limited to off-the-shelf training programmes until recently.

Summary

The introduction of centres into a maturing region, riding on the back of a still-evolving human resources profession, has been a gradual and step-by-step process, much like eating an elephant. In many instances, the concepts of competency-definition and assessment were novel, and therefore it was daunting to consider the task holistically. We still have a way to go if we are to gain common ground for professionally run competency-based exercises and centres. There has been much learning along the way, and no doubt more to come.

Where Next?

The issues around pre- and post-centre activities are a natural consequence of implementing centres within an organization. However, these are all the more challenging in the recently matured human resource function in east Africa, where they have had to shift their focus from short-term people-management to thinking about talent more strategically and holistically. By and large, organizations in the region see the greatest future usage coming from centres for internal development, linked to other strategic interventions such as 360 degree feedback programmes and executive coaching. Again, this emphasizes an environment maturing to the point where objective and sometimes challenging feedback is seen as an important part of growing the organization's future leaders; a move away from the 'closed door' business leadership-style of the recent past.

Looking to the future, many organizations expressed a desire to see more exercises that focus on assessing integrity or innovation. Furthermore, whilst they wished they could include more exercises in centres this was balanced against the desire to somehow make the processes more time-efficient, perhaps through greater use of technology – a reflection of the increasing pace of business across the globe.

Ironically, the fact that using Assessment and Development Centres is now seen as a sign of being 'an employer of choice', means that 'the market has moved towards using centres' and this has created a hierarchy of aspiring organizations who are now trying to climb that ladder'. A concern is that these late adopters are short-cutting the process by using homemade basic exercises; untrained and too few assessors; with no guides for assessors or proper understanding of competencies, and that they are not following the behavioural assessment process. In many cases, these are assessment centres in name only and are most likely not delivering accurate or meaningful feedback for selection or development. This runs the risk of 'tarring all centres with the same brush' in the eyes of users and participants. Our future challenge in east Africa, therefore, is to educate a wider section of businesses to the value of adhering to best practice when using these potentially business transformative methodologies.

References

Ballantyne, I. and Povah, N. 2004. *Assessment and Development Centres* (2nd Edition). UK: Gower.

Bold, T., Mwabu, G., Kimenyi, M. and Sandefur, J. 2009. *Free primary education in Kenya: enrolment, achievement and local accountability*. [online]. Available at www.iig.ox.ac.uk/output/presentations/pdfs/12a-randomized-eval-policies-kenya-presentation-01.pdf [accessed: 6 June 2010].

Mahajan, V. 2009. *Africa Rising: How 900 Million African Consumers Offer More Than You Think* (2nd Edition). USA: Pearson.

Povah, N., Crabb, S. and McGarrigle, R. 2008. *The Global Research Questionnaire: An International Survey of Assessment Center Practices*. [Online: A&DC]. Available at: http://www.adc.uk.com/page.aspx/239/Research_Findings [accessed: 9 February 2011].

Roodt, G. and Schlebusch, S. 2008. *Assessment Centres: Unlocking Potential for Growth*. Randburg: Knowres.

Teferra, D. 2008, February. *African higher education: capturing the recent past, projecting the future*. [online]. Available at www.bc.edu/bc_org/avp/soe/cihe/inhea/editorial.htm [accessed: 6 June 2010].

Teferra, D. 2009, December. *Mobilizing MNCs to advance higher education and research in Africa*. [online]. Available at www.bc.edu/bc_org/avp/soe/cihe/inhea/editorial.htm [accessed: 6 June 2010].

Teferra, D. 2009, November. *Building capacity in Africa: The need for coherent policy and informed action*. [online]. Available at www.bc.edu/bc_org/avp/soe/cihe/inhea/editorial.htm [accessed: 6 June 2010].

Uwezo Kenya. 2010. *Are Our Children Learning? Annual Learning Assessment*. Nairobi: Women Education Researchers of Kenya.

Woodruffe, C. 2000. *Development and Assessment Centres* (3rd Edition). UK: The Chartered Institute of Personnel and Development (CIPD).

28 The Application of the Assessment Center Method in China

KAI-GUANG LIANG AND YING LIU

Globalization, as an all-pervasive phenomenon, has extensively influenced the human resource management practices in many nations. In China, due to the country's extraordinary economic growth in the past 30 years, selection and development of talent are at the heart of the burgeoning stream of research. Chinese organizations have witnessed an increasing use of various assessment techniques including the assessment center (AC) method as an integrated part of their talent selection and development process (Luo and Meng 2005). At the same time, various scholars have given a new impetus to AC research in China. The aim of this chapter is to inform practitioners and researchers of these recent, intriguing developments. In particular, we provide an overview of the development of ACs in China. To identify these recent developments we examine the evolution of ACs in China, current practices in different economic sectors of China based firms, as well as some cultural and operational issues in implementing ACs in China.

Evolution of Assessment Centers in China

China has a long history in assessing and selecting civil service officials, which can be traced back to the Sui Dynasty (605 AD). However, the AC method was first applied to China during the time of World War II (1943–1946). It was used to select and train intelligence agents by the Cross-nation Military Intelligence established in Chongqing, which was known as the "Sino-American Cooperation Organization" (SACO) (OSS Assessment Staff 1948).

In the mid 1980s, simulations were reintroduced by Lu Hongjun to select senior managers for Chinese state-owned companies, which caught the attention of central and local governments in China (Lu 1986). The International Labor Organization sent experts to Beijing in the late 1980s to train Chinese officials and professionals on assessment methods (Beijing Municipal Organization Department 1987).

In 1992, Liang and his colleagues applied AC techniques to selection and promotion for managers in some widely known private enterprises (for example, Stone Group Co., Lido Holiday Inn) and published the first paper about the validity of the in-basket simulation in the *Chinese Journal of Applied Psychology* (Liang, Xu and Fu 1992). In 1996, the department of selection in the Ministry of Human Resource successfully implemented an AC. The modern AC method was widely imported from the west and it grew in popularity during the late 1990s when some large multinational firms, such as Motorola, Alcatel, Coca Cola, Nokia, Philips, and GM, amongst others, brought their headquarters' practices to their Chinese operations to help select and develop their future leaders. At the same time, some well-known consulting firms, such as DDI, PDI, SHL, and Hay, started to establish offices in China. Now, ACs have become more and more popular and are becoming well accepted in China, to the point that they have extended and replaced the concept of traditional civil service examinations.

Application of the Assessment Center Methods in Chinese Settings

As one of the most valid selection tools, the assessment center method is very well accepted in Chinese society today. This is mainly because there is a long history of civil service examination usage in China, and assessment centers are an extension of that concept. In China, the use of AC techniques is mainly for employee selection. Many of the top 100 Chinese companies use some version of the AC method, with various combinations of elements, including psychological tests, simulations, and structured interviews.

In 2010, a local consultancy called China Select, conducted a nationwide survey of selection and assessment issues in 1,315 organizations, including firms in both public and private sectors employing a total of more than 1 million people. About 17 percent of these organizations use ACs as an assessment tool in selecting various kinds of employees. The type of assessees, the length of AC, and the frequencies of tools used in an AC are listed in Table 28.1.

Table 28.1 Survey of AC practices in China

Who is the AC for?	
Level of assessee	**%**
Senior managers	65
Middle level managers	69
Management trainees	35
Employees	24
Operators	9
Length of AC	
No. of days	**%**
½ or less	28
1	34
1½-2	21
>2	16

Tools used in AC	
Tools	**%**
Structured interviews	74
Leaderless group discussions	58
Personality tests	58
Case analysis exercises	57
Role play simulations	50
Cognitive ability tests	49
Group discussion with assigned roles	36
Presentations	36
In-basket exercises	30

Based on 196 companies who use ACs as a selection tool; adapted from China Select (2010), China Talent Selection Survey 2010.

As shown in the table, the AC is mostly used for assessing and selecting middle managers (69 percent) or senior managers (65 percent) and the most frequently used AC techniques are structured interviews (74 percent), leaderless group discussions (58 percent), personality tests (58 percent), and case analysis exercises (57 percent). Most of the ACs (63 percent) in these organizations last no more than 1 day.

In China, there are four different types of organizations in terms of ownership: the public sector, state-owned enterprises, private companies, and foreign invested firms including multinational companies (MNCs). AC practices are quite different in these four types of firms. A number of other studies found differences in how AC techniques were applied in different organizations within the country (Wang 1990; Liang 2008; 2010). Different applications of AC in different types of organizations are summarized in Table 28.2.

First, ACs are widely applied in multinational firms. Large MNCs tend to transfer their home HRM practices including ACs to their Chinese subsidiaries (Zhu 2005). Compared with the other three types of Chinese companies, the AC practices in MNCs are more comprehensive and the AC tools more elaborate. Liang and Xu (2010) found that more than 50 percent of the multinational firms used AC methods for employee selection. Many well-known MNCs such as Unilever, Philips, AkzoNobel, Shell, General Motor, AstraZeneca, and Danone have set up an AC specifically for campus recruiting and management trainee selection. The leaderless group discussion is often used as a screening tool when a large number of candidates apply for entry level jobs. The most sophisticated use of ACs in MNCs is for early identification of high-potential employees in key functions. According to a recent survey on succession management practices with a sample of 20 MNCs in China (Xu and Liang 2010), approximately one-third of MNCs use an AC to identify and develop their high potential employees. Table 28.3 summarizes key features of a developmental assessment center in a multinational pharmaceutical company in China.

Table 28.2   AC applications in different types of organizations in China

	Multinational corporations	Private companies	State-owned companies	Public sector
Purpose	Both for selection and development	Mostly for selection or promotion with a few trials for development centers	Mostly for selection or promotion with a few trials for development	For selection or promotion only
Participants	Almost all important jobs including management trainees, middle level managers, senior executives and high potentials	Management trainees, middle level managers and senior executives	Management traineess and senior executives	Middle and lower level employees
AC Techniques	All AC techniques. Simulations may be developed based on job analysis and critical incidents	Structured interview, psychological tests, off-the-shelf simulations (including in-basket, leaderless group discussion) may be used; Simulations are rarely developed based on the job analysis	Panel structured interview, psychological tests, personal history data, background investigation, off-the-shelf simulations (including in-basket, leaderless group discussion) may be used; Simulations are rarely developed based on the job analysis	Panel situational interview, psychological tests, SJTs, personal history data, background investigation, off-the-shelf simulations (including in-basket, leaderless group discussion) may be used; Simulations are rarely developed based on the job analysis
Length	½–2 days	½–1 day	Rarely exceed ½ day	Rarely exceed ½ day
Validation	A few	Rare	Never	Never; focus on objectivity and fairness

Table 28.3 A case of a Developmental Assessment Center in a MNC

DAC Features	Descriptions
High fidelity of the simulations	Simulations are developed based on critical incidents faced by sales managers. They are integrated, realistic, "day-in-the-life" simulations of key challenges of higher level positions (one level above the candidates' current position).
Multiple assessment tools	The simulations include multiple exercises such as an in-basket, client role play, and business plan presentation.
Internal assessors	Multiple, well-trained internal role players and observers are used (3–4 assessors for each candidate).
Job competency model	Evaluations are made against objective behavioral competencies which are developed based on critical incident interviews with subject matter experts of the target job (supervisors, high performers, and other job stakeholders).
Follow-up development activities	A half-day self-development strategy workshop is conducted for all assessees; a detailed written assessment report as well as one-on-one feedback is provided to each assessee; each assessee is required to prepare an individual development plan which may be reviewed by their supervisor.

Concerning the private companies, we cannot assume there is a uniform pattern of AC use in this sector. This is because the private sector has grown rapidly over the last three decades. In 2010, one-in-five employees in China worked in the private sector. The number of private companies had reached 7.5 million, accounting for half of China's gross domestic product (All-China Federation of Industry and Commerce). Nevertheless, the predominant forms in the private sector are small and medium sized companies. Similar to other countries, many of these small and medium-sized companies are managed on a less systematic basis and lack sophisticated HRM practices. Thus, ACs are rarely used in these small and medium-sized companies. However, many well-managed private firms have started to gain market share in every industrial sector in China (for example, Vanke, LiNing, MetersBonwe) or even in the international market (for example, Lenovo, Huawei, and BYD). Many of them became publicly traded companies. A large number of people who had previously been working in MNCs are now working or seeking jobs in these fast growing companies. Therefore, AC use is growing in popularity in recent years among some large and fast growing private firms. First, there is a growing need for ACs to be used as an assessment tool to enhance the match between experienced external candidates and the job and organization requirements. Second, there is a growing need for ACs to be used as a component in their campus recruitment effort. The campus recruiting methods including AC tools practiced in MNCs in China are more visible and therefore tend to be quickly learned by these private companies.

Occasionally, a few private companies may use ACs as an OD intervention to help solve their people problems. One of the authors once received a request from a CEO in a private hi-tech company to help reduce the gulf between the CEO and one of his key direct reports. The CEO volunteered to be assessed and his key direct report and 5 other managers participated in the assessment center. Both the CEO and the key manager were provided with written assessment reports with detailed descriptions of their strengths and development needs followed by coaching sessions. The two regained trust immediately after the coaching sessions.

To better understand AC applications in China, we need to truly understand the essence of human resource management in China, particularly in public organizations and state-owned companies. Almost without exception, all of the top managers we have interviewed pointed out that the major difference between state-owned companies and private or foreign companies lies in the human resource regulations. You would find the same practices in marketing, manufacturing, or sales departments in Chinese state-owned companies as those in foreign companies, but you would not find the same practices in the human resource department. Human resource functions such as selection, promotion and performance management are usually based on job analysis and competency modeling. However, selections for senior level civil servants or CEOs are not merely based on job analysis and competency modeling. The government has special means for selecting this group of people which include political concerns.

In the public sector, there are two different systems of selecting people. For middle and lower-level employees, competency-based human resource practices are widely used; however, top managers go through the special selection process by the Organization Department of the Communist Party. The criteria and processes of the two different selection systems are different. The selection criteria of the Organization Department of the Communist Party include *de* (morality), *neng* (ability), *qin* (diligence), *ji* (performance), and *lian* (probity), and AC practices are seldom used in this selection process.

In Chinese state-owned companies, the human resource department has more power than the HR department in private or foreign companies. Selection, promotion, or human resource allocations are not necessarily based on requirements of the position, and may be based on "guanxi" inside the companies. Furthermore, a new position could be developed just for a certain person. Therefore, open and transparent communication is not a characteristic of the HR department; rather, HR professionals are expected to keep confidential secrets. In many cases managers do not use norms and regulations to manage people; they use some special interpersonal relations skills to make sure things are done well. When managing the same group of people under the same circumstances, managers with better interpersonal skills will be more effective. This makes interpersonal skills almost the most important skill in public sector and state-owned companies. Thus, special attention is needed to design sessions to assess communication and interpersonal skills. Thus, simulation context design should be aligned with the local business environment, reflecting business environments and challenges in China.

About 20 percent of state-owned enterprises (SOEs) use AC methods in China, where the AC is primarily used for selection of senior executives as well as campus recruiting efforts. Unlike the private sector, the state-owned enterprises consist of the 128 largest SOEs directly controlled by the central government and close to 154,000 SOEs supervised by local governments. Although only 3.1 percent of enterprises are SOEs, the average assets of SOEs are 13.4 times of that of non-SOEs (Xu 2010). Due to their protected position in China's huge market, many of the largest SOEs such as China Mobile Communications, China National Petroleum and China Petrochemical have been listed as the most profitable companies in China. However, the competition is getting intense in the domestic market as well as in the international market, and the state authorities acknowledge these SOEs lag behind foreign rivals in skills and efficiency. Therefore, the government has launched several campaigns in recent years in global talent searches of executives to help strengthen these companies' international competitiveness (McDonald 2010). Thus, the AC is called upon to help assess the fit between the candidates from home and abroad and the job requirements. The AC tools may include a case study, personality test, and structured interview. It's interesting to note that, while the panel interview is rarely used in MNCs and private companies probably due to concerns of efficiency, many SOEs prefer a panel-interview format to conduct a selection interview where the CEOs and Party bosses, human resource directors as well as some university professors or external consultants serve as interviewers. Special screening, primarily based on candidates' personal history data (for example, whether the candidates have written, spoken, or done anything that is against the Party), may be conducted to make sure these candidates are loyal to the Party.

In the public sector, AC methods are not as widely used, because the China Communist Party maintains control of leaders by using a selection process "behind closed doors." For those public sector organizations that have been using AC methods, in most cases, they use them to select middle and lower-level employees instead of senior-level managers. Specifically, paper and pencil tests in civil service examinations are used only for entry-level government employees, the contents of which cover logical reasoning, verbal ability, and knowledge of government regulations and policies and current affairs. Situational judgment tests (SJTs) have been developed since 2003 (Qi and Dai 2003) and adopted by the China Centre for Leadership Assessment (CCLA) under the Central Organization Department in 2006.

Personality inventories are used in some cases. Only the in-basket exercise and leaderless group discussion are sometimes used for government positions beyond the entry level, and the structured interview is a must for senior level of government officials. The dominant method is the situational interview which is a highly structured, standardized process (Hong and Tu 2006).

The format of situational interview developed by the China Centre for Leadership Assessment (CCLA) is more like a traditional exam with the following features:

- A script with standard situational interview questions.
- A display which is used to show the interview questions read by the principal interviewer to the candidate in some cases.
- The interview session lasts approximately 40 minutes per candidate.
- The interview panel usually consists of one principal interviewer and five to seven judges. The principal interviewer is normally a senior official two levels above the target positions, while judges are professors or management consultants from universities, management consulting firms and other departments of the government agencies.
- The panel of the interviewers and judges complete the rating forms which cover six to seven leadership dimensions.
- Examples of commonly assessed leadership dimensions include: Organizing and Influencing, Analytical Thinking and Innovation, Flexibility in Decision-making, Learning and Adaptability, Interpersonal Sensitivity, Motivating Others, Communication.

Although the Party maintains control of the selection of local government leaders, the "behind closed doors" selection process is widely criticized as hotbeds for corruption, nepotism, and the selection of incompetent leaders. A new process termed "open recommendation and selection" (ORS) has recently attracted attention when ORS was carried out in selecting leaders at the county, district, and bureau levels in several provinces across China. The essence of ORS is that candidates now go through a competitive and transparent instead of "behind closed doors" selection process. The new tools used in ORS encourage public feedback through telephone hotlines, official websites, and mail in comments (Song 2008). For example, the capital of Guizhou province, Guiyang City, has recently selected Party secretaries at the county and district levels through ORS procedures after a mass riot took place in an adjacent county in 2008. The ORS process in Guiyang is illustrated in Figure 28.1 (Liang 2008).

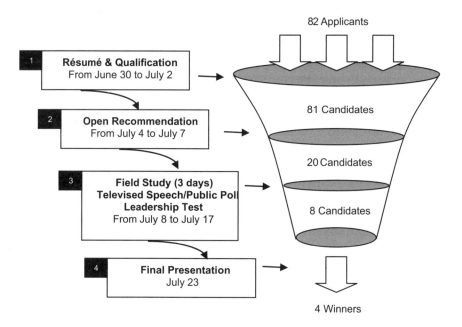

Figure 28.1 ORS in action: Guiyang case

It should be noted that the selection process in the public sector is based more on fairness rather than predictive validity. The AC tools adopted in the selection process such as the situational interview, situational judgment tests and other tools, are all favored because they are readily standardized. The assessors' proficiencies in assessment tools such as probing skills in a structured behavioral interview are less valued. The assessors would never be allowed to operate alone to conduct assessments of candidates, as there is a risk they would easily be influenced by the personal connections of the candidates. As a matter of fact, the concept of validity has not been well understood in China, especially in the public sector. Very few empirical studies have been carried out to collect validation evidence on various selection tools used in the public sector.

In a selection assignment for a central government agency, one of the authors of this chapter personally had a very interesting experience when he was enlisted to be one of the external assessors for a promotional assessment for a senior government official position.

The government agency did not understand the value of behavioral observations during the assessment. Among the nine assessors, he was the only one who took any detailed notes during the interview process. The rest of the assessors only marked the scores on the so-called competency rating scales. Several of them were curious about the note-taking behavior and asked why he did this.

Cultural Issues in Implementing Assessment Centers in China

As Byham (2004) indicated, an AC is an easily adaptable evaluation system, not an evaluation instrument; it is a standardized procedure for evaluating participants to predict future behaviors specific to a particular organization and environment. Therefore, AC practices in China are very similar to those in the West. As a standard procedure or system, AC practices influence: how job analysis is conducted, the nature of job requirements, defining the target group, the assessment techniques (exercises) to be employed, who should be assessors, and the content of the assessor training.

However, culture affects behavior, and people from different culture are socialized to behave in different ways. Therefore, in AC practices, observational systems, self- and peer-ratings, information policy toward participants, data-integration processes, feedback processes, and the evaluation of the AC, are country-specific. In addition, cross-cultural issues should concern AC processes such as competency modeling, assessment of people's competencies, simulation design, and feedback. For example, the same psychological tests may not be valid in Chinese settings because of different social norms.

Since people from different cultures may interpret behaviors in different ways, the effects of cultural values across different countries should not be ignored. In fact, a lack of well-trained specialists for interpreting AC results has always been a problem in Chinese organizations. Liu and Davis (2010) summarized a number of cross-cultural studies and found that compared to Americans, Chinese are higher in power distance, lower in individualism, higher in collectivism, higher in uncertainty avoidance, less internal and less self-enhancing for achievement events, and exhibit less universalism. The study performed by the Chinese Culture Connection (1987) shows that the Chinese might be characterized as high on identification with their various in-groups, which means they tend to keep high harmony within groups. Hofstede's IBM survey and Bond's Chinese value survey showed that Chinese, more so than Americans, are likely to choose long-term rather than short-term orientation decisions (Hofstede 1991).

Members of collectivist cultures were more likely to be affected by relational aspects than were members of individualist cultures (Dong and Liu 2010; Hofstede 1991). There are many differences in behavioral competencies, especially in interpersonal interactions, between Chinese and Westerners. Compared to the west, the Chinese adopt a more subtle approach when dealing with difficult interpersonal issues such as negative feedback in performance appraisal, demotion, or removing an old colleague from a position in an organization. Some actions considered ineffective in the West might be perceived as moderately effective, especially in very traditional Chinese organizations such as state-owned enterprises. For example, a top management team would select members representing different stake-holders rather than selecting the most competent members.

Power distance is another cultural value that will affect AC applications. Chinese society is characterized as high power distance. Most decision-making processes involve the approval of the upper-level managers. Managers, especially in public sectors and state-owned companies prefer to select subordinates who show the characteristic of high power distance above any other knowledge, skills and competencies. For example, in an in-basket exercise, Chinese civil servant candidates will probably choose decisions reflecting their supervisors' opinion rather than choosing the ones they believe to be right. Top managers are usually selected from outside the organization, and only people above certain administrative hierarchy could become candidates for selection.

Chinese people give special priority to "saving face." They are not only concerned with threats to their own loss of face, but also carefully avoid causing a "loss of face" for others. Acting to preserve the face of others will enhance their own. Therefore, in Chinese society, indirectness is favored, so statements are made tentatively and unpleasant truths tend to be avoided.

Providing feedback is an important output from an AC. Feedback given to candidates after attending an AC usually focuses not just on the decision, but also on development plans for the individuals concerned (Fletcher and Kerslake 1992). However, this kind of formal feedback process is a big challenge in Chinese culture. The cultural value of power distance and harmony make seeking and giving feedback more difficult in Chinese settings (Liang, Pan, Lu and Li 2002). Given that Chinese culture places more emphasis on saving face, people in China are not used to asking for and providing feedback, for they are concerned with any damage to one's face. Negative feedback could pose a serious problem to the smooth functioning of the team, if not given appropriately (Liu and Davis 2006). Thus, the question arises as to what extent candidates are able to display an accurate impression of their performance during the AC itself. In fact, because most ACs are used for selection purposes, feedback is rarely given to the candidates. In China, no one would question the results as long as it is standardized. There is a misunderstanding in China that if a selection tool is standardized, then it must be fair (Liang and Yang 2007). One possible solution is to engage in small talk to show your concern and care before getting to the subject of constructive feedback, which means a longer time is required to conduct a feedback session, than might be the case in the west.

Trust building is important in any workplace, and especially so in China. This shows up in assessment, for example, in a role-play exercise, where one has to be very careful not to be too direct. Even when having different opinions, Chinese people tend to keep silent rather than express different opinions openly. Additionally, in a high power distance society like China, you have to choose a senior person to play the role of "boss" since people talk differently to a younger person than to an older, senior manager. It is therefore very difficult for candidates who have been given the brief of a new boss to tackle sensitive issues, such as a performance issue, with one of their subordinates in a first meeting.

One major characteristic unique to China is the Chinese concept of "guanxi" (Cheng 2000). A rough translation of this term is that it exists everywhere in the Chinese workplace and one could not do business without it; perhaps similar to the western term "atmosphere." Chinese supervisors often go out of their way to help subordinates who share high-quality relationships with them. It is important to maintain good "guanxi" with the customers and colleagues since providing backup support, which refers to filling in for team members when they are absent, and trust in a working team are highly affected by "guanxi." This means that every time someone returns from an assessment, his friends and colleagues would expect him to share all that he knows, otherwise their relationships would be damaged. Therefore, we have to change the simulation exercises from time to time, in order to maintain confidentiality and security.

In sum, the design of simulations, standards of evaluation, and the execution of AC techniques should be aligned with the Chinese working environment in order to obtain a better understanding and more accurate assessment of candidates. For example, text messages or SMS are quite popular in China and everyone uses them very often but no one uses voice mail. Therefore the medium used for communication in an AC should be considered carefully. As another example, exchanging gifts is also a popular custom in China. Usually the value of the gift is an indication of how important the receiver is in the sender's eyes. In simulation designs, this custom would need to be covered.

Challenges and Future Trends in Assessment Centers in China

Despite the apparent need for assessment tools and methodologies in China, there are several challenges that need to be addressed in AC practices in Chinese organizations. The most critical challenge for AC applications in Chinese organizations is validity of inferences of AC results (Chen and Wang 2002), mainly because managers in Chinese organizations do not have the sense of validity in general. Validity focuses on the inferences drawn from test scores (Guion and Highhouse 2006), thus ensuring the appropriateness and prediction of selection and promotion procedures (Schleicher and Day 2002). Without validation research, misguided selection tools such as graphology and horoscopes will prevail. As a matter of fact, about 12–16 percent of Chinese organizations use graphology as a selection tool, and 7 percent use horoscopes in their employee selection.

There are regulations on equal employment opportunities in China, but with little impact on employment practices. There are no legal risks for using invalid testing devices at present. The most important value of a selection tool is to provide a process with face validity and standardization, like the college entry exam (Liang and Yang 2007).

A second challenge regarding AC practices is the relative difficulty in developing a valid competency model in private Chinese companies using traditional job analysis or competency modeling methods. Most of the private companies have a relatively short history and they are very dynamic in terms of growth rate as well as strategic direction. Many people are promoted very fast and the job requirements are constantly changing. While "learning on the fly" is definitely a key characteristic for managers and employees alike in the private sector, it is indeed difficult to develop a job competency model in such a dynamic business context. Without a solid competency model as a basis, the AC method will be less effective.

Third, moral character has been an essential attribute of leaders in Chinese organizations throughout Chinese history, in both political and business organizations. Several studies have demonstrated that the moral character dimension is significantly related to the leadership effectiveness in Chinese organizations (Ling 1989, Hui and Tan 1999). However, this competency is often confused with loyalty to the Party, which is a prerequisite for executives in state-owned enterprises and government agencies. As operational definitions of leaders' moral character vary among different organizations and across different sectors, it poses a great challenge for the Chinese AC practitioners to effectively assess this leadership dimension.

Future Trends of AC Practices in China

There is an apparent trend that more companies, especially the largest and best-managed private and state-owned Chinese companies are using ACs to develop their future leaders. There are several reasons for the emerging interest in this practice. First, many best-managed and well-known MNCs in China are using ACs to develop high potential talent and this "best practice" tends to be transferred to the domestic Chinese companies. Second, more and more private Chinese firms are paying attention to succession management, after their founders have run the businesses for two or three decades, and now the first generation entrepreneurs are near retirement. Third, as China continues being a growth market, the demand for experienced and talented people is growing accordingly. Various approaches including ACs are coming into play to help address the talent development issues.

The necessity to demonstrate adequate psychometric evidence of construct validity of AC ratings should be recognized by more people in Chinese organizations. More valid AC techniques need to be developed and applied widely in different types of organizations in China.

To improve cross-cultural sensitivity, more cultural training needs to be undertaken. Dong and Liu (2010) argued that cross-cultural training should cover personal space (the proximity between people during interactions), differences in terminology/language, body language/mannerisms/gestures, the hierarchy in organizations, physical dress/wardrobe, determination of leadership, personality characteristics, and providing positive and negative feedback.

Summary and Conclusions

In sum, the design of Chinese organizational assessment systems has been changing. The capabilities of individuals are the primary focus. These capabilities cause organizations to be managed in a way that develops organizational capabilities and provides competitive advantage. The best approach to selection for a competency-based organization would be to include realistic assessments of whether individuals are capable of learning the types of skills that are needed by the organization (Thornton and Mueller-Hanson 2004). AC methods are most appropriate for that purpose. In the past, Chinese practitioners have brought in Western tools and test materials and conducted AC practices in China in a standardized way, consistent with how they are used internationally. Having reviewed many issues concerning the ways in which culture can be associated with AC practices, in the future more AC exercises that reflect Chinese culture should be developed to serve the rapidly changing nature of the working environment within China. It is important for researchers and practitioners to design and validate more AC techniques in Chinese settings.

References

Byham, W.C. 2004. What is an Assessment Center? The Assessment Center Method, Applications, and Technologies. [Online]. Available at: http://www.assessmentcenters.org/articles/whatisassess3.asp [accessed: 2 July 2010].

Chen, M.K. and Wang, C.M. 2002. Assessment center: Development procedures and construct validity. *Chinese Journal of Ergonomics*, 8, 27–30.

Cheng, S.M. 2000. Globalization and job search strategies: The use of "Guanxi" among Chinese business students. *Management Research News*, 23, 69–70.

China Australia Governance Program 2007. China Development Brief. [Online]. Available at: http://www.chinadevelopmentbrief.com/node/925 [accessed: 2 July 2010].

China Select. 2010. China Talent Selection Survey 2010. [Online]. Available at: http://www.chinaselect.cn [accessed: 2 July 2010].

Chinese Culture Connection. 1987. Chinese values and the search for culture-free dimensions of culture. *Journal of Cross-Cultural Psychology*, 18, 143–164.

Dong, K. and Liu, Y. 2010. Cross-cultural management in China. *Journal of Cross-cultural Management*, 17, 223–243.

Fletcher, C. and Kerslake, C. 1992. The impact of assessment centers and their outcomes on participants' self-assessment. *Human Relations*, 45, 281–289.

Guion, R.M. and Highhouse, S. 2006. *Essentials of Personnel Assessment and Selection*. Mahwah, NJ: Lawrence Erlbaum Associates.

Hofstede, G. 1991. *Cultures and Organizations: Software of the Mind*. London: McGraw-Hill.

Hong, Z. and Tu, D. 2006. Reliability analysis of structured interview: A multivariate generalizability theory approach. *Psychological Exploration*, 26, 85–90, 95.

Hui, C.H. and Tan, G.C. 1999. The moral component of effective leadership: The Chinese case. In *Advances in Global Leadership, Volume 1*, edited by W.H. Mobley. JAI Press, 249–266.

Liang, K.G. 2010. *Assessment Center in China: What is the Difference?* [Online]. Available at: http://www.cndgroup.com/Article/ShowClass.asp?ClassID=12 [accessed: 2 July 2010].

Liang, K.G., Pan, D.H., Lu, Y.J. and Li, Z.L. 2002. 360-degree feedback as a leadership development process: The Chinese cases. *The first Symposium on the organizational behavior and human resource development of both sides of the Taiwan Straits, Shanghai, China*, 1, 1–10.

Liang, K.G. and Xu, Y.L. 2010. Talent Recruiting and Selection at Post-Crisis Period in China. The 46th CnD Leadership Forum.

Liang, K.G., Xu, Y.L. and Fu, Y.H. 1992. Assessment center method: An application in assessment center management and construct validity. *Chinese Journal of Applied Psychology*, 4, 50–57.

Liang, K.G. and Yang, X. 2007. *Challenges in Implementing Personality Assessment in Chinese Firms*. Paper presented at the Practice Forum chaired by R. Arvey: The Generalizability of Personality Assessment Techniques in Non-Western Cultures. The 22nd annual conference of Society for Industrial and Organizational Psychology, New York, New York, US.

Liang, K.G. 2008. *Government Selection in China: Past, Present and Future*. Presentation at the 34th International Congress on Assessment Center Methods, Washington, DC.

Lievens, F. and Thornton, G.C. III. 2005. Assessment centers: recent developments in practice and research. In *Handbook of Personnel Selection*, edited by A. Evers, O. Smit-Voskuijl, and N. Anderson. Malden, MA: Blackwell Publishing, 243–264.

Ling, W.Q. 1989. Pattern of leadership behavior assessment in China. *Psychologia: An International Journal of Psychology in the Orient*, 32, 128–134.

Liu, Y. and Davis, D. 2006. Teamwork in China. *Dissertation Abstract*, August, 2006.

Lu, H.J. 1986. A tentative study of the situational simulation method in the appraisal and selection of managerial cadres. *Psychological Science*, 9, 45–50.

Lu, H.J. 2005. *Human Resource Assessment Center*. Tsinghua University Press.

Luo, F. and Meng, Q.M. 2005. A research on how different types of graded dimensions affect the construct validity of the assessment center. *Psychological Science*, 28, 1437–1439.

McDonald, J. 2010. China's State-Owned Companies In Global Talent Search For Execs. The Huffington Post. [Online]. Available at: http://www.huffingtonpost.com/2010/08/30. [accessed: 2 July 2010].

OSS Assessment Staff. 1948. *Assessment of Men: Selection of Personnel for the Office of Strategic Services*. NY: Rinehart and Co.

Qi, S. and Dai, H. 2003. The concept, function and development of SJT. *Psychological Exploration*, 23, 43–46.

Schleicher, D.J. and Day, D.V. 2002. A new frame for frame-of-reference training: Enhancing the construct validity of assessment centers. *Journal of Applied Psychology*, 87, 735–746.

Song, N. 2008. Nanjing experiments yet again with new method of promoting officials. TIPS and LINKS, Issue 28, April 10, 2008, China Program, The Carter Center. [Online]. Available at: http://chinaelectionsblog.net/?p=13416 [accessed: 2 July 2010].

Thornton, G.C. III and Mueller-Hanson, R.A. 2004. *Developing Organizational Simulations: A Guide for Practitioners and Students*. Mahwah, NJ: Erlbaum.

Wang, L. 1997. *Organization Management Psychology*. Peking: Peking University Press.

Wang Z. 1990. *Research Methods in Psychology*. Peking: Renmin Education Press.

Wu, Z.M. 1999. *Psychometric Research of Assessment Center*. Unpublished doctoral dissertations, Beijing Normal University.

Xu, G. 2010. State-owned enterprises in China: How big are they? [Online]. Available at: http://blogs.worldbank.org/eastasiapacific 2010–01–19 [accessed: 2 July 2010].

Xu, Y.L. and Liang, K.G. 2010. A survey report on high potential identification and development in China. The 48th CnD Leadership Forum.

Yin, L. 2007. The basic characteristics and developmental trend of the assessment center. *Psychological Science*, 30, 1276–1279.

Zhu, C.J. 2005. *Human Resource Management in China – Past, Current and Future HR Practices in the Industrial Sector*. London and New York: RoutledgeCurzon.

CHAPTER

29 *The Use of Assessment and Development Centres in Russia*

SVETLANA SIMONENKO

This chapter describes the Russian HR market and more specifically the application of Assessment Centre (AC) methodology. It examines some of the cultural features that are evident in the behaviour of participants attending ACs, particularly with regard to simulation exercises such as role plays and fact-finding exercises. It also includes a case study which provides a detailed description of how a Development Centre (DC) was implemented according to best practice principles and the key role of line managers in this process.

A Brief Review of the HR Market in Russia

Examining Russia and most of the adjacent countries which were part of the former Soviet Union, this huge territory is comprised of several very different markets. There is no doubt that the largest and the most developed one is Russia, followed by Ukraine and then Kazakhstan. When we focus on how this effects assessment centre practices across the region, it is evident that there are a number of significant differences caused not only by the geography, but also by the different economic conditions in the major cities and the provinces, different levels of awareness of such methods amongst HR experts and different levels of understanding of the benefits of applying such assessment methods amongst company managers. These differences become apparent in a number of ways, ranging from how the levels of knowledge and prevailing attitudes towards HR assessment methods determine the way they are used and for what purposes, the impact that costs have on how such assessments are conducted, and how the results of these assessments are used. This chapter discusses some of these assessment issues in the context of the HR market within Russia.

The Emergence of the Assessment Centre Method

We start by looking at how the assessment centre method has evolved within the region, based largely on the level of knowledge that exists amongst practitioners. The use of assessment centres (ACs) commenced in Russia less than 20 years ago, in the early 1990s, when western companies started opening their representative offices bringing with them the methods they used in their head offices in the US, the UK and Germany. This demand led to the appearance of consulting companies, made up mainly of psychologists, who offered the use of psychological methods of personality assessment to assess personnel within these private sector companies. Very few of the consultants at that time had any idea what assessment centres were actually like, as there were no training courses or Russian language books devoted to the subject. The little knowledge that did exist came from the stories of those who had witnessed such activities or had been through assessment centres abroad.

This limited knowledge, coupled with a good psychological education and experience of carrying out therapeutic and skill-based training, enabled the consultants to visualize and create assessment centres, based on their own interpretation of the AC method, and this approach is still popular with some practitioners today. As word spread that the assessment centre is the most reliable assessment method (Ballantyne and Povah 1995, 2004), ACs became a victim of their own success in Russia, as many people now trust this method but very few really understand what an AC is like. This has resulted in the rapid development of various derivatives of the AC method, some of which are worlds apart from the way they should be, according to the established international standards (International Task Force on Assessment Center Guidelines 2009; British Psychological Society: Psychological Testing Centre 2003).

SOME QUESTIONABLE ASSESSMENT PRACTICES

In some cases it is like comparing the small medical bag of a rural doctor in the nineteenth century with the surgical equipment found in a modern hospital. For example, some ACs require 10–12 participants to sit in a semi-circle in one big room and everyone in turn stands up and makes a self-presentation, having not been given a brief or any detailed instructions. Sometimes, a time limit is set, stating that the presentation should not exceed three or five minutes. The more participants that are involved, the less time is allocated for the presentation. It is obvious that this approach has many flaws, as the participants are all able to observe each other and they are clearly not been treated equally, as the circumstances are different for each participant, depending on when they get their turn. Assessors represented by consultants, HR-experts and sometimes line managers, score the competencies at their discretion, since they usually don't have any scoring guidelines.

In such so-called ACs, all of the participants are often involved in a group discussion simultaneously. It is not unusual for them to be given a common task bearing a strong resemblance to a training exercise or a simple, elementary school mathematical problem. For example, a peasant bought a horse for RUB600 in a market and sold it for RUB800, then bought it again for RUB700 and this time sold it for RUB900. Was the deal profitable and what was the gain? The discussion tends to focus on two possible solutions to this task; namely, a gain of either RUB300 or RUB400. The whole discussion is devoted to arriving at a single answer. The correct answer is RUB400 and the answer RUB300 is a simple mathematical mistake, based on viewing this as a single transaction rather than two separate transactions, each of which makes a profit. The interesting point is that this very narrow exercise attempts to measure the Commercial Awareness competency and worse still it is also used to assess mid- and top-level managers.

Another example of inappropriate practice often occurs with role plays, where a participant has to interview a subordinate. The participants split into pairs and go to different parts of the room. The exercise is conducted with one of the participants acting as a subordinate and the other one acting as a manager and then they switch the roles. Before the role play starts, everyone is provided with a concise half-page description of his/her role. The participants read through it and start acting. When they switch roles they simply hand over the role descriptions to each other. The assessor supervises this process, gives instructions and makes notes. There are also cases when one assessor watches two or more pairs simultaneously, by simply walking from one pair to another one during the role play. Notes are made in a free format. Classifying the competency-based behaviours displayed while watching them is considered appropriate. This practice like many others is driven by a lack of appreciation of what is required to ensure an objective, fair and reliable assessment process and the wish to minimize costs. For example, to save the participants' time and the HR department's budget, it is quite popular to assess managers during training, by asking the trainer to generate each participant's profile and score some competencies based on such training results.

In order to assess senior managers, consultants are quite often asked to attend a genuine strategic planning session and observe the managers and score the competencies. Unfortunately, it has to be admitted that consultants practically always agree to such work, despite the fact that such sessions lack a suitable structure and format to make them suitable assessment activities. Moreover, some consulting companies have made such services standard, and promote them on the market as a new innovative assessment method. For example, during the recent economic crisis in 2008/09, the use of business simulations as a means of conducting assessments became widespread. A typical approach entailed 10–12 participants playing a board game devoted to one particular business aspect, such as human resource management. The consultant will often actively participate in the group and discusses their decisions, guides the participants, asks questions, throws in new information, and so on. At the end, the consultant scores the group participants against the competencies and gives descriptions of their behaviour. Thus, one consultant handles 10–12 participants. The consulting company promoting this technique will assess as many as 50–100 employees in a single day, using only 5–8 consultants. This approach has become very popular, as major Russian companies often have tens of thousands of employees and conducting talent-management programmes would otherwise take several years and cost a lot of money. Assessing 100 people within 1 day reduces both the timeframe and the budget.

Unfortunately, it is practically impossible to stop these poorly run AC imposters because of the general lack of knowledge and skill of HR experts in the personnel assessment area. Also there is usually a time lag of about 3 years before the company becomes aware that the assessment was ineffective. During the first year, steps are taken to develop those employees who scored highest against the competencies and to involve them in fast-track training programmes aimed at delivering quick improvements. However, during the second year it starts to become apparent that those who were scored high do not always show good results in work, and those who were scored lower will sometimes outperform them. The third year is devoted to understanding the reasons why these differences have arisen and this often leads to the gradual realization that it was due to the assessment methods used. Unfortunately, this results in the company management and employees being disappointed in ACs and personnel assessment in general and they decide to reject any further use of ACs.

Repairing the Reputation of ACs in the Russian Market

These blatant misrepresentations of the AC method have undoubtedly given it a 'bad name' and one of the major challenges facing the serious AC practitioner is how to overcome this problem. In our experience there are a number of things one can do, such as attempt to educate the HR market about why the AC method works and the importance of best practice if you want to realize the benefits, demonstrate the effectiveness of a well-run AC by conducting appropriate validation research, and be sensitive to how ACs are perceived in an organization that has experienced such malpractice and adopt strategies that will help to overcome any misplaced prejudices.

For example, 3 years ago we were approached by a major metallurgical company with the request to hold an AC for top executives. Two years before, the company had run a large-scale project aimed at selecting the most talented employees in all of their business units and branches. However, the poor quality of the assessment process had an extremely negative effect on the HR department's image and gave rise to great mistrust in such activities. When we started dealing with this company, it was agreed that the events would be called Development Centres, as the HR Director wanted us to avoid mentioning 'assessment', so as not to trigger negative reactions in the employees. We therefore agreed that we would refer exclusively to Development Centres and their purpose would be to identify development areas and to define personal development programmes. Clearly there is always the unethical risk that using the term Development Centre is a misrepresentation of the purpose of the centre but fortunately in this case, whilst the event entailed assessing the participants, the purpose was to develop them.

Another case illustrating the same problem of the tainted image of ACs happened as recently as 2009. The HR Director of a large Russian investment corporation asked for a presentation for their Management Committee that would illustrate how the assessment of its management team would enable predictions to be made about the company's future effectiveness. Upon viewing the draft presentation in which the AC was strongly recommended, the HR Director asked for this term to be avoided because some of the senior managers were very suspicious about ACs and did not see them as a serious approach. This was very strange, as only a year earlier they had widely employed ACs within their Talent Management process. After speaking with some managers, it emerged that the AC had been designed in-house and had some of the inappropriate characteristics described above. To avoid the predictable resistance of the managers we dropped any references to the term 'Assessment Centre' and instead referred to 'Simulation Exercises'. We also provided brief explanations and samples to demonstrate some of these exercises and emphasized that we offered a different methodology from what they had used previously.

It was clearly evident that the poor quality of the so-called AC which had been designed in-house had led HR specialists and managers to look for alternative ways of conducting personnel assessment, such as assessing people during training or whilst participating in real management meetings, and so on. This experience reinforced the need to educate the target audience and to sell the benefits of AC best practices. One particular lesson we learned from this was the possible emotional reaction that some senior managers have to the word 'assessment', so we decided to modify our sales presentations by replacing the term 'Assessment Centre' with 'Simulation Exercises'.

AC Cost-Related Issues

With such a wide variation in different approaches to how ACs are conducted, it is no surprise that the costs vary significantly as well. Furthermore, the standard of living in Moscow and St. Petersburg is much higher than in other cities and regions of Russia, and this is reflected in the prices charged for conducting ACs. For example, in 2010 in Moscow the price for carrying out an AC for one person varies from US$300 to almost US$4,000. The price depends on the level of employee being assessed and the methods used. Higher prices tend to be charged by the companies with access to western assessment techniques. The average price for conducting an in-company AC is within the range of US$400–1,200 per person. Whereas in other regions US$500 per person is the maximum price and the most frequent price range is from US$20 to US$100 per person. The same situation exists in Ukraine where the prices in Kiev are essentially higher than in other cities, as it is where most companies have their head offices. However, in general the prices in Ukraine are approximately half of those in Russia. In both Russia and Ukraine, personnel assessment services are offered by nearly all consulting companies who have an HR consulting department. For example, the services of financial audit, organizational development, business processes analysis, rerouting, and so on, can be offered at the same time. Most recruitment and training companies also offer ACs.

The price difference is also influenced by the fact that in Russia, as well as in all of the former Soviet territories, a considerable number of 'free techniques' are circulating, for example, MBTI, MMPI, 16PF, Lüscher-Color-Test and CPI, amongst others. All these questionnaires can be downloaded free of charge from the Internet. These techniques are used everywhere, both by HR staff of Russian companies and assessment consultants. Moreover, large companies use software developers to create special HR assessment software that includes such questionnaires and openly advertise it, as they are not afraid that any action will be brought against them. At universities where psychology is taught, practically any psychometric technique can be taken from the library and photocopied and even more worrying this includes the result processing keys. Copying and illegal use of books, training materials and assessment centre exercises once acquired, illustrate that the legislation designed to protect intellectual property rights does not work.

Cultural Influences

When using ACs in Russia and other CIS countries, we start by considering the typical features of standard exercises, as described in various sources such as Ballantyne and Povah (1995; 2004), British Psychological Society: Psychological Testing Centre (2003), and many others. These features make us think about the extent to which the western HR assessment approaches are applicable and how the standard exercises of ACs have to be adapted for use in Russia.

Such features, for example, include people's attitude to their private life, their desire to keep it low-key and to conceal their problems. As a rule, employees do not tend to discuss any details of their private life with managers, especially when they don't have a well-established relationship with that person. This naturally has an impact on the way participants play the role of a manager in a role play, as they tend to carefully avoid any personal issues and if such issues arise, any discussion of work-related issues stops. This is strongly evident in role plays where one of the subordinate's relatives is sick, as this type of personal problem is regarded as a totally justified explanation of the subordinate's decline in performance. Thus when encountering such a problem, the participant feels at a loss and is either afraid of asking further questions for fear of hurting his/her feelings or instead focuses on offering help and support, without seeing any need to tackle the sub-standard performance.

Another cultural difference emerges in people's attitude to decision-making. For example, having read the instructions and brief description of the situation in a fact-finding exercise, participants are sometimes ready to make decisions at once without asking any additional questions. Often while getting prepared, they develop their hypothesis of developments and make their decision based on their own experience. When the time comes to questioning, they ask only two or three questions to confirm their hypothesis and make their decision at once. The person administering the exercise will often have to remind the participant that there is time for fact-finding and there is quite a lot of information, in order to prompt them to ask questions. However, not all participants, even having received such a reminder, choose to continue asking questions, but instead insist that they are content with what they have and everything is clear. Sometimes after such reminders, the participants simply repeat questions they have already asked and then stop as they are ready to make their decision. It is safe to say that fact-finding is perceived by participants as one of the most complex and ambiguous exercises. People complain that they are not provided with the information they need so the case cannot be solved or refer to their experience rejecting any decisions other than the one made by them.

Indeed this pattern is so pronounced, with about one-third of AC participants typically behaving this way, that we decided to investigate why this happened when we provided feedback. We found that participants were often surprised how many facts could have been obtained for decision-making and they tended to say that such information was not needed by them, as in their opinion they had identified the key facts by asking those two to three questions. According to their comments, managers are perceived to be incompetent if they have to ask too many questions, as it indicates they are unable to make decisions. Prompt insight into the situation on the basis of very brief information is considered more professional than to admit that you understand nothing and to start asking many questions.

The same quality is displayed in role plays when the participants base their hypothesis of what is happening on the information provided in their brief and they merely see the role play as an opportunity to verify it. They also choose to disregard or play down any facts which challenge their initial conclusion.

Also when completing the ability tests, participants often tended to ignore the response option 'I cannot answer' even though it was a perfectly valid response if the table or the text did not provide sufficient information to be able to answer the question. This is probably because such answers were perceived negatively by candidates, as they implied that they were incapable of solving the problem.

It can be assumed that such behaviour is somehow related to the fact that fast decision-making and riskiness is socially desirable behaviour. For example, in Russia the proverbs 'the one who takes no risks has no champagne', 'nothing ventured, nothing gained' or 'there's honour in taking risks' are extremely popular.

In 2006, we carried out some research among Russian and western companies operating in the Russian and Ukrainian markets to identify the key competencies of mid-level managers (Simonenko and Khrenov 2010). We conducted over 150 interviews with managers of companies in different business sectors to analyse their work. During this research, 20 competencies were identified including such obvious competencies as Leadership, Interpersonal Sensitivity, Planning and Organizing, Problem Analysis, and so forth; however, there was no Resoluteness competency. Moreover, such behavioural indicators as 'makes decisions promptly on the basis of limited information' and 'is ready to run reasonable risk' were not included in any of the identified competencies because our respondents did not mention them in the interviews. Probably these qualities are available in plenty, and senior managers did not consider them as factors for success but as behaviours which hindered effective work. From our experience of competency modelling for different companies, managers often value diligence and the ability to be dutiful, more than decisiveness. They wish to see their subordinates as being disciplined and tolerant. However, about two to three years after implementing such competency models they often realize there is an absence of initiative and they blame their subordinates for a huge lack of independent decision-making and for failing to take responsibility. This contradiction appears to be due to the subordinate's lack of data-gathering and structured problem-solving skills. Based on poor analysis, quick decisions often end up being ineffective, so senior managers prefer to control the majority of decisions made by subordinates. Usually senior managers simply approve the decisions that they agree with and block the decisions which appear wrong from their point of view, rather than taking the time to discuss them before deciding. By acting in this manner, senior managers do not delegate authority and responsibility to their subordinates and they unconsciously discourage an environment in which they could develop their analytical and decision-making skills. This creates a vicious circle, which can only be broken by improving people-management skills, so that managers become more enlightened and recognize the need to provide the necessary developmental opportunities for their staff. Implementing AC methodology in organizations could play an important role in taking one of the first steps to tackle this particular deficiency.

A Development Centre Case Study

Fortunately it is possible to demonstrate that assessment and development centres based on the well-established and recommended methodology (International Task Force on Assessment Center Guidelines 2009; British Psychological Society: Psychological Testing Centre 2003) undoubtedly pays off and delivers high validity, if sufficient time is invested in doing things properly.

The history of carrying out development centres (DCs) in the Russian branch of Svenska Cellulosa Aktiebolaget (SCA) is interesting as it can be used as a rare illustration of the way to derive the maximum benefit from such an activity. The positive effect was achieved due to the proper organization of the assessment procedure and the active involvement of the manager in his subordinates' development.

SCA is the major European manufacturer of wood and paper products. The company manufactures and sells personal-care products, paper products and packaging solutions. The key trademarks are TENA, Libero, Libresse, Zewa, and Tork.

In 2007, we were asked to conduct a DC for six customer-contact managers. The main objective of the DC was to identify each employee's competencies requiring development. There was also a possibility that based on the assessment results, decisions would be made to promote these individuals. The DC preparation included several key tasks: drawing up the assessment matrix, creating SCA competency scoring sheets and designing the timetable for the centre. While drawing up the Assessment Matrix (see Table 29.1), we followed two key principles: each competency should be assessed in at least two exercises, and the DC should consist of as few techniques as possible.

In designing the timetable, we applied the following rules:

- Assessors should see all participants. The participant should be engaged in each subsequent exercise with a different assessor. It is necessary to minimize any opportunity for the assessors to display subjectivity or bias.
- Interactive exercises should be combined, whenever possible, with written ones.
- Sufficient numbers of breaks should be provided for the assessors to complete the scoring sheets.
- Participants should not have any long breaks between exercises.

We used seven different tools to assess the eight competencies and we suggested that the participants completed the ability tests and the personality questionnaire online, several days before the DC, which meant they only had to complete five exercises during the DC, thus enabling us to run it within 1 day.

Table 29.1 The assessment matrix

Competencies \ Technique	RPI	RPE	AP	ARG	INB	AT	15FQ+
Effective Communication	■	■			▒		▒
Cooperation	■				▒		▒
Decision-Making			■		■	▒	
Interpersonal Sensitivity	■		■				▒
Negotiating Skills	■	■					▒
Planning and Organizing	▒	▒	▒		■		▒
Problem Analysis		▒	■			■	▒
Customer Focus		■					▒

■ = This technique provides *strong* evidence of this competency.
▒ = This technique can provide *some* evidence of this competency.

RPI = Role Play (Internal) with a subordinate; RPE = Role Play (External) with a customer; AP = Analytical Presentation Exercise; ARG = Assigned Role Group Discussion; INB = In-Basket Exercise; AT = Ability Tests; 15FQ+ = Personality Questionnaire

Feedback Preparation and Delivery

Based on the assessment results and after feedback reports had been prepared, a feedback meeting was held with each participant and the sales department manager. The sales department manager was actively involved, during the assessment of the employees (attendance of separate exercises undertaken by his subordinates during the DC) and discussion of their development options.

Prior to the feedback meeting we had a discussion with the sales department manager where we presented each employee's results, the consolidated results of the business unit as a whole (covering both strengths and weaknesses) and discussed in detail what actions should be undertaken by the manager to develop each subordinate. He asked us to advise him how the results could be used in the most effective way and we suggested that the sales manager be present during the discussion of the individual development plan with each of the subordinates.

The feedback meetings, which were focused on creating individual development plans, were attended by three people: the consultant, the employee and the sales department manager (the employee's immediate superior). The consultant ran the meeting with the employee, and the manager added to the discussion as required. The feedback meeting started by focusing on the competencies that the employee planned to develop during the year. This choice is based on the DC results, the employee's preferences, the consultant's recommendations, and the business needs (Woo et al. 2009; Thornton and Rupp 2006).

However, there were frequent differences between the employee's preferences and the business needs, and the manager's vision. There were cases when the participant wished to develop the competency with the highest score, despite the fact that the DC results and the immediate superior highlighted more obvious gaps in other competencies, which would have a greater impact on his effectiveness.

In order to identify appropriate development actions, the consultant and the participant discussed which working situations and projects the employee would find most beneficial to work on, so as to develop the relevant competencies. The presence of his direct manager was of immeasurable value in this situation, as the participant was able to immediately agree the specific actions he would complete on his own and the manager would be able to supervise and ensure they were performed properly. Jointly they would also agree a plan for ongoing review and feedback. For example, when the consultant discussed the opportunity to develop the Decision-Making On-Site competency with one of the participants, the sales manager offered his help by saying that he was ready to go with the subordinate to the meeting and give him feedback after it. This action was included in the individual development plan. This action was clearly quite motivational and the subordinate was very surprised, for as he said later, he had never expected that his manager would be willing to devote so much of his time to his development.

Thus, the individual development plan was actually prepared by the employee together with his manager. The consultant provided only methodological and facilitative support. Now the employee had to put this plan into practice and the manager had to provide appropriate assistance when required and to monitor the competency development progress.

We were fortunate enough to be able to check their success of following this approach 2 years later, when we were asked to conduct another DC for them. This time the participants included the employees who had participated in the Development Centre

2 years earlier. We found it interesting to see the result of their joint efforts to develop the competencies, both of the subordinates and the manager. During this time, some of the employees' roles had changed: some were promoted, others' areas of responsibility extended or objectives had become more complex. Therefore, this time the Development Centre included more complex assessment techniques, although the objective remained more or less the same; namely, competency development, albeit within an environment with more complex objectives, and the promotion opportunity for several employees.

Table 29.2 provides an indication of the progress made in developing five different competencies between two DCs which were run in 2007 and 2009. The table contains only the data on each participant's competencies included in their 2007 individual development plans.

Table 29.2 Comparing competency development progress between two DCs

	Participant 1		Participant 2		Participant 3	
Competencies	**2007**	**2009**	**2007**	**2009**	**2007**	**2009**
Cooperation	2	3				
Decision-Making	2	3			2	2.5
Interpersonal Sensitivity			2	3		
Planning and Organizing	2	2.5	2	2		

The table demonstrates that the participants appear to have made progress on all of the competencies except one. It is also important to keep in mind that the participants faced more challenging exercises in the DC in 2009, and this meant that the same competencies were assessed at a more complex level. It is therefore not unreasonable to assume that had the same exercises been used as in 2007, the participants would have probably performed at an even higher level. During the feedback, the participants and their manager confirmed that they had actively implemented the individual development plans they had generated 2 years before, although not everybody managed to fully complete their plan.

Thus this case study illustrates that a properly conducted competency assessment procedure provides valuable information about an employee's capabilities, strengths and weaknesses. It also shows that the employee's ability to successfully complete his or her individual development plans benefits from being created and executed by the employee in conjunction with his/her manager. This results in the employee demonstrating an improvement in ability to display job-related competencies, which enables him or her to achieve higher levels of performance in work. We cannot of course claim any statistical evidence, due to the very limited sample of just three people. But we can point to the fact that this seems to provide some indication that there is a good argument for doing personnel assessment properly and there also appears to be an obvious impact of involving the manager in developing his/her subordinates' competencies and thus increasing their effectiveness.

Conclusions

As the world continues to become a smaller place and more and more multinational companies start to operate within the Russian market, there will be increasing pressure for HR technologies and services of the same quality that they get in Europe and the US. Managers who have had a working experience in multinational companies and then joined local organizations have raised the profile of HR best practices and AC methodology and have introduced them into domestic business. This has created an interest and impetus to explore these practices in Russia, Ukraine and Kazakhstan. But as the saying goes: 'a little knowledge is a dangerous thing' and the lack of familiarity with objective, systematic, merit-based HR procedures, and the absence of any national occupational standards, means that we see a lot of ill-conceived assessment events which fail to conform to the International Guidelines that define what constitutes a genuine AC or DC.

It is also important to recognize that 'western' assessment methods cannot simply be transferred in their current form, as they need to be modified to accommodate specific cultural norms and behaviours. For example, we cannot ignore tendencies such as valuing relationships more than regulations and business, valuing risk-taking and being willing to take a chance and rely on a bit of luck, and so on. Thus it is necessary to adapt assessment centre exercises (participant booklets and assessment manuals), before they can be used in any local Russian AC or DC. However, once this has been done we should be able to obtain very positive results from implementing behaviour based assessment methodology in a large, growing market such as Russia.

References

Ballantyne, I. and Povah, N. 1995. *Assessment & Development Centres* (1st Edition). Aldershot: Gower.

Ballantyne, I. and Povah, N. 2004. *Assessment and Development Centres* (2nd Edition). Aldershot: Gower.

British Psychological Society: Psychological Testing Centre. 2003. *Design, Implementation and Evaluation of Assessment and Development Centres. Best Practice Guidelines.* [Online]. Available at: http://www.psychtesting.org.uk/the-ptc/guidelinesandinformation.cfm [accessed: 19 April 2010].

International Task Force on Assessment Center Guidelines. 2009. Guidelines and ethical considerations for assessment center operations. *International Journal of Selection and Assessment,* 17, 243–254.

Simonenko, S. and Khrenov, D. 2010. *Сказки и были о методах оценки персонала. [Fairy Tales and True Stories about Assessment Methods of Personnel.]* Москва, РФ: DeTech.

Thornton, G.C. III and Rupp, D.R. 2006. *Assessment Centres in Human Resource Management: Strategies for Prediction, Diagnosis, and Development.* Mahwah, NJ: Lawrence Erlbaum.

Woo, S., Sims, C., Rupp, D. and Gibbons, A.M. 2009. Correction to 'Development engagement within and following developmental assessment centers: Considering feedback favorability and self-assessor agreement.' *Personnel Psychology,* 62, 199–200.

30 Assessment Center Practices in Japan: A Brief History and Challenges[1]

SHINICHI HIROSE

In this chapter, I briefly review over 30 years of history and the current status of assessment center (AC) practices in Japan. The way Japanese organizations utilize ACs is quite different from the practices observed in the countries where they originated, that is, the US, Canada, and the UK. This is explained mainly by cultural differences, especially in the context of the individualism and collectivism characteristics of each culture. Although most of this chapter focuses on AC practices in the private sector, some practices in the public sector will also be shared. Also, I briefly discuss the challenge of development and deployment of multicultural ACs, which are highly important for many Japanese companies facing the needs of further globalization. Finally, the issues and future outlook of AC practices by organizations operating in Japan are discussed.

Early Days of AC Adoption

Several consulting companies and training providers began exploring the potential feasibility of applying ACs in Japan in the early 1970s. They invited AC practitioners and researchers mainly from the US during this period, including Douglas W. Bray and William C. Byham, and started accumulating knowledge and capabilities of conducting ACs in Japan. However, when they started promoting selection-oriented AC programs, these weren't welcomed by most prospects. On the other hand, Japanese organizations showed much more interest in utilizing ACs for developmental purposes, which are what we now call Development Centers (DCs).

---

1   Sources of information used in this chapter are, unless otherwise clearly cited, based on interviews with professional AC/DC practitioners with considerable years of experiences as assessors and/or program administrators. I appreciate the cooperation of these people who in the interest of commercial confidentiality have chosen to remain anonymous.

WHY SELECTION ACs WEREN'T WELCOMED

In the dawn of the Japanese industrial recovery after World War II, Abegglen (1958) pointed out that the philosophy of Japanese companies is lifetime employment and the workplace is not simply a place to earn wages but a symbiotic community. Since each *kaisha* (company) was regarded as a closed community in which all members share a common destiny, it was hesitant to let outside consultants evaluate its internal members. People in the kaisha believed that they know each other extremely well, and they did not feel the need to ask outside parties to evaluate their "family" members. They were quite confident about making judgments about promotions by themselves. On the other hand, in the midst of a high-growth economy, they were very eager to see their people grow in other ways, such as through developmental programs, which weren't explicitly connected with promotional decisions.

Japanese culture also had to be considered in the interpretation of certain behaviors in certain exercises. For example, it is often noted that Japanese assessees tend to withhold many critical decisions in the in-basket exercise in order to ensure that a consensus is reached later. Under the US scheme, such behavior is very likely to be judged as "indecisive," whereas reaching consensus for major issues is a norm in Japanese corporations.

In addition to the kaisha culture, the Equal Employment Opportunity Act was passed in 1972. Companies gradually started to consider the renovation of their internal HR systems which at that time were quite seniority-based and male-dominated, and some of them began to use outside consultants for the introduction of new programs.

ADOPTION OF DCs IN THE 1980s

Although the early adopters signed up to DCs in the late 1970s, many companies didn't introduce them until the 1980s. Japan was in the bubble economy in the late 1980s and many companies reported record-high revenues and profits. In this cash-rich situation, many Japanese companies started new initiatives in employee development and, in their pursuit of new goals, a number of companies decided to embrace DCs. The typical companies who adopted DCs were Japan-based companies or Japanese subsidiaries of foreign-based companies employing over 10,000 workers. Examples include NTT (Nippon Telegraph and Telephone Corporation), Panasonic (previously Matsushita), Toyota, and Prudential Life Insurance. Most of these companies developed internal assessors in addition to getting help from professional assessors to conduct DCs. They embedded the DC into their formal human resource management (HRM) process.

The introduction of a DC typically started at the level of junior managers (Kacho) with 20 to 40 participants per session, and then moved up to the senior manager level (Bucho), though rarely to the executive level. In most of these companies, the first decision-maker for the introduction of the DC was the Director of Human Resources who was also a member of the corporate executive board. The strategic importance of the DC was well communicated by the HR Director to the top management group. AC/DC practitioners commonly believe that the practice of DCs introduced in 1980s is still continuing in most of these organizations. During design and implementation, many modifications and adaptations were made to fit ACs originated in the US into Japanese corporate culture, as in the case of Wacoal described in Taylor and Frank (1988).

Formats of ACs and DCs in Japan

The notable features of a Japanese program are most clearly observed in the DC for junior managers. Though programs targeted for other layers also carry the flavor of Japanese corporate/national culture, relatively speaking they seem to be similar to the US practices.

DCs FOR JUNIOR MANAGERS

In the DC program for junior managers, almost all exercises except the individual role playing involve group work and a peer-feedback process. Typically the participants are assigned to three groups, and two groups are instructed to observe the third group whilst they participate in an exercise. When that group finishes their exercise, the next group participates in the exercise under the observation of the other two groups, and so on. At the end of each exercise, feedback is given by members of the two observing groups, and by the formally assigned and trained assessors. In other words, all participants are asked to play the role of "informal assessors," while experiencing the exercises themselves. To accommodate this arrangement, the session schedule is designed as shown in Figure 30.1.

	DAY 1		DAY 2		DAY 3	
9:00	Orientation • Purpose and process 1. Role of Manager and Required Skills/ Dimensions		4. In-Basket (cont'd) • Group discussion • Presentation of group's recommendations • Assessor feedback & debrief		6. Analysis & Presentation (cont'd) • Presentation • Watch video • Assessor feedback & debrief	
12:15	Lunch		Lunch		Lunch	
13:00	2. Group Discussion #1		5. Group Discussion #3		7. Coaching Interaction (cont'd) • Watch video • Assessor feedback & debrief	
	(Group 1) • Group discussion • Watch video • Peer feedback	(Groups 2 & 3) • Observe & record behaviors • Complete FB form	(Group 3) • Group discussion • Watch video • Peer feedback	(Groups 1 & 2) • Observe & record behaviors • Complete FB form		
					8. Drafting Personal Development Plan	
	3. Group Discussion #2		6. Analysis & Presentation	7. Coaching Interaction		Individual Feedback Sessions
	(Group 2) • Group discussion • Watch video • Peer feedback	(Groups 1 & 3) • Observe & record behaviors • Complete FB form	• Individual analysis	• Preparation • Coaching role play		
						17:00
18:00	Dinner		Dinner			
19:00	4. In-Basket • Individual work		6. Analysis & Presentation (cont'd) • Individual analysis			

Figure 30.1 Typical three-day DC schedule for junior managers

Source: Takeuchi (2010).

Group-oriented program design can be seen in many parts of Figure 30.1. On the morning of Day 1, the orientation session is held. Here, in addition to the general program explanation, the key dimensions that need to be observed are clearly presented. Brief training for peer assessment skills is also given. The group discussions are videotaped so that participants can watch it while getting feedback from peers. Even with the in-basket exercise, a group activity is added. After completion of the individual in-basket exercise, there is a group discussion session, where the participants are asked to jointly evaluate each person's output and to develop group recommendations as collective outputs.

The layout of the room is also specially arranged to allow peer observation and feedback, as seen in Figure 30.2. In this figure, six people in group 1 conduct a group discussion under the observation of the people in groups 2 and 3. Under this arrangement, participant 2A, who belongs to group 2 and participant 3A in group 3 are instructed to observe the behavior of participant 1A in group 1 (Takeuchi 2010).

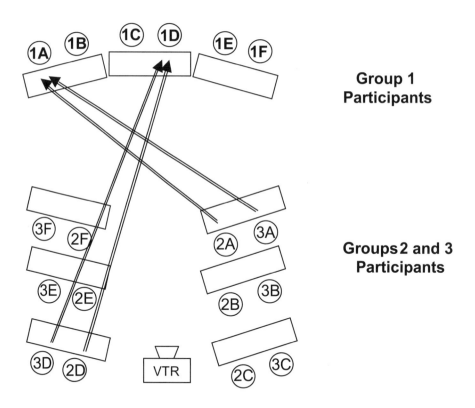

Figure 30.2 Group discussion layout for peer observation and feedback
Source: Takeuchi (2010).

It is widely believed that the heavy use of peer feedback in these DCs is effective and successful owing to the Japanese corporate and national culture. As many researchers pointed out, the Japanese workplace is dominated by collectivism, in contrast to individualism. For example, in his global survey of business culture, Hofstede (1980) found that Japan is one of the least individualistic countries. Triandis (1995) and Huff and Kelley (2003) argued that in-group trust is strong in collectivist cultures like Japan, and Howard, Shudo and Umeshima (1983) found that Japanese put importance on the outward-oriented values such as a world of beauty and being cheerful, while Americans value personal independence and autonomy (Cole 1979). Although there are some indications that Japanese are gradually becoming more individualistic (Miyanaga 1991), Japanese are still much more collectivistic than Americans (Ralston, Holt, Terpstra and Kai-Cheng 2008).

A collectivistic atmosphere is evident in Japanese offices. There are no partitions in the room, and the staff can see each other all day. Everyone knows who's doing well and who's not, and extends help to others when needed. In this environment, a competitive motivation among peers is almost non-existent and peers are open and positive in helping others grow. Also, organizational citizenship behavior is prevalent within collectivistic cultures (Moorman and Blakely 1995). This cultural setting nurtured the development of Japanese DCs for junior managers, where the participants are asked to provide each other with peer feedback. In this context, the peer feedback becomes as important as the advice made by trained assessors.

The set of dimensions was also reconsidered and modified to fit the Japanese societal and workplace value set shared in most companies. For example, when the 25 dimensions developed for AT&T's Management Progress Study (Bray, Campbell and Grant 1974) were considered for application to the Japanese programs, several dimensions were dropped, including the dimension of "Ability to Delay Gratification." This decision was made because some dimensions did not have discriminative power when applied to a Japanese sample, that is, samples showed very homogeneous responses. Analytically, while Arthur, Day, McNelly and Eden (2003) boiled down 168 dimension labels into 6 overriding dimensions in their meta-analysis, Toshima (2001) in Japan grouped 18 original dimensions into three categories by using the factor analysis method. Three factors, accounting for 28 per cent of the variance, were named problem-handling, autonomous decision-making, and interpersonal effectiveness.

In recent years, however, there have been discussions to put some eliminated dimensions back into the commonly used dimension sets. This trend is because there are some indications that the mindset of Japanese people is gradually becoming more individualistic (Miyanaga 1991), and because many foreigners, who have joined the Japanese workforce to make up for the shortage of the domestic working population, have introduced more diversity to the Japanese workforce.

Some companies prefer offering DCs for all manager candidates before promotion selection, so that they can provide equal growth opportunity to all qualified employees. In such cases, the DCs have two purposes: the explicit purpose is preparatory development of managerial skills: the implicit purpose is to collect supplementary performance data to be used when making promotion decisions. Other major components for promotional consideration are the accumulated annual performance appraisal data and semi-structured interviews conducted by junior executives (who are not in the reporting line of the assessee) at the end of the promotional consideration process. As such, this type of pre-promotion DC may be better termed an Assessment-Development Center. However, many companies still use DCs as post-promotion training, to make those who got promoted ready for their new position and job requirements. This type of DC typically does not rigorously collect individual performance data.

AC/ADC FOR SENIOR MANAGERS

In the programs targeted at senior managers, the main purposes are evaluation and selection, rather than development. Therefore the programs are more AC-like rather than DC-like. In general, the peer observation system is not used in such programs. The majority of exercises are individualized, and only a few group assignments are given. For executive-level assessment, "A Day in the Life" style of totally integrated exercises are conducted in simulated executive suites which have been provided by professional assessment firms in recent years. Some companies conduct ACs for top-level executives (the C-suite) in English, with a non-Japanese dimension set, so they can select globally capable and adaptable leaders who can operate in an environment with global competition and alliances. Japanese companies use senior manager/executive ACs for internal promotion in almost all cases, while the Japanese subsidiaries of foreign-based MNCs sometimes use them as methods for external hiring.

ASSESSOR EXPERIENCE AS A GROWING/EDUCATIONAL OPPORTUNITY

Japanese companies often consider that the role of an AC/DC assessor provides their internal assessors with opportunities for growth. Companies expect their internal assessors to become more familiar with the company's developmental dimensions, more skilled to analytically evaluate and lead/mentor their subordinates, and more sensitive to their own growth. Based on these expectations, some companies prefer to assign the assessor role to the high-potential group, or make the assessor experience almost mandatory for their senior managers.

ACs FOR SCHOOL GRADUATES

The idea of applying group exercises in the process of recruiting new school graduates can be traced back to 1953 (Shimamura). Since then, some companies have used group exercises as a part of the selection procedure, but it was not until the early 2000s that a number of companies introduced AC-like exercise(s) into their recruitment programs.

Companies generally start the selection process by screening the applicants based on bio-data and essays, and then invite the most promising applicants to participate in exercises such as leaderless group discussions and/or team-based problem-solving. Companies who have reported on the web the use of AC-like exercise(s) include Japan Post, Goldman Sachs, Nippon Life Insurance Company, IBM Japan, SoftBank, The Asahi Shimbun Company (newspaper), AGF (Ajinomoto General Foods), Glaxo SmithKline K.K., P&G Japan, Toshiba, Hitachi, Samsung Japan, JR (Japan Rail) Tokai, Seven-Eleven Japan, Fast Retailing Co. Ltd. (UNIQLO), McDonald's Holdings Company (Japan), Ltd., Accenture, ANA (All Nippon Airways), JICA (Japan International Cooperation Agency), and many more.

By observing the exercises, assessors evaluate the predefined dimensions in addition to the potential cultural fit to the company. The topics and instructions given to the groups vary greatly from case to case. However, based on the numerous blog and website reports by the student-applicants, the topics can be categorized into three general genres. The first category includes morals and values. Questions about the requirements to be a respectable professional, an admirable company, or a stable and prosperous country are presented. Clearly there are no right answers but assessors can observe how each applicant talks and behaves, and whether each one possesses a good fit with the corporate culture and value set. A second category focuses on situation analysis, problem-solving, and solution-planning. Each group of applicants is asked to discuss, decide, and develop an integrated solution. Topics may be the desirable future of the company, the industry, the country, or the world with regard to economic development, equal employment opportunity, global diversity, humane healthcare, and fairness and human rights. In this category of topics, a certain amount of fact-based common sense, or sometimes subject matter insight to the company and industry, is required on top of the demonstration of desirable behavioral dimensions. The last category is characterized by the keyword "puzzle." Each team is given a real jigsaw puzzle, some other kind of puzzle, or a problem set to be solved. In this type of exercise, it is assumed that the assessors mainly focus on observing the behavioral dimensions related to cooperation, team building, and relationship maintenance.

Although the application of AC-like exercise sessions in school graduate recruiting became very popular, some concerns and unresolved issues remained. Assessors aren't always trained, and in some cases observation is not made by multiple assessors (that is, only one person is observing). Moreover, in many cases companies conduct just one exercise, which is inconsistent with the AC Guidelines (International Task Force on Assessment Center 2009) which require multiple exercises for the program to be a valid AC. Also, since Japanese companies hire new school graduates without predefining the job category, the dimension sets are not job specific, but rather generic. Thus, there are discussions about the validity and reliability of such AC-like practices among Japanese practitioners and researchers.

Nevertheless, conducting such an AC-like exercise still has a certain benefit both to the companies and the student-applicants, because it functions as a mechanism for two-way communication and education. Needless to say, companies can acquire rich evaluation data by adding exercises on top of final interviews. For applicants, it serves as a place to better understand the companies in terms of the underlying culture and values, which often guide them to select the companies with a better fit. Although an internship program (commonly two to five days) is more welcomed by students to experience the workplace atmosphere, many large corporations realize that conducting an internship program for many students is not operationally realistic. In that sense, too, the AC-like exercise has become a favored component in the process of hiring new graduates.

Integrating Assessment Scores

Integration of dimensional scores into one single overall assessment rating is conducted in most of the cases discussed so far, except for the "pure" DCs which do not aim to record and utilize performance data for future appraisal purposes. The consensus-based integration method is strongly favored over formula-based methods. Assessees are typically rated on a 5-point scale, and therefore many receive the same rating in large samples. However, there are two special situations where rank-ordering is undertaken instead of the 5-point scaling. One case is the emergent lay-off situation, in which participants are rank-ordered and those who receive the lowest scores are laid off. Another situation is either the start up of new Japanese subsidiaries or the up-scaling of promising ventures, where companies need to hire many capable managers in a short period, and hiring decisions are made based on rank-ordered scores.

In general, there is a tendency for both companies and assessees to prefer narrative reports to simple scores. Many companies have difficulties in utilizing dimension scores, since these scores do not provide straightforward explanations. The integrated scores deliver a simple message, and the narrative reports communicate subtle and rich behavioral observations. To overcome the lack of ability to understand and use dimension-level scores, some researcher-practitioners have begun to help the HR divisions in some companies.

The Role of DC/AC Results in Making Promotion Decisions

In many large Japanese companies, lifetime employment is the norm even today. In this circumstance, companies can accumulate many years of annual performance appraisal data for every staff member. Therefore, promotion decisions were traditionally based on the cumulative daily performance scores. After the introduction of DC/AC programs, how has this tradition changed? The answer, in short, is: not much.

The method of utilizing DC/AC data varies from company to company but, in general, it can be said that DC/AC data are being used as supplementary and/or confirmatory evidence for promotion consideration. In one company, the initial promotion nominee list for Kacho is developed on the base of cumulative annual appraisal data. Then, these nominees attend an AC. If a person gets dimension scores of 2 or 1 on a 5-point scale in more than two dimensions, that person is eliminated from the nominee list. Nominees who pass this screening move on to the next step, where they are interviewed by skilled interviewers from the HR department and then are interviewed by junior executives for the final call. Such use of an AC can be considered a means to acquire confirmatory evidence for promotion.

Another company uses the cumulative annual appraisal data for the initial nomination of new managers. In addition, they also look into the past DC performance data, and very often pick up several additional nominees, who, although they are not considered excellent on the basis of formal appraisal data, have demonstrated exceptional performance in some dimensions in the DC. In this way, this company uses DC data as supplementary evidence in the promotion process.

In many cases, the DC/AC is positioned as an auxiliary device to identify high-potential individuals. The basis for internal promotions in almost all companies is the cumulative performance appraisal data. Japanese companies tend to identify high-potential people by the third year after employment, which is well before the period for manager selection; they then provide those high-potentials with better job opportunities to foster their career growth. Wakabayashi, Graen and Uhl-Bien (1990) named such corporate conduct as "hidden investment."

ACs/DCs in the Public Sector

Traditionally, government ministries and agencies hired school graduates only on the basis of written exams and interviews. Recently there were discussions of the need to hire highly experienced mid-career personnel from the private sector pool to revitalize public offices. From 2006, the National Personnel Authority (Jinji-in), which is responsible for developing exams for hiring government personnel, started providing in-basket types of exams for mid-career hiring of chief-of-subunit (Kakaricho) class managers. However, since the choice of the type of exam was at the discretion of each ministry and agency, this did not mean that the in-basket was introduced to all government sectors. In August 2010, the Jinji-in announced that government ministries and agencies will formally introduce the AC-type exams for mid-career hires in 2012. The types of exercises used in these exams will be group discussions and/or in-baskets, in addition to essays. Since the announced exams are the open, competitive selection ACs which are going to be introduced in the public sector for the first time in Japan, the Authority is taking extra care to assure fairness. By March 2011, more details about the exams had yet to be formally announced. It would be highly desirable for researcher-practitioners to closely watch these forthcoming events.

Contrary to common practice in the US and other countries, in the police and fire departments there are no known records of using ACs for selection and promotion. However, the police and fire academy have long-established courses of DC-like programs for post-promotional personnel education.

The New Requirements Associated with Globalization

Owing to the shrinking and aging domestic population in Japan, it is urgent and critical for Japanese companies to expand overseas operations by sending more expatriates to other countries and by hiring more foreign employees. Historically, only a handful of large corporations had a certain level of presence overseas. However, globalization is becoming a survival issue even for smaller companies these days. It means that companies need to send out more Japanese employees as expatriates, and that they need to hire many foreign expatriates living in Japan who are qualified from the viewpoint of the culture of foreign countries where Japanese companies operate, as well as of the values of each company.

In the past, many Japanese companies made expatriate selection mainly on the basis of language proficiency. Some expatriates did a great job, but there were many who did not. A study of multinational companies (MNCs) found that the success factors were family situation, flexibility/adaptability, job-knowledge and motivation, relational skills, and extra-cultural openness, rather than language proficiency (Arthur and Bennett 1995). In a study conducted for the selection of European managers to be cross-cultural trainees to Japan, Lievens, Harris, Van Keer and Bisqueret (2003) found that openness was significantly related to performance in training, while cognitive ability contributed to the acquisition of language; and adaptability, teamwork, and communication had supplementary effects on performance. Harris and Lievens (2005) named a higher level of construct "cultural intelligence," which involves most of the dimensions described above. They also argued that the assessment center could be the most promising method in measuring cultural intelligence, assuming further development of culture-sensitive assessment centers. Owing to the high demand from clients to deliver expatriate selection programs, Japanese professional assessment firms began developing programs to identify the qualified expatriate candidates from the pool of the client's employee body.

In addition to the issue of expatriate selection, Japanese companies are having difficulties in implementing their DC/ACs overseas. They found that their Japanese version of DC/ACs are not always appropriate in other countries, just as the US MNCs long ago found that their home-made programs were not necessarily applicable abroad. Japanese companies are trying to modify their Japanese version of DC/ACs into a version appropriate for other countries and regions by conducting cultural checks to modify content so the programs provide effective assessments. However, it is still important for these companies to retain the core elements of their corporate value in the program, even after the cultural check.

In the US, researchers and practitioners historically have paid close attention to the need to remove cultural biases from AC/DCs, to ensure equal employment opportunity in what is a diverse, domestic labor market. On the other hand, when hiring local employees out of the company's home country, cultural diversity plays a major, positive role to help select or develop people in the right way, based on the underlying culture. Triandis (1996) argued that historically a majority of psychological constructs were developed solely based on the Western culture, and that there should be a different set of psychological concepts derived from Eastern culture. He also made the point that the development of universally non-biased AC content would be difficult or impossible, which means the development of content for each target culture is unavoidable. Briscoe's (1997) discussion of the issues involved in the development of cross-cultural AC/DCs, and the many potential problems associated with multicultural AC/DC deployment, is still applicable today.

Issues and Outlook

As Japanese corporations become more globalized, even junior managers must be prepared to deal with hetero-cultural situations. Collectivism-based DCs, adapted to Japanese culture, will need to be redesigned so that the programs can evaluate non-traditional dimensions such as the adoption of diversity and openness.

On the other hand, even in hetero-cultural settings, it is expected that more emphasis will be put on education into corporate values and culture. Even though socialization efforts to inculcate corporate values are now evident, more sophisticated programs will be needed when Japanese companies hire and train more managers in foreign countries. Many consider it critical that all global employees share common corporate values and norms despite coming from different cultural backgrounds. Furthermore, under the assumption of lifetime employment, companies need to consider the career path of those who did not get promoted. It is essential that companies do not severely demotivate those people by failing to present them with acceptable and attractive career paths. This requirement will need the close cooperation among AC/DC practices and other HRM functions.

Researchers and practitioners will need to continue to pay attention to organizational developments in the near future, for example, monitoring the use of mid-career hiring-exams in the public sector, as well as the validity of AC-like programs for new school graduate recruiting in the private sector.

Finally, this review found that professionally acceptable research into the predictive accuracy and validity of Japanese AC/DCs is lacking. To date there have been no movements among professional assessment firms to provide scientifically robust evidence to prove the appropriateness of their practices, and nor have there been any proposals to cooperate in establishing a set of standards such as those published by the International Task Force. It is becoming critical that researchers and practitioners conduct empirical studies of Japanese AC/DCs, given that the Japanese companies must extend their AC/DC programs beyond the country border.

References

Abegglen, J.C. 1958. *The Japanese Factory: Aspects of Its Social Organization*. Glencoe, IL: Free Press.

Arthur, W. and Bennett, W. 1995. The international assignee: The relative importance of factors perceived to contribute to Success. *Personnel Psychology*, 48, 99–114.

Arthur, W., Day, E.A., McNelly, T.L. and Edens, P.S. 2003. A meta-analysis of the criterion-related validity of assessment center dimensions. *Personnel Psychology*, 56, 125–154.

Bray, D.W., Campbell, R.J. and Grant, D.L. 1974. *Formative Years in Business: A Long-Term AT&T Study of Managerial Lives*. New York: Wiley.

Briscoe, D.R. 1997. Assessment centers: Cross-cultural and cross-national issues. *Journal of Social Behavior & Personality*, 12, 261–270.

Cole, R.E. 1979. *Work, Mobility, and Participation: A Comparative Study of American and Japanese Industry*. Berkeley: University of California Press.

Harris, M.M. and Lievens, F. 2005. Selecting employees for global assignments: Can assessment centers measure cultural intelligence? In *Current Topics in Management*, edited by M.A. Rahim and R.T. Golembiewski. New Brunswick, NJ: Transaction Publishers, 221–240.

Hofstede, G.H. 1980. *Culture's Consequences: International Differences in Work-Related Values*. Beverly Hills, CA: Sage Publications.

Howard, A., Shudo, K. and Umeshima, M. 1983. Motivation and values among Japanese and American managers. *Personnel Psychology*, 36, 883–898.

Huff, L. and Kelley, L. 2003. Levels of organizational trust in individualist versus collectivist societies: A seven-nation study. *Organization Science*, 14, 81–90.

International Task Force on Assessment Center Guidelines. 2009. Guidelines and ethical considerations for assessment center operations. *International Journal of Selection and Assessment*, 17, 243–253.

Lievens, F., Harris, M.M., Van Keer, E. and Bisqueret, C. 2003. Predicting cross-cultural training performance: The validity of personality, cognitive ability, and dimensions measured by an assessment center and a behavior description interview. *Journal of Applied Psychology*, 88, 476–489.

Miyanaga, K. 1991. *The Creative Edge: Emerging Individualism in Japan*. New Brunswick (USA): Transaction Publishers.

Moorman, R.H. and Blakely, G.L. 1995. Individualism-collectivism as an individual difference predictor of organizational citizenship behavior. *Journal of Organizational Behavior*, 16, 127–142.

Ralston, D.A., Holt, D.H., Terpstra, R.H. and Kai-Cheng, Y. 2008. The impact of national culture and economic ideology on managerial work values: A study of the United States, Russia, Japan, and China. *Journal of International Business Studies*, 39, 8–26.

Shimamura, H. 1953. The Application of Group Discussion in Recruitment Exam. *Keieisha [The Executives]*, 7, 50–52.

Takeuchi, K. 2010. *Assessment Center Methods in Japan*. 35th International Congress on Assessment Center Methods, Singapore, 19–21 October.

Taylor, C. and Frank, F. 1988. Assessment centers in Japan. *Training and Development Journal*, 42, 54.

Toshima, Y. 2001. S3–5 Factor structure of assessment center dimensions and personality traits. *Conference Proceedings of Japan Society of Personality Psychology*, 10, 58–59.

Triandis, H.C. 1995. *Individualism and Collectivism*. Boulder: Westview Press.

Triandis, H.C. 1996. The psychological measurement of cultural syndromes. *American Psychologist*, 51, 407–415.

Wakabayashi, M., Graen, G. and Uhl-Bien, M. 1990. The generalizability of the hidden investment hypothesis in leading Japanese corporations. *Human Relations*, 43, 1099–1116.

31 *Assessment Centers in Israel: Some Practices and Perspectives*

SHAUL FOX AND SOLY HABOUCHA

Local folklore has it that Israelis are the most psychologically assessed people in the world. It is certainly true that psychological selection procedures are deeply ingrained in the national ethos of personnel recruitment and it has been claimed that a jobseeker's chances of undergoing an Assessment Center-type selection process are nowhere greater than they are in Israel.

We thought it appropriate to begin this chapter with a cursory, bird's-eye survey of Assessment Center (AC) practice in Israel as we know it. Lacking an empirical descriptive study, we present our own perspective of local patterns, based on over 30 years of experience in the field of personnel selection in general, and in the development and implementation of ACs in particular. Due to the scarcity of developmental centers in Israel, we address selection and promotion centers only.

The second part of the chapter recounts some of the objections to ACs we have encountered, most notably decrying breaches of standardization. We propose that standardization in the context of ACs may be less critical than commonly assumed, whereas oft-ignored parameters, such as participant "stage time" and assessor "observation time", deserve more attention as contributors to AC quality.

Finally, we share with the reader our own practical approach to issues we have raised, focusing on applications we deem conducive to the quality of assessment.

A Brief History

As was the case in the United States (Ben-Shalom and Fox 2009), the military in Israel has served as a prolific hotbed for the development of psychological selection and classification systems. The high priority afforded effective placement and deployment of personnel has driven military psychologists to spearhead the development of assessment procedures, long before the civilian market defined a clear demand for such services.

For over five decades, psychometric cognitive tests, structured behavioral interviews and biodata have been the core of a primary classification system for all prospective military inductees, as well as of selection systems for specific specialties. The earliest adaptation of Assessment Center Methodology (ACM) for evaluating leadership potential occurred in the 1950s, as obstacle courses and classical AC exercises such as Leaderless Group Discussions were introduced as part of the officer selection system. Concurrently, special service units such as commandos, aircrew and paratroopers, incorporated field-screening in their selection procedures, like the Office of Strategic Services in the US. Typical activities entail intense group and individual missions, requiring cooperation, physical endurance, problem-solving abilities and tenacity in the face of rigorous mental and emotional stress. In these ACs, veteran non-commissioned officers or officers serve as assessors, with psychologists responsible for their training and for the proper application of exercises, observation and evaluation procedures.

A development of significant importance occurred in the 1980s, with the introduction of two-day ACs for the assessment of promotion potential to senior officer rank (Lt. Colonel). A short decade later, an additional AC screening station was established, for promotion from Lt. Colonel to full Colonel.

In the early 1990s, the practice of ACs gradually spread to other security organizations (such as the police, the prison authority, and the national security services), creating a natural overflow into the civilian sector, most notably in governmental organizations.

In a country where military service is compulsory, such pervasive use of psychological screening procedures in the armed forces has bred habituation in large segments of the population, as well as among those ex-military HR officers who enter the civilian market with an affinity for psychological assessment scores as decision-support systems. Sow this fertile soil with ex-military psychologists eager to continue practicing their trade, and it is no surprise that psychological selection procedures in general, and ACM in particular, proliferate in the country as a whole.

Among the central agents of personnel assessment are "psychological screening services" (PSS) companies, which offer the full gamut of psychological assessment tools and procedures. These companies cater to all sectors of the market and annually process tens of thousands of job applicants for prospective employers. Over the past two decades, PSSs have embraced ACM with avid enthusiasm, for both selection and promotion purposes. In some cases, the practice of ACM in PSS screening processes differs somewhat from that adopted in in-house ACs, as will be pointed out.

Some Current Practices

With time, local AC practice has developed certain distinctive characteristics, some of which are presented here.

DIVERSITY OF TARGET POSITIONS

In addition to the classic application for assessing managerial and promotion potential, ACM is routinely used for entry-level selection. Target positions are varied and diversified: aircrews, policemen, medical school applicants, sales and marketing personnel, foreign service cadets, civil servants, overseas emissaries, high-tech professionals, call-center staff and security guards, to name but a few. So common is the use of simulations and situational tests in screening procedures, that the term "Assessment Center" has been embraced and integrated into the everyday language of HR specialists, recruiters, personnel agencies and even the job applicants themselves.

DIVERSITY OF METHODOLOGIES

The gamut of uses, of users and of applications, has created a kaleidoscope of practices that significantly stretch and challenge the limits of the term "Assessment Center." At one end of the continuum are classic AC programs that closely adhere to the International Task Force on Assessment Center Guidelines (2009). They are based on thorough job analyses, target-specific exercises, assessment teams that include trained senior managers and experienced psychologists, and common observer-participant ratios of one to two. They involve six-to-eight participants, last one or two days, include cognitive and personality tests as well as interviews and peer evaluations, and produce detailed summary reports written by psychologists.

At the other end of the spectrum are selection procedures that are widely, and erroneously, labeled "assessment centers" in the popular jargon, but are best defined as stand-alone examination components or single hurdles in multi-hurdle screening processes. One may find a group of 10–12 candidates, varying in age and experience and competing for different positions in different organizations, undergoing testing in a PSS company. Grouped together for "situational testing" by loose common denominators of the target positions, they may undergo two generic exercises of 30–40 minutes each, under the observation of one or two junior psychologists who rate each participant on a set of dimensions derived from his/her specific target position.

From crude, preliminary screening to in-depth, wide-bandwidth assessment, actual AC applications run the entire gamut. As a rule, when selection ratios are high and the required competencies not very intricate, cursory ACM procedures are deemed to be a cost-effective method for skimming off lower-potential candidates. On the other hand, when the skills and abilities required are relatively complex and when selection errors incur significant costs to the organization, "full power" and well-invested ACs are usually implemented.

MULTI-METHOD APPROACH

In most cases, Israeli ACs integrate a broad methodological diversity. The use of cognitive and personality tests, personal interviews, biographical questionnaires and peer evaluations as part of the AC process is common practice. The prevailing view of an AC is that of a panoramic scanning procedure which enhances diagnostic power by superimposing images of the participant obtained from different diagnostic tools.

THE AC AS A "PSYCHOLOGICAL TOOL"

In contrast to the North American template, where most ACs do not engage psychologists as assessors (Eurich, Krause, Cigularov and Thornton 2009; Krause and Thornton 2009), the dominant view in Israel is of an AC as a *psychological* assessment procedure. As such, it is most often considered the realm of the psychologist, who typically designs the exercises, trains and heads the team of assessors, leads the summary discussion, writes the final reports and is subsequently held accountable for the validity of the results.

RATING DIMENSIONS

The Israeli practitioner is not truly preoccupied with the "dimensions vs. exercises" controversy. Once categorized as a psychological tool, it is perhaps natural for the Israeli AC to address dimensions, and sometimes even traits. Moreover, some promotion ACs report results exclusively in terms of dimension scores, without a final, aggregate overall score. This uncommon practice is implemented only when an AC targets an organizational *level* as opposed to a specific position, as there may not be a single "ideal profile" to serve as an anchor. The aim of such ACs is the accurate portrayal of the candidate's abilities, strengths and weaknesses, while the responsibility for profile integration is left to decision-makers.

EXERCISES

In choosing exercises, Israeli practitioners resemble their European (as opposed to American) counterparts in their reliance on group exercises (Krause and Thornton 2009), frequently employing more than one in the same AC. Although classic exercise formats are common, they often display a flair for creativity, most notably when designing in-house ACs. The authors too have employed novel exercise formats for special purposes. In one case, the target population was mid-level managers with significant prior AC experience. Two weeks prior to the AC, candidates were tasked with a home assignment: to prepare a position paper, including practical recommendations, regarding a carefully selected policy issue actually facing the organization. In the AC, each participant made a presentation before a "board" of fellow participants, who then deliberated the merits of each proposal and formulated a consensus policy.

Another exercise was designed for the selection of detectives and interrogators. Each participant was to recount his/her personal biography to his/her peers, weaving in certain fictitious facts or events, dictated to them in advance. Each peer, individually, then questioned the speaker in an effort to determine whether s/he "lied" at all, and if so, to identify the fallacious information reported. On other occasions, in-basket exercises were adapted to an intranet-mail format, which enabled observers to selectively respond to participants' emails in the name of the intended recipients, thus creating more dynamic and stressful interactions.

The impression of both assessors and participants is that, when methodologically sound, such high-fidelity simulations (bordering on work samples) often elicit highly revealing and informative behaviors.

Objections to ACs

The introduction of a promotional AC in an organization is not a mere technical change in HR management practice. It is a major, perhaps even strategic, change with significant implications for organizational life. In some organizations with which we have worked, promotional ACs have encountered stiff resistance from both managers and employees, for a variety of reasons. In a society with a rich socialistic history and active workers' unions, ACs have sometimes been perceived as an invasive, threatening intrusion into the delicate balance of workers' interests. The significant cost of constructing and operating an AC is always a serious consideration, while its incremental contribution beyond workers' performance history has sometimes been questioned. It is our impression that some workers' resistance to ACs has stemmed from concern that objective assessment would jeopardize the fruits expected from years of nurturing ties with superiors, whereas some managers with "political clout" feared it would reduce their influence in promotion decisions. For those and other reasons, there have been cases in which grass-root resistance has thwarted the introduction of a new AC or led to the annulment of an established one. Even in less extreme cases, workers' opposition to an *existing* AC may impair its efficiency, as negative attitudes towards a test are known to have a detrimental effect on testees' motivation to succeed, their feeling of self-efficacy and their actual performance (Hausknecht, Day and Thomas 2004; McCarthy, Hrabluik and Jelley 2009).

In line with Gilliland's (1993) model and Shaw, Wild and Colquitt's (2003) recommendations, our policy has been to identify and address potential sources of resistance as early as possible and to provide the organization (workers and managers) with essential information regarding AC procedures, content and utilities. This includes a well-substantiated rationale for its use, backed by evidence of validity from both the professional literature (for example, Dayan, Kasten and Fox 2002; Gaugler, Rosenthal, Thornton and Bentson 1987) and from other organizations. We have found the testimony of managers and workers' representatives in corresponding organizations to be of great persuasive value.

Over the years, as the academic and professional training of young HR managers has evolved to include psychological and methodological coursework, we have encountered a new, challenging line of criticism. The major claim is that ACs, at least in Israel, suffer from an integral flaw; namely the lack of standardization, as participants' scores may be contingent on a number of factors that the examiner cannot control. Such an unstandardized instrument, the claimants argue, can be neither accurate nor fair.

Standardization is indeed a fundamental principle of psychological testing, recognized as a precondition for objectivity, fairness, reliability and validity. It calls for applying identical testing conditions and scoring procedures for all testees (Brennan 2006), parameters of critical importance in high-stakes testing procedures due to their potential legal and professional implications (Thornton and Gibbons 2009).

The major grounds on which critics have challenged AC standardization are presented below.

INFORMATION LEAKAGE

Among the fundamental requirements for any test is the presentation of stimuli that are equally novel to all examinees. Advance knowledge regarding a test introduces construct-irrelevant variance that may warp the information holder's scores, to the detriment of the test's reliability and validity. Although "leaks" of AC procedures and content are always a concern, the unique characteristics in Israel make it especially vulnerable to this breach: a small country in both size and population, widespread use of AC methodology, a tendency for repetitive applications of overused exercises by PSSs and the accessibility of coaching services. Due to the incremental effects of factors such as previous personal experience with ACs, tips and information passed on by word-of-mouth and available coaching options, a large number of Israeli examinees aren't truly naïve.

Since most ACs are high-stake tests, it is natural for motivated candidates to invest considerable effort in self-preparation, including information-gathering. An allegedly substantial threat to the purity of AC assessments arises from commercially available coaching programs, which may be differentiated in terms of their aim, scope, intensity, methodology and duration. Some ambitious, broad-range programs aim beyond improving AC performance and strive to actually enhance managerial skills. If successful, such efforts may raise AC scores beyond pre-coaching levels by *actually improving ability*, with no detrimental effect on their utility as predictors (Kulik, Bangert-Drowns and Kulik 1984). However, we are not familiar with such sophisticated programs in Israel, where typical coaching classes are brief and tend to focus on situational-specific tension-reduction and impression-management techniques. How does this limited-scope coaching affect AC scores? The literature does not appear to address the issue in the context of full-scale AC programs. Available evidence suggests that test-focused coaching enhances results in certain single-method assessment procedures, such as LGDs (Kurecka, Austin, Johnson, and Mendoza 1982) and situational interviews (Campion and Campion 1987, Maurer, Solamon, Andrews and Troxtel 2001, Maurer, Solamon and Troxtel 1998). What, then, are the repercussions of mixing "naïve" participants with experienced or "coached" participants in the same AC? Is this not a major breach of standardization?

Lacking conclusive empirical evidence, some local practitioners seem to rely on certain impressionistic assumptions:

1. The widespread use of ACM in screening processes has created a test-wise population. Actual variance in the degree of performance-affecting familiarity with ACM is not as large as may be feared.
2. Impression-management tips and techniques taught in coaching programs may, at best, be applied and "acted" in single, short-duration exercises. In full-length, intensive AC programs, however, participants eventually succumb to their natural behavioral styles.
3. Effective self-preparation reflects motivation, initiative and self-monitoring capabilities, all characteristics that will affect on-the-job performance no less than AC ratings. Thus, coaching does not necessarily decrease validity. In some instances (cognitive tests, interviews), it is known to actually enhance it (Allalouf and Ben-Shakhar 1998, Maurer, Solamon and Lippstreu 2008).

Thus in Israel, the issue of pre-test familiarity with ACs is not a major source of concern. Many practitioners seem to surmise that in full-scale ACs, it does not significantly hamper validity. Some indications from the field seem to support this assumption. Several ACs the authors are familiar with maintain predictive validities in the $.30 \le r \le .40$ range, in spite of being in-house procedures (and thus particularly prone to information leaks, see Dodd 1977), which have undergone few significant changes in exercise form or content in many years (see also Dayan, Kasten, and Fox 2002). Similarly, the predictive validities of several OSS-type military selection procedures have remained relatively stable over decades, despite the fact that their core format and contents have not undergone substantial changes, while increasing numbers of participants partake in preparatory coaching programs every year.

One of the authors recently designed and administered a rather unusual AC program, at the commission of military HR. Participants were none other than 20 senior psychologists and consultants (many of whom had significant experience as assessors in ACs), who were vying for promotion to Lt. Colonel rank. Undoubtedly, this group was highly "contaminated" in terms of pre-knowledge. Interestingly, our most notable impression of this AC was its lack of distinction relative to more "ordinary" ACs, in terms of group dynamics, participants' behaviors, coping styles and problem-solving efficiency, score distributions and the feedback obtained from both participants and evaluators (three senior psychologists and two very senior officers). Observers reported encountering no unusual difficulties in evaluating their examinees, while the majority of participants reported feeling "essentially no different" than they imagine non-psychologists would feel under similar circumstances. Participants with extensive AC experience appeared to have no notable advantage over their less experienced peers.

These and other experiences seem to hint that prior acquaintance with AC methodology, procedures and exercise paradigms may not necessarily have a major impact on AC reliability and validity.

PRIOR ACQUAINTANCES

Given the relatively limited size of organizations in Israel, in-house promotional ACs often grapple with cases of prior acquaintance between participants or between assessors and participants. When candidates are of similar backgrounds and age groups, similar difficulties occasionally arise in selection ACs as well.

Clearly, encounters between familiar "others" in an AC introduces extraneous influences of unknown impact and valence, which, although extraneous to the setting and to the test situation, are likely to impact both and affect the behavior of the participants concerned. In a high-stakes situation of tension and uncertainty, the effect of the presence of familiar others may run the gamut, from reassuring to intimidating or even threatening, depending on a large number of factors. Prior acquaintance between an assessor and an assessee may compromise the objectivity as well as the integrity of the ratings, as a priori opinions and implicit attitudes affect perceptions of behaviors and their evaluation.

Attempting to define the term "acquaintance" (see Colvin and Funder 1991) further complicates matters. Firstly, the degree of familiarity between individuals, as well as the emotions accompanying such familiarity, runs along broad spectra. Secondly, neither of these parameters can be assumed to be reciprocal, as one's acquaintance with, and feelings about, a person may differ significantly from that person's familiarity with, and feelings about one. If we add the fact that the *number* of acquaintances within a given group can also vary, it becomes clear that group composition may introduce construct-irrelevant variance, affecting participant performance and scores. Once again, we are treading on the, by now, wobbly ground of AC standardization.

There seems to be a dearth of research regarding the influence of familiarity between AC participants on their ratings. Van Scotter, Moustafa, Burnett, and Michael (2007) report that prior acquaintance between evaluators and ratees produced performance appraisals that were both more positive and more accurate. This seems to indicate that, although familiarity may engender a positive bias, it provides a richer basis of information and yields more accurate assessments. Additional studies also report that closer familiarity yields more agreement among assessors and higher validities (for example, Colvin and Funder 1991; Funder, Kolar and Blackman 1995; Paulhus and Bruce 1992). Although not conducted in AC settings, these studies seem to hint that, in terms of pure utility (if not methodological purity), prior acquaintance may not necessarily harm the validity of ratings.

On a practical level, almost all ACs we are familiar with invest effort to prevent, or minimize, prior acquaintances. When necessary, the assignment of participants to groups is carefully monitored so as to assure optimal "balance" between groups, in terms of sensitive parameters, including prior acquaintances. Many AC organizers conduct advance verification with assessors, leading to the occasional replacement of a particular assessor or to the rearrangement of the rotation plan so as to prevent the assessment of a specific participant by a particular assessor.

When intra-group acquaintances are unavoidable, we have found it helpful to conduct a special "debriefing" in the summary interview commonly performed at the conclusion of the AC. Each participant's impression of their influence on his/her own and others' behavior is obtained and considered. There have been cases in which post-hoc illuminations, thus obtained, have affected the interpretation of some interpersonal dynamics observed during an AC.

GROUP HETEROGENEITY

Considering that Israel is a melting-pot society of Jews and Arabs, still absorbing immigration from dozens of countries as diversified as Ethiopia and the former Soviet Union, it is naturally common for local ACs to be demographically heterogeneous. Insofar as heterogeneity is a microcosmic reflection of actual workgroup compositions on the job, it may contribute positively to the evaluation process. The concern, however, regards the adverse effects of heterogeneity on those minority candidates "suffering" from linguistic, cultural, gender, or other relative "disadvantages", similar to those reported by Dean, Roth and Bobko (2008) regarding Afro-American AC participants.

Moreover, group diversity arouses fundamental questions regarding ACs in general. How does group composition affect individual behavior? Does performance vary as a function of the particular makeup of the group with which one is tested? These questions are especially relevant to local ACM practices, in which group exercises predominate.

Heterogeneity of AC groups may stem from any number of parameters, including *racioethnic background, gender, personal attributes* (for example, abilities, personality, attitudes), and even the *target positions* for which participants are being screened.

The amalgam of applicants competing for *different positions* in different organizations in the same AC is entirely a PSS phenomenon. It typically stems from a lack of sufficient candidates for any given position to allow target-specific ACs. This sort of group blend need not be a major obstacle to diagnostic efficiency, if the positions in question share common abilities and the simulations used, as well as the dimensions measured, are relevant to them all. Unfortunately, due to technical and commercial considerations, this condition is not always met. There are ACs in which participants are evaluated differentially, each within the prism of their specific target position. This practice is questionable at best and may be condoned only when the sole other alternative is to forego interactive situational assessment entirely.

Ostensibly, *racioethnic and gender diversity* would appear to be the more formidable obstacles to AC reliability and validity, as existing preconceptions, schemas, attitudes, and biases of all protagonists taint and warp both intergroup dynamics and observers' evaluations. What has been termed the "diversity-validity dilemma" (Pyburn, Ployhart and Kravitz 2008) reflects the fact that some of the most valid predictors of job performance, including ACs, are also associated with racioethnic and gender score differences. Over 40 years of struggle with adverse impact have yielded no panacea for this troublesome phenomenon (Dean, Roth and Bobko 2008), leading Ployhart and Holtz (2008) and Kravitz (2008) to propose HR policies and decision strategies aimed at circumventing those undesirable group differences that apparently cannot be totally overcome in the screening procedures themselves.

As for the effects of subgroup representation on assessee scores, some indication may be obtained from studies of workers' performance ratings. After controlling for differences in abilities, education and experience, Sackett, DuBois and Noe (1991) found that the relative ratings of men and women varied as a function of their proportion in the workgroup, while that of whites and blacks did not. Comparable results are reported in Pazy and Oron's (2001) study on the performance ratings of senior officers in the Israel Defense Forces. Female officers' ratings varied in direct relation to their proportion in the unit, while those of male officers did not. In contrast, Schmitt (1993) found only marginal effects of group composition (gender and race proportions) on the final AC ratings of participants, replicating earlier findings (Schmitt and Hill 1977).

As heterogeneous groups become more common in global-village societies, it appears that racioethnic and gender "disturbances" of AC standardization are here to stay. It may be somewhat comforting that, compared to other selection methods, ACs are among those instruments found to *reduce* racioethnic differences, especially when the effects of cognitive ability are neutralized (Cascio and Aguinis 2005; Ployhart and Holtz 2008, Schmitt and Mills 2001).

Since interpersonal differences in attributes are inevitable, every AC group presents an idiosyncratic, unique environment with which its members are to cope in interactive exercises. A common assumption is that since this diversity reflects reality – in their work environments individuals interact with a blend of different personalities and backgrounds – it should not lower validity and may even contribute to it. However, this does not attenuate the potential impact of lack of standardization among groups on reliability. In terms of trait-activation theory (Tett and Burnett 2003), group composition may prime the relevance of different traits in group interaction. Thus, whether group dynamics activate a dominant candidate's competitive-hostile inclination or his supportive-cohesive mode may depend on the presence or absence of other dominant, competitive participants. Practically, this source of heterogeneity is unavoidable and appears to be a primary violation of standardization in ACM.

Can an AC Be Totally Standardized and Should It Be?

While some of the violations of standardization discussed above are the product of circumstantial, local conditions, which may or may not exist in other contexts and countries, others, such as the effects of group composition, are indigenous to ACM itself. Also indigenous to ACM are the breaches of standardization inherent to interactive activities of all kinds, including group discussions and role plays, which are standard AC exercises. In any interaction, unavoidable variations in individual's behavior and idiosyncrasies trigger ripples of reactions and counter-reactions in the interpersonal dynamics, creating a different challenge for every participant. Such *variability* of test conditions leads to the inescapable conclusion that, in orthodox psychometric terms, classic ACs cannot be fully standardized. Does the solution lie in the elimination of interactive exercises from the practitioner's toolbox?

In order to place this question in its proper perspective, we suggest considering the special place of the AC in the wider context of assessment methods in general. The pursuit of standardization in assessment has engendered diagnostic instruments such as multiple-choice examinations, multiple choice closed biodata questionnaires, self-report behavioral inventories and structured interviews. While these useful techniques have contributed to the psychometric attributes of the scores they engender, they have been found lacking in the assessment of important facets of human performance, such as initiative, creativity, leadership qualities, motivation, interpersonal relations and other valuable attributes.

In many ways then, ACM is the product of the practitioner's search for assessment procedures that transcend these limits and complement the information provided by the standardized tests. We have embraced role plays and group exercises, precisely because they are dynamic, stimulus-rich replicas of real-life situations that cannot be tapped by rigidly structured test items and scoring procedures of the totally objective kind. Unlike the standardized objective test, the human-encounter exercise presents the examinee with a complex, multifaceted situation of some ambiguity and variation, with the precise aim of eliciting the subjective interpretations and response choices that are of diagnostic value to the observer. It appears to us that this is a core contribution of the AC to assessment, which we should make every effort to exploit and to perfect, not to forsake.

There is no question that a great many aspects of the AC (such as exercise format and procedures, observation techniques, scoring instruments and integration methods) should be standardized to an adequate degree. We propose, however, to refrain from overzealous structuring of those components that are less "standardizable" by nature, for fear of truncating what may be their most significant contribution to the assessment process. Rigid structuring of interactive exercises risks reducing them to "closed questionnaires", just as over-meticulous concretization of evaluation forms may sacrifice the observer's insight and free judgment of human behavior. In fact, why bother to engage senior managers and experienced psychologists as refined and sophisticated assessors, only to reduce their judgmental decisions to marking "X" in meticulously predefined boxes?

This raises the inevitable question: Is validity possible without standardization? On the one hand, it may be claimed that the traditional ACs of the past were more "interactive" than present day procedures (Lievens and Thornton 2005), and yet impressively valid (Gaugler et al. 1987). Yet, in the face of longstanding psychometric theory and tradition, such a claim cannot be sustained without some conceptual rationale, however tentative. Could there be an explanation for the validity-without-standardization phenomenon?

One possibility is that, in best-practice ACs, the multiplicity and heterogeneity of observations, of context-relevant test situations and of evaluators produce a wealth of behavioral samples and judgmental perspectives that compensate for lack of standardization. These conditions may be providing an alternate "mechanism" for attenuating sources of measurement error elsewhere contained by standardization. Support for the notion that the "multiplicity and heterogeneity" principle entails some compensative quality may perhaps be sought in another assessment method practiced in some Israeli organizations, namely peer evaluations. Members of each unit or department are asked to rate co-workers on a list of personal characteristics and/or to evaluate their potential for promotion. Ostensibly, such evaluations are plagued by a multitude of faults. Objectivity is undermined by personal friendships and rivalries, while raters are untrained in assessment and are oftentimes unfamiliar with, or even informed of, the criteria to be predicted. And yet, "evidence supports peer ratings as reliable, valid, and useful forms of performance criteria" (Dierdorff and Surface 2007: 93).

The explanation being what it may, it seems justified to propose that standardization is not a precondition for validity (Brennan 2006), provided the intrinsic advantages of ACM over more standardized tools are maximized and meticulously applied. Unfortunately, it is our impression that we are moving in the opposite direction. Recent trends in Israel, and apparently in other countries as well, seem to be gnawing at a fundamental parameter of AC quality, which is the amount of information upon which assessments are based.

Stage Time and Observation Time

The eminent decline of AC validities over the past decades has been the object of some concern (Thornton and Gibbons 2009). A variety of possible explanations have been proposed, including the gradual "reduction" of AC methodology and procedures (Schuler 2008). Noting the growing tendency for shorter ACs, Lievens and Thornton (2005: 250) surmise that the drive towards ever "leaner" assessments "may affect the accuracy and effectiveness of the AC." It is our concern that this ostensibly laudable, relentless drive for increased efficiency may lead some practitioners on the path of the proverbial farmer, whose horse died just before mastering the art of making do without food entirely.

Among the notable characteristics of the "leaner" ACs encountered in Israel are shorter programs, more participants in each group, and lower observer/participant ratios. Attempts to bolster efficiency have often also led to an increase in the number of exercises, in line with findings regarding the positive relation between the number of exercises and AC validity (Gaugler et al. 1987).

What appears to have been neglected, however, is the accumulated impact of these changes on three important characteristics of ACs, which may be assumed to have a significant effect on the reliability and the validity of its results: the "stage time" allotted to each participant, the efficient "observation time" per participant allotted to each observer, and the "aggregate observation time" of each participant from all assessors. Although we have not encountered direct references to these terms in the literature, they appear to warrant attention in our analysis of AC quality.

"Stage time" may be defined as the time allotted to each participant by the AC program to display active and observable coping behavior with the tasks assigned to him/her. A prerequisite for accurate and reliable assessment is the adequate sampling of relevant behaviors. Although silence, passivity and body language are also behaviors to be noticed and evaluated, it is primarily from *active* participation that interpretable diagnostic information is obtained. An efficient AC design must provide each participant sufficient time to express him/herself on each of the exercises and dimensions measured. All else being equal, the more opportunity to "show one's wares," the richer the behavioral samples on which evaluations will be based, resulting in more reliable and valid evaluations. It thus follows that the total "stage time" allotted by an AC program to the individual participant is among the determinants of the reliability and validity of the assessments generated.

Numerous factors influence the "stage time" allotted in a particular exercise. Most notable among them:

1. The duration of the exercise and the number of participants.
    While an individual exercise is almost entirely "personal stage time", group exercises are time-sharing activities. Given a specific time frame, the fewer participants in an activity, the more "stage time" allotted to each.
2. The proportion of "data-generating time" as opposed to "administration time".
    In each exercise, time spent on instructions, reading background information, self-preparation, breaks, and the like, is devoid of diagnostic value and is thus essentially lost. Compressing more exercises in a given time frame often increases total administration time, reducing overall data-generating time, and consequently, the individual participant's stage-time.

It is thus clear that AC duration, the number of participants, the number of exercises and exercise methodology interact to exert a major impact on the total "stage time" allotted to each participant. Is it possible that the quest for leaner ACs has reduced the values of this important parameter, to the detriment of the reliability and validity of our results?

The complement to the participant's "stage time" is the observer's effective "observation time" per participant – the net time allotted to observe the participant's performance. Reliable assessments require not only that the participant display behavior, but that there be someone there with sufficient time and cognitive resources to observe and assess this behavior. Under the best of conditions, assessors are under substantial cognitive load. As we increase the number of AC participants, shorten "data-producing time" and/or require them to divide their attention among more participants, cross-subject interference reduces their "observation time" of each participant, seriously hampering the reliability of their assessments. As the assessor's reliability deteriorates, so does score validity.

Finally, we ought to consider also each participant's "aggregate observation time", or the combined, accumulated time that *all* assessors were granted to observe the participant throughout the AC. As a rule, more "aggregate observation time" should produce more reliable and more valid AC scores, making this parameter an additional important indication of AC quality.

Our underlying premise is that, as a rule, more information fosters higher reliabilities and validities. The implications of the "thin slice" literature which suggests that accurate assessments of some traits can be made on the basis of very brief observations (for example, Ambady and Rosenthal 1992; Carney, Colvin and Hall 2007), are beyond the scope of the present chapter. Suffice it to say that we believe those competencies and dimensions targeted by ACs to be significantly more complex than those sampled in the thin slice literature, are thus governed by entirely different standards.

Personally Preferred Practices

What then, are the essential features of the ACM we deem important to preserve quality? How do we attempt to circumvent the pitfalls we have decried here?

Over time, every practitioner tends to develop "personally preferred practices" (PPPs). Typically, these are the product of a progressive synthesis of several factors, including interpretation of the literature one is familiar with, applications that "have worked", solutions to practical obstacles, as well as acquired habits. Expectedly, many of our own

PPPs address issues we have raised here and reflect applications we deem conducive to the quality of assessment.

PPPS AFFECTING STAGE TIME, OBSERVATION TIME AND COGNITIVE LOAD

In order to provide sufficient information for each observer to independently evaluate all participants on all dimensions with a fair degree of confidence, we strive to optimize a number of parameters:

Number of participants

Six participants in one-day, eight to ten hour ACs and eight participants in two-day ACs are maximums we try not to surpass. Larger numbers invariably result in observers reporting difficulty assessing at least some of the participants.

Observer/participant ratio

We have found the (1:2) +1 formula to work best. The "+1" is the AC administrator, usually the most experienced psychologist, who also serves as a part-time evaluator.

Observation schedule

Observers evaluate only two participants in group exercises and up to three in individual exercises, provided these are performed serially. Over an entire AC, observers evaluate every participant in at least two distinct activities, preferably in one group and one individual exercise.

Exercise duration

Assuring adequate stage and observation times is a leading consideration in setting the duration of each exercise. A balance is sought between the pressure for efficiency in testing time, on the one hand, versus the desire to allow participants who thrive on longer "incubation time" an opportunity to express themselves, on the other.

Number of dimensions

Typically, evaluation forms tap only two interpersonal dimensions, two performance dimensions, and some estimate of practical cognitive ability, all derived from job analysis. Among other advantages, fewer dimensions help reduce observer cognitive load.

Evaluation time

Observers are allotted ample time between exercises to complete their evaluations calmly and thoroughly, while participants are occupied completing questionnaires or preparing their next activity.

OBSERVER TEAMS

Observers are almost always a mixed team of psychologists and senior managers, the former often outnumbering the latter. More often than not, the psychologist in charge is influential in determining the pool of "eligible" managers, based on their previous performance as observers.

INCREASING FAIRNESS AND REDUCING OBJECTIONS

Efforts to assure optimal fairness include:

1. Providing participants with advance information regarding the format of the AC, its aims and organizational uses, preferably in a frontal group briefing.
2. Striving for homogeneous group composition to the extent possible.
3. Avoiding the evaluation of participants by any observer sufficiently familiar with them so as to have an a priori opinion of their character or abilities. In some organizations, participants may request not to be evaluated by specific observers.
4. Debriefing participants at the conclusion of the AC, thus providing them an opportunity to report any factor which may have hampered performance.
5. Providing feedback to participants.
6. Granting the "right of appeal" of AC results, in which case the participant's claims and AC file are reviewed by an independent senior psychologist. Although AC scores cannot be retroactively altered, legitimate claims are acknowledged and practical recommendations made to decision-makers.

HOW MUCH STANDARDIZATION?

Our approach to the role of standardization is intimately related to our use of situational tests, not as a stand-alone omnipotent assessment technique but as a primary component of a multi-method AC procedure, which also includes cognitive and personality tests, bio-data questionnaires and peer evaluations. Anchored to such an array of steadfast support measures, we believe the situational test may be allowed to venture into the more turbulent waters of dynamic, interactional testing, wherein the standardization of *method* still reigns, but not necessarily the standardization of *content*.

This differentiation is best illustrated with some examples:

1. Whereas care is taken to ensure standard exercise formats, observation methods and evaluation forms, precise exercise content may vary. As different contents may be equally effective in eliciting a behavior of interest, we believe it legitimate for different participants or groups to face different situations of the same type.
2. The precise dynamics of interactional exercises may also vary, as a function of participants' responses to initial stimuli. Thus, an actor playing the role of a well-defined character initially behaves in a standard, predetermined manner, but may eventually challenge a dominant participant very differently than a more submissive one, as would happen in real life. Similarly, in an interactional in-basket exercise, a participant who appears to be serially avoiding conflict may be confronted head-on by his "superior" to see how he does handle conflict when it is inescapable. Despite

the fact that it cannot be standardized, we consider such differential probing to be of significant value to assessment, provided it is executed in a professional manner.

3. While significant effort is applied to ensure observers have a clear conceptual understanding of the AC dimensions and rating scales, we encourage and expect assessments that transcend predefined dimension components and offer a significantly richer and deeper view of any relevant candidate characteristic.

4. Final data integration is performed using a methodical procedure in which the results of all assessment tools employed, including the distribution of evaluations on every dimension and every exercise, are systematically reviewed. Yet, final scores are the product of a holistic judgment attained by consensus discussion, led by the head psychologist. The "agenda" may include any aspect of the participant's attributes bearing possible implications on his suitability to the target position.

Concluding Remarks

The practice of ACM in Israel goes back over five decades and is both widespread and deeply rooted. Yet objections to the method persist and practitioners still struggle with basic methodological issues, of which standardization is perhaps the most central. We have attempted to address some of the practical and theoretical intricacies of classic standardization in the context of ACs, questioning the centrality of its role and proposing the "multiplicity and heterogeneity principle" as a possible compensating mechanism. We have also suggested the concepts of "stage time" and "observation time" as parameters of importance to AC quality, and presented some of the practical principles that guide our own work in designing ACs. We hope some of the ideas presented here will be of heuristic value to the professional community and contribute to our understanding of the AC as well as to its practical implementation.

References

Allalouf, A. and Ben-Shakhar, G. 1998. The effect of coaching on the predictive validity of scholastic aptitude tests. *Journal of Educational Measurement*, 35, 31–47.

Ambady, N. and Rosenthal, R. 1992. Thin slices of expressive behavior as predictors of interpersonal consequences: A meta-analysis. *Psychological Bulletin*, 111, 256–274.

Ben-Shalom, U. and Fox, S. 2009. Military Psychology in the Israel Defense Forces: A perspective of continuity and change. *Armed Forces & Society*, 36, 103–119.

Brennan, R.L. 2006. Perspectives on the evolution and future of educational measurement. In *Educational Measurement*, edited by R.L. Brennan. American Council on Education (4th Edition), 1–16.

Campion, M.A. and Campion, J.E. 1987. Evaluation of an interviewee skills training program in a natural field experiment. *Personnel Psychology*, 40, 675–691.

Carney, D.R., Colvin, R.C. and Hall, J.A. 2007. A thin slice perspective on the accuracy of first impression. *Journal of Research in Personality*, 41, 1054–1072.

Cascio, W.F. and Aguinis, H. 2005. *Applied Psychology in Human Resource Management* (6th Edition). Englewood Cliffs, NJ: Prentice-Hall.

Colvin, R.C. and Funder, D.C. 1991. Predicting personality and behavior: A boundary on the acquaintanceship effect. *Journal of Personality and Social Psychology*, 60, 884–894.

Dayan, K., Fox, S. and Kasten, R. 2008. The preliminary employment interview as a predictor of assessment center outcomes. *International Journal of Selection and Assessment*, 16, 102–111.

Dayan, K., Kasten, R. and Fox, S. 2002. Entry-level police candidate assessment center: An efficient tool or hammer to kill a fly? *Personnel Psychology*, 55, 827–849.

Dean, M.A., Roth, P.L. and Bobko, P. 2008. Ethnic and gender subgroup differences in assessment center ratings: A meta-analysis. *Journal of Applied Psychology*, 93, 685–691.

Dierdorff, E.C. and Surface, E.A. 2007. Placing peer ratings in context: Systematic influences beyond rate performance. *Personnel Psychology*, 60, 93–126.

Dodd, W.E. 1977. Attitudes toward assessment center programs. In *Applying the Assessment Center Methods*, edited by J.L. Moses and W.C. Byham. New York: Pergamon Press, 262–283.

Eurich, T.L., Krause, D., Cigularov, K. and Thornton, G.C. III. 2009. Assessment centers: Current practices in the United States. *Journal of Business & Psychology*, 24, 387–407.

Funder, D.C., Kolar, D.C. and Blackman, M.C. 1995. Agreement among judges of personality: Interpersonal relations, similarity, & acquaintanceship. *Journal of Personality and Social Psychology*, 69, 656–672.

Gaugler, B.B., Rosenthal, D.B., Thornton, G.C. III and Bentson, C. 1987. Meta-analysis of assessment center validity [Monograph]. *Journal of Applied Psychology*, 72, 493–511.

Gilliland, S.W. 1993. The perceived fairness of selection systems: An organizational justice perspective. *Academy of Management Review*, 18, 694–735.

Hausknecht, J.P., Day, D.V. and Thomas, S.C. 2004. Applicant reactions to selection procedures: An updated model and meta-analysis. *Personnel Psychology*, 57, 639–683.

International Task Force on Assessment Center Guidelines. 2009. Guidelines and ethical considerations for assessment operations. *International Journal of Selection and Assessment*, 17, 243–253.

Krause, D.E. and Thornton, C.G. III. 2009. A cross-cultural look at Assessment Center practices: Survey results from Western Europe and North America. *Applied Psychology: An International Review*, 58, 557–585.

Kravitz, D.A. 2008. The diversity-validity dilemma: beyond selection – the role of affirmative action. *Personnel Psychology*, 61, 173–194.

Kulik, J.A., Bangert-Drowns, R.L. and Kulik, C.C. 1984. Effectiveness of coaching for aptitude tests. *Psychological Bulletin*, 95, 179–188.

Kurecka, P.M., Austin, J.M., Johnson, W. and Mendoza, J.L. 1982. Full and errant coaching effects on assigned role leaderless group discussion performance. *Personnel Psychology*, 35, 805–881.

Lievens, F. and Thornton, C.G. III. 2005. Assessment Centers: Recent developments in practice and research. In *The Blackwell Handbook of Personnel Selection*, edited by A. Evers, N. Anderson and O. Voskuijl. Malden, MA: Blackwell, 243–264.

Maurer, T.J., Solamon, J.M. Andrews, K.D. and Troxel, D. 2001. Interviewee coaching, preparation strategies, and response strategies in relation to performance in situational employment interviews: An extension of Maurer, Solamon and Troxel (1998). *Journal of Applied Psychology*, 86, 709–717.

Maurer, T.J., Solamon, J.M. and Lippstreu, M. 2008. How does coaching interviewees affect the validity of a structured interview? *Journal of Organizational Behavior*, 29, 355–371.

Maurer, T.J., Solamon, J. and Troxel, D. 1998. Relationship of coaching with performance in situational employment interviews. *Journal of Applied Psychology*, 83, 128–136.

McCarthy, J, Hrabluik, C. and Jelley, B.R. 2009. Progression through the ranks: Assessing employee reactions to high stakes employment testing. *Personnel Psychology*, 62, 793–832.

Paulhus, D.L. and Bruce, N.M. 1992. The effect of acquaintanceship on the validity of personality impression: A longitudinal study. *Journal of Personality and Social Psychology*, 63, 816–824.

Pazy, A. and Oron, I. 2001. Sex proportion and performance evaluation among high-ranking military officers. *Journal of Organizational Behavior*, 22, 689–702.

Ployhart, R.E. and Holtz, B.C. 2008. The Diversity-validity dilemma: Strategies for reducing racioethnic and sex subgroup differences and adverse impact in selection. *Personnel Psychology*, 61, 153–172.

Pyburn K.M. Jr., Ployhart, R.E. and Kravitz, D.A. 2008. The diversity-validity dilemma: Overview and legal context. *Personnel Psychology*, 61, 143–151.

Sackett, P.R., DuBois, C.L.Z. and Noe, A.W. 1991. Tokenism in performance evaluation: The effects of work group representation on male-female and white – black differences in performance ratings. *Journal of Applied Psychology*, 76, 263–267.

Schmitt, N. 1993. Group composition, gender, and race effects on assessment center ratings. In *Personnel Selection and Assessment: Individual and Organizational Perspectives*, edited by H. Schuler, J.L. Farr and M. Smith. Hillsdale, NJ: Lawrence Erlbaum, 315–332.

Schmitt, N. and Hill, T.E. 1977. Sex and race composition of assessment center groups as determinant of peer and assessor ratings. *Journal of Applied Psychology*, 62, 261–264.

Schmitt, N. and Mills, A.E. 2001. Traditional tests and job simulations: Minority and majority performance and test validities. *Journal of Applied Psychology*, 86, 451–458.

Schuler, H. 2008. Improving assessment centers by the trimodal concept of personnel assessment. *Industrial and Organizational Psychology*, 1, 128–130.

Shaw, J.C., Wild, E. and Colquitt, J.A. 2003. To justify or excuse? A meta- analytic review of the effects of explanations. *Journal of Applied Psychology*, 88, 444–458.

Tett, R.P. and Burnett, D.D. 2003. A personality trait-based interactionist model of job performance. *Journal of Applied Psychology*, 88, 500–517.

Thornton, G.C. III and Gibbons, A.M. 2009. Validity of assessment centers for personnel selection. *Human Resources Management Review*, 19, 169–187.

Van Scotter, J.R., Moustafa, K., Burnett, J.R. and Michael, P.G. 2007. Influence of prior acquaintance with the rate on rater accuracy and halo. *Journal of Management Development*, 26, 790–803.

32 *Assessment Centers in Organizational and Cultural Contexts: Evidence of the Versatility of a Proven Human Resource Intervention*

GEORGE C. THORNTON III AND NIGEL POVAH

The authors of the chapters in this book reinforce and enhance our passion for assessment centers. In line with each of the three themes of the book we see new evidence that the assessment center (AC) method can contribute to individual and organizational effectiveness. We invited the contributors to tell the stories of their involvement in ACs because we were aware of their special contributions. We were not disappointed to read the descriptions of their programs. We were gratified to learn about their research, how they dealt with special demands in their organizations and their countries, and how they integrated the AC method into broader talent-management programs.

The chapters exceeded our expectations. We learned many new ideas. Each author provided unique, rich, and useful information. The chapters in this book teach us many lessons about the AC method and how it can be shaped to contribute to many aspects of corporate strategy, and specifically talent management. Even after over 50 years of experience with and research on ACs (Thornton Chapter 11), we are still learning new things about this versatile method. In this chapter we describe several lessons we have learned, and then outline areas where more research is needed to teach us additional lessons.

ACs Continue to Flourish

The first lesson is that ACs continue to flourish, as evidenced by the surveys of AC practices around the world (Povah Chapter 22; Krause Chapter 23). There is also increasing activity in those countries (in addition to the US and UK) where AC practices are well established, such as South Africa (Buckett Chapter 13) and Israel (Fox and Haboucha Chapter 31). ACs are also growing in developing countries such as Brazil (Betti and Monobe Chapter 18) and Kenya (Manji and Dunford Chapter 27) where previously organizations may not have had the resources to support expensive human resource management practices, and in countries, such as China (Liang and Liu Chapter 28), Russia (Simonenko Chapter 29) and Indonesia (Pendit Chapter 24) where merit-based selection and promotion were not the norm. Lievens and Thornton (2005) documented the spread of ACs around the world up to 2000. That growth continues, as was apparent at the 35th International Congress on Assessment Center Methods in Singapore in October 2010, when there were over 160 delegates. This was the largest number of attendees at the Congress, with people coming from 25 countries, including those typically not represented, such as Russia, Botswana, India, Macau, and Hong Kong.

Traditional designs of the AC method continue to be used in each of the three most common applications: selection/promotion, diagnosis and developmental planning, and training and development. Classic ACs assessing standard management dimensions using paper-and-pencil materials to present common simulation exercises are used throughout the US to help make promotion decisions in police and fire departments and elsewhere. While there is a trend for companies to use consultants as assessors because of limited time available from middle managers, other ACs follow the traditional use of managers as assessors. Managers are used in Gothenburg in Sweden (Bergvall Chapter 16), Credit Suisse in Switzerland, (Birri and Melcher Chapter 12). In Singapore (Ng and Nosworthy Chapter 26), ACs have been used since 1999 to select school principals, graduates for the foreign service, and university scholarship winners. ACs using a combination of line managers, HR managers, academics, and consultants as assessors are being used to diagnose strengths and weaknesses in participants and to prescribe development plans. ACs are being adapted to promote learning and change within the confines of the AC itself.

The AC Method is Highly Flexible

The second lesson is that the AC method is highly flexible. Howard (1997) used the term "plastic" to imply the notion that ACs can be molded and shaped to fit various needs of the organization. That term may have negative connotations of "second class" or "cheap," and we know ACs are not inexpensive. We prefer to use terms such as versatile, flexible, and adaptable. The authors here report many different uses of ACs with a variety of different design features:

- Assessing new jobs: certifying competence of human resource managers (Premarajan Chapter 15); the placement of physicians in internships (Rupp and Searle Chapter 14).
- Different dimensions are being assessed: learning agility (Livings and Mitchell Chapter 17), resoluteness (Simonenko Chapter 29), morals and values (Hirose Chapter 30).
- Innovative exercises are being designed: a "Day in the Life" scenario with two stages: a calm stage followed by a crisis stage (Livings and Mitchell Chapter 17). Pritchard and Riley (Chapter 5) provide thorough analyses of the advantages and disadvantages of off-the-shelf, custom-built, and hybrid exercises. Lievens and Schollaert (Chapter 4)

describe how the introduction of situational cues into role player briefs for one-to-one exercises can elicit valuable behavioral evidence from participants.

- Other assessment methods may be used in conjunction with simulation exercises: personality tests in Brazil (Betti and Monobe Chapter 18), ability tests and personality questionnaires in Russia (Simonenko Chapter 29).
- Different ways of observing and integrating behavioral observations are being used, for example, task-based ACs (Jackson, Grace, Ahmad, and Yoon Chapter 3).
- Special modes of feedback are employed: combined groups of fellow-participants and assessors give feedback to each participant in Japan (Hirose Chapter 30); video recordings were made of the group and one-to-one exercises, so line managers could review them with their participants to aid post-center development activity (Purdy Chapter 19).
- Technology is converting the process from paper-and-pencil to virtual administration (Meiring and van der Westhuizen Chapter 6).

And yet all of these variations still conform to the basic required elements of the AC method laid out in the *International Guidelines and Ethical Considerations for the Assessment Center Method* (International Task Force 2009).

Cross-Cultural Adaptations May or May Not Be Necessary

A third lesson is that there may, or MAY NOT, need to be adjustments in AC methods in the light of cross-cultural differences in various organizations in various countries. The recent version of the International Guidelines (International Task Force 2009: 251) admonishes "Practitioners using assessment center methods beyond the boundaries of the country/region from which the assessment center program originated should determine the extent to which cultural accommodations may be necessary." Beyond such general statements, little guidance is provided on what factors to consider and what actions to take. Examples of adaptations to accommodate specific cultural considerations abound in the chapters in this book.

- Hirose (Chapter 30) explains why group feedback is given in Japan.
- Pendit (Chapter 24) explains why in Indonesia figures and illustrations are needed in the background material for complex exercises and why additional reading time is needed.
- Manji and Dunford (Chapter 27) show how the notion of timekeeping affects ACs in East Africa.
- In Russia (Simonenko Chapter 29) supervisors avoid talking with subordinates about personal matters and thus role players in one-on-one interview simulations would not be expected to have relevant plausible background information at hand, in sharp contrast with the typical interaction in many other countries where the role player must be prepared to respond about family and other matters off the work site.

We often think first about the need for cross-cultural sensitivity when ACs are moved from countries with a long-standing AC tradition (such as the US, UK, or Germany) to new countries. An extension of this need is presented by Hirose (Chapter 30) who points out that Japanese consultants need to make cultural checks when they export their ACs to other countries.

On the other hand, a comparison of the lists of dimensions across many countries shows many similarities, such as competencies in communication, problem-solving, interpersonal effectiveness, and leadership. For example, Betti and Monobe (Chapter 18) express surprise that the traditional managerial performance dimensions used in other countries are quite applicable in Brazil, as well as their applicability when the Brazil programs were moved to other countries.

ACs Thrive in and Augment Systems of Talent Management

A fourth lesson is that ACs tend to thrive in organizations where they are part of a well planned, complex, integrated system addressing the issues of talent management. Whereas the designers and implementers of the AC method benefit from the opportunity to play a central role in the strategic systems of selecting and developing talent, the broader talent-management system benefits from the unique information provided by the AC method. Whereas talent-management programs typically rely on evaluation of past experience and performance indicators, the AC provides information about competency to perform in future roles. Organizations frequently make promotions to upper management positions on the basis of considering both performance and potential. Evaluation of performance is readily available, but assessment of potential is often very difficult. Here is where the AC method can provide better information than is typically available.

Chapters by Boyle (Chapter 20), Betti and Monobe (Chapter18), Livings and Mitchell (Chapter 17) and Purdy (Chapter 19) describe how ACs have been integrated into systematic talent-management programs. Birri and Melcher (Chapter 12) describe how ACs in Credit Suisse survived and changed over a 25-year history of intimate cooperation with the broader programs in talent management and human capital management. Thornton and Birri (Chapter 21) point out that whereas the early demise of ACs is often due to technological flaws, sustainability of ACs over time is more a function of placing the AC into a fully integrated HR management system. Other insights into how ACs have been sustained over time are provided by Nosworthy and Ng (Chapter 26). Boyle (Chapter 20) is particularly helpful in providing insights into how to influence decisions about the use of ACs.

ACs and Social Change

A fifth lesson is much broader in scope: the assessment center method has been an integral part of major social changes at the national level in a number of countries in recent years. In South Korea (Kim Chapter 25), Singapore (Nosworthy and Ng Chapter 26) and Gothenburg in Sweden (Bergvall Chapter 16), the AC method has been a part of reforms in promotion practices in national and local civil service organizations. In South Korea, the AC method provides a means of implementing merit-based talent-management programs, including promotion to key levels of management in a government ministry and the city of Seoul, and developmental experiences for managers in a national training facility. In Singapore, however, the AC has not only become an established means of making objective appointment or promotion decisions within the Civil Service, but it has also started to gain acceptance as a tool for the diagnosis and development of future leaders. In Sweden, the city of Gothenburg adopted ACs for the last decade as a means of appointing all managers so as to ensure an objective, transparent, and equitable process. In South Africa, the AC method has been used to conduct thorough and fair talent-assessment of candidates for several levels of administrators in a key government organization (Buckett Chapter 13). The program is one of several talent-management programs that help with the peaceful transition from apartheid to democratic practices in government. In Indonesia, after years of oppressive regimes, democratic government emerged in the late 1990s, accompanied by many pressures to install transparency in government and business organizations (Pendit Chapter 24). Close scrutiny of business operations came with increased global business and pressure from regional trade agreements. The AC method provided a means to reduce corruption and nepotism, and to introduce transparency in human resource management in, first, government-owned companies such a PT Telkom, and subsequently private-sector corporations.

Research is Practical

A final lesson we learn from these chapters is twofold: continuing research has practical pay-offs, and we still have a lot to learn. Original research reported in this book shows the practical pay-offs from empirical studies. Bergvall (Chapter 16) found that AC ratings predicted both managerial and subordinate ratings, and that running an in-house operation was more cost effective than contracting with outside consultants. Lievens and Schollaert (Chapter 4) summarize theory and research which shows that the use of Trait Activation Theory leads to practical pay-offs in exercise design: specific instructions and role-player prompts elicit behavior particularly germane to evaluations of specified assessment dimensions. Guenole, Chernyshenko, Cockerill, Stark, and Drasgow (Chapter 2) show that thorough assessor-training yields assessment center ratings that possess construct validity, that is, ratings show the statistical properties that support the inference that dimension ratings are measuring the intended managerial performance dimensions. Their chapter contains an explicit, extensive description of the assessor training needed to attain these levels of accuracy. Fletcher (Chapter 8) summarizes his and others' research on the impact of ACs and DCs on motivation and well-being. Dewberry (Chapter 7) analyzes conversations in the consensus discussion and provides qualitative evidence of assessor biases. Woodruffe (Chapter 9) finds evidence of ethnic and racial bias and argues for greater diversity awareness in the design and implementation of ACs.

MORE RESEARCH IS NEEDED

The authors highlight a number of unanswered questions and so we make no apologies for repeating the much quoted mantra: "More research is needed."

Some topics will be relatively easy to study. For example, the extensive applications of the AC method in countries with diverse populations, such as China, India and Indonesia, offer fertile soil for studies of performance of different groups, potential rater biases, and rater–ratee interactions. On the last point: are there same-race biases in AC ratings?

Do assessors of a race rate participants of the same race higher than they rate participants of another race? A first study along these lines in the AC context was reported by Gibbons, Vanhove and Thornton (2010). In a study of 50 assessors and 209 candidates, they found that same-race and same-sex biases accounted for less than 2 percent of variance in ratings. We are aware of the highly sensitive nature of such studies, but if biases in AC ratings exist, they need to be addressed, with the hope of revising materials or training raters in different ways.

More research is also needed to understand the effect of repeated participation in the AC method in programs like the one described by Rupp and Searle (Chapter 14). We might expect that performance would improve with repeated assessment. Simonenko (Chapter 29) demonstrated with a small number of participants that improvement occurred on selected dimensions over a two-year period; studies with larger samples are clearly needed.

Two chapters provide contrasting views of the effects of participating in an assessment center on the unsuccessful candidates. Fletcher (Chapter 8) reports a number of negative outcomes, including diminished motivation and well-being. By contrast, Birri and Melcher (Chapter 12) provide longitudinal data which shows no evidence of a "loser syndrome," that is, there is there is no indication that candidates became discouraged or reported negative psychological effects after a negative AC result. Although the differences were not statistically different, candidates with negative AC results reported somewhat lower engagement before the AC compared to those with positive results. More importantly, both groups of candidates showed increases in engagement scores. Further research is needed to understand why we see these disparate results.

ACs are favored because they have high fidelity. But fidelity is quite complex (Thornton and Kedharnath, in press) encompassing a match of several features of the test or AC with features of the job, for example, stimulus material, content of the problems, response requirements, level of difficulty, situational characteristics such as the industry, stress, and so forth. More research would be helpful to understand the importance of different aspects of fidelity.

Other needed research will be much harder to conduct. True comparisons of "dimension-based ACs" with "exercise-based ACs" or "task-based ACs" (Jackson, Ahmed, Grace, and Yoon Chapter 3) require that ACs are developed from scratch using the rationale and methods that differentiate them.

There is still a relative dearth of evidence about how participants follow up after ACs where the purpose is diagnosis of strengths and weaknesses followed by developmental planning. Existing studies show not much is done. This has been labeled the Achilles heel of developmental ACs. Studies of the lasting behavioral and performance impact of developmental ACs requires longitudinal designs to follow participants over periods of at least 12 to 18 months.

Even more difficult will be empirical research into the most effective ways of gaining influence in high-level decision-making where AC information might be effective in helping organizations improve complex talent-management programs. Hollenbeck (1994) pointed out that we know little about how CEOs and boards of directors make decisions about management succession. Those who implement ACs and feedback results from ACs to high levels of management are in a good position to provide descriptions of how CEOs and boards of directors make decisions about leadership selection. Insights into these processes are provided by authors in this book, for example, Boyle

(Chapter 20). They provide fertile ground for others to engage in empirical studies. Studies of these matters require research where the organization, not the individual, is the unit of analysis. That is, we want to understand what organization-wide and environmental variables are related to effective use of the AC method to foster talent management. The case study method detailing the evolution of the use of ACs in different organizations using different AC methods may be fruitful. The beginnings of such studies are an integral part of this process.

Challenges to the Traditional AC Method

A number of chapters in the book raise serious questions about the efficacy of the AC method. We believe that healthy skepticism of the method will do much to set parameters on what ACs can and cannot do, identify areas of weakness, lead to modifications, and ultimately benefit the integrity of the AC method. A few examples of authors who raise tough questions will suffice. Jackson and colleagues in Chapter 3 raise the basic question of whether dimensions are viable and necessary as the core focal element of the AC method, or whether tasks and roles are more appropriate. Fletcher (Chapter 8) alerts us to the potential negative effects that an AC may have on participants' anxiety, attitudes, and self-esteem. Woodruffe (Chapter 9) points out ways that ACs may not be welcoming to participants who are not white, male, and graduates of elite schools. Dewberry (Chapter 7) expresses concern that potential biases can enter the group decision-making process of the integration session, sometimes called "the wash-up" session. Hoffman and Baldwin (Chapter 10) note that the traditional interpretation of AC performance has not considered the contextual effects on performance as thoroughly as might be productive, in contrast to the related method of MSPRs.

How Evidence-Based is AC Practice?

There has been a regular and rich interchange of science and practice in the AC method over the past 50 years (Thornton Chapter 11). Reading the chapters in this book, we have asked ourselves again: to what extent is the practice of ACs an example of evidence-based management (EBM, Briner and Rousseau 2011)? According to Briner and Rousseau, EBM is present when a practice (a) integrates practitioners' expertise and evidence from research, (b) uses evidence even if it is inconvenient, and (c) relies on systematic reviews rather than a single study. Four sources of evidence are used in evidence-based management (Briner and Rousseau; 6–7): "practitioner expertise and judgment, evidence from the local context, a critical evaluation of the best available research evidence, and the perspective of those people who might be affected." Table 32.1 summarizes key characteristics of evidence-based practice and shows our appraisal of the extent to which the practice of ACs satisfies these characteristics.

Table 32.1 Characteristics of evidence-based practice and the state of AC practice

Characteristics of evidence-based practice	Practiced in AC applications?
The term "evidence based" is used or well known.	While the term may be new to some people in the AC field, AC adherents have used related terms, for example, the influence of science on AC practice.
The latest research findings and research summaries are accessible.	Hundreds of books, articles, reports, conference presentations, and so forth have been published on the AC method in core and bridge journals; they provide significant support for selection/promotion applications, and an ever increasing amount for diagnostic and developmental applications.
Articles reporting primary research and traditional literature reviews are accessible to practitioners.	Qualitative and quantitative reviews have been published over the past 30 years. An early review was written explicitly for managers and published in *Harvard Business Review*, and a special issue of *The Psychologist Manager*, a bridge journal for psychologists, published several articles on developmental assessment centers.
"Cutting edge" practices, panaceas, and fashionable new ideas are treated with healthy skepticism.	Pressures to streamline, make virtual, reduce behavioral fidelity, use technology, assess overly broad dimensions and competencies, and making ACs task-based rather than dimension-based have been challenged strongly, but accepted when supported by subsequent evidence.
There is a demand for evidence-based practice from clients and customers.	Clients have demanded evidence for validity and fairness for selection/promotion, partly based on the need to defend selection practices in employment litigation. There has not been the same demand for evidence of the effects of diagnostic and developmental ACs.
Practical decisions are integrative and draw on the four sources of information and evidence described above.	Practitioner expertise and the perspective of those affected are used. Two examples: local job analysis/competency modeling is standard practice; and taking consequential validity into consideration. Collecting local validity evidence and critical evaluation of the best research evidence are used far less frequently.
Initial training and continuing professional development (CPD) adopt evidence-based approaches.	Select universities have offered graduate training in how to validate and evaluate ACs for different purposes. Annual conferences report research evidences on the AC method. There is little CPD on how to conduct and use evidence-based studies of developmental ACs.

This table is an adaptation of Table 2 in Briner and Rousseau (2011). All statements in column one are quotations from page 9 in that source.

Our analysis suggests a somewhat contrasting set of answers to the question "How evidence-based is AC practice?" On the one hand, the practice of ACs for the purposes of selection, identification of long-range potential, and promotion is based on extensive research showing the predictive validity, incremental validity, utility, and lack of bias of overall assessment ratings. On the other hand, the practice of ACs for the purposes of differentially diagnosing strengths and weaknesses in specified dimensions, laying out developmental plans, and motivating participants to undertake training activities seems to rely on a relatively small but growing set of construct validity studies. Practitioners seem to be unfamiliar with or immune to another segment of construct validity studies which question the ability of the AC method to differentiate among the dimensions supposedly being assessed. To be sure, there is emerging research on the elements of developmental assessment centers. For examples of these studies, please see the references to publications authored by each of the team of Gibbons, Rupp, Kim and Woo. Although there is this set of several studies, the practice of using ACs to develop skills is still in its infancy and there are, as yet, no summaries of research evidence. One reason for the relative lack of evidence in this area is that the AC itself is only one part of what makes a successful developmental intervention. Other factors include the feedback reports, follow-up management of subsequent interventions, and insistence on measurement of outcomes. There does not appear to be a demand from clients for evidence to support the diagnostic and developmental applications of the AC method, namely differential diagnosis and skill training.

More generally, we conclude that the practice of ACs is to a large extent evidence-based, due to the substantial research showing the importance of several elements of the AC method, namely the methods used to design the exercises, how assessors are trained, and how the method is implemented and monitored. All of these well-supported practices are recommended in the widely followed sets of guidelines and ethical standards for assessment center operations in various countries.

Conclusions

We are heartened by the cumulative experience and insights of the authors in this book. They have reinforced our passion for the potential of the many opportunities for the assessment center method to contribute to individual development and organizational effectiveness. From our years of exposure to colleagues and assessment center research and practice around the world, we were aware of many of these contributions. But, in reading these chapters we came away with many other new insights.

The authors show us, in various ways, how assessment centers and development centers can play a central role in talent-management programs, how they are adaptable to many different purposes, and how they provide fair methods of dealing with diverse workforces in various countries. These assessment and development programs have both benefited from solid empirical research and provided rich, real-life settings for basic and applied research. We envisage future research will be stimulated by the many questions raised and contributions made in the chapters in this book.

Lastly, we hope that like us, you are excited by the prospect of adding to the growing body of knowledge that has been accumulated about ACs over the last 50-plus years. Regardless of whether you are a researcher who is stimulated to conduct some interesting and much-needed further research, or a practitioner who is inspired to implement an AC for the first time or to embrace some new features within the design of your existing AC, we hope this book has helped to fuel your passion for this all-embracing and versatile methodology.

References

Briner, R.B. and Rousseau, D.M. 2011. Evidence-based I-O psychology: Not there yet. *Industrial and Organizational Psychology: Perspectives on Science and Practice*, 4, 3–22.

Gibbons, A.M., Rupp, D.E., Kim, M.J. and Woo, S.E., 2006. Perceptions of managerial performance dimensions in Korea. *Psychologist-Manager Journal*, 9, 125–143.

Gibbons, A.M., Rupp, D.E., Snyder, L.A., Holub, A.S. and Woo, S.E. 2006. A preliminary investigation of developable dimensions. *Psychologist-ManagerJournal*, 9, 99–123.

Gibbons, A.M., Vanhove, A.J. and Thornton, G.C. III. 2010. *Untangling the effects of candidate and assessor race and gender on assessment center ratings.* Paper to the 35th International Congress on Assessment Center Methods: Putting the Pieces Together, Singapore, 20–21 October 2010.

Hollenbeck, G.P. 1994. *CEO Selection: A Street-Smart Review.* Greensboro, NC: Center for Creative Leadership.

Howard, A. 1997. A reassessment of assessment centers: Challenges for the 21st century. *Journal of Social Behavior and Personality*, 12, 13–52.

Rupp, D.E., Baldwin, A.M. and Bashshur, M.R. 2006. Using developmental assessment centers to foster workplace fairness. *Psychologist-Manager Journal*, 9, 145–170.

Rupp, D.E., Gibbons, A.M., Baldwin, A.M., Snyder, L.A., Spain, S.M., Woo, S.E., Brummel, B., Sims, C. and Kim, M.J. 2006. An initial validation of developmental assessment centers as accurate assessments and effective training interventions. *Psychologist-Manager Journal*, 9, 171–200.

Rupp, D.E., Snyder, L.A., Gibbons, A.M. and Thornton, G.C. III 2006. What should developmental assessment centers be developing? *Psychologist-Manager Journal*, 9, 75–98.

International Task Force on Assessment Center Guidelines. 2009. Guidelines and ethical considerations for assessment center operations. *International Journal of Selection and Assessment*, 17, 243–254.

Lievens, F. and Thornton, G.C. III. 2005. Assessment centers: Recent developments in practice and research. In *Handbook of Personnel Selection*, edited by A. Evers, N. Anderson and O. Voskuijl. Malden, MA: Blackwell, 243–264.

Thornton, G.C. III and Kedharnath, U. In press. Work sample tests. In *Handbook of Testing and Assessment in Psychology*, edited by K.F. Geisinger. Washington, DC: American Psychological Association, xxx.

Woo, S., Sims, C., Rupp, D. and Gibbons, A.M. 2008. Development engagement within and following developmental assessment centers: Considering feedback favorability and self-assessor agreement. *Personnel Psychology*, 61, 727–759.

Woo, S., Sims, C., Rupp, D. and Gibbons, A.M. 2009. Correction to "Development engagement within and following developmental assessment centers: Considering feedback favorability and self-assessor agreement." *Personnel Psychology*, 62, 199–200.

Subject Index

Author Index

If you have found this book useful you may be interested in other titles from Gower

Assessment and Development Centres
Second Edition
Iain Ballantyne and Nigel Povah
Hardback: 978-0-566-08599-4

Cultural Differences and Improving Performance
How Values and Beliefs Influence Organizational Performance
Bryan Hopkins
Hardback: 978-0-566-08907-7
Ebook: 978-0-566-08908-4

Developing HR Talent
Building a Strategic Partnership with the Business
Kirsty Saddler and Jan Hills
Paperback: 978-0-566-08829-2
Ebook: 978-0-7546-8167-0

Enterprise Growth Strategy
Vision, Planning and Execution
Dhirendra Kumar
Hardback: 978-0-566-09198-8
Ebook: 978-0-566-09199-5

Going Global
Managing the HR Function Across Countries and Cultures
Cat Rickard, Jodi Baker and Yonca Crew
Paperback: 978-0-566-08823-0
Ebook: 978-0-7546-8134-2

Gower Handbook of Internal Communication
Second Edition
Edited by Marc Wright
Hardback: 978-0-566-08689-2
Ebook: 978-0-7546-9097-9

GOWER

Gower Handbook of Leadership and Management Development
Fifth Edition
Edited by Jeff Gold, Richard Thorpe and Alan Mumford
Hardback: 978-0-566-08858-2
Ebook: 978-0-7546-9213-3

Project Success
Critical Factors and Behaviours
Emanuel Camilleri
Hardback: 978-0-566-09228-2
Ebook: 978-0-566-09229-9

Service Led Design
Planning the New HR Function
Jane Saunders and Ian Hunter
Paperback: 978-0-566-08826-1
Ebook: 978-0-7546-8161-8

Six Sigma in HR Transformation
Achieving Excellence in Service Delivery
Mircea Albeanu and Ian Hunter with Jo Radford
Paperback: 978-0-566-09164-3
Ebook: 978-0-566-09165-0

Talent Management in the Developing World
Adopting a Global Perspective
Joel Alemibola Elegbe
Hardback: 978-1-4094-1813-9
Ebook: 978-1-4094-1814-6

Visit **www.gowerpublishing.com** and

- search the entire catalogue of Gower books in print
- order titles online at 10% discount
- take advantage of special offers
- sign up for our monthly e-mail update service
- download free sample chapters from all recent titles
- download or order our catalogue